CAMBRIDGE LATIN AMERICAN STUDIES

EDITORS
DAVID JOSLIN   JOHN STREET

6

THE ABOLITION OF THE
BRAZILIAN SLAVE TRADE

THE SERIES

THE ABOLITION OF THE BRAZILIAN SLAVE TRADE

BRITAIN, BRAZIL AND THE SLAVE TRADE QUESTION
1807–1869

BY

LESLIE BETHELL

Lecturer in Hispanic American and Brazilian History
University College London

CAMBRIDGE
AT THE UNIVERSITY PRESS
1970

CAMBRIDGE UNIVERSITY PRESS
Cambridge, New York, Melbourne, Madrid, Cape Town, Singapore, São Paulo, Delhi

Cambridge University Press
The Edinburgh Building, Cambridge CB2 8RU, UK

Published in the United States of America by Cambridge University Press, New York

www.cambridge.org
Information on this title: www.cambridge.org/9780521075831

© Cambridge University Press 1970

First published 1970
This digitally printed version 2008

A catalogue record for this publication is available from the British Library

Library of Congress Catalogue Card Number: 79–98696

ISBN 978-0-521-07583-1 hardback
ISBN 978-0-521-10113-4 paperback

She [Brazil] wants cheap labour . . . the African is the cheapest labourer . . . we have undertaken to prevent her getting that labour. Is it possible for two states to be beset by any question more completely by the ears?

James Hudson, lately British minister at Rio de Janeiro, in September 1852

Two irreconcilable currents . . . the first took us to Africa in search of slaves to satisfy the increasing needs of our agricultural development . . . the second . . . moved us away from Africa because of the English insistence on [the] abolition of . . . the slave trade . . . This clash between national needs and English demands was the very essence of our history in the first fifty years of the nineteenth century.

José Honório Rodrigues, *Brazil and Africa* (1965), p. 115

To Valerie

CONTENTS

PREFACE

For 300 years, from the beginning of the sixteenth to the beginning of the nineteenth century, the transatlantic slave trade—the forced migration of Africans to work as slaves on the plantations and in the mines of British, French, Spanish, Portuguese and Dutch colonies in North and South America and the Caribbean—was carried on, legally, and on an ever-increasing scale, by the merchants of most Western European countries and their colonial counterparts, aided and abetted by African middlemen. Indeed, until the second half of the eighteenth century, when (at a conservative estimate) 70–75,000 slaves were being transported annually across the Atlantic, scarcely a voice was raised against it. On 25 March 1807, however, after a lengthy and bitter struggle, inside and outside Parliament, it was declared illegal for British subjects (and at this point during the Napoleonic Wars at least half the trade was in British hands) to trade in slaves after 1 May 1808: opposition to the slave trade on moral and intellectual grounds had gathered momentum during the preceding twenty years and changing economic conditions, which to some extent reduced the importance to the British economy of the West Indian colonies, for whom the slave trade was a major lifeline, while at the same time creating new interest groups unconnected with and even hostile to them, had greatly facilitated its abolition. Encouraged by this success the British abolitionist movement brought pressure to bear on the British government to go further in expiating Britain's own guilt by using all the means at their command to persuade other, 'morally inferior', nations to follow Britain's lead. (At the time, only Denmark, by a royal decree of 1792 which came into effect in 1804, and the United States, by the law of 2 March 1807 which came into force on 1 January 1808, had already prohibited the trade.) In addition to moral considerations there were sound economic reasons why Britain should pursue such a policy. With the British West Indian sugar planters now deprived of their regular supply of cheap labour, it was important that their rivals, especially those in Cuba and Brazil who already enjoyed many advantages over them, should be put on an equal footing in this one respect at least. And if the African continent were to be opened up as a market for manufactured goods and a source of raw materials (besides being 'civilised' and 'Christianised'), as many in Britain hoped, it was essential that every effort should be made to bring about the slave trade's total destruction. Thus it was that for more than half a century after Britain herself had abolished the slave trade, and especially from the end of the Napoleonic Wars in 1815 to the beginning of the Crimean War in 1853—a period of almost unbroken peace, stability and British pre-eminence in international affairs—successive British Foreign Secretaries, notably George Canning (1807–9, 1822–7), Lord Castlereagh (1812–22), Lord Aberdeen (1828–30, 1841–6) and, above all, Lord Palmerston (1830–4, 1835–41, 1846–51), devoted much of their time and energies towards securing the *international* abolition of the transatlantic trade in African slaves. By means of a 'judicious mixture of bullying and bribery' (to use Sir Charles Webster's phrase) strenuous efforts were made to coax or coerce the European, American and African states which retained an interest in the trade to enter into abolition agreements with Britain, to introduce and enforce their own anti-slave trade legislation and to permit the British navy to police slaving areas on both sides of the Atlantic. It was not to prove an easy task: few other nations shared Britain's newly acquired abolitionist sentiments and, for some, vital economic interests were at stake. Moreover, British interference in their internal affairs was deeply resented. Not until the late 1830s had the slave trade been prohibited by all the major European and American states. Even then a trade which had for centuries been the mainstay of the 'Atlantic economy' and closely linked with powerful interests in Europe, Africa and the Americas was not to be readily suppressed. During the 1840s the transatlantic slave trade probably reached an all-time peak. And two of the trade's most important branches—the

Preface

Brazilian (illegal since 1830) and the Cuban (illegal since 1820)—continued into the second half of the nineteenth century. The Brazilian slave trade was eventually stamped out during the years 1850-1 (although a few isolated landings of slaves from Africa occurred as late as 1855); the slave trade to Cuba was finally brought to an end in 1865.

The history of the international abolition and suppression of the transatlantic slave trade in the nineteenth century has still to be written, although W. L. Mathieson, *Great Britain and the Slave Trade, 1839-1865* (London 1929) and Christopher Lloyd, *The Navy and the Slave Trade* (London 1949), for example, are useful pioneer works. My own aim has been to provide, within a general framework, a detailed study of one important aspect of the subject—the struggle for the abolition of the slave trade to Brazil. (It has *not* been my purpose to write a history of the Brazilian slave trade itself in its later and largely illegal stages, although I have been compelled to make some necessarily tentative calculations as to its volume.) I have tried to answer three basic questions: first, how did the Brazilian slave trade, one of the major pillars of the Brazilian economy, come to be declared illegal? (chapters 1-2); secondly, why for twenty years did it prove impossible to suppress the trade once it had been declared illegal? (chapters 3-10); and thirdly, how was it finally abolished? (chapters 11-12). Although Britain's anti-slave trade efforts have necessarily received the closest attention, I have tried to look at the slave trade question from the Brazilian as well as the British point of view with the result that my book is, I hope, as much a contribution to Brazilian as to British history. In a more modest way, it is also a contribution to Portuguese history since, until 1822, Brazil was a colony of Portugal, during the 1830s the illegal slave trade to Brazil continued to be carried on under the Portuguese flag, and Portuguese Africa remained to the end the main supplier of slaves to Brazil. Above all, perhaps, it is a study in Anglo-Brazilian relations which were dominated—and damaged—by the slave trade question during the thirty years after Brazil's assertion of her independence

xi

Preface

from Portugal in 1822—and, indeed, long after the trade had been suppressed (see chapter 13). In this book I have confined my attention to the abolition of the Brazilian slave trade. It is my present intention to write a second volume on the struggle for the abolition of slavery in Brazil in the second half of the nineteenth century.

It is a great pleasure to be able to acknowledge here the great debt I owe Professor R. A. Humphreys, who during my undergraduate years first aroused my interest in Latin American history, who closely supervised my postgraduate research and training as an historian, and who encouraged me to write this book. I should also like to mention Christopher Fyfe, who stimulated my interest in African history and the slave trade, Kenneth Timings, who guided the early stages of my research in the Public Record Office, and Professor William Ashworth, who on more than one occasion gave me friendly support when I despaired of ever finishing the book. Professor José Honório Rodrigues took an interest in my work, helped me in numerous ways during my visits to Brazil, and fired my enthusiasm for Brazilian history and for Brazil. Like all students of Anglo-Brazilian relations I am indebted to Professor Alan K. Manchester whose book *British Preëminence in Brazil. Its Rise and Decline*, first published in 1933, remains the most notable contribution to the subject.

For the financial assistance which made it possible for me to spend two short periods of research and travel in Brazil I wish to express my gratitude to Dr Celso da Rocha Miranda, the William Waldorf Astor Foundation, the Anglo-Brazilian Society in London, the Brazilian Ministry of Foreign Affairs and the University of Bristol. I should also like to record my gratitude to the staffs of the following libraries and archives: in England, Public Record Office, British Museum, University of London Library, University College London Library, Institute of Historical Research, Leeds City Library and National Register of Archives; in Brazil, Arquivo Histórico do Itamaratí, Arquivo Nacional, Biblioteca

Preface

Nacional, Instituto Histórico e Geográfico Brasileiro and Arquivo do Museu Imperial, Petrópolis. For permission to consult the Palmerston Papers in the National Register of Archives, London, I am indebted to the Trustees of the Broadlands Archives. While teaching at the University of Bristol grants from the Colston Research Fund enabled me to continue my research in London. An award from the Twenty-Seven Foundation facilitated the final preparation of the manuscript for publication. Mrs Doreen Nunn typed the whole of the final draft—in difficult circumstances. My greatest debt, however, is to my wife. Without her constant help and encouragement this book would never have seen the light of day: she read, criticised and typed successive drafts and somehow learned to live with it—and with me. She also read the proofs and helped prepare the index.

Rio de Janeiro   L. B.
August 1969

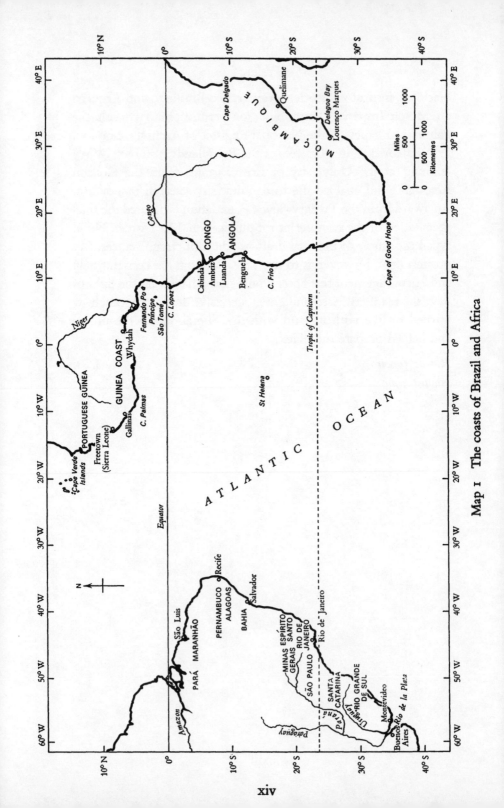

Map 1 The coasts of Brazil and Africa

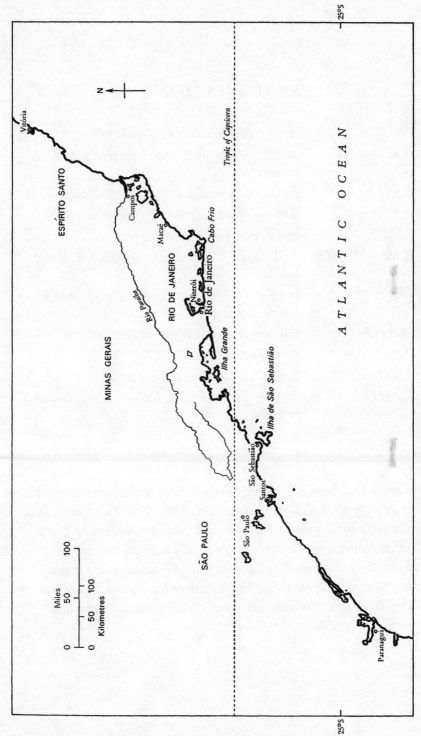

Map 2 The Brazilian coastline north and south of Rio de Janeiro

ABBREVIATIONS

A.D.I.	*Archivo Diplomatico da Independencia*
A.H.I.	Arquivo Histórico do Itamaratí, Rio de Janeiro
A.M.I.P.	Arquivo do Museu Imperial, Petrópolis
A.N.	Arquivo Nacional, Rio de Janeiro
B.F.S.P.	*British and Foreign State Papers*
B.M. Add. MSS	Additional Manuscripts, British Museum, London
F.O.	Foreign Offices Archives, Public Record Office, London
H.A.H.R.	*Hispanic American Historical Review*
P.P.	*Parliamentary Papers*
P.R.O.	Public Record Office, London
R.I.H.G.B.	*Revista do Instituto Histórico e Geográfico Brasileiro*

PORTUGUESE ORTHOGRAPHY

It has, I fear, been impossible to avoid completely inconsistencies of orthography and accentuation in the use of Portuguese. In general, I have preserved the original 'old' Portuguese in citing nineteenth-century books, pamphlets and newspapers (except for the well-known *Jornal do Comércio*). Ships' names, of course, appear in their original form. Proper names have for the most part been modernised in accordance with current Brazilian practice.

FIRST STEPS TOWARDS ABOLITION, 1807–1822

At the beginning of the nineteenth century when Britain launched her crusade against the transatlantic slave trade, there was no nation more deeply involved in the exportation, transportation and importation of African slaves than Portugal. Although the African territory effectively occupied or controlled by the Portuguese (who had first discovered and explored the coastline of Africa three and a half centuries before) scarcely extended beyond a few scattered towns, settlements and fortified trading posts along the coast and along the banks of the great rivers, thousands of slaves were annually exported to the New World from those parts of the African continent claimed by the Portuguese Crown as part of its vast overseas dominions. Bissão and Cacheu in what is now Portuguese Guinea, which were governed from the Cape Verde Islands, had already been virtually 'slaved out' and the Portuguese had long since lost to the English, the French, the Dutch and the Danes their monopoly of trade on the *Costa da Mina* (the coastline north of, and parallel with, the equator, stretching from Cape Palmas to the Cameroons and embracing the Ivory, Gold and Slave Coasts, sometimes collectively known as the Guinea Coast). But they retained the islands of São Tomé and Príncipe in the Gulf of Guinea, through which a great number of slaves were exported, and the fortified post of São João Baptista de Ajudá at Whydah in Dahomey, perhaps the most important slave port north of the equator. Moreover, Portuguese and Portuguese-claimed territories south of the equator—the Congo and Angola—constituted one of the largest areas of slave supply, and São Paulo de Luanda and São Filipe de Benguela (both in Angola) two of the greatest slave ports, on the west coast of Africa. Angola had fallen sadly short of its early economic promise and since the middle of the seventeenth century its exports had been almost exclusively of slaves; indeed, the slave trade had become the colony's only important commercial activity and the export tax on slaves provided as much as four-fifths of the public revenue. Since the middle of the eighteenth century, an increasing number of slaves had also been transported round the Cape and across the Atlantic from Portuguese settlements in Moçambique on the east coast of Africa—notably from Quelimane, Inhambane, Ibo and the fortified island of Moçambique itself; there, too, the trade in slaves had become the most successful branch of commerce and the greatest source of public revenue.[1]

Across the South Atlantic, only 35–50 days sail from the west coast of Africa, the Portuguese colony of Brazil was one of the greatest importers of African slaves in the New World. For more than two and a half centuries the Portuguese in America, faced · with the problem of *a falta de braços* (the shortage of labour: literally, the lack of arms), had been heavily dependent on Negro slave labour. (Amerindian labour was used, particularly in the more backward, remote areas of the north and in São Paulo, but the Brazilian Amerindian was ill equipped for regular field labour. Moreover, in Brazil, as in Spanish America, both Church and State had traditionally—and illogically—shown a greater concern for the welfare of the Amerindian than of the African; indeed, during the years 1755–8 the enslavement of Amerindians had been finally prohibited in Brazil.) In almost every part of Brazil Negro slavery was the most characteristic aspect of both the rural and the urban scene. The Portuguese had pioneered large-scale plantation (*fazenda*) agriculture in the New World and slavery was the cornerstone of the plantation economy and plantation society. The sugar industry, upon which Brazil had originally been built, had suffered a slow decline since the middle of the seventeenth century when Brazil's virtual monopoly of the world sugar market had been broken by the British and French West Indies, but sugar remained the colony's major cash crop and large concentrations of slaves were still to be found on the sugar plantations (in the cane fields, the mills and the Big Houses) in, for

---

[1] For the slave trade in Portuguese Africa, see, for example, James Duffy, *Portuguese Africa* (Harvard, 1959), pp. 137, 142, 146; James Duffy, *A Question of Slavery* (Oxford, 1967), pp. 1–2; R. J. Hammond, *Portugal and Africa, 1815–1910* (Stanford, 1966), pp. 37–8, 42, 55–6, 68–9; Mabel V. Jackson, *European Powers and South-East Africa* (London, 1942), pp. 84–7, 188–9.

example, the Recôncavo (the fertile coastal area) of Bahia, in Pernambuco, in the *baixada fluminense* (the coastal strip of what is now the state of Rio de Janeiro), and, a more recent development, in São Paulo. Slaves also worked both the cotton plantations of south-west Maranhão and Pernambuco (cotton represented 20% of the value of Brazil's exports at the beginning of the nineteenth century) and the tobacco and cacao plantations of Bahia and Alagoas. In the far south—Rio Grande de São Pedro (Rio Grande do Sul) and Santa Catarina—Negro slaves were employed on a considerable scale in stockraising (for hides and *carne sêca*), in cereal production and in subsistence agriculture. There were also large numbers of slaves engaged in subsistence agriculture in Minas Gerais, where the gold and diamond mines, which had flourished during the first half of the eighteenth century but which were now in decline, had originally attracted slave labour to the area. In Rio de Janeiro, the viceregal capital since 1763, in Bahia, the former capital, and, indeed, in every town from São Luís in the north to Porto Alegre and Pelotas in the south, slaves were widely employed as domestic servants, and *negros de ganho*—individual slaves who were hired out by their masters and paid wages—were to be found working, for example, as stevedores and porters in the docks, water and refuse carriers, and even as masons and carpenters. The Church—monasteries, convents and hospitals—owned slaves. The State owned and hired slaves for the building and maintenance of public works.[1]

It is impossible to calculate with any degree of accuracy either the total population of Brazil in 1800, or its racial composition, or the proportion of free persons to slave. However, a reasonable estimate of the population (excluding unreduced Amerindians, numbering perhaps as many as 800,000) would seem to be between 2 million and 2½ million. Two-thirds, perhaps three-quarters, of the population were coloured and between one-third and one-half were slaves. In the areas of greatest slave concentration—Bahia,

[1] For the structure of the Brazilian economy and Brazilian society at the end of the colonial period see, for example, Caio Prado Júnior, *Formação do Brasil Contemporâneo* (5th ed., São Paulo, 1957); Eng. trans., *The Colonial Background of Modern Brazil* (Univ. of Calif. Press, 1967), *passim*; Sérgio Buarque de Holanda (ed.), *História Geral da Civilização Brasileira*. tomo I, vol. ii, *A Época Colonial. Administração, Economia, Sociedade* (São Paulo, 1960), *passim*; Celso Furtado, *Formação Econômica do Brasil* (Rio de Janeiro, 1959); Eng. trans., *The Economic Growth of Brazil* (Univ. of Calif. Press, 1963), pp. 79–106.

First steps towards abolition, 1807-1822

Pernambuco, Minas Gerais, Rio de Janeiro and Maranhão—slaves were in the majority.[1] The slave population of Brazil, like that of other slave societies in the New World, required regular replenishment through the transatlantic slave trade. One reason for this was the very high slave mortality rate. Many slaves never survived their initial acclimatisation and training; others died as a result of poor diet, insanitary living conditions and disease (slave *senzalas* were especially susceptible to epidemics of cholera and smallpox). More important, since it was considered most economic to 'work out' slaves (or at least those slaves employed in the fields) and then to replace them with others, a great many Africans died from illtreatment and sheer exhaustion. A field slave was not expected to last indefinitely. At the same time, the rate of natural reproduction amongst slaves was extremely low: there were, on average, eight male to every two female slaves, slave women were not conspicuously fecund and, given the conditions under which most births took place, it is hardly surprising that the infant mortality rate was high—even by the standards of the time. Thus, the annual importation of considerable numbers of slaves from Africa was necessary simply in order to maintain the *existing* slave population of Brazil. In periods of economic expansion *additional* supplies of labour were required—and at the beginning of the nineteenth century the Brazilian economy was (if only temporarily) in an unusually healthy state. Population growth and the beginnings of industrialisation and urbanisation in Western Europe had increased the demand for foodstuffs (including sugar) and raw materials (especially cotton), while at the same time political events—the American Revolutionary Wars, the French Revolutionary Wars, the Napoleonic Wars and, not least, the bloody uprising in the Caribbean sugar island of Santo Domingo—had crippled many of Brazil's economic rivals and raised world prices for tropical produce. Even the old sugar areas of the north-east were temporarily

[1] The most thorough examination of the available evidence on the size, distribution and racial composition of the Brazilian population at the end of the colonial period is Dauril Alden, 'The Population of Brazil in the late eighteenth century: a preliminary study', *H.A.H.R.* xliii (1963), pp. 173–205. See also José Honório Rodrigues, *Brasil e África: outro horizonte* (2nd ed., Rio de Janeiro, 1964); Eng. trans., *Brazil and Africa* (Univ. of Calif. Press, 1965), pp. 52–4; Arthur Ramos, *O Negro na Civilização Brasileira* (Rio de Janeiro, 1956), pp. 24–7.

4

restored to something resembling their former prosperity. In contrast with the British West Indies, Brazil had plenty of fertile virgin land available for cultivation at times when world demand for Brazilian produce was at a high level. A *falta de negros*, however, remained a constant problem, despite the internal slave trade from areas in relative economic decline. As a result more slaves than ever before—15,000 to 20,000 annually—were being imported into Brazil, principally into Rio de Janeiro (mostly from Angola, the Congo and Moçambique) and Bahia (from Whydah and other points on the *Costa da Mina*), but also into Pernambuco and Maranhão.[1]

With the entire economic life of Portugal's overseas empire in Africa and America organised around the slave trade, abolitionist feeling was notably weak throughout the Luso-Brazilian world. In the past individual voices had been raised against the worst evils associated with slavery and the slave trade: for example, those of Padre Antônio Vieira (1608–97), the celebrated Jesuit diplomat and publicist, and André João Antonil (1649–1716), author of the famous treatise *Cultura e Opulência do Brasil* (published in Lisbon in 1711), both of whom spent the greater part of their adult lives in Brazil. Amelioration, not abolition, however, had been their aim. In the curiously entitled *Ethiope Resgatado, Empenhado, Sustentado, Corregido, Instruido e Libertado* (The Ethiopian Ransomed, Indentured, Sustained, Corrected, Educated and Liberated), which was published in Lisbon in 1758, Padre Manuel Ribeiro da Rocha, a Lisbon-born secular priest who had lived for much of his life in Bahia, went further and advocated the end of the slave trade and the gradual substitution of free for slave labour in Brazil. His, however, was very much a minority viewpoint. In 1761 slavery was abolished in Portugal itself (and the transportation of Negroes to territories outside the Portuguese Empire was prohibited), but no moves were, or could be, made either to emancipate the slaves in Portugal's overseas territories or to abolish the slave trade to Brazil. The vast majority of white Portuguese—planters, merchants, officials, even priests—were deeply prejudiced on the subject of slavery and the slave trade, believing that Africans were born

---

[1] Mauricio Goulart, *Escravidão Africana no Brasil: das origins à extinção do tráfico* (São Paulo, 1950), pp. 265–70. During the colonial period as a whole it is probable that as many as three million slaves were imported into Brazil.

to serve and that through the slave trade they were rescued from barbarism in Africa and introduced to the benefits of Christianity in Brazil.[1] Even those who came into contact with the progressive ideas of the late eighteenth century and, in particular, the attacks being made on both the morality and the legality of slavery, could envisage no alternative basis for the economic life of the Empire and felt compelled to defend both the system and the trade which sustained it as necessary evils which, at best, could only be reformed. For example, Bishop José Joaquim da Cunha de Azeredo Coutinho (1742–1821), a leading figure of the Portuguese 'Enlightenment', identified himself with the landed interest in Brazil, and frequently argued that both slavery and the slave trade (he described the latter as a 'lawful business' and a 'form of commerce') were indispensable for the agricultural development of Brazil, where land was plentiful and labour in short supply, and thus for the prosperity and security of Portugal and the Empire as a whole.[2]

Not surprisingly, early appeals by Britain to the Portuguese government in Lisbon for the immediate abolition of the transatlantic slave trade fell upon deaf ears. When, in April 1807, within three weeks of Britain's own abolition bill receiving the royal assent, Lord Strangford, the British minister to the Portuguese court, acting under instructions from George Canning, the British Foreign Secretary, urged the Portuguese to follow Britain's lead or at the very least ensure that the Portuguese trade remained confined strictly within its existing limits, Antônio de Araújo Azevedo, the Portuguese Foreign Minister, replied that it was 'utterly impracticable' for Portugal to adopt any measures to discourage, much less to abolish, the trade in slaves.[3] Historically,

[1] See C. R. Boxer, *Race Relations in the Portuguese Colonial Empire, 1415–1825* (Oxford, 1963), pp. 101–21.

[2] J. J. da Cunha de Azeredo Coutinho, *Analyse sobre a justiça do commercio do resgate dos escravos da Costa da Africa* (1798: 2nd ed., Lisbon, 1808). See also Sônia Aparecida Siqueira, 'A escravidão negra no pensamento do bispo Azeredo Coutinho. Contribuição ao estudo da mentalidade do último Inquisidor', *Revista da História* (São Paulo), 56 (1963), pp. 349–65, 57 (1964), pp. 141–76.

[3] Canning to Strangford, 15 April 1807, quoted in James Bandinel, *Some account of the trade in slaves from Africa* (London, 1842), p. 126; Strangford to Canning, no. 31, 4 June 1807, F.O. 63/54. Bandinel's book is an invaluable abstract of Foreign Office slave trade papers; the author was chief clerk and superintendent of the Slave Trade Department of the Foreign Office, 1819–45.

however, as a result of treaties going back to the middle of the seventeenth century, Britain enjoyed a special relationship, economic and political, with Portugal and, because of the enormous disparity in wealth and power between the two nations, a relationship in which Britain played very much the dominant role. Moreover, towards the end of the year, Portugal's position of semi-dependence on Britain was to be dramatically underlined and Britain thereby afforded a rare opportunity for securing from Portugal an initial, if limited, concession on the question of abolition. In August 1807 Napoleon had issued an ultimatum to Dom João, the Prince Regent of Portugal, acting on behalf of his demented mother, Queen Maria I: he must close his ports to English ships and thus bring Portugal into the Continental System which was aimed at destroying Britain's trade with Europe, or else face the consequence of a French invasion. By threatening, on the one hand, to destroy the Portuguese fleet in the Tagus and seize Portugal's colonies if he gave way, while promising, on the other, to renew Britain's existing obligations to defend the House of Bragança and its dominions against external attack if he stood firm, Lord Strangford was able to pressure Dom João into rejecting the ultimatum, and when, in November, General Junot marched on Lisbon, the Portuguese royal family and the Portuguese court, escorted by four British warships, sought refuge across the Atlantic in Brazil.[1] In January 1808 Dom João landed briefly at Bahia where he issued his *Carta Régia* opening the ports of Brazil to the trade of all friendly nations (which in practice meant British trade). By March he was safely installed in Rio de Janeiro which, unexpectedly, had become the seat of the Portuguese government and capital of the Portuguese empire. Dom João, however, was now entirely dependent upon British troops and arms for the defence of Portugal against the French and upon the British navy for the protection of Brazil and the rest of Portugal's overseas empire. Thus Britain was in a position to make demands upon Portugal which could not easily be refused. By the secret Convention of October 1807 it had already been established that

---

[1] For the transfer of the Portuguese court from Lisbon to Rio de Janeiro, see Caio de Freitas, *George Canning e o Brasil* (2 vols., Rio de Janeiro, 1958), i. 32–96; Alan K. Manchester, *British Preëminence in Brazil: Its Rise and Decline* (Univ. of North Carolina Press, 1933), pp. 54–68.

in the event of the Portuguese court's moving to Rio de Janeiro the price of British protection would be not only the opening up of Brazil (an important market in itself and a convenient back door to Spanish America) to direct British trade, at a time when British goods were being excluded from Europe and were threatened with exclusion from North America, but also the transfer by treaty of Britain's extensive commercial privileges from Portugal to Brazil.[1] Canning now made it clear that a new Anglo-Portuguese treaty must also include an engagement by Portugal for the 'gradual disuse and ultimate and not distant abolition of the [slave] trade'; in the meantime, he considered that the Portuguese should stop exporting slaves to non-Portuguese territories in the New World and refrain from extending their trade into areas on the African coast which were being abandoned by British traders.[2]

After lengthy negotiations in Rio de Janeiro, Lord Strangford, who had followed the Portuguese court to Brazil, finally persuaded Dom João to sign, on 19 February 1810, two treaties with Britain. The first was a treaty of commerce and navigation, to be renewed after fifteen years, which, amongst the many privileges it con-ferred upon British trade, fixed a maximum tariff of 15% *ad valorem* on British goods entering Brazil (article 9) and allowed the British government to appoint judges conservators, that is, special magistrates who would be responsible for dealing with cases involving British citizens in Brazil (article 10).[3] The second was a treaty of alliance and friendship, the tenth article of which referred to the slave trade: convinced of the 'injustice and dis-utility' of the trade and especially the disadvantages arising from 'introducing and continually renewing a foreign and factitious population' in Brazil, the Prince Regent agreed to co-operate with Britain 'by adopting the most efficacious measures for bringing about the gradual abolition of the slave trade throughout the whole of his dominions', and, in the meantime, undertook that the trade should not be permitted 'on any part of the coast of Africa not actually belonging to His Royal Highness's dominions

---

[1] Caio de Freitas, *op. cit.* i. 45–6.
[2] Canning to Strangford, 17 April 1808, quoted in Bandinel, *op. cit.* p. 127.
[3] For a discussion of the Anglo-Portuguese commercial treaty of 1810, see Manchester, *op. cit.* pp. 86–90; Caio de Freitas, *op. cit.* i. 167–99, 255–88.

8

in which that trade has been discontinued and abandoned by the Powers and States of Europe which formerly traded there'. Portuguese subjects, however, retained the right to trade in slaves 'within the African dominions of the Crown of Portugal', and it was made clear that neither the rights of the Portuguese Crown— which had in the past been in dispute—to the territories of Cabinda and Molembo (5° 12′ to 8° S.) from just north of the mouth of the Congo to the northern boundary of Angola, nor the right of the Portuguese to trade with Ajudá (Dahomey) and other parts of the *Costa da Mina* north of the equator belonging to or claimed by the Portuguese Crown, were in any way invalidated.[1] Thus Portugal had entered into her first obligation to restrict and gradually to abolish the slave trade—and British pressure for its fulfilment would henceforth be unrelenting. For the time being, however, Britain had recognised the right of the Portuguese to continue the trade within their own dominions. In short, the treaty was less than a notable victory for the anti-slave trade cause. Throughout the negotiations, however, Strangford had been faced with stubborn opposition from Dom João and several of his leading ministers to *any* concession on the slave trade question.[2] And it is worth noting that the British government was unable to squeeze even this much out of Spain, which was, like Portugal, dependent upon British support in the struggle against Napoleon, but which, also like Portugal, had colonies in the New World, notably Cuba and, to a lesser extent, Puerto Rico, whose sugar, tobacco and coffee plantations were heavily dependent on imported slave labour.[3]

---

[1] *B.F.S.P.* i. 555–7. A Portuguese *alvará* of 24 November 1813 limited the number of slaves a vessel could carry (5 slaves per 2 tons) and introduced new regulations concerning hygiene, food etc. (Bandinel, *op. cit.* p. 128): 'this traffic', it declared, 'was ignominious and impossible to envisage without horror and indignation, and was carried on in defiance of all natural and divine laws'.

[2] Manuel de Oliveira Lima, *Dom João VI no Brasil, 1808–21* (2nd ed., 3 vols., Rio de Janeiro, 1945), ii. 438. Oliveira Lima quotes from the correspondence of the French consul Maler who reported that Dom João always discussed the slave trade question *com calor*.

[3] For almost three centuries plantation agriculture had been relatively neglected in Spanish Cuba. From the last quarter of the eighteenth century, however, and especially following the disruption by revolution and war of the sugar economy of Santo Domingo, the island had achieved a new level of economic prosperity based on the production and export of sugar, tobacco and coffee and the Cuban slave trade had expanded considerably as a result. For an examination of Britain's relations with Spain over the slave trade

First steps towards abolition, 1807–1822

Whilst the war continued, Britain, in full command of the seas, was able to exert some control over the foreign transatlantic slave trade, although not as much as Lord Grenville, leader of the government which finally abolished the British slave trade, had envisaged. 'Did not the noble and learned Lord see', he had written to Lord Eldon in May 1806, 'that if we gave up the trade it was not possible for any State without our permission to take it up? Did we not ride everywhere unrivalled on the ocean? Could any power pretend to engross this trade, while we commanded from the shores of Africa to the Western extremities of the Atlantic?'[1] In the event it was not possible for the British navy, simultaneously engaged in several theatres of war and never able to spare more than four or five vessels for special anti-slave trade duties, to suppress a trade carried on over so wide an area and on so great a scale. It was, however, at least possible to keep it within acceptable bounds. Not only were enemy colonies—French and Dutch—seized and the importation of slaves considerably reduced, but under Orders in Council issued in March 1808 British warships were able to make full use of the belligerent right of search to identify and capture enemy slave ships and send them as prizes of war for adjudication before a British vice-admiralty court, most frequently that sitting in the Colony of Sierra Leone, which in 1807 had been taken over by the Crown from the bankrupt Sierra Leone Company.[2] For this service bounty or head money at the generous rate of £60 a male, £30 a female and £10 a child was offered for each slave captured and subsequently liberated, although after the flag officer, the governor of Sierra Leone, informers, agents, attorneys—and even Greenwich Hospital—had taken a share, only a small proportion reached the officers and crew of the vessel which had made the capture.[3] For a while the

question during the first half of the nineteenth century, see David Robert Murray, 'Britain, Spain and the slave trade to Cuba, 1807–45' (unpublished Ph.D. thesis, Cambridge, 1967); Arthur F. Corwin, *Spain and the Abolition of Slavery in Cuba, 1817–1886* (Univ. of Texas Press, 1967); H. H. S. Aimes, *A History of Slavery in Cuba, 1511–1868*(New York, 1907); Eric Williams, 'The Negro Slave Trade in Anglo-Spanish Relations', *Caribbean Historical Review*, i (1950), pp. 22–45.
[1] Grenville to Eldon, 16 May 1806, quoted in João Pandiá Calógeras, *A Política Exterior do Império* (2 vols., Rio de Janeiro, 1927–8), i. 371–2.
[2] See E. I. Herrington, 'British Measures for the Suppression of the Slave Trade from the West Coast of Africa, 1807–1833' (unpublished M.A. thesis, London, 1923), chapter 1.
[3] See Christopher Lloyd, *The Navy and the Slave Trade* (London, 1949), pp. 79–80.

British navy also took it upon itself (with doubtful legality) to visit, search and capture slave vessels of all maritime nations—American vessels, for example—which had declared the slave trade illegal.[1] And, for a short period, British naval officers mistakenly interpreted the ambiguous tenth article of the Anglo-Portuguese treaty of February 1810 as meaning that Portuguese slave trading was illegal north of the equator, and that they were therefore entitled to suppress it: several Portuguese slave ships were captured and a number of important commercial houses in Bahia and Pernambuco which had enjoyed particularly close links with the Guinea Coast suffered heavy losses.[2] In 1813, however, the Admiralty issued strict instructions that Portuguese ships sailing between Portuguese ports in Africa and Brazil were not to be molested (leaving the vexed question of which ports in Africa belonged to Portugal unanswered).[3]

During the later stages of the war Sweden and the Netherlands —the latter had been recently liberated from French rule and the restored House of Orange was therefore indebted to Britain— were prevailed upon to sign bilateral conventions with Britain outlawing the slave trade. But Portugal continued to hold out against British demands for immediate and total abolition, and Spain was prepared to do no more than Portugal had done in 1810, that is, to restrict the trade to its own dominions.[4] The British abolitionists were angry at this failure to bring into line friendly but dependent nations like Spain and Portugal: 'It happens quite providentially', William Wilberforce wrote to James Stephen in April 1814, 'that the only powers which are interested in carrying the slave trade on are Spain and Portugal, and they may surely be compelled into assent.'[5] They were also

[1] See Herrington, unpublished thesis, pp. 44 ff.; Hugo Fischer, 'The Suppression of Slavery in International Law', *International Law Quarterly*, iii (1950), pp. 32 ff.

[2] See *Representation of the Brazilian Merchants against the insults offered to the Portuguese flag and against the violent and oppressive capture of several of their vessels by some officers belonging to the English navy* (London, 1813); Strangford to Castlereagh, 20 February 1814, printed in C. K. Webster, ed., *Britain and the Independence of Latin America, 1812–1830. Select Documents from the Foreign Office Archives* (London, 1938), i. 171; Manchester, *op. cit.* p. 168.

[3] See Herrington, unpublished thesis, pp. 76–80.

[4] See Corwin, *op. cit.* p. 25; Bandinel, *op. cit.* pp. 131–2.

[5] Wilberforce to Stephen, 18 April 1814, in R. I. and S. Wilberforce, *Life of William Wilberforce* (London, 1838), iv. 175.

bitterly disappointed with the terms of the first treaty of Paris (30 May 1814). France had been defeated; yet its captured West Indian colonies were now to be returned and, restored to the throne of France, Louis XVIII merely engaged to abolish the trade 'in the course of five years' and in the meantime to confine it to his own dominions. In view of the fact that the French slave trade had been severely curtailed during the war, it seemed as though Britain was actually permitting its revival, albeit temporarily.[1] Lord Castlereagh, however, Britain's Foreign Secretary, preoccupied with the wider political settlement with France, had been content to secure the principle of abolition and an agreement as to a terminal date.

The forthcoming Congress of European states in Vienna seemed to offer the best opportunity so far of Britain's securing a general condemnation and renunciation of the transatlantic slave trade. Wilberforce and his friends, determined that the issue would not be neglected, mounted a propaganda campaign so frenzied that it seemed to the Duke of Wellington, British ambassador in Paris at the time, that 'the people in general appear to think it would suit the policy of the nation to go to war to put an end to that *abominable* traffic, and many wish that we should take the field on this new crusade'.[2] Castlereagh, who himself represented Britain at Vienna and who considered his main task was the re-shaping of Europe and the establishment of a lasting peace, was irritated by this abolitionist pressure. Moreover, it was his personal opinion that it was wrong 'to force it [the abolition of the slave trade] upon nations, at the expense of their honour and of the tranquility of the world. Morals were never well taught by the sword.'[3] However, public opinion at home compelled him to make the slave trade a major issue at the conference and to use both threats and bribes to secure its total abolition, or at least its abolition north of the equator, where it was largely carried on. The three Central Powers—Russia, Austria and Prussia—were ready to co-operate:

---

[1] *B.F.S.P.* i. 172–5; C. K. Webster, *The Foreign Policy of Castlereagh, 1812–15* (London, 1931), pp. 271–2; *Life of Wilberforce*, iv. 187–9; F. J. Klingberg, *The Anti-Slavery Movement in England* (New Haven, 1926), p. 146.

[2] Wellington to Sir Henry Wellesley, his brother, 29 July 1814, quoted in Betty Fladeland, 'Abolitionist Pressures on the Concert of Europe, 1814–1822', *Journal of Modern History*, xxxviii (1966), p. 361.

[3] Quoted in Klingberg, *op. cit.* p. 144.

they had no colonial interests. But Castlereagh had less success in his dealings with the major offenders. He failed to persuade France—no longer a suppliant—to abolish the trade immediately and Spain—no longer dependent—to prohibit the trade north of the equator immediately and south of the line within a maximum period of five years. Both spurned his offers of financial indemnity and colonial territory by way of compensation. Led by the Conde de Palmella, the Portuguese delegation also felt five years afforded them insufficient time to prepare for the abolition of the trade; they apparently offered to abolish it within a period of eight years, but only on condition that Britain gave up the commercial treaty of 1810 and Castlereagh was not empowered to negotiate along these lines.[1] Under considerable pressure, however, with the British army under General Beresford in effective control of Portugal at the end of the Peninsular War while the Portuguese court continued to reside in Brazil, and relying on Britain to defend Portugal's wider interests at Vienna, the Portuguese finally agreed to end the trade north of the equator in return for a substantial financial indemnity. Under a Convention signed on 21 January 1815, Britain agreed to pay the sum of £300,000, thereby discharging all claims in respect of the illegal detention and capture of Portuguese ships by British warships and their condemnation in British vice-admiralty courts before 1 June 1814. Under a separate treaty signed the following day, 22 January 1815, Britain also remitted further payments due on a loan of £600,000 which had been negotiated in 1809 (about half remained to be paid) and Dom João engaged to declare the slave trade north of the equator illegal and to adopt whatever measures were necessary to enforce the partial ban on the trade.[2] This arrangement constituted something of a triumph for Palmella. Only part of the Portuguese slave trade to Brazil—and by this time the less substantial part, that

[1] On the slave trade issue at the Vienna Congress, see Webster, *Castlereagh, 1812–15*, pp. 413–26. Portugal did not *promise* to abolish the slave trade after eight years: cf. Webster, *op. cit.* pp. 459–60, and Manchester, *op. cit.* p. 171, n. 30; see also later correspondence on Portuguese policy at Vienna, e.g. Palmerston to Moncorvo (Portuguese minister in London), 30 April 1836, F.O. 84/202 and Palmerston to Howard de Walden (British minister in Lisbon), no. 13, 20 April, no. 14, 29 April 1839, F.O. 84/281.

[2] B.F.S.P. ii. 348–55; Antônio Pereira Pinto, *Apontamentos para o Direito Internacional; ou Collecção Completa dos Tratados celebrados pelo Brazil com differentes Nações Estrangeiras* (Rio de Janeiro, 1864–69), i. 124–37.

to Bahia, Pernambuco and Maranhão—was carried on from the African coast north of the equator. The treaty expressly permitted Portuguese subjects to transport slaves to Brazil from Portuguese territories in Africa south of the line. Dom João was merely called upon to reiterate his pledge gradually to abolish the entire slave trade throughout his dominions. In doing so he engaged to negotiate separately a further treaty fixing the date by which the trade south of the equator would be prohibited. Two weeks later, on 8 February 1815, Portugal joined with Britain, France, Spain, Sweden, Austria, Prussia and Russia in an Eight Power Declaration that the slave trade was 'repugnant to the principles of humanity and universal morality', that 'the public voice in all civilised countries calls aloud for its prompt suppression', and that all the Powers possessing colonies acknowledged the 'duty and necessity' of abolishing it as soon as practicable. It was, however, agreed that 'the period for universal cessation must be the subject of negotiation between the Powers concerned'.[1] In June 1815 this declaration was annexed to the *Acte Final* of the Congress of Vienna: it was to serve as a basis for the Conferences of European ministers held in London on more than a dozen occasions between 1816 and 1819—'a sort of permanent European Congress'—at which information on the slave trade was collected and means for suppressing it discussed. In the meantime France had joined the ranks of those powers which had agreed completely to abolish the slave trade. In March 1815, during his Hundred Days, Napoleon, hoping to win over British opinion, had decreed the immediate cessation of the French slave trade. In July Louis XVIII was, therefore, obliged to announce that he would do the same: as Lord Liverpool wrote to Castlereagh, 'he owes it to us who will have restored him to his throne a second time'.[2] And in November, after Waterloo, an anti-slave trade article was added to the second treaty of Paris: the Big Five—Britain, Russia, Austria, Prussia *and France*—engaged to concert their efforts for the 'entire and definite abolition' of a trade 'so odious and so strongly condemned by the laws of religion and nature'.[3]

[1] Declaration . . . relative a l'abolition universelle de la traite des nègres, 8 February 1815, *B.F.S.P.* iii, 971–2.
[2] Bandinel, *op. cit.* p. 169; Liverpool to Castlereagh, 7 July 1815, quoted in Fladeland, *op. cit.* p. 366.   [3] *B.F.S.P.* iii. 292–3.

First steps towards abolition, 1807–1822

France, the Netherlands and Sweden, besides Britain, the United States and Denmark, had now prohibited or agreed to prohibit the transatlantic trade in African slaves. Furthermore, many of the revolutionary Spanish American régimes had outlawed the trade or had indicated a willingness to do so.[1] Of the major slaving countries, Spain and Portugal alone clung to their share of the trade, and even Portugal had abolished it north of the equator. Prohibition, however, was by no means synonymous with suppression. Neither treaties nor laws are self-enforcing and, whether from lack of power or lack of purpose (in some cases treaty obligations were no doubt undertaken which it was never intended should be honoured) few governments took the necessary steps to enforce the ban on the trade, which continued to expand in response to the New World's growing demand for slaves. In Brazil, for example, where the opening of the ports in January 1808 had accelerated the process of integration into the international economy and stimulated the production of sugar, cotton and, for the first time on any sizable scale, coffee, the demand for fresh supplies of African slaves was insatiable and the trade continued illegally north of the line (though on a reduced scale) and legally to the south.[2] From Rio de Janeiro, in December 1817, Henry Chamberlain, the British consul-general and *chargé d'affaires* (Strangford had returned home in 1815), wrote of the 'system of doing nothing which characterizes the administration'; he thought that the trade, legal and illegal, would continue and flourish 'until some great pressure either of interest or inconvenience forces the ministry to put a stop to it'.[3]

Britain was prepared to assume the role of international policeman and to add the interception of slave vessels attempting an illegal crossing of the Atlantic to the peacetime duties of the Royal Navy. It seemed, however, that in time of peace, British naval officers were not entitled under customary international law to carry out the preliminary visit and search which were necessary

[1] See J. F. King, 'The Latin American Republics and the Suppression of the Slave Trade', *H.A.H.R.* xxiv (1944), pp. 388–9.
[2] For some estimates of the size of the Brazilian slave trade in the period after 1808, see Edmundo Correia Lopes, *A Escravatura: Subsídios para a sua história* (Lisbon, 1944), pp. 139–47.
[3] Chamberlain to Castlereagh, 24 December 1817, F.O. 63/204.

to discover whether or not ships of other nations were carrying slaves illegally, much less to detain them—even in cases where the trade had been declared illegal by treaty with Britain.[1] This opinion was stated in its classic form in the High Court of Admiralty on 15 December 1817 when Sir William Scott (later Lord Stowell), a leading authority on international maritime law, gave judgement in an appeal case concerning *Le Louis*, a French ship out from Martinique, captured in March 1816 by a British vessel near Sierra Leone, taken before the vice-admiralty court sitting there and subsequently condemned. Scott's famous judgement in which, with great reluctance, he reversed the decision of the Sierra Leone court, was to be quoted frequently both at home and abroad by opponents of Britain's more high-handed anti-slave trade measures during the next fifty years. 'No doubt could exist', he declared,

that this was a French ship intentionally engaged in the slave trade. But these were facts which were ascertained in consequence of its seizure; before the seizer could avail himself of his discovery it was necessary to enquire whether he possessed any right of visitation and search; because if the discovery was unlawfully produced he could not be allowed to take advantage of the consequences of his own wrong ... I can find no authority that gives the right of interruption to the navigation of the states in amity upon the High Seas, excepting that which the rights of war give to both belligerents against neutrals ... if this right of war is to be imported into a state of peace [for the purpose of suppressing the slave trade] it must be done by convention.

France had never assented to the visit, search and capture of French ships engaged in the slave trade by the ships of Britain or any other power. 'To force the way to the liberation of Africa by trampling on the independence of other states in Europe ... to procure an eminent good by means that are unlawful', Scott concluded, 'is as little consonant to private morality as to public justice.'[2]

As leading abolitionists like Lord Brougham had been arguing

[1] See, for example, Robinson (King's Advocate) to Bathurst, 28 June 1816, printed in C. W. Newbury (ed.), *British Policy towards West Africa. Select Documents, 1786–1874* (Oxford, 1965), p. 139.
[2] J. Dodson, *Report of cases argued and determined in the High Court of Admiralty* (London, 1828), ii. 236–64.

for years, if the slave trade were to be effectively suppressed it was necessary not only for Britain to persuade the maritime powers to agree by treaty to its abolition and to enact and enforce anti-slave trade legislation, but also to put teeth into existing and projected anti-slave trade treaties by inserting a limited right of visit and search on the High Seas and by making arrangements for the adjudication of captured vessels and the liberation of the slaves they carried.[1] The right of search question had been raised at Vienna without success. Britain therefore was obliged to fall back upon negotiations for bilateral agreements with the individual powers concerned—a laborious process which added vastly to the work of the Foreign Office and which, combined with the need to furnish information for the London Conferences on the Slave Trade, made necessary the establishment in 1819 of a separate Slave Trade Department. If, however, it had proved, and was still proving, difficult to persuade other states to abolish the trade, it was likely to be even more difficult to persuade them to grant to British warships the right to search any of their merchant vessels suspected of engaging in the trade. For although the right of search could be—and was—dressed up as a mutual right, reciprocity from the outset was bound to be largely a myth: Britain alone had the ships available to patrol the coasts of Africa and America and, in any case, the slave trade was no longer carried on in British merchant vessels. It was, therefore, feared that Castlereagh's plan for 'the vigilant superintendence of an *armed international* police force on the coast of Africa' would in practice mean, in peace-time, the kind of high-handed interference by the British navy with merchant shipping on the High Seas which had been so resented during the war years. Moreover, it was essential that no one state with an interest in the slave trade should be left out of a right of search treaty system. As Castlereagh wrote in February 1818,

the system of obtaining fraudulent papers and concealing the real ownership . . . makes it easy for the subjects of all states to carry on the traffic whilst the trade in slaves remains legal for the subjects of any one state . . . even were the traffic abolished by all states, whilst the flag of one state precludes the visit of all other states the illicit slave

---

[1] E.g. Brougham speeches of 14 June 1810, 9 July 1817, quoted in C. W. New, *Henry Brougham* (London, 1961), pp. 129–30, 140.

trader will always have the means of concealing himself under the disguise of the nation whose cruiser there is no chance of his meeting on the coast.[1]

Slave traders were already in the habit of employing fictitious bills of sale, double sets of papers, alternative flags, fraudulent logbooks etc., to protect where necessary their illegal activities—practices which were to add considerably to Britain's difficulties in attempting to suppress the international slave trade during the next fifty years.

British pressure for a right of search treaty was first brought to bear on Portugal, of all the remaining slave trading powers the one most dependent on Britain and already bound by the second article of the treaty of 22 January 1815 to adopt measures necessary for the suppression of the illegal trade. On 28 July 1817, after *um grande receio e hesitação*, the Conde de Palmella, now Portuguese minister in London, was prevailed upon to sign an Additional Convention to the treaty of 1815.[2] It defined more precisely that part of the Portuguese slave trade which remained legal, that is, the trade carried on in *bona fide* Portuguese vessels between ports within the dominions of the Portuguese Crown south of the equator, and Portuguese territory on the African coast south of the line, namely 'between Cabo Delgado and the Bay of Lourenço Marques' on the east coast and both the areas 5° 12' to 8° S. (Molembo and Cabinda) and 8° to 18° S. on the west. It was then agreed that, outside ports and roadsteads and beyond the cannon-shot of shore batteries, ships of war of either power, furnished with the necessary special warrants, might visit and search merchant vessels of either power suspected on reasonable grounds of having on board slaves which had been shipped from prohibited areas on the African coast (that is, north of the equator) and to detain them if slaves were actually found on board. It was further agreed that a captured ship would be taken for adjudication before one of two

[1] Memorandum, 4 February 1818, Annex to 10th Protocol of London Conferences on the Slave Trade, F.O. 84/2. Cf. Thomas Fowell Buxton, *The African Slave Trade and its Remedy* (2nd ed., London, 1840), p. 209, quoted below, ch. 6, p. 152.

[2] *B.F.S.P.* iv. 85–115 and Pereira Pinto, i. 155–87; Palmella to Conde da Barca, no. 32, 29 July 1817, Reservado, A.H.I. 58/3. A Portuguese *alvará* of 26 January 1818 prohibited the trade north of the equator and laid down severe penalties for illicit trading (Pereira Pinto, i. 398–404; Chamberlain to Canning, no. 85, 23 August 1818, F.O. 63/212).

mixed commissions, one sitting in British territory in west Africa, the other across the Atlantic in Brazil. Each commission was to be composed of a commissary judge and commissioner of arbitration from each nation, and a secretary or registrar appointed by the government in whose territory the commission was situated. The commission would decide—without right of appeal—whether or not a vessel brought before it was a slave ship trading illicitly and legally captured, and would, accordingly, either 'condemn' it as a lawful prize, confiscate it and liberate the slaves it carried, or else 'acquit' it, restore both vessel and slaves to the owners, and order the captors to make good any losses arising from its illegal detention. The mixed commissions, however, were given no jurisdiction over the owners, master or crew of a condemned vessel: individuals were to be handed over to their own authorities for trial and punishment in their own courts and according to their own laws. Portugal undertook to introduce legislation for the punishment of illicit slave trading, agreed to prohibit the importation of slaves into Brazil under any but the Portuguese flag and once again promised—rather half-heartedly—to abolish the trade completely in the not too distant future. By a separate article, signed on 11 September 1817, it was agreed that directly the entire Portuguese slave trade was prohibited, steps would be taken to adapt the Convention to the new cirumstances. In default of any agreed emendation, it would remain in force for fifteen years from the day on which the trade was abolished.[1] Despite the fact that a limited right of search had been secured from Portugal, critics of the Convention could reasonably complain that it would provide 'legalised protection' for the Portuguese slave trade. As Palmella was quick to realise at the time, south of the equator, sheltered by treaty from interference by the British navy, the trade could continue *tranquilamente* until Portugal herself chose to abolish it, while north of the line some little time would elapse before mixed commissions could be set up and even then the activities of British cruisers would be so severely circumscribed by the terms of the Convention that it could well prove to be a deterrent rather than an encouragement to naval enterprise.[2]

[1] *B.F.S.P.* iv. 115–16; Pereira Pinto, i. 187–8.
[2] Palmella to Conde da Barca, 29 July 1817.

First steps towards abolition, 1807–1822

The Anglo-Portuguese Convention of 28 July 1817 was to form the basis for right of search conventions with many other maritime powers. On 23 September 1817, for example, in return for a generous indemnification of £400,000, Spain finally agreed immediately to abolish the slave trade north of the equator, where the greater part of the Cuban trade was carried on and, from May 1820, south of the equator as well; the Spanish government also conceded to British cruisers the right to visit, search and detain ships suspected of illegal slave trading.[1] On 4 May 1818 the Netherlands, which had already prohibited the trade as a result of an earlier treaty with Britain, signed a similar right of search Convention.[2] In 1819 appointments were made to an Anglo-Portuguese mixed commission in Rio de Janeiro, an Anglo-Spanish commission in Havana, an Anglo-Dutch commission in Surinam, and to Anglo-Portuguese, Anglo-Spanish and Anglo-Dutch commissions which the Foreign Office decided should all sit in Freetown, Sierra Leone. By the end of the following year all six mixed commissions were fully operational.[3] With the signing of the first right of search treaties, warrants authorising the search of Portuguese, Spanish and Dutch ships suspected of slaving had been issued by the Admiralty to British warships on all foreign stations, and in November 1819 the west coast of Africa became for the first time a separate naval station comprising a frigate, three sloops and two gun brigs (albeit less than half the number of ships engaged in keeping Napoleon on St Helena), with Sir George Collier as its first commander and as its *raison d'être* the protection of British settlements and legitimate trade and, most important, the suppression of the illegal slave trade.[4] The West African coast was to remain an independent command for the next fifty years, except for the periods 1832–9 and 1857–60 when it was temporarily combined with the Cape station.

---

[1] B.F.S.P. iv. 33–68; Bandinel, *op. cit.* pp. 159–60. For a thorough examination of the negotiations leading to the Anglo-Spanish anti-slave trade treaty of 1817, see Murray, unpublished thesis, pp. 60–116.

[2] B.F.S.P. v. 125–43; Bandinel, *op. cit.* pp. 163–4.

[3] For a general view of the various mixed commissions for the adjudication of captured slave ships, see Leslie Bethell, 'The Mixed Commissions for the Suppression of the Transatlantic Slave Trade in the Nineteenth Century', *Journal of African History*, vii (1966), 79–93.

[4] Lloyd, *op. cit.* pp. 67–8, Appendix D.

First steps towards abolition, 1807–1822

Meanwhile, at the Congress of Aix-la-Chapelle in the autumn of 1818, another opportunity for effecting joint European action against the slave trade had been missed. A proposal by Castlereagh that the Great Powers should jointly agree to concede a limited right of search for the purpose of suppressing the slave trade was defeated largely by French opposition. By way of an alternative he urged a joint declaration that the slave trade be declared piracy: once the trade was regarded as piratical and the trader as *hostis humani generis* by the general law of nations, the warships of any power could search and capture slave ships on the High Seas whatever flag they flew and they could then be condemned in the captor's own tribunals. This was a suggestion originally made at Vienna and again during the London Conferences, but never properly discussed; it made little progress on this occasion. A major difficulty was that, whereas piracy ran contrary to the interests of all civilised nations and was therefore universally condemned, the slave trade was still partially permitted and, indeed, protected—by Portugal, for example. Moreover, to declare the slave trade piracy, it was argued, would be to grant to British cruisers even greater powers to interfere with international commerce.[1] The only result of the Congress so far as the slave trade was concerned was the adoption by the Big Five of a resolution in favour of pressure upon Portugal to fulfil earlier promises, renewed in 1817, to prohibit the trade south as well as north of the line. Of the powers represented at Vienna in 1815, Portugal alone had not yet completely abolished or even set a date for the complete abolition of the slave trade.[2]

On more than one occasion during 1819 Palmella wrote from London to the Portuguese government, which was still resident

[1] From Washington, Stratford Canning pointed out that an international agreement to regard the slave trade as piracy would in fact be less satisfactory from the British point of view than the *right* conceded by treaty to the British navy to search *all* vessels *suspected* of being engaged in the slave trade. In searching for pirates, he argued, 'no particular exercise of the right could be justified but by the fact of the vessel so searched proving to be a pirate. It is evident that the responsibility of the searching officer would be thereby so greatly increased as to make him unwilling to act except in cases of very clear and positive information', Stratford Canning to Canning, 10 March 1823, quoted in H. G. Soulsby, *The Right of Search and the Slave Trade in Anglo-American Relations* (Baltimore, 1933), p. 27.

[2] On the slave trade question at the Congress of Aix-la-Chapelle, see C. K. Webster, *The Foreign Policy of Castlereagh, 1815–22* (London, 1929), pp. 463–4; Fladeland, *op. cit.* pp. 367–9.

21

in Brazil, that the slave trade was now bound to end sooner or later and that Britain appeared ready to adopt any measures, not excluding the use of force, for its early suppression.[1] His warnings, however, went unheeded. Nor was Sir Edward Thornton, British minister to the Portuguese court, able to make any progress. In April 1821, following successful liberal-nationalist revolts in Lisbon and Oporto during the previous August, Dom João, afraid of losing Portugal, was finally prevailed upon to leave Brazil and return home after an absence of thirteen years. But Thornton, who followed him, was no more successful in Lisbon than he had been in Rio de Janeiro in persuading the Portuguese government to prohibit the slave trade south of the equator.

The slave trade question and, in particular, Portugal's refusal to come into line with the other maritime powers was again on the agenda when, in the autumn of 1822, the European powers met at Verona. George Canning, who returned to the Foreign Office in September following Castlereagh's suicide, was anxious that every effort should be made to devise some means of extinguishing 'that scandal of the civilised world', although he was not very hopeful given what he called 'the lowered tone of sentiment throughout Europe upon subjects appealing to the feelings of mankind' and the widespread mistrust of British motives.[2] Once again, as Canning anticipated, France blocked all schemes for collective preventive measures (like, for example, declaring the slave trade piracy) and as at Aix-la-Chapelle all discussion on the slave trade proved fruitless. A British suggestion, originally made at Vienna in 1815, that the exports of slave-trading states, and sugar in particular, should be excluded from the European market—to the obvious advantage of British West Indian sugar—was apparently 'met . . . with a smile'.[3] In the end little was achieved beyond a reaffirmation, on 28 November 1822, of the Vienna Declaration and a promise to take all steps to put down the trade which were compatible with national rights and interests—'vague generalities

---

[1] Oliveira Lima, *op. cit.* ii. 455–6; Goulart, *op. cit.* pp. 238–40.

[2] Canning to Wellington, 30 September 1822, printed in *Despatches, Correspondence and Memoranda of the Duke of Wellington edited by his son* (London, 1867–80), i. 322.

[3] Cabinet memorandum, 15 November 1822, Canning Papers, 131; extracts printed in Webster, *Britain and the Independence of Latin America*, ii. 393–8.

of verbal reprobation', declared the directors of the influential African Institution (founded in Britain in 1807 to promote the 'civilisation' of Africa and, incidentally, the abolition of the foreign slave trade), 'which, as experience teaches, bind them to no specific efficient measure'.[1]

Spurred on by abolitionists at home, the British government not only maintained its diplomatic pressure on Portugal for the final abolition of the trade and on other foreign governments for the enforcement of existing abolition treaties, but also continued to press for the extension and reinforcement of the right of search treaties. From the outset it had been necessary to give assurances that only vessels with slaves on board would be liable to search and capture. In 1818, for example, when an initial approach was made to the United States, which under Article 10 of the treaty of Ghent (1814) had agreed to co-operate with Britain in suppressing the slave trade, Richard Rush, the American minister in London, reported that 'no peculiar structure or previous appearance in the vessel searched; no presence of irons or other presumptions of criminal intention; nothing but the actual finding of slaves on board was ever to authorise a seizure or detention'.[2] As soon became clear, however, the fact that slave ships were free from any interference until the moment they took on slaves constituted the most serious weakness of the right of search treaties. It seemed to the British government that the slave trade would never be suppressed until British cruisers were allowed to detain slave vessels outward as well as homeward bound and they therefore began to press for the addition to the right of search treaties of an 'equipment clause' as a result of which any one or more of a pre-scribed list of 'equipment articles'—shackles and handcuffs, spare planks for a slave deck, open hatches, unusual quantities of fresh water, food, disinfectant etc.—would constitute *prima facie* evidence that a ship setting out for, on its way to or arriving at the African coast was employed in the slave trade and, unless satisfactorily accounted for by the owner or master, the presence of such equipment would constitute sufficient grounds for

[1] 17th Annual Report of the Directors of the African Institution, quoted in Fladeland, *op. cit.* p. 373. On the slave trade question at the Congress of Verona, see Wellington's *Despatches*, i *passim*.
[2] Rush to Adams, 18 April 1818, quoted in Soulsby, *op. cit.* p. 16.

23

condemnation; that is to say, ships would be dealt with as if the act for which they were equipped had already been committed. Few nations, however, were yet prepared to concede to the British navy such an extensive right to interfere with their merchant shipping. In any case, it was argued, was it not unjust to make no distinction between the possible intention of committing a crime and the crime itself? During the years 1822–3 Spain, the Netherlands and Portugal eventually signed additional articles to their anti-slave trade treaties with Britain whereby vessels could be detained if there was 'clear and undeniable proof' that slaves embarked in prohibited areas (that is, north of the equator only in the case of Portugal) had been on board at some time during the ship's voyage. In short, ships could be taken after they had landed their cargoes of slaves. But of the three only the Netherlands, whose flag had already almost disappeared from the trade as a result of the efforts of the Dutch authorities, was prepared to allow the capture of ships which were simply equipped for the trade.[1]

Throughout these years, two of the great maritime nations, France and the United States, both of which had prohibited the slave trade, steadfastly refused to concede to Britain even the limited right to search vessels suspected of actually having slaves on board. As Canning told Wellington in October 1822, on the slave trade question France was 'hostile', the United States 'lukewarm, if not indifferent'.[2] As a result of her experiences during the French Revolutionary Wars and during the War of 1812, when the right of search was abused for the purposes of impressment, the United States had become the most outspoken champion of maritime rights and of the freedom of the seas. Nevertheless, on 13 March 1824, after length negotiations, a convention was signed in London under which Britain and the United States agreed between themselves to regard the slave trade as piracy, even though

---

[1] Anglo-Spanish treaty, 10 December 1822, *B.F.S.P.* xi. 713–14; Anglo-Dutch treaty, 31 December 1822, *B.F.S.P.* x. 554–7; Anglo-Portuguese treaty, 15 March 1823, *B.F.S.P.* xi. 23–6 and Pereira Pinto, i. 191–3; Anglo-Dutch treaty, 25 January 1823, *B.F.S.P.* x. 557–61. In November 1824 Sweden signed a right of search treaty which included an equipment clause. Illegal since 1813, the slave trade was no longer carried on under the Swedish flag and, in the circumstances, it was not felt necessary to establish any Anglo-Swedish mixed commissions.

[2] Canning to Wellington, 10 October 1822, quoted in Fladeland, *op. cit.* p. 372.

it had not yet been declared piracy in international law, thereby making British and American slave ships liable to search and capture by British and American cruisers—although they were to be handed over for adjudication to their own national tribunals. In the United States Senate, however, the question of an anti-slave trade treaty became entangled with the issue of domestic slavery and the Convention of 1824 was never ratified.[1] On the other hand, the United States administration, armed with more stringent anti-slave trade legislation and able temporarily to send a small American naval force to the West African coast, had considerable success in preventing the importation of slaves into the United States despite the growing demand for slaves in the cotton states and, for the time being at least, controlled the use of American ships and the American flag in the foreign slave trade.[2] During the twenties, France, too, passed and enforced more severe anti-slave trade legislation and reduced to a trickle the number of slaves being imported into Martinique and Guadeloupe, although the absence of a right of search treaty with Britain and of a permanent French squadron on the African coast enabled traders of other nations in, for example, the Cuban trade to make use of the French flag.[3]

By the mid-1820s, almost twenty years after the first effective steps had been taken for the abolition of the transatlantic slave trade, few, if any, African slaves were being imported into the British, French and Dutch West Indies, the new Spanish American republics or even the southern United States. There was still, however, an extensive—and entirely illegal—trade from Africa (largely from the West African coast north of the equator) to the Spanish sugar colonies of Cuba and Puerto Rico. On an even greater and expanding scale—for the most part legal and, in spite of the capture of a number of Portuguese slave ships sailing north of the equator by warships of the British West African

---

[1] For Anglo-American anti-slave trade negotiations in this period, see Soulsby, *op. cit.* pp. 15–38; Bandinel, *op. cit.* pp. 176–91.
[2] Peter Duignan and Clarence Clendenen, *The United States and the African Slave Trade, 1619–1862* (Stanford, 1963), pp. 28–30; Warren S. Howard, *American Slavers and the Federal Law, 1837–1862* (Univ. of Calif. Press, 1963), pp. 26–7, 30.
Bandinel, *op. cit.* p. 172; Herrington, unpublished thesis, pp. 151–5.

25

squadron,[1] virtually undisturbed—the trade in slaves continued from Africa (and especially from Portuguese Africa south of the equator) to Brazil, which had in 1822 declared its independence from Portugal.

[1] Two were condemned and 1 released by the Anglo-Portuguese mixed commission sitting in Freetown in 1820; 4 condemned and 1 released in 1821; 2 condemned and 2 released in 1823; 5 condemned in 1824; 4 condemned in 1825. Only one ship—the *Emilia* condemned in August 1821—came before the Anglo-Portuguese mixed commission in Rio de Janeiro during these years; for this case, see Manchester, *op. cit.* pp. 180–3.

CHAPTER 2

INDEPENDENCE AND ABOLITION, 1822–1826

The independence of Brazil was essentially the result of a hopeless attempt by Portugal during the years 1821–2, following Dom João's return to Lisbon after an absence of thirteen years, to put back the clock and reduce Brazil, politically and economically, to its former colonial status. Brazil had progressed too far since the flight of the Portuguese court to Rio de Janeiro in 1807–8 for anything less than complete political and economic equality with the mother country to be any longer acceptable: Brazilian ports had been open to world, and especially British, trade, and the influx of 'new people, new capital, new ideas' had stimulated economic development and modernisation; Brazil had been governed from Rio de Janeiro, not Lisbon—indeed since December 1815 its status had been that of a kingdom equal with Portugal; the development of Brazilian self-consciousness had been considerably accelerated. When, therefore, Portugal proved intransigent in her demand for Brazil's capitulation to Portuguese rule, many Brazilians—and some Portuguese whose roots and interests were now in Brazil—saw no alternative to secession from the Portuguese empire. Left behind in Rio de Janeiro as Prince Regent, Dom João's eldest son, the twenty-four-year-old Dom Pedro, choosing to lead rather than be overwhelmed by the growing movement for independence, threw in his lot with the Brazilians and, when ordered to do so, refused to return to Portugal. 'Fico' ('I remain'), he announced on 9 January 1822. Thereafter, guided in the later stages by the distinguished *paulista* José Bonifácio de Andrada e Silva events moved swiftly towards a complete break with Portugal until finally, on 7 September 1822, on the banks of the Ipiranga near São Paulo, Dom Pedro proclaimed 'Independence or Death'. Once independence had been declared the financial and military weakness of the mother country was such that there was never any question of her being able to reassert her authority over Brazil

27

by force, although a short *Guerra da Independência* was necessary to remove the Portuguese troops and the Portuguese naval squadron stationed at Bahia and to secure the allegiance of Bahia and the northern provinces of Brazil to Dom Pedro in Rio de Janeiro.[1]

Brazil's assertion of her independence from Portugal had far-reaching consequences for the future of the Brazilian slave trade. The Portuguese had repeatedly declared that their transatlantic colonial interests alone made it impracticable to prohibit the trade south of the equator. It was therefore possible to argue, as did George Canning, who became Foreign Secretary just one week after Dom Pedro had announced the separation of Brazil and Portugal, that Portugal's one excuse for not fulfilling her treaty engagements of 1810, 1815 and 1817 (to abolish, at some future date, the entire slave trade) was now 'abolutely and *ipso facto* abrogated and annulled by an event which abolishes altogether the colonial character of the Brazils'. Moreover, Canning could fairly argue that the entire Portuguese transatlantic slave trade had become *de facto* illegal from the moment Brazil and Portugal were separated: transporting slaves to territories outside the Portuguese empire had been prohibited as long ago as 1761; under article 4 of the treaty of 1815, Dom João had specifically engaged not to permit the Portuguese flag to be used in the slave trade except for the purpose of supplying with labour 'the transatlantic possessions belonging to the Crown of Portugal'; and article 1 of the Additional Convention of 1817 had defined as illicit that trade carried on by Portuguese vessels to ports outside the dominions of the Portuguese Crown.[2] The Duc de Palmella, now head of the Portuguese government in Lisbon, seemed disposed to agree with

---

[1] For the independence of Brazil, see John Armitage, *The History of Brazil from the Period of the Arrival of the Braganza Family in 1808 to the Abdication of Dom Pedro the First in 1831* (2 vols., London, 1836); Francisco Adolfo de Varnhagen, 'História da independência do Brasil', *R.I.H.G.B.* 79 (1916), 25–594; Manuel de Oliveira Lima, *O movimento da independência, 1821–1822* (São Paulo, 1922); Tobias do Rego Monteiro, *História do império: A elaboração da independência* (Rio de Janeiro, 1927); João Pandiá Calógeras, *A History of Brazil*, trans. Percy A. Martin (Univ. of North Carolina Press, 1939), pp. 72–83; Alan K. Manchester, 'Paradoxical Pedro—First Emperor of Brazil', *H.A.H.R.* xii (1932), pp. 179–86; *História Geral da Civilização Brasileira*, tomo II, vol. i, *O Brasil Monárquico. O Processo de Emancipação* (São Paulo, 1962).

[2] Canning to Ward (Lisbon), no. 8, 18 October 1822, printed in C. K. Webster, ed., *Britain and the Independence of Latin America, 1812–1830. Select Documents from the Foreign*

Canning: 'the time for pressing for total abolition under the Portuguese flag', he told Edward Ward, the British *chargé*, privately, in July 1823, 'may perhaps soon arrive', and in the following March he agreed with Sir Edward Thornton, the British minister, that 'Portugal could have no interest in it [the slave trade] in the case of the independence of Brazil'.[1] But since to acknowledge that the Portuguese slave trade was in fact abolished under the terms of the existing treaties would be to imply that they recognised the independence of Brazil, the Portuguese government felt that any such agreement would at that stage be premature. So far as Canning was concerned, however, the point had been gained: the trade to Brazil carried on by Portuguese merchants in Portuguese vessels was at last illegal south as well as north of the equator. Moreover, he maintained that the Royal Navy had the right to suppress it since article II of the treaty of 1815 expressly exempted from British interference those Portuguese ships trading with Portuguese dominions south of the line *only so long as the trade was permitted by law and treaty.*

Thus, so far as the abolition of the Brazilian slave trade was concerned, the independence of Brazil seemed to constitute a valuable step forward. But did it, at least in the short run, also mean two steps back? Britain was now confronted with a new state which was possibly more deeply involved in the trade than any other—Brazil was certainly the greatest remaining importer of African slaves—and which had no commitment of any kind to abolish it. Native Brazilians and Portuguese assuming Brazilian nationality would be able legally to trade in slaves to Brazil—even north of the equator—without the slightest fear of interference from the Brazilian authorities or from the British Navy. The Portuguese flag might soon be driven out of the trade, but Portuguese traders, and indeed the traders of all nationalities, would no doubt take advantage of the new Brazilian flag, where necessary,

Office Archives (London, 1938), ii. 234–5. See also Canning to Wellington, 15 October, printed in Wellington's *Despatches*, i. 358; Canning to Wilberforce, 19 October, 24 October, Canning Papers, 80*a*. Instructions to cruisers concerning slave ships flying the Portuguese flag should not be delayed long after Wellington had reported from Verona on the slave trade question, Canning told Bathurst, Secretary for War and Colonies, 6 December 1822, Canning Papers, 106.

[1] Ward to Canning, 20 July 1823, Private, Canning Papers, 132; Thornton to Canning, 8 March 1824, F.O. 63/285; see also Bandinel, *Some account of the trade in slaves*, pp. 157–8.

to avoid search and capture by British warships. If all Britain's diplomatic efforts since 1807 were not to be nullified, it was essential that Brazil should be persuaded to prohibit the trade and to sign an anti-slave trade treaty with Britain. Canning was fully aware that, under normal circumstances, negotiations with Brazil for the abolition of the slave trade might well be protracted and ultimately fruitless: Portugal had held out for fifteen years against British persuasion and threats because the trade served her *colonial* interests; Brazil, for whom the trade was an integral part of her *domestic* economy, was likely to prove even more intransigent. But just as Britain had squeezed anti-slave trade agreements, however limited in their scope, from a reluctant Portugal as the price for British support during the war and immediate post-war years, so Britain's pre-eminence in Europe and the world at large, and her influence over Portugal in particular, now appeared to present her with an opportunity to wring concessions from an even more reluctant Brazil. The new Brazilian government would be anxious to secure international recognition of Brazil's independence and this, Canning immediately realised, would 'put Brazil at our mercy as to the continuance of the slave trade'; Brazil was now in the position of having to 'solicit from other nations a recognition to which may be annexed what conditions those nations may think fit, and specifically, a renunciation of the slave trade'.[1]

Despite the view deeply held by King George IV and many ultra-Tory members of the Cabinet that the principle of legitimacy should not be violated by any over-hasty recognition of revolutionary régimes in the New World, the British government was moving slowly in the direction of recognising several of the new Spanish American republics—those at least whose *de facto* independence from Spain was now beyond question and with whom Britain had close commercial ties. Recognition was, as Castlereagh had said shortly before his death, only 'a matter of time, not principle'. Canning was even more sympathetic than his predecessor towards a policy of recognising the independent American states—which now included Brazil.[2] Nevertheless he

[1] Canning to Wellington, 15 October 1822, two separate despatches printed in Wellington's *Despatches*, i. 355, 358.
[2] On the policies of Castlereagh and Canning towards Latin American independence in general, see Webster, *Britain and the Independence of Latin America*, i. intro.

instructed the Duke of Wellington, who led the British delegation at Verona, to assure the Allied Powers that 'no state in the New World will be recognised by Great Britain which has not frankly and completely abolished the trade in slaves'.[1] Most of the new Spanish American states, whose interest in the slave trade had been relatively small, had long ago demonstrated their willingness to abolish it—and this was one more argument in favour of recognising them.[2] Brazil had not yet done so. As early as 30 September 1822, Canning wrote to Wellington, 'it is needless to observe that . . . recognition [of Brazil] can only be purchased by a frank surrender of the slave trade'.[3] A month later he told William Wilberforce, who had been in the habit of corresponding regularly with Lord Castlereagh on slave trade matters and who had now transferred his attention to Castlereagh's successor, that he anticipated receiving any day an application from Brazil for the acknowledgment of its independence. 'Shall we be justified', he wondered, 'in making the abolition of the slave trade a *sine qua non* condition of any such acknowledgment?', and concluded, 'I incline to think so', although in view of Britain's commercial interests in Brazil he felt it would be necessary to proceed 'with caution and good heed' and satisfy 'the commercial as well as the moral feelings of the country'. Pressed by Wilberforce to clarify his position, Canning was inclined to agree with him that Brazil (regarded by Wilberforce as 'the very child and champion of the slave trade, nay the slave trade personified') should be 'purged from its impurity before we take it into our embraces'; possibly anticipating pressure from commercial circles for unconditional recognition, however, he was prepared to give by way of an assurance to Wilberforce no more than a promise that 'the slave trade shall not be *established* by a new compact even if it cannot be

---

[1] Canning to Wellington, no. 4, 27 September 1822, printed in Webster, ii. 74; quoted in King, *H.A.H.R.* (1944), p. 391.

[2] When in 1823 Canning finally sent out consuls and commissioners to look into the ripeness of various Spanish American states for recognition, along with questions as to a new state's *de facto* independence he always asked, 'has it abjured and abolished the slave trade?' (Instructions, 10 October 1823, printed in Webster, i. 433). The first three states with whom Britain signed reciprocal commercial treaties comprising recognition—Buenos Aires (February 1825), Colombia (April 1825) and Mexico (December 1826)—had all done so; standard anti-slave trade articles were incorporated into the treaties. See King, *H.A.H.R.* (1944), pp. 391–3.

[3] Canning to Wellington, 30 September 1822, printed in Wellington's *Despatches*, i. 329.

extinguished by one', that is to say, an independent Brazil would, at the very least, have to agree to accept the restrictions imposed on the trade by the anti-slave trade treaties contracted by Portugal when the Portuguese court was resident in Rio de Janeiro.[1]

At the beginning of November, Canning was approached by a Brazilian agent, General Felisberto Caldeira Brant Pontes (the future Marquês de Barbacena), who had been in London since June 1821 furthering the interests of the Prince Regent, Dom Pedro. Brant had recently received instructions, dated 12 August 1822, to enter into negotiations for the recognition of Dom Pedro's separate authority.[2] Through the good offices of Baron de Neumann, the Austrian *chargé d'affaires*, General Brant, *acting as a private individual*, arranged a meeting with Canning for Friday, 8 November, at which he emphasised the mutual benefits to be derived from early recognition by Britain of Brazil's independence. Although displaying a great interest in what Brant had to say, Canning made it clear that he was not free to act as he wished in the matter: as was the case with the new Spanish-American republics, both King and Cabinet would have to be consulted and the reaction of Britain's ancient ally Portugal, as well as other European powers, would require careful consideration. There was a further obstacle, Canning added: Brazil's involvement in the slave trade. Now Brant was personally opposed to the slave trade and the slave system on economic and social as well as on moral grounds and several months earlier had suggested to José Bonifácio de Andrada e Silva that an offer to abolish the trade within a fixed period (he had in mind four years) could prove immensely helpful: Britain would almost certainly be prepared to pay a substantial indemnity, he thought, and might even facilitate the admission of Brazilian sugar into the British home market; besides, the Brazilian government could conveniently allow the odium for a measure as unpopular as abolition to fall upon the English.[3] It now

[1] Canning to Wilberforce, 24 October 1822, printed in *Correspondence of William Wilberforce*, ed. by R. I. and S. Wilberforce (2 vols., London, 1840), ii. 466; Wilberforce to Canning, 25 October 1822, Canning Papers, 80*a*; Canning to Wilberforce, 31 October 1822, printed in Wellington's *Despatches*, i. 474.

[2] 12 August 1822, Instructions, *A.D.I.* i. 9. See Caio de Freitas, *George Canning e o Brasil*, i. 338–40, 344–6. The instructions followed Dom Pedro's manifesto of 6 August, printed in Wellington's *Despatches*, i. 439–48.

[3] Brant to José Bonifácio, 6 May 1822, printed in *Publicações do Arquivo Nacional*, vii (1907), pp. 245–6.

seemed from his discussions with Canning that abolition would also facilitate early British recognition. Brant, however, had still not received instructions on this point and contented himself with the observation that in his opinion neither Dom Pedro nor José Bonifácio, in contrast with the majority of Brazilians, wished to see the slave trade continue and they might well be prepared to abolish it entirely *in return for recognition.* Directly he made this suggestion, Brant reported, Canning's attitude changed completely—the complete and immediate abolition of the trade was, after all, more than he had dared hope for—and he asked Brant to put his request for recognition in writing immediately.[1] Brant did so on the following day (9 November), including in his list of reasons why Britain should consider recognition the fact that the Brazilians 'finding themselves honoured and favoured by His Britannic Majesty in their hour of need . . . would look for every means of showing their appreciation and none would be so proper as the abolition of the slave trade'. At any other time, Brant continued, abolition would be impossible, but 'under present circumstances it will perhaps be easy with slight modifications (*com ligeiras modificações*)'; popular resistance to the measure would presumably be weakened 'from motives of gratitude' if Brazil were to obtain immediately the recognition of her independence.[2] Canning and Brant met again on the following Thursday (14 November) when, according to the latter, Canning said that if Brant could guarantee that Dom Pedro would abolish the slave trade in return for recognition he could almost promise (*quasi posso afirmar*) that Britain would immediately recognise Brazil. Brant, however, was obliged to say that he was not in a position to guarantee anything, although he was prepared to wager that if immediate recognition were forthcoming, and especially if Britain would also agree to the admission of Brazilian sugar, the slave trade would cease entirely *within four years.*[3] A second letter setting out his views on the recognition question (in terms almost identical with those of 9 November) was submitted to Canning

---

[1] Brant to José Bonifácio, 12 November 1822, *A.D.I.* i. 198–9; also Hipólito José da Costa to José Bonifácio, no. 3, 12 November 1822, *A.D.I.* i. 203–5.
[2] Brant to Canning, 9 November, enclosed in Brant to José Bonifácio, 12 November 1822, *A.D.I.* i. 200–3.
[3] Brant to José Bonifácio, 16 November 1822, *A.D.I.* i. 208–9.

after the meeting.[1] Yet another meeting was held on the following Saturday (16 November) at which Canning again insisted on linking recognition with the ending of the slave trade. But Brant asserted that recognition must be unconditional, although he still believed that *in return* the slave trade would almost certainly be brought to an end within four years.[2]

At each of these meetings Canning had emphasised that he was expressing his own, private views to, so far as he was concerned, a private individual. In the meantime, however, he had decided to bring the matter before the Cabinet. Brant's overtures seemed to provide a remarkable, indeed unique, opportunity for securing the complete abolition of the Brazilian slave trade. And this possibility, together with the continued existence of the monarchy in Brazil, should, Canning felt, help reconcile the more reactionary members of the Tory Cabinet to immediate recognition of Portugal's former colony, which in turn would facilitate the early recognition of the more stable of the Spanish American republics —another of Canning's objectives. He wrote to Lord Liverpool, the Prime Minister, that Brant's letter of 14 November was 'one of the best for its purpose that I ever read'.[3] On 15 November a long memorandum was circulated to the members of the Cabinet on the need for British recognition of certain states in the New World. In respect of Brazil, as in the case of the Spanish American republics, commercial considerations were given some prominence. But was there not, Canning asked, 'a more direct and powerful motive for wishing to be able to recognise Brazil?'—to secure in return the abolition of the slave trade. 'The one great question which hangs about the neck of this country is that of the slave trade. The great mart of the legal slave trade is Brazil. The continuance of that legal slave trade is the cover and pretext for all the slave trade that is carried on illegally and in violation of treaty as well as law.' The Duke of Wellington's not unexpected failure at Verona to secure agreement on joint action by the Great Powers against the trade served to underline the fact that 'the voluntary

---

[1] Brant to Canning, 14 November, enclosed in *ibid*. Also printed (in English) in Wellington's *Despatches*, i. 573–5 (in full) and Webster, ii. 393 (extracts).
[2] Brant to José Bonifácio, 17 November 1822, *A.D.I.* i. 209.
[3] Canning to Liverpool, 16 November 1822, Canning Papers, 70. Also Canning to Liverpool, 18 November, *ibid*.

relinquishment of the slave trade by Brazil is the single chance for its final and total abolition'. Brant's overtures, Canning went on, suggested that it might be possible to end the Brazilian trade in return for recognition of Brazilian independence, provided they took action at once. If Britain did nothing, Canning added, they might miss irrevocably

an opportunity of effecting the greatest moral good of which human society is now susceptible, of getting rid of the most perplexing discussion with which the Councils of this country are embarrassed and finally of saving from utter ruin our own West Indian Colonies. For *them*, assuredly, there is no prospect of being saved, but through the general abolition of the slave trade and the slave trade can be abolished only through Brazil.

He therefore proposed that, directly Brant received full powers, he (Canning) should be given authority to negotiate a treaty on the basis of 'an acknowledgment on our part (properly qualified with respect to the rights of the King of Portugal) of the separate and independent Government of Brazil; and of an engagement on the part of the Prince Regent of Brazil to abolish absolutely and totally (at a time to be specified) the Brazilian Slave Trade'.[1]

A few days later, in the belief that Canning was anxious to recognise Brazil and was satisfied with the assurances he had been given on the slave trade question, Brant let it be known that he was in fact empowered to sign a treaty by which Britain would recognise Brazil. Canning at once invited him to call at the Foreign Office on Tuesday, 19 November, immediately prior to a Cabinet meeting called to discuss this very question.[2] On this occasion Lord Liverpool also joined in the discussions and, according to Brant, both Canning and Liverpool again insisted that British recognition of Brazil and mediation with Portugal (for the suspension of all schemes for an expedition against Brazil and the withdrawal of all existing Portuguese troops) must be closely tied to abolition within a very short time (*dentro em mui curto prazo*). When Brant replied that he had no authority to enter

---

[1] 15 November 1822, Cabinet Memorandum, Canning Papers, 131. Extracts printed in Webster, ii. 393–8. See also Caio de Freitas, *op. cit.* i. 349–52.

[2] Canning to Liverpool, 18 November 1822, Canning Papers, 70; Hipólito to José Bonifácio, no. 5, 18 November 1822, *A.D.I.* i. 212–13.

into any agreement along such lines, Lord Liverpool apparently invited him to follow the normal procedure of signing a provisional agreement *sub spe rati*. Still Brant hesitated, with the result that the British ministers declared that nothing further could be achieved and the question would now have to be transferred to Rio de Janeiro.[1]

For more than a week Brant remained in a torment of indecision, lamenting the fact that he had received no clear instructions, despite his having first warned José Bonifácio more than six months before that the slave trade might become a major issue in the negotiations with Britain. He seemed to have been presented with an excellent opportunity of securing a definite commitment by Britain to recognise Brazilian independence, but an equally definite commitment by Brazil in respect of the abolition of the slave trade was clearly a *sine qua non* of this; whatever he decided to do he risked being accused either of retarding recognition or of compromising the Brazilian government on a very delicate issue. After consulting Hipólito José da Costa, editor of the *Correio Brasiliense* (a Portuguese language newspaper published in London since 1808) and well known as an abolitionist, who had also been instructed to act on behalf of the Prince Regent, on 28 November Brant decided to accept the British proposal for an agreement to be signed *sub spe rati*: it could always, he decided, be rejected by Dom Pedro if he thought fit. Canning, however, now announced that he was waiting for a response to a recent despatch to Lisbon— which Brant and Hipólito took to mean that Canning had decided, after all, to delay recognition in deference to Portugal.[2] In fact the contrary was true: on 21 November, two days after the Cabinet had discussed the issue, Canning had instructed Edward Ward in Lisbon to explain to the Portuguese government that, while no engagement of any kind had yet been contracted with the Brazilian government, circumstances had arisen which might make it expedient for Britain 'to acknowledge more or less formally the

[1] Brant to José Bonifácio, 20–30 November 1822, *A.D.I.* i. 216–21; Hipólito to José Bonifácio, no. 6, 30 November 1822, *A.D.I.* i. 213–16. There was clearly some confusion over what the British ministers were demanding. Whereas Brant recalled that they had asked for abolition *dentro em mui curto prazo* Hipólito in his despatch referred to abolition *dentro em dous anos* and, at another point, *dentro um ano*.
[2] Brant to José Bonifácio, 20–30 November 1822; Hipólito no. 6; Hipólito to Brant, 21 November 1822, enclosed in Hipólito no. 6.

de facto establishment of the new Brazilian Government'; it was to be understood, however, that this should in no way be taken to mean that the British government was relinquishing its equal and impartial interest in, and desire to maintain friendly relations with, both kingdoms, nor that this precluded an amicable adjustment between the two nations which would preserve the crowns of both kingdoms for the House of Bragança.[1] At the end of November, however, news arrived that on 12 October Dom Pedro had been proclaimed Emperor of Brazil, a title with popular, Napoleonic, overtones which suggested a protest against the principle of legitimacy and an assertion of superiority over the King of Portugal, and which, moreover, seemed inconsistent with Dom Pedro's earlier declaration that he intended to conserve the monarchy in Brazil. In the light of this news, Canning felt compelled to declare a 'pause' in his discussions with Brant until he had had a chance to study the real intention and meaning of the proclamation and its effect upon the internal situation in Brazil, upon the attitude of Portugal and of the other European powers, and upon the ultra-Tories in the Cabinet who, while not rejecting out of hand the idea of early recognition, had no doubt already warned Canning to move with caution. When, early in the new year, Canning had once again satisfied himself that the new order in Brazil was well established and accepted by the overwhelming majority of the people, he agreed to pick up the threads of the negotiations with General Brant—only to discover that Brant had received no further instructions on the slave trade question and, indeed, that as a result of the political changes that had taken place in Brazil since August there was now some doubt concerning his credentials as Brazilian agent in London.[2] Canning therefore went ahead with the proposal for transferring the talks to Rio de Janeiro where, following the return of the Portuguese court to Lisbon, Britain was represented by her consul-general, Henry Chamberlain, whom Canning regarded as 'a sort of *chargé d'affaires*'.

On 15 February 1823, Chamberlain was instructed by Canning

---

[1] Canning to Ward, no. 14, 21 November 1822, printed in Webster, ii. 235–6.
[2] Hipólito no. 7, 15 December 1822, *A.D.I.* i. 223–4; Brant no. 8, 15 January 1823, *A.D.I.* i. 234–7; Canning to Chamberlain (Rio), no. 5, 15 February 1823, Secret, printed in Webster, i. 220–1. See also Brant no. 30, 6 May, no. 36, 1 June, no. 42, 1 July 1823, *A.D.I.* i. 252, 264, 271.

to inform the Brazilian government that recognition would be 'principally a question of time' were it not for 'one consideration which was clearly stated to General Brant as a governing consideration in British policy'—the abolition of the slave trade. Britain was not prepared to recognise a state 'distinguished from all other states in the vast extent of the New World by its solitary adherence to the slave trade'. Canning then went on, 'Let the Brazilian Government announce to us their renunciation [of the trade] and M. de Andrada may depend upon it, that single and sole condition will decide the disposition of this country and greatly facilitate the establishment of a cordial amity and intercourse between Great Britain and Brazil.' Chamberlain was authorised to tell José Bonifácio—in confidence—that 'if the Recognition of the New Empire by Great Britain be an object of interest to his Sovereign, you are persuaded that he may best find his way to it through an offer on the part of Brazil to consent to a renunciation of the slave trade'.[1] In this, the first *official* statement of his views on the subject of recognition and abolition, Canning was far less willing to commit himself and far more ambiguous than he had been three months earlier in the talks he had had with Brant (if Brant's own reports are to be believed). Was Canning now officially offering to recognise Brazil in return for abolition? Or was he saying nothing more than that abolition was a necessary preliminary step, a *sine qua non*, of recognition? It seems on the face of it as though, using recognition as bait, Canning was fishing for a prior commitment by Brazil to abolish the slave trade whilst carefully avoiding any firm promise that recognition would follow, at any rate immediately. On the other hand, it is interesting to note that he told Lord Liverpool that he had instructed Chamberlain to suggest to Andrada that he submit to Britain 'a treaty . . . on the basis of an abolition'. And he went on to suggest that they might usefully employ the services of Lord Amherst who would soon be calling at Rio de Janeiro *en route* for India, where he was to take up the post of governor-general. Amherst's visit, Canning felt, would provide an additional opportunity to urge upon Dom Pedro personally and upon the Brazilian government 'the project we had so nearly concluded with Brandt (*sic*)' without

[1] Canning no. 5, Secret.

exciting any attention in London.[1] Lord Liverpool agreed that it was an opportunity not to be lost.[2] In the event, however, perhaps because he still lacked confidence that the Cabinet would fully support his actions, Canning's instructions to Amherst were even more ambiguous than his instructions to Chamberlain had been. He was to make it absolutely clear in Rio de Janeiro that all future Anglo-Brazilian relations turned on the question of abolition: 'the whole difference as to the manner in which a close connection with the new government of Brazil would be viewed in this country depends upon the single consideration, whether that government shall or shall not have proclaimed the abolition of the slave trade'. He was to exploit the insecurity of the new state and its anxiety to secure British favours, making it known that if Brazil were to agree to abolish the trade immediately Britain would do all in her power to ensure that a satisfactory settlement with Portugal was reached and that the independence of Brazil was generally recognised ('that sacrifice once frankly offered, all arrangements will be comparatively easy'). Moreover, when the commercial treaty of 1810 came up for revision in two years' time, Britain might feel disposed to its revision 'on principles less disadvantageous to Brazilian commerce'. The Brazilian government should therefore send full powers to their agent in London to enter into 'an arrangement, of which the renunciation of the slave trade shall be the first condition: and in all other conditions of which it will be the earnest desire of Great Britain to consult, on principles of fair reciprocity, the welfare and prosperity of both nations'.[3] Should the Brazilian government prove obstinate, Amherst was told to avoid any suggestion of menace or intimidation, but nevertheless to warn them of the consequences of refusal: 'an object so desirable should be brought about rather by the voluntary act of the Brazilian Government *and in anticipation of the wish of Great Britain*, than that the question of obtaining the concession from her *by other means* should ever become a matter of joint deliberation with the cabinets of Europe' (my italics).[4]

---

[1] Canning to Liverpool, 17 February 1823, Secret, Canning Papers, 70.
[2] Canning to Amherst, 18 February 1823, Canning Papers, 80.
[3] Canning to Amherst, no. 1, 28 February 1823, Conf., F.O. 84/24.
[4] Canning to Amherst, no. 2, 28 February 1823, F.O. 84/24. I have examined in some detail the question of whether or not in 1822–3 Canning made a direct offer of immediate

Independence and abolition, 1822-1826

At the beginning of 1823, the Brazilian Emperor, Dom Pedro, and his leading minister, José Bonifácio, were faced with a major dilemma. They were well aware of the urgent need to gain recognition of Brazil's independence, both as a means of averting any attempt by Portugal, encouraged and possibly assisted by the Holy Alliance Powers, to reassert her authority, and of avoiding internal instability and disintegration (there were separatist and republican as well as loyalist elements in the north and south of the country). Failure to establish the Emperor's authority beyond all possible doubt could have grave political consequences for Brazil. Prompt recognition by, and support from, Britain, whose navy commanded the Atlantic, whose capital and commerce sustained the new Empire, and who moreover exercised great influence in Lisbon, would clearly be decisive. As Brant was to write from London in July, 'With England's friendship we can snap our fingers at the rest of the world . . . it will not be necessary to go begging for recognition from any other power for all will wish our friendship.'[1] On the basis of Brant's earlier despatches, Dom Pedro and José Bonifácio had formed the clear impression that the British government had offered to recognise Brazil *immediately*—but only if the Brazilian government at the same time agreed to abolish the slave trade. Since there was a distinct possibility that Britain would forcibly suppress the trade if Brazilian co-operation were not forthcoming, they reasoned, might it not be expedient to agree to British demands and thereby secure positive benefits in return?

As Brant had indicated in his discussions with Canning in London, both José Bonifácio and Dom Pedro personally abhorred the institution of slavery and were far more favourably disposed towards the abolition of the trade which sustained it than any Portuguese government had been. For José Bonifácio and indeed for other leading figures of the 'Generation of Independence', influenced by the liberal and humanitarian ideas of the European Enlightenment and by the theories of classical economists, slavery

recognition of Brazil's independence in return for the abolition of the slave trade by Brazil because in the past it has been a matter of some little controversy: see, for example, Manchester, *British Preeminence in Brazil*, pp. 211, 213; Manchester, 'The Rise of the Brazilian Aristocracy', *H.A.H.R.* xi (1931), pp. 141-5; Calógeras, *A Política Exterior do Império*, i. 346; Antônio Augusto de Aguiar, *A Vida do Marquez de Barbacena* (Rio de Janeiro, 1896), p. 37; Webster, *Britain and the Independence of Latin America*, i. 58.

[1] Brant to José Bonifácio, 5 July 1823, quoted in Manchester, *British Preëminence*, p. 193.

40

had lost both its moral and its economic *raison d'être*. Not only did they regard it as an affront to Natural Law and Human Rights, but in the long run the slave system (the 'canker of the state' and the 'gangrene of our prosperity', José Bonifácio called it) was now thought to be less productive than a system based on free labour. Moreover, as events in Santo Domingo had amply demonstrated (and their impact throughout the slave-owning world cannot be exaggerated), the existence in any society of large numbers of African slaves posed a serious threat to internal security; in the view of José Bonifácio, 'their [the white population's] safety as well as their interests require that the number [of slaves] should not be increased'. Finally, Brazil's new leaders, like their counterparts in the United States fifty years earlier, found it difficult to reconcile, on the one hand, liberty and independence with, on the other, a neo-colonial economic and social system based on slavery and the slave trade. Brazilian independence, however, had been won relatively peacefully (in contrast with Spanish America) without any economic or social dislocation, and Brazil's system of large-scale plantations producing sugar, cotton, tobacco, coffee and other tropical produce for the international market and wholly dependent on slave labour, had never been more firmly established nor more central to the Brazilian economy as a whole. The population of Brazil now numbered almost 4 million, between a quarter and a third of whom were slaves—three-quarters of them concentrated in Bahia, Minas Gerais, Rio de Janeiro (province and capital), Pernambuco, Maranhão and Espírito Santo.[1] Apart from its role in supplying labour for future economic expansion, the transatlantic slave trade was essential, as it had always been, as the only means of replenishing the existing slave population (the annual importation of slaves into Brazil had risen from 15,000–20,000 at the beginning of the century to 30,000 by the early twenties[2]). 'The annual mortality on many sugar plantations is so great', wrote Charles Pennell, the British consul in Bahia, in 1827,

---

[1] Stanley J. Stein, *Vassouras. A Brazilian Coffee County, 1850–1900* (Harvard Univ. Press, 1957), p. 295: Free and slave population of Brazil by province, 1823 and 1872.

[2] In his book *Notices of Brazil in 1828 and 1829* (2 vols., London, 1830), ii. 322, the Rev. R. Walsh gives the following figures for landings of slaves in the area of Rio de Janeiro: 1822, 27,363; 1823, 20,349; 1824, 29,503; 1825, 26,254. The following estimates of slaves landed during the years 1822–5 are taken from the quarterly returns sent to the Foreign Office by British consuls in Brazil. Rio de Janeiro: 1822, 28,246; 1823, 18,922;

'that unless their numbers were augmented from abroad the whole slave population would become extinct in the course of about twenty years; the proprietors act on the calculation that it is cheaper to buy male slaves than to rear Negro children.'[1] Until it became possible to recruit free European immigrants in large numbers—'the poor, the wretched, the industrious of Europe', as José Bonifácio called them—Brazilian agriculture had no alternative source of labour. Few Brazilians, even amongst those of enlightened views, believed that the immediate abolition of the slave trade could be other than an economic disaster and, since a large proportion of government revenue came from import duties on slaves and export duties on slave produce, a financial disaster as well. Moreover, the Brazilian *fazendeiros*, the majority of whom, Henry Chamberlain believed, now recognised that it would be impossible to continue the trade indefinitely but who anticipated that it would last for at least another ten or twenty years,[2] could be expected to resist strongly any move towards abolition in the immediate future. Earlier limited concessions to Britain under the treaties of 1810, 1815 and 1817, which the Portuguese court temporarily resident in Brazil had made in return for British support for Portuguese interests in Europe, had been at the expense of Brazilian interests and had been deeply resented by the Brazilian landowners, especially in the north-east, which was most directly affected by the prohibition of trading north of the equator. Indeed, it could be argued that one important reason why the Brazilian landowners and slaveholders had given their support to an independent monarchy in Brazil was precisely because they saw independence as a means of escaping from Britain's unrelenting pressure on Portugal for the complete and immediate abolition of the slave trade. It was in the light of such considerations that Dom Pedro and José Bonifácio calculated that the political dangers which were likely to arise from premature abolition would be even greater than those that might result

1824, 26,712; 1825, 25,769. Bahia: 1822, 7,656; 1823, 2,672; 1824, 3,137; 1825, 3,840. Smaller numbers of slaves were also landed in Pernambuco and Maranhão, but the figures are incomplete. See also Affonso de E. Taunay, *Subsídios para a história do tráfico africano no Brasil* (São Paulo, 1941), pp. 275–6.
[1] Pennell to Canning, 9 January 1827, F.O. 84/71.
[2] Chamberlain to Canning, no. 55, 26 April 1823, Secret, F.O. 63/259.

from non-recognition: they would find themselves opposed by the most powerful economic interests in the country and, whereas they might resist the pressure exerted by the traders (most of whom were Portuguese), to alienate the great Brazilian plantation owners could endanger the stability and perhaps the very existence of the new régime.

In February 1823, in reply to his repeated requests for clear instructions, José Bonifácio had finally told Brant in London that no decision could be taken on the slave trade question until the Constituent Assembly had met, although for their part the government were in favour of gradual abolition *em tempo razoável proporcionado a falta de braços*.[1] (José Bonifácio himself was in the process of preparing a remarkable memorial to be presented to the Assembly in which he advocated not only the gradual abolition of the slave trade within a period of four or five years, but also the abolition of the slave system itself 'by slow degree' and large scale immigration from Europe to meet Brazil's demand for labour.[2]) At the same time José Bonifácio had informed Chamberlain that the Brazilian government would make every effort to end the trade 'at the earliest possible period consistent with the state of the country and the prejudiced feelings and opinions of its inhabitants'—a period he optimistically put at five or six years—but had emphasised that there was no prospect of immediate action.[3] In an interview with José Bonifácio on 17 April, the day the Constituent Assembly met for the first time, Chamberlain reported the contents of Canning's important despatch of 15 February which set out his views on abolition and recognition. While not explicitly offering recognition in exchange for abolition (his instructions did not warrant this), Chamberlain did express his personal belief that 'the renunciation of this trade on the part of Brazil would secure the recognition of the New Empire by Great Britain'. Abolition should come first, he explained, simply in order that it might have the appearance of a voluntary act performed by Brazil in the furtherance of its own interests and inspired by humanitarian feelings, rather than a forced bargain,

[1] José Bonifácio to Brant, 24 February 1823, *A.D.I.* i. 24 and Pereira Pinto, i. 312.
[2] *Representação a Assembleia Geral Constituinte e Legislativa do Imperio do Brazil sobre a Escravatura* (Paris, 1825; Eng. trans., London, 1826).
[3] Chamberlain to Canning, 2 April 1823, Secret, F.O. 63/259.

43

a concession reluctantly afforded to Britain. For his part José Bonifácio reaffirmed that he was anxious to fix a date for the end of the slave trade and no less anxious to secure British recognition, but that the immediate abolition of the trade would be political suicide; 'a little patience' was needed.[1] The two men met again on the 23rd, following a meeting of the Council of State (with Dom Pedro himself in the chair) at which José Bonifácio had been authorised to say that it was the unanimous wish of the government that the slave trade should cease but that for a combination of political and economic reasons abolition could not take place immediately: 'a reasonable term' was needed to prepare public opinion for the change, to enable merchants to withdraw their capital from the trade, and to provide for alternative supplies of labour. 'The old Government', José Bonifácio told Chamberlain, '... did nothing, absolutely nothing, to prepare the country ... it all remains to be done now.' In order that the position should be made absolutely clear, Chamberlain asked him whether he was 'resolved not to consent to immediate abolition in return for recognition', to which José Bonifácio replied, 'Exactly so.' When pressed on the number of years required to prepare the country for the end of the trade he replied, 'Five years as a maximum.' The Brazilian government, he then declared, were prepared to abolish the slave trade within a fixed period—by treaty, which would, of course, constitute recognition by Britain.[2]

A few weeks later Lord Amherst arrived in Rio de Janeiro. In his discussions and communications with José Bonifácio on 16 May he went further than Chamberlain: Britain was anxious to establish political relations with Brazil, he declared, and since everything hinged on the slave trade question he was, he said, authorised to invite José Bonifácio to send his agent in London full powers to settle the terms of a treaty between Britain and Brazil, the first article of which would take the form of a renunciation of the slave trade by Brazil. Amherst received a strong impression that the Brazilian government really did intend to end the slave trade 'at

[1] Chamberlain no. 55, Secret; extracts printed in Webster, i. 223–5. See also Caio de Freitas, *op. cit.* ii. 411–14; Manchester, *British Preëminence*, pp. 212–13.
[2] Chamberlain no. 55, Secret. An article in *O Espelho*, 30 May, by O *Philanthropo* (the Emperor Dom Pedro himself) recommended abolition after two years (enclosed in Chamberlain to Canning, 6 June 1823, F.O. 63/259).

no very distant period' but, like Chamberlain, he was compelled to report that immediate abolition was out of the question—even if immediate recognition were offered.[1] In the meantime José Bonifácio had informed Chamberlain that it was the Emperor's intention 'to observe religiously' the Anglo-Portuguese anti-slave trade treaties of 1815 and 1817: Brazilians had become accustomed to the restrictions which were already imposed on the trade.[2] Thus, without a struggle, one of Canning's objectives was achieved: at least there was to be no extension of the area in which the slave trade to Brazil could be legally carried on as a result of the separation of Portugal and Brazil. North of the equator British cruisers could visit and search Brazilian as well as Portuguese ships (José Bonifácio had privately expressed a wish to Chamberlain that British cruisers would take 'every slave ship they fall in with at sea'[3]) and the mixed commission in Rio de Janeiro would continue to function—as an Anglo-Brazilian commission.[4] Moreover, once the Brazilian government had accepted the treaties of 1815 and 1817 it was, like the Portuguese government, obliged by treaty with Britain to move towards complete abolition.

Shortly after his discussions with Chamberlain and Amherst, José Bonifácio was forced out of office—in part because of his advanced views on slavery and the slave trade—and, to Chamberlain's consternation, Dom Pedro permitted the slave trade question to be debated openly by the Constituent Assembly. However, the members of the Assembly proved for the most part to be remarkably liberal, enlightened and, significantly, urban in outlook. In secret session the abolitionists, led by José Bonifácio, his two brothers (Antônio Carlos and Martim Francisco) and General

[1] Amherst to José Bonifácio, 17 May 1823, *A.D.I.* ii. 444; Amherst to Canning, 17 May, Secret, F.O. 84/24; Amherst to Canning, 21 May, Private, Canning Papers, 80.
[2] José Bonifácio to Chamberlain, 23 May, enclosed in Chamberlain to Canning, no. 62, 24 May 1823, F.O. 63/259. This decision was confirmed by José Bonifácio's successors, e.g. Antônio Luís Pereira da Cunha (Márquês de Inhambupe), to Chamberlain, 13 July, enclosed in Chamberlain no. 14, 19 July 1826, F.O. 84/55. The Brazilian government also accepted the Anglo-Portuguese additional anti-slave trade convention of March 1823 (Hayne to Canning, 5 April 1825, F.O. 84/40).
[3] Chamberlain to Canning, 2 April 1823, Secret.
[4] A Brazilian commissioner had joined the Rio de Janeiro mixed commission soon after independence (Hayne to Canning, no. 34, 5 March, no. 35, 28 March 1823, F.O. 84/23). Apart from one isolated case, however, that of the *Cerqueira* in 1825, the commission was not called upon to function for a number of years.

Brant (who had by this time returned to Brazil), managed to secure a majority in favour of abolition and the negotiation of an anti-slave trade treaty with Britain. After rejecting proposals for ten years and for one year, however, the Assembly insisted upon a minimum period of four years for the gradual abolition of the trade.[1] Some audacious proposals for the elimination of slavery were also made, but failed to win over a majority of the Assembly. Even so, article 254 of the draft Constitution of 4 September 1823 condemned slavery in principle and proposed *a emancipação lenta dos negros*. The Constitution, however—far too liberal for Dom Pedro—was never adopted and on 12 November 1823 the Assembly was dissolved. The Constitution which was eventually promulgated by the Emperor, in March 1824, ignored the issue of slavery, although references to *libertos* presupposed the continued existence of *escravos*.[2] In the meantime, in October 1823, José Joaquim Carneiro de Campos, Foreign Minister in a new Brazilian government, had assured Chamberlain, 'We are ready to do anything, everything, within our power, even beyond what the commonest prudence would authorise to show how much we prize, how really we are desirous to obtain the friendship of England and her acknowledgment of our independence.' Nevertheless, they were prepared to abolish the slave trade only 'at the earliest possible period consistent with the safety of the Imperial Government' (now understood to be at least four years) and only in return for immediate recognition and a guarantee by Britain of the territorial integrity of the Brazilian Empire.[3] In London Canning remained unimpressed by vague proposals for *abolição gradual*. Even the idea of negotiating on the basis of recognition in return for abolition after five years failed to interest him. Only *immediate* abolition, he declared, would satisfy him, although he was ready to allow one year for the completion of slaving enterprises actually undertaken when the trade became illegal. If the Brazilians were prepared to agree to this, he had little doubt that 'other matters

[1] Chamberlain to Canning, 21 October 1823, Sep. and Secret, F.O. 84/24.
[2] João Luis Alves, 'A Questão do Elemento Servil', *R.I.H.G.B.* tomo esp. 1914, pt. IV, pp. 190–1. This article contains a most valuable digest of Brazilian anti-slave trade legislation and an equally valuable summary of debates on the slave trade question in the Brazilian legislature.
[3] Chamberlain to Canning, 21 October 1823, Secret, F.O. 84/24.

between Great Britain and Brazil may be settled to their mutual satisfaction'.[1]

During the summer of 1823 it became apparent to Canning that there was little hope of quickly reaching a satisfactory agreement with Brazil for the *immediate* abolition of the slave trade—a *sine qua non* of British recognition. He had also had time to reflect further on the positive advantages to be gained—not least the maintenance of Britain's political and economic supremacy in Portugal—from delaying recognition until an attempt had been made to persuade Portugal herself to recognise Brazilian independence.[2] In August Canning made his first definite proposals for reconciling Portugal to the inevitable, and a month later Portugal formally requested Britain's 'good offices' in her dispute with her former colony. It was subsequently agreed that talks would be held in London and the Brazilian government nominated as their representatives Felisberto Caldeira Brant and Manuel Rodrigues Gameiro Pessôa (later Visconde de Itabayana), the Brazilian agent in Paris. While the terms of their instructions were under discussion in Rio de Janeiro, Chamberlain repeatedly warned the new Brazilian Foreign Minister, Luís José de Carvalho e Melo, that an agreement to abolish the slave trade remained the essential pre-condition upon which British recognition depended.[3] In the event, in January 1824 Brant and Gameiro were instructed to seek recognition by Britain without prior conditions but to concede separately abolition *dentro de um conveniente espaço de tempo*. Secretly they were authorised to offer abolition after eight years, but were this to appear to stand in the way of recognition by Britain, they could, as a last resort, drop to four years and demand 800 *contos de reis* in indemnity for each of the four years lost; they were not authorised to reduce further the four year period stipulated by the Constituent

---

[1] Canning to Chamberlain, no. 10, 5 August 1823, F.O. 84/24; Brant to José Bonifácio, no. 32, 10 May 1823, *A.D.I.* i. 254–5; Caio de Freitas, *op. cit.* i. 396–7. Before leaving London Brant now suggested that for Britain to allow an interim period of *ten years* before abolition would be the best way of securing an anti-slave trade agreement with Brazil (Brant to Canning, 3 August, enclosed in Brant to Carneiro de Campos, 13 October 1823, Rio de Janeiro, *A.D.I.* i. 289–90).

[2] See Manchester, *British Preëminence in Brazil*, pp. 193–4.

[3] Chamberlain to Canning, no. 164, 31 December 1823, Secret, printed in Webster, *Britain and the Independence of Latin America*, i. 232–3; Chamberlain to Canning, no. 3, 7 January 1824, Secret, Webster, i. 235.

Assembly. A little later, they were to receive additional instructions to demand from Britain a guarantee for Brazil's territorial integrity as well.[1]

On his arrival in London in April 1824, Brant at first read all the signs as being so favourable to the recognition of Brazil by both Portugal and Britain that it seemed possible that Brazil would not be called upon to make any sacrifices to attain it. Certainly little mention was made of the slave trade. But although the question was to be shelved temporarily while the Brazilians negotiated directly with the Portuguese, Brant was clearly given to understand that abolition remained the price of Britain's own recognition.[2] Officially opened in July, the London Conference quickly deteriorated into an endless wrangle as to the meaning of 'sovereignty' and 'independence' with Canning urging moderation on both sides. He failed, however, to reconcile Portuguese and Brazilian interests and, although Brazil did not break off negotiations until the following February, talks were suspended in November.[3] Having fulfilled, if unsuccessfully, its obligations to mediate, the British government, which was on the verge of recognising several of the Spanish American republics, at last felt itself able to come to terms unilaterally with Brazil. Further delay could only endanger British commercial interests and political influence in Brazil, as well as constituting a threat to the unity of the country and the stability of monarchical institutions which Canning was anxious to preserve as a valuable link between the New World and the Old. More particularly, as Canning had warned the Portuguese, the Anglo-Portuguese commercial treaty of 1810 which, like the anti-slave trade treaties of 1815 and 1817, had been accepted by Brazil after independence, came up for revision in 1825 and negotiations could no longer be avoided with the Brazilian government for a new treaty, or alternatively, the

[1] Instructions, 3 January 1824,*A.D.I.* i. 39–53; Luís José de Carvalho e Melo to Brant and Gameiro Pessôa, 16 February 1824, A.H.I. 268/1/14; Carvalho e Melo to Brant and Pessôa, 28 August 1824, *A.D.I.* i. 89–90. See also Caio de Freitas, *op. cit.* ii. 64–8; Calógeras, *A Política Exterior do Império*, ii. 78–84.

[2] Brant and Gameiro Pessôa to Carvalho e Melo, 6 June 1824, *A.D.I.* ii. 57; see also Caio de Freitas, *op. cit.* ii. 85.

[3] For British mediation between Portugal and Brazil and the London Conferences, see Manchester, *British Preëminence in Brazil*, pp. 192–8; Caio de Freitas, *op. cit.* ii. 72–136; Calógeras, *op. cit.* ii. 111; Oliveira Lima, *O Reconhecimento do Império (1822–7)* (Rio de Janeiro, 1902), pp. 73–166.

renewal of the existing treaty, the signing of which would, of course, constitute recognition by Britain.

At the beginning of 1825 Canning decided to send Sir Charles Stuart, who had been British minister in Lisbon during the Peninsular War and ambassador in Paris since 1815, on a special and urgent mission to Lisbon and Rio de Janeiro. In March Stuart received the first part of his instructions: he was to make a final effort to persuade the Portuguese to come to terms with Brazilian separatism but, whether or not he was successful in this task, he was to proceed to Rio and enter into negotiations for an Anglo-Brazilian commercial treaty.[1] In the event Stuart managed to persuade the Portuguese that recognition could no longer be avoided, and in May he was empowered—as Canning had hoped—to negotiate with the Brazilian government on behalf of Portugal as well.[2] On 18 July 1825 he arrived in Rio de Janeiro; on 29 August he signed the treaty by which Portugal recognised the independence of Brazil.[3] One feature of this treaty—a pledge by Dom Pedro never to permit any other Portuguese colony to unite with Brazil—had some bearing on the slave trade question. If Angola, for example, were allowed to detach itself from Portugal and form some sort of association with Brazil (there had been moves to this end in Luanda and Benguela which historically had enjoyed such close ties with Brazil) then the slave trade from Angola to Brazil would no longer be *de facto* illegal simply as a result of the separation of Portugal and Brazil. In addition to other, broader considerations, Britain therefore had sound abolitionist reasons for supporting Portugal in the defence of the territorial integrity of the rest of the Portuguese Empire once the independence of Brazil had been recognised.[4]

[1] Canning to Stuart, no. 1, 14 March 1825, F.O. 13/1, extracts printed in Webster, i. 262–72; also Caio de Freitas, *op. cit.* ii. 193–217.
[2] For Stuart's mission to Lisbon, see Caio de Freitas, *op. cit.* ii. 221–58; Manchester, 'The Recognition of Brazilian Independence', *H.A.H.R.* xxxi (1951), pp. 94–5.
[3] For Stuart's negotiations in Rio on behalf of Portugal, see Caio de Freitas, *op. cit.* ii. 271–302; Manchester, *H.A.H.R.* (1951), pp. 95–6; Manchester, *British Preeminence*, pp. 201–3. The text of the August 1825 treaty can be found in E. Bradford Burns, *A Documentary History of Brazil* (New York, 1966), pp. 219–22. The United States had recognised Brazil a year earlier although only after being assured that among other things Brazil considered herself bound by the Anglo-Portuguese anti-slave trade treaties (Addington to Canning no. 31, 31 May 1824, Webster, ii. 511).
[4] As early as February 1823, José Bonifácio had told Chamberlain, 'With regard to colonies on the coast of Africa, we want none, nor anywhere else; Brazil is quite large

Independence and abolition, 1822–1826

In the meantime, Stuart had received from London more explicit instructions concerning his negotiations on behalf of the British government. Canning was now disposed to delay the signing of an entirely new commercial treaty since commercial negotiations were in progress, or would shortly be opened, with several Spanish American republics as well as with Portugal and other European states, and the main lines of future British commercial policy had not yet been finally formulated; it was not impossible that Britain might wish to liberalise its commercial relations with Brazil. Consequently Stuart was advised simply to secure a Convention permitting the treaty of 1810 to continue in force for two years during which time it could be properly revised and renewed. This Convention, Canning was careful to add, should include a stipulation that in the revised treaty there would be an article for the 'immediate and effectual abolition by Brazil of the Brazilian slave trade'. The point which Britain had been making for the past two and a half years was once again underlined: 'it would be impossible for us to sign any treaty with the new American states in which such a stipulation was not included'. It would seem, however, that Canning had at last reconciled himself to the fact that the Brazilians would find *immediate* abolition difficult, if not impossible, to concede, although he was still not prepared to grant them the interim period of at least four years that they themselves had indicated might be acceptable: the interval which would elapse before the new commercial treaty was signed (that is, up to two years), he told Stuart, would afford Brazil ample time to prepare for the end of the slave trade.[1]

On 25 July, within a week of his arrival in Rio, Stuart had put

enough and productive enough for us, and we are content with what Providence has given us' (Chamberlain to Canning, 2 April 1823, Secret, Webster, i. 222). See José Honório Rodrigues, *Brazil and Africa*, pp. 126, 138, 141–2, 148–9, 154–5, 165, 170, 173, for the unconvincing argument that 'the great idea' of British diplomacy was not so much the abolition of the slave trade as the separation of Brazil and Africa so as to clear the way for British imperial expansion and the development of Africa as an economic rival of Brazil.

[1] Canning to Stuart, 7 May 1825, 12 May 1825, F.O. 13/1. In November Canning indicated that he would be satisfied with a separate abolition treaty signed at the same time as the commercial treaty, and he hinted that Britain might even give up its commercial privileges in Brazil if their loss were compensated by the simultaneous attainment of such a 'great moral and political good' (Canning to Stuart, 28 November 1825, F.O. 13/2).

Britain's demands for abolition before the Emperor, Dom Pedro.[1] Thanks entirely to Britain's efforts, he argued, Portugal was about to recognise Brazil and Britain herself would soon follow suit. Brazil therefore had clear, if unwritten, obligations to come to some agreement with Britain for the abolition of the slave trade since throughout all the talks and negotiations since 1822 a bargain had been implied: abolition for recognition. Moreover, since she had already accepted the treaties of 1815 and 1817 Brazil, like Portugal, was committed to fixing a date for its final and total abolition. The Brazilian government might just as well concede the point, Stuart added, since once Brazil and Portugal were formally separated the bulk of the slave trade to Brazil would in any case become illegal: as Canning had first pointed out in November 1822, Portugal, whose African territories south of the line supplied the Brazilian market with an increasing proportion of its slaves now that the trade north of the equator was illegal, was bound by treaties which Britain had every intention of enforcing not to export slaves to non-Portuguese territories across the Atlantic. Stuart already enjoyed a reputation for pursuing his own policies, regardless of instructions from London—as ambassador in Paris he had frequently caused Canning considerable embarrassment—and he now saw within his grasp a great opportunity for securing two separate treaties: one abolishing the slave trade after two years, the other a commercial treaty based on that of 1810 with all the privileges it conferred on British commerce, including a maximum tariff of 15% on imported British goods. Although they came as no great surprise, the Brazilian plenipotentiaries, Visconde de Paranaguá and Marquês de Santo Amaro, were disappointed with the terms of the treaties which Stuart now offered them; they felt, however, that they could not refuse Stuart's demands, linked as they were both to services rendered and to recognition by Britain. Nevertheless they managed to secure important concessions from Stuart who believed that the prevailing pro-British mood would not last indefinitely now that recognition was assured, and therefore regarded the negotiations as a race against time. (He might also have been influenced by his desire to leave Rio—'this detestable place', he called it—at the

[1] Stuart to Canning, 25 July 1825, F.O. 13/4.

earliest possible moment.) In the negotiations for a commercial treaty, for example, he dropped his demand for the retention of the judges conservators, the existence of which, the Brazilians claimed, was incompatible with the new Brazilian Constitution of 1824. In negotiating the anti-slave trade treaty, in order to appease the traders and, more particularly, the *fazendeiros*, Stuart agreed that there should be an interim period of four, not two, years before the slave trade became entirely illegal; in their earlier proposals, he acknowledged, Brazilian governments had never promised more than abolition after four years, and they were being hard pressed to continue the trade for very much longer. When it came to the question of what form the preamble to the treaty should take, Dom Pedro refused to accept that he was bound by any treaties made by Portugal, insisting that the abolition of the slave trade should be the result of a voluntary act by the head of the new Brazilian state, and Stuart saw no reason to press the point. On 18 October 1825, acting entirely on his own initiative, he signed separately a commercial treaty and an abolition treaty. The preamble to the latter suggested that it sprang from, on the one hand, 'the separation of the Empire of Brazil from the Kingdom of Portugal' which had 'enabled His Britannic Majesty to claim the execution on the part of His Most Faithful Majesty [the King of Portugal] of the treaties concluded in 1815 and 1817 which prohibit the exportation of slaves to foreign countries from the coast of Africa' and, on the other, 'His Majesty, the Emperor of Brazil, being anxious to put an end to the slave trade'. The trade was to become entirely illegal for Brazilian subjects four years after the ratification of the treaty (article 1) and was thereafter to be considered piracy (article 2). In the meantime the trade was to remain legal to and from Portuguese and Portuguese-claimed territories on the west and east African coasts south of the equator but illegal north of the line. The rest of the treaty, the work of Henry Chamberlain, the British consul-general, consisted of a number of articles setting out the ways in which the illegal trade was to be put down and including the grant of the right of search to British warships. In return, the Brazilians asked for three guarantees: first, that Britain would ensure that Portugal did not prohibit the export of slaves from its territories in Africa during the four-year interim period; secondly, that neither Britain nor the nations with whom Britain already had negotiated abolition treaties would interfere with Brazilian slavers during that period; and thirdly, that Britain would not see the Brazilian Government overthrown as a result of internal political disturbances arising from opposition to the treaty. All of them Stuart rejected—Brazilian fears on every point, he said, were groundless—but he agreed to refer them to London for separate consideration along with the two treaties.[1]

Canning received Stuart's treaties, which bore so little resemblance to what he had envisaged, with extreme irritation. 'This comes of a man thinking himself cleverer than all the rest of mankind', he wrote to Granville, 'and believing himself to be protected by the King against the responsible Minister under whom he is acting.'[2] After consulting his Law Officers and William Huskisson, President of the Board of Trade, Canning refused to ratify either treaty and recalled Stuart to London. He was not in the event displeased at the preferential nature of the commercial treaty Stuart had secured but he regarded many other aspects of it—not least the abolition of the judges conservators—as 'foolish and mischievous'.[3] He objected no less strongly to certain features of Stuart's anti-slave trade treaty. The lack of any reference to previous engagements to abolish the slave trade was, he thought, 'a most serious defect'. The preamble appeared 'to attribute the

---

[1] On the negotiation of the abolition treaty of October 1825, Stuart to Canning, 25 July, 24 August, 30 August 1825, F.O. 13/4, 18 October 1825, F.O. 128/4, 21 October 1825, F.O. 13/6, 11 February 1826, Private, Webster i. 297–8; Stuart to Planta (F.O.), 5 September 1825, Planta to Canning, 5 October 1826, Private, Canning Papers, 109; Stuart to Paranaguá, 15 October, Santo Amaro and Paranaguá to Stuart, 18 October, Stuart to Santo Amaro and Paranaguá, 20 October 1825, A.D.I. vi. 159–60, 161–2, 163–5; Carvalho e Melo to Gameira Pessôa, 28 September 1825, Inhambupe to V. de Itabayana (Gameira Pessôa), no. 118, 3 February 1826, A.H.I. 268/1/14; Stuart to Inhambupe, 15 April 1826, A.H.I. 273/1/8. Brazil's request for guarantees appears in Calógeras, *A Política Exterior*, ii. 489–91. On the negotiations for the commercial treaty of October 1825, see A. J. Pryor, 'Anglo-Brazilian Commercial Relations and the Evolution of Brazilian Tariff Policy, 1822–1850' (unpublished Ph.D. thesis, Cambridge, 1965), pp. 32–44; Manchester, *British Preëminence*, pp. 203–4; Caio de Freitas, *op. cit.* ii. 348–68. The treaties were published in the *Diario Fluminense* (Rio de Janeiro) 14 November 1825, and subsequently in the London press—much to Canning's annoyance.
[2] Quoted in H. V. Temperley, *The Foreign Policy of Canning, 1822–7* (London, 1925), pp. 508–9.
[3] Canning to Liverpool, 27 November 1825, printed in *Some Official Correspondence of George Canning*, ed. Edward J. Stapleton (2 vols., London, 1887), i. 334.

concurrence of the Emperor of Brazil to His Imperial Majesty's own mere motion, as if it were entirely optional with His Imperial Majesty to admit or disclaim those obligations'. Canning believed that the basis of any Anglo-Brazilian abolition treaty should be the 'unquestioned principle' that, when one state became divided into separate independent states, each state retained the obligations of the original. The principle seemed particularly valid in this case since the Portuguese court had been resident in Rio de Janeiro when the treaties of 1810, 1815 and 1817 were signed. 'Each of the monarchies into which the dominions of the House of Braganza are now divided', Canning claimed, 'inherits the engagements and obligations which were contracted during their union by their common sovereign.'[1] This was much more than a legal quibble, a mere objection to the re-negotiation of engagements thought to be already in force. Canning's basic concern was the preservation of the Brazilian monarchy (even though he was not prepared to guarantee it) and the maintenance of British influence in Brazil, and he feared that the reaction of the Brazilian landed interest to a treaty of total abolition would be so hostile that both Britain and the Brazilian Emperor would come badly out of the manoeuvre. Moreover, Brazil would have a ready-made excuse for the renunciation of the treaty at a later date: Brazil's vital economic interests had been jeopardised, it would be argued, by an Imperial Government which, in its anxiety to secure diplomatic recognition, had totally capitulated to the demands of a foreign power. Canning therefore concluded that it would be sound policy to encourage amongst Brazilians the idea that abolition was a necessary corollary of independence from Portugal, and that Brazilian obligations under the treaties with Portugal were the basis of British demands. He surmised that it should be easier for Brazilians to accept abolition if it appeared to arise 'out of a positive engagement rather than out of a demand on our part and an uncondi-

---

[1] Canning to Stuart, no. 1, 12 January 1826, F.O. 84/56. Also Canning to Huskisson, 22 November, 26 November, 30 December 1825, Canning Papers, 117; Inhambupe to Paranaguá, 9 January 1826, *A.D.I.* ii. p. 324; Canning to Stuart, no. 2, 12 January 1826, F.O. 13/17. The Law Officers of the Crown supported this 'generally recognised principle', 8 December 1825, F.O. 83/2343. Dr Stephen Lushington, a well-known abolitionist M.P. and lawyer, could not recall that the principle had ever been maintained by any writer on international law, nor upheld by any state, Memorandum, 26 January 1826, F.O. 84/60.

tional surrender on his [the Emperor's]'.[1] Moreover, if abolition by Brazil were regarded as a concession to Britain rather than as the acceptance of engagements already subsisting and obligatory, it would be more difficult for the British government to refuse future requests for an extension of the interim period before abolition as well as the Brazilian Emperor's demand for guarantees as a *quid pro quo*.

From the more practical viewpoint, Canning did not now object to a four year period before total abolition; he was satisfied that Stuart had secured the shortest possible period and he did not wish to reopen negotiations on this point. But he was inclined to agree with Huskisson that Stuart's treaty was a confused jumble of the regulations which were to take effect when the Brazilian slave trade became entirely illegal and those under which the trade was to be carried on in the meantime. Like many British abolitionist leaders, Huskisson was somewhat disenchanted with the kind of limited right of search treaty Britain had signed with Portugal, Spain, the Netherlands and now, it seemed, with Brazil. 'This treaty', he wrote, 'does appear to me a far worse farrago than anything of the sort which I have looked into. Impossible to reconcile its contradictions. To understand or put in motion its complicated machinery equally impossible. If you attempt it you will be worried to death by the abolitionists here and complaints from Brazil.' Far simpler and less ambiguous, he persuaded Canning, would be to say that the Anglo-Portuguese treaties of 1815 and 1817 would remain in force for four years, after which period the trade would be entirely prohibited and treated as piracy.[2]

Canning's rejection of Stuart's treaty meant that negotiations for the final abolition of the Brazilian slave trade would have to be reopened. Yet with every year the situation in Brazil became less propitious. The Emperor was still in favour of abolition and aware of the importance to Brazil of British friendship and support. His ministers, however, were more than ever concerned with the possible economic and political repercussions of abolition and Henry Chamberlain, who was again British *chargé d'affaires* from

[1] Canning to Stuart, no. 1, F.O. 84/56.
[2] Huskisson Memorandum, 1 January 1826, F.O. 13/33; Huskisson to Canning, 1 January 1826, Private, Canning Papers, 68; Canning to Stuart no. 1, F.O. 84/56; Canning to A'Court (Lisbon), 22 December 1825, Private, Canning Papers, 117.

May 1826, following Stuart's departure, no longer had any confidence in their desire to end the trade. In July 1826 he wrote to Canning, 'This present bias of the Government towards those who carry on the slave trade . . . this legal forbearance on the one hand and fostering care on the other but ill accord with the declared desire of the Government to co-operate in the repression of the trade and their wish for its abolition. Their present acts differ wholly from their professions'; in September, 'The Government themselves notwithstanding their official declarations encourage the continuation and extension of the trade'; in November, 'Whatever may be said of this Government I look for very little being done.'[1] There was clearly a danger that, as the Brazilian government became more self-confident, they would become less persuaded of the need to pay so heavy a price for the formal diplomatic recognition of their by now well-established independence. (After all, despite Canning's refusal to ratify the Stuart treaties, recognition by Britain as well as Portugal had now in effect been achieved: at the end of January 1826 Manuel Rodrigues Gameiro Pessôa had been received as Brazilian minister in London and preparations were being made to send to Rio as British minister Robert Gordon, a younger brother of Lord Aberdeen.) And there was yet another danger. In May 1826 the Brazilian Chamber of Deputies, in which representatives of the landed interest were much more prominent than they had been in the Constituent Assembly, had met for the first time, and they had taken up the issue of the slave trade. José Clemente Pereira, one of the influential deputies for Rio de Janeiro province, had immediately introduced a bill for the total abolition of the slave trade— by 31 December 1840! If the government really believed that the slave trade was no longer in Brazil's interests, he declared, they should enact legislation for its *gradual* abolition: they should not compromise national independence and national interests by signing a treaty for its immediate abolition simply because a powerful foreign nation demanded it. After studying the question, however, the Chamber's *Comissão de Legislação e de Justiça* gave as its opinion that as an interim period before abolition

[1] Chamberlain to Canning, 31 July, Private, 9 September, 17 November, 1826, F.O. 84/55.

fourteen years was too long. Before the deputies dispersed for the recess, however, Nicolau Pereira de Campos Vergueiro (São Paulo) submitted for discussion at the beginning of the next session another proposal for the abolition of the slave trade—this time after six years.[1] Thus a speedy settlement of the slave trade question was becoming urgent and, rather than transfer the negotiations to London as he had first intended, Canning decided that Gordon should be empowered to sign in Rio de Janeiro first a new anti-slave trade treaty—which Canning now recognised would be a case of 'uncompensated concession on the part of Brazil'— and then a new commercial treaty.[2]

Robert Gordon, a proud, hard man and a tough negotiator, whom Dom Pedro was to refer to as 'that ill mannered and obstinate Scot',[3] arrived in Rio de Janeiro on 13 October 1826 and after, with some difficulty, persuading the Emperor to bypass the Chamber of Deputies, reopened negotiations for an Anglo-Brazilian anti-slave trade treaty. On 31 October, Gordon had his first conference with the Brazilian plenipotentiaries, Antônio Luís Pereira da Cunha (Marquês de Inhambupe), Senator, Councillor of State and Minister of Foreign Affairs, and his immediate predecessor, José Egídio Álvares de Almeida (Marquês de Santo Amaro), also a Councillor of State. Insisting that he was asking for 'no more than the execution of His Imperial Majesty's engagements', Gordon reminded them that in 1823 Brazil had been prepared to enter negotiations for the early abolition of the trade in return for recognition and that only 'motives of delicacy' had prevented Britain's accepting this offer. The British government had nevertheless continued to work for the recognition of Brazilian independence on the understanding, he claimed, that Brazil would then 'spontaneously' abolish its slave trade; the Brazilian government, he hoped, would now, with good grace, agree to abolition within two years. And, in case they should entertain lingering thoughts of evading their obligations, again he

---

[1] Alves, *R.I.H.G.B.* (1914), pp. 192–3.
[2] Canning to Gordon, no. 1, 1 August, no. 3, 1 August 1826, F.O. 13/25.
[3] Quoted in Calógeras, *op. cit.* ii. p. 497. Canning had equally strong views on the Brazilian Emperor. 'You have a difficult person to deal with in the Emperor of Brazil', he wrote to Gordon. 'But . . . all such violent and wayward tempers are usually accessible to fear when better motives fail of effect upon them' (Canning to Gordon, 18 December 1826, Private, Canning Papers, 126).

emphasised the point that the Brazilian slave trade would soon come to an end in any case directly the British government prevailed upon Portugal to fulfil her existing treaty obligations to stop the export of slaves from her African territories. (On 2 October, Sir William A'Court, British minister in Lisbon, had finally extracted from the Portuguese government an official acknowledgment that with the irrevocable loss of Brazil the time had now come to prohibit the slave trade south of the equator.[1]) Rather to Gordon's surprise the Brazilians again agreed—reluctantly, but without too much protest—to sign a treaty abolishing the slave trade. They accepted that Brazil was obliged to end the trade almost at once in return for services rendered by Britain; they recognised that Brazil's long-term interests demanded a gradual end to the trade: and they realised that it would be impossible for Brazil to resist indefinitely an international movement against the slave trade backed by British power. Their overriding fear was that a refusal to co-operate might lead to a withdrawal of British support followed by the suppression of the trade in any case—by force. Yet the Brazilian plenipotentiaries were no less apprehensive about the consequences of abolition than their predecessors had been a year ago and they asked for six years (the period under consideration in the Chamber of Deputies) before the entire trade finally became illegal. Gordon refused to give way. The trade, he said, had become *de facto* illegal with the separation of Brazil and Portugal, and 'it would be inconsistent to sanction for a long period a trade which is actually prohibited'. At a second conference on 2 November, Gordon also vigorously rejected a further request that the negotiations be postponed until the Chamber reassembled in the following May. When, on 17 November, the two sides met for a third time, the Brazilians came with authorisation from the Emperor and the Council of State to propose an interim period of *four* years, together with some indemnification for loss of revenue. Gordon rejected the idea of indemnification but said he was willing to agree to a period of *three* years before final abolition. In doing so he pointed out that as recently as October 1825 the Emperor had been prepared to accept a period

[1] A'Court to Canning, 3 October 1826, F.O. 84/54; see also Bandinel, *op. cit.* pp. 157-8.

58

of four years; one year, however, had since been lost in negotiation and the trade would thus become illegal at approximately the time originally intended. During the next few days there were rumours that the Emperor was about to leave the capital and, on 20 November, in a strongly worded note, Gordon asked the Brazilians to consider the unfavourable impression they would make on the British government if they now refused to sign immediately a treaty substantially the same as that signed a year ago, and concluded by reminding them of the 'consequences of procrastination'. In a conference held on the following day he made the point yet again that 'six months hence there might be no port [in Portuguese Africa] left open in which the trade could be carried on by Brazil, except by contraband'. The Brazilians finally proposed that the trade be abolished three years after the ratification of the treaty and, on the understanding that ratification would be immediate, Gordon announced his acceptance. In view of the fact that the last proposal put before the Chamber of Deputies had been for abolition after six years, the Brazilian representatives, however, still wanted an understanding that negotiations would be continued in London for a reasonable prolongation of the time limit. For his part Gordon could see no reason for a change in the date now set for final abolition, and merely agreed to pass on the request as an 'observation'. It was at this point that the Brazilians chose to object once again to the principle, set out in the preamble of the new British treaty draft, that the independent state of Brazil was obliged to accept engagements undertaken by Portugal in 1815 and 1817. In view of the attitude Canning had adopted to Stuart's treaty, however, Gordon was not prepared to abandon 'the first basis of our present negotiations . . . the mutual obligation to confirm what had been agreed upon previous to the separation of Brazil from Portugal', although he went on to assure the Brazilians that this was by no means a general principle and applied only to the anti-slave trade treaties. The Brazilians also sought the same guarantees referred home by Stuart in the previous year, namely that the legal trade would not be interrupted by other nations during the interim period prior to complete abolition, and that the existing political system in Brazil would not be overthrown when the terms of the treaty became known. Gordon, however, had no hesitation in rejecting these demands.[1]

An Anglo-Brazilian anti-slave trade treaty was finally signed on 23 November 1826, and ratified by Dom Pedro on board a warship sailing out of Rio harbour for Rio Grande do Sul. Gordon had secured precisely what Canning required. The preamble to the treaty declared that, with the separation of Brazil from Portugal, Britain and Brazil acknowledged 'the obligation which devolves upon them to renew, confirm and give full effect to the stipulations of the treaties subsisting between the Crowns of Great Britain and Portugal for the regulation and final abolition of the African slave trade, in so far as these stipulations are binding on Brazil', and desired 'to fix and define the period at which the total abolition of the said trade, so far as relates to the dominions and subjects of the Brazilian Empire, shall take place'. Article 1 read,

At the expiration of three years to be reckoned from the exchange of ratifications of the present treaty [Britain ratified the treaty on 13 March 1827] it shall not be lawful for the subjects of the Emperor of Brazil to be concerned in the carrying on of the African slave trade under any pretext or in any manner whatever and the carrying on of such trade after that period by any person, subject of His Imperial Majesty, shall be deemed and treated as piracy.

Considering the crucial importance it was to have later, remarkably little had been made in the negotiations of the phrase 'deemed and treated as piracy'. It seems that the Brazilians did query its use but accepted Gordon's rather vague explanation that Britain now insisted upon its inclusion in all anti-slave trade treaties. Its implications for the future were hardly discussed. The remaining articles of the treaty were concerned with the regulation of the slave trade carried on north of the equator, which the Brazilian government had already acknowledged was illegal, during the interim period before total abolition. For this purpose the Anglo-Portuguese

[1] Gordon to Canning, no. 1, 27 November, no. 2, 27 November, 1826, F.O. 84/56; Gordon to Canning no. 5, 27 November, no. 6, 27 November, no. 7, 27 November, 1826, F.O. 13/26; Inhambupe to Itabayana, 27 November, 4 December, 1826, A.H.I. 268/1/14; see also Caio de Freitas, *op. cit.* ii. 371–5; Manchester, *British Preëminence*, pp. 214–15.

treaties of 1815 and 1817 were adopted and renewed by the two powers 'as effectually as if the same were inserted, word for word, in this convention'.[1] On 17 August 1827, after some hard bargaining, the Brazilians accepted a commercial treaty couched in precisely the terms which Canning desired: that is to say, a treaty which included both the 15% maximum tariff on imported British goods and the judges conservators.[2] The process was thus completed whereby, in return for the recognition of Brazilian independence, Britain secured the consolidation of a highly privileged economic position in Brazil, together with an engagement by Brazil to abolish the slave trade in 1830.

[1] Treaty of 23 November 1826, *B.F.S.P.* xiv. 609–12; Pereira Pinto, i. 389–93.
[2] On the final negotiation of the Anglo-Brazilian commercial treaty, see Pryor, 'Anglo-Brazilian Commercial Relations', pp. 45–7; Caio de Freitas, *op. cit.* ii. 375–7; Manchester, *British Preëminence*, pp. 206–11.

CHAPTER 3

BRAZIL AND THE SLAVE TRADE,
1827-1839

On 26 November 1826, a few days after the negotiations for an
Anglo-Brazilian abolition treaty had been brought to a successful
conclusion, Robert Gordon, the British minister in Rio de Janeiro,
warned George Canning, the British Foreign Secretary, that the
treaty was bound to be 'in the highest degree unpopular' in
Brazil; it had been, he later admitted, 'ceded at our request in
opposition to the views and wishes of the whole Empire'.[1] It was,
however, six months before the Brazilian Chamber of Deputies
was given an opportunity to voice the strongly anti-abolitionist
opinions which the vast majority of influential white Brazilians
undoubtedly held. In May 1827 the Chamber reassembled after a
recess lasting almost twelve months and on 22 May the new
Brazilian Foreign Minister, Marquês de Queluz (João Severiano
Maciel da Costa)—himself the author of an abolitionist tract,
*Memoria sobre a necessidade de abolir a introducção dos escravos africanos
no Brazil* (published in Coimbra in 1821), in which he had argued
that the trade would nevertheless be necessary for some little time
to come—presented a report on the recent treaty negotiations
with Britain in which he maintained that the Brazilian government had been *forced* to sign the treaty of 23 November 1826
entirely against their will.[2] On 16 June 1827, the treaty was put in
the hands of the Chamber's *Comissão de Diplomacia* which
narrowly, by three votes to two, agreed to accept it.[3] Those in

[1] Gordon to Canning, no. 2, 27 November 1826, F.O. 84/56; Gordon to Dudley, no. 1,
17 May 1828, F.O. 84/84.
[2] Queluz to José Antônio da Silva Maia, Secretary to the Chamber, 22 May 1827, quoted
in Alves, *R.I.H.G.B.* (1914), pp. 194–5; Rodrigues, *Brazil and Africa*, p. 144; Manchester,
British Preëminence in Brazil, pp. 215–16. Britain, Queluz suggested, had threatened not
only to force Portugal to close her African ports to Brazilian traders but also to instruct
her navy forcibly to prevent Brazilian ships from trading on the Portuguese African
coast. When Gordon protested at this account of the treaty negotiations Queluz privately
admitted that Gordon had never made such a threat in so many words but insisted that
this had been understood from what had been said (Gordon to Dudley, 17 July, 18
August 1827, F.O. 13/38).   [3] Alves, *op. cit.* p. 195; Rodrigues, *op. cit.* pp. 145, 147.

favour of the treaty—Luís de Araújo Basto (deputy for Bahia), Romualdo Antônio de Seixas (the bishop of Bahia and deputy for Pará), and Marcos Antônio de Sousa (bishop elect of Maranhão and deputy for Bahia)—while objecting to the way in which an abolition agreement had been extracted from Brazil, condemned the slave trade, expressed the belief that Brazil was obliged to fulfil earlier engagements to abolish it and declared that to do so would be to act in the country's best long-term interests. The two dissenting members of the Commission—Brigadier Raimundo José da Cunha Matos (Goiás) and Luís Augusto May (Minas Gerais)—openly identified themselves with the interests of the *fazendeiros* and were in favour of rejecting a treaty which was, in the words of Cunha Matos, 'derogatory to the honour, interest, dignity, independence and sovereignty of the Brazilian nation'. For three successive days, 2, 3 and 4 July, the slave trade question was then hotly debated by the Chamber as a whole.[1] Significantly, perhaps, the trade was at no time openly defended on the time-honoured grounds of 'converting the heathen' (Dom Romualdo was loudly applauded when he denounced the hypocrisy of those who argued that the trade rescued Negroes from war and slavery in Africa and bestowed upon them the benefits of Christianity in Brazil), nor, surprisingly, did anyone except José Lino Coutinho (Bahia) defend it on the grounds of the Negro's alleged racial inferiority. Lip-service at least was paid to the progressive ideas of the age, and little attempt was made to justify an indefinite continuation of the slave trade. Indeed a surprising number of deputies acknowledged that abolition was ultimately in Brazil's interests, both social and economic. Nevertheless the great majority of speakers considered that abolition within the short space of three years would be premature and likely seriously to prejudice Brazil's basic national interests—namely, agriculture ('the vital foundation of the nation's existence', as Cunha Matos called it), commerce and shipping—to say nothing of undermining the already precarious state of the country's finances. 'The moment has not arrived for us

[1] The following summary of the debate on the abolition treaty in the Chamber of Deputies, 2–4 July 1827, is taken from Rodrigues, *op. cit.* pp. 145–55; Alves, *op. cit.* pp. 195–203; Gordon to Dudley, no. 3, 14 July 1827, F.O. 13/38. For the debate on the Anglo-Brazilian commercial treaty, see Pryor, 'Anglo-Brazilian Commercial Relations', pp. 54–62.

to abandon the importation of slaves', declared Cunha Matos, who led the attack on the treaty throughout the debate, 'for although it is an evil, it is a lesser evil than not importing them'. Speaker after speaker emphasised the country's need for a steady supply of unskilled African labour, 'the number of deaths among slaves being equal to or greater than the number of births', as one of them reminded the Chamber. 'As this commerce so directly and indirectly influences all the sources of national wealth, is it fitting that it shall cease at the time stipulated without plans to replenish the great void that it will necessarily leave?', asked Nicolau Pereira de Campos Vergueiro (São Paulo), who later became a pioneer in the importation of free European labour into Brazil. European immigration was ultimately the only real alternative to the African slave trade, but few Brazilian planters had yet seriously considered the possibility of employing free white labour, assuming it to be available, in large-scale plantation agriculture in the tropics. Earlier in the century there had been a few attempts to promote European, mainly German and Swiss, colonisation on a small scale (a decree of 25 November 1808, promulgated during Dom João's first twelve months in Brazil, had granted foreigners the right to own land), but even these modest experiments had proved extremely costly and the results had been disappointing.[1] Another solution to the problem and one frequently advanced by abolitionists at the time, seemed to lie in the use of surplus Indian labour. But in the light of the experience of three centuries few Brazilian landowners believed either that there were sufficient numbers of Indians or that Indian could be an adequate, much less an immediate, substitute for African labour. 'Let us concede that the Indian can be civilised', declared José Clemente Pereira (Rio de Janeiro); 'when will his labour be profitable to Brazil? No doubt that will come late and very slowly, while the shortage of Africans is immediate and sudden'. In the event only one deputy, Dom Romualdo, a man with a profound belief in the need both to 'civilise' the Indian and to introduce 'honest families and hard-working men from Europe', spoke in favour of the *immediate* abolition of the slave trade. The cries of those who com-

[1] See João Pandiá Calógeras, *A History of Brazil* (Univ. of North Carolina Press, 1939), pp. 108–9.

plained that abolition would mean the ruin of Brazil were, he declared, 'the complaints and pretexts which avarice and selfishness generally urge against reform and innovation which are salutary and necessary but which clash with the profits and advantages of a few individuals'; even if a period of twenty years were allowed for the run-down of the slave trade, he went on, nothing would be done to prepare for abolition and, at the end of that time, the same arguments would again be heard in favour of its continuation. But Romualdo's was a voice crying in the wilderness. The great majority of Brazilian deputies remained convinced that the abolition of the slave trade was an unmitigated disaster. Moreover, they objected strongly to the fact that the Brazilian government, or so it seemed, had abolished the trade not because they judged such a move to be in Brazil's best interests but because a powerful foreign nation judged it to be in theirs. (Few Brazilians accepted at face value the humanitarian basis of Britain's anti-slave trade campaign; its purpose, they firmly believed, was first, to ruin Brazilian agriculture to the advantage of British West Indian interests and, secondly, to break Brazil's links with Africa in order to facilitate British expansion there and the subsequent development of the African continent as an economic rival of Brazil.) Most deputies were disposed to agree with Cunha Matos that they had been 'forced by threats of hostilities in case of opposition on our side ... forced, obliged, necessitated, subjected and compelled by the British government to conclude an onerous and degrading Convention upon affairs which are internal, domestic and purely national, and exclusively the competence of the free and sovereign legislative body and of the august head of the Brazilian nation'. They were angry with the Emperor and his government on two counts: in the first place, by agreeing to abolish the slave trade after a period of only three years, they had, at the instigation of the British minister, ignored the fact that the Chamber itself was considering various proposals for ending the slave trade within a more reasonable period of time (for example, Vergueiro's proposal for abolition after six years); in the second place, they had entirely disregarded the Chamber's general claim to be consulted on all treaties with foreign powers. Nor were the deputies blind to the serious implications of the first article of the treaty which declared the slave trade piracy. Cunha Matos, Clemente Pereira and Dom Romualdo were all agreed that this was an attempt, in violation of Brazilian law and without the sanction of the Brazilian legislature, to deny to Brazilians found to be engaged in the illegal slave trade access to their own national courts, subjecting them instead to the jurisdiction of foreign (that is, British) tribunals. It was, Clemente Pereira declared, 'the most direct attack that could be made upon the Constitution, upon national dignity and honour and upon the individual rights of Brazilian citizens'. But their anger was to little purpose. Since the abolition treaty had already been ratified by Brazil, the Chamber had no choice but to accept it.

Concerned at the extent and vehemence of the opposition to the abolition treaty both in the legislature and throughout the country, the Brazilian government made several attempts to persuade the British government to postpone the date now set for abolition.[1] George Canning, the author of the treaty, was now dead, and Lord Aberdeen, British Foreign Secretary (1828–30), was prepared to consider it, although he suspected that a proposal to extend the interim period in which the Brazilian slave trade was legally permitted to continue south of the equator 'would not be listened to in the House of Commons'.[2] Wellington, the Prime Minister, completely rejected the idea. 'The whole question', he wrote to Aberdeen in September 1828, 'is one of impression. We shall never succeed in abolishing the foreign slave trade. But we must take care to avoid to take any step (*sic*) which may induce the people of England to believe that we do not do everything in our power to discourage and put it down as soon as possible.'[3] In the event, therefore, the British government were prepared to yield on one point only: Brazilian slave ships could continue to trade on the African coast south of the line until the date when the trade became finally and completely illegal—13 March 1830— after which they would be allowed a further six months in which they could legitimately return to Brazil.

The British government, however, can have had few expecta-

[1] See Manchester, *op. cit.* pp. 224–5.
[2] Aberdeen to Wellington, 27 August 1828, printed in Wellington's *Despatches*, iv, p. 674.
[3] Wellington to Aberdeen, 4 September 1828, *ibid.* v. p. 14.

tions that when the treaty of 1826 eventually came into force the Brazilian government would fulfil their obligations to abolish the trade. Robert Gordon had already expressed the opinion that the slave trade would be carried on tenfold during the three-year period up to 1830 and that it would then be continued illicitly with the connivance of the Brazilian government.[1] In April 1828 a British merchant, W. A. Kentish, who had lived in Bahia for twelve years, advised Wellington that the abolition treaty was

an agreement which that [the Brazilian] government could not carry into execution, even if it were *candid* in its professions, which on this point I can aver it is not . . . The government *may prohibit* [the] importation [of slaves] at the *principal* ports . . . but I am certain it will *leave it to be understood* at the time that *liberty will be given to land them on any contiguous part of the coast*, because the nation to a man . . . would acquiesce in nothing short of this. If the government there can gain any important *point* by *professing* to discountenance the traffic, or by *pretending* to enforce its abolition I have no doubt of its professions; but never while the Brazils shall depend upon the fruits of agriculture for its support will there be any diminution in this trade.[2]

Charles Pennell, British consul in Bahia and later consul-general in Rio de Janeiro, had anticipated that the treaty would be regarded by Brazilian governments as 'a dictation of a superior authority from which it is lawful to escape, rather than as a compact which they are bound to enforce'. 'To bribe and intimidate this government into the adoption of our sentiments or of our measures (and that we have done both is a popular conviction) . . .', Pennell added later, 'is a fruitless task.'[3]

On 3 May 1830, in his annual *Falla do Throno*, Dom Pedro announced that under the terms of the Anglo-Brazilian treaty of 1826, the Brazilian slave trade was now illegal and that his government intended to take all necessary measures to prevent its continuation: 'the slave trade has ceased', he declared, rather

[1] Gordon to Canning, no. 2, 27 November 1826, F.O. 84/56.
[2] Kentish to Wellington, 13 April 1828, printed in Wellington's *Despatches*, iv. pp. 370–1.
[3] Pennell to Canning, 8 June 1827, Pennell to Dudley, 22 August 1827, quoted in Manchester, *op. cit.* pp. 222–3; Pennell to Palmerston, 12 February 1831, F.O. 84/122.

3-2

Brazil and the slave trade, 1827–1839

prematurely.[1] In the event the trade was to receive very little attention during the next twelve months which saw a series of political crises in Brazil, culminating on 7 April 1831 in the emperor's abdication and the appointment of three Regents to exercise power on behalf of his six-year-old son, the future Dom Pedro II.[2] Among the factors which had contributed to the deepening rift between Dom Pedro and the majority of his subjects, besides his unconstitutional, autocratic, methods of government, his heavy dependence on Portuguese ministers and advisers, his unsuccessful foreign policy in the Río de la Plata and, not least, his scandalous private life, had been the price he had been prepared to pay for the international recognition of Brazil's independence, and especially the abolition treaty with Britain, which had tended to confirm the widely held view that the Emperor put dynastic considerations before Brazilian national interests. Yet no attempt was made to reverse Brazilian policy on the slave trade question after the abdication crisis. On the contrary, on 21 May 1831 the Minister of Justice in the new government, Manuel José de Sousa França, instructed the Municipal Council of Rio de Janeiro (and his instruction was subsequently issued to all Municipal Councils and Provincial Presidents) to do all that they could to prevent the importation of slaves into Brazil, which he reminded them was now entirely illegal.[3] Moreover, he went on to point out that, under Article 179 of the new Criminal Code of 16 September 1830 which prohibited the reduction of free persons to slavery, the authorities already had the power to liberate any illegally imported slaves seized by them and to institute criminal proceedings against both the *contrabandistas* and any person henceforth purchasing Africans imported direct from Africa.

[1] Quoted in João Dornas Filho, *A Escravidão no Brasil* (Rio de Janeiro, 1939), p. 79. On 11 October 1829 the Minister of Marine had announced that no ship would be allowed to leave a Brazilian port for the slave trade after 15 November (Aston to Aberdeen, no. 2, 27 March 1830, F.O. 84/111). See also earlier announcement, 1 October 1829, printed in *B.F.S.P.* xvii, 743.
[2] For the political crisis culminating in the abdication of Dom Pedro I, see Calógeras, *History of Brazil*, pp. 94–118; Manchester, *H.A.H.R.* xii (1932), pp. 186, 190–7; Manchester, *H.A.H.R.* xi (1931), pp. 162–8; C. H. Haring, *Empire in Brazil* (Harvard, 1958), pp. 30–42. The Regents were General Lima e Silva, Senator Vergueiro and the Marquês de Caravelas. On 17 June 1831 the last two were replaced by deputy José da Costa Carvalho and deputy João Bráulio Muniz.
[3] See Agostinho Marques Perdigão Malheiro, *A Escravidão no Brasil: Ensaio histórico-jurídico-social* (2nd ed., São Paulo, 1944), ii. 49–50; *B.F.S.P.* xix. 531.

68

Brazil and the slave trade, 1827–1839

On 31 May 1831 Felisberto Caldeira Brant, now Marquês de Barbacena, introduced into the Brazilian Senate an anti-slave trade bill which found ready approval. It was immediately sent to the lower Chamber where several deputies had already spoken in favour of some kind of preventive legislation and where Honório Hermeto Carneiro Leão, a young *mineiro* politician who was later to become Marquês de Paraná and a leader of the Conservative Party, had actually proposed the setting up of a Commission to look into the question. Father Diogo Antônio Feijó, the liberal priest, deputy and, from July, Minister of Justice, was largely responsible for steering Barbacena's bill through the Chamber (though not without some amendments) and it finally became law on 7 November 1831.[1] The first article declared categorically that *all slaves entering Brazil would henceforth be legally free.* The law then went on to identify a wide range of persons connected with the illegal importation of slaves—the commander, master and mate of a slave ship, the owner and, if he were knowingly party to the transaction, the previous owner of the vessel, those financing the venture or assisting in any way with its preparation, those involved in the disembarkation of slaves and those knowingly buying newly imported (*boçal*) slaves—who, while they were not deemed and treated as pirates as the treaty of 1826 prescribed, became liable to between three and nine years imprisonment and corporal punishment under Article 179 of the Criminal Code and to a fine of two hundred *milreis* for each slave imported as well as to the expense of re-exporting the liberated slaves to Africa. Finally, a small reward of 30 *milreis* in respect of each slave apprehended was offered to informers or, where a slave ship was taken at sea, to the commander, officers and crew of the Brazilian vessel responsible for the capture.[2] In April 1832 further regulations were introduced which provided for the inspection by the police and by the local justices of the peace (*juizes de paz*) of all ships entering or leaving a Brazilian port and for the more careful

---

[1] For the origins and passage of the Brazilian anti-slave trade law of 1831, see Alves, *op. cit.* pp. 208–11. The *Anais do Senado* and *Anais da Câmara* unfortunately contain only brief summaries of the debates on this important bill.

[2] Law of 7 November 1831, printed in Perdigão Malheiro, ii. 239–40 and Pereira Pinto, i. 404–7. See also Alves, *op. cit.* pp. 210–11, n. 21; Manchester, *British Preëminence*, pp. 242–3.

scrutiny of slaves offered for sale in Brazil in order to verify that they had been imported before 13 March 1830.[1] The Brazilian Chamber of Deputies had accepted an anti-slave trade bill, like the treaty from which it sprang, fatalistically. The abolition of the Brazilian slave trade was a *fait accompli*. How much better that Brazilians attempting to continue the trade should be promptly dealt with by their own authorities in their own courts and under Brazilian law rather than that the British navy should assume responsibility for the suppression of the Brazilian slave trade—and that British courts should possibly treat Brazilians engaged in the trade as pirates. This attitude was summed up by José Lino Coutinho (Bahia), Minister of Empire (Internal Affairs) July 1831 to January 1832, who declared that Brazilian legislation was necessary if only *para salvar a decência nacional*.[2] (Many deputies never seriously anticipated that the Brazilian law would actually be enforced: it was *uma lei para inglês ver*.) At the same time, the passage of the law of November 1831 was undoubtedly facilitated by the political mood—liberal and reformist—in Brazil following the forced abdication of Dom Pedro I and, more important, by a temporary falling off in the demand for slaves and a certain revulsion (albeit short-lived) against the slave trade. The Brazilian slave trade both legal (south of the Equator) and illegal (north of the line) had increased markedly (if not quite tenfold, as Robert Gordon had anticipated) during the period

---

[1] Decree of 12 April 1832, printed in Pereira Pinto, i. 408–11; see also Alves, *op. cit.* p. 218; Manchester, *op. cit.* p. 243, n. 94. When it became clear that it was not practicable to repatriate slaves liberated by the Brazilian authorities two *avisos*, 29 October 1834 and 19 November 1835, were issued to guarantee their freedom and to regulate their hire to persons of *reconhecida probidade e inteireza* (printed in Pereira Pinto, i, pp. 411–15, 415–19). In the event most *Africanos livres* quickly reverted to slavery. British representations on their behalf, and on behalf of Africans freed by the Rio de Janeiro mixed court, proved in vain—at least until the second half of the nineteenth century (see below, ch. 13, pp. 380–3). For the story of the 'free Africans', see W. D. Christie, *Notes on Brazilian Questions* (London, 1865), pp. 1–50; A. C. Tavares Bastos, *Cartas do Solitario* (Rio de Janeiro, 1863), pp. 125–45.

[2] Quoted in Alves, *op. cit.* p. 208. A bill for the termination of the slave trade on 31 December 1829 presented to the Chamber by Pedro de Araújo Lima as early as 14 May 1827 (before the debate on the treaty of 1826) had been defended on the grounds that '*éste negócio é do Brasil, a decisão deve ser brasileira*' (see Luís Henrique Dias Tavares, 'As Soluções Brasileiras na Extinção do Tráfico Negreiro', *Journal of Inter-American Studies*, ix (1967), p. 373). During the period 1827–31 a number of bills were also introduced into the Brazilian legislature, notably by Antônio Ferreira França in May 1830, for the gradual abolition of slavery (see Alves, *op cit.* pp. 213–17, Calógeras, *Política Exterior*, ii. pp. 514–516).

immediately prior to its abolition: whereas during the years 1822–7 an average of sixty ships had landed approximately 25,000 slaves annually in the province of Rio de Janeiro, in 1828 over one hundred and ten ships landed approximately 45,000 slaves, a similar number were landed in 1829, and in the first six months of 1830 seventy-six ships landed over 30,000 slaves. In the province of Bahia, where in recent years some fifteen ships had annually landed between 3,000 and 4,000 slaves, in 1829 forty-three ships landed over 17,000, while in the same year a further 5,000 were landed by twenty-two ships in Pernambuco.[1] Besides more than satisfying the current needs of the Brazilian planters—the average price of a young, healthy male slave fell from £70 before March 1830 to £55 in April 1831 to £35 in July 1831[2]—and thus in the short run diminishing Brazil's dependence on the slave trade, this unprecedented influx of more than 175,000 slaves in a period of three years before final abolition aroused in a more extreme form an emotion which was always present, if for the most part dormant, in Brazil: the fear of Africanisation. In a country where Negro slaves formed such a large proportion of the total population, far more effective than conventional abolitionist arguments about the immorality of the trade or the superiority of free labour and machinery over slave labour was the argument that the continued wholesale importation of Africans degraded and barbarised an already backward country and, since slaves were the natural enemies of their masters, constituted an ever increasing threat to internal security and to white domination. 'Heaping barrels of gunpowder into the Brazilian mine' was the metaphor most frequently employed by opponents of the slave trade in Brazil. As Evaristo da Veiga, the editor of that most influential newspaper, the *Aurora Fluminense*, and one of the founders of the abolitionist

[1] Estimates from quarterly returns of British consuls to the Foreign Office. See also Walsh, *Notices of Brazil*, ii. p. 322: 1828, 43, 555; 1829, 52, 600 (figures for Rio de Janeiro only); Luís Vianna Filho, *O Negro na Bahia* (Rio de Janeiro, 1946), p. 98: 1828, 8, 127; 1829, 12, 808; 1830, 8, 425 (figures for Bahia); the Rev. C. S. Stewart, *A visit to the South Seas... during the years 1829 and 1830* (London, 1832), i. pp. 80–1. In May 1829 the U.S. minister in Rio de Janeiro reported that the trade which had doubled between 1820 and 1827 had since trebled (see Lawrence F. Hill, 'The Abolition of the African Slave Trade to Brazil', *H.A.H.R.* xi. (1931), p. 171, n. 8). Similarly the trade to Cuba had increased sharply during the three years before legal abolition in May 1820. See Corwin, *Spain and the Abolition of Slavery in Cuba*, p. 15.

[2] Pennell to Palmerston, no. 7, 23 July 1831, F.O. 84/122; see Manchester, *op. cit.* p. 239.

Brazil and the slave trade, 1827–1839

Sociedade Defensora da Liberdade e Independencia Nacional, argued, 'our country is inundated without measure by a rude and stupid race, the number of whom already existing ought to alarm us'.[1] It is a curious fact that in the public debate over the slave trade the abolitionists revealed the most overt racial prejudice: the population Brazil wanted was a white one, José Bonifácio had declared.[2] The defenders of the slave trade, on the other hand, argued that Africans were needed to 'civilise' Brazil.[3]

When the Brazilian law of 7 November 1831 came into force the Brazilian slave trade was virtually at a standstill as a result of the glut on the slave market which followed several years of unusually heavy imports (in anticipation of the end of the trade) and uncertainty in trading circles as to what measures the British and Brazilian governments might adopt once slaving became illegal and, what was more alarming, piratical. For more than two years, from the middle of 1830 to the end of 1832, very few slaves were imported into Brazil.[4] The demand for fresh supplies of slaves quickly revived, however, and, as had been widely expected, the Brazilian slave trade was reorganised on an illegal—and highly profitable—basis.

During the 1830s the plantation sector of the Brazilian economy was considerably strengthened and extended. For the first time since its initial boom during the last quarter of the eighteenth century, cotton production in Brazil stagnated in the period after 1830 (it was to revive only during the American Civil War), but sugar production, despite Cuban competition and the growth of the European sugar beet industry, increased steadily both in the traditional sugar regions of the north-east and, more particularly,

---

[1] *Aurora Fluminense*, 10 March 1834. Cf. 30 November 1831, 10 May 1834. The *Sociedade* sponsored the publication of an outstanding abolitionist tract by F. L. C. Burlamaque, *Memoria analytica acerca do commercio de escravos e acerca dos males da escravidão domestica* (Rio de Janeiro, 1837).

[2] Quoted in Chamberlain to Canning, 2 April 1823, Secret, printed in Webster, *Britain and the Independence of Latin America*, i. p. 222.

[3] On this point, see Rodrigues, *op. cit.* pp. 149–50.

[4] See, for example, Pennell to Aberdeen, 15 October 1830, F.O. 84/112; Pennell to Palmerston, 12 February, 2 March, 23 July, 27 August 1831, F.O. 84/122; Cunningham and Grigg (mixed commissioners, Rio de Janeiro) to Palmerston, 7 December 1831, F.O. 84/120; Grigg to Palmerston, 6 December 1832, F.O. 84/129; *Aurora Fluminense*, 22 August 1831, 30 November 1831; *Relatório do Ministério da Justiça* (Rio de Janeiro, 1832). Also reports from British consuls in Bahia, Pernambuco, Maranhão etc.

in São Paulo and the Campos area of Rio de Janeiro province.[1] Of even greater significance was the quite spectacular expansion in coffee production in Rio de Janeiro province and, to a lesser extent, in Minas Gerais and São Paulo. Coffee had been introduced into the northern province of Pará from Cayenne at the beginning of the eighteenth century. Later it was cultivated in the immediate neighbourhood of Rio de Janeiro—almost entirely for local consumption; the port of Rio exported little more than one ton of coffee in 1779 and only 1,400 tons as late as 1806.[2] During the first quarter of the nineteenth century, however, as a taste for coffee developed among the growing urban populations of Western Europe and North America, and its commercial possibilities became more apparent, the coffee bush gradually spread across the virgin highlands of northern Rio de Janeiro and southern Minas Gerais, eventually penetrating São Paulo. It was above all in the valley of the river Paraíba that topography, soil and climate combined to create exceptionally favourable conditions for the cultivation of coffee.[3] Land values were inflated, landholdings consolidated and the pattern of large *fazendas*, already so familiar in the areas of sugar cultivation, was reproduced in the new and expanding coffee region of south-east Brazil. During the late twenties, coffee established itself as Brazil's third most important cash crop. During the thirties it outstripped sugar and cotton to become the country's principal export,[4] accounting for 40% of

[1] See Furtado, *Economic Growth of Brazil*, pp. 116–24. For the development of the sugar plantation economy in São Paulo, see Roger Bastide and Florestan Fernandes, *Brancos e Negros em São Paulo* (2nd ed., São Paulo, 1959), pp. 23–7. Since completing this book my attention has been drawn to an interesting new monograph, Maria Thereza Schorer Petrone, *A Lavoura Canavieira em São Paulo. Expansão e Declínio (1765–1851)* (São Paulo, 1968).

[2] Richard Morse, *From Community to Metropolis. A biography of São Paulo, Brazil* (Gainsville, 1958), p. 111.

[3] For the development of coffee production in the Paraíba valley, see Stein, *Vassouras*, pp. vii, 3–26. Also Emília Viotti da Costa, *Da Senzala à Colônia* (São Paulo, 1966), pp. 19–24; Furtado, *op. cit.* pp. 123–8.

[4] See Furtado, *op. cit.* pp. 123–4. Stein gives the following figures for exports of coffee from Rio de Janeiro (in *arrobas*; *arroba* = 31·7 lb.):

1792	160	1830	1,958,925
1817	318,032	1835	3,237,190
1820	539,000	1840–1	4,982,221
1826	1,304,450		

(Stein, *op. cit.* p. 53, Table 4: production, export and price of coffee of the Rio area, 1792–1860)

73

Brazil and the slave trade, 1827-1839

Brazil's total exports by the end of the decade. An important new chapter in the economic history of Brazil had been opened.

From the outset the coffee *fazendas* were worked by African slave labour. Slaves cleared the forest, planted the bushes, harvested and processed the coffee, maintained the plantation and served in the Big House. And once established, a slave labour force required regular replenishment so high was the rate of slave mortality, the result of punishing work schedules, brutal discipline and disease.[1] On a typical coffee *fazenda* in the *município* of Vassouras in the Paraíba valley in 1835, for example, as Professor Stanley Stein has shown, 26 out of a total of 136 slaves—almost 20%—were found to be defective or sick, and during a period of only 16 months (1835-7) 16% of the *fazenda's* slaves died.[2] It was not uncommon for a planter to have only 25 acclimatised, trained and working slaves three years after buying a lot of 100.[3] A number of slaves were recruited through the internal slave trade from area to area within Brazil (Minas Gerais, for example, had under-utilised labour resources), but only the trade across the Atlantic could provide the coffee planters of the Paraíba valley with the regular supplies of field labour they so urgently required. 'America devours the blacks', wrote the French émigré Charles Auguste Taunay in his *Manual do agricultor brasileiro*, 'If continued importation were not supplying them, the race would shortly disappear from our midst'.[4] Legal or illegal, there seemed to be no alternative to the Atlantic slave trade. Brazilian non-slave labour—white, mulatto and Negro—was not readily available in sufficient quantity and, so it was believed, like Amerindian labour, unsuitable for large-scale plantation agriculture.[5] Renewed efforts to encourage European immigration had produced only meagre results: never more than 2,500 and frequently less than 1,000 Europeans were attracted to Brazil in any one year, and they did not choose to travel thousands of miles in order to work alongside African slaves on sugar, cotton or coffee plantations.[6] During the late twenties rumours had circulated in Rio de Janeiro and in Bahia

[1] See Stein, *op. cit.* pp. 132-47, 161-95.
[2] *Ibid.* p. 185.　　　　　　　　　　　[3] *Ibid.* p. 70.
[4] Quoted in *ibid.* p. 227.　　　　　　[5] See Furtado, *op. cit.* pp. 134-6.
[6] José Fernando Carneiro, *Imigração e Colonização no Brasil* (Rio de Janeiro, 1949), Appendix.

74

that Brazilian and Portuguese merchants were planning to introduce 'free black colonists' into Brazil directly the slave trade became illegal and, provided contracts were voluntarily made and
'colonists' were not reduced to slavery on their arrival, there
seemed to be no legal impediment to the scheme. Britain's representatives in Brazil could not see how the British government
could deny the right of the Negro to leave Africa of his own free
will if sufficient inducement and adequate guarantees were
offered.[1] Lord Aberdeen, however, British Foreign Secretary at
the time, saw in this only a rather obvious attempt to continue
the slave trade under another guise since in his view it would be
impossible to guarantee the freedom of African colonists in a
society so completely based upon African slavery. In December
1829 Aberdeen had therefore made it known that since the treaty
of 1826 rendered the trade illegal 'under any pretext and in any
manner whatever', Brazilian ships carrying 'free blacks' would be
'liable to be treated and dealt with in the same manner as if they
had been more openly engaged in the traffic for slaves'.[2] The idea
was therefore dropped.

As early as November 1833, George Jackson and Frederick
Grigg, the British commissioners in the Rio de Janeiro mixed
court, wrote that, after a lull of two or three years, and in spite of
the law of 1831 which declared it illegal, the Brazilian slave trade
had started to grow at an alarming rate.[3] Ostensibly bound for the
west African coast with tobacco and rum for the legitimate
African trade, or for Montevideo and the Río de la Plata, or simply
for another Brazilian port, ships regularly left Rio de Janeiro and
neighbouring ports for the African slave trade. On their return,
with the aid of an elaborate system of shore signals, they landed
their illicit cargoes of slaves at various points along the Brazilian
coast: between Rio de Janeiro and Vitória—at Guarapari, Macaé,
São João da Barra (at the mouth of the River Paraíba down-
stream from Campos), Rio das Ostras, Manguinhas, Ilha de Santa
Anna, Maricá Islands, Cabo Frio; between Rio de Janeiro and
Santos—at Mangaratiba, Restinga de Marambaia, Dois Rios,

[1] E.g. Pennell to Aberdeen, 23 January, 23 April 1830, F.O. 84/112.
[2] Aberdeen to Aston, 7 December 1829, F.O. 84/95.
[3] Jackson and Grigg to Palmerston, 12 November 1833, F.O. 84/138.

Brazil and the slave trade, 1827–1839

Angra dos Reis, Ilha Grande, Parati, Ubatuba, Ilhas dos Porcos, Ilha de São Sebastião, Ilha de Santo Amaro, Periqué, Sombrio; in Rio itself on the quiet beaches of Copacabana, Glória and Botofogo; across the bay on the beaches of Niterói and Jurujuba; and even beneath the guns of the fortress of Santa Cruz at the entrance to Rio harbour. The empty vessels then proceeded to the port of Rio de Janeiro or, with increasing frequency, to one of the smaller Brazilian ports where they entered *em castro* (in ballast) or *quase em castro*, or with a small cargo of wax, ivory and oil from West Africa, and immediately began refitting for the slave trade. *Boçal* or *nôvo* Negroes who were not immediately transferred to plantations near the coast after disembarkation were housed in recently established depots (some of the largest were to be found in the Rua de Rosário near the docks in Rio de Janeiro) where attempts were made, without much success, to teach them the rudiments of the Portuguese language so that they might be auctioned along with *ladinos* (slaves already acclimatised and trained) and *crioulos* (slaves born in Brazil). Upcountry planters, in Vassouras, Valença, Paraíba do Sul, Juiz de Fora, Leopoldina and other *municípios* of the Paraíba valley were supplied with slaves either by the agents and middlemen (*comissários*), many of them Portuguese, who marketed their produce and supplied them with consumer goods, or by travelling slave pedlars (*comboieiros*).[1] 'Again and again while travelling in the interior . . .', wrote George Gardner in his *Travels in the Interior of Brazil*, 'I have seen troops of slaves of both sexes who could not speak a single word of Portuguese, varying from 20 to 100 individuals, marched inland for sale, or already belonging to proprietors of plantations.'[2] Illegal landings were also regularly made in and near Bahia (at Itaparica, Ilha dos Frades, Santo Amaro do Ipitanga and the beautiful beach of Itapoan),[3] in Pernambuco and, less frequently, at Paranaguá (200 miles south of Santos), and in the provinces of Santa Catarina and Rio Grande do Sul. Even the Bahian trade, however, now constituted only a minor branch of the growing metropolitan trade which served the sugar plantations of Rio and São Paulo and, most important, the developing coffee areas of the Paraíba valley.

[1] See Stein, *op. cit.* pp. 69–73.
[2] George Gardner, *Travels in the Interior of Brazil . . . during the years 1836–41* (London, 1846), p. 12.   [3] See Vianna Filho, *op. cit.* p. 86.

Brazil and the slave trade, 1827–1839

Successive Brazilian governments proved incapable of enforcing the law of 7 November 1831 and thus of preventing the revival and expansion of the slave trade after it had become illegal. They were, for the most part, weak and short-lived, lacking adequate financial, military or naval resources, and preoccupied with the constitutional and political conflicts which inevitably followed upon Dom Pedro's abdication and with a series of provincial revolts which threatened to destroy the unity and stability achieved at independence.[1] For a short time a Brazilian naval squadron patrolled the coast of Rio de Janeiro province, and during the years 1834–5 captured six slave ships.[2] However, the Brazilian navy was needed for more urgent duties when, in 1835, provincial revolts with distinct separatist overtones broke out in the extreme north and the extreme south of the country (in Pará and Rio Grande do Sul). All serious efforts to suppress, or at least to obstruct, the trade at sea were henceforth abandoned. Meanwhile, a stream of orders to the presidents of maritime provinces, demanding more determined efforts to prevent slaves being landed and the punishment of slave importers and those who abetted them, issued forth from the Ministry of Justice in Rio de Janeiro, notably during Aureliano de Sousa e Oliveira Coutinho's term of office (June 1833 to January 1835).[3] The administration of justice and law enforcement at the local level, however, was in the hands of elected *juizes de paz* and officers of the National Guard, few of whom were above accepting bribes and most of whom were themselves landowners or else were linked by family and interest to the landed class which had a stake in the continuation of the slave trade.[4] With rare exceptions they were therefore prepared to connive at slave landings. Once clear of the coast newly imported

[1] For a brief account of political developments during the thirties—'a decade of extraordinary confusion and commotion'—see Haring op. cit. pp. 45–52. For a fuller treatment see Sérgio Buarque de Holanda (ed.), *História Geral da Civilização Brasileira*, tomo II, vol. ii *O Brasil Monárquico. Dispersão e Unidade* (São Paulo, 1964).

[2] See below, ch. 5, pp. 138–9, 140–1.

[3] See list of government orders and decrees for the suppression of the slave trade (most of them issued during the years 1834–5), enclosed in Hamilton (Rio de Janeiro) to Aberdeen, no. 36, 13 August 1842, F.O. 84/408. Also *Relatórios do Ministério da Justiça* (Rio de Janeiro, 1832–7).

[4] The administrative history of Brazil during the period of the Regency remains to be written. But see T. W. Pa´mer, 'A Momentous Decade in Brazilian Administrative History, 1831–40', H.A.H.R. xxx (1950), pp. 209–17; *História Geral da Civilização Brasileira*, tomo II, vol. ii, chapter I.

77

slaves were in any case beyond the reach of the law: *fazendeiros de café* and *senhores de engenho* (sugar planters) exercised virtually supreme senhorial authority over their own estates. On those rare occasions when a case was brought to court, the ends of justice were invariably defeated by a combination of shameless bribery and intimidation. Moreover, trial was by jury in all criminal cases and jurors were for the most part chosen from the ranks of the propertied slave-owning section of society. Carefully selected special magistrates (*juizes de direito*) who were sent periodically by the provincial authorities to look into the evasion of the law were impotent. In November 1834 Agostinho Moreira Guerra was confined to his home on Ilha Grande 'as in a besieged citadel in constant fear of assassination, not daring to stir out unless accompanied by an armed force'.[1] The suppression of the slave trade, he declared, was 'totally impracticable in the present circumstances'.[2] In January 1835, Joaquim José Rodrigues Tôrres, president of Rio de Janeiro province, complained to Aureliano, the Minister of Justice, that he was 'almost reduced to the character of a mere spectator of crimes which I can neither check nor punish'; it was, he wrote, 'impossible to withstand the torrent which every day hurries us nearer to the brink of a horrible abyss'.[3] Only for a short period early in 1835 was there any discernible reaction against the slave trade. This followed a major slave insurrection in Bahia which, combined with threats of similar revolts elsewhere, served to remind white Brazilians of the dangers inherent in the annual importation of thousands of fresh slaves from Africa.[4]

In October 1835 the period during which three Regents had

---

[1] Jackson and Grigg to Palmerston, no. 34, 18 December 1834, F.O. 84/153.

[2] Agostinho Moreira Guerra to Joaquim José Rodrigues Torres, President of Rio de Janeiro province, 12 November 1834, enclosed in *ibid*. For a very similar case, see José Antônio Pimenta Bueno, *juiz de direito* in São Sebastião, to Rafael Tobias de Aguiar, President of São Paulo province, 8 March, enclosed in Jackson and Grigg no. 7, 28 March 1834, F.O. 84/152.

[3] Rodrigues Torres to Aureliano, 16 January, enclosed in Jackson and Grigg, no. 4, 24 January 1835, F.O. 84/174.

[4] See speech of president of Bahia to Bahia legislative assembly, 1 March, and representation of Rio de Janeiro legislative assembly, 17 March, enclosed in Jackson and Grigg, no. 15, 23 March 1835, F.O. 84/174; representation of Bahia legislative assembly, 11 May, enclosed in Jackson and Grigg, no. 35, 6 July 1835, F.O. 84/175. For an account of the Bahian slave revolt see R. Nina Rodrigues, *Os Africanos no Brasil* (Rio de Janeiro, 1932), pp. 79–83; Donald Pierson, *Negroes in Brazil: a study of race contact at Bahia* (Chicago, 1942), pp. 43–5.

exercised power on behalf of the young Dom Pedro II came to an end and Father Feijó elected in April, took office as single Regent of Brazil. Feijó had himself been in part responsible for the passage of the 1831 anti-slave trade law and among the ministers he appointed were a number with abolitionist inclinations, including Antônio Paulino Limpo de Abreu (Minister of Empire, October 1835 to February 1836, June to September 1836, March to May 1837, Minister of Justice, October 1835 to June 1836, Minister of Foreign Affairs, June to November 1836, February to May 1837) and Manuel Alves Branco (Minister of Foreign Affairs, October 1835 to February 1836, Minister of Empire and Minister of Finance, May to September 1837). However, no government in Rio de Janeiro exercised effective control over the country as a whole—indeed as a result of changes embodied in an *Ato Adicional* of 12 August 1834 the power of the central government was now to a considerable extent *constitutionally* curtailed.[1] During the mid-thirties the slave trade continued to expand steadily with little or no interference from the Brazilian local authorities along the coast until it eventually reached and passed its pre-1826 level. In September 1836 the British commissioners wrote that 'at no period has it perhaps been ever carried on with greater activity and daring'.[2] In November Hamilton Hamilton, the British minister, reported that there were 3,500 slaves gathered in depots at Campos, 3,000 at Macaé, 2,000 at São Sebastião, and 3,000 in Rio de Janeiro, and that in consequence slave prices were falling for the first time in five years.[3] Nevertheless, during the last quarter of 1836 thirty-six slave ships left Rio de Janeiro for Africa and twenty-nine ships arrived with slave cargoes (fourteen of them landed over 6,000 slaves during the last six weeks of the year).[4] And by April 1837 there had been a further 'great and lamentable increase' in the trade.[5] Approximately 46,000 slaves, most of them from Angola, the Congo and Moçambique, were illegally landed from nearly 100 ships in the provinces of Rio de Janeiro and São Paulo alone during 1837.[6]

[1] See Palmer, *op. cit.* pp. 213 ff.
[2] Jackson and Grigg, no. 24, 30 September 1836, F.O. 84/199.
[3] Hamilton, no. 12, 11 November 1836, F.O. 84/204. Hamilton Charles James Hamilton was British minister in Rio de Janeiro, May 1836 to August 1846 (although absent on extended leave, December 1837 to July 1841).
[4] See Appendix.
[5] Grigg, no. 11, 5 April 1837, F.O. 84/215.   [6] See Appendix.

Brazil and the slave trade, 1827–1839

During the years 1834–7 there were sporadic attempts to strengthen the Brazilian anti-slave trade law of 7 November 1831. Bills were introduced which, for example, would have enabled the Brazilian government to authorise the capture and condemnation of vessels which, while not actually in the process of importing slaves, had clearly done so, which would have taken cases of slave trading out of the hands of the *juizes de paz*, which would have imposed stiffer penalties on those convicted of importing or attempting to import slaves, and which would have imposed stricter controls over the departure and arrival of ships in the African trade. Without exception all came to grief in the Chamber of Deputies which during the period of the Regency (1831–40) found itself in an unusually powerful position and which, particularly after the elections of 1833 (the first since the abdication of Dom Pedro I), came firmly under the control of land-owning and slave-owning interests.[1] The Chamber proved far more responsive to the opposite demand, made with increasing frequency during this period, that all existing anti-slave trade legislation should be repealed. As early as May 1834 the municipal council of Bananal (São Paulo) had addressed a resolution to the legislature in Rio de Janeiro in favour of repealing the law of 1831.[2] During the next three years a flood of similar petitions reached the capital from municipalities throughout Rio de Janeiro, São Paulo and Minas Gerais. A law so completely out of touch with the realities of Brazilian life, it was argued, could not possibly be enforced and any attempt to do so could only bring the law as a whole into contempt. Of more immediate importance to the Brazilian planters was the fact that although the law of 1831 could not prevent their obtaining all the slaves they needed, it did mean that the thousands of Negroes who had been and were still being imported into

[1] Alves, *op. cit.* pp. 220–1; *Relatório do Ministério da Justiça*, 1834, 1835, 1836; Jackson and Grigg, no. 14, 17 November 1833, F.O. 84/138, no. 14, 6 June, no. 18, 28 June 1834, F.O. 84/152, no. 26, 14 October, no. 29, 10 November 1834, F.O. 84/153, no. 36, 27 July 1835, F.O. 84/175, no. 24, 30 September, no. 28, 2 November 1836, F.O. 84/199. Until 1855 the Brazilian Chamber of Deputies consisted of approximately 100 members elected on a limited class franchise. The provinces most heavily represented were Minas Gerais (20), Bahia (13), Pernambuco (13), São Paulo (9), Rio de Janeiro (8). Members of the second legislative chamber, the Senate, were nominated by the emperor for life.
[2] Enclosed in Jackson and Grigg, no. 14, 6 June 1834, F.O. 84/152. The question had been discussed in government circles as early as January 1834 (Jackson and Grigg, no. 3, 15 January 1834, F.O. 84/152).

Brazil came to them legally free. This created a potentially dangerous situation and it was for this reason that the planters and their spokesmen in the capital demanded not only the repeal of the law but also a general amnesty for those who had already infringed it. As well as seeking to safeguard their future needs they also sought security for the 'property' they already held. The question of whether the law of 1831 should be repealed was discussed in the Chamber itself on more than one occasion, but successive governments somehow managed to avoid a step which would so greatly antagonise Britain.

On 30 June 1837, conceding that the anti-slave trade law he had fostered had proved entirely inadequate for its purpose, the Marquês de Barbacena introduced into the Senate a new bill which he hoped would be accepted as a realistic compromise by opposing interests.[1] On the one hand, Barbacena sympathised with the manpower problems of the plantation owners, 'peaceful landlords, heads of respectable families, men full of industry and virtue, who promote public and private prosperity with their labour': without the slave trade, he agreed, they faced—at least in the short run—the possibility of a steady decline in their labour force 'as sickness, old age and mortality make an end of the largest army when not recruited'. Moreover, it was unreasonable, Barbacena believed, to punish the planters for not looking too closely into the origin of the slaves they bought; there had never been an infraction of the law, he said, 'with such plausible reasons for being excused, if not forgiven'. It was also impracticable to punish slave owners for having violated the law in the past. 'Endeavouring to bring to justice the parties guilty of purchasing Negroes illegally introduced into this Empire', Barbacena was to tell W. G. Ouseley, the British *chargé d'affaires*, a year later, 'would be . . . worse than Civil War.'[2] On the other hand, he was more convinced than ever that the slave trade was not only immoral but

---

[1] *Anais do Senado de 1837*, 175–81; *Jornal do Comércio*, 1 July 1837; Hesketh and Grigg, no. 22, 2 July 1837, F.O. 84/218; Hamilton, no. 15, 3 July 1837, F.O. 84/222. See also Alves, *op. cit.* pp. 225–8; Antônio Augusto de Aguiar, *Vida do Marquez de Barbacena* (Rio de Janeiro, 1896), pp. 953–6; João Pandiá Calógeras, *Da Regência à Queda de Rozas* (São Paulo, 1933), pp. 345–8.

[2] Quoted in Ouseley to Palmerston, no. 1, 9 July 1838, F.O. 84/253. William Gore Ouseley was secretary to the legation in Rio de Janeiro 1833–45 and served as *chargé d'affaires* January to August 1833, January to May 1836, June 1838 to July 1841.

that, in the long run, it constituted a serious threat to Brazil's internal peace, stability and racial equilibrium. If the trade were to continue at its present level, he told the Senate, 'Brazil will very soon be not the imitator and rival of civilized nations but the imitator and rival of the coast of Africa.' He therefore proposed, first, that more effective measures should be taken to prevent the importation of slaves but, secondly, that the purchase of slaves, once they had been imported, should no longer be a punishable offence. Under Barbacena's bill, which was designed to replace the law of 1831, the importation into Brazil of either slaves or 'free blacks' was prohibited; Brazilian ships and foreign ships in Brazilian ports found with slaves on board *or even equipped for the slave trade* would be liable to capture and, if condemned, would be broken up and sold; the proceeds would go to the captors and informers in the form of higher rewards; anyone found guilty of transporting and landing slaves or concealing newly imported slaves would continue to face imprisonment, fines and the expense of re-exporting the liberated slaves; the examination of ships arriving at or departing from a Brazilian port would be further tightened up and clearances for the African coast refused unless bond were given to the value of the ship and its cargo, returnable after eighteen months only if the ship had not in the meantime engaged in the slave trade. Under the final article, however, the existing law of November 1831, which had declared automatically free all Africans entering Brazil as slaves and which had made the purchase of illegally imported slaves a punishable offence, was to be revoked.[1]

Despite opposition from several members, Barbacena's bill was approved by the Senate.[2] On 9 August it was sent to the Chamber where it came up for discussion on 2 September. The Brazilian deputies were deeply divided in their attitudes towards the bill.[3] For those who favoured the repeal of the 1831 law (the majority) it brought partial satisfaction, but they objected to the remainder

[1] For the text of the bill, see Alves, *op. cit.* pp. 226–8.
[2] *Jornal do Comércio*, 5 August 1837; Hesketh and Grigg, no. 30, 14 August 1837, F.O. 84/219.
[3] Debates reported in Hesketh and Grigg, no. 33, 4 September, no. 35, 19 September, no. 40, 3 November 1837, F.O. 84/219, and Hamilton, no. 27, 28 November 1837, F.O. 84/223.

of the bill directed as it was at the more efficient suppression of the slave trade. Those who wished to see the slave trade suppressed (the minority) were seriously disturbed by the bill's final article: taken as a whole, they insisted, the bill could only serve to encourage the trade since it simply put a premium on the ingenuity of the slave smuggler; moreover, it amounted to an amnesty for all those who had been breaking the law in the past and deprived those Africans who had been landed in Brazil and sold into slavery since 1830 of all hope of asserting their legal right to liberty. Nor was the British legation in Rio de Janeiro slow to make it known how much the British government would deplore the passage of Barbacena's bill—despite its many welcome features—if it were to include the repeal of existing anti-slave trade legislation.[1] In the event, however, the *Comissão de Diplomacia* was no less divided than the Chamber to whom it reported on 30 September, and the session ended in mid-October without any progress having been made.

Meanwhile, in September 1837, a major political crisis had ended with the resignation of Father Feijó and the elevation to the Regency of the President of the Chamber of Deputies, Pedro de Araújo Lima (*a pernambucano* and the future Marquês de Olinda). It also brought to power a government composed of, and strongly supported by, politicians who, like Bernardo Pereira de Vasconcelos of Minas Gerais, Joaquim José Rodrigues Tôrres of Rio de Janeiro (the future Visconde de Itaboraí), José da Costa Carvalho of São Paulo (a former Regent and the future Marquês de Monte Alegre), Miguel Calmon du Pin e Almeida of Bahia (the future Marquês de Abrantes) and Araújo Lima himself, had progressively dissociated themselves not only from Feijó but also from what they had come to regard as the extreme liberalism, federalism and decentralisation of the years since the *Ato Adicional* of 1834, and who were eventually to advocate a return (*regresso*) to order, authority and a stronger central executive. United by close family ties and common interests, these *regressistas*, together with younger politicians like Honório Hermeto Carneiro Leão (Minas Gerais) and Paulino José Soares de Sousa (Rio de Janeiro), were to form for a generation to come the nucleus of the *Partido Conservador*.

[1] Hesketh and Grigg, no. 30, 14 August 1837.

Brazil and the slave trade, 1827–1839

At the same time the government of 19 September 1837,[1] which
remained in office until 16 April 1839, was much closer than its
predecessors had been to the views of the majority of deputies in
the Chamber (it has frequently been described as the *gabinete
parlamentar*) and even more in tune with the interests of the sugar
and coffee *fazendeiros*. Bernardo Pereira de Vasconcelos, the dominant force in the government, who combined the posts of Minister
of Empire and Minister of Justice, had from the outset opposed the
abolition treaty of 1826[2] and since 1836 had campaigned both inside
and outside the Chamber for the repeal of the law of 1831. His
position had been made clear in a public speech a month before
taking office when he had declared: 'Let the English carry into execution this treaty which they have forced upon us by abusing their
superior power, but to expect that we should co-operate with the
English in these speculations gilded with the name of humanity is
unreasonable.'[3] Frankly acknowledging that even had they wished
to they were powerless to suppress the slave trade,[4] the new government made no attempt to enforce the law of 1831 and, moreover,
abandoned many of the administrative measures which previous
governments had found it convenient to adopt. One of Vasconcelos's first acts as Minister of Justice, for example, was to revoke a
decree of 6 June 1837 for the more scrupulous examination of ships
arriving from Africa and to release three ships already detained.[5]
Even Antônio Peregrino Maciel Monteiro, the Foreign Minister,
who, almost alone amongst senior ministers, was known to oppose
the slave trade and who deplored publicly 'the torrent of frauds
and abuses' which surrounded it,[6] could see little point in institut-
ing proceedings against those involved in the illegal trade since, as
he told George Gordon, the British *chargé d'affaires*, in February
1838, 'it may be safely predicted from experience that no court of
justice will be found to give sentence against them'.[7] A few months

---

[1] I have adopted the Brazilian practice of referring to governments during the period of
the empire (1822–89) by the date on which they assumed office.
[2] See Walsh, *op. cit.* ii. pp. 217–19.   [3] Quoted in *Jornal do Comércio*, 19 August 1837.
[4] *Relatório do Ministério da Justiça*, May 1838.
[5] Hamilton, no. 26, 28 November 1837, F.O. 84/223; Hesketh and Grigg, no. 45,
17 November 1837, F.O. 84/219.
[6] *Relatório do Ministério dos Negócios Estrangeiros*, May 1838.
[7] Monteiro to Gordon, 12 February, enclosed in Gordon to Palmerston, no. 4, 28 February
1838, F.O. 84/252. Gordon was *chargé d'affaires* from the departure of Hamilton in
December 1837 to the return of Ouseley in June 1838.

later Francisco Gé Acaiaba de Montezuma, a former Minister of Justice and Minister of Foreign Affairs (May to September 1837), declared:

The law of 7 November is a complete nullity. The object of putting a stop to the traffic has not been attained, nor have the government any hopes that it will be. The speculators in it rely on a total impunity the moment the landing is effected. Many of the local authorities protect the disembarkation of the slaves and their passage from one point to another. In several places this is going on in the face of open day and at any hour without concealment. Woe to the magistrate who should attempt to interfere. He becomes an object of hatred, his life is in danger and some have been assassinated. No captures are made at sea for the promised reward is no longer paid to the captors. In a word, all conspire in favour of the traffic and against the law to repress it.[1]

Indeed the law of 1831 was so patently a dead letter that even the demand for its repeal was beginning to subside a little. As for Barbacena's bill with its provisions for stricter preventive measures, this was quietly forgotten.

The Brazilian government were under constant pressure from the British legation in Rio de Janeiro (which virtually assumed the role of an abolitionist society in Brazil) to enforce the law of 1831 and to introduce more effective anti-slave trade legislation: in May and again in September 1838, for example, Britain formally demanded the fulfilment of Brazil's engagement of 1826 to declare the slave trade piracy and to treat the traders as pirates.[2] Britain's representatives in Brazil, however, reported, with increasing irritation, that far from doing all in their power to suppress the slave trade the Brazilian government were shamelessly protecting it. In January 1838 Gordon wrote that the trade had reached 'fearful and impressive' proportions;[3] and during the next twelve months another 40,000 or so slaves from the Congo, Angola and Moçambique were landed in the area to the north and south of Rio de Janeiro—notably at São Sebastião, Campos, Ilha Grande and in

---

[1] Quoted in Jackson and Grigg, no. 3, 9 April 1838, F.O. 84/241.
[2] Gordon to Monteiro, 28 May, enclosed in Gordon to Palmerston, no. 14, 15 June 1838, F.O. 84/253; Ouseley to Monteiro, 5 September, enclosed in Ouseley to Palmerston, no. 16, 24 September 1838, F.O. 84/254 (following Palmerston to Hamilton, 28 February 1838, F.O. 84/254).
[3] Gordon to Palmerston, no. 1, 19 January 1838, F.O. 84/252.

the capital itself.[1] A mass of evidence regarding slave landings, the individuals concerned and the location of their establishments was patiently gathered by the British legation and by British consulates and regularly transmitted to the Brazilian authorities. Nothing was done, however, to prevent ships fitting out and leaving Brazil for the African coast or from landing their slave cargoes on their return. Public sales of newly imported slaves took place almost every day in Rio de Janeiro. The Brazilian government, as Luís Vianna Filho has said, simply resorted to a policy of neither seeing nor hearing (*não ver e não ouvir*)—blind to the vast illegal importation of slaves and deaf to British protests against it.[2]

In April 1839 the Cabinet of 19 September 1837 was forced out of office. The three which followed—in rapid succession—contained at least a few genuine opponents of the trade, notably Cândido Batista de Oliveira, Foreign Minister and Finance Minister *ad interim* in the Cabinet of 16 April 1839, and Caetano Maria Lopes Gama, Foreign Minister in the Cabinet of 1 September 1839 and Minister of Empire as well as Foreign Minister in the Cabinet of 18 May 1840. For more than a year the slave trade was less openly protected; indeed some hesitant steps were taken to check its growth.[3] On 23 July 1840 the 'parliamentary *coup d'état*', which brought to an end the Regency of Pedro de Araújo Lima and invested the fifteen year old Dom Pedro with Imperial authority, also gave Brazil eight months of enlightened, liberal—and strongly abolitionist—government. Led by Antônio Carlos de Andrada Machado e Silva, a brother of José Bonifácio (who died in 1838), the liberal *gabinete da maioridade* included the third of the remarkable Andrada brothers, Martim Francisco, as Finance Minister, together with Limpo de Abreu as Minister of Justice, and Antônio Francisco de Paula e Holanda Cavalcanti de Albuquerque as Minister of Marine. This government successfully resisted renewed pressure from the provincial assemblies of Minas Gerais,

[1] See Appendix.
[2] Vianna Filho, *op. cit.* p. 88. In June 1827, referring to the continuation of the illegal trade north of the equator, Charles Pennell in Bahia had accused the local authorities of 'perverse blindness and diseased optics' (Pennell to Canning, no. 11, 1 June 1827, F.O. 84/71).
[3] Ouseley to Palmerston, no. 50, 28 September 1839, F.O. 84/287.

Brazil and the slave trade, 1827–1839

Bahia and Rio de Janeiro, as well as from the Chamber of Deputies, for the repeal of the law of 1831. Circulars calling for tighter restrictions on the trade were dispatched to the presidents of maritime provinces and although the warships available for anti-slave trade duties remained extremely few in number and poor in quality, for a few months the Brazilian navy enjoyed modest success. The press was virulent in its opposition to these moves and local authorities again failed to give the government their full support. Nevertheless, W. G. Ouseley had no doubt that the change of attitude in government circles went some way towards discouraging the slave traders for the first time in many years. He even detected, or so he imagined, a gradual but perceptible change in Brazilian public opinion towards the slave trade.[1] The situation was soon to change, however: on 23 March 1841 the Cabinet of the Majority was replaced by a *gabinete conservador* and the Conservatives remained in power for three years. Once again Brazilian governments in Rio de Janeiro gave their blessing to the illegal slave trade or at least did little to obstruct it. The Cabinet of 1 February 1844, broadly Liberal in composition, and the Cabinets which succeeded it during the *qüinqüênio liberal* (1844–8), in which politicians like Alves Branco and Limpo de Abreu (who had been closely identified with the Feijó régime) as well as Holanda Caval-canti, José Carlos Pereira de Almeida Tôrres (Visconde de Macaé) and Francisco de Paula Sousa e Melo were prominent, felt obliged to compete with the Conservatives in their willingness to permit the slave trade.[2] For almost a decade, with the exception of a brief period of two months (August to September 1848),[3] no serious attempt was made to enforce the law of 1831. It was 1850 before a Brazilian government was fully prepared—and, it should be added, fully able—to fulfil its treaty engagements of 1826 and launch a full-scale and ultimately successful effort to suppress the illegal slave trade.[4]

---

[1] Ouseley, no. 32, 12 August 1839, F.O. 84/324; Ouseley, no. 46, 16 October 1840, F.O. 84/325. Also F.O. memorandum on the indications in Brazil of a spirit hostile to the slave trade, 2 June 1842, F.O. 84/445.

[2] See Paula Beiguelman, 'Aspectos da organização político—partidária no Império Brasileiro', *Revista de História* (São Paulo), xxv. (1962), no. 51, pp. 6–7; *História Geral da Civilização Brasileira* II, iii, pp. 195–6.

[3] See below ch. 10, pp. 292–4.   [4] See below ch. 12.

CHAPTER 4

TREATY NEGOTIATIONS, 1830–1839

So long as Brazilian governments proved unable or unwilling to enforce their own legislation prohibiting the importation of slaves into Brazil in the period after 1830, Britain, or to be more precise the British navy, represented the only serious threat to the continued existence of the illegal Brazilian slave trade. And the navy's success or failure in containing the Brazilian slave trade—it was doubtful whether, without the co-operation of Brazil, the British navy could ever completely suppress it—was not dependent solely on the number of warships available for anti-slave trade duties. It was also, and more immediately, dependent on the extent to which the necessary powers to visit, search and capture slave vessels in the Brazilian trade had been accorded British warships under the various anti-slave trade treaties which Britain had signed with Brazil and other foreign powers.

Considering the attention Canning had devoted to the precise nature of the treaty Britain had extracted from Brazil in 1826, it is remarkable how little thought he seems to have given to the crucial question of how the Brazilian slave trade, once illegal, could be suppressed by the British navy if, as seemed likely even at the time, the Brazilian government failed to fulfil its treaty obligations. For three years (1827–30) the Brazilian trade remained illegal only north of the equator and the treaty of 1826 provided that, during this period, British cruisers should continue to operate under the Anglo-Portuguese Right of Search Convention of 1817; an Act of 2 July 1827 (7 and 8 Geo. IV cap. 74) authorised Anglo-Brazilian mixed commissions, which were to sit in Rio de Janeiro and Sierra Leone, to adjudicate any Brazilian ships captured north of the line —provided they were carrying slaves.[1] In August 1827 Gordon (still in Rio de Janeiro) had been instructed by Lord Dudley (Foreign Secretary 1827–8) to demand an article, to be added to

[1] Hertslet's *Treaties*, iii. 33–40.

the treaty of 1817, 'establishing the illicit employment of the vessels by their fitting-up and by other general circumstances . . . in lieu of the clause requiring proof of slaves having been actually embarked'.[1] The Brazilian government, however, had rejected all Gordon's approaches. The nearest the British government came to securing an 'equipment clause' was when they toyed with the idea of allowing the slave trade to continue south of the equator for a further six months as a *quid pro quo*. Negotiations in London, however, broke down over the details of what comprised equipment for slaving purposes and thereby justified a ship's seizure and condemnation.[2] The treaty of 1817, and the British navy's powers under it, therefore remained unchanged.

But what was to happen after 13 March 1830 when the entire Brazilian slave trade became illegal? Under article 1 of the treaty of 1826 the slave trade carried on by Brazilians was to be 'deemed and treated as piracy'. By whom? By both parties to the treaty? Could British cruisers search and capture Brazilian slave ships anywhere on the high seas? With or without slaves on board? Could British courts adjudicate upon them as pirate vessels? Could individuals concerned in the trade be tried and punished as pirates? There was a remarkable degree of confusion over the exact meaning of the treaty's first and most important article.

In January 1826 Stephen Lushington, a prominent abolitionist lawyer and M.P., criticising the abolition treaty negotiated by Sir Charles Stuart and eventually rejected by Canning, had emphasised the importance of declaring the Brazilian slave trade piracy in order that 'any British cruiser might seize a Brazilian ship so engaged and the crew would be liable to be brought to trial as pirates and their property confiscated'.[3] During the debate on the treaty of 1826 in the Brazilian Chamber of Deputies, several

---

[1] Dudley no. 5, 31 August 1827, F.O. 84/71 (James Bandinel, apparently alone, had suggested that it would be wise to secure the addition of an equipment clause to the Treaty of 1817 *before* signing an abolition treaty with Brazil: comments on Lushington memorandum, 26 January 1826, F.O. 84/60).

[2] Gordon to Aracaty, 17 December 1826, enclosed in Gordon to Dudley, no. 1, 17 May 1828, F.O. 84/84; 'Memorandum on the grounds on which it might be advisable to take into consideration the proposal of M. d'Itabayana to prolong the period at present fixed for the final abolition of the Brazilian slave trade', 2 September 1828, F.O. 84/71; Itabayana to Aberdeen, 9 May 1829, F.O. 84/95.

[3] Memorandum, 26 January 1826, F.O. 84/60.

speakers had anticipated, with some anxiety, that Brazilian slave ships captured by the British navy would be dealt with as pirate ships in British courts.[1] And more than one British official concerned with the abolition of the slave trade interpreted the first article of the treaty of 1826 in the same light. For instance, Henry Hayne, commissary judge in Rio de Janeiro, exulted over 'that valuable and important word, piracy', adding, 'It would [also] appear to be an important object to get that little word piracy inserted in the Portuguese treaty as soon as possible.'[2] Looking to the period after 1830, William Smith, commissioner of arbitration in Freetown, urged the immediate creation of a court there competent to take cognisance of Brazilian subjects charged with piracy.[3] Before leaving London for the north of Brazil as British consul in São Luís de Maranhão, Robert Hesketh also expressed himself strongly on the meaning of the treaty of 1826: Brazilian slavers (even those without slaves on board) could be detained off the Brazilian coast, he thought, and tribunals competent to try both crew and vessel could be set up in any port where there was a British consul; the owner, master and crew of a condemned vessel would be liable to severe punishment for piracy; their offence could even be a capital one if they had resisted capture by force.[4] This was also the view expressed by the Rev. Robert Walsh, chaplain to the British legation in Rio de Janeiro, in his well known book *Notices of Brazil in 1828 and 1829*: after 23 March 1830 (*sic*), he wrote, the trade would no longer be permitted and 'the whole of this ransacked and harassed coast will then be protected and every slaver on any part of it will be seized and tried as a pirate'.[5] Even the slave traders apparently feared the worst: during 1830 they left the west African coast in convoys, convinced that if they were detained by a British cruiser they would be dealt with as pirates in British admiralty courts.[6] For the first time, it seemed, their lives as well as their property were at stake.

---

[1] See above, ch. 3, p. 65-6.
[2] Hayne to Aberdeen, 29 September 1829, Private, F.O. 84/93.
[3] Smith to Aberdeen, 19 August 1829, F.O. 84/88.
[4] Memorandum, 3 August 1831, F.O. 84/122.
[5] R. R. Walsh, *Notices of Brazil in 1828 and 1829* (London, 1830), p. 491.
[6] Pennell to Aberdeen, no. 5, 20 April 1830, F.O. 84/122.

For more than a year the British government did indeed discuss with their legal advisers whether or not they were entitled to treat Brazilian slave traders as pirates as soon as the Brazilian trade became illegal. The legal complexities of the question, however, were not inconsiderable. In March 1830 Sir Herbert Jenner, the Advocate General, warned the government that

as the traffic in slaves is not piracy by the Law of Nations, and as the right of punishing the subjects of foreign states who may engage in it can only be acquired by treaty, the ordinary courts in this country are not competent to take cognizance of such offences; the sanction of the legislature will be necessary to the establishment of a court for the trial of such Brazilian subjects as may be found carrying on the slave trade after the period fixed by the treaty for its abolition.[1]

Legislation designed to replace the Act of 2 July 1827 (which authorised Anglo-Brazilian mixed commissions *alone* to adjudicate upon captured Brazilian ships) was actually drafted, but the British government decided not to proceed with it. They were reluctant to enforce so extreme an interpretation of their rights under the first article of the treaty of 1826 unless it proved absolutely necessary to do so, and there was at the time evidence of a willingness on the part of the Brazilian government to fulfil their treaty engagements and bring the slave trade to a halt. The British government recognised, too, that the time required to secure the passage of a new bill would afford the traders an invaluable breathing space. There was, moreover, an alternative course of action available to them: to persuade the Brazilian government to allow the Anglo-Portuguese right of search treaty of 1817, modified so as to bring it into line with the purpose of the Anglo-Brazilian treaty of 1826 (the abolition of the trade south as well as north of the equator), to continue in force.

The Brazilian government's interpretation of the first article of the treaty of 1826 was by no means clear. A *portaria* issued on 4 November 1829, announcing that the British government had

[1] Jenner, 8 March 1830, quoted in Cabinet memorandum, 7 July 1845, B.M. Add. MSS. 43125 (Aberdeen Papers), at the time when Aberdeen's Brazil (Slave Trade) bill was being prepared, see below, ch. 9, p. 256, n.1.

agreed that Brazilians might legally continue the slave trade on the African coast south of the equator until 13 March 1830 and were instructing British naval officers accordingly, concluded that vessels leaving the coast on or before that date could therefore complete their voyages 'without incurring the liability of being treated as pirates, according to the Convention'.[1] It was not stated by whom these vessels might be treated as pirates after that date. In July 1830, Eustáquio Adolpho de Mello Mattos, the Brazilian *chargé d'affaires* in London, was instructed to ask the British government for the dissolution of the Anglo-Brazilian mixed commissions in Rio de Janeiro and Freetown on the grounds that, having been established in 1828 on a temporary basis in order to judge the legality of captures during the period when the slave trade was in part legal, they were superfluous now that the trade was entirely illegal. Cases of illegal slave trading by Brazilians, it was suggested, should in future be regarded as piracy and dealt with by competent Brazilian tribunals (*os tribunais competentes do Paiz*).[2] However, in a note dated 4 October 1830 to Lord Aberdeen, the British Foreign Secretary, Mello Mattos wrote, 'le commerce d'esclaves dans la côte d'Afrique étant absolument interdit aux sujets brésiliens depuis le 13 mars derrière et ceux qui l'entreprendront à l'avenir, devant être punis d'après les stipulations du Traité du 23 novembre 1826 *par les tribunaux ordinaires des deux Hautes Parties Contractantes*' (my italics).[3] The Brazilian government, it seems, was demanding the dissolution of the mixed commissions in an attempt to ensure that in future Brazilian courts, and Brazilian courts alone, would deal with Brazilians engaged in the slave trade. However, on the strength of the words of the *portaria* of 4 November 1829 and, more important, of the note sent by Mello Mattos to Aberdeen on 4 October 1830, it was henceforth possible for the British government to argue—as fifteen years later they were to argue during the debates on the legality of certain extreme measures proposed by Lord Aberdeen (once again Foreign Secretary) for the suppression of the Brazilian slave trade—that the Brazilian government had acknowledged that under article 1 of

---

[1] Quoted in Cabinet memorandum, 7 July 1845.
[2] Miguel Calmon du Pin e Almeida to Mello Mattos, no. 31, 3 July 1830, A.H.I. 268/1/15.
[3] Mello Mattos to Aberdeen, 4 October 1830, F.O. 84/111.

the treaty of 1826 Britain had indeed the right to treat the Brazilian slave trade as piracy.

For the time being, the British government remained unwilling to assert this right. At the same time, having gone to a great deal of trouble to secure an abolition treaty from Brazil they were certainly not prepared to relinquish their responsibilities and leave the suppression of the illegal Brazilian slave trade to the Brazilian authorities alone. Lord Palmerston, who became Foreign Secretary in November 1830 and who, apart from one brief interval in opposition, was to remain at the Foreign Office until 1841, told Mello Mattos in December that it was absolutely essential that the mixed commissions should continue in existence to adjudicate upon captured Brazilian vessels since the Brazilian trade would doubtless be pursued for some time to come and 'some considerable time will elapse before arrangements can finally be made for the constitution of tribunals for exercising criminal jurisdiction in cases of piracy under the provisions of the treaty'.[1] (Palmerston, too, was thereby guilty of ambiguous phrasing: deliberately or otherwise, he did not make it clear whether he considered that, under the treaty, it was the responsibility of Brazil alone or of both Britain and Brazil to set up these tribunals.) In reply, Mello Mattos admitted that the immediate dissolution of the mixed commissions would be 'attended with considerable inconvenience', but felt that 'the necessary remedies must be had recourse to' rather than that they should sanction 'the illegal protraction of tribunals whose functions have ceased of right'.[2]

In the meantime rumours had begun to circulate amongst British naval officers on the west African coast that captured Brazilian slave ships could no longer be adjudicated in the mixed court at Sierra Leone. In March 1831 Commodore Hayes commanding the British West African squadron finally sought clarification from the Anglo-Brazilian mixed commission itself, whereupon the acting British judge, the Brazilian judge, and the British arbitrator decided unanimously that henceforth Brazilian slavers 'would undoubtedly be guilty of piracy but no authority is delegated to the British and Brazilian court of mixed commission by the treaty

[1] Palmerston to Mello Mattos, 10 December 1830, F.O. 84/111.
[2] Mello Mattos to Palmerston, 30 March 1831, F.O. 84/122.

of 23 November 1826 to take cognizance thereof'; in their view the treaty of 1817 under which the commission functioned had been prolonged only until the slave trade was finally abolished in March 1830.[1] Thus, the British navy was in danger of being paralysed for want of clear instructions as to its powers at the very moment when it was needed to enforce one of the British government's greatest diplomatic successes of recent years, the illegalisation of the Brazilian branch of the transatlantic slave trade.

In London, Palmerston conferred once again with the government's legal advisers, and they provided the way out for which he was looking. They reminded him of the existence of a separate article to the treaty of 1817 (which seems until then to have been overlooked) according to which, in the absence of a further agreement between the two contracting powers, the treaty could remain in force for fifteen years after the final abolition of the trade.[2] On 16 August 1831, therefore, Palmerston informed Mello Mattos that in the British government's view the Anglo-Brazilian mixed commissions in Rio de Janeiro and Sierra Leone could legally continue to adjudicate upon captured Brazilian slave ships and since the Brazilian trade was now entirely illegal the mutual right of search should no longer be restricted to the area north of the equator; appropriate instructions would, he said, be issued to British naval officers and commissioners. Cases of slave trading, Palmerston added, by way of explanation, could be 'much more conveniently as well as speedily and effectively disposed of in these courts than by any tribunals which may be constituted for the trial of Brazilian subjects engaged in carrying on the slave trade'.[3] Again the question arises, constituted by whom? Was Palmerston deliberately leaving open the possibility of authorising British courts to deal with cases of Brazilian 'piracy' if Brazil refused to agree to the continuation of the mixed commissions? Or, as the Brazilians were to argue when the issue was resurrected in 1845 with the passage of Lord Aberdeen's notorious Slave Trade

---

[1] Hayes to Sierra Leone commissioners, 10 March, Findlay, Smith and Paiva to Hayes, 15 March, enclosed in Findlay and Smith to Palmerston, Brazil no. 29, 18 March 1831, F.O. 84/118.
[2] Jenner to Palmerston, 28 July 1831, F.O. 83/2345.
[3] Palmerston to Mello Mattos, 16 August 1831, F.O. 84/131.

(Brazil) Act, had Palmerston admitted, at least by implication, that Brazil alone had the right to treat Brazilians as pirates? In any event, whether because they were unable to refute Palmerston's interpretation of the treaty of 1817, or because they realised (as Palmerston at first seemed not to realise) that, since it lacked an equipment clause, for example, the treaty of 1817 imposed certain important restrictions on the anti-slave trade activities of British warships, or because they were aware that the alternative was for Britain simply to treat the Brazilian slave trade as piracy, the Brazilian government decided not to contest the British assertion that the treaty should continue in force for a further fifteen years. José de Paiva, the Brazilian commissary judge in Sierra Leone, who in July 1830 had been instructed to leave Freetown, was subsequently told to stay at his post since negotiations in London had not 'produced the desired effect'.[1] It was not until 1845, fifteen years later, when the Brazilian government invoked their right to terminate the treaty of 1817, that Britain again invoked its right, under article 1 of the treaty of 1826, to treat the Brazilian slave trade as piracy.

In 1831 Lord Palmerston had successfully asserted Britain's right to participate in the capture and adjudication of Brazilian ships carrying on a trade which was now entirely illegal. But was this enough? As had happened so often in the past, as soon as positive steps were taken to suppress the slave trade under one flag, it was liable to rear its head under another: the traders could always make use of the papers and colours of a state with whom Britain had no right of search treaty or one that was more limited in its scope. Even before they knew how far the Brazilian authorities would enforce the ban on the trade or what action Britain was preparing to take under the treaty of 1826, the traders realised that after 1830 the Brazilian flag could no longer provide the kind of protection for the slave trade to Brazil that it had done in the past. And they wasted no time in looking around for one that would be safer.

[1] Instructions to Paiva, 3 July 1830, 26 February 1831, A.H.I. 57/3; Paiva to Findlay and Smith, 20 June, Findlay and Smith to Paiva 21 June, enclosed in Findlay and Smith, Brazil no. 34, 23 June 1831, F.O. 84/118; Paiva to Findlay and Smith, 27 July, enclosed in Findlay and Smith no. 46, 27 July 1831, F.O. 84/118.

They did not have far to look. There was, for example, the French flag which already protected a great part of the trade to Cuba. Although the slave trade was prohibited by French law, and during the late twenties French anti-slave trade legislation had been strengthened, the British navy had no powers to interfere with ships flying the French flag. Unfortunately for prospective speculators in the Brazilian trade, this and many other possible solutions to their difficulties were speedily denied them by Lord Palmerston who, on taking office, had immediately initiated a new round of negotiations with every maritime power, including France, which had not yet signed an adequate right of search treaty with Britain. In November 1831 the liberal government of Louis Philippe, anxious for British support, finally conceded the mutual right of search within specific geographic limits with the proviso, however, that captured ships were to be adjudicated not in courts of mixed commission—this no French government could ever permit—but in their own national courts. A second convention signed in March 1833 extended the area in which the right of search operated and, moreover, included both an equipment clause and a provision concerning the break-up of condemned slave ships.[1] Illegal slave trading under French colours henceforth became too great a risk. Another flag had been almost entirely eliminated from the transatlantic slave trade.

One obvious alternative to the Brazilian flag did, however, remain: the Portuguese flag. By 1830 the bulk of the Brazilian slave trade had been driven south of the equator and despite their many promises, the Portuguese still had not declared slaving there illegal—much less conceded to British warships a more extensive right of search. It was less than ten years since Brazil had been a Portuguese colony and the Brazilian slave trade still harboured many Portuguese traders resident in Lisbon, Oporto, Portuguese Africa, Rio de Janeiro and Bahia who had found the Brazilian flag so convenient for slaving purposes after 1822 since for a while it seemed to provide almost total protection from the British navy: they could all now revert to their own flag. Moreover, merchants

[1] 30 November 1831 (*B.F.S.P.* xviii, 641–4); 22 March 1833 (*B.F.S.P.* xx, 286–301). See Bandinel, *Some account of the trade in slaves*, pp. 242–3. Slave traders in Brazil had planned to make use of the French flag (Hayne to Aberdeen, 29 September 1829, F.O. 84/93).

who at independence had assumed Brazilian nationality had no difficulty in transferring their ships to fictitious Portuguese owners, or merely providing them with false Portuguese papers and a Portuguese flag. Portuguese diplomatic and consular officials in Brazil and Portuguese colonial authorities in Africa were usually willing to co-operate, provided adequate bribes were offered. And because Brazilians and Portuguese spoke the same language British naval officers found it particularly difficult to differentiate between genuine and fictitious Portuguese vessels. As early as 1829 traders in Brazil and Africa were preparing to take advantage of the Portuguese flag; by 1833, after so many years in which it had almost disappeared from the trade, it was being used as extensively as when Brazil was a Portuguese colony. Thus, within a few years of its conclusion, the Anglo-Brazilian treaty of 1826 had become virtually irrelevant to the British navy's efforts to suppress the Brazilian slave trade. The slave traders, 'whose perception of the means of fraud', the Sierra Leone commissioners wrote in January 1833, 'appears to become keener the more their schemes are opposed',[1] had apparently triumphed again.

It would seem that Britain had never envisaged this turn of events. Canning, for example, had believed that the Portuguese slave trade to Brazil could never again be a live issue since it had become *de facto* illegal as a result of the independence of Brazil in 1822 and, moreover, under existing treaties Britain had the right to suppress it.[2] With the sharp rise after 1830 in the trade carried on under the Portuguese flag, this view was now to be put to the test. Could British warships search and capture Portuguese slave ships south as well as north of the equator? The Law Officers of the Crown whose opinion on this point was sought by Aberdeen in November 1830 and again by Palmerston in January 1832 thought not. Irrespective of whether or not the Portuguese slave trade had become illegal with the independence of Brazil, they argued, British naval action was still confined within the straightjacket of the treaty of 1817: only Portuguese ships found north of the line with slaves on board could be captured and taken before the one remaining Anglo-Portuguese mixed commission sitting

---

[1] Smith and Macaulay to Palmerston, General no. 12, 5 January 1833 (Report on 1832), F.O. 84/134.   [2] See above, ch. 2, pp. 28–9.

at Sierra Leone. Even if the Portuguese government were to declare the entire slave trade illegal (and they had not yet officially done so), it would still be necessary to reach agreement with them before the right of search could be extended to all ships flying the Portuguese flag. And a further agreement would certainly be needed before British cruisers could capture Portuguese ships simply fitted out for the slave trade.[1] In short, if the British navy were to make any immediate impression on the slave trade to Brazil, now that it was increasingly protected by the Portuguese flag, a new Anglo-Portuguese anti-slave trade treaty was a first priority. Thus, after an interval of almost a decade, negotiations with Portugal for the abolition of the slave trade once more became a major concern of the British government.

In his dealings with Portugal during the 1830s, Lord Palmerston had two principal aims: first, to persuade the Portuguese government to enact stiffer and more comprehensive legislation which would make all slaving illegal and liable to severe punishment both in Portugal itself and throughout Portuguese territories in Africa; secondly, and more important, to secure a new anti-slave trade treaty so that the British navy would be in a position to prevent the evasion of Portuguese regulations both by the Portuguese and by any other traders assuming Portuguese nationality, if the Portuguese authorities themselves proved unable or unwilling to enforce the law. Although pressure was again brought to bear on Portugal from the beginning of 1832,[2] no real progress was possible until the autumn of 1834, when, with the assistance of Britain and France, the young Queen Maria II, the daughter of Dom Pedro I of Brazil, was restored to the throne and liberal, constitutional government re-established in Portugal after the eight years of violent political conflict and civil war which had followed the death of Dom João in 1826.[3] A succession of weak, unstable

---

[1] Jenner to Aberdeen, 19 November 1830, F.O. 83/2345; Jenner to Palmerston, 18 January 1832, F.O. 83/2346.

[2] See Bandinel, *op. cit.*, pp. 214–15.

[3] See H.V., Livermore, *A New History of Portugal* (London, 1967), pp. 268–79. In 1826 Dom Pedro chose to remain in Brazil and abdicated in favour of his daughter. Following his own abdication in 1831 he returned to Portugal and threw his support behind Queen Maria. For British policy in Portugal and the formation of the Quadruple Alliance of Britain, France, Portugal and Spain (1834), see C. K. Webster, *The Foreign Policy of Lord Palmerston 1830–1841* (London, 1951), i. 237–53, 370–410, and H. C. F. Bell, *Lord Palmerston* (London, 1936), i. 139–50.

Portuguese governments, however, were understandably anxious to avoid unpopular and controversial measures like the abolition of the slave trade. There was little abolitionist feeling in the country and in Lisbon there was still a powerful slave trade interest. Furthermore, any attempt to curtail the trade could be expected to provoke discontent and possibly insurrection in Angola and Moçambique, where slaves remained the only important export commodity and the only source of revenue, and where the great body of Portuguese officials, whose salaries were small and often months, even years, in arrears, protected and encouraged the trade for their own profit.[1] On the other hand, the new Portuguese régime, which owed its very existence to British support, could ill afford to antagonise Britain. Both Conde de Villa Real and the Duc de Palmella, successive heads of government during 1835, admitted that Portugal had engaged by treaty to abolish the slave trade in its entirety and accepted the argument that, as a result of the independence of Brazil, it was in fact already illegal, both by treaty with Britain and by Portuguese laws prohibiting participation in the foreign slave trade which went back to the middle of the eighteenth century.[2] Moreover, now that the trade was no longer supplying Portuguese territories in America with labour, more enlightened ministers could more easily face the fact it was retarding the economic development of Portuguese territories in Africa.

Prompted by Lord Howard de Walden, who had taken up his post as British minister in Lisbon at the end of 1834, Villa Real offered to declare the slave trade piracy, and for several months Palmella actually pretended that a bill had been approved by the Council of State and would soon be submitted to the Chamber of Deputies. The most the Portuguese government could manage, however, was instructions to colonial governors in Africa not to grant passports to ships intending to carry slaves to countries which had prohibited the slave trade and, on 22 October 1835, a circular to all Portuguese consuls, including those in Brazil, demanding

[1] See Duffy, *Portuguese Africa*, pp. 73–8, 146–7.
[2] Howard de Walden to Palmerston, no. 1, 8 February, no. 7, 7 April 1835, F.O. 84/178; Palmella to Howard de Walden, 10 July, enclosed in Howard de Walden no. 9, 18 July 1835, F.O. 84/178. Charles Augustus Ellis, 6th Baron Howard de Walden, was minister in Lisbon 1834–46.

4-2

stricter measures against the Portuguese slave trade which, they were reminded, had been illegal for more than a decade.[1] Now that, at least in practice, the Portuguese government had agreed that the slave trade carried on by Portuguese subjects and under the Portuguese flag was illicit, it occurred to Rear Admiral Sir Graham Eden Hammond, commander-in-chief of the South American naval station (and both W. G. Ouseley, the British *chargé d'affaires*, and George Jackson, the British commissary judge in Rio de Janeiro, agreed with him) that British cruisers might seize slave ships flying the Portuguese flag. In the face of their own declaration that such ships were engaged in illegal activities, the Portuguese government could hardly complain.[2] Palmerston would have liked to accept this view, but was warned by Sir John Dodson, the Advocate General, that such a course of action would be illegal. The recent Portuguese ordinance was intended to discourage the slave trade, Dodson agreed, but did not confer additional powers on British cruisers whose activities, pending the negotiation of a new anti-slave trade treaty, remained within the limits prescribed by the existing Anglo-Portuguese treaties.[3]

In September 1834, on the eve of his departure for Lisbon, Lord Howard de Walden had been furnished with the draft of a new anti-slave trade treaty,[4] but successive Portuguese governments managed to delay the opening of serious negotiations until October 1835. Thereafter, however, despite a series of political changes in Portugal and the delaying tactics which successive governments adopted—as a major difficulty was settled with one government it was reintroduced by the next, and as one proposition was agreed upon another was recontested—Howard de

[1] Enclosed in Howard de Walden to Palmerston, 31 October 1835, F.O. 84/178.
[2] Hammond to Ouseley, 26 January, Ouseley to Hammond, 30 January, enclosed in Ouseley to Palmerston, no. 2, 31 January 1836, F.O. 84/204; Jackson and Grigg no. 4, 10 February 1836, F.O. 84/198.
[3] Palmerston to Howard de Walden, no. 15, 10 August 1836, F.O. 84/203; Dodson to Palmerston, 15 August 1836, F.O. 83/2347 (cf. his predecessor Jenner's views, see above, pp. 97–8); Palmerston to Hamilton, no. 9, 1 September 1836, F.O. 84/204.
[4] Palmerston to Howard de Walden, no. 3, 8 September 1834, F.O. 84/155. The question was first raised by Howard de Walden at the beginning of 1835 (Howard de Walden to Wellington, no. 1, 8 February 1835, F.O. 84/178).

Walden skilfully reached agreement, with only minor emendations, on all the more controversial points in the draft: the unlimited duration of the treaty (the Portuguese were inclined to concede the right of search for only eight or ten years in the first instance); the right of search both north and south of the equator;[1] the equipment clause; the adjudication of captured ships by Anglo-Portuguese mixed commissions (the Portuguese wanted captured vessels to be taken before their own national courts in the same way that under the Anglo-French treaties French ships were taken before French tribunals); a break-up clause (in order to prevent the slave dealers themselves buying condemned slave vessels which were up for auction the British government now insisted in all its anti-slave trade treaty negotiations that they should be broken up and sold in separate lots); and the disposal of liberated slaves by the captors and not by the government in whose territory the mixed commission was sitting (the British government could never agree that liberated slaves should remain in Portuguese Africa where slavery persisted and where they could expect little protection from the Portuguese authorities against slave traders). In April 1836 Howard de Walden was able to report that he hoped to sign a treaty within a few days.[2] In July in reply to a question from Thomas Fowell Buxton, Wilberforce's successor as leader of the anti-slavery group in Parliament, Palmerston told the House of Commons that he expected to hear at any time that a treaty with Portugal had been completed.[3] Howard de Walden, however, had been over-optimistic. Another change of government in Portugal led to yet another round of negotiations. These too were on the point of conclusion when a major political

---

1 As early as July 1835 Palmella had conceded that the treaty of 1817 remained in force 'with a latitude far more ample than that which it formerly had', and he had proposed that a declaration to this effect should be added to the treaty (Palmella to Howard de Walden, 10 July, enclosed in Howard de Walden no. 9). Palmerston, however, had insisted upon a completely new anti-slave trade treaty which would include equipment and break-up clauses as well as the right of search in all latitudes (Palmerston to Howard de Walden, no. 7, 25 August 1835, F.O. 84/178).

2 Howard de Walden no. 10, 15 April 1836, F.O. 84/202. By this time Palmerston was beginning to lose patience with the Portuguese. His notes to the Portuguese minister in London were becoming noticeably sharper in tone (e.g. Palmerston to Moncorvo, 30 April 1836, F.O. 84/202—'a long and painful recital' of Portuguese bad faith on the slave trade question going back 30 years).

3 Hansard's *Parliamentary Debates*, 3rd series, xxxiv, 1266, 5 July 1836.

upheaval, the Septembrist Revolution of 1836,[1] led to further frustrating delays.

However, the President of the Council of Ministers in the government which now took office was Marquês de Sá da Bandeira, a man of principle, an opponent of the slave trade and a firm believer in the economic development of Portuguese Africa who hoped, as the Portuguese historian Oliveira Martins has written, 'to construct a Brazil in Africa'.[2] An abolition bill which Sá da Bandeira himself had first introduced in March, when he was Minister of Marine and Colonies, was pushed quickly through the legislature. The bill which became law on 10 December 1836 prohibited the import and export of slaves throughout Portugal's dominions (with two exceptions: Portuguese subjects could take up to ten slaves with them from one Portuguese territory to another and slaves could be imported into Portuguese territories in Africa by land). It also prescribed severe penalties both for Portuguese subjects who continued to engage in the slave trade and for Portuguese officials who facilitated or connived at it.[3] In some English circles in Lisbon the new law was regarded as the death blow to the Portuguese slave trade.[4] There was, however, still a long way to go: like all previous Portuguese anti-slave trade laws and decrees it proved to be a dead letter from the start. The new law met with implacable resistance in Africa, where it was suspended both by the Marquês de Aracaty, governor-general of Moçambique, and Manoel Bernardo Vidal, governor-general of Angola, on the grounds that it would ruin their territories and was in any case impossible to enforce; neither was able to take any effective steps to prevent the continuing shipment of thousands of slaves to Brazil each year.[5] Indeed, in the mid-thirties

---

[1] See Livermore, *op. cit.* p. 424; Webster, *Foreign Policy of Palmerston*, i, p. 485; Hammond, *op. cit.* p. 22.   [2] Quoted in Hammond, *op. cit.* p. 44.

[3] *Diario do Governo*, 21 December, enclosed in Howard de Walden no. 32, 22 December 1836, F.O. 84/203. Decree of 10 December 1836 printed in Julio Firmino Judice Biker, *Supplemento a Collecção dos Tratados, Convenções, Contratos e Actos Publicos celebrados entre a Coroa de Portugal e as mais Potencias desde 1640 compilado pelo Visconde de Borges de Castro* (Lisbon, 1872–9), xxviii, pp. 633–59; B.F.S.P. xxiv, 782–9.

[4] Smith to Palmerston, no. 40, 24 December, F.O. 84/203.

[5] Aracaty circular, 11 November 1837, and Sá da Bandeirat o Howard de Walden, 8 May, enclosed in Howard de Walden no. 10, 10 May 1838, F.O. 84/249 (printed in Biker, xxviii, 66–83); Jackson, *European Powers and South-East Africa*, pp. 196–7; Duffy, *op. cit.* pp. 76, 144, 147; Hammond *op. cit.* pp. 45–6.

Portuguese subjects and Portuguese ships were more extensively engaged in the Brazilian slave trade than ever before and, moreover, Portuguese papers and colours were used on an ever increasing scale by traders of other nations. Not only was the Portuguese flag, genuine and assumed, used to cover practically the whole of the illegal slave trade to Brazil, but following the signing of a new and more effective treaty between Britain and Spain in June 1835, an increasing proportion of the illegal Cuban trade as well.[1] 'The ships of Portugal', Palmerston told the House of Commons, 'now prowl about the ocean pandering to the crimes of other nations; and when her own ships are not sufficiently numerous for the purpose, her flag is lent as a shield to protect the misdeeds of foreign pirates.'[2]

Furthermore, a successful conclusion to the negotiations between Britain and Portugal for an anti-slave trade treaty which the British navy could enforce seemed as far away as ever. Even Sá da Bandeira, who was both President of the Council of Ministers and Foreign Minister for a great part of the period from September 1836 to April 1839, approached the question of an anti-slave trade treaty with extreme caution. His political position was extremely precarious and he had to consider the reactions of the slave trade interest in Lisbon. More important, he was only too well aware of the likelihood of serious disturbances and insurrections in Portuguese Africa. He was also naturally unwilling to accept *in toto* any treaty dictated by Britain, and especially one which he felt failed to safeguard the rights and legitimate interests of Portuguese citizens, as well as the freedom of lawful commerce under the Portuguese flag. Moreover, now that the Portuguese government had demonstrated their good intentions by prohibiting the trade he felt that a different kind of treaty was required from that which had almost been signed in 1836. In May 1837 Sá da Bandeira produced as an unofficial guide to Portuguese thinking (he was temporarily absent from the Foreign Ministry) a counter-draft which

[1] For the negotiations leading to the Anglo-Spanish treaty of 1835, see Murray, 'Britain, Spain and the slave trade to Cuba', pp. 145–64; Bandinel, *op. cit.* pp. 227–31. The Cuban slave trade continued but the trade to Puerto Rico virtually came to a halt in the mid-thirties. (See Corwin, *Spain and the Abolition of Slavery in Cuba*, p. 155.)
[2] Quoted in W. L. Mathieson, *Great Britain and the Slave Trade 1839–1865* (London, 1929), pp. 21–2.

inter alia limited the right of search to an area 100 miles off the coasts of Africa, South America and Cuba (and for an experimental period only), replaced the Anglo-Portuguese mixed commissions for the adjudication of captured Portuguese ships with Portuguese national courts and permitted captured slaves to be liberated in Portuguese Africa. Furthermore, concerned to ensure that British efforts to put down the Portuguese slave trade should lead neither to the secession of Portugal's colonies in Africa nor to an expansion of British influence there, Sá da Bandeira included in his counter-draft a provision for the renewal of the ancient treaties of alliance and friendship by which Britain undertook to defend the territorial integrity of Portugal and its overseas dominions.[1] Howard de Walden found some of Sá's proposals, and especially that concerning the dissolution of the mixed commissions, 'somewhat astounding', considering the extent of the Portuguese involvement in the transatlantic trade and the fact that Portuguese law courts were 'in a more notorious disorganised state than any in Europe'. In his view the counter-draft differed from the treaty proposed by Britain 'as to principle, spirit and efficiency'.[2] Not surprisingly, Palmerston found it 'completely inadmissible'.[3] When, therefore, in November Sá da Bandeira returned to the Foreign Ministry and offered to reopen negotiations on the basis of this draft Howard de Walden, under instructions from Palmerston, stood firmly by the original British treaty proposals and refused to re-negotiate points which had been agreed upon in 1836.[4] Nor in this context was Palmerston prepared to renew earlier Anglo-Portuguese treaties of alliance and friendship; he saw this as a move by Portugal to secure recognition of its long-standing claim to the Lower Congo and its adjoining coast (5° 12′ to 8° S.) which once—but no longer—Britain had been prepared to consider. In this area were to be

---

[1] Sá's 'Observations on the draft of treaty proposed by the British government . . . for the abolition of the slave trade', and his own counter-proposals, 3 May, enclosed in Howard de Walden no. 13, 5 May 1837, F.O. 84/215; counter-proposals printed in Biker, xxviii, 54–65. [2] Howard de Walden no. 13.

[3] Palmerston to Howard de Walden, no. 12, 27 October 1837, F.O. 84/215.

[4] Howard de Walden no. 18, 14 November 1837, F.O. 84/215; Howard de Walden 1 February 1838, Broadlands MSS (Palmerston Papers), GC/HO/492; Howard de Walden no. 2, 25 February 1838, F.O. 84/248. I am indebted to the Trustees of the Broadlands Archives for their permission to use the Palmerston Papers.

found such notorious slave trading centres as Kabenda (or Cabinda) and Ambriz, and it now seemed that the cause of the suppression of the slave trade—as well as the interests of British commerce—were best served by keeping Portugal out of this disputed territory.[1]

It was during the winter of 1837–8 that Lord Palmerston finally came to the conclusion that Portugal would co-operate with Britain for the suppression of the slave trade only if threatened with coercion and that if threats should fail it might indeed be necessary for Britain, as he told Hamilton Hamilton, British minister in Rio de Janeiro, to take matters into its own hands and treat slave ships flying the Portuguese flag 'summarily and by its own authority as pirates and outlaws'.[2] Palmerston had already warned the Portuguese government—in May 1837—that they should not be surprised if the Portuguese flag, so extensively used to cover an illegal and inhuman trade, should one day cease to be respected by the British navy.[3] In March 1838 Lord Howard de Walden in Lisbon was instructed to make it absolutely clear that if Portugal refused to sign the British treaty draft 'word for word as it now stands' without further delay, the British government would be obliged to take 'what the Americans call high-handed measures' and 'deal unceremoniously' with the Portuguese flag.[4] This was regarded by the Foreign Office as 'almost if not entirely the ultimatum.'[5] 'Not a crusado will we ever pay [in compensation]', Palmerston wrote privately to Howard de Walden, 'and if Portugal chuses to make war with us on that account we shall settle the question most effectively by taking possession of all her African settlements and colonies.' 'If like the wife in Molière', he added a little later, 'they like and chuse to be beat, so let it be.'[6]

1 See R. T. Anstey, *Britain and the Congo in the Nineteenth Century* (Oxford, 1962), pp. 40–3; Hammond, *op. cit.* pp. 53–5.
2 Palmerston to Hamilton, no. 6, 30 November 1837, F.O. 84/223. Also Palmerston memorandum, 31 January 1838, F.O. 84/248; Palmerston to Howard de Walden, no. 4, 3 March 1838, F.O. 84/248; Palmerston to Howard de Walden, 10 February 1838, Broadlands MSS, GC/HO/816.
3 Palmerston to Howard de Walden, no. 6, 10 May 1837, F.O. 84/215.
4 Palmerston to Howard de Walden, no. 6, 24 March 1838, F.O. 84/248; Palmerston to Howard de Walden, 24 March, 7 April 1838, Broadlands MSS, GC/HO/821, 823.
5 Memorandum attached to Palmerston to Howard de Walden, no. 15, 19 May 1838, F.O. 84/249.
6 Palmerston to Howard de Walden, 10 March, 28 April 1838, Broadlands MSS, GC/HO/819, 825.

On 15 April 1838, Howard de Walden and Sá da Bandeira began a fresh round of treaty negotiations, and during the next few weeks met almost daily; it was, as the British minister said, 'a very uphill game'.[1] While Sá da Bandeira now conceded most of the more important points sought by Britain—the right of search north and south of the equator, an equipment clause, a break-up clause and new Anglo-Portuguese mixed commissions to adjudicate captured vessels—he continued to demand that Britain too should make concessions. In order to secure the treaty and at the same time make it acceptable to the Portuguese Côrtes, Howard de Walden ventured beyond the limits of his instructions (he had been authorised to sign nothing short of the British draft as it stood) and agreed to certain modifications which he believed were unlikely to reduce the effectiveness of the treaty. He conceded, for instance, the right of either power to revise the treaty after fourteen years; he also accepted the regulations Portugal proposed for the treatment of liberated slaves in her own colonies, and agreed that *emancipados* should be handed over to the government in whose territory the mixed commission was sitting, rather than to the government of the captors.[2] As a result, after three weeks' discussion, he was able to report that 'no principle remains to be discussed or contested' and that he and Sá da Bandeira had initialled the articles of a treaty which, though imperfect, on the whole would do.[3]

At the eleventh hour, however, the Portuguese minister refused finally to sign the treaty unless there were inserted into it a 'formal and explicit' guarantee of substantial British land and sea support in the event of disturbances or separatist uprisings in Portuguese African territories when its terms became known.[4] Sá da Bandeira had first asked for this in November of the previous year at which time Howard de Walden had been instructed to say that in the unlikely event of Angola or Moçambique's attempting to join Brazil or Spain within two years of the ratification of the treaty,

[1] Howard de Walden to Palmerston, 2 May 1838, Broadlands MSS, GC/HO/516.
[2] Howard de Walden no. 6, 24 April, F.O. 84/248, no. 8, 7 May, Conf., F.O. 84/249; Howard de Walden 24 April, 5 May 1838, Broadlands MSS, GC/HO/515, 518.
[3] Howard de Walden no. 7, 7 May, F.O. 84/249; Howard de Walden 7 May 1838, Broadlands MSS, GC/HO/519.
[4] Sá da Bandeira to Howard de Walden, 8 May 1838, enclosed in Howard de Walden no. 10, 10 May, F.O. 84/249.

the British government was at most prepared to afford Portugal limited naval assistance.[1] When, during the recent talks, Sá da Bandeira had raised the matter again, Howard de Walden had offered to sign a declaratory note along these lines which could form a basis for future negotiations.[2] It seemed, therefore, that in bringing up the question of a guarantee yet again and at so critical a point in the negotiations, Sá da Bandeira was deliberately trying to delay the signature of the treaty.[3] Palmerston, meanwhile, was pressing Howard de Walden for an immediate and distinct answer as to whether the Portuguese would or would not sign.[4] In the circumstances, on 9 May Howard de Walden decided to end the negotiations;[5] his departure for home and a well-earned leave were in any case long overdue.

In the event, however, Sá da Bandeira persuaded him to stay in Lisbon for one more week:[6] Sá was well aware of the consequences of a final and total breakdown in negotiations, and Howard de Walden was equally aware that there would never be a better chance of securing a treaty. During that week, the articles which had already been agreed upon were signed *sub spe rati*, on the understanding that agreement would subsequently be reached on outstanding differences—principally the question of a guarantee—and that the signing would be kept secret and considered not to have taken place if the treaty were rejected by Lord Palmerston.[7] But Sá da Bandeira remained adamant on the need for a guarantee

[1] Palmerston to Howard de Walden, no. 14, 9 December 1837, F.O. 84/215.

[2] Confidential memorandum delivered to Sá da Bandeira, enclosed in Howard de Walden no. 6.

[3] Two years later, when asked in the Senate why he had not signed a treaty in April–May 1838, Sá replied, 'I was afraid of Lord Palmerston. I could not get it out of my head that he wanted to obtain possession of our African colonies and I was determined not to sign any treaty for the abolition of the slave trade without obtaining a guarantee of the most complete and comprehensive nature for our African colonies' (quoted in Howard de Walden no. 18, 24 January 1840, Conf., F.O. 84/320).

[4] Palmerston to Howard de Walden, no. 10; Palmerston to Howard de Walden, 28 April 1838, Private.

[5] Howard de Walden to Sá, 9 May, enclosed in Howard de Walden no. 10.

[6] Sá to Howard de Walden, 12 May, enclosed in Howard de Walden no. 12, 14 May, 1838, Conf., F.O. 84/249.

[7] Copy of undated confidential memorandum read to Sá in May, enclosed in Howard de Walden no. 24, 18 December 1838, F.O. 84/251. The events of this week also recalled in Barão de Ribeira da Sabrosa (Sá's successor) to Howard de Walden, 11 September, and Howard de Walden to Ribeira da Sabrosa, 16 September, enclosed in Howard de Walden no. 46, 20 September 1839, F.O. 84/282.

in respect of Portuguese territories in Africa: and he insisted that the Côrtes would certainly reject any treaty which did not include one. He had in mind an additional article which would detail the assistance to be provided by Britain—two or three boats and 400–500 men from the Cape, Mauritius or Bombay in the event of disturbances in Moçambique, and three or four boats and 800 men from the Cape, St Helena or Sierra Leone if trouble broke out in Angola.[1] Palmerston had recently repeated, however, that the British government were willing to promise no more than 'contingent assistance limited both as to its nature and as to the time within which it is to be afforded'.[2] Howard de Walden was therefore unable to do more than offer to sign *sub spe rati* a very general article promising 'an effectual aid . . . the object, nature, amount and duration of such assistance to be regulated by special arrangements subject to immediate negotiations'. In addition to a guarantee, Sá da Bandeira now began to demand that not one month but six, and possibly longer, should be allowed for the ratification of the treaty, and also that it should not come into operation on the west coast of Africa until a further four months after ratification and until six months after ratification on the east coast.[3] These last demands finally nullified all Howard de Walden's efforts to prevent the negotiations from breaking down: he knew that only the fact that a treaty had been signed and would become operative immediately could possibly persuade Palmerston to overlook the concessions he had made to the Portuguese in respect of the limited duration of the treaty and the disposal of liberated slaves. Moreover, he had just received another despatch from Palmerston instructing him to bring matters to a head. Parliament and the Cabinet, Palmerston wrote, were in 'the proper mood', and he was prepared to wait only one more week before proceeding with tougher measures: 'the steam's up, and if

---

[1] Draft of article delivered by Sá da Bandeira at an interview on 18 May, enclosed in Howard de Walden no. 13, 20 May 1838, F.O. 84/249.

[2] Palmerston to Howard de Walden, no. 13, 5 May, F.O. 84/249; counter-proposal delivered to Sá on 19 May, enclosed in Howard de Walden no. 13, 20 May, 1838, F.O. 84/249.

[3] Howard de Walden to Ribeira da Sabrosa, n.d. (29 September to 4 October), enclosed in Howard de Walden no. 50, 4 October 1839, F.O. 84/283. Moreover, Sá always contended that the treaty could not be ratified until the Côrtes had approved it, and the Côrtes was not due to meet again until January 1839.

Portugal will not do her duty, we shall do ours'.[1] On 22 May, after a final unsatisfactory interview with Sá da Bandeira, Howard de Walden left Lisbon for home to discuss the situation with Palmerston, convinced that only his departure could bring the Portuguese to their senses and make them 'knock under'.[2]

The Portuguese later claimed that had Howard de Walden stayed in Lisbon a few days more, or even a few hours, the outstanding difficulties would easily have been resolved and a treaty duly signed. Even if this were true—and there is no particular reason to think so—the treaty would never have been ratified by Lord Palmerston who, as might have been expected, not only rejected outright Portuguese demands for a comprehensive guarantee of their African colonies and an extension of the period allowed for ratification, but also strongly disapproved of most of the concessions that Howard de Walden had made. In particular, he refused to limit the duration of the treaty or allow a right of revision, and the adoption of the British proposals for the disposal of liberated slaves by the captors was, he said, a *sine qua non* of any agreement.[3] Palmerston had no sympathy with Sá da Bandeira's very real difficulties: he was convinced that any proposal put forward by Portugal—a country whose subjects were 'habitually and systematically addicted to the slave trade'[4]—must be aimed at defeating the purpose of the treaty. (On another occasion Palmerston was to write to Lord John Russell, 'The plain truth is that the Portuguese are of all European nations the lowest in the moral scale.'[5]) However, since the latest news from Lisbon suggested that Portugal might at last be on the point of capitulation, he decided to make one final attempt to secure by treaty the necessary powers to suppress the slave trade carried on under the Portuguese

[1] Palmerston to Howard de Walden, 12 May 1838, Broadlands MSS, GC/HO/827; Palmerston to Howard de Walden, no. 14, 12 May, F.O. 84/249.

[2] Howard de Walden no. 15, 22 May, F.O. 84/249, enclosing treaty draft as it then stood (printed in Biker, xxviii, 100–23); Howard de Walden 23 May 1838, Broadlands MSS, GC/HO/521.

[3] Palmerston to Jerningham, no. 20, 23 July 1838, F.O. 84/250, enclosing a paper divided into four columns: (i) British draft and passages objected to; (ii) omissions, additions and alterations suggested by Portugal; (iii) reasons for agreeing or dissenting; (iv) final draft as it then stood.

[4] Palmerston to Howard de Walden, no. 15, 19 May 1838, F.O. 84/249.

[5] Quoted by Christopher Lloyd, *The Navy and the Slave Trade* (London, 1949), p. 148; also James Duffy, *A Question of Slavery* (Oxford, 1967), p. 3.

flag. If the Portuguese again refused to co-operate, unilateral action would then seem more than ever justified.

At the end of July 1838 the British treaty draft, with only a few minor alterations, was sent back to Lisbon. George Jerningham, the British *chargé*, was empowered to sign a treaty, but not to negotiate: any further delay or any fresh proposals, Palmerston said, would be considered as 'tantamount to a refusal' to sign.[1] On 1 August the draft was again presented to the Portuguese government, but this time as an ultimatum.[2] Sá da Bandeira was now more than willing to sign the treaty draft as it had stood in May when Howard de Walden left for home and was even prepared to negotiate separately the question of a guarantee. But he was still unable to accept the draft in what was virtually its original form and again expressed his objections to, for example, the treaty's unlimited duration without any right of revision (an 'insurmountable obstacle'), its failure to renew and confirm earlier treaties of alliance, friendship and guarantee, and the use of the word 'piratical' in describing the trade ('absolutely inadmissible').[3] On his return to Lisbon in November, Howard de Walden was again disposed to make concessions on all these points: they would, he felt, put Portuguese sincerity to the test and weaken Sá da Bandeira's position when he had to explain the final collapse of negotiations.[4] But Palmerston was irritated by the obstinacy of the Portuguese government and he wholeheartedly distrusted Sá da Bandeira. 'Sá, wholly unprincipled and dishonest himself', he wrote privately and without the slightest justification, 'protects the criminals [the slave traders] because they support him, and all he says about national honour and dignity is nothing but a mask assumed to hide his real motives.'[5] Palmerston was not prepared to make any concessions and distinctly warned Howard de Walden not to let the Portuguese think that he took a 'softer'

[1] Palmerston to Jerningham, no. 20.
[2] Jerningham to Sá da Bandeira, 1 August, enclosed in Jerningham no. 8, 6 August 1838, F.O. 84/250; printed in Biker, xxviii, 167–95.
[3] Sá da Bandeira to Jerningham, 6 October, enclosed in Jerningham no. 15, 8 October 1838, F.O. 84/251; printed in Biker, xxviii, 196–241. Also Jerningham no. 16, 8 October 1838, Conf.
[4] Howard de Walden no. 23, 8 December 1838, F.O. 84/251; Howard de Walden 16 December 1838, 6 January 1839, Broadlands MSS, GC/HO/539, 541.
[5] Palmerston to Howard de Walden, 24 December 1838, Broadlands MSS, GC/HO/829.

line towards the treaty than did the British government.[1] On 16 February 1839, after a 'warm scene' with Howard de Walden, who warned him that Britain was proposing to take the 'strongest measures' against the Portuguese slave trade unless Portugal complied with British demands, Sá da Bandeira again positively refused to sign the British treaty draft as it stood.[2] As a result, another round of negotiations finally broke down, the Anglo-Portuguese anti-slave trade treaty which Lord Palmerston so desperately required remained unsigned, and Portugal prepared to face the consequences.

Although treaty negotiations with Portugal were of greater immediate concern to Palmerston throughout the 1830s, negotiations with Brazil were not neglected. If and when the slave trade was driven from under the Portuguese flag the Brazilian flag could still be expected to give a certain amount of protection to Brazilian slave ships and to those of other nations unless preventive measures were taken in advance. Under the treaty of 1817 (suitably modified in the light of the treaty of 1826) British warships were authorised to visit and search all suspicious vessels flying the Brazilian flag, although only those actually carrying slaves could be detained. Brazilian ships could not be seized on account of their equipment alone—even when they were found in notorious slaving areas. It was therefore important, Palmerston realised, for Britain to persuade Brazil no less than Portugal to concede an 'equipment clause'. In October 1831 Arthur Aston, *chargé d'affaires* in Rio de Janeiro, was instructed to reopen the question of the need for an equipment clause to be added to the treaty of 1817[3]—a matter first raised, without success, by Robert Gordon four years earlier. Unsettled political conditions, however, made negotiations impossible until September 1832 when Bento da Silva Lisboa, well known as an abolitionist, took charge of Brazilian foreign policy. In the event Silva Lisboa argued that it was unnecessary to strengthen the anti-slave trade treaty with Britain since the strict enforcement of the new Brazilian legislation of

[1] *Ibid.* Also Palmerston no. 2, 19 January 1839, F.O. 84/281.
[2] Howard de Walden no. 9, 15 February, no. 10, 17 February, no. 11, 18 February, F.O. 84/281; Howard de Walden 26 February 1839, Broadlands MSS, GC/HO/550.
[3] Palmerston to Aston, no. 9, 8 October 1831, F.O. 84/122.

November 1831 would be 'sufficient in itself to cause a cessation of the slave trade'. Indeed he again raised the possibility of actually terminating the right of search and dissolving the mixed commissions in view of their 'utter uselessness'.[1] As well as an equipment clause, Palmerston was also anxious to secure an agreement for the break-up of Brazilian vessels condemned by the Anglo-Brazilian mixed commissions,[2] but to Silva Lisboa this seemed a wanton destruction of valuable Brazilian property and he rejected this second proposal too. (Later the Brazilian government was to put forward an alternative proposal: condemned slavers should be sold to one of the two governments for conversion into anti-slave trade cruisers. Palmerston was prepared to agree to this provided slave ships not required by either government were broken up; during the 1820s the British navy had already purchased some condemned slave ships and the idea of slavers acting against their former partners in crime always had a certain appeal for British abolitionists.)

As the illegal Brazilian slave trade began to show signs of expansion, despite all the Brazilian government's efforts to prevent it, Silva Lisboa decided, reluctantly, that Britain must after all be given greater powers for its suppression. In his *Relatório* (annual report) of May 1833 he recommended that the Chamber of Deputies should now seriously consider the British proposals for a more effective anti-slave trade treaty which would include an equipment clause.[3] In July he vaguely intimated to William Gore Ouseley, the British *chargé d'affaires*, his own willingness to start negotiations at once,[4] but he was never given authority to make any really positive moves in this direction. Throughout the following year Palmerston urged Henry Stephen Fox, who was for a short period minister in Rio before going to Washington, to try and reach agreement on the addition of equipment and break-up clauses to the right of search treaty of 1817. Alternatively, it was suggested he might join with the French *chargé* in persuading Brazil to accede to the Anglo-French treaties of 1831 and 1833

[1] Silva Lisboa to Aston, 9 October, enclosed in Aston no. 7, 22 October 1832, F.O. 84/130; Ouseley to Palmerston, 16 February 1833, Broadlands MSS, GC/OU/19.
[2] Palmerston to Fox, 26 December 1832, F.O. 84/130.
[3] *Relatório do Ministério dos Negócios Estrangeiros* (Rio de Janeiro, May 1833).
[4] Silva Lisboa to Ouseley, 8 July, enclosed in Ouseley no. 18, 29 July 1833, F.O. 84/141.

which included both these clauses but which, Palmerston seemed to forget, provided for the adjudication of captured vessels by national courts and not by mixed commissions.[1] Twice during 1834 Aureliano de Souza Oliveira Coutinho, Silva Lisboa's successor at the Foreign Ministry (and also Minister of Justice), applied to the newly elected Chamber of Deputies, over which the landed interest had such complete control, for authority to open further treaty negotiations with Britain. The Brazilian government's proposals for a more efficient policing of the illegal Brazilian slave trade by the British navy on the African coast and on the High Seas were, however, as ill received as their proposals made at the same time for more effective controls in Brazil and in Brazilian waters. Moreover, after Aureliano had foolishly read to a packed Chamber one of Henry Fox's more strongly worded notes demanding Brazilian co-operation against the slave trade, a violent attack was launched against Britain for continuing to meddle in Brazilian affairs.[2] Far from wishing to grant Britain greater powers to interfere with Brazilian merchant vessels—as slave ships were widely regarded—the Brazilian deputies (who were also beginning to agitate for the repeal of the law of 1831) revived the demand for the termination of the existing right of search and the immediate abolition of the Anglo-Brazilian mixed commissions in Rio de Janeiro and Freetown. The government were forced to back down and Fox, like Aston and Ouseley before him, was informed that the Brazilian legislation already in force combined with the existing Anglo-Brazilian treaties were sufficient to suppress the slave trade—at least they would be, Aureliano commented bitterly, were it not for the protection given to the trade by the Portuguese flag and by Portuguese colonial and consular officials (which was a matter for negotiation with Portugal).[3]

A change of government in England had little effect on the diplomatic struggle for the addition of equipment and break-up clauses to the treaty of 1817. The Duke of Wellington, Foreign Secretary in Peel's short-lived Conservative government (1834–5), sent to Rio de Janeiro a draft of two articles, and Fox was given

[1] Palmerston to Fox, no. 3, 25 July 1834, F.O. 84/156.
[2] Jackson and Grigg no. 26, 14 October 1834, F.O. 84/153; Fox no. 6, 15 October 1834, F.O. 84/156; Alves, 'A Questão do Elemento Servil', *R.I.G.H.B.* (1914), p. 220.
[3] Aureliano to Fox, 2 October, enclosed in Fox no. 6.

full powers to negotiate upon them.[1] This time, to his own surprise, he was successful. The slave insurrection in Bahia early in 1835 had stiffened the Brazilian government in their determination to strengthen the abolition treaty with Britain as well as their own anti-slave trade legislation. And for the first time they could go ahead with some confidence secure in the knowledge that the insurrection had also opened the eyes of many planters to the dangers of permitting the unrestricted importation of Negroes into Brazil. As it happened, Manuel Alves Branco, Brazilian Foreign Minister at the time, had already been given full powers to solicit stronger measures from Britain. In May he informed the Chamber of Deputies of his intention to re-open negotiations with Britain for improvements to the treaty of 1817.[2] But before agreeing to Britain's treaty proposals, Alves Branco put forward three demands of his own: first, and most important, that Britain should agree to pay the indemnities which the Brazilian government claimed for the illegal capture during the period 1826–30 of the slave ships *Activo*, *Perpetuo Defensor*, *Heroina* plus another dozen or so Brazilian vessels (with a few doubtful exceptions, they had clearly been engaged in the illegal slave trade but they had not been carrying slaves at the time and had therefore been acquitted by the mixed commission in Sierra Leone and awarded damages—provided the two governments agreed that damages were merited); secondly, that Britain should accept any Africans liberated in future by the Rio mixed commission and transport them to her own colonies; and thirdly, that Britain should co-operate with Brazil in persuading other South American states to sign anti-slave trade treaties.[3] Alves Branco did not press these points, however, when Fox said he had no powers to negotiate along these lines, and additional articles to the treaty of 1817, almost identical with those drafted by Wellington, were signed in Rio de Janeiro on 27 July 1835. A Brazilian merchant vessel could now be detained and taken before one of the mixed commissions

[1] Wellington to Fox, no. 10, 31 December 1834, F.O. 84/156.
[2] Fox no. 4, 25 March 1835, F.O. 84/179; *Relatório do Ministério dos Negócios Estrangeiros* (Rio de Janeiro, May 1835).
[3] Fox no. 12, 4 August 1833, Conf., F.O. 84/179. On the claims question, see F.O. Memorandum, 14 January 1842, F.O. 84/445 and Manchester, *British Preëminence in Brazil*, pp. 233–6.

whether or not slaves had actually been shipped, provided there was evidence on board of an intention to trade in slaves (that is, provided the ship carried 'any one or more' of what had by now become a standard list of 'equipment articles'), and could be condemned unless the owner satisfied the commission of its legitimate trading purpose (article 1). All condemned vessels were in future to be broken up and sold in separate lots (article 2). A third additional article stipulated that the first two would be ratified within a period of eight months.[1]

Back at the Foreign Office after his brief spell in opposition, Palmerston was well satisfied with Fox's work. As to the Brazilian government's own propositions he declared first, repeating the by now familiar British view, that while vessels illegally captured should, of course, be released by the mixed commissions, no compensation could ever be paid to those proved to have been engaged in the illegal slave trade even though they might have been illegally obstructed; secondly, that Britain might be willing to take care of all slaves liberated by the commission in Rio de Janeiro if Brazil were prepared to foot the bill; and, thirdly, that he would gladly join in anti-slave trade negotiations with the Spanish American governments.[2] It was Palmerston's aim, as he told the House of Commons in August 1836, to unite against the trade 'all the maritime powers whose flags could be abused or prostituted', whether or not they were directly involved in the trade.[3] As the net closed in around the traders and they were forced to relinquish flag after flag which had previously protected them, there was always a danger that they would resort to the Stars and Stripes and to the flags of the few remaining European states which had not yet signed right of search treaties with Britain. Failing these—and there was now every hope that the European states, if not the United States, would co-operate with Britain[4]—it was possible

---

[1] Fox no. 11, 4 August 1835, F.O. 84/179. For the text of the additional articles, see Pereira Pinto, i, 394–8.
[2] Palmerston to Fox, no. 14, 3 November 1835, F.O. 84/179.
[3] Hansard, xxxv, 939, 5 August 1836.
[4] Palmerston persuaded the Hanse Towns (1837), Tuscany (1837) and the Two Sicilies (1838) to accede to the Anglo-French right of search treaties of 1831 and 1833 as Sweden and Denmark had already done in 1834 (see Bandinel, *op. cit.* pp. 245–7). At several conferences held between 1838 and 1841, Austria, Prussia and Russia refused to do the same. A comprehensive Quintuple Treaty (Britain, Austria, Prussia, Russia and France)

they might make more systematic use of the flags of the new Spanish American republics. In the event, however, Brazilian representatives abroad gave Palmerston no more than nominal support in his efforts to close the remaining gaps in the preventive system.[1]

Additional articles to the treaty of 1817 had now been signed. They were still not ratified, however, and a Brazilian law of 14 June 1831, which had been enacted following the abdication of Dom Pedro I and in the light of the treaties he had signed on his own initiative, stipulated that in future all agreements with foreign powers should be referred to the *Comissão de Diplomacia* of the Chamber of Deputies and ratified only after the agreement of both the Chamber and the Senate had been secured.[2] Hence the necessity for successive Brazilian ministers to test the temper of the Chamber and to wait until 1835 before taking steps to strengthen the anti-slave trade treaty. The additional articles of 27 July 1835 were duly referred to the *Comissão*, but public affairs were so chaotic in the period up to October when Father Feijó became Regent that the Brazilian government were able to push very little through the Chamber, and certainly nothing so controversial; they were not even discussed before the end of the session. Obviously ratification was not going to be easy, particularly since, as Ouseley had anticipated, the widespread concern at the slave revolt in Bahia soon faded and was forgotten. Only further disturbances of a similar nature, Ouseley believed, could have kept alive the first stirrings of a more widespread abolitionist sentiment, but by the end of 1835 the situation was calm. Once again influential voices inside and outside the Chamber were raised in favour of the slave trade as, at worse, a necessary evil, and Alves Branco was now widely criticised for having agreed in the first place to sign

was finally signed in London on 20 December 1841 which France alone failed to ratify (*ibid.* pp. 244, 247–50).

[1] On Britain's negotiations with Spanish American governments, see J. F. King, 'The Latin American Republics and the Suppression of the Slave Trade', *H.A.H.R.*, xxiv, (1944), pp. 387–411. Ouseley doubted whether right of search treaties with Spanish American states were necessary. 'Doubtless theoretically and legally a treaty is required', he had written in January 1835 with reference to Uruguay, 'but we are mistaken if we regard South American republics as much better in organisation, national faith and civilisation than the Barbary States' (Ouseley to Backhouse (F.O.), 10 January 1835, Conf., F.O. 84/179).

[2] Alves, *R.I.H.G.B.* (1914), p. 222.

additional articles to the anti-slave trade treaty. Some Brazilians, it is true, wanted to strengthen Britain's hand against the slave trade but at the same time they were genuinely concerned to ensure that British warships did not overstep their rights in the future, as they had undoubtedly done in the past. Others, more unscrupulous, aroused for their own purposes those nationalistic suspicions and prejudices which most Brazilians now held about any treaty with a European power, one with Britain and directed against the slave trade most of all. Having freed themselves from Portugal in 1822, it was widely argued, Brazilians should declare their independence from their new master, Britain. It was time to call a halt to 'our accustomed obedience to the British Cabinet' and to the idea that 'they [the British] have the squadron, they have the money, their will therefore be done!', as one Rio newspaper pronounced.[1] Alves Branco came under fire most of all for not having made a settlement of Brazilian claims against the British government the *sine qua non* of further concessions. The owners of vessels illegally captured before 1830, and notably the *bahianos* José and Manoel Cerqueira Lima who had £250,000 at stake, made strong representations to the Chamber that there should be no ratification of the additional articles until Britain recognised the validity of Brazilian claims.[2]

Towards the end of 1835, the Marquês de Barbacena was sent on a special mission to London.[3] The main purpose of the mission was the revision of the Anglo-Brazilian commercial treaty of 1827, but Barbacena was also authorised to discuss with the British government the suppression of the slave trade at sea as well as ways and means of encouraging free white emigration from Europe to Brazil. In March 1836 Barbacena was instructed to sound out

[1] See letters and press cuttings from Rio de Janeiro, enclosed in Jackson to Palmerston, London, 4 February 1837, F.O. 84/218. The Brazilians, wrote William Hunter, the American *chargé* in Rio, saw Britain's 'over and constant pressure' on the slave trade issue as 'a method of intervention in their domestic affairs and a control over them not only as to the direct but as to collateral subjects' (Hunter to Forsyth, Secretary of State, 29 August 1837, printed in W. R. Manning, ed., *Diplomatic Correspondence of the United States. Inter-American Affairs, 1831–60* (Washington, 1932–9), ii, 218. 'Their most liberal minded statesmen', he later wrote, 'seem to speak of Portugal and Brazil as though they were English colonies' (Hunter to Forsyth, 25 November 1839, *ibid.* ii, 238).

[2] Jackson and Grigg no. 54, 28 October 1835, F.O. 84/175; Pierre Verger, *Bahia and the West African Trade, 1549–1851* (Ibadan, 1964), pp. 34–5.

[3] For the Barbacena mission, see Antônio Augusto de Aguiar, *Vida do Marquez de Barbacena* (Rio de Janeiro, 1896), pp. 890 ff.

Lord Palmerston on the idea of a new three-way anti-slave trade Convention between Britain, Portugal and Brazil which would provide for more effective joint cruising on the African and Brazilian coasts and possibly for the imposition of stiffer penalties for slave trading.[1] Palmerston, however, was unwilling to interrupt Lord Howard de Walden's treaty negotiations in Lisbon which he believed (wrongly) were nearing completion. Nor did he see what would be gained from a new convention of the kind proposed by Barbacena until additional articles to the existing right of search treaty had been conceded. Throughout the legislative session of 1836, however, the Fox-Alves Branco agreement remained on the table of the Brazilian Chamber—even though the session was extended to deal with urgent outstanding business. At the beginning of the following session, the Brazilian government again asked for its ratification, but again the question was shelved. (Besides their personal, although for the most part indirect, interest in the slave trade, many deputies had in mind the forthcoming elections.) Hamilton Hamilton, who had replaced Henry Fox as British minister in May 1836, was assured by successive Brazilian Foreign Ministers that the government were impotent in face of an intransigent Chamber, but as yet another session came to a close Hamilton began to question whether they were genuinely trying to push through the ratification of the 1835 agreement. Were they perhaps taking the easy way out by formally requesting it in their annual reports to the Chamber and then taking no further action? In June 1837, Hamilton suggested that Francisco Gé Acaiaba de Montezuma, Foreign Minister at the time, should at least submit the question to the Chamber and attempt to deal with any opposition, if he were not to incur the imputation of bad faith and political dishonesty.[2] Britain wanted a repetition of 1826: an agreement with the Brazilian government allowing the British navy a greater measure of freedom to crush the slave trade, regardless of public opinion—and Brazilian interests. But it was precisely because of

---

[1] José Ignácio Borges to Barbacena, no. 2, 17 March 1836, A.H.I. 268/1/15.
[2] Hamilton to Montezuma, 5 June, enclosed in Hamilton no. 12, 24 June 1837, F.O. 84/222. During the previous twelve months Hamilton had demanded the ratification of the additional articles on at least ten separate occasions: 29 June, 23 August, 4 September, 4 December 1836, 7 January, 18 February, 22 February, 18 March, 8 April, 30 April 1837.

the emperor's total capitulation to British demands in 1826 that the Chamber of Deputies had first secured and now clung to its new powers, and, like their counterparts in Portugal, Brazilian ministers were reluctant to look for trouble at a time when few governments survived for more than six months in any case.

In September 1837 when the Chamber was preoccupied with another aspect of the slave trade question, Barbacena's anti-slave trade bill to replace the law of November 1831, the *Comissão de Diplomacia* did at last produce a report on the additional articles of July 1835, but one which, significantly, dealt with Brazilian claims against Britain as well. The Commission admitted that the slave trade was on the increase and that the addition of an equipment clause to the treaty of 1817 would probably do more than any other single measure to check its growth. But they also maintained that it was illogical to concede yet more extensive powers to British cruisers when indemnities for earlier abuses had still not been awarded. At the very least the Brazilian government should be given 'guarantees that such abuses would be avoided or remedied and no occasion be given in future for further representations'. One means of preventing unjust sentences on Brazilian vessels, the Commission felt, would be to remove the Anglo-Brazilian mixed commission from Sierra Leone to a Brazilian port, or else dissolve it and transfer its duties to the commission sitting in Rio de Janeiro. The Freetown commission had been, and would continue to be, heavily weighted in favour of the British captor, whereas in Brazil the demands of justice—and the interests of Brazilian subjects—were less easily ignored.[1] The adoption of this report by the Chamber would have deferred ratification of the additional articles indefinitely since the British government had frequently and flatly rejected Brazil's financial claims for illegal captures in the past and would certainly not be prepared to see the work of the Freetown commission transferred to Rio de Janeiro. Palmerston now made it clear that he would not take kindly to the Brazilian government's attaching impossible conditions to the fulfilment of an engagement which they had already undertaken unconditionally.[2] The Conservative Cabinet of September 1837,

---

[1] *Jornal do Comércio*, 12 September 1837. On the performance of the mixed commissions, see ch. 5. [2] Palmerston to Hamilton, no. 6, 30 November 1837, F.O. 84/223.

the *gabinete parlamentar*, led by Bernardo Pereira de Vasconcelos were more closely identified with *fazendeiro* interests and more openly sympathetic to the continuation of the slave trade than any previous Brazilian government, and they proved to be as unwilling to extend the scope of Brazil's anti-slave trade treaty with Britain as they were to strengthen Brazil's own anti-slave trade legislation. The government successfully managed to avoid a discussion of the Commission's report when the new Chamber assembled early in 1838. They did nothing, however, to secure the ratification of the additional articles of 1835, which, for the first time were not even mentioned in the Foreign Minister's *Relatório*. The frequent assurances to Hamilton Hamilton and George Gordon, acting British *chargé d'affaires* during the first half of 1838 in the absence of both Hamilton and Ouseley, that the additional articles would be ratified at the first opportunity were beginning to wear thin.

During a visit to London in April 1838, Ouseley suggested to Palmerston that financial inducements, 'the offer of a certain sum', might prove 'the promptest and ultimately the most economical mode of gaining the point' (the ratification of the anti-slave trade agreement of 1835).[1] Secrecy, Ouseley wrote, was the only condition: the Brazilians liked to be bribed, but they did not like it known that they were being bribed. Palmerston's response was to write: 'I can authorise nothing on this point except a private hint that if the articles are not ratified we may possibly act as if they were.'[2] Ouseley himself had long been a forthright advocate of coercive measures. Force was something Brazilians—'vain, mediocre and ostentatious people of Portuguese origin', as he contemptuously described them[3]—could understand. Once the preventive squadrons on the coast of west Africa and Brazil had been reinforced, he argued, the British government should 'take matters into their own hands'. It might soon be necessary, he wrote on another occasion, to act 'without the fetters imposed at present by the treaty and the constitution of the mixed court', to

---

[1] Memorandum on the slave trade instructions to the Rio mission, London, 24 April 1838, F.O. 84/252. Later Ouseley again advocated a policy of bribing deputies and senators properly instead of simply giving them 'bad dinners and evening parties' (Ouseley to Palmerston, 21 May 1839, Broadlands MSS, GC/OU/33).

[2] Minute added to Ouseley's memorandum, dated 27 April.

[3] Ouseley 21 May 1839, Private.

'do away with the defective machinery hitherto employed' and to 'send them [Brazilian slavers] elsewhere for adjudication'.[1] In September 1838, during an interview with Maciel Monteiro, the Brazilian Foreign Minister, Ouseley went so far as to threaten him openly that if Brazil persisted in her refusal to co-operate with Britain for the suppression of the slave trade and 'conciliatory and amicable means were found useless', measures might be adopted which would be highly disagreeable to the Brazilian government. When, a few months later, Ouseley again made it clear in a note to Monteiro that Britain was resolved to end the slave trade and would not be deterred 'by any obstacles of whatever nature and however painful to the friendly feelings which actuate her towards Brazil from promptly using the means she possesses in order to carry into effect this resolution dictated at once by justice, humanity and policy', he was echoing Lord Palmerston's own words.[2] For the time being, however, Britain refrained from taking any unilateral action against Brazilian slave vessels.

Thus, at the end of almost a decade of negotiations with Portugal and Brazil, no effective Anglo-Portuguese anti-slave trade treaty had been signed, nor had essential equipment and break-up articles been added to the Anglo-Brazilian treaty. As a result, throughout this period the British navy's powers to suppress, or even to contain, the illegal slave trade to Brazil remained severely limited.

[1] Ouseley to Palmerston, 21 August, 26 September 1838, Private, F.O. 84/254.
[2] Ouseley no. 16, 24 September 1838, F.O. 84/254; Ouseley to Monteiro, 15 January, enclosed in Ouseley no. 5, 19 January 1839, Conf., F.O. 84/283.

CHAPTER 5

THE BRITISH NAVY AND THE MIXED COMMISSIONS, 1830–1839

During the 1830s, as indeed throughout the long and costly campaign which lasted for more than half a century from 1807 to the mid-sixties, Britain's efforts for the suppression of the transatlantic slave trade at sea were concentrated on the coast of west Africa. Since 1807, when the sloops *Pheasant* and *Derwent* were first sent out to enforce Britain's own anti-slave trade legislation, a number of ships of the Royal Navy had been stationed on the west African coast where their duties had also come to include the suppression of the illegal foreign slave trade. After 1819, following the signing of the first right of search treaties with Portugal, Spain and the Netherlands, the coast from Cape Verde in the north to Benguela in the south (3,000 miles) had constituted a separate naval station. But from 1832 to 1839 the West African squadron came under the orders of the commanders-in-chief of the Cape of Good Hope station, successively Rear Admiral Frederick Warren (1831–4), Rear Admiral Sir Patrick Campbell (1834–7) and Rear Admiral George Elliot (1837–40). This combined West African and Cape station covered an enormous area from 26°W. to 75°E., and as far north as 23° 30′N. in the Atlantic and 10°S. in the Indian Ocean. Yet in 1836, for example, it accounted for only 14 of the 100 or so ships and a little over 1,000 of the 17,000 men on all foreign stations. The number of ships was increased to 17 in 1838 and to 19 in 1839, but at any one time there were never more than eight of them patrolling the entire west coast of Africa north of the equator from Cape Verde to the Bights of Benin and Biafra—where, moreover, their duties included the protection of British settlements and legitimate commerce as well as the interception of slavers.[1] Not a single ship was permanently stationed on the west

[1] For the boundaries of the West African and Cape naval stations, and the number of ships attached to them, see Christopher Lloyd, *The Navy and the Slave Trade* (London, 1949), Appendix C, Appendix D; C. J. Bartlett, *Great Britain and Sea Power, 1815–1853* Oxford, 1963), Appendix II.

122

African coast south of the line between Cape Lopez and Benguela, nor indeed on the east African coast. There was little point: British cruisers were not empowered to search and capture Portuguese vessels south of the equator and almost without exception ships operating in southern latitudes, whether Portuguese or not, sheltered under the Portuguese flag. Consequently, most slave ships, even north of the equator, completed their voyages to and from the African coast without ever sighting a British warship: the captain of a slaver taken off Gallinas in 1833, for example, told the mixed court in Sierra Leone that he had already made thirteen voyages without the slightest difficulty.[1]

Not only were there too few ships stationed in slave-trading areas but the west African coast tended to be a dumping ground for the worst ships in the Royal Navy. Many were virtually useless for the duties assigned to them: large, slow, fifth- and sixth-rate frigates, veterans of the Napoleonic wars, with their tall, easily sighted masts, and smaller Seppings brigs which, it was generally agreed, sailed like haystacks, were easily outmanoeuvred and outsailed by most of the slave ships they did encounter, an increasing number of which were fast, sleek American-built clippers. The only two cruisers to prove a match for the slave ships, at least in the early thirties, were significantly themselves ex-slavers which had been bought by the navy after their condemnation in the Sierra Leone mixed court. The *Black Joke* and the *Fair Rosamund*, which served as tenders to Commodore Hayes' flagship *Dryad*, captured nine of the eleven slave ships which the squadron took between November 1830 and March 1832. When, later in 1832, the *Black Joke* was declared unseaworthy, Peter Leonard, who had served as surgeon on the *Dryad* during 1831 and later wrote an interesting account of his voyage, lamented the destruction of a ship 'which has done more towards putting an end to the vile traffic in slaves than all the ships of the station put together'.[2]

[1] Christopher Fyfe, *A History of Sierra Leone* (Oxford, 1962), p. 197.
[2] Lloyd, *op. cit.* pp. 71–3; Peter Leonard, *A Voyage to the West Coast of Africa in H.M.S. Dryad* (London, 1833), p. 104. See also Sir Henry Huntley, *Seven Years' Service on the Slave Coast* (2 vols., London, 1836). Huntley, who served on a number of ships, including the *Fair Rosamund*, during this period, came to believe that 'to keep up a squadron for the purpose of suppressing the slave trade is a monotonous and idle absurdity', quoted in Lloyd, pp. 72–3. For the success story of the *Black Joke*, see J. Holland Rose, *Man and the Sea* (Cambridge, 1935), p. 245, and W. L. Clowes, *The Royal Navy* (London, 1903), vi. p. 269.

British navy and mixed commissions, 1830–1839

Every year, in their annual reports, the British commissioners in Sierra Leone urged the British government to increase the number and quality of the cruisers which could give their undivided attention to the suppression of the slave trade.[1] The claims of the West African squadron to a greater number of ships and men were consistently upheld by Lord Palmerston at the Foreign Office, who frequently complained of the Admiralty's lack of enthusiasm for his anti-slave trade policies. In 1862, when his career was nearing its end, Palmerston was to write:

No First Lord, and no Board of Admiralty, have ever felt any interest in the suppression of the slave trade, or taken of their own free will any steps towards its accomplishment, and whatever they have done in compliance with the wishes of others they have done grudgingly and imperfectly. If there was a particularly old slow-going tub in the Navy she was sure to be sent to the coast of Africa to try and catch the fast sailing American clippers; and if there was an officer notoriously addicted to drinking, he was sent to a station where rum is a deadly poison.[2]

For their part, the Admiralty could point to the limited resources at their disposal and to the many calls made upon them as a result of the increase in the number of peacetime services, other than the suppression of the slave trade, which the navy was required to perform in every part of the world—the promotion and protection of Britain's expanding commerce and colonial interests, the suppression of smuggling and piracy, the protection of the fisheries, the transportation of convicts, the packet service, and oceanic surveying. Throughout this period, as in any other, the overall strength of the navy was determined by a compromise between, on the one hand, what seemed desirable in the light of the demands of these miscellaneous services and the state of Britain's relations with other powers and, on the other, what was practicable from a political and financial standpoint, bearing in mind the continual pressure, both inside and outside Parliament, for cuts in government spending.[3]

[1] E.g., Smith and Macaulay to Palmerston, General no. 12, 5 January 1833 (Report on 1832), F.O. 84/134; Macaulay to Palmerston, General no. 4, 5 January 1835 (Report on 1834), F.O. 84/166; Macaulay and Doherty to Palmerston, General no. 111, 31 December 1838 (Report on 1838), F.O. 84/231.
[2] Quoted in A. E. M. Ashley, *Life of Henry John Temple, Viscount Palmerston, 1846–1865* (London, 1876), ii, 227; also Lloyd, p. 155.   [3] See Bartlett, *op. cit. passim.*

British navy and mixed commissions, 1830–1839

The tactics employed by the small West African squadron were not the most effective that might, in theory, have been devised. British warships allowed slave ships to reach the African coast unmolested and to ship their cargoes at their leisure; for the most part they cruised thirty or forty miles offshore between well-known points of embarkation, and confined themselves to forcing the slavers to run the gauntlet on their return to Cuba or Brazil (which they usually accomplished without much difficulty). Foreign critics of Britain's anti-slave trade policies suggested that the navy was only interested in slavers which had taken on their slaves because of the use that could be made of liberated slaves as labourers in Britain's own colonies both in Africa (Sierra Leone) and later in the West Indies. Some of the squadron's English critics suggested that since naval officers earned bounty money for each slave captured and liberated (though with increasing captures head money had been cut in 1824 from £60 a male, £30 a female and £10 a child to a flat £10 and in 1830 to £5 per slave[1]) but not a penny for capturing an empty ship, they were encouraged to defer any action against a slave ship until slaves had been taken on board; as Lord Brougham pointed out, while their duty was to suppress the slave trade they were rewarded in proportion to the height which the trade was suffered to reach.[2] None of these charges—which the Admiralty strenuously denied—was ever adequately substantiated. In fact British officers turned a blind eye on empty slave ships less because the necessary financial incentives were lacking than because they were not authorised to capture ships flying the Spanish or Portuguese flags unless they were actually carrying slaves and, almost without exception, the slavers which British warships met during this period sailed under one or other of these two flags. After the signing of a new Anglo-Spanish treaty in June 1835, naval officers were empowered to capture Spanish ships which were equipped for the trade, and for a few months during 1836–7 they took every opportunity of doing so—even though there was no financial reward and there was a

---

1 Lloyd, op. cit. p. 80; Michael Lewis, The Navy in Transition. A Social History, 1814–64 (London, 1965), p. 236.
2 Hansard, xi, 599, House of Lords, 29 January 1838. The trade, Brougham argued, 'flourishes under the very expedients adopted to crush it and increases in consequence of those very measures resorted to for its extinction'.

considerable risk of mistaken capture and subsequent acquittal by an Anglo-Spanish mixed commission.[1] It was not long, however, before Spanish traders sought the protection of the Portuguese flag and although it was still occasionally possible to divest a Spanish ship of its assumed Portuguese nationality and, on the basis of its equipment, secure its condemnation, the almost universal use of the Portuguese flag in the Cuban as well as the Brazilian trade forced the British navy to revert to its earlier, unsatisfactory, offshore tactics.

In view of its size and quality and the severe limitations which the anti-slave trade treaties imposed upon its activities, it is perhaps remarkable how many slave ships were captured by the West African squadron. During the five years from the summer of 1830 to the summer of 1835, an average of only ten slavers a year were taken—all with slaves on board. However, the next four years, and particularly 1836 when the new Anglo-Spanish treaty was enforced, were years of unprecedented success for the squadron: on average thirty-five slave ships were captured each year.[2] The great majority of these ships were engaged in the illegal trade to Cuba, now the principal market for slaves shipped north of the line; some of them, however, were owned by Portuguese residents in Bahia and others had at one time or another made successful trips to Brazil (usually to Bahia or Pernambuco). The *Tamega*, with 440 slaves on board, taken off Lagos by H.M.S. *Charybdis* in June 1834, was the first slaver actually heading for Brazil which the West African squadron had captured since the entire Brazilian slave trade had been declared illegal four years earlier.[3] The next few years saw the occasional capture of other ships returning to Brazil: two in 1835—the *Atrevida* and the *Legitimo Africano*; four in 1836—the *Mindello*, the *Esperanza*, the *Quatro de Abril* and the *Veloz*; three in 1837—the *Lafayette*, the *Amelia* and the *Providencia*; and four in 1838—the *Deixa Falar*, the *Gratidão*, the *Veloz* and the *Camões*.[4] However, fewer than one in ten of the ships captured

[1] During 1836 British cruisers captured thirty-seven Spanish slave ships on the west coast of Africa—twenty-four equipped for the trade (Campbell and Lewis to Palmerston, General no. 4, 5 January 1837 (Report on 1836), F.O. 84/212).
[2] See annual reports of British commissioners in Sierra Leone.
[3] Macaulay to Palmerston, Portugal no. 2, 5 January 1835, F.O. 84/169.
[4] Macaulay and Lewis to Palmerston, Portugal no. 3, 2 January 1836, F.O. 84/194;

by the West African squadron during the thirties were actually engaged in the Brazilian slave trade. Several thousand slaves were lost to the Brazilian market, but this was only a tiny proportion of the number of slaves annually transported across the Atlantic to Brazil. The trade between Bahia and the Bights was the hardest hit, as indeed it had been during the previous twenty years, but it was by now a relatively insignificant part of the Brazilian trade. The greater part of the trade—that carried on south of the line from the Congo, Angola and Moçambique to the area north and south of Rio de Janeiro—the West African squadron was obliged to ignore almost completely. Indeed, between the spring of 1830 and the autumn of 1839 only one slave ship sailing for Brazil was captured south of the line. This was the *Incomprehensivel*, bound for Rio de Janeiro with almost 600 slaves from Moçambique, which H.M.S. *Dolphin* happened to meet on the high seas (24° S. 16° W.) in December 1836.[1]

With the exception of a very small number handed over to their own authorities all the slave vessels captured by the British West African squadron during the thirties were despatched (with prize crews on board) to Sierra Leone for adjudication in the mixed court there. In 1819 Sierra Leone had been an obvious choice for the seat of the mixed commissions on the west African coast: a vice-admiralty court had already been established there for the adjudication of British—and occasionally foreign—slave ships captured by British cruisers during the Napoleonic wars; as a settlement for liberated Africans, it was well suited to receive slaves from condemned ships; and British commissioners could be easily and quickly replaced by colonial officers in cases of illness or death. But Sierra Leone had proved to have two serious drawbacks. First, it was a notorious white man's grave: four British commissary judges—two of them in 1826—and numerous lesser officials in the mixed court were to die at their posts. Secondly, although two important centres of slave trade activity—the

Campbell and Lewis, Portugal no. 2, 5 January 1837, F.O. 84/212; Macaulay and Lewis, Portugal no. 118, 1 January 1838, F.O. 84/235; Macaulay and Doherty, Portugal no. 109, 31 December 1838, F.O. 84/237.
[1] Macaulay and Lewis, Brazil no. 120, 1 January 1838, F.O. 84/238.

interconnecting systems of the Rio Nunez, Rio Pongas and adjoining rivers to the north, and the Sherbro and Gallinas estuaries to the south—were within easy reach of the colony, most captures were in fact made 1,000 miles away in the Bights of Benin and Biafra. During the 1830s there were moves to transfer the mixed commissions from Sierra Leone to the island of Fernando Po, ceded to Spain by Portugal in 1778 but never settled. Fernando Po occupied a commanding position opposite the Niger Delta only two or three days sail from the Bights, and in 1827 Captain W. F. W. Owen was sent to the island, with Spain's permission, in order to start a settlement there and to erect suitable buildings for a mixed court. Three years later, a Parliamentary Select Committee under the chairmanship of Joseph Hume, who represented interests hostile to Sierra Leone, recommended the immediate removal of the mixed commissions from Sierra Leone to Fernando Po. In the event, however, Spain refused to transfer to Britain its sovereignty over the island without which there would have been no guarantee for the freedom of slaves liberated there, and the Treasury turned down an offer from Spain to sell the island for £100,000. To the disappointment of British naval officers—and British merchants in the expanding palm oil trade of the Niger Delta—the Fernando Po scheme was abandoned in 1832, and the mixed commissions remained in Freetown.[1]

After several minor disagreements between British and foreign commissioners, and between commissioners and the first British naval officers to arrive with prizes, a uniform procedure for adjudicating captured ships brought before the mixed commissions in Sierra Leone—and those across the Atlantic—had eventually been hammered out.[2] On arrival in port, the captured slave ship, together with any slaves it carried, became the responsibility of the

---

[1] For the Fernando Po scheme, see Fyfe, *op. cit.* pp. 165, 175, 178, 187–8; K. Onwuka Dike, *Trade and Politics in the Niger Delta, 1830–85* (Oxford, 1956), 55–60; *Cambridge History of the British Empire* (Cambridge, 1940), ii, 650–2; C. W. Newbury (ed.), *British Policy towards West Africa* (Oxford, 1965), pp. 10–11.

[2] Largely in conformity with the directives contained in the lengthy printed memorandum issued to all British commissioners to assist them in the performance of their unfamiliar duties (Castlereagh to H.M. commissioners, 20 February 1819, F.O. 315/1; *B.F.S.P.* viii, 25–49). On the preparation of this memorandum, see Leslie Bethell, 'The Mixed Commissions for the Suppression of the Transatlantic Slave Trade in the Nineteenth Century' *Journal of African History*, vii (1966), p. 84, n. 20.

marshal or bailiff of the court. The slaves normally remained on board throughout the period of adjudication, although in Sierra Leone, at the discretion of the court, the sick and dying were sometimes taken ashore. The naval officer who had made the capture (if he had accompanied the ship) or else the officer in command of the prize crew had first to make an affidavit before the registrar of the court, and then hand over any papers found on board the captured vessel together with a declaration or certificate, drawn up at the time of capture, describing when and where the ship had been searched, the condition in which it was found and the number of slaves on board. Interested parties were then called upon to appear before the court in order to demonstrate why the vessel should not be condemned; unless it could be proved to the contrary, it was assumed that a vessel was guilty of illegal slaving activities and that it had been legally captured. There followed an examination by the registrar of the master, crew (in practice usually the mate and boatswain) and any other witnesses, which usually took the form of a series of set questions. The evidence was then put in the hands of proctors (or attorneys) representing the captors and the claimants, who argued the case before the two commissary judges. The commissioners, like many of the proctors, were not always legally qualified (not that lawyers necessarily make the best international judges). George Jackson, for instance, who was British commissary judge successively in Sierra Leone (1828–32), Rio de Janeiro (1832–41), Surinam (1841–5) and Luanda (1845–59), had previously spent twenty years in the diplomatic service. Some of those who served on the British side of the mixed court in Freetown, however, had formerly held the position of King's Advocate or Chief Justice in the colony, and most had gained valuable experience, first as registrar to the court and then as commissioner of arbitration, before being promoted to commissary judge.[1]

In cases where a ship had been taken as it left Africa with its cargo of slaves, a mixed commission needed no further proof of a vessel's character; it was necessary only to establish that the slaves had been shipped from a prohibited area (in the case of 'Portuguese' ships, for instance, that they were trading north of the

[1] *Journal of African History*, vii (1966), p. 85, n. 22.

equator), and that the search and capture had been both legal and executed in the appropriate manner. In such cases most of the disputes between commissioners arose largely over the nationality of a captured slave ship. However, when empty ships suspected of being equipped for the slave trade were brought before a commission for adjudication, which was increasingly the case after 1835, and proof of slaving became more difficult to establish with any certainty, disputes became much more common. British commissioners were specifically instructed that in reaching a verdict they should never lose sight of their judicial character, and that they should 'uniformly endeavour to combine a fair and conscientious zeal for the prevention of the illegal traffic in slaves with the maintenance of the strictest justice towards the parties concerned'.[1] In practice, however, it frequently happened that the British representative on the mixed commission assumed the role of prosecutor while his foreign colleague spoke for the defence: British commissioners naturally tended to be more hostile towards the slave trade and more sympathetic towards the British officers who had made the capture; foreign commissioners, if not overtly sympathetic to the slave traders, were at least more concerned to safeguard the rights and freedom of those of their country's merchant vessels which were engaged in legitimate commerce.

In the event, foreign governments were represented only intermittently in the so-called 'mixed' commissions sitting in Sierra Leone: they had difficulty in filling the posts in the first place and subsequently experienced even greater difficulty in finding replacements when the need arose. Nominees often refused the appointment or unduly delayed their departure for Africa; once there, the climate and disease invariably caused them to suffer long periods of ill-health which necessitated equally long periods of convalescence in the Canaries or some other suitably healthy spot. In cases where there was a vacancy in the mixed commission when a ship was brought in, the remaining members of the commission were authorised to proceed with the adjudication; thus in the absence of both a foreign commissary judge and a foreign commissioner

[1] Castlereagh to Thomas Gregory, first commissary judge in Freetown, 19 February 1819, F.O. 315/1.

of arbitration—as was not infrequently the case—the British commissioners acted alone. For their part, the British government never experienced any difficulty in filling the temporary vacancies which retirement, illness or death created on their side of the mixed commissions: in Havana and Rio de Janeiro they could call upon the British consul-general or vice-consul; in Sierra Leone the Governor or Lieutenant-Governor, Chief Justice or Secretary of the Colony could take over. All commissions were required by treaty to give sentence 'as summarily as possible', preferably within twenty days of the captured vessel's arrival in port, and certainly within two months, but only those sitting in Sierra Leone consistently met this requirement. One reason for the greater speed of adjudication at Freetown in comparison with Havana or Rio de Janeiro—and also for the lower incidence of acquittals—was the fact that British officials in the 'mixed' commissions frequently found themselves sitting alone.

When a commission decided in favour of acquittal as, for instance, in the case of the *Camões* which in 1838 came before the Anglo-Portuguese commission in Sierra Leone,[1] the ship, its cargo, and any slaves on board were generally restored at once to the owners, who were entitled to claim the costs of the suit and all losses and damages sustained as a result of the capture and detention of their vessel. The commissioners in Sierra Leone usually appointed one or two 'respectable merchants' to assist the registrar of the court in assessing the amount for which the captors, or if they defaulted, their government, were liable. Under the right of search treaties, the two contracting powers undertook to ensure the payment of damages within a period of twelve months. The British government, however, as we have seen, refused to consider any claims for compensation in cases where it was satisfied that the vessel, though illegally captured, had in fact been engaged in the illicit slave trade. Vessels condemned by a mixed commission—and only a small minority were not condemned—were publicly auctioned: some were bought by local merchants and shopkeepers, usually at bargain prices—to be resold at a profit; some, like the *Black Joke* and the *Fair Rosamund*, were purchased by the

[1] Macaulay and Doherty to Palmerston, Portugal no. 109, 31 December 1838, F.O. 84/237.

Admiralty and subsequently converted into cruisers for anti-slave trade patrol; and some were bought on behalf of slave traders (sometimes the original owners) and re-entered the trade. The proceeds of a sale, which might amount to anything from £100 to £5,000, were divided between the two governments concerned. This income helped to meet the contingent expenses of the mixed commissions—the rent of the courthouse, the cost of furniture, the fees of interpreter, translator, copyist, marshal, auctioneer, shipbreaker, assessor, and the wages of porters, servants and messengers—which at Rio de Janeiro, Havana, and Surinam were shared equally between the governments concerned and at Freetown were divided between Britain (two-sixths) and Portugal, Spain, Brazil and the Netherlands (one sixth each). In Britain's case the income from the sale of slave ships could also be set against the prize money awarded to the captors. In accordance with the anti-slave trade treaties, slaves from condemned vessels were liberated and delivered over to the government in whose territory the commission sat, to be employed as free labourers or servants. In Sierra Leone liberated slaves—35,000 of them during the thirties—were registered at King's Yard as British citizens and became the responsibility of the Liberated African Department, which sent most of them to live and work in villages near Freetown, although some were persuaded to emigrate to the West Indies as free apprentices.[1]

During the 1830s, four mixed commissions sat in Sierra Leone: the Anglo-Spanish, Anglo-Portuguese and Anglo-Dutch commissions which had been established in 1819 and the Anglo-Brazilian set up in 1828. However, of approximately 200 ships to come up for adjudication during the period from the middle of 1830 to the middle of 1839—fifty-one of them in one year, 1836— two-thirds were dealt with by the Anglo-Spanish commission and, with one exception, the remainder by the Anglo-Portuguese commission. The Dutch slave trade had been suppressed in the late twenties and after 1829 only one Dutch ship—the barque *Jane*

---

[1] On the Liberated African Department, see Fyfe, *op. cit.* pp. 138–9. Liberated African establishments were severely curtailed after 1843, *ibid.* pp. 229–30. A Danish scholar, Richs Meyer-Heiselberg, is now making a study of the liberated Africans in Sierra Leone. See, for example, *Notes from Liberated African Department* (Scandinavian Institute of African Studies, Research Report no. 1, Uppsala, 1967).

in 1862—was brought into Sierra Leone. Because of the almost universal assumption of Portuguese nationality by ships in the Brazilian trade every ship intercepted north of the equator on its way to Brazil was taken before the Anglo-Portuguese commission. The only case adjudicated by the Anglo-Brazilian commission in this period was that of the *Incomprehensivel* captured in 1836. Ostensibly a Portuguese ship taken south of the equator, the Anglo-Portuguese commission was bound to acquit it on the grounds of illegal capture. In the hope of proving it Brazilian, therefore, the prize crew brought it before the Anglo-Brazilian commission. There were, at the time—February 1837—no Brazilian commissioners resident in Freetown. José de Paiva had served as Brazilian commissary judge from 1828 until his death in June 1834. His successor, Mathias Egídio da Silveira, who had been appointed commissioner of arbitration in February 1832 but who had only taken up his post in December 1833, and Manuel de Oliveira Santos, the newly appointed commissioner of arbitration, both left Freetown for health reasons during 1836, the former in March and the latter in June, neither of them to return to their posts. The case was therefore put in the hands of Lieutenant-Governor Campbell, acting British commissary judge in the absence of Henry Macaulay (one of Zachary Macaulay's sons and brother of the historian), and W. W. Lewis, the British commissioner of arbitration. The defendants proved the ship Portuguese-owned but, as a result of precedents already established in the Anglo-Brazilian mixed court in Rio de Janeiro, the commissioners felt justified in condemning it on the grounds that the owner was permanently resident in Brazil, exclusively engaged in the Brazilian slave trade and to all intents and purposes Brazilian.[1] Even so, it was another three years before further captures were made south of the equator by ships of the West African and Cape station and before the Anglo-Brazilian commission in Sierra Leone was again called upon to act.

The British navy did not confine itself exclusively to the west African coast in its efforts to suppress the illegal slave trade. British warships on the South American and West Indies stations, for

[1] Macaulay and Lewis, Brazil no. 120, 1 January 1838, F.O. 84/238.

example, were issued with warrants to search ships suspected of slaving, although few were ever specifically commissioned for this task and their role was, for the most part, secondary to that played by ships of the West African squadron. In the mid-thirties, there were some fifteen ships attached to the South American station which embraced both the Atlantic and the Pacific coasts of the continent.[1] Fewer than half, however, were stationed on the Atlantic and their major task of protecting British interests took them as far afield as the Falkland Islands, the Río de la Plata, Rio de Janeiro and the north-east coast of Brazil. The British legation in Rio de Janeiro and the British commissioners in the Anglo-Brazilian mixed court (who, like their colleagues in Surinam and Havana, enjoyed what were virtually sinecures) continually urged the need for more British warships permanently engaged in suppressing the slave trade—a *cordon sanitaire* along the coast of Brazil with a particularly close surveillance of the well-known landing places between São Sebastião and Vitória.[2] But if the Admiralty was unable to spare the men and the ships to strengthen the West African squadron, it was certainly unable to find extra ships for South America. In any case, stationed as they were south of the line, British cruisers off the Brazilian coast were not only unauthorised to interfere with slave ships setting out from Brazilian ports, whether under the Brazilian flag or the Portuguese, but they did not even have the authority to detain ships when they returned loaded with slaves if, as was invariably the case, they had hoisted the Portuguese flag. At the same time, with the revival of the Brazilian slave trade after the short lull which followed its legal abolition in 1830, British cruisers could hardly fail to come across the occasional slave ship, if only by accident, and it was hard for naval officers to ignore their existence—certainly when they had slaves on board. It was, after all, a rare opportunity for them to earn bounty money. Some slavers were stopped and searched; a few were seized and sent before the Anglo-Brazilian commission in

---

[1] See Bartlett, *op. cit.* Appendix II; Lloyd, *op. cit.* p. 78.
[2] E.g., Jackson and Grigg to Palmerston, no. 7, 16 May 1832, Grigg no. 15, 6 December 1832, F.O. 84/129; Jackson and Grigg no. 13, 12 November 1833, F.O. 84/138; Ouseley no. 8, 21 May 1833, F.O. 84/141; Jackson and Grigg no. 15, 23 March 1835, no. 24, 30 September 1835, F.O. 84/199; Gordon no. 1, 19 January 1838, F.O. 84/252; Jackson and Grigg no. 27, 14 August 1838, F.O. 84/242; Ouseley 10 August, 26 September, Private, F.O. 84/254.

Rio de Janeiro either because the officer concerned hoped to tear aside the Portuguese disguise and prove a ship Brazilian, or because he was imperfectly acquainted with the terms of the anti-slave trade treaties. Inevitably mistakes were made, but as a result of a series of test cases British cruisers on the South American station were gradually able to extend their powers and reduce, if only slightly, the value of the Portuguese flag to the illicit trader operating south of the equator where at first it had afforded him complete protection.

In November 1833 H.M. sloop *Snake* stopped and searched the *Maria da Gloria* outside Rio harbour and found she was carrying over 400 slaves (more than half of them children under twelve) from Luanda. Even though the Portuguese flag had been hoisted the ship was detained and taken before the Anglo-Brazilian mixed commission in Rio de Janeiro—which had not adjudicated a case for almost three years. There the owner of the vessel and its cargo, Anastácio José Ribeira, claimed Portuguese nationality. Born a Portuguese subject in Brazil, he was resident there when Brazil became independent and so, under the Brazilian constitution, he could claim Brazilian nationality. He had, however, fought on the Portuguese side in the skirmishes which had taken place between loyalists and independents in Bahia during 1822–3, and had then lived in Lisbon until 1830. He now lived on Ilha Grande, south of Rio de Janeiro, and traded as a Portuguese merchant to and from the capital. Speculators in the Brazilian slave trade like Ribeira were able to call themselves Portuguese or Brazilian as the circumstances dictated, like the bat in the fable which called itself a mouse at one time and a bird at another, according to its convenience. During the lengthy proceedings which ensued, the British commissary judge, George Jackson, who had recently been transferred from Freetown to Rio de Janeiro, almost laid himself open to the charge of trying to fix Brazilian nationality on the *Maria da Gloria*, but in the end he had to agree with the Brazilian judge João Carneiro de Campos that it was in fact a *bona fide* Portuguese vessel. Already, in March 1831, it had been established—in the case of the *Destimado* captured by H.M.S. *Druid* off Bahia and that of the *Africano Oriental* seized by the Brazilian authorities— that the Anglo-Brazilian commission had no jurisdiction over

Portuguese vessels.[1] So on 20 December the *Maria da Gloria* was acquitted[2]—but not released. No appeal was possible against the decision of a mixed commission, but there was nothing to prevent the captors from transferring a case to another commission. The *Maria da Gloria* was therefore despatched with a prize crew on board to the mixed court in Sierra Leone.[3] On 22 February 1834, however, the judges in the Anglo-Portuguese commission reluctantly acquitted and released the vessel on the grounds that, under the treaty of 1817, no British cruiser could legally detain a *bona fide* Portuguese slave ship south of the equator.[4] By this time over a hundred of the slaves had died, sixty-four more were too sick to leave Sierra Leone and the rest were emaciated and diseased.[5] The *Maria da Gloria*—'a floating charnal house'—set off on another miserable voyage across the Atlantic—her third in six months. Some of the slaves were being landed on the coast of Bahia several weeks later when the ship was picked up by a Brazilian cruiser, but after another long legal enquiry she was again released. The slaves were freed in accordance with the Brazilian law of November 1831, but by then most had been transported to plantations inland, well beyond the reach of the law.[6]

In the course of this disastrous affair, however, certain important precedents were established in the mixed court at Rio de Janeiro. The judges had not challenged the right of a British cruiser to visit and search a Portuguese vessel south of the equator

[1] Cunningham and Grigg to Palmerston, no. 9, 25 March 1831, F.O. 84/120. The slaves were liberated, but both ships were acquitted and restored to their owners, although no costs or damages were awarded. Two more slave ships—the *Eliza* and the *D'Estevão de Athaide*—had been acquitted in December 1830 on the grounds that they had taken on slaves during the period in which the trade was still legally permitted.

[2] On the *Maria da Gloria* case, Jackson and Grigg to Palmerston, nos. 15, 16 and 17, 12, 26 and 27 December 1833, F.O. 84/138. For the ship's early history, Macaulay to Palmerston, General no. 4, 5 January 1835, F.O. 84/166.

[3] Fox to Palmerston, 13 January 1834, Private, F.O. 84/156.

[4] Smith and Macaulay to Palmerston, Portugal no. 19, 31 March 1834, F.O. 84/149; Macaulay, General no. 4, F.O. 84/166.

[5] Smith and Macaulay, Portugal no. 20, 19 April 1834, F.O. 84/149. For a graphic description of the *Maria da Gloria's* condition at this time, see Captain Joseph Denman, *Practical Remarks on the Slave Trade and on the Existing Treaties with Portugal* (2nd ed., London, 1839), pp. 17–21. Denman, who later became famous for his anti-slave trade exploits on the west African coast, had served on board the *Snake* and was a member of the *Maria da Gloria's* prize crew.

[6] Jackson and Grigg to Palmerston, 17 September 1834, F.O. 84/153; Parkinson (consul in Bahia) to Palmerston, no. 5, 16 May 1834, F.O. 84/157.

where there were grounds for suspecting that it might be a slave
ship and of Brazilian nationality. Nor had they refused to take
cognisance of a captured ship which was ostensibly Portuguese. It
appeared that they were prepared at least to try and differentiate
between genuine Portuguese slavers and Brazilian vessels pretending to be Portuguese, and although a ship which proved to be
Portuguese would have to be released the court was ready to condemn a ship which was shown to be Brazilian, provided that it had
slaves on board. It was taken for granted by both the British and
Brazilian judges that British cruisers had the right to search and
capture Brazilian ships carrying slaves south of the equator. The
'Portuguese' slaver, *Paquete do Sul*, which had been captured by
H.M. sloop *Satellite* at the same time as the *Maria da Gloria* soon
after it had landed its slaves on the Brazilian coast, was proved to
have a Brazilian owner and, after some hesitation on the part of
the Brazilian judge (no slaves had been found on board at the time
of capture, and although the Anglo-Portuguese convention of
March 1823 permitting the capture of ships which had recently
had slaves on board had been accepted by Brazil in 1825 it formed
no part of the Anglo-Brazilian treaty of 1826) it was condemned
on 30 January 1834.[1] In July of the same year the schooner *Duqueza
de Braganza* with nearly 300 slaves on board, also captured by the
Satellite, was proved Brazilian-owned despite its Portuguese flag,
Portuguese master and fictitious Portuguese papers; it too was
condemned and the Africans were given certificates of emancipation and found work as free labourers or apprentices.[2] It was hoped
that the condemnation of the *Paquete do Sul* and the *Duqueza de
Braganza* would act as a deterrent to Brazilians (and others) who
were hoping to cover their illegal enterprises with the Portuguese
flag and, at the same time, would encourage the British navy to
persevere with its efforts. 'Annoyed and baffled', however, by the
release of the *Maria da Gloria*, British officers were reluctant to

---

[1] Jackson and Grigg, no. 4, 30 January 1834, F.O. 84/152.
[2] Jackson and Grigg, no. 20, 24 July 1834, F.O. 84/152. Like the Africans liberated by the
Brazilian authorities under the law of November 1831, the Africans liberated by the
Anglo-Brazilian mixed commission at Rio de Janeiro under the treaties of 1817 and 1826
were, for the most part, gradually absorbed into the existing slave population. The fate
of these *Africanos livres* or *emancipados* became a major cause of conflict between
the British and Brazilian governments (see above, ch. 3, p. 70, and below ch. 13,
pp. 380–3.

detain any slaver which was not patently Brazilian[1]—and few of them were. In the event, with the exception of the *Rio de la Plata* captured by the *Raleigh* in November 1834 with 523 slaves from Angola on board, they did not risk another capture for over eighteen months. The *Rio de la Plata* was flying the Uruguayan flag at the time and carried a licence to import 'black colonists' into Montevideo, but in the Rio mixed court Jackson eventually succeeded in proving it Brazilian-owned. The vessel was condemned in February 1835 and those slaves still alive (by this time over half the cargo had died) were liberated.[2]

In the spring and summer of 1834 the Brazilian navy began to have some success against the slave trade. The *Cacique* chased and the *Fluminense* finally captured the slaver *Dous de Março* soon after it had landed slaves at São Sebastião, and the *Libre* captured the slaver *Santo Antonio* with almost 150 slaves off Ilha Grande: both were ostensibly Portuguese ships.[3] The Brazilian law of November 1831, which had been introduced at a time when the Brazilians were demanding the dissolution of the mixed commissions, stipulated that vessels captured by Brazilian warships should be taken for adjudication before the ordinary Brazilian courts, but George Jackson suggested to Henry Fox, the British minister, that they would be dealt with more effectively in the mixed court and, after some discussion with Fox, the Brazilian Minister of Justice agreed to issue orders that the *Dous de Março* and the *Santo Antonio* as well as similar cases in the future should be taken in the first instance before the mixed commission in Rio de Janeiro.[4] The two vessels came before the British and Brazilian commissioners on 23 July 1834. In the case of the *Dous de Março*, Jackson took the view that the ship was really Brazilian—she had sailed from Brazil the previous year as a Brazilian ship and there was no proof of any subsequent sale—but Carneiro de Campos, the Brazilian commissioner, accepted her Portuguese character. In the

[1] Fox to Palmerston, no. 2, 24 July 1834, F.O. 84/156.
[2] On the *Rio de la Plata* case, Fox to Palmerston, 23 December 1834, F.O. 84/157; Jackson and Grigg to Wellington, no. 6, 9 February 1835, F.O. 84/174; Dodson to Palmerston, 25 May 1835, F.O. 83/2346. Also J. F. King, 'The Latin American Republics and the Suppression of the Slave Trade', *H.A.H.R.* xxiv (1944), p. 396.
[3] Jackson and Grigg no. 12, no. 16, 5 June, 26 June 1834, F.O. 84/152.
[4] Jackson to Fox, 14 June 1834, enclosed in Jackson and Grigg no. 16; Fox to Palmerston, no. 2, 24 July 1834, F.O. 84/156.

event of two commissary judges failing to agree either on a ship's guilt or on the legitimacy of the capture, lots were drawn to decide which of the two commissioners of arbitration should consider the case: the final verdict was then a majority decision. Arbitrators, however, usually—although by no means always—agreed with their senior partners on the commission. This case proved no exception: the Brazilian arbitrator, successful in the draw, favoured acquittal and the *Dous de Março* was restored to its owners. On the other hand it was quickly established to the satisfaction of both judges that the *Santo Antonio* was a Brazilian ship which had merely gone through the process of a fictitious sale; it was condemned on 4 September.[1]

Meanwhile Lord Palmerston at the Foreign Office was still not satisfied with the acquittal of the *Maria da Gloria*. He submitted all the relevant information on the case to Sir Herbert Jenner, the Advocate General, who replied that the Anglo-Portuguese commission at Sierra Leone had rightly decided in favour of acquittal but that the vessel should have been condemned in the first place by the Anglo-Brazilian court in Rio de Janeiro: the enterprise was Brazilian throughout (the ship was fitted in Rio de Janeiro and was on its way back there) and the owner was a merchant resident in Brazil. Jenner accepted the view put forward at the time by the proctor for the captors, David Stevenson, an English lawyer resident in Rio, that in international law the national character of a merchant derived from the location of his residence and mercantile establishment and not from his place of birth. Thus a Portuguese living in Brazil was bound by Brazilian law and treaties and could be punished for contravening them.[2] Palmerston immediately passed this opinion on to the Admiralty and to George Jackson in Rio de Janeiro, with instructions that he should in future condemn ships like the *Maria da Gloria*. At the same time Henry Fox was ordered to urge the Brazilian government to give similar directives to Brazilian commissary judges.[3] Alves Branco,

---

[1] Jackson and Grigg no. 21, no. 23, 8 September, 16 September 1834, F.O. 84/153.

[2] Jenner to Palmerston, 29 September 1834, F.O. 83/2346. This opinion was reinforced by Jenner's successor, Sir John Dodson, when he criticised the views of the Brazilian judge and arbitrator in the *Dous de Março* case; this vessel, too, he believed, should have been condemned (Dodson to Wellington, 20 January 1835, F.O. 83/2346).

[3] Palmerston to Rio commissioners, no. 4, 8 October 1834, F.O. 84/153; Palmerston to Fox, no. 7, 8 October 1834, F.O. 84/156. Jackson's position was that in fact the owner of

the Brazilian Foreign Minister at the time, found the proposal inadmissible: while he accepted that subjects of friendly nations such as Portugal, living temporarily in Brazil, were subject to the country's laws, he did not consider that they could be brought before special tribunals established as a result of treaties with foreign powers.[1]

During 1835 five more 'Portuguese' ships were brought before the mixed commission in Rio—all of them captured by Brazilian cruisers—but although the commissary judges now had conflicting instructions for dealing with cases where a ship claimed Portuguese nationality, an open breach between the two sides of the court was avoided. There was no doubt that the *Amizade Feliz* and the *Angelica* were slave ships: both carried over 300 slaves from Ambriz and the former had already successfully crossed the Atlantic with slaves on at least one previous occasion. The problem was the usual one of national character. Both claimed Portuguese nationality but their real ownership was not easy to establish and Brazilians certainly were involved. When once again the Brazilian judge accepted and the British judge rejected their claim of Portuguese owership, lots were drawn for arbitration and this time the final decision fell to the English arbitrator, Frederick Grigg. The lack of evidence concerning their ownership, however, obliged him to question the competence of the commission to adjudicate, and in both cases the ships were handed over to the Brazilian government. The patacho *Continente*, flying the Brazilian flag and captured with sixty-two slaves on board in the harbour at São Sebastião, was one of the few cases of a slave ship which did not even pretend to be Portuguese; it was condemned on 28 July 1835. The *Aventura*, which was taken at the same time immediately after landing its cargo, had hoisted the Portuguese flag only just before it was captured; it was easily proved Brazilian and quickly condemned. And the Brazilian smack *Novo Destino* was acquitted on 1 September after the judges had agreed that it was a coastal trader which had been captured by mistake, and that

the *Maria da Gloria* was not an established merchant resident in Brazil, but an independent dealer always on the move (Jackson and Grigg no. 26, 14 October 1834, F.O. 84/153).

[1] Alves Branco to Fox, 7 February, enclosed in Fox to Palmerston, no. 2, 13 March 1835, F.O. 84/179.

the owners were not aware of the existence of two slaves found on board.[1]

In October 1835 the Brazilian government finally accepted the British view of the *Maria da Gloria* case: they instructed the Brazilian commissary judge that Portuguese citizens resident in Brazil should henceforth be regarded as Brazilian and that their ships therefore came within the jurisdiction of the Anglo-Brazilian mixed commission.[2] The two governments had already agreed that *per se* the Portuguese flag could not protect slave ships trading south of the equator from interference by British and Brazilian cruisers. Moreover, a slave ship claiming to be Portuguese would be condemned in the Anglo-Brazilian court if it could be proved that it was carrying or had carried slaves, that its Portuguese colours and papers were fraudulent, and that it was really Brazilian-owned. Another step forward had now been taken: whatever their nationality, ships owned by slave traders operating from Brazil were now liable to be treated as Brazilian ships. Rear Admiral Hammond, commander-in-chief of the South American station, immediately issued fresh instructions to his officers,[3] and within a month H.M. sloop *Satellite*, patrolling off the coast of Bahia, chased and captured the brig *Orion* with a valuable cargo of nearly 250 young slaves. In January 1836 the *Orion* was strongly defended in the Rio de Janeiro mixed court as a Portuguese-owned vessel carrying colonists from Angola to Moçambique, which had been illegally searched and captured south of the equator. To the surprise of the defendants, however, Jackson and Carneiro de Campos, acting in accordance with their new instructions, condemned it on the grounds that the owner, though not Brazilian,

[1] On the *Amizade Feliz*, Jackson and Grigg no. 12, 16 March, no. 22, 22 May 1835, F.O. 84/174; on the *Angelica*, Jackson and Grigg no. 16, 11 April, no. 28, 19 June 1835, F.O. 84/174. In both cases Grigg's decision was approved (Palmerston no. 18, 24 December 1835, F.O. 84/173, based on Dodson 17 December 1835, F.O. 83/2346). On the *Continente*, Jackson and Grigg no. 35, 13 July, no. 39, 29 July 1835, F.O. 84/175; on the *Aventura*, Jackson and Grigg no. 35, 13 July, no. 40, 31 July 1835, F.O. 84/175; on the *Novo Destino*, Jackson and Grigg no. 46, 21 September 1835, F.O. 84/175.

[2] Alves Branco to Fox, 27 October, enclosed in Fox to Palmerston, no. 22, 8 November 1835, F.O. 84/179; order of 29 October, enclosed in Jackson and Grigg no. 57, 10 November 1835, F.O. 84/175.

[3] Hammond circular, 24 November, enclosed in Jackson and Grigg no. 4, 10 February 1836, F.O. 84/198.

was resident in Brazil.[1] Since the Brazilian government had never officially published details of their recent understanding with Britain on this point, this judgement created a considerable stir in slave-trading circles in Rio de Janeiro. Only a few weeks later another 'Portuguese' ship, the *Vencedora*, would probably have been condemned on the same grounds had it not been for a technical irregularity in the capture. The *Hornet*, a packet ship running between Rio de Janeiro and the Río de la Plata, was not carrying the necessary search warrant when it fell in with the *Vencedora*, and the commissary judges had to declare the capture illegal and restore the ship to its owners.[2] However, the case did have one beneficial result. It served to remind the British government of the importance of issuing the warrants required by the right of search treaties to every ship which might at any time come across an illegal slaver. It also raised one very important question which, since the ship was acquitted on other grounds, was never satisfactorily answered. The *Hornet* had captured the *Vencedora* as it was at anchor just off the Maricá islands near Rio de Janeiro; that is, in Brazilian territorial waters. Jackson and Grigg mentioned this in a despatch to Lord Palmerston because, they said, if the British government wanted cruisers to make captures in such circumstances the clause in the treaty of 1817 restricting the right of search to the high seas should be omitted if and when the Anglo-Brazilian treaty were modified. If, in the meantime, such captures were illegal, naval officers ought clearly to be cautioned.[3] Nothing was done, however, and the question of whether or not the British navy had the right to obstruct the illegal slave trade in Brazilian territorial waters was to lead to serious disputes between the two governments throughout the next decade.

In the mid-thirties there were still too few British cruisers stationed on the Brazilian coast to make any real impact on the Brazilian slave trade. Moreover, although in theory many 'Portuguese' ships—perhaps the majority—now came within the juris-

---

[1] On the *Orion*, Jackson and Grigg no. 4, 10 February 1836, F.O. 84/198. The Portuguese minister in London, Barão de Moncorvo, protested vigorously at this capture.
[2] Jackson and Grigg no. 7, 5 March 1836, F.O. 84/198.
[3] *Ibid.* For an interesting comment on the territorial waters issue, see Hugo Fischer, 'The Suppression of Slavery in International Law', *International Law Quarterly*, iii (1950), p. 40.

diction of the Anglo-Brazilian mixed commission, in practice, even in cases where a slave ship was known to have fitted out and set off from a Brazilian port, it was never easy to invalidate its Portuguese papers and establish with certainty that the owners were Brazilians or Brazilian residents. Some owners claimed to be resident in Portugal or Africa; others appeared to be travelling merchants of no fixed address and only occasionally resident in Brazil. In some cases the maze of false sales and transfers made it impossible to discover any but a nominal owner. A naval officer detaining a 'Portuguese' slave ship south of the equator was still taking a great risk. Furthermore, relations between British naval officers and the Anglo-Brazilian mixed commission in Rio de Janeiro remained, from the point of view of the former, less than satisfactory. As well as the many legal complexities arising out of the treaties which were beyond the comprehension of most naval officers there were, too, seemingly endless and frustrating delays between their bringing a case before the commission for adjudication and the execution of its sentence—caused by, amongst other things, the inertia of Brazilian officials and the frequency of Brazilian holidays as well as disputes between the two commissioners. Between November 1833 and April 1838, fifteen cases came before the Anglo-Brazilian commission in Rio: it took, on average, 6 days before proceedings were opened, 37 days for the commission to pass sentence, a further 70 days for the sentence to be executed in cases where the vessel was condemned and 28 days more before any slaves were actually liberated. During this time prize crews were not only prevented from returning to their anti-slave trade (and other) duties; they were also responsible for the safety both of the prisoners and of the slaves, who, in Rio de Janeiro, remained in the crowded and disease-ridden ships throughout the period of adjudication. The duties of the prize crew were not only unpleasant—they were also dangerous: several desperate attempts were made by armed parties from the shore to release the prisoners and recapture the slaves awaiting their liberation. The Brazilian government failed to provide accommodation on shore for either slaves or prisoners and at the same time insisted that they had no hulk of sufficient size and in an adequate state of repair which could be used in the harbour. Eventually, having despatched the *Romney* to Havana harbour for a similar purpose, the British government in 1840 sent out an old sloop the *Crescent* to act as a floating hospital and prison ship in Rio harbour.

For two years after the acquittal of the *Vencedora* in 1836 not a single slave ship was captured on the Brazilian coast. The slave dealers, accustomed to operating with complete freedom, were therefore taken completely by surprise when, in April 1838, H.M. sloop *Rover*, cruising off the Maricá islands, captured first the *Flor de Loanda* as it was landing its cargo of nearly 300 slaves, and then the *Cesar* with over 200 slaves on board. The arrival of these two prizes in Rio harbour caused great consternation; crowds were openly hostile towards the prize crews and the Brazilian government had to provide an armed guard in case attempts should be made to rescue the prisoners. The excitement increased when, a month later, a prize crew from H.M.S. *Wizard* arrived with the slaver *Brilhante* and her 250 slaves. Three successive captures close to Rio de Janeiro, combined with subsequent rumours that the British squadron would soon be substantially reinforced, succeeded in paralysing the slave trade for some little time.[1] When, however, the *Flor de Loanda* came before the mixed court, the two judges decided that the supposed Portuguese owner, Manuel Antonio Teixeira Barboza, could not reasonably be said to reside in Brazil and they therefore had no alternative but to declare that, although the *Flor de Loanda* was engaged in an illegal enterprise—the Portuguese had at last legally abolished the slave trade in December 1836—the court had no jurisdiction over an apparently *bona fide* Portuguese ship. The *Flor de Loanda* was acquitted on 15 May.[2] It was important, however, that so notorious a slave ship should not escape condemnation. Th edecision in its favour had already resulted in a renewal of slaving activity in Rio de Janeiro and Jackson and Grigg therefore suggested to George Gordon, acting British *chargé d'affaires*, that it should be handed over to the Brazilian authorities for violating the Brazilian law of November 1831, or else to the Portuguese consul-general and acting *chargé*, João Baptista Moreira, for violating the Portu-

---

[1] Jackson and Grigg no. 5, 21 May, no. 7, 31 May, no. 14, 29 June, no. 19, 11 July, no. 40, 27 October 1838, F.O. 84/241–242; Gordon no. 10, 21 April, no. 14, 15 June, 1838, F.O. 84/252–253.

[2] Jackson and Grigg no. 5, 21 May, no. 11, 20 June 1838, F.O. 84/241.

guese law of December 1836.[1] After two notes from the British legation and long delays, Maciel Monteiro, the Brazilian Foreign Minister, decided not to interfere; a slaver captured by a British cruiser, he said, could only be adjudicated by a mixed commission.[2] This led Gordon to consider releasing the *Flor de Loanda* and allowing it to land the rest of its cargo. The Brazilian government would then be forced to act, he reasoned, or else stand accused of conniving at the slave trade. Instead, however, he turned to Moreira, but the Portuguese consul-general, notorious for the help he gave Brazilian slavers needing Portuguese colours and papers, replied that the law of 1836 was concerned only with Portuguese slavers taken by Portuguese cruisers—and, in any case, he had no funds with which to send it to Lisbon.[3] The British *chargé d'affaires*, W. G. Ouseley, later discovered that Moreira had intended to take custody of the *Flor de Loanda*, pretend to despatch it to Lisbon, land the slaves up the coast and then announce that the ship had been wrecked and its cargo drowned. Ouseley claimed, however, that the slave traders in Rio de Janeiro had threatened and bribed Moreira into refusing to take cognisance of the case; they realised that his acceptance of a Portuguese cruiser might establish a precedent and that a similar fraud would not always be as easy to pull off.[4] It appeared then that the only remaining alternative was to send the *Flor de Loanda* to the mixed court at Freetown, but it proved unfit for another voyage across the Atlantic, and within a few days of setting off was forced to turn back. Instead Lieutenant Armitage of the *Rover* was sent to Sierra Leone with all the relevant evidence on board H.M.S. *Waterwitch*. On his arrival Armitage was clearly warned by Henry Macaulay, the British commissary judge, that the *Flor de Loanda* would not be condemned.[5] Had it been prosecuted before the Anglo-Brazilian

[1] Gordon to Palmerston, 21 May 1838, F.O. 84/253.
[2] Monteiro to Gordon, 2 June, enclosed in Gordon to Palmerston, no. 15, 15 June 1838, F.O. 84/253.   [3] Ouseley to Palmerston, 26 July 1838, F.O. 84/253.
[4] Ouseley no. 12, Conf., 21 August 1838, F.O. 84/254. Moreira made a small fortune out of the slave trade during 1838. When the Brazilian government finally withdrew his exequatur in May 1839 Ouseley called it 'the greatest blow given to the slave trade for many years' (Ouseley no. 15, Conf., 7 May 1839, F.O. 84/286). Intrigue in Lisbon and in Rio de Janeiro for his reinstatement continued for months afterwards.
[5] Macaulay and Lewis no. 66, 27 May 1839, F.O. 84/269. The Portuguese government had protested at the capture of the *Flor de Loanda* 'in violation of international maritime law' (Howard de Walden no. 18, 27 November 1838, F.O. 84/251).

mixed commission at Sierra Leone in the first place, Macaulay said, the vessel would have been condemned without hesitation (Palmerston had recently told Macaulay that Jackson should have decided in favour of condemnation since, in his view, the Portuguese owner of the *Flor de Loanda* was undoubtedly a resident of Rio de Janeiro; he had bought the ship there and it was from Rio that he had conducted his slaving operations).[1] However, the decision of the mixed commission in Rio not to treat the *Flor de Loanda* as a Brazilian slaver could not now be reversed, Macaulay insisted, and it therefore came before the court in Freetown as a Portuguese ship captured south of the line. As such it must be acquitted by the Anglo-Portuguese mixed commission. In every respect the case was almost exactly parallel with that of the *Maria da Gloria* five years earlier; but the captors, the British commissioners in Rio de Janeiro and the members of the British legation in Rio de Janeiro all seem to have been unaware of this important precedent. In the event, therefore, the case of the *Flor de Loanda* was never brought before the court in Freetown. And it was now twelve months since its acquittal in Rio de Janeiro. During this time Ouseley had provided for the welfare of the slaves and finally arranged for them to be hired out privately under strict contracts; eighty-five of them were entrusted to the Santa Casa da Misericórdia, a charitable hospital in Rio de Janeiro.[2] As for the ship itself, since there was no hope of a successful prosecution, the British government abandoned all claim to it at the end of 1839.

In the meantime, the other ships which appeared before the mixed court in Rio de Janeiro at the same time as the *Flor de Loanda* had both been condemned. Jackson and Carneiro de Campos had no difficulty in satisfying themselves that the *Cesar* was a Brazilian ship fraudulently using the Portuguese flag after a fictitious sale.[3] They were also able to agree that the owner of the *Brilhante* was a Portuguese, José Vieira de Mattos, but they were not of one mind as to whether or not he could be said to reside in Brazil. In the end the British arbitrator, Grigg, who was called

[1] Palmerston to H.M. commissioners, 5 December 1838, F.O. 84/242, based on Dodson, 30 November 1838, F.O. 83/2347.
[2] Ubaldo Soares, *A Escravatura na Misericórdia* (Rio de Janeiro, 1958) pp. 107–9. They were finally released in 1846.
[3] Jackson and Grigg no. 7, 31 May 1838, F.O. 84/241.

upon to make the casting vote, agreed with Jackson in favouring condemnation.[1] These two cases, however, together with that of the *Flor de Loanda*, had once again demonstrated how difficult it was to determine the real ownership of so-called Portuguese slave ships and the problem of establishing the grounds on which the owners could be said to be resident in Brazil.

It now occurred to Lord Palmerston that it would be much more satisfactory to concentrate on trying to establish that a slave ship had no claim to Portuguese nationality rather than attempt to prove it Brazilian. If a ship were clearly not Portuguese and provided some sort of case for Brazilian ownership could be made out—even though it could not be proved—the Anglo-Brazilian mixed commission might be prepared to condemn it. During the proceedings in the *Aventura* case in 1835 Jackson and Carneiro de Campos had recognised the principle that even though a ship carried a Portuguese flag and passport it could not be recognised as Portuguese by the court unless it also satisfied the requirements of the Portuguese commercial code of 1833. If it did not, the court could assume that the ship had fraudulently taken on a Portuguese character solely for the purpose of slaving and, if it seemed to be really Brazilian, it would be liable to condemnation. One of the arguments in favour of condemning both the *Aventura* and the *Orion* in the following year had been their inability to produce a Portuguese certificate of registry and other documents proving their Portuguese nationality. This new principle was strengthened by the Portuguese decrees of 17 December 1836 and 16 January 1837 which specifically laid down that only ships strictly complying with the requirements set out in the Portuguese commercial code of 1833 were entitled to claim Portuguese nationality: a ship must either have been built in the Portuguese dominions or, if foreign built, purchased before the decree of January 1837 had been promulgated, having sailed under the Portuguese flag and no other prior to that decree (only foreign built steamers could be purchased after the decree, and then only for a period of three years); the ship must belong to Portuguese subjects and be navigated in conformity with Portuguese common law; it must carry a certificate of registry, showing the name of the owner, his place

[1] Jackson and Grigg no. 19, 11 July 1838, F.O. 84/242.

of residence, the tonnage and build of the ship and recording all sales and purchases.[1] In April 1838, after he had heard that the Portuguese Minister of Marine was urging Portuguese consuls in Brazil to enforce these decrees in order to prevent the illegal use of the Portuguese flag and Portuguese papers,[2] Palmerston instructed the British commissioners in Rio de Janeiro and Freetown that no ship in the Brazilian slave trade should be regarded as Portuguese unless it came within the terms of the recent Portuguese decrees. Since a ship which did not do so would not enjoy the protection of the Portuguese government it could be safely condemned provided there was evidence to suggest Brazilian nationality.[3] When Palmerston heard that the *Flor de Loanda* had been acquitted before his new instructions reached Rio de Janeiro, he was doubly annoyed: not only did he regard its owner as a Brazilian resident conducting an essentially Brazilian trade, but in any case the ship itself fulfilled none of the requirements of Portuguese nationality.[4]

In October 1838, after numerous demands from the British legation, Maciel Monteiro finally instructed Carneiro de Campos that he, too, could take cognisance of and condemn all 'Portuguese' ships taken in the act of conveying slaves to Brazil in which Brazilians or foreigners resident in Brazil had an interest, with the exception of those coming strictly within the terms of the Portuguese commercial code.[5] Until such time as Portugal conceded to Britain the right of search south of the equator, British cruisers were still virtually powerless to interfere in any way with genuine

[1] See Queries addressed to Moreira on the significance of the decrees with regard to the slave trade, 7 August, 10 November, Replies 26 August, 8 December, Observations of Stevenson, 27 August, 8 December, all enclosed in Hamilton to Palmerston, 31 December, 1837, Conf., F.O. 84/223.
[2] Sá da Bandeira to Barão Bomfim (Minister of Marine), 2 March, and circular to Portuguese consuls, 2 March, enclosed in Howard de Walden to Palmerston, no. 3, 8 March 1838, F.O. 84/248.
[3] Palmerston to Rio commissioners, no. 4, 30 April 1838, F.O. 84/241; Palmerston to Sierra Leone commissioners, no. 12, 30 April 1838.
[4] Palmerston to H.M. commissioners, 5 December 1838, F.O. 84/242.
[5] Order of 19 October and Monteiro to Ouseley, 22 October, enclosed in Ouseley to Palmerston, no. 19, 23 October 1838, F.O. 84/254. The British legation also continued to demand that the Brazilian government take measures to regulate the sale of Brazilian and foreign ships to Portuguese subjects and instruct customs officials that no Portuguese ships should be allowed to enter or clear any Brazilian port unless the master produced a certificate of registry in the form prescribed by the Portuguese maritime code.

Portuguese vessels in the slave trade to Brazil. And they still could
not capture vessels leaving Brazil for Africa or arriving in African
waters, even where Brazilian ownership could be proved; neither
Brazil nor Portugal had yet conceded the vital equipment clause.
But as the qualifications for recognition as a *bona fide* Portuguese
vessel were gradually more strictly defined, British cruisers on the
South American station—there were still no cruisers stationed on
the west African coast south of the equator—could with greater
certainty capture what they believed to be Brazilian vessels sailing
under the Portuguese flag, provided they were carrying slaves or
had recently done so, secure in the knowledge that they would
probably be condemned by the mixed commission in Rio de
Janeiro. Before the end of 1838 H.M.S. *Electra* had picked up the
slave ship *Diligente* and H.M.S. *Wizard* the slave ship *Feliz*. In
March of the following year the *Electra* captured a further two
slavers—the *Carolina* and the *Especulador*—and in April H.M.S.
Grecian cruising off Cabo Frio fell in with the *Ganges* and the *Leal*.
Each of the six carried between 200 and 400 slaves and all had
hoisted the Portuguese flag. By the middle of 1839 they had all
been condemned and their slaves liberated.[1] The Anglo-Brazilian
mixed commission in Rio de Janeiro which had known years without a single adjudication and which had rarely dealt with as many
as five cases in any one year had never had a busier six months.
So intense was the hostility in Rio at the British navy's latest
efforts against the slave trade that George Jackson and Frederick
Grigg had frequently to call upon the national guard to escort
them through the angry crowds which were inclined to hurl stones
at the courthouse when the mixed commission was in session.[2]
The British commissioners in Rio might not in normal circumstances be called upon to do as much work as their colleagues
in Sierra Leone, but in many respects they lived more dangerously.

Although the efforts of the small British naval squadron on the
South American coast to place some curb on the illegal Brazilian

[1] Jackson and Grigg no. 43, 12 December 1838, F.O. 84/242; Jackson and Grigg no. 5,
15 January, no. 10, 31 January, no. 15, 3 April, no. 16, 11 April, no. 17, 17 April, no. 19,
20 April 1839, F.O. 84/275. All these cases, like those before them, were subject to great
delays in the Rio mixed court, see Hesketh to Ouseley, 31 May 1839, F.O. 84/286.
[2] Jackson and Grigg no. 21, 24 April 1839, F.O. 84/275.

slave trade met with some little success in the late thirties, it is well to remember that the vessels seized and the slaves liberated constituted only a tiny fraction of the trade being carried on at this time. During the three and a half years from December 1835 to April 1839 when British cruisers captured eleven vessels off the Brazilian coast—and the West African squadron captured only one, the *Incomprehensivel*, south of the line and a dozen or so to the north—slave ships made at least 300 successful voyages from the Congo, Angola and Moçambique besides many more from the *Costa da Mina* and landed at least 125,000 slaves in Brazil.

There is little doubt that during the thirties both the British West African and South American squadrons lacked the necessary numbers of ships (and the speed) to prevent the alarming expansion which occurred in the illegal Brazilian slave trade. The British cruisers which were available for anti-slave trade patrol could, however, have been considerably more effective than they were had not their activities been so severely circumscribed by the absence of any right to search—much less capture—most of the ships engaged in the slave trade to Brazil south of the equator, protected as they were by the Portuguese flag; nor could they detain those they encountered north of the equator unless they had slaves on board at the time. Indeed without a great increase in its powers a much stronger maritime police force would have found itself equally frustrated. Unless the anti-slave trade treaty system within which the British navy operated were considerably extended, or the British government adopted tougher measures unilaterally, Lord Minto, First Lord of the Admiralty, told the House of Lords in January 1838 in reply to criticism of the navy's performance, it would be absolutely impossible to put down the slave trade.[1]

[1] Hansard, xl, 610, 29 January 1838.

CHAPTER 6

THE EXTENSION OF BRITAIN'S POWERS, 1839

By the late 1830s the failure of Britain's efforts to contain, much less to suppress, the illegal transatlantic slave trade—the Cuban trade as well as the Brazilian continued to flourish—was causing increasing concern amongst English abolitionists. Many were coming round to the view, frequently expressed by diplomats, commissioners and naval officers directly concerned with improving and implementing the anti-slave trade treaties, that Britain would soon have to resort to more drastic measures, if necessary without the consent of the three major offenders, Portugal, Spain and Brazil.[1] Lord Brougham, for instance, addressing the House of Lords in January 1838, expressed the hope that the final suppression of the trade would be the earliest and most enduring glory of Queen Victoria's reign. For how much longer, he asked, with heavy irony, would Britain continue to 'pause and falter, and blanch and quail before the ancient and consecrated monarchy of Brazil, the awful might of Portugal, the compact, consolidated, overwhelming power of Spain' while Africa was ravaged?[2] When on 10 May 1838, for the first time in three years, the Commons debated the slave trade question, a motion demanding that greater pressure should be brought to bear on foreign powers, and especially on Portugal, found support on both sides of the House and

[1] E.g. Ouseley no. 13, 17 June 1836, F.O. 84/204; Hamilton no. 17, 15 August 1837, F.O. 84/223; Howard de Walden no. 1, 14 February, no. 2, 25 February 1838, F.O. 84/248; Macaulay and Doherty, General no. 111, 31 December 1838, F.O. 84/231; Jackson and Grigg no. 3, 9 April 1838, F.O. 84/241. The most extreme measures were frequently advocated by naval officers. For example, Lieut. James of H.M.S. *Spry* suggested 'hanging the whole crew [of a slave ship] at the yard-arms of their own vessel . . . let her float about the ocean like a spectre ship as a floating example to others painting on her sides in large letters "THIS WAS A SLAVER"'(James, 1 May 1837, enclosed in Admiralty to F.O., 25 May 1837, F.O. 84/228).

[2] Hansard, xl, 608, 29 January 1838. Cf. preface to the second edition of Thomas Clarkson, *History of the Rise, Progress and Accomplishment of the Abolition of the African Slave Trade by the British Parliament* (London, 1839): 'there are yearly transported to Cuba and Brazil above 100,000 unhappy beings by the two weakest nations in Europe, and those two most entirely subject to the influence and even direct control of England'.

was carried without a division. Sir Robert Inglis, a Tory abolitionist, trusted that 'the time was not far distant when the House
would sanction such measures that the carrying on the slave
trade . . . should be treated as piracy', and a Whig, Sir Henry
Verney, hoped the government 'would not shrink from enforcing
the treaties entered into on the subject, even by war if necessary'.[1]
At the same time a number of leading abolitionists were beginning
to lose faith in British diplomacy and British naval action as a
means of suppressing the foreign slave trade. For the first time on
any significant scale the very foundations of Britain's traditional
anti-slave trade policies were being called into question.

During the summer of 1837, Thomas Fowell Buxton transferred his attention from the issue of emancipation and apprenticeship in the West Indies, which had been the main concern of the
abolitionist movement since the founding of the Anti-Slavery
Society in 1823, to that of the slave trade.[2] He did not under-
estimate the value of 'maritime exertions' for its suppression, but
he was concerned to show that the efforts made by the Foreign
Office and the Admiralty since 1807 had been largely futile because they relied *solely* on 'force and a strong hand'. He had little
faith in the existing network of anti-slave trade treaties designed
to empower the British navy to suppress the trade: 'this con-
federation', he wrote, 'must either be universally binding or it is
of no avail. It will avail us little that ninety-nine doors are closed
if one remains open. To that outlet the whole slave trade of Africa
will rush.' And even if every door were bolted and Britain's
entire naval resources mobilised against the trade, it would still
continue: it was, he understood, an axiom at the Customs House
that 'no illicit trade can be suppressed where the profit exceeds
30%'. Only if the slave trade were declared piracy and made a
capital offence would the traders be deterred; and there was not
the remotest possibility of all the slave-trading powers agreeing to
this—much less of their being able to enforce it. Buxton nevertheless believed that 'strong external measures ought still to be
resorted to' and supported the growing demand for a bigger preventive squadron on the West African station combined with

[1] Hansard, xlii, 1034, 1139, 10 May 1838.
[2] C. Buxton (ed.), *Memoirs of Sir Thomas Fowell Buxton* (London, 1848), pp. 429–30.

stronger measures against slave ships sailing under the Portuguese flag, more effective blockading tactics on the African coast, and, a new idea this, the extension of the anti-slave trade treaty system to the African chiefs. Such measures might at least impede the trade in the short run. But for its total eradication he argued that diplomacy and naval action must be supplemented by measures to end the slave trade at its source—in Africa. Buxton therefore set out to revive the 'positive' ideas for the economic, social and moral regeneration of Africa which had first been advanced by the eighteenth-century humanitarians, Granville Sharp and the Sierra Leone Company, the African Institution, the geographer James McQueen as well as numerous explorers: Africa should be 'civilised', ran the argument, and weaned from its adherence to slavery and the slave trade by means of Christianity, agriculture and legitimate commerce. The deliverance of Africa was to be effected *by calling out her own resources*, Buxton wrote. His views on the slave trade, which were eventually published in *The African Slave Trade and its Remedy*, were put before the Cabinet in the summer of 1838, and in the following year the Society for the Extinction of the Slave Trade and the Civilization of Africa was formed to mobilise public support for a new approach towards Africa, and especially to promote the opening up of the Niger to agriculture, settlement and trade.[1]

Less important at the time but more significant for the future, another abolitionist society, the British and Foreign Anti-Slavery Society, was also founded in 1839. Its leader, Joseph Sturge of Birmingham, a radical Quaker, believed that the best hope for the eventual abolition of the slave trade lay not in the civilisation of Africa but in the abolition of slavery in the New World—and it was necessary for Britain to persuade the remaining slave states of the evils of slavery as a social system. Moreover, Sturge repudiated altogether Britain's use of force for the suppression of the slave trade; his 'Christian conscience' was revolted by the idea of 'trying to promote philanthropic ends by violence and blood' instead of by 'moral, religious and pacific means'—and he was

---

[1] See Thomas Fowell Buxton, *The African Slave Trade and its Remedy* (2nd ed., London, 1840); J. Gallagher, 'Fowell Buxton and the New African Policy, 1838–1842', *Cambridge Historical Journal* x (1950), 36–58; also Philip D. Curtin, *The Image of Africa. British Ideas and Action, 1780–1850* (Wisconsin, 1964), pp. 298–302.

appalled, too, by the cost, both in lives and money, of maintaining the African blockade. If the West African squadron had failed in its purpose, Sturge and his followers argued, then the answer was to remove, not strengthen it.[1] In 1839 the first shots were fired in a long campaign, led by the Anti-Slavery Society and taken up by radical free traders in the House of Commons, aimed at dismantling the entire British preventive system.

During the years 1838–9 the Melbourne administration could ill afford to risk the loss of Radical and Nonconformist support and, although on the whole unimpressed by them, was obliged to show at least some interest in Buxton's audacious schemes for a forward policy in West Africa, despite the fact that they clearly violated all the canons of Britain's colonial policy at the time. An anti-slave trade treaty which might be offered to African rulers—based on the agreement already signed with the Sultan of Muscat—was drafted in the Slave Trade Department of the Foreign Office, and the government went so far as to sanction plans which eventually led, in 1841, to the ill-fated Niger Expedition.[2] Lord Palmerston, however, regarded Buxton's schemes as 'wild and crude'. While conscious of the need to open up markets for British manufactured goods in new continents, he considered that as far as Africa was concerned the destruction of the slave trade must come first. 'It is Europe and not Africa which takes the lead in the intercourse between these two quarters of the globe', Palmerston wrote to Glenelg, the Colonial Secretary. 'We want to sell our commodities to Africa and we send them thither. The Africans who want to buy will pay us whatever we like. If we insist on having slaves, slaves they will produce . . . If . . . we can prevent Europeans from bringing slaves away from Africa we will convert the trade into one of barter of commodities.'[3] In other words, the extension of legitimate trade with Africa would be not the cause but the consequence of the suppression of the slave trade, and Palmerston remained convinced, despite many disappointments in the past,

---

[1] H. Richard, *Memoirs of Joseph Sturge* (London, 1864), pp. 203–19; Mathieson, *Britain and the Slave Trade*, pp. 47–8.

[2] Gallagher, *op. cit.*; Curtin, *op. cit.* p. 302 ff.

[3] Palmerston to Glenelg, 10 October 1838, quoted in R. J. Gavin, 'Palmerston's Policy towards East and West Africa 1830–1865' (unpublished Ph.D. thesis, Cambridge, 1958), pp. 136–7. Chapter 4 of this thesis contains a most interesting discussion of the development of Palmerston's African policies.

that if the existing preventive system could be brought into full operation by strengthening the squadron on the west African coast and simultaneously extending its powers for dealing with Portuguese and Brazilian slavers, then the trade might yet be suppressed, or at least substantially reduced, and Britain's traditional anti-slave trade policies vindicated.

After several years of almost continuous, but nonetheless fruitless, negotiations in Lisbon, Palmerston had come to despair of ever persuading the Portuguese government to concede a satisfactory anti-slave trade treaty. Confident of support in the Cabinet and in Parliament, throughout 1837 and 1838 he had frequently, and increasingly, threatened to take matters into his own hands if the Portuguese persisted in refusing co-operation on his terms.[1] Finally, in December 1838, although negotiations were still going on—they were not to break down finally until February 1839—he decided to 'cut the knot' and authorise the navy to seize all ships flying the Portuguese flag found carrying slaves or equipped for the slave trade. If as a result Portugal chose to declare war, he wrote privately to Howard de Walden—almost repeating what he had said nine months earlier—'so much the better . . . There are several of her colonies which would suit us remarkably well, and having taken them in war we should retain them at the peace which she would beg on her knees to obtain from us . . . We shall not care a fig for Sá [da Bandeira's] pride and national dignity. We shall not be so foolish as to send a squadron to the Tagus to force the Portuguese government to sign a treaty but shall simply take the leave they will not give.' And a month later he wrote in even stronger terms, 'We cannot class Portugal among [the] powers with which England is on terms of friendly alliance. We consider Portugal as morally at war with us and if she does not take good care and look well ahead she will be physically at war with us also.' He also took the opportunity of including Portuguese possessions in India in the list of colonies Britain would seize if Portugal were foolish enough to go to war.[2]

---

[1] See above, ch. 4.

[2] Palmerston to Howard de Walden, 24 December 1838, 24 January 1839, Broadlands MSS, GC/HO/829, 831. The East India Company was eager to buy Portugal's possessions in India because of loss of revenue resulting from extensive smuggling. If the

Clearly if British naval officers were to be ordered to search and and capture ships flying the Portuguese flag legislation would be needed to protect them against actions brought by Portuguese nationals. As Palmerston had said in May it was necessary to 'appeal to Parliament for powers to do ourselves and on our own authority that which Portugal refused to permit us to do by treaty',[1] and at the beginning of December he had requested the Treasury to prepare a bill.[2] It was several months, however, before the bill came before Parliament. Other urgent matters requiring the government's attention, in particular the Bedchamber Crisis, were responsible for the delay and no progress was made on the bill until the end of the following May. In the meantime (in reply to a question from Sir Robert Inglis) Palmerston told the House of Commons that the government had every intention of taking the measures they had so long threatened, and in the Lords the news that a plan of action was being prepared was welcomed by Lord Brougham who declared that 'the more vigorous it was the better pleased with it he should be and the more heartily would he support it'.[3]

When Palmerston was again free to take up the Portuguese slave trade question, the final drafting of the bill for which the Queen's Advocate, the Solicitor General and Stephen Lushington were responsible proved to be a more complicated matter than he had originally anticipated. It was, for instance, necessary to authorise some court to adjudicate upon Portuguese ships captured by British cruisers and to liberate any slaves they carried. Palmerston had originally wanted a bill that would simply authorise naval officers to search and capture any slave ships flying the Portuguese flag, and empower British commissioners to try and condemn them. It was soon realised, however, that the Anglo-Portuguese mixed commission at Freetown could not be relied upon to condemn all the slave ships brought before it: where a ship was cap-

dispute with Portugal over the slave trade were to lead to war, Palmerston declared, 'we shall help ourselves to their Indian settlements and keep them without payment' (Palmerston to Howard de Walden, 20 January Private).

[1] Hansard, xiii, 1,150–1, 10 May 1838.
[2] See L. M. Bethell, 'Britain, Portugal and the suppression of the Brazilian slave trade: the origins of Lord Palmerston's Act of 1839' *English Historical Review*, lxxx (1965), p. 776, nn. 2, 4.
[3] Hansard, xlvi, 145–6 (8 March 1839), xlvii, 718 (2 May 1839).

tured south of the line or only equipped for the trade the Portuguese judge and arbitrator, even if they took cognisance of the case, were bound to decide in favour of acquittal and award damages. The solution eventually arrived at was to empower British vice-admiralty courts to adjudicate upon Portuguese ships (as they did ships belonging to British subjects). It was decided moreover that the bill should also include, first, a list of all 'equipment articles' which, singly or collectively, would constitute *prima facie* evidence of slaving and grounds for condemnation unless the owner could offer a satisfactory explanation for their presence on board; secondly, a stipulation that condemned ships should either be bought by the navy or broken up and sold in separate lots; and, thirdly, a clause to the effect that bounty money would be paid to naval officers capturing Portuguese slavers south as well as north of the line.[1]

One further addition was made. It was brought to Palmerston's attention by Lord Minto, First Lord of the Admiralty, that if as a result of the bill's passage the slave trade were driven from under the cover of the Portuguese flag, the alternatives open to the Portuguese and Brazilian traders were by now rather limited since one by one the loopholes in the suppression system had been successfully plugged. In the last resort, Minto concluded, they would no doubt dispense with flag and papers altogether—as indeed a few had already done. If a ship's nationality could not be established with any certainty, neither a mixed commission nor a national court had any jursidiction over it, and it could not therefore be condemned. On the other hand, neither was it in a position to claim the protection of any government, and Palmerston agreed with Minto that the bill he was preparing should empower British cruisers to search and capture slave ships without nationality, and to take them, too, before British vice-admiralty courts.[2]

A great deal of time was spent assembling and printing the vast correspondence on the treaty negotiations with Portugal, and in drafting a long preamble to the bill which detailed the circum-

[1] See Palmerston's comments on the bill as first drafted on 2 February, enclosed in F.O. to Harrison (Treasury), 22 May 1839, F.O. 84/297; also statements by Palmerston in House of Commons, Hansard, xlvi, 146 (8 March 1839), l, 119-32 (8 August 1839).
[2] Minto to Palmerston, 19 April 1839, Private, F.O. 84/301. Palmerston wrote in the margin, 'to be attended to in preparing bill'.

stances occasioning and justifying the measures proposed for the suppression of the slave trade carried on under the Portuguese flag. Palmerston was throughout prepared to contend that British naval operations against slave ships flying the Portuguese flag could be extended without infringing the existing Anglo-Portuguese treaties of 1815 and 1817. The arguments first used by Canning fifteen years earlier were paraded once again, but this time with a great deal more subtlety. The declared object of these treaties, it was argued, had been to suppress the illicit Portuguese slave trade and at the same time prevent interference with that part of the trade still permitted by treaty and law, that is, the trade carried on for the supply of Portugal's transatlantic possessions south of the equator. Article 2 of the treaty of 1815 laid down that there should be no interference with Portuguese ships trading between Portuguese territories south of the line 'during such further period as the same might be permitted to be carried on by the laws of Portugal, and under the treaties subsisting between the two Crowns'. Palmerston argued that 'the treaty of 1815 admits the previous existence of a right of interruption on the part of Great Britain because the treaty stipulates for a suspension of that right'. With the independence of Brazil, the entire Portuguese trade had necessarily become illegal, although it was not until December 1836 that the Portuguese had formally recognised the fact and legislated accordingly. As a result, he concluded, British cruisers were released from their temporary engagement not to capture Portuguese slavers south of the equator.[1] It was not until the end of June that William Rothery, legal adviser to the Treasury on slave trade matters, prevailed upon Palmerston to drop these unconvincing

[1] Palmerston to Howard de Walden, no. 4, 3 March, no. 14, 12 May 1838, F.O. 84/248–9; Howard de Walden to Ribeira da Sabrosa, 28 April 1839, printed in Biker xxviii, 244–97 (based on draft enclosed in Palmerston to Howard de Walden, no. 13, 20 April 1839, F.O. 84/281); draft of preamble to proposed bill, enclosed in F.O. to Harrison, 22 May 1839, F.O. 84/297. The preamble concluded that Britain had no alternative but to resort to the exercise of 'that right of interruption which she consented to suspend for a time upon conditions which Portugal has not fulfilled'. Canning had been the first to argue along these lines (see ch. 2, p. 29), David Stevenson, unofficial legal adviser to the Rio legation on slave trade questions, most recently and ingeniously (memorandum, 17 January 1838, enclosed in Hamilton to Palmerston, London, 1 May 1838, F.O. 84/253). Palmerston was prepared to adopt Stevenson's arguments 'as a defence of measures to which the British government may be pushed by the continued refusal of Portugal to act up to the spirit of previous engagements' (memorandum, 1 June 1838, F.O. 84/253).

arguments, so often aired and as often refuted.[1] Palmerston was well aware that the law officers of the Crown had always disputed this admittedly convenient interpretation of the Anglo-Portuguese treaties: they had consistently maintained that until the Portuguese formally conceded a more extensive right of search, British cruisers could only legally search and capture Portuguese ships carrying slaves shipped on the African coast north of the equator.[2] All that the preamble to the new bill could therefore hope to demonstrate was that Britain was justified in resorting unilaterally to tougher anti-slave trade measures on the grounds that Portugal had not merely failed to enforce its anti-slave trade legislation—that was an internal matter—but had also failed to fulfil the letter and spirit of its treaty engagements with Britain. In contravention of article 10 of the treaty of 1810, for instance, Portugal had failed to adopt the most effective means for bringing about a final abolition of the slave trade, and had allowed it to continue in Portuguese ships and under the Portuguese flag in those parts of Africa 'where the Powers and States of Europe which formerly traded there have discontinued and abandoned it'. In violation of article 4 of the treaty of 1815, she had permitted her flag to be used 'for supplying with slaves other places than the transatlantic possessions of Portugal' (that is, independent Brazil). In violation of articles 2 and 3 of the treaty of 1817, she had sought to prevent the British navy from putting down the illicit exportation of slaves from 'ports not possessed or claimed by Portugal in Africa' and the illicit importation of slaves in Portuguese vessels into 'ports not in the dominion of His Most Faithful Majesty', and in violation of the separate article of the same treaty she had refused to adapt the provisions of the treaty to the altered state of affairs which resulted from the Portuguese law of December 1836 entirely abolishing the slave trade. In the event the final version of the preamble made no attempt to claim that the existing treaties empowered the British navy to extend its operations against the Portuguese flag south of the equator. Lord Palmerston's bill was clearly intended to authorise the navy to go beyond its treaty rights.

On 10 July 1839 the Slave Trade (Portugal) Bill which Palmerston

---

1 Following Rothery to Chancellor of Exchequer, 25 June 1839. F.O. 84/305.
2 See ch. 4, pp. 97–8, 100.

expected to be received 'with acclamation' was finally introduced into the House of Commons. It went through in a fortnight
without a debate. Peel, the leader of the Opposition, felt the bill
entirely justified. After the second reading, James Bandinel of the
Slave Trade Department at the Foreign Office sent a copy of the
bill to Howard de Walden in Lisbon in readiness for the moment
when it became law, which he thought would probably be before
the end of the following week.[1] (Palmerston had already arranged
with Lord Minto to send an extra warship to Lisbon in case of
trouble: as he explained to Howard de Walden, the British squadron in the Tagus was in need of summer exercise and 'it may as
well exercise itself by bringing Portugal to their senses'.[2]) A storm
broke unexpectedly, however, when Lord Minto moved the bill's
second reading in the House of Lords on 1 August. The Duke of
Wellington opposed it. In the first place, he objected to the government's manner of proceeding: Parliament was being asked to
pronounce on Britain's differences with Portugal and to authorise
officers of the Crown to capture, and British courts to adjudicate
upon, Portuguese ships and subjects engaging in activities which
were breaches of Portuguese municipal law alone. Wellington
reminded the House that 'the greatest judge who ever presided in
an Admiralty Court' (Lord Stowell) had laid down in the *Le
Louis* case (1817) that in peace-time the right of search was illegal
and contrary to the law of nations, unless that right had been conceded by treaty. In reality British officers were being authorised to
adopt 'measures of hostility against Portugal and other operations
of war'. If all demands for the fulfilment of Portugal's treaty obligations had been ignored and all negotiations for a new treaty had
proved futile, Britain had the right to adopt extreme measures.
But it was the executive's place to declare war on Portugal and to
initiate naval or military action by order in council. 'War was all
very well when directed by the executive,' Wellington declared,
'not by the legislative.'[3] Of those previously consulted by Palmerston in the preparation of the bill, only Glenelg, the former Colonial Secretary, had questioned the manner of proceeding. Would
it not be more usual, he had asked, for the Crown to issue orders

---

[1] Bandinel to Howard de Walden, 18 July, 1839, Private, F.O. 84/282.
[2] Palmerston to Howard de Walden, 22 June 1839, Broadlands MSS, GC/HO/837.
[3] Hansard, xlix, 1,063–7.

to British cruisers and then approach Parliament for a bill of indemnity? In his reply Palmerston had argued that the government was already pledged to both Houses to adopt the proposed course of action which was given more force and solemnity by being made an Act of Parliament.[1]

Wellington's quarrel, however, was not only with the procedures the government proposed to adopt, but also with the measures themselves—particularly when they were directed against Britain's old ally Portugal. Whilst roundly condemning the slave trade, he feared that Britain's attitude towards it was increasingly inconsistent with its traditional policy of peace and of respect for the rights and independence of other states. During recent years, he claimed, British cruisers had begun to exercise what amounted to a general right to stop and search suspicious ships of any nation, regardless of the terms of the anti-slave trade treaties, and even in cases where no treaty existed (he probably had in mind the capture a few months earlier of some Spanish vessels navigating under American papers and colours which led to a major dispute with the U.S. government[2]). Many maritime nations, he said, were beginning to resent the activities and presumptions of the British navy: they might soon resist or retaliate, and there was even a risk of 'universal war'. Palmerston's bill which authorised British cruisers to seize Portuguese vessels and vessels 'without nationality' could not fail to aggravate the situation. Lord Minto, for the government, supported by the Prime Minister, Lord Melbourne, said that it was 'too much to be endured' that Britain should be frustrated by the 'surreptitious or daring practices of a single nation'. Yet if the navy were to succeed in driving the trade from under the Portuguese flag and if, at the same time, an outright declaration of war with Portugal were to be avoided—as they sincerely hoped that it would be—the passage of Palmerston's bill was absolutely essential. They were not trying to substitute the authority of Parliament for the prerogative of the Crown: they were merely asking Parliament

---

[1] Glenelg to Palmerston, 17 June, Palmerston to Glenelg, 18 June 1839, Broadlands MSS, GC/GL/218.

[2] See Hugh G. Soulsby, *The Right of Search and the Slave Trade in Anglo-American Relations, 1814–1862* (Baltimore, 1933), pp. 46–51; Warren S. Howard, *American Slavers and the Federal Law, 1837–1862* (Univ. of Calif. Press, 1963), pp. 37–40.

to pass the legislation necessary to enable the Crown to exercise its prerogative.[1]

Despite the government's efforts the Tory peers threw the bill out by 38 votes to 32. And *The Times* the next day commented that it was 'a very tyrannical measure—the insolent assumption of supremacy of a great power over a small one. The Lords acted with dignity in not consenting to be backers of a cowardly system of bullying. Would Lord Palmerston venture to treat France as he does Portugal!'[2] For their part the Portuguese press exulted at the 'ruin' of the Melbourne government, lauded Wellington and rhapsodised about the valuable role played in a 'democracy' by a second legislative chamber and an independent, dispassionate aristocracy.[3] When two months later the news of the Lords' decision reached Rio de Janeiro, the Brazilian press was also loud in praise of Wellington and the Tories, who were portrayed as the champions of slavery in Brazil and the Portuguese colonies.[4]

On the day following the defeat of Palmerston's bill, Lord Brougham had moved an address to the Queen proposing that British officers should first be ordered to capture Portuguese slavers and then both Houses would concur in whatever measures of indemnification were necessary. This proposal seemed to satisfy some Tory peers who, while favouring strong measures to put down the Portuguese slave trade, objected to the way the government had handled the matter and were concerned about the constitutional principle at issue. Brougham's resolution was agreed to, although Wellington himself said he would refuse to vote for it if it were his last act in the House.[5] On 3 August the Cabinet therefore decided to go ahead with the measures they proposed against Portuguese slave ships—on the understanding, however, that a 'protecting bill' would still be necessary. It was Palmerston's impression, however, that the Cabinet were prepared to proceed 'without it if none can be got', and he affirmed in a private letter to Lord Howard de Walden that 'if we cannot get a Bill we shall

[1] Hansard, xlix, 1,067–71, 1,072–3.
[2] *The Times*, 2 August 1839.
[3] *O Diario do Governo*, 9 August, *O Nacional*, 10 August, enclosed in Howard de Walden to Palmerston, 10 August 1839, F.O. 84/282.
[4] Ouseley to Palmerston, 14 October 1839, F.O. 84/288.
[5] Hansard, xlix, 1,128–30, 1131.

proceed without one'.[1] But when he suggested to the Law Officers of the Crown that the government could simply order naval officers to capture Portuguese slavers, land the slaves at a suitable British colony, and then scuttle the ships or break them up and sell them as old timber without submitting them to formal adjudication and that a bill was in fact unnecessary, they reminded him that 'the destruction of or any unnecessary injury to [Portuguese] ships or [their] crews would subject the parties concerned to an action in our courts at the suit of the persons aggrieved ... It is [therefore] very expedient that before any steps are taken for detaining ships not now authorised to be detained express authority should be given by Act of Parliament so as to indemnify all Parties concerned'.[2]

On 8–9 August, Palmerston's bill, with an amended and very much shorter preamble which simply stated that orders had now been given to the navy and that protecting legislation was therefore necessary, passed briskly through the Commons with the blessing of both sides of the House. On 15 August—the day on which Melbourne moved the second reading in the Lords—Palmerston instructed the Admiralty to authorise naval officers to search all suspicious ships flying the Portuguese flag wherever they were met, and to detain those carrying slaves or fitted out for the purpose.[3] Further instructions were promised regarding the disposal of the ships and the slaves they carried. There was still a possibility that the Lords might again reject the bill but, as Palmerston pointed out, if actions were brought against British naval officers 'none could come to issue before next session and then we should certainly get a protecting Bill'.[4] In the event fewer Tory peers opposed the bill this time and it passed its second reading, without significant alteration, by 39 votes to 28. Wellington and twenty other Tory peers, however, filed a protest comprising

---

[1] Palmerston to Russell, 3 August, *Early Correspondence of Lord John Russell, 1805–1840* (London, 1913), ii, 253–5; Palmerston to Howard de Walden, 3 August 1839, Broadlands MSS, GC/HO/840. Also Lord Broughton (J. C. Hobhouse), *Some account of a long life* (London, 1867), v, p. 6.

[2] Palmerston to Law Officers, 6 August, F.O. 83/2348 (drafted 3 August); Dodson, Campbell and Rolfe to Palmerston, 8 August 1839, Broadlands MSS, SLT/15.

[3] Palmerston to Admiralty, 15 August 1839, F.O. 84/302.

[4] Palmerston to Howard de Walden, 10 August 1839, Broadlands MSS, GC/HO/841.

thirteen reasons why even now they were unable to support it.[1] At the third reading Wellington and eight of his closest political friends again made a formal protest but, to the dismay and anger of the Portuguese, the bill became law on 24 August 1839 (over eighteen months after Palmerston had first given it consideration).[2] Three weeks later, British naval officers were instructed to send captured Portuguese ships—and those without nationality—to the nearest British vice-admiralty court for adjudication; to land any slaves at the nearest British settlement; and to hand over masters and crews to their own authorities for trial (the British government did not intend to go so far as to try Portuguese subjects in British courts). The Admiralty was required to establish vice-admiralty courts wherever they were found necessary and to instruct judges to arrange for the break up and sale of those condemned ships which the navy did not propose to purchase.[3] With this Act and subsequent measures for its implementation, Lord Palmerston had struck what Captain Henry J. Matson, who commanded H.M.S. *Waterwitch* on the west African coast from 1839 to 1843, later called 'the first great blow in the suppression of the slave trade'.[4]

In Lisbon *o bill Palmerston* was regarded as 'a gross usurpation of power' and 'a flagrant violation of international law'. And one, moreover, that was completely without justification. In denying all responsibility for the failure of early treaty negotiations with Britain and thus for the present state of affairs, the Portuguese government argued that they had always been prepared to sign a reasonable anti-slave trade treaty but that Palmerston and Howard de Walden between them had deliberately sabotaged the negotiations by presenting, in the form of an ultimatum, a treaty draft which they knew would be unacceptable in Lisbon. ('There existed a system regularly followed up for the purpose of injuring

[1] Hansard, l, 336–9. There is an eye witness account of the debate in the Lords on 15 August by a leading participant, see Sir Joseph Arnould, *Memoir of Thomas, First Lord Denman* (London, 1873), ii, pp. 98–102. It was the view of Denman, a future Lord Chief Justice, that 'when once it has been established that the slave trade is illegal the restraints which treaties have put upon its abolition ought to be looked at with a jealous eye'.
[2] 2 and 3 Vict. cap 73; Hertslet's *Treaties* v (1840), 427–31.
[3] Palmerston to Admiralty, 31 August, 14 September, 1 October 1839, F.O. 84/302–3.
[4] *P.P.* 1847–8, xxii (272), House of Commons Select Committee on the Slave Trade, 1st Report, par. 1,258.

the negotiations', wrote Barão de Ribeira da Sobroza, who succeeded Sá da Bandeira as head of the Portuguese government and whom Howard de Walden regarded as 'a thorough blackguard'.) Portugal's refusal to accept Britain's treaty proposals was then made a pretext for the recent bill which authorised British warships to behave like pirates and freebooters in their efforts to suppress the slave trade, ignoring existing treaties and Portugal's rights as an independent state, and which, at the same time, it was said, ensured that Britain's own colonies were furnished with a regular and plentiful supply of Negroes from captured Portuguese slave vessels.[1]

Despite popular demands for resistance and retaliation, the Portuguese government recognised that they were virtually powerless in this matter and soon became anxious to reopen negotiations for an anti-slave trade treaty which would replace Palmerston's Act.[2] For his part that 'iniquitous and malevolent personage', Lord Palmerston,[3] considered that any treaty, however stringent, would now constitute a concession to Portugal. He was content to let the matter rest unless the Portuguese were ready to sign, without question, the original British treaty draft, with the addition of a further article requiring Portugal to declare the slave trade piracy.[4] To the Portuguese, the very existence of the Act was 'tantamount to, indeed worse than, war'[5] and they had no alternative but to abandon most of their earlier demands for concessions. They held out only over the duration of the treaty; the right of search, they insisted, must be liable to termination, by

[1] Howard de Walden to Palmerston, no. 42, 26 August, Howard de Walden to Bandinel, 20 September, Private, F.O. 84/282; Ribeira da Sobroza to Howard de Walden, 11 September, enclosed in Howard de Walden no. 46, 20 September, F.O. 84/282 (printed in Biker xxviii, 456–523); Moncorvo to Palmerston 1 August, 14 August, F.O. 84/284 (printed in Biker xxviii, 378–85, 410–15); memorial by Visconde da Carreira, Portuguese minister in Paris, 13 August, Biker xxviii, 392–409; Sá da Bandeira, *O trafico da escravatura e o bill de Lord Palmerston* (Lisbon, 1840: written December 1839); Ananias Dortano Brasahemeco, *Rights of Portugal in reference to Great Britain and the question of the slave trade* (2 vols., 1840).
[2] Howard de Walden to Palmerston, no. 47, 20 September, F.O. 84/282. Sá was now widely criticised for not having signed a treaty in 1838 (Howard de Walden no. 8, 3 February 1840, F.O. 84/320).
[3] Brasahemeco, *op. cit.* p. 414.
[4] Palmerston to Howard de Walden, no. 27, 16 October 1839, F.O. 84/283; Palmerston no. 10, 23 May 1840, F.O. 84/321.
[5] Howard de Walden to Palmerston, no. 13, 13 February 1840, F.O. 84/320.

common consent, within a fixed period after the cessation of the Portuguese slave trade, with an understanding that should the trade revive the right of search would immediately come back into force. This demand seemed reasonable enough, but Lord Palmerston was prepared to agree that the right of search should be given up only when slavery was abolished throughout the world![1] With his Act in force Palmerston could afford to allow treaty negotiations with Portugal to be suspended, indefinitely if need be.

Lord Palmerston had always known that, when the British navy was finally authorised to capture all slave vessels flying the Portuguese flag, both Portuguese and Brazilian ships would revert once again to the Brazilian flag and thus continue to avoid capture, at least on their outward voyage and up to the moment when their slaves were embarked, unless British warships were at the same time empowered to seize Brazilian slavers on the basis of their fittings alone. In July 1835 the Brazilian government had signed additional articles to the treaty of 1817, one of which was an equipment clause, but these the Brazilian Chamber of Deputies had steadfastly refused to ratify. Like Portugal Brazil had been warned that Britain's patience could not be expected to last forever. But in the case of Brazil outright coercion was to prove unnecessary. In 1839 the British commissioners in Rio de Janeiro and Sierra Leone who, independently of each other, had been studying the Anglo-Brazilian and Anglo-Portuguese anti-slave trade treaties together with the relevant printed correspondence, discovered what they and the British government had been seeking for so long: a justification, within both the letter and the spirit of the treaties *as they stood*, for the search and capture by the British navy of Brazilian ships equipped for the slave trade, and for their condemnation by the Anglo-Brazilian mixed commissions.

[1] Howard de Walden no. 28, 6 August, Palmerston no. 27, 20 August 1841, F.O. 84/362. On the treaty negotiations intermittently carried on during the twelve months following the passage of the Palmerston Act and taken up again in August 1841, see memorandum, 'Negotiations with Portugal upon the draft of treaty submitted to the Portuguese government through Mr Jerningham on 1 August 1838', 26 November 1841, F.O. 84/388.

In January 1839 H.M.S. *Wizard* brought into Rio de Janeiro the Portuguese slave ship *Feliz* with 236 slaves on board. From the British legation W. G. Ouseley forwarded to George Jackson and Frederick Grigg, the British commissioners, an extract from the *Wizard's* log which mentioned the boarding of a Brazilian slaver the *Feliz Aurora* on 9 October of the previous year and her subsequent release when it was discovered that, although equipped for the trade, she was not carrying any slaves.[1] Ouseley thought the *Feliz* might be the *Feliz Aurora* homeward bound: if so, the *Wizard's* log would help to prove the captured vessel Brazilian and not Portuguese as she was now claiming. In the event, the mixed commission condemned the *Feliz* even though it could not be established with any degree of certainty that she had previously sailed as the *Feliz Aurora*. What was more significant, however, was that in their reply to Ouseley the British commissioners regretted that the *Feliz Aurora* itself had not been detained as they had 'little doubt of her liability to condemnation on proof of the alleged equipment being given'.[2] Ten days later they explained in a despatch to Lord Palmerston that, in their view, British naval officers were mistaken in thinking that they could not detain Brazilian slave ships outward bound. They certainly had no right to capture Portuguese ships on their outward journeys (they in fact had no power as yet to interfere with them, with or without slaves, south of the equator), but the mixed commission could and would condemn any genuine Brazilian slavers brought before it including those that might at first sight appear to be Portuguese.[3]

Ouseley immediately saw the significance of this opinion, and was soon in touch with British naval officers stationed on the Brazilian coast.[4] They were reluctant to act, however: their previous relations with the mixed court in Rio de Janeiro had been a long story of frustrating delay, with all the disagreeable duties that this entailed. Moreover, on more than one occasion they had been compelled to witness the release of notorious slavers with full cargoes of Negroes on board. Now they were being asked to

---

[1] Ouseley to Jackson and Grigg, 9 January, enclosed in Ouseley to Palmerston, no. 4, 15 January 1839, F.O. 84/285.
[2] Jackson and Grigg to Ouseley, 12 January, *ibid.*
[3] Jackson and Grigg to Palmerston, no. 8, 22 January 1839, F.O. 84/275.
[4] Ouseley to Palmerston, no. 4, 15 January, no. 6, 1 February 1839, F.O. 84/285.

capture Brazilian ships they merely suspected of intending to trade in slaves; the chances of mistakes were high and the legal position by no means clear. Only Commander Smyth of H.M.S. *Grecian* was prepared to risk a test case. On 30 May he brought into Rio harbour the barque *Maria Carlota* and the schooner *Recuperador*. Both had set out from the Brazilian coast fully equipped for slaving, one destined for Moçambique, the other for Angola, and both sailing under the Portuguese flag.[1] The unprecedented seizure of ships off the coast of Brazil simply on the strength of their apparent intention to cross the Atlantic and bring back African slaves caused a sensation in Rio de Janeiro and great consternation within the slaving community. Both the traders and their opponents realised that if the mixed commission were to recognise the legality of these captures a decisive blow would be dealt the Brazilian slave trade. The crucial but elusive equipment clause would in practice have been secured, and Brazilian slave ships would, for the first time, be liable to search and capture not only on their homeward journey but also as they left Brazil and—presumably—as they arrived off the African slave ports.[2]

As the captors were on the point of bringing their two prizes before the mixed court, João Carneiro de Campos, the Brazilian commissary judge, refused to take cognisance of either case.[3] Ouseley had to bring pressure to bear on Cândido Batista de Oliveira, Foreign Minister in the Cabinet of 16 April 1839, before the Brazilian judge was directed at least to examine the evidence, and even then the Brazilian government emphasised that this did not necessarily imply that they considered the court competent to deal with cases of this kind.[4] George Jackson, however, refused to open proceedings until the competence of the court to adjudicate on the *Maria Carlota* and the *Recuperador* had been officially admitted and throughout June and July Ouseley kept up the pressure on Cândido Batista for his co-operation. To condemn such flagrant instances of slaving, Ouseley argued, would be a great step forward in the struggle for the suppression of the Brazilian slave trade; failure to condemn on the other hand would

[1] Jackson and Grigg, no. 41, 22 June 1839, F.O. 84/276.
[2] Ouseley no. 22, Conf., 22 June 1839, F.O. 84/286. [3] Jackson and Grigg, no. 41.
[4] Ouseley to Cândido Batista, 9 June, enclosed in Ouseley no. 22; Cândido Batista to Carneiro de Campos, 14 June, enclosed in Jackson and Grigg no. 41.

be a serious step backward, making inevitable 'more severe and active measures' by the British navy. Cândido Batista, a deputy from the state of Rio Grande do Sul where there was rather less interest in the slave trade than in other economically more important areas of the country, was personally inclined to embrace this excellent opportunity of bypassing the Chamber of Deputies on the issue of the equipment clause. Convinced that the introduction of growing numbers of slaves into Brazil was both inimical to the real interests of the planters and a threat to internal security, he was prepared to consider seriously Ouseley's opinion that it was in his power to interpret the treaties in such a way as to ensure that their purpose, the suppression of the trade, was not obstructed by 'legal technicalities'. Unfortunately, Cândido Batista's Cabinet colleagues were less favourably disposed on slave trade matters, and were painfully aware that a decision as controversial as the one they were being asked to take would be violently opposed by powerful slaving and land-owning interests which they were not in a position to disregard.[1]

While these discussions continued a number of slave trade enterprises were held up (over twenty ships, all fitted out, waited anxiously in Rio Bay alone) and insurance rates rose steeply.[2] For the first time in years slave traders operating from Brazil were genuinely alarmed. They enjoyed one brief moment of relief—almost elation—at the news from London that the Melbourne administration had resigned, but Ouseley quickly made it known that no British government, Whig or Conservative, would in any way ease the pressure on the Brazilian slave trade. And in the event the Whig government survived the Bedchamber Crisis and its notorious Foreign Secretary remained in office for a further two years.

When, on 27 July, the Brazilian commissary judge was finally instructed to take cognisance of all prizes brought before him the traders saw this as the death blow to their activities. Their fears were exaggerated. All that the decision meant was that the Brazilian government and its legal advisers had realised that without the mixed court's first adjudicating a case a capture could not

---

[1] Ouseley no. 31, 20 July 1839, Conf., F.O. 84/287.
[2] Ouseley no. 37, 29 July 1839, F.O. 84/287.

be declared illegal and a ship could not be restored to its owners with indemnities. Far from concurring in the British view that all Brazilian ships in the slave trade, whether or not they carried slaves, were liable to capture and condemnation, the Brazilian government studiously avoided all reference to the treaty of 1826 and, mindful of the two cases about to come before the court, made a point of reiterating their view that according to a strict interpretation of the letter of the treaty of 1817—which had continued in force after 1830 at the express wish of Lord Palmerston—the visit and search of Brazilian vessels except where there was a reasonable suspicion of their having slaves on board was unquestionably illegal.[1]

Despite the owners' claim that she was fitted for the transportation of 'free colonists', there was no doubt that the *Maria Carlota*, the first of the two cases to come before the mixed court was a notorious slave ship. Furthermore, her owners were undoubtedly Brazilian, or at least Portuguese resident in Brazil, despite the usual claim that the ship was Portuguese property. Only the question of the legality of the capture was therefore open to dispute and it was on this point that the two judges now differed in their interpretation of the Anglo-Brazilian abolition treaty. On 31 August Carneiro de Campos delivered his verdict in favour of acquittal: the *Maria Carlota* had been illegally searched and detained since she was neither carrying slaves nor had she had slaves on board at any stage of her voyage.[2] By this time, even Jackson had begun to have doubts. How far was the position he had adopted justified? His responsibility was, he realised, very great since it was his reading of the anti-slave trade treaties that had led directly to the *Grecian*'s two controversial captures. But now the Brazilians had rejected this interpretation and the Foreign Office in London had still not accepted it. He was, however, strongly supported by Ouseley who undertook to share the responsibility with him: Ouseley fully agreed with Jackson's view of the treaties and had no doubt that it would eventually receive official approval.[3] And so, on 2 September Jackson declared himself in favour of

[1] Jackson and Grigg, no. 48, 30 July 1839, F.O. 84/277.
[2] Jackson and Grigg, no. 53, 23 September 1839, F.O. 84/277.
[3] Jackson to Ouseley, 30 August, Ouseley to Jackson, 31 August, enclosed in Ouseley to Palmerston, 16 September 1839, separate and conf., F.O. 84/287.

condemning the *Maria Carlota*.[1] Ouseley reported to Palmerston that Jackson had supported his verdict with 'able and well-considered arguments'.[2] In fact he was on this occasion even more confused and incoherent than usual, although the core of his argument was relatively simple. The Anglo-Portuguese treaty of 1817 had been signed when the Portuguese-Brazilian slave trade was only partially illegal (that is, north of the equator) and, as a result, it had been necessary to protect the legal trade from improper interference. In two important respects, then, this treaty differed from and was 'weaker' than Britain's treaties with the Netherlands (1818 and 1823), France (1831 and 1833), Spain (1817 and 1835) and the other maritime powers which had declared the entire trade illegal. First, in no circumstances could a Portuguese slave ship be detained nor, strictly speaking, could it even be searched by a British cruiser south of the equator; secondly, a Portuguese slaver could not be searched and detained north of the equator unless slaves were actually on board. The treaty of 1817 was incorporated 'word for word' into the Anglo-Brazilian treaty of 1826 in order to regulate the Brazilian trade (also illegal only north of the equator) until March 1830 when it became entirely illegal. The treaty of 1817 would then have ceased to apply to the Brazilian trade but for the separate article of September 1817 which permitted the continuation of the treaty for fifteen years after total abolition in order that the two governments might have time to adapt its provisions to the new situation. Some modification was obviously required since the treaty of 1817 was in conflict with and to some extent even nullified article 1 of the treaty of 1826, which expressly prohibited Brazilians from carrying on the slave trade, north or south of the equator. Jackson took the view that even though the two governments had failed to negotiate the necessary alterations to the treaty of 1817, the British and Brazilian commissioners, with the approval of their governments, could in practice disregard the limitations which the treaty imposed upon British and Brazilian cruisers thus bringing the stipulations of the treaty of 1817 into line with the intention of

[1] Jackson and Grigg, no. 53. See also Jackson's earlier opinion on *Maria Carlota* case, 5 June, enclosed in Jackson and Grigg no. 41.
[2] Ouseley 16 September, separate and conf., F.O. 84/287.

the treaty of 1826, that is, the immediate and effective suppression of the Brazilian slave trade. In fact the Anglo-Brazilian mixed commission in Rio de Janeiro had already condemned Brazilian slave ships captured off the Brazilian coast, that is south of the line, and one Brazilian ship—the *Incomprehensivel*—taken in mid-Atlantic also south of the line had been condemned in the court at Freetown. Thus in practice the treaty of 1817 had been interpreted in the light of the treaty of 1826, and with the acquiescence of the Brazilian government. Now, Jackson argued, the same principle which had removed one restriction on the right of British cruisers to search Brazilian slavers—that the search must be north of the equator—could equally well apply to the other—that the vessel searched must be suspected of having slaves on board. (Jackson also made great play of the fact that empty Brazilian slavers— two of them captured by the Brazilians themselves—had already been condemned in the Rio court with the apparent approval of the Brazilian government. But what he failed to add was that all the ships in question had recently landed slaves in Brazil whereas the main purpose of his interpretation of the treaties was to enable British cruisers to capture Brazilian slave ships as they left Brazilian ports or arrived in African waters on their *outward* journey.) The most obvious flaw in Jackson's argument (which the Brazilians did not miss) was that if the right to search and capture outward-bound slavers came within the terms of the existing treaty stipulations why, for more than a decade, had the British government gone to such trouble to try and negotiate additional articles, including an equipment article, to the treaty of 1817. Jackson's only response was to claim, unconvincingly, that such an article would not have given cruisers and mixed commissions *new* powers but would merely have helped to avoid dissension by establishing what fittings should be accepted as *prima facie* evidence of slaving in cases where outward bound ships were detained.

Since the two commissary judges were unable to agree on the fate of the *Maria Carlota*, lots were drawn for an arbitrator, and it fell to Frederick Grigg to have the last word. His mind riddled with doubts about the validity of Jackson's reasoning, he was reluctant to declare his verdict—which led the exasperated Ouseley to write to James Bandinel at the Foreign Office that 'when our senior commissioner goes right, the other bolts'.[1] Ouseley had now to overcome Grigg's scruples without appearing openly to dictate to him and, in a strongly worded memorandum, he once again set out the grounds for condemning the *Maria Carlota*.[2] Grigg eventually allowed himself to be overwhelmed. On 13 September he decided in favour of condemnation.[3] Ouseley had gained his 'immense point': the verdict on the *Maria Carlota* he triumphantly described as 'the greatest blow the slave trade has experienced since the commission was established in this capital'.[4] The renewed consternation among the slave traders in Rio seemed to prove his point.

But once again both Ouseley's enthusiasm and the traders' despair were a little premature. On 24 September the mixed commission acquitted the *Recuperador*, the second of the two ships brought in by the *Grecian*. The verdict was not even the outcome of a Brazilian success in the draw for arbitration—it never came to that. On this occasion Jackson agreed with Carneiro de Campos. It was a 'most extraordinary and unexpected decision' and one which astonished not only Ouseley and Robert Hesketh, the British consul and proctor in both cases, but also Figuanière, the Portuguese minister in Rio, and Lopes Gama, the Brazilian Foreign Minister. All along the two cases had been regarded as identical; if anything the evidence against the *Recuperador* was even stronger than that against the *Maria Carlota*. As the *Feliz*, the *Recuperador* had already been captured with slaves on board and condemned in the Rio court earlier in the year. The owners—Brazilians—had bought it back again (another example of the need to break up condemned slavers when they could not be used by either government), renamed it, and sent it off on another slaving voyage. The ship had been built in Sardinia and so, quite apart from the question of ownership, could not possibly qualify for Portuguese nationality. The few documents found on board had been issued by João Baptista Moreira, the former Portuguese consul-general and *chargé d'affaires* in Rio de Janeiro, whose exequatur had been

[1] Ouseley to Bandinel, 18 September 1839, Private, F.O. 84/287.
[2] Ouseley to Grigg, 5 September, enclosed in Ouseley to Palmerston, 18 September 1839. Private, F.O. 84/287.
[3] Jackson and Grigg, no. 53.
[4] Ouseley to Palmerston, 18 September, Private.

withdrawn a month before the date of signature. The *Recuperador* was fully equipped for the slave trade and it was less than a fortnight earlier that the court had condemned the *Maria Carlota* on identical grounds.

The judges, however, decided that the evidence of the *Recuperador*'s intention to trade in slaves was not entirely convincing. There was here a genuine problem. If a ship were to be punished before it had actually committed the illegal act of trading in slaves, the only conclusive evidence, the existence of slaves or clear signs of their recent presence, would obviously not be found. Thus the circumstantial evidence would have to be overwhelming if judges—and the Brazilian judge in particular—were to be persuaded of a ship's guilt (especially when the capture had been made on the Brazilian coast). In the case of the *Recuperador* there was slaving equipment on board but it was claimed that it had been there when, as the *Feliz*, the ship was sold after its earlier condemnation. Even if this were the case (and the captors denied it) the judges made no attempt to explain why cargo and fittings common only to slaving vessels had been left on board when the *Recuperador* left Brazil apparently on its way back to the African coast.[1]

The acquittal of the *Recuperador* enabled Brazilian traders to breathe freely again and had a depressing effect on the enthusiasm, so recently aroused, of the British squadron on the Brazilian coast. Yet the *Maria Carlota* verdict had not been reversed: the *Recuperador* had not been released on the grounds that cruisers were not empowered to capture Brazilian ships fitted for the slave trade; the legality or illegality of the capture had not been discussed. Carneiro de Campos had made it clear that he still opposed in principle the British interpretation of the abolition treaty; Jackson, however, did not anticipate that the precedent of the *Maria Carlota* would be disturbed in future cases brought before the court.[2] In practice, it seemed, the equipment clause had been secured.

[1] On the *Recuperador* case, Jackson and Grigg, no. 55, 25 September 1839, F.O. 84/277; Ouseley no. 57, 20 October 1839, F.O. 84/288; Smyth to Commodore Sullivan, 10 October, Hesketh to Ouseley, 11 October, enclosed in Ouseley no. 57; Ouseley to Palmerston, 21 December 1839, Secret, F.O. 84/288.
[2] Jackson and Grigg, no. 62, 7 November 1839, F.O. 84/277.

On the other side of the Atlantic an opportunity for establishing a similar precedent had presented itself in the summer of 1839 when the brig *Emprehendedor* arrived in Freetown with a prize crew from H.M.S. *Wolverine* on board. It had been captured on 23 June while at anchor in the roadstead off Whydah, preparing to take on board a cargo of slaves. In the course of the search the master had produced Portuguese papers, but there was evidence that the ship was trading to and from Cuba where presumably the owner operated, and as a 'Spanish' ship its cargo and fittings alone made it liable to seizure and condemnation under the Anglo-Spanish treaty of 1835. On 28 August the Anglo-Spanish mixed commission in Freetown had no difficulty in deciding that the *Emprehendedor* was a slave ship, but the captors were unsuccessful in their efforts to prove it Spanish. It transpired that the ship had for some time been engaged in the illegal slave trade to Bahia where the owner, Andre Pinto da Silveira, resided. In order, therefore, to avoid restoring the slaver to its owner, with damages, the case was transferred to the Anglo-Brazilian mixed commission. It was the first ship to appear before that commission since the *Incomprehensivel* two and a half years earlier and, as on that occasion, no Brazilian commissioner was available to deal with the case. Since July 1836 there had been only one Brazilian official in Freetown, Joaquim Feliciano Gomes, who was appointed commissioner of arbitration in May 1837, arrived in February 1838 and left in July of the same year without ever being called upon to adjudicate a single case. Thus the case of the *Emprehendedor*, like so many cases in the Sierra Leone mixed court, came before the British commissioners acting alone. They quickly agreed that despite its Portuguese papers the *Emprehendedor* could properly be treated as a Brazilian ship and that as such it was contravening both Brazilian law and the Anglo-Brazilian abolition treaty. But the crucial question, which was also at issue in the mixed court in Rio de Janeiro, still remained to be answered: could a Brazilian slaver legally be seized by a British cruiser and condemned by an Anglo-Brazilian mixed court when evidence of its illegal activities was only circumstantial, that is, when the ship was equipped for the slave trade (and in this case lying off a notorious slave port) but before any slaves had been taken on board? During the previous months Henry Macaulay, the British commissary judge, had slowly come round to the conclusion that it could. His argument was in part similar to that used by George Jackson in the case of the *Maria Carlota*. He went further, however, and declared that regardless of whether the existing treaties empowered British cruisers to capture Brazilian ships fitted for slaving, no Brazilian ship brought before an Anglo-Brazilian commission need ever be acquitted if it could be proved a slave ship. No party could be wronged by the commission in such cases since none could claim the right to carry on a trade declared illegal by the Anglo-Brazilian treaty of 1826 and the Brazilian law of 1831. It did not matter, therefore, at what stage of a slaving enterprise a ship was captured, 'whether in the inception, or the prosecution or the consummation'. Unless satisfactorily accounted for, the existence of equipment for the illegal slave trade on board a ship could thus be treated as *prima facie* evidence of illegal activities. Without hesitation the *Emprehendedor* was condemned on 31 August under 'the comprehensive terms' of the treaty of 1826 'fairly and liberally interpreted'[1]—the same day as the Brazilian commissary judge in the Rio de Janeiro mixed court declared that the *Maria Carlota* had been illegally captured. In Freetown, however, no Brazilian judge was present to contest the new interpretation of the Anglo-Brazilian treaty. Macaulay, like Jackson, was well aware of the extent of his responsibility: he anticipated that several Brazilian slavers would be captured and condemned on the same grounds as the *Emprehendedor*—perhaps as many as thirty—before news of Palmerston's approval, or disapproval, arrived in Freetown.[2]

The issue would in any case have thrust itself upon the mixed court in Freetown even without Macaulay's deliberately taking advantage of the *Emprehendedor* case to establish the precedent he sought. Captain Tucker, senior naval officer on the west African coast north of the equator, now had a stronger squadron at his disposal, and was prevented from operating more efficiently because his officers were not authorised to capture Brazilian ships before they had taken on slaves. He felt it his duty to check the growing Brazilian trade and from his own reading of the treaties

---

[1] On the *Emprehendedor* case, Macaulay and Doherty to Palmerston, Brazil no. 105, 2 September 1839, F.O. 84/271.   [2] *Ibid.*

of 1817 and 1826, became convinced that there was no good reason why Brazilian slavers should not be captured at any stage of their enterprise. A month after he had captured the empty Portuguese slaver *Emprehendedor*—believing it to be Spanish—he decided to take a chance and, on 25 July, he seized the Portuguese brig *Firmeza*, also at anchor off Whydah waiting for slaves, in the belief that it was really Brazilian.[1] At the same time he ordered the officers under his command to follow his example and seize all 'Portuguese' ships equipped for the slave trade where they had reasonable grounds for believing them Brazilian: two days later the *Lynx* took the *Simpathia* as it, too, waited at anchor for its human cargo to be loaded. When the *Firmeza* and the *Simpathia* came before the Anglo-Brazilian commission at Sierra Leone, the British commissioners readily condemned them.[2] They even went so far as to express surprise that Captain Tucker and his officers should ever have doubted that the commission would condemn Brazilian ships captured in such circumstances.[3] Officers of the West African squadron stationed north of the equator were now in no doubt that Brazilian slave ships would be condemned on the strength of their equipment alone. Before the close of the year nine more empty slavers were brought before the Anglo-Brazilian commission in Sierra Leone. Although three had assumed Portuguese nationality, all were proved Brazilian—most of them in the Bahian trade—and all nine were condemned.[4] There was still no Brazilian judge in Freetown to dispute these verdicts.

How did Lord Palmerston react to the initiative taken by British naval officers and British commissioners in Rio de Janeiro and Freetown? On hearing from Ouseley about Jackson's views on the Anglo-Brazilian treaties he had asked Sir John Dodson, the Advocate General, whether they had any validity and, if so, what new instructions should be issued to the navy. On 3 April 1839

[1] Tucker to Macaulay, 25 July, 18 October, enclosed in Macaulay and Doherty to Palmerston, General no. 180, 31 December 1839, F.O. 84/273.
[2] Macaulay and Doherty, Brazil no. 189, 31 December 1839, F.O. 84/273.
[3] Bidwell (registrar of the court) to Tucker, 14 September, enclosed in Macaulay and Doherty, General no. 180; Macaulay and Doherty to Tucker, 31 December 1839, F.O. 315/13.
[4] Macaulay and Doherty, Brazil no. 189.

Dodson had firmly stated that in his view Jackson's opinions were *not* consistent with the terms of the treaty of 1826 and that no new instructions were warranted. When, later in the month, he was asked to reconsider this opinion, Dodson saw no reason to change his mind. At the same time, however, he admitted that the treaty of 1817 and the first article of the treaty of 1826 were to some extent in conflict and that their meaning was ambiguous. In the circumstances he thought that, *provided the Brazilian government were agreeable*, Jackson's interpretation might legitimately be adopted since it certainly accorded with the purpose of the two governments in signing the treaty—the complete suppression of the Brazilian slave trade.[1] On 31 August, as proceedings in the *Maria Carlota* case were being wound up at Rio de Janeiro and in Freetown the *Emprehendedor* was being condemned, Palmerston instructed Jackson to try and persuade the Brazilian government to concur in his interpretation of the treaty; failing this he was given clear instructions that he should not act upon it.[2] Had this despatch arrived in Rio earlier, Jackson and Grigg were to admit in November, the *Maria Carlota* would have been acquitted.[3] But at the time they assumed that the point at issue was settled, with Brazilian acquiescence, and so kept quiet about Palmerston's instructions. It was November before Palmerston heard that both the *Emprehendedor* and the *Maria Carlota* had been condemned. He gladly accepted the *fait accompli* and approved both verdicts without hesitation.[4] The next day he advised the Admiralty that in the light of the spirit and intention of the first article of the Anglo-Brazilian abolition treaty, Brazilian slave ships leaving Brazilian ports or arriving off the African coast were now liable to capture and condemnation.[5] Two months earlier, under Lord Palmerston's Act of August 1839, British cruisers had been authorised to capture all Portuguese slave ships and ships without nationality at any stage of their voyage and send them to British vice-admiralty

---

[1] Palmerston to Dodson, 2 April, Dodson to Palmerston, 3 April, Palmerston to Dodson, 17 April, Dodson to Palmerston, 20 August 1839, F.O. 83/2348.
[2] Palmerston to Rio commissioners, no. 12, 31 August 1839, F.O. 84/276.
[3] Jackson and Grigg, no. 62, 7 November 1839, F.O. 84/277.
[4] Palmerston to Sierra Leone commissioners, no. 36, 22 November, F.O. 84/266 (printed in Newbury, *op. cit.* pp. 149–50); Palmerston to Rio commissioners, no. 22, 22 November 1839, F.O. 84/277.
[5] Palmerston to Admiralty, 23 November 1839, F.O. 84/303.

courts for adjudication. Now they received similar instructions to capture all Brazilian ships they encountered and to send them for adjudication to one or other of the Anglo-Brazilian courts of mixed commission where, it was hoped, even if they were only equipped for the trade, they would henceforth be condemned. During 1839 real progress had been made—or so it seemed— towards the final suppression of the Brazilian slave trade.

CHAPTER 7

BRITAIN AND THE SLAVE TRADE, 1839–1845

As Captain Joseph Denman, one of the most experienced British naval officers to serve in the anti-slave trade blockade of the west African coast, was later to recall, the year 1839 opened 'an era in the history of the slave trade when for the first time suppression [by the British navy] became possible'.[1] Ships of the Royal Navy were at last empowered to search and capture Portuguese and Brazilian (as well as Spanish) vessels—together with those without nationality—carrying slaves or simply equipped for the trade in southern as well as northern latitudes. Moreover, the activities of the navy—at least on the African side of the Atlantic where Britain's efforts for the suppression of the foreign transatlantic slave trade were still concentrated—were no longer confined to the high seas. Lord Palmerston had already advised the Admiralty that, in the opinion of Sir John Dodson, the Advocate General, if British warships were to enter African waters and rivers it was unlikely that local chiefs would, or were entitled to, claim that their territorial rights had been violated.[2] In 1841 he confirmed that his Act of 24 August 1839 authorised British officers to search and detain slavers found at anchor off ports in Portuguese Africa and in Portuguese African waters: where there were Portuguese authorities in the vicinity prior permission should be sought but, even if it were refused, an officer should not be deterred from doing his duty provided that he did not expose his ship to attack from Portuguese shore batteries.[3] Thus, not only was the British navy able to extend its anti-slave trade operations to the African coast south of the line, but it was able to adopt new and considerably more effective tactics: for the first time instead of operating out at sea as though slave ships arose from the depths of the ocean, British

---

[1] Evidence before Anglo-French (Broglie-Lushington) committee on the slave trade, 1 April 1845, B.M. Add. MSS (Aberdeen Papers), 43557.
[2] Dodson to Palmerston, 3 August 1838, F.O. 83/2347.
[3] Leveson (F.O.) to Admiralty, 28 July, 6 August 1841, F.O. 84/384.

warships could cruise inshore and blockade the more notorious slave ports and points of embarkation along the coast, picking up vessels as they arrived and even as they lay at anchor as well as on their return voyage. And there was, too, every incentive for the navy to exercise its new powers. Following the treaty of 1835 with Spain and in anticipation of changes in the treaties with Portugal and Brazil making possible the seizure of empty slave vessels, the bounty system had been modified: the Tonnage Act of 1838 provided for the payment where a ship was captured with slaves on board of £1 10s. a ton plus £5 a head (only £2 10s. if the slave died before the prize reached port) and a straight £4 a ton in cases where the captured slave vessel was empty.[1] Moreover, naval officers had now less reason to fear either that their prize would be acquitted or that undue delay would occur before it was condemned. Henceforth Portuguese ships would be taken before a British vice-admiralty court instead of the Anglo-Portuguese mixed commission in Sierra Leone. As for Brazilian ships, naval officers on the west African coast were well aware that in the Anglo-Brazilian commission at Sierra Leone there was rarely a Brazilian commissioner present to contest the British view that even where they were only equipped for the trade they were now liable to capture and condemnation.

In 1840 the west coast of Africa once again became a separate naval station and its southern boundary was extended to Cape Frio, thus encompassing both the Congo and Angola. The coast south of Cabo Frio (from which slaves were hardly ever exported) and Portuguese Moçambique on the east African coast remained the responsibility of the Cape squadron.[2] Increases in the navy estimates during the late thirties resulted in a slight rise in the number of ships on the west African coast—to twelve in 1840 and thirteen in 1841.[3] It was, of course, far short of what was needed for the task in hand, but was nevertheless welcomed by those who believed that the slave trade would diminish in proportion to the strength of the British preventive squadron. More important, the additions to the squadron included, besides one steamship, some sailing ships of better design such as the *Waterwitch*, a small ten-

---

[1] Lloyd, *Navy and the Slave Trade*, p. 81; Lewis, *Navy in Transition*, p. 236.
[2] Lloyd, *op. cit.* Appendix D.
[3] Lloyd, *op. cit.* Appendix C; Bartlett, *Britain and Sea Power*, Appendix II.

gun brig privately built and purchased by the navy in 1834, the first really fast ship attached to the West African squadron which was not itself an ex-slaver.

In November 1839 the first capture authorised by the Palmerston Act—that of the barque *Veloz* flying the Portuguese flag and fitted for carrying slaves—was made by H.M.S. *Wolverine* at the mouth of the Congo. After twenty years in which, with the exception of the few that were handed over to their own authorities, all foreign slave ships had been taken by their British captors for adjudication before mixed commissions, the *Veloz* was despatched to the British vice-admiralty court sitting in Freetown, Sierra Leone where on 2 January 1840 it was condemned. The *Columbine* was also active in the Congo area, capturing three empty Portuguese slavers before the end of the year, while the *Bonetta* took two off the coast of Angola; these, too, were condemned in the Sierra Leone vice-admiralty court. Cruisers on the Cape station were also for the first time engaged in anti-slave trade patrol: H.M.S. *Modeste* captured two ships (one carrying 716 slaves) on the east coast of Africa which in February 1840 were condemned in the vice-admiralty court at the Cape of Good Hope. During 1840 ten more Portuguese ships were condemned in the Freetown court after they had been detained—seven of them south of the equator—by cruisers on the west African station. And in the same year a further nineteen vessels—most of them captured on the east African coast—were condemned in the court at Cape Town. In June 1840 ships were taken for the first time to the vice-admiralty court at St Helena; before the end of the year thirteen had been condemned, eight with no nationality and all captured on the west African coast between 7° and 12° S. During 1841 and the first half of 1842 a further dozen Portuguese ships were captured (mostly north of the line) and condemned in the Freetown court, and around fifty slave ships and auxiliary vessels, both Portuguese and with no known nationality, were condemned at St Helena; many of the latter had been captured south of the line by the *Waterwitch* under Captain H. J. Matson and the *Fantome* under Captain E. H. Butterfield.[1] Furthermore, after

[1] List of captures adjudicated at St Helena, F.O. 84/748; list of captures adjudicated in the Cape vice-admiralty court, August 1839 to September 1849, F.O. 84/824; list of adjudi-

eight years in which only one case—that of the *Incomprehensivel*—
had come before the Anglo-Brazilian mixed commission in
Freetown, eleven Brazilian ships were taken there in the last six
months of 1839, a further eight in 1840 and eight more during the
first six months of 1841—most of them on suspicion of being
equipped for the slave trade. In the absence of any Brazilian commissioner all were condemned without hesitation by the British
commissioners acting alone.[1]

Many of the ships adjudicated in Sierra Leone had been captured by cruisers under the command of Captain Denman, senior
officer on the northern division of the West African station which
stretched from Cape Verde to Cape Palmas. Between May and
December 1840 they had maintained an effective blockade of
Gallinas, an estuary 150 miles south of Sierra Leone, emerging
with fifteen captures to their credit. It was at this point that
Denman made the important and far reaching decision to land a
small force at Gallinas, destroy eight of its slave barracoons
together with the stores belonging to European slave dealers and
liberate the slaves—over 800 of them—awaiting transportation.
This exercise, which Denman considered 'the most severe blow
ever struck at the slave trade', was fully supported by the Colonial
Secretary Lord John Russell, who in 1841 recommended its repetition on 'all parts of the coast not belonging to any civilised power'.
Palmerston approved: 'taking a wasp's nest', he told Lord Minto,
First Lord of the Admiralty, '. . . is more effective than catching
the wasps one by one'. Within a short period similar tactics had
been adopted elsewhere along the African coast to the north and
south of Sierra Leone where, as at Gallinas, traders in the Cuban
trade were most directly affected, and also south of the equator at
Cabinda and Ambriz where landing parties from the *Waterwitch*
and the *Madagascar* destroyed eight barracoons and liberated over
1,300 slaves destined for Brazil.[2]

cations in the Freetown vice-admiralty court, 1840–4, enclosed in Melville to Bandinel,
1 January 1845, F.O. 44/556. For some of the more exciting exploits of Matson, Denman,
Butterfield etc. during this period, see Lloyd, *op. cit.* 91–6.
1 · Macaulay and Doherty, Brazil no. 189, 31 December 1839 (report on 1839), F.O.
84/273; Jeremie and Lewis, Brazil no. 136, 31 December 1840 (report on 1840), F.O.
84/310; Melville, Brazil no. 117, 31 December 1841 (report on 1841), F.O. 84/346.
2 For the Gallinas incident and subsequent developments, see Gavin, 'Palmerston's Policy
towards East and West Africa', pp. 138–40; Lloyd, *op. cit.* p. 95; Fyfe, *History of Sierra*

Britain and the slave trade, 1839–1845

With more than 150 ships engaged in the slave trade to Brazil captured (besides a large number in the Cuban trade) and heavy losses inflicted upon the slave traders on land as well as at sea, the years from the middle of 1839 to the middle of 1842 constituted a period of unprecedented success for the British West African and Cape squadrons. And their efforts were largely responsible for a sharp downturn in the volume of the Brazilian slave trade after several years of steady expansion. There were, however, other factors as well: the glut of slaves in the Brazilian market following the enormous imports of the late thirties, the reduced demand for Brazilian produce in Western Europe and North America, as a result of a temporary decline in world trade, and, not least, the adoption of certain anti-slave trade measures by the Brazilian governments themselves during the period after April 1839 and especially in the months following *A Maioridade* in July 1840.[1] Between January and April 1839 at least 15,000 slaves had been landed along the coast between São Sebastião and Vitória; fewer than 15,000 were landed in the last eight months of 1839 and an even smaller number during the following twelve months.[2] In October 1840 Ouseley wrote that the traders of Rio de Janeiro 'had not for many years been so completely discouraged, nor have their speculations been so completely unsuccessful as during the last six months'.[3] Only about 10,000 slaves were imported into the area to the north and south of Rio de Janeiro during 1841 and a further 10,000 during the first three quarters of 1842. A comparable decline took place in imports to Bahia: only 1,500 were landed in 1840, 1,500 in 1841 and 2,500 in 1842.[4]

Nevertheless, the Brazilian slave trade had by no means been suppressed and from the end of 1842 there were signs of a marked revival: it would seem that during the three years 1843–5 as many as 80,000 slaves—possibly more—were successfully landed in the provinces of Rio de Janeiro and São Paulo and at least another 15,000 in Bahia and Pernambuco.[5] There were several reasons for this resurgence. In the first place, the Brazilian economy, and

Leone, p. 220; *P.P.* 1847–8, XXII (272), House of Commons Select Committee on the Slave Trade, 1st Report, Denman evidence; Anstey, *Britain and the Congo*, p. 13.
[1] See above, ch. 3, pp. 86–7.   [2] See Appendix.
[3] Ouseley to Palmerston, no. 46, 16 October 1840, F.O. 84/325.
[4] See Appendix.   [5] See Appendix.

especially the coffee sector, resumed its expansion after its temporary setback during the years 1840–1. Secondly, as we have seen, the Brazilian government's own efforts to suppress the trade were relaxed following the resignation in March 1841 of the abolitionist *Gabinete da Maioridade*.[1] Finally, British pressure on the slave trade was also eased as the powers of the British navy were in some respects curtailed and as traders began to discover new ways of shielding their illegal activities from British interference.

In November 1841 a Conservative government had taken office in England and Lord Palmerston had been replaced at the Foreign Office by Lord Aberdeen who, personally, was perhaps slightly less committed on the slave trade question than his predecessor and politically less inclined to assert British power to the full for its suppression, more anxious to avoid unnecessary disputes with other powers and more wedded to the principles of legality. By this time the Law Officers of the Crown had had second thoughts about the legality of Captain Denman's activities at Gallinas in 1841 and similar actions taken by other British naval officers along the west African coast and in May 1842 Aberdeen felt bound to advise the Admiralty Lords that, in the opinion of the Queen's Advocate,

blockading the rivers, landing and destroying buildings and carrying off persons held in slavery in countries with which Great Britain is not at war cannot be considered as sanctioned by the law of nations or by the provisions of any existing treaties . . . however desirable it may be to put an end to the slave trade, a good, however eminent, should not be attained otherwise than by lawful means.[2]

There was no alternative, it seemed but to pursue the policy, begun a few years earlier, of persuading west African chiefs to sign bilateral treaties with Britain for the abolition of the slave trade and, incidentally, for the protection and furtherance of legitimate commerce. (Palmerston, on the other hand, felt that the Law of Nations governed the relations between European and American states and was not applicable to 'half naked and

[1] See above, ch. 3, p. 87.
[2] Aberdeen to Admiralty, 20 May 1842, F.O. 84/436; printed in Newbury, *British Policy towards West Africa: Select Documents*, pp. 162–3.

uncivilised' Africans who should be compelled to abandon the slave trade where they were too barbarous to sign anti-slave trade treaties.[1]) New instructions were consequently issued from the Admiralty forbidding the destruction of slave barracoons on the African coast and the liberation of slaves without authorisation by treaty or written agreement and, in particular, totally forbidding the destruction of merchandise and property belonging to foreign traders. In short, the navy should act in African territorial waters with a greater concern for legality than had been displayed in the recent past. Inevitably these instructions bred a new caution amongst British naval officers on the west African station which, the traders explained to the African chiefs, was the consequence of a revolution in England and the overthrow of Lord Palmerston and his anti-slave trade policies.[2] The publication of Aberdeen's letter of May 1842 to the Admiralty also led directly to the famous action for damages amounting to some £300,000 which was brought by the slave traders of Gallinas against Captain Denman and which served as yet a further deterrent to the British navy. It was six years before the case was settled—in favour of Denman.[3]

The attitude of the new Conservative government towards Lord Palmerston's Act of 1839 was also a matter of no little concern both to its author and to leading abolitionists who feared a further relaxation of the anti-slave trade measures which had been adopted—with such striking results—by the previous Whig government. In 1839 a number of Tory peers led by the Duke of Wellington, now a prominent figure in Peel's Cabinet, had been bitterly opposed to the Act and it was known that Aberdeen himself was highly critical of it, believing that relations with Portugal were 'of a character entirely different from those of any other country'; the Tagus, it seemed to him, was 'by far the most important spot in Europe for us outside our own Dominions' and it was his sincere hope that the English might once again be 'not

---

[1] Hansard, lxxvi, 940–1 (16 July 1844), lxxx, 207–8 (5 May 1845). In his evidence to the House of Lords Select Committee on the Slave Trade in 1850 Denman expressed the view that it was 'utterly absurd' to invest 'petty barbarians' with the rights of civilised powers: 'the position England should assume towards them is of a grown up person towards a child'. *P.P.* 1850 (Lords) xxiv (35), 1st Report, par. 4517.

[2] *P.P.* 1847–8, xxii (272), House of Commons Select Committee on the Slave Trade, 1st Report, Matson evidence, par. 1258.

[3] Fyfe, *op. cit.* p. 224; Lloyd, *op. cit.* pp. 97–9.

only masters there but at home there'.[1] Palmerston's Act which the Portuguese so detested had now been in force for almost three years and the Portuguese government were very anxious to reach a settlement on an anti-slave trade treaty which would replace it, although they remained determined that the treaty should be one of limited duration. Aberdeen, who also wished to see the Act replaced by a treaty, was ready to offer a sop to Portuguese pride: he conceded an imprecisely worded additional article under which the two governments agreed to consult with each other if, at any time after the suppression of the slave trade, it seemed necessary to revise the treaty in order to avoid inconveniencing legitimate commerce. As a result, on 3 July 1842, Howard de Walden and the Duc de Palmella reached agreement in Lisbon on a new Anglo-Portuguese anti-slave trade treaty. Based on the British treaty draft of August 1838 and closely resembling the Anglo-Spanish treaty of 1835, the new treaty satisfied the British government on every important point in dispute for almost a decade, including equipment and break-up clauses. Moreover, in accordance with the terms of a memorandum which was signed at the same time, on 25 July the Portuguese government promulgated a decree prescribing severe penalties for slave trading, now described as piracy.[2] Two weeks later the Act of 1839 was suspended in so far as it applied to ships flying the Portuguese flag; it remained in force only in respect of those without nationality.[3] 'It was', Aberdeen said in the House of Lords, 'an act very little consistent with the friendly relations that subsisted between England and Portugal; indeed it was rather an act of hostility and one which might have led to interminable war had it been directed against any power of greater weight and better able to cope with us.'[4] While the suspension of part of the Act of 1839 and its replacement by an Anglo-Portuguese treaty in no way affected the right of British cruisers to search and capture slave ships flying the

---

[1] Aberdeen to Ripon, 14 December 1842, quoted in W. D. Jones, *Lord Aberdeen and the Americas* (Univ. of Georgia Press, 1958), p. 5, n. 3.

[2] Howard de Walden to Aberdeen, no. 22, 3 July 1842, F.O. 84/403; *B.F.S.P.* xxx, 527–81; *B.F.S.P.* xxxi, 450.

[3] 5 and 6 Vict. cap 114, 12 August 1842; Lord Canning (F.O.) to Admiralty, 6 September 1842, F.O. 84/436.

[4] Hansard, lxv, 936, 2 August 1842; cf. Aberdeen to Peel, 18 October 1844, quoted below, ch. 9, p. 244.

Portuguese flag on the high seas, article 3 of the treaty clearly stated that they no longer had the right to search or detain slave ships which were at anchor in a roadstead or within cannon shot of shore batteries along the coast of Portuguese Africa unless expressly requested to do so by the local Portuguese authorities. Accordingly, at the beginning of 1843 fresh instructions were sent to British naval officers ordering the exercise of even greater caution in Portuguese territorial waters than elsewhere along the African coast.[1] Furthermore, under the terms of the new treaty captured Portuguese vessels were in future to be adjudicated not by British judges in British vice-admiralty courts but once again by Anglo-Portuguese mixed commissions. Four new commissions—two in British and two in Portuguese territory—were to be established and, in the meantime, the Anglo-Portuguese commission in Sierra Leone, which had dealt with only three cases in over three years, was to resume its earlier functions. By 1842, however, when the Brazilian trade was beginning to revive again after its slight setback, the British navy had already gone a long way towards ensuring that the Portuguese flag, so extensively employed during the thirties, would no longer be used in the Brazilian trade: the Anglo-Portuguese mixed commissions which were eventually set up in Luanda (Angola), Boa Vista (Cape Verde), Spanish Town (Jamaica) and the Cape of Good Hope (on this occasion the British government chose the Cape in preference to Sierra Leone because of its proximity to both Portuguese East and West Africa)—all of which were functioning by the spring of 1844—were never very active.[2]

A number of Portuguese traders who had formerly sailed under their own colours now preferred to sail without flag or papers. They were thus still liable to capture under the Act of 1839, but British vice-admiralty courts were not empowered to punish the master and crew of a condemned ship whereas if the vessel could be proved to be Portuguese and taken before an Anglo-Portuguese mixed commission and condemned the master and crew could be handed over to the Portuguese authorities and would then as pirates, under the decree of July 1842, face severe penalties. For

[1] Canning to Admiralty, 23 January, 26 January 1843, F.O. 84/292.
[2] See Bethell, *Journal of African History* (1966), p. 91, n. 42.

their part British naval officers made no great effort to prove apparently stateless vessels Portuguese because they knew captured vessels would be dealt with more summarily in British vice-admiralty courts, where there was no foreign judge to question either the legality of the capture or the character of the vessel in question, than they would in any of the Anglo-Portuguese mixed commissions. During the three years from the end of 1842 more than thirty ships without flags or papers—most of them engaged in the Brazilian trade south of the equator—were captured and subsequently condemned in the vice-admiralty courts at St Helena, the Cape and Sierra Leone.[1]

A great many of the slave traders (Portuguese, Brazilians and others) who chose to seek a safe alternative to the Portuguese flag found it in the Stars and Stripes. Despite all Palmerston's efforts the United States remained the one great maritime power outside the network of right of search treaties and British cruisers were therefore powerless to search or capture vessels flying American colours and carrying American papers.[2] Nor were American vessels adequately policed by the American navy: since the early twenties American warships had visited the African coast rarely and only a small American squadron was stationed, and this intermittently, on the coast of Brazil. The American flag began to appear regularly in the foreign slave trade when it was introduced into the Cuban trade following the signing of the comprehensive Anglo-Spanish treaty of 1835. From 1838 there were reports of its appearance in the Brazilian trade and its use increased rapidly during the years 1840–1.[3] Despite federal laws prohibiting the participation of American citizens and American vessels in the slave trade, American-built ships left Baltimore, New York, Providence, Boston, Salem and other New England ports for Brazil where they were either sold to Americans acting as front men for slave dealers, or sold directly to dealers who agreed to take delivery only when a vessel reached the African coast, or

[1] See above, p. 182, n. 1.
[2] Negotiations between Britain and the United States over the right of search have been thoroughly examined in H. G. Soulsby, *The Right of Search and the Slave Trade in Anglo-American Relations 1814–62* (Baltimore, 1933).
[3] Ouseley to Palmerston, no. 47, 16 October 1840, F.O. 84/325; Ouseley no. 7, 28 February 1841, F.O. 84/364; Ouseley no. 97, 31 August, no. 98, 31 August 1841, F.O. 84/366.

189

simply chartered for the slave trade. These vessels then sailed for Africa protected by the American flag—and often with an American master and crew on board—carrying 'coast goods' (slaving equipment and goods to be exchanged for slaves) and 'passengers' (additional slave crew). For some American vessels—those acting simply as 'auxiliaries'—this concluded their involvement in the slave trade. Others made the return journey with a slave cargo— either as American vessels or, more frequently, after changing their flag and papers, as Brazilian or Portuguese vessels, since once slaves had been embarked American vessels and crew ran the risk under American law of being treated as pirates if they were unlucky enough to encounter an American warship; in the circumstances they preferred to chance capture by the British navy. What was even more serious from the British point of view was the fact that increasing numbers of Brazilian and Portuguese vessels outward bound from Brazilian ports fraudulently assumed American nationality by simply hoisting the American flag in order to avoid being searched by ships of the British West African squadron when they arrived off the coast of Africa.[1] At the end of 1841, in his annual Message to Congress, President Tyler admitted that the American flag was being 'grossly abused by the abandoned and profligate of other nations'[2] for slave trade purposes.

While readily acknowledging that the Royal Navy had as yet no right to visit and search *bona fide* American vessels, from the middle of 1839 the British government had authorised British officers, at their own discretion, to visit slave vessels flying the American flag where there were reasonable grounds for suspecting fraud, in order to ascertain their true nationality and, if they could easily be proved Spanish, Brazilian or Portuguese, to seize and send them for adjudication. In practice, however, it proved extremely difficult to differentiate between genuine and spurious

---

[1] American participation in the Brazilian slave trade during the 1840s has been well documented. On the activities of the *Agnes*, the *Montevideo* and the *Sea Eagle* during 1844, for example, see Lawrence F. Hill, *Diplomatic Relations between the United States and Brazil* (Duke Univ. Press, 1932), ch. 5, 'The Abolition of the African Slave Trade to Brazil' (originally published in *H.A.H.R.* xi (1931), 169–97), pp. 122–7. During the years 1841–5, 64 American vessels were sold in Rio de Janeiro, 56 left for Africa, 40 arrived from Africa, *ibid.* p. 129. Also Warren S. Howard, *American Slavers and the Federal Law, 1837–1862* (Univ. of Calif. Press, 1963), Appendix G, 'Some American Slavers in the Brazilian trade, 1840–1850.'

[2] Soulsby, *op. cit.* p. 47.

American vessels. Inevitably there were mistakes, and in any case the United States refused to recognise Britain's attempts to distinguish between the right of visit (in order to establish nationality) and the right of search in International Law.[1] In March 1840, at Sierra Leone, two senior naval officers, one American, Lieutenant John S. Paine of U.S.S. *Grampus*, and one British, Commander William Tucker of H.M.S. *Wolverine*, on their own initiative established a working arrangement for the suppression of the slave trade carried on under the American flag: they agreed that the ships of their respective squadrons would investigate every vessel found flying American colours and detain all those equipped for slaving or carrying slaves; if a vessel proved to be American it would be handed over to an American cruiser; if Spanish, Brazilian, Portuguese (or British) to a British cruiser. The following June, however, this *ad hoc* arrangement for joint Anglo-American cruising was repudiated in Washington.[2] At the same time the American government remained intransigent in its attitude towards the British navy and the right of search.

Lord Aberdeen was no more able to make progress on this crucial question than Palmerston had been. He therefore decided to settle for a more effective policing of American merchant ships by the American navy. Under Article 8 of the Webster-Ashburton Treaty, signed in Washington on 9 August 1842, the United States agreed to station a permanent naval force of not less than 80 guns on the west African coast.[3] The first American West African squadron under Commodore Matthew Perry (famous later for opening Japan to western trade) arrived on the coast in August 1843. Comprising only four ships, however—the frigate *Macedonia*, the brig *Porpoise* and two sloops—it established its base at Porto Praia in the Cape Verde Islands a considerable distance from the slave areas of the Guinea Coast and a month's sailing from the Congo. Moreover, Perry and his successors were instructed to make the protection and promotion of a legitimate American trade rather than the suppression of the slave trade their

[1] For the dispute over the difference between the right of visit and the right of search in international law, *ibid.* pp. 58–77.
[2] *Ibid.* p. 56; Peter Duignan and Clarence Clendenen, *The United States and the African Slave Trade 1619–1862* (Stanford Univ. Press, 1963), pp. 42–3.
[3] Soulsby, *op. cit.* pp. 78–88; Duignan and Clendenen, *op. cit.*, pp. 37–8.

first concern. As a result, the American squadron did little to reduce American participation in the transatlantic slave trade.[1] In February 1844 George H. Profitt, American minister in Rio de Janeiro, wrote to the American Secretary of State in Washington:

the slave traders laugh at our African squadron and more than one trader to the coast has openly avowed that he could sail round the frigate *Macedonia* three times in three miles, that they would not care if there were twenty such frigates on that coast, that they had never yet seen one of the American squadron although they had visited the coast for hundreds of miles and that the only cruisers they meet with are British and to them they have but to display American colours.[2]

Although the Conservative government in Britain never formally renounced their claim that British warships could at least exercise the right to visit vessels suspected of illegally hoisting the Stars and Stripes so as to avoid legitimate search, in practice it fell into disuse after the treaty of 1842 came into force; henceforth British naval officers were given strict instructions to approach vessels flying the American flag only when they were absolutely certain that they were not American.

Throughout the years 1843–5 British officers complained that their anti-slave trade efforts were being paralysed by the widespread use of the American flag.[3] Of the Brazilian slave trade Profitt wrote from Rio de Janeiro—with some little exaggeration:

it is a fact not to be disguised or denied that the slave trade is almost entirely carried on under our flag and in American built vessels sold here, chartered for the coast of Africa for slave traders. Indeed the scandalous traffic could not be carried on to any extent were it not for the use made of our flag, and the facilities given by the chartering of American vessels to carry to the coast of Africa the outfit for the trade and the materials for purchasing slaves.[4]

A year later, in February 1845, his successor Henry A. Wise, a Virginian and a friend of slavery (although at the same time an enemy of the slave trade) commented:

[1] Duignan and Clendenen, *op. cit.* pp. 38–9; Howard, *op. cit.* pp. 40–3 and Appendix E, 'The African Squadron'.   [2] Quoted in Hill, *op. cit.* p. 122.
[3] E.g. Foote (H.M.S. *Madagascar*) to Admiralty, 29 September 1843, F.O. 84/548; Commodore Jones (H.M.S. *Penelope*) to Admiralty, 31 December 1844, F.O. 84/609; Bosanquet (H.M.S. *Alert*) to Jones, 2 July 1845, F.O. 84/612.
[4] Quoted in Hill, *op. cit.* p. 121.

We are a 'byword among nations'—the only people who can now fetch and carry any and everything for the slave trade, without fear of English cruisers; and because we are the only people who can, are we to allow our proudest privilege to be perverted, and to pervert our own glorious flag into the pirate's flag—the slaver's protection—the Brazilian and Portuguese and Spanish passport to a criminal commerce against our own laws and the municipal laws of almost every civilised nation upon earth? . . . our flag alone can give the requisite protection against the right of visit, search and seizure and our citizens . . . are concerned in the business and partake of the profits of the African slave trade to and from the ports of Brazil, as fully as the Brazilians themselves and others, in conjunction with whom they carry it on. In fact, without the aid of our citizens and our flag it could not be carried on with success at all.[1]

Again the gravity of the situation was understandably exaggerated though clearly the refusal of the United States to concede a right of search treaty threatened to undermine the entire British preventive system.

In the meantime, the Brazilian flag had made a reappearance in the Brazilian slave trade and for a while afforded it an unexpected measure of protection. Many Brazilian and Portuguese traders who had come to recognise that they could no longer continue to use the Portuguese flag as they had done in the thirties, who felt that to sail without colours was too risky a business and who did not consider it worth the trouble and expense involved in securing American papers and colours (particularly since British cruisers for a time seemed fully prepared to search and capture Brazilian and Portuguese vessels which had simply assumed American nationality for slaving purposes) began to show a marked preference for the Brazilian flag. At first Brazilian colours and Brazilian papers simply ensured that, if captured leaving Brazil, a ship would be taken before the Anglo-Brazilian commission in Rio de Janeiro where there was at least a reasonable chance of acquittal. On the African coast, the Brazilian flag offered no more protection than the Portuguese if a ship were unfortunate enough—or slow enough—to be caught by a British cruiser: thanks to the absence of Brazilian commissioners, condemnation by the mixed com-

---

[1] Quoted in Hill, *op. cit.* p. 128.

mission sitting at Sierra Leone was as certain as in any British vice-admiralty court. At the beginning of October 1841, however, a new Brazilian commissary judge, José Hermenegildo Frederico Nitheroy, and a new commissioner of arbitration, Joaquim Tomás do Amaral, arrived in Sierra Leone and it was only a matter of time before the right of British cruisers under the terms of the Anglo-Brazilian treaties to capture Brazilian ships on the basis of their fittings alone (a right which had first been established in the case of the *Emprehendedor* two years previously, which was reaffirmed by the new Conservative government at the end of 1841, but which was still contested by Brazil[1]) was challenged in open court. On 9 December 1841 a prize crew from H.M.S. *Waterwitch* brought into Freetown the Brazilian *Ermelinda*, captured six weeks earlier off the coast of Angola. On the following day a prize crew from H.M.S. *Cygnet* brought in the Brazilian *Galianna*, captured two weeks before in the Bight of Benin. Both vessels came up before the Anglo-Brazilian commission and for the first time since 1831 there was a full complement of commissioners in court to deal with them. From the very outset—or so it seemed to Dr William Fergusson, the acting Governor of the colony, who was standing in for W. W. Lewis, the British commissary judge—Nitheroy assumed the role of adviser to, and counsel for, the Brazilian traders, and when he finally came to give his opinion he declared that since there were no slaves on board the ships had in each case been illegally detained. Fergusson on the other hand favoured the condemnation of both vessels: the case of the *Emprehendedor* constituted a precedent for such a decision and there was reason to assume the Brazilian government's tacit approval of subsequent condemnations by the Anglo-Brazilian commission since they had been informed of every verdict that the commission had reached and accepted half of the proceeds of every ship sold. The failure of the judges to agree meant that as both arbitrators were present it was necessary in both cases to draw lots for arbitration. When, on 11 January 1842, the English arbitrator, Michael Melville, won the toss the *Galianna* was condemned. When, on 20 January, the Brazilian Tomás do Amaral won, the *Ermelinda*, almost identical in terms

[1] Canning to Admiralty, 23 December 1841, F.O. 84/385.

of its fittings, was released.[1] It was a most unsatisfactory outcome which led to a noticeable increase in the use of the Brazilian flag and which seriously undermined the confidence of British naval officers in the Anglo-Brazilian commission at Sierra Leone.

It was June 1842 before another Brazilian ship, the *Santo Antonio*, was brought before the mixed commission. By this time neither of the Brazilian commissioners was in Freetown: Nitheroy had gone to the Canaries for health reasons in May; at about the same time Amaral also left for reasons that are not clear—never to return. The British commissioners therefore speedily dealt with and condemned the *Santo Antonio*.[2] They went on to condemn three more Brazilian ships before the end of 1842 and three more early in 1843—none of them actually carrying slaves. On his return to Sierra Leone in May 1843, however, Nitheroy again made it clear that he had never been instructed to accept the British interpretation of the Anglo-Brazilian abolition treaty; moreover, he not only believed that such instructions would never be issued, but even if they were, he declared, he personally would ignore them, continue to adjudicate upon cases in the light of his own interpretation of the treaty, and indict before the Brazilian Chamber of Deputies any minister responsible for their issue.[3] Clearly there was a danger of open dispute in the mixed court every time a Brazilian ship suspected of intending to trade in slaves was captured by a British cruiser. Under the 'toss-up' system condemnation or liberation would in every case depend on chance with the result that Brazilian slave ships were bound to be released and British naval officers further deterred from detaining slave ships flying the Brazilian flag except where they were caught in the act of transporting slaves. The British commissioners therefore suggested to Lord Aberdeen that a case should be submitted to arbitration only when the two judges differed about the nationality or the character of a ship.[4] In September 1843, on Sir John Dodson's

---

1 Fergusson and Melville to Aberdeen, Brazil no. 3, 13 January, no. 10, 25 January 1842, F.O. 84/391. In London Sir John Dodson agreed with Fergusson that the *Ermelinda* should have been condemned (Dodson to Aberdeen, 27 September 1842, F.O. 83/2350).
2 Melville and Hook to Aberdeen, Brazil no. 86, 31 December 1842 (report on 1842), F.O. 84/393.
3 Nitheroy, 5 July 1843, enclosed in Melville to Aberdeen, Brazil, separate, 18 February 1844, F.O. 84/504.
4 McDonald and Hook, Brazil no. 24, 28 June 1843, F.O. 84/449.

advice, Aberdeen specifically instructed British commissioners to 'resist the call for arbitration' in cases where a Brazilian ship was found to be equipped for slaving purposes; all Brazilian slavers, he agreed, were engaged in an illegal trade and were therefore liable to capture and to condemnation.[1] The decision was regarded by the British officials in the court at Sierra Leone as one of great consequence for the future of the Brazilian slave trade, 'a wound from which we hope it will never recover'. In their annual report for 1843 they enthused over 'this noble instruction' which they described as 'one of the most important events in the annals of abolition'.[2] The truth was, however, that little real progress had been made. The British commissary judge soon realised what should have been obvious all along that since he could not pass sentence on a captured slaver without the concurrence of his Brazilian colleague an absolute refusal on his part to go to arbitration in disputed cases would simply mean that they would be frozen until the two governments came to some agreement over the equipment clause.[3]

Fortunately, the problem arose only when a refusal by a Brazilian judge to condemn a Brazilian slave ship on the basis of its appearance and fittings coincided with the presence in court of a Brazilian arbitrator. This had been the situation in the winter of 1841–2 when the *Galianna* was condemned and the *Ermelinda* acquitted. In fact it never recurred. When during the summer of 1843 the Brazilian ships *Confidencia*, captured in March by H.M.S. *Lily* off Quelimane on the east African coast, and *Esperança*, captured in May by H.M.S. *Spy* off Little Popo, arrived in Freetown as prizes both commissary judges were present and failed to agree on a verdict. The British judge, however, was perfectly willing to accept arbitration since the Brazilian arbitrator was still absent from the court, as he had been since May of the previous year. The casting vote automatically went to the British arbitrator who, without hesitation, condemned both ships.[4] In the autumn of 1843

---

[1] Aberdeen to Sierra Leone commissioners, no. 14, 11 September 1843, F.O. 84/448.
[2] H.M. commissioners to Foote, senior naval officer, 6 November 1843, enclosed in Melville 18 February 1844; McDonald and Hook, Brazil no. 82, 31 December 1843 (report on 1843), F.O. 84/450.
[3] Melville 18 February 1844; Dodson to Aberdeen, 11 May 1844, F.O. 83/2352.
[4] McDonald and Hook no. 82.

Nitheroy took a further two months leave. He returned to learn of the instructions Lord Aberdeen had issued on the question of arbitration and, considering his judicial functions would be seriously impaired, resigned his post on 9 November.[1] Once again Brazil had no representative in the mixed court to contest the legality of British captures. During the winter of 1843-4 more than a dozen Brazilian ships came before the mixed court—only three of them carrying slaves. Acting alone the British judge and the British arbitrator condemned all except two, the *Conceição Flora* and the *Prudencia*, which they released for lack of sufficient proof of their criminal intentions.[2] Two acquittals within a few months suggest that British officials did not summarily condemn all the Brazilian ships brought before them.

In May 1844, to the consternation of both British commissioners and British naval officers, Manuel de Oliveira Santos, who had been Brazilian commissioner of arbitration in the mid-thirties, returned to Sierra Leone in the same capacity empowered, if necessary, to act as commissary judge. In the event there was again no need for alarm. Remarkably, Oliveira Santos seems not to have received any clear instructions from the Brazilian government as to how he should act and in the first case to come before the court—that of the slave ship *Izabel* captured by H.M.S. *Larne*—he allowed himself to be guided throughout the whole proceedings by Michael Melville, the new British commissary judge, whom he knew well from his previous stay in Freetown. After a hearing lasting only eight days the ship was condemned unanimously even though there was nothing to indicate that slaves had ever been near her.[3] It was the first time that a Brazilian judge had condemned a Brazilian ship on the strength of its equipment alone. In his routine despatches Melville treated the verdict as a matter of course, but, privately, he expressed to James Bandinel at the Slave Trade Department at the Foreign Office his elation at achieving the break-through for which they had been hoping. It was, he thought, the most remarkable event of the year.[4]

[1] Melville and Hook, Brazil no. 52, 10 November 1843, F.O. 84/450.
[2] McDonald and Hook, Brazil no. 82; Melville and Hook to Aberdeen, Brazil no. 102, 31 December 1844 (report on 1844), F.O. 84/507.
[3] Melville and Hook, Brazil no. 102.
[4] Melville to Bandinel, 21 August 1844, Private, F.O. 84/504.

Britain and the slave trade, 1839-1845

In September and November 1844 Oliveira Santos condemned two more Brazilian ships equipped for the slave trade—the *Aventureiro* and the *Virginia*—besides two which had been captured carrying slaves.[1] It was at this point that he learnt to his consternation that the Brazilian minister in London, José Marques Lisboa, had forcibly denied that the Brazilian government had ever, even tacitly, acceded to the principle that *all* Brazilian slave ships were liable to condemnation by the mixed commissions.[2] During the winter of 1844-5 six Brazilian ships accused of intending to trade in slaves were brought before the Freetown court. Oliveira Santos was absent for the adjudication of one case—that of the *Esperança* (previously condemned in June 1842 as the *Santo Antonio*)—and there was no delay in bringing in a verdict of guilty. On every other occasion, however, he failed to agree with the British judge and gave a verdict in favour of acquittal. Until they actually took slaves on board, he now argued, there was bound to be serious doubt about the intentions of these and similar ships and he went on to accuse Britain of trying to ruin Brazil's legitimate trade with Africa. But since no other Brazilian official was present in the court the British judge could still afford to agree to arbitration and the five Brazilian ships were condemned on the casting vote of James Hook, the British arbitrator.[3] Before leaving Sierra Leone on 1 April 1845 suffering from fever and what a medical certificate described as 'Dry Belly Ake' Oliveira Santos reaffirmed his belief that no verdict other than 'not guilty' should be brought in against Brazilian ships captured before they had shipped any slaves. And from London on 5 August he actually retracted the verdicts he had given in such cases in the past.[4] Conversations with Lisboa had served to persuade him that he had been mistaken in letting himself be guided by precedents which had been established in the Anglo-Brazilian mixed commission in the absence of a Brazilian commissioner and without the sanction of the Brazilian government.

[1] Melville and Hook, Brazil no. 102.
[2] Lisboa to Aberdeen, 27 June 1844, F.O. 84/524.
[3] Melville and Hook, Brazil no. 102; Melville and Hook, Brazil no. 133, 31 December 1845 (report on 1845), F.O. 84/560.
[4] Melville and Hook, Brazil no. 29, 2 April 1845, F.O. 84/558; Oliveira Santos to França Ferreira (Brazilian Foreign Minister), 24 May 1845, A.H.I. 57/2; Melville and Hook, Brazil no. 116, 8 October 1845, F.O. 84/560.

In the meantime, some important decisions had been taken in London about the future of Britain's anti-slave trade campaign. In December 1842 the Conservative government had set up a commission consisting of Stephen Lushington, James Bandinel, Captain Joseph Denman and William Rothery whose task it was to look into the overall role of the British navy in the suppression of the slave trade, to make recommendations as to the tactics it should employ and to draw up new and comprehensive instructions for the guidance of British naval officers. Their report, which was ready by the spring of 1844, recommended a much greater effort on the west African coast and the more systematic adoption by the West African squadron of inshore cruising and blockading tactics like those pursued during the years 1840–2—though with a rather less cavalier attitude towards legality.[1] In accepting these recommendations the government agreed to increase the number of ships on the West African station to the greatest possible extent with the result that during the next twelve months the squadron was almost doubled. By 1845 it consisted of twenty-one ships, including seven steamers—the flagship *Penelope*, the *Gorgon*, the *Hydra*, the *Growler*, the *Ardent*, the *Albert* and the *Prometheus* (not all of them suitable for the anti-slave trade patrol, however) and a few fast sloops and Symondite brigs.[2] (And following a successful cruise by the *Cleopatra* in 1842 a greater number of ships of the Cape squadron were despatched on anti-slave trade patrol along the east coast of Africa.[3]) The full impact of these changes began to be felt during the period immediately following the departure of Oliveira Santos from Sierra Leone in April 1845. The British West African squadron enjoyed a greater degree of success than for some years past: in less than four months fifteen Brazilian ships were brought before the Anglo-Brazilian mixed commission—all

---

[1] B.M. Add. MSS 40453 (Peel Papers). One outcome of the commission's report was the compilation, long overdue, of a digest of anti-slave trade treaties, acts, instructions etc., which could be issued in book form to naval officers engaged in the suppression of the trade: *Instructions for the Guidance of Her Majesty's Naval Officers Employed in the Suppression of the Slave Trade* (London, 1844).

[2] Lloyd, *op. cit.* p. 101 and Appendix C. The West African squadron was still concentrated north of the equator, however: 2 ships north of Sierra Leone, 6 between Sierra Leone and Gallinas, 4 in the Bights, 4 in the Congo, 2 at Benguela (Jones to Admiralty, 28 August 1845, F.O. 84/612).

[3] For the British Navy's anti-slave trade patrol of the east African coast, see G. S. Graham, *Great Britain in the Indian Ocean* (Oxford, 1967), p. 134 ff.

of them captured before they had taken any slaves on board—
and all of them were condemned by the British commissioners.[1]
It was at this point, however, in August 1845, that the mixed
commission was declared no longer competent to adjudicate upon
captured slave vessels and the whole question of the British
navy's rights *vis-a-vis* Brazilian slave ships was once again thrown
wide open.[2]

Across the Atlantic British warships stationed on the coast of
Brazil played a secondary role in the suppression of the Brazilian
slave trade during the period after 1839, as they had done throughout the eighteen thirties. When, at the end of 1839, the navy's
anti-slave trade powers were first extended, the bulk of the squadron on the east coast of the South American station (which for a
brief period during 1840–1 was combined with the Cape station
under Rear Admiral Sir Edward King) had been, or was about to
be, despatched to the Río de la Plata for the purpose of protecting
British commercial interests in the area and keeping the peace
which Juan Manuel de Rosas, the Argentinian dictator (1835–52),
seemed intent on disturbing. And it was to remain there for the
best part of a decade.[3] Repeated demands from the British legation
and from the British commissioners in Rio de Janeiro, and on one
notable occasion in October 1841 from a former Brazilian first
minister, Antônio Carlos de Andrada,[4] for the systematic patrol of
the Brazilian coast by a permanent British preventive squadron
went unheeded in London. During the early forties three or four
cruisers were from time to time available to protect British
interests in Brazil during what W. G. Ouseley, the British *chargé*
in Rio liked to call 'these ticklish times' (a reference to the fact that
the central government had still not yet asserted its authority over

[1] Melville and Hook, Brazil no. 133.
[2] See below, ch. 9.
[3] For the political struggle in Uruguay between Colorados and Blancos during the
thirties and forties, the interference of Rosas and Anglo-French intervention in the
interests of political stability and trade, see, for example, John F. Cady, *Foreign Intervention
in the Río de la Plata, 1838–1850* (Univ. of Pennsylvania Press, 1929), *passim*, and H. S.
Ferns, *Britain and Argentina in the Nineteenth Century* (Oxford, 1960), pp. 240–80.
[4] Hamilton to Aberdeen, no. 12, 20 October 1841, F.O. 84/366. News of the Andrada-
Hamilton interview caused a political scandal in Brazil; see A. C. Tavares Bastos, *Cartas
do Solitário* (Rio de Janeiro, 1863), p. 174.

all parts of the vast country and provincial revolts were still not uncommon) and, incidentally, to keep a look out for slave ships. From the very outset, however, they were subjected to restrictions of a kind that warships on the other side of the Atlantic experienced only after 1842. For example, the British navy could not institute a blockade of the Brazilian coast without interfering with the legitimate coastal trade which bound together Brazil's geographically isolated provinces and without violating Brazilian territorial waters. There was also the problem of local Brazilian civil and military authorities who, apart from the fact of their protecting or conniving at the trade, were bound to resent any infringement of Brazil's rights as an independent state; where they were able to do so they could reasonably be expected to repel British cruisers—by force. Moreover, in the case of vessels captured on the Brazilian coast condemnation was much less certain in the mixed court at Rio de Janeiro than it was in the mixed court at Sierra Leone. Unlike Freetown, there was always a Brazilian commissary judge present in Rio and, as the case of the *Recuperador* had clearly shown in 1839, where a Brazilian vessel was taken outward bound and in the absence of any conclusive proof of its guilt, circumstantial evidence of its intention of trading in slaves would have to be overwhelming to convince a Brazilian judge of its criminal character. For him, no single piece of slaving equipment could justify the condemnation of a ship captured off the Brazilian coast where hundreds of vessels were daily engaged in perfectly legitimate trading activities. Furthermore, despite the precedent of the *Maria Carlota*, the Brazilian judge could be expected always to dispute the legality of the capture itself in such cases. Nor could British naval officers rely with any confidence upon the support of Sir George Jackson, the British commissary judge. In 1838, he had been criticised by Lord Palmerston for his acquiescence in the release of the *Flor de Loanda* and, more recently, severely reprimanded and threatened with recall for his verdict on the *Recuperador*. W. G. Ouseley, Robert Hesketh, the British consul, and more than one naval officer had all commented on his querulous, unstable temperament and complained of his dilatory conduct in court. It was also said—although never entirely substantiated—that like Carneiro de Campos he accepted bribes from the traders, that the Brazilian judge had 'a complete and powerful influence over him' and that he himself employed, and ill-treated, liberated slaves. He was, Ouseley wrote, 'more than a little cracked . . . it is a pity that he should be here now. We should have crushed the rascals completely with almost any sane Commission . . . as long as he is in the Commission here, all our difficulties will be doubled'. And, with a touch of malice, he added, 'Nor do I think he wishes to put an end to the slave trade, his occupation would be gone perhaps he thinks.'[1] Perhaps the complaints and the malicious rumours surrounding Jackson arose simply from a desire to get rid of a man who, despite his conduct in the *Maria Carlota* case, had in truth shown himself too scrupulous in discharging his judicial functions, neither sufficiently sympathetic towards the captors nor hostile enough towards the captured. Certainly his presence in Rio was another good reason why British naval officers on the South American station were reluctant to seize Brazilian slave ships. At the same time, because of their proximity to the headquarters of the slave trade, any captures which the British navy was able to make could be expected to have a singularly dramatic impact on the trade. In the event, British naval operations on the Brazilian coast during the years 1840–2 did play a part—if only a small part—in reducing the Brazilian slave trade to its lowest level for almost a decade. Whether, in view of the resentment and hostility they aroused in Brazil, they made it more difficult in the long run for the Brazilian government to co-operate with Britain in suppressing the trade remains an open question.

The *Congresso* detained in January 1840 by H.M.S. *Wizard* a few miles outside Rio harbour was the first ship to be picked up as it left the Brazilian coast for Africa after the navy had received its new instructions to search and capture *all* Brazilian and Portuguese slave vessels. A few months earlier the *Congresso*, which had hoisted the Portuguese flag, would undoubtedly have been taken before the Anglo-Brazilian mixed commission in Rio de Janeiro where the captors would have attempted to prove it Brazilian. As a result

[1] Ouseley to Palmerston, 15 November 1839, Private and Conf., F.O. 84/288; Ouseley to Palmerston, 9 January 1840, Private, F.O. 84/323; Ouseley 17 April 1841, Private, Secret and Conf., F.O. 84/364; Ouseley 6 May 1841, Private and Conf, F.O. 84/365. See also 'Memorandum on the causes leading to Jackson's removal from Rio', 13 March 1842, F.O. 84/445 (in July 1841 Palmerston had decided to transfer Jackson to Surinam).

of the Palmerston Act, however, it was now more expedient to accept a ship's apparent Portuguese character at its face value, even where it would have been easy to prove it Brazilian, or to prove that it was not legally entitled to claim any nationality, so that it might be taken before a British vice-admiralty court where condemnation was more certain and, even allowing for another transatlantic voyage, more rapid than in the Rio de Janeiro mixed court. W. G. Ouseley and Captain Freemantle, the senior naval officer on the Brazilian coast, therefore decided to send the *Congresso* to the vice-admiralty court sitting at the Cape of Good Hope.[1] Four other slave ships captured during the early months of 1840—the *Saudade*, the *Roza*, the *Treze de Junho* and the *Tentador* —could also have been taken before the mixed commission in Rio, but instead were despatched with prize crews to British vice-admiralty courts, three to the Cape and one to Barbados.[2] It was originally the intention of both Ouseley and the captain of the *Wizard* to send the *Tentador* at least to Rio, since it was known to have actually landed a cargo of slaves, but as the capture had been made inside Brazilian territorial waters, they finally decided that fewer difficulties would arise if this case like the others were to come before a British vice-admiralty court.

These proceedings did not fail to arouse comment. Figuanière e Morão, the Portuguese minister in Rio de Janeiro, protested to Ouseley about the illegal captures of Portuguese ships by British cruisers 'acting like freebooters' and to the Brazilian Foreign Minister, Caetano Maria Lopes Gama, for his failure to prevent 'violent and illegal acts considered piratical' in Brazilian waters. In particular, Figuanière called for the punishment of the commanders of two Brazilian warships and of the Santa Cruz fortress (which stood at the entrance of Rio harbour) for failing to prevent the British 'attack' on the *Saudade* after it had been cleared by Brazilian customs officials.[3] Lopes Gama, however, no friend of

---

[1] Freemantle to Ouseley, 18 January, Ouseley to Freemantle, 19 January, Ouseley to Rear Admiral George Elliot (commander-in-chief on the Cape and West African naval station), 19 January, enclosed in Ouseley to Palmerston, no. 6, 17 February 1840, F.O. 84/323.

[2] Ouseley no. 7, 17 February 1840, F.O. 84/323; Ouseley no. 23, 28 May, no. 25, 1 June 1840, F.O. 84/324. All five ships were condemned.

[3] Figuanière to Ouseley, 28 January, Figuanière to Lopes Gama, 22 January, 4 February, enclosed in Ouseley no. 6, 17 February 1840, F.O. 84/323.

the slave trade, managed to maintain tolerably good relations with the British legation throughout his period of office (September 1839 to July 1840); and although in his *Relatório* of May 1840 he deplored the deterioration which had taken place in Anglo-Portuguese relations as a result of the passage of the Palmerston Act, he considered that the operation of the Act in no way affected Brazil.[1] His successors, however, adopted a much tougher attitude towards British naval action on the Brazilian coast: Aureliano de Souza e Oliveira Coutinho, for example, Foreign Minister in the Cabinet of the Majority and in the Conservative Cabinet which succeeded it in March 1841, was concerned lest some of the ships, ostensibly Portuguese, which British naval officers were now despatching to British vice-admiralty courts—there were seven more such cases in 1841—might in fact be Brazilian. Moreover, one at least had been taken inside Brazilian territorial waters. In August 1841, Aureliano supported the action of the commander of the Santa Cruz fortress in firing on H.M.S. *Grecian* in the very act of towing the Portuguese slaver *Constante* out of Rio harbour, prior to sending it to the Cape. After an investigation, however, he announced in November 1841 that Brazil was in no way responsible for either the *Constante* or any other ship recently seized by a British cruiser under the authority of the Palmerston Act.[2]

The majority of slave ships encountered by the British navy off the coast of Brazil during this period, however, had either adopted American colours, and could not without risk be touched, or else sailed under the Brazilian flag in order that they would have to be taken before the mixed commission in Rio where there was always a good chance of acquittal. (Only after 1842, as we have seen, when a Brazilian commissioner was occasionally present in Freetown, did the Brazilian flag afford a measure of protection on the African coast as well.) Indeed it was not unknown for the owner of a ship taken as it left Brazil to offer the captors large sums of money if they would promise to take their prize before the

[1] *Relatório do Ministério dos Negócios Estrangeiros* (Rio de Janeiro, May 1840).
[2] *Relatório do Ministério dos Negócios Estrangeiros* (Rio de Janeiro, May 1841); Aureliano to Ouseley, 20 August, enclosed in Hamilton to Aberdeen, no. 6, Conf., 20 October 1841; report of speech by Aureliano in Senate, 3 November, enclosed in Hamilton no. 15, 29 November 1841, F.O. 84/367.

mixed commission in Rio instead of a British vice-admiralty court. During the two years 1840–1 seven Brazilian ships were captured by cruisers of the South American squadron and taken into Rio as British prizes. Three, the *Dom João de Castro* which had already landed its cargo, the *Paquete de Benguela* with 280 slaves on board and the *Asseiceira* with 332 slaves, were condemned, although only after the usual delays; for example, thirteen weeks elapsed before the mixed court gave its verdict on the *Dom João de Castro*.[1] The remaining four—the *Alexandre*, the *Nova Aurora*, the *Castro* and the *Convenção*—all of which had been seized as they were leaving Brazilian ports for Africa were restored to their owners and in three cases awarded damages: there was insufficient evidence of their criminal character and it was agreed that they were probably engaged in the Brazilian coastal trade.[2] Four acquittals by the Rio mixed commission within a period of twelve months were hardly calculated to increase the enthusiasm of British naval officers for the chase. Furthermore, while Carneiro de Campos, the Brazilian judge, had taken cognisance of every case brought before him, he had made it clear that he rejected the British view of the anti-slave trade treaties and made a point of protesting at what he regarded as the illegal capture of Brazilian ships on account of their equipment alone.

In making these relatively few captures (several of which turned out to be mistaken) British warships visited and searched a great many innocent Brazilian ships as they left Brazilian ports; the steamer *Ardent*, for example, was said to have searched a total of fifty-four ships during a ten day visit she paid to Bahia and

[1] On the *Dom João de Castro*, Jackson and Grigg, no. 67, 15 November, no. 75, 21 December 1839, F.O. 84/277; Jackson and Grigg, no. 8, 31 January 1840, F.O. 84/314; Ouseley no. 16, 24 March 1840, F.O. 84/323. On the *Paquete de Benguela*, Jackson and Grigg, no. 2, 2 January 1841, F.O. 84/350. On the *Asseiceira*, Jackson and Grigg, no. 34, 9 July 1841, F.O. 84/351.

[2] On the *Alexandre*, Jackson and Grigg, no. 2; Ouseley 17 April 1841, Private, Secret and Conf., F.O. 84/364. On the *Nova Aurora*, Jackson and Grigg, no. 16, 17 April 1841, F.O. 84/350; Jackson and Grigg, no. 34. On the *Castro* Jackson and Grigg no. 34. Dodson approved the verdict (Dodson to Aberdeen, 13 September 1841, F.O. 83/2349). He confirmed the right of British warships to detain Brazilian ships equipped for the slave trade—*but not in Brazilian territorial waters*. On the *Convenção* Hesketh and Grigg, no. 3, 15 January 1842, F.O. 84/397; Hamilton no. 2, 18 January 1842, F.O. 84/406. After some hesitation Dodson withheld approval of the *Convenção*'s acquittal (Dodson to Aberdeen, 31 May 1842, F.O. 83/2350), but given the complexities of the case Grigg was not reprimanded.

Pernambuco at the beginning of 1842.[1] Some of these searches took place in Brazilian territorial waters and indeed in Rio harbour itself, within sight of the fort at Santa Cruz and of Brazilian warships; occasionally shots were fired; vessels were boarded by force; masters and crews were, it was alleged, insulted and treated like prisoners; hatches were forced open and cargoes brought on deck; seals of official despatches were broken. As a result, British naval officers—and British commissioners—were subjected to 'the most virulent calumnies and abuse' and personal threats of assault', which, Ouseley advised, should be treated 'with entire contempt'.[2] The Brazilian Foreign Minister himself repeatedly protested at what virtually amounted to a British blockade of Rio de Janeiro and neighbouring ports.[3]

More serious still were the direct clashes which took place between Brazilian local authorities and the armed boats which British cruisers sent on anti-slave trade patrol amongst the off-shore islands, along the coast and sometimes up river as well. Typical of these was an incident involving H.M.S. *Clio*.[4] On 12 May 1841, the captain sent a boat with a crew of twelve men under Lieutenant Cox to cruise amongst the Piumas Islands (half a mile from the Brazilian coast near Campos), well known as a favourite spot for landing slaves. Lieutenant Cox had strict instructions not to give any offence to the inhabitants of the islands and not to become involved in any dispute with them: at the first signs of opposition he was to retire. On their first day out, his crew boarded and seized a brig with 300 slaves on board, but six or seven small craft, each carrying a dozen men, set out from one of the islands, attacked the British boat and wounded four British seamen. They succeeded in releasing and subsequently destroying the captured slave ship. When, a week later, the British boat put into Campos for water and provisions, Lieutenant Cox and his crew found themselves detained by the local authorities, accused of piracy, publicly exposed to the insults of a violent mob—which

---

[1] Cowper (consul in Pernambuco) to Aberdeen, no. 3, 31 March 1842, F.O. 84/411.
[2] Ouseley to Palmerston, no. 61, 24 May 1841, F.O. 84/365.
[3] E.g. Aureliano to Ouseley, 3 July, enclosed in Hamilton to Aberdeen no. 6, 20 October 1841, F.O. 84/366.
[4] Ouseley to Palmerston, no. 65, 15 June 1841, F.O. 84/365; Admiralty memorandum, 7 September 1841, F.O. 84/385.

was demanding their lives—and eventually imprisoned in irons. The news soon reached Rio de Janeiro where Ouseley was, as usual, eager to take 'prompt and strong measures' and, what is more, he did so, causing in Rio the 'satisfactory and salutary sensation' he sought by despatching all available British warships to Campos. In fact, their presence was unnecessary, since the Brazilian government had already ordered the release of the British seamen after they had spent a week in prison. Aureliano expressed regret at the 'disagreeable occurrence' at Campos, but nevertheless took the opportunity of reminding Ouseley that it was the direct result of an act of violence in Brazilian territorial waters by a British boat which, like too many others, failed to confine its activities within the terms of the Anglo-Brazilian anti-slave trade treaty.[1] In the case in question, the English lieutenant had not even had the courtesy to inform the authorities in Campos why he was present in the area and why he was proposing to send men ashore. 'I would prefer', Aureliano wrote to Ouseley, 'that Brazil should be erased from the list of nations rather than she should subject herself to the disgraceful tutelage of another which should arrogate to itself the right of interfering imperiously in the internal administration of my country.'[2] For his part, Ouseley was not prepared to let the matter drop. He thanked Aureliano for his prompt intervention on behalf of Lieutenant Cox and his men, but strongly deplored the hostile attitude of the Brazilian local authorities in general 'who seemed to think . . . that they are authorised to consider themselves as at war with English officers and subjects'. And, typically, Ouseley concluded with a threat: in future, he wrote, British naval officers would be justified in considering 'all subaltern authorities guilty of such outrages as having *ipso facto* forfeited their title to be treated as belonging to a civilised government'.[3] When news of the incident finally reached London, Lord Palmerston fully supported all that Ouseley had said and done. He had already (in August) instructed Hamilton Hamilton, who was returning to Brazil as British minister after more than three years' leave, to demand the punishment of those who

[1] Aureliano to Ouseley, 24 May, enclosed in Ouseley no. 65.
[2] Aureliano to Ouseley, 31 May, enclosed in Ouseley no. 65.
[3] Ouseley to Aureliano, 4 June, enclosed in Ouseley no. 79, 7 July 1841, F.O. 84/365.

had attacked the British boat and of the local authorities at Campos who had committed the alleged outrage against a British officer and British seamen: if the Brazilian government could not, or would not, afford redress, then Hamilton was told to warn the Brazilian government that the British navy would in future be ordered to 'treat the people on the coast who may commit such acts as pirates or *banditti* subject to no law and obeying no legal authority'.[1]

Nevertheless, clashes with the Brazilian authorities along the coast continued to occur as British boats patrolled Brazilian territorial waters, occasionally occupying offshore islands and sometimes landing men in pursuit of the traders and their slaves. Insults and shots were exchanged, English seamen were wounded and occasionally they ended up in prison. Several of the crew of H.M.S. *Rose*, for example, were seized by the Campos authorities in March 1842, and in July of the same year one of the *Fantome's* boats was attacked whilst at anchor near Ilha Grande. In November there were incidents at Santos involving the officers and men of H.M.S. *Curlew* and at Macaé where a boat belonging to the *Partridge* tried to detain the slaver *Leopoldina* under the batteries of the local fort.[2] Each incident was magnified by interested parties in the Brazilian legislature, in the provincial assemblies and in the press, in order to inflame still further Brazilian opinion which was becoming increasingly anti-British. Indeed some authorities were not above inventing offences in order to excite ill-feeling. Thus, outraged national sentiment was successfully grafted on to economic interest in defence of the slave trade. Aureliano put the blame for the incidents on the British officers who, despite the fact that there had been no formal declaration of war, abused their already excessive powers, affected 'the manners and the language of enemies' and engaged in 'absolute hostilities'. It was not surprising, therefore, that they were sometimes treated as such. Britain's campaign for the suppression of the illegal Brazilian slave trade, Aureliano had written to Hamilton in January 1842,

[1] Palmerston to Hamilton, no. 37, 26 August, 1841, F.O. 84/366, based on memorandum of 12 August (F.O. 84/365).
[2] For a discussion of these and other incidents, see Hamilton to Paulino, 1 September 1843, enclosed in Hamilton to Aberdeen, no. 9, 27 February 1844, F.O. 84/523.

ought not to be transformed by a false or excessive zeal into a covert war against a nation which on the question of the trade especially is the ally and not the adversary of England, and which it cannot be supposed has embraced this cause with the intention of becoming its victim or of being treated with a rigour which could not be tolerable on the part of a declared enemy.[1]

Hamilton for his part voiced the British government's anger at, first, the behaviour of the local civil and military authorities who, by opposing the British navy's anti-slaving operations, were in fact defending the slave trade, and secondly, the laxity of the central government who, by refusing to punish them, were 'accessories after the fact'. While ever the Brazilian authorities refused to fulfil their treaty engagements and allowed increasing numbers of illegal slave ships to go to and from Brazilian ports under cover of the coastal trade, there were bound to be occasional disputes and cases of mistaken search and capture, he said, unless the British navy were to abandon the patrol of the Brazilian coast altogether.[2]

The British legation in Rio de Janeiro was now being regularly supplied with reliable information on the movements of slave ships in and out of Brazilian ports. In December 1840 'a person high in the Imperial administration' had recommended to Ouseley a young man, formerly a first mate in the Brazilian mercantile marine and with some slaving experience, who was capable of furnishing valuable information on the slave trade and who, for both humanitarian and financial motives, was prepared to work for the legation. Privately, he was put in touch with individual naval officers and most of the captures made during 1841 resulted from information he had supplied for which he was paid a percentage of the prize money on the vessels condemned. During 1842, as the slave trade began to revive, the British government also agreed to pay him a monthly salary.[3] But there were now too few

[1] Aureliano to Hamilton, 15 January, enclosed in Hamilton no. 14, 22 February 1842, F.O. 84/406.
[2] Hamilton to Aureliano, 18 July, enclosed in Hamilton no. 88, 12 October 1842, F.O. 84/408.
[3] Gordon memorandum, 21 November, enclosed in Hamilton no. 17, Secret, 29 November, 1841, F.O. 84/367; Aberdeen to Hamilton, no. 3, 2 March 1842, F.O. 84/410; Hamilton no 42, Secret, 20 September 1842, F.O. 84/408.

British cruisers available for anti-slave trade duties for really effective use to be made of him. From 1842 the small British naval force on the Brazilian coast, already hopelessly inadequate for the job in hand, was further depleted by the transfer of ships to the Río de la Plata—and across the Atlantic when the decision was taken to strengthen the West African squadron—with the result that there were times when only one vessel was stationed on the entire coast of Brazil.[1] Moreover, British naval officers were by now understandably reluctant to seize Brazilian ships which were not actually carrying slaves. Most of the empty slave vessels detained by British cruisers—three in 1842 and six in 1843—were said to have no nationality and were despatched to British vice-admiralty courts. Some of these, like the *Vencedora* captured by one of H.M.S. *Frolic's* boats in September 1843, were unquestionably Brazilian and should have been adjudicated by the mixed commission at Rio de Janeiro. In the course of 1842 only one ship, the *Aracaty*, came before the commission—and that had been captured by a Brazilian cruiser, the *Fidelidade*, after landing its cargo of slaves in Alagoas; it was condemned in July 1842 after Pereira da Silva, the Brazilian proctor and a man who repeatedly denounced 'the exaggerated pretensions and continued insults of Britain' in the Rio provincial assembly, had made an extraordinarily spirited, if unsuccessful, bid to persuade the commission that it was not competent to adjudicate upon Brazilian prizes, particularly those captured inside Brazilian territorial waters.[2] During the three years 1842–4 only three British prizes came before the Anglo-Brazilian commission in Rio de Janeiro—the *Dous Amigos*, the *Bom Destino* and the *Nova Granada*—and of these only the second, captured in September 1843 by H.M.S. *Racer* off Bahia after it had landed a cargo of slaves, was condemned.[3]

---

[1] As early as August 1841 Rear Admiral Sir Edward King had recommended that the navy concentrate all its efforts on the west African coast (King to Admiralty, 7 August 1841, F.O. 84/385). Hamilton deeply regretted the decision to strengthen the West African squadron alone in 1844 (Hamilton no. 20, 18 May 1844, F.O. 84/528).

[2] Hesketh and Grigg, no. 22, 1 August 1842, F.O. 84/397. One particularly violent speech of Pereira da Silva's was reported in Hesketh and Grigg, 20 April 1842, Conf., F.O. 84/394 and Hamilton no. 32, 23 April 1842, F.O. 13/180. Pereira da Silva later wrote a number of historical works, including *Historia da Fundação do Imperio Brasileiro* (7 vols., Rio, 1864), *Historia do Brazil durante a minoridade de Dom Pedro II* (Rio, 1888) and *Memorias do Meu Tempo* (2 vols., Rio, 1898).

[3] Samo and Grigg, no. 3, 5 January 1844, F.O. 84/510.

The capture of the *Dous Amigos* brought the issue of captures in Brazilian territorial waters to a head. In June 1843 the *Curlew*'s boats had followed the Brazilian brig out of Rio harbour and immediately detained her. After the two judges in the mixed court had disagreed about the precise place of capture, the Brazilian arbitrator won the toss and released the ship on the grounds that, in violation of article 2 of the treaty of 1817, it had been captured in territorial waters.[1] Six months later, H.M.S. *Dolphin* took the *Maria Theresa* at anchor off the Porcos Islands near Ubatuba; the ship appeared to be Brazilian but Commander Hoare was dissatisfied with its papers and sent it to the vice-admiralty court sitting in British Guiana where in due course it was condemned.[2] (On a visit to Bahia later the same year, Hoare was warned not to go ashore: three thousand dollars had been offered to anyone who succeeded in knifing him.[3]) In January 1844, incensed by these latest incidents, the Brazilian Foreign Minister, Paulino José Soares de Sousa, delivered one of the strongest protests Brazil had so far made against the 'clear and manifest violation of the treaties' and of the law of the nations by the British navy and 'the violation of its [Brazil's] rights and the outrages practised upon it'. He deplored the capture of Brazilian vessels merely on the suspicion that they intended to engage in the slave trade, the despatch of Brazilian ships to British tribunals and, most of all, the interference of the British navy in territorial waters where under International Law the Brazilian authorities alone had the right to exercise jurisdiction. This right was, he said, 'an indispensable guarantee of the territory of the Empire; without it the latter would not exist and as often as it be violated that independence will also be violated'. The British navy continued to act on the Brazilian coast, he went on, in a way that since Aberdeen's letter to the Admiralty of May 1842 was not even sanctioned on the coast of west Africa. And he

[1] Samo and Grigg, no. 26, 18 July 1843, F.O. 84/453.
[2] Hamilton no. 10, 27 February 1844, F.O. 84/523.
[3] *P.P.* 1847-8, xxii (536), House of Commons Select Committee on the Slave Trade, 3rd Report, Hoare evidence, 1 June 1848, par. 6031. Assaults on naval officers were now quite common: the commander, master and steward of the *Frolic* were severely beaten up in Santos in January 1844; the crew of the *Growler* were attacked in Pernambuco in March; sailors from Hoare's own gig were seized and imprisoned when ashore seeking supplies at Ubatuba in February (see Manchester, *British Preëminence in Brazil*, p. 295).

took the opportunity to remind the British government how impolitic were such proceedings:

[They] necessarily excite national susceptibility and rouse the feelings even of those who are not interested in the traffic . . . in the midst of the difficulties which must necessarily attend the extinction of the traffic in a country the population of which has been accustomed for ages scarcely to possess any other riches except those drawn from the earth by the labour of slaves, it [the Brazilian government] laments that the imprudent and violent proceedings of the British cruisers accumulate new embarrassments and excite sympathy for the traffickers by the feeling of offended national self love.[1]

As it happened, Sir John Dodson had already ruled that British cruisers could not visit or detain Brazilian ships within the roadsteads of Brazil. The capture of the *Dous Amigos*, he declared, had therefore been technically illegal since the *Curlew's* boats were despatched from within Rio harbour. The owners of the *Maria Theresa*, too, were entitled to damages since in his opinion neither the Palmerston Act nor the treaty of 1817 permitted British cruisers to capture ships found within the recognised territorial jurisdiction of a civilised power. As a result, in July 1844 naval officers were instructed categorically that no captures should be made in either Brazilian or African territorial waters without the prior consent of the local authorities.[2]

The *Nova Granada*, the last prize to come before the mixed commission in Rio de Janeiro, provoked towards the end of 1844 the most bitter and lengthy controversy to take place over the 'equipment clause' since the question had first been raised by the capture and condemnation of the *Maria Carlota* more than five years before. Carneiro de Campos was in favour of acquitting the *Nova Granada* because the ship was said to be a legal trader plying between Santos and Recife and, more important, because as in every case of this nature which came before him, he contested the legality of the capture. John Samo, the new British commissary judge—George Jackson had by this time been transferred to the

[1] Paulino to Hamilton, 11 January, enclosed in Hamilton to Aberdeen, no. 9, 27 February 1844, F.O. 84/523; printed in Perdigão Malheiro, ii, 244–52, and Pereira Pinto, i. 445 ff.
[2] Dodson to Aberdeen, 29 September 1843, F.O. 83/2351; Dodson to Aberdeen, 9 May 1844, F.O. 83/2352; Aberdeen to Admiralty, 4 July 1844, F.O. 84/547; Aberdeen to Hamilton, no. 12, 2 July 1844, F.O. 84/524; Manchester, *op. cit.* p. 241.

Anglo-Dutch commission in Surinam where he could do no damage (since no cases came before it)—cited recent cases in the court at Freetown as well as the precedent of the *Maria Carlota* and pleaded forcibly for condemnation. And bearing in mind Aberdeen's instructions of September 1843 to the Freetown commissioners, he refused to see the problem shelved yet again by allowing the question to go to arbitration.[1] The case dragged on for months, and eventually involved both the Brazilian government and the British legation.[2] In the event, the Anglo-Brazilian mixed commission in Rio de Janeiro, like that in Sierra Leone, ceased to function in the middle of 1845 and no verdict on the *Nova Granada* was ever given. Whereas in Sierra Leone the closing of the commission interrupted a run of successful prosecutions against Brazilian slave ships, in Rio de Janeiro it simply brought to a timely end the stalemate reached in the *Nova Granada* case. In December, when it was almost impossible to keep the ship afloat, the captors (the officers and crew of H.M.S. *Viper*) abandoned their prize and ran it ashore at a spot indicated by the Commissioner of the Imperial Dockyard.[3]

[1] Samo and Grigg, no. 33, 11 December 1844, F.O. 84/511.
[2] E.g., for the British point of view, Hamilton to França Ferreira, 4 December, enclosed in Hamilton no. 47, 14 December 1844, F.O. 84/525, and for the Brazilian view, Limpo de Abreu to Hamilton, 5 July, enclosed in Hamilton no. 30, 29 July 1845, F.O. 84/582.
[3] Hamilton no. 53, 22 December 1845, F.O. 84/582.

CHAPTER 8

SLAVE TRADE, SLAVERY AND SUGAR DUTIES, 1839–1844

Throughout the period 1839–44 the British government persisted in their efforts, which already went back more than a decade, to strengthen the Anglo-Brazilian anti-slave trade treaty of 1826. In 1839 it had seemed as though the stalemate which had arisen from the refusal of the Brazilian Chamber of Deputies to ratify the additional equipment and break-up articles signed by Henry Fox and Manuel Alves Branco in July 1835, and vital to any effective British preventive system, had at last been broken: British commissary judges in Rio de Janeiro and Freetown, eventually supported by the British government, had reinterpreted the treaty *as it stood* and argued that British warships already had the right to search and capture Brazilian vessels suspected of intending to trade in slaves.[1] Successive Brazilian governments, however, refused to accept the validity of the British reinterpretation of the treaty. As a result, disputes over the legality of British captures were endemic in both the Anglo-Brazilian mixed commissions, and British naval officers could never rely with any confidence on the condemnation of their prizes.[2] It was a thoroughly unsatisfactory state of affairs and, while ever the British government was reluctant to resort to the kind of measures which had been taken against the Portuguese slave trade (including the adjudication of prizes by British admiralty courts), one which could only be remedied by agreement with Brazil. Treaty negotiations therefore continued and, with every year, a settlement of some kind became more urgent as, with the gradual elimination of the Portuguese flag from the Brazilian trade, traders resorted to the Brazilian flag on an ever-increasing scale. And as if anti-slave trade treaty negotiations were not difficult and complicated enough, from 1841 they became entangled with negotiations for a new commercial treaty and such controversial issues as, on the one hand, the future of

[1] See above, ch. 6.   [2] See above, ch. 7.

slavery in Brazil and, on the other, British imperial preference and, in particular, the British sugar duties.

In the summer of 1839—before the condemnation of the *Maria Carlota* in Rio de Janeiro and the *Emprehendedor* in Freetown and before the passage of Lord Palmerston's Act—the Brazilians themselves had initiated a new round of anti-slave trade treaty negotiations. Cândido Batista de Oliveira, Foreign Minister in the Cabinet of April 1839, was determined to take whatever measures he could to bring the trade to an end and on 22 June, in a confidential memorandum, he suggested to W. G. Ouseley, the British *chargé*, that rather than continue the attempt to patch up the existing treaty by the adoption, for example, of the additional articles of 1835 it would be more expedient to remodel the entire suppression system. He suggested, first, that the capture of Brazilian slave ships *on the high seas* should henceforth be 'exclusively the duty of the English cruisers' and that there was no longer any need to take them for adjudication before Anglo-Brazilian mixed commissions —which could therefore be abolished; secondly, within the area of their own jurisdiction, the Brazilian government would be responsible for enforcing their own legislation; and thirdly, slaves liberated by either government would be transported to a British colony.[1] It seemed to Ouseley that the scheme offered the British government a *carte blanche*: it would allow them, with the consent of the Brazilian government, to deal with Brazilian slave ships in the same way that they were planning, without the consent of the Portuguese government, to deal with Portuguese slave ships.[2] Cândido Batista's position in the government was weak, however, and Ouseley, anxious to secure an official exchange of notes on the subject in order that future Brazilian Foreign Ministers might feel themselves committed, tried to elicit from him a more precise statement to the effect that ships involved in the slave trade *in any way* had no claim on the protection of the Brazilian flag, and that

[1] Memorandum, 22 June, enclosed in Ouseley to Palmerston, 22 June 1839, Private, F.O. 84/286; Cândido Batista to José Marques Lisboa (*chargé* in London), no. 17, 22 June 1839, A.H.I. 268/1/15; Cândido Batista letter in *Jornal do Comércio*, 9 March 1846. See also Alves, *R.I.H.G.B.* (1914), pp. 228–9. The additional articles of 1835 were not mentioned in Cândido Batista's *Relatório* of May 1839.

[2] Ouseley to Palmerston, no. 40, 9 August 1839, F.O. 84/287.

British cruisers were entitled to capture them and deal with them as they thought fit.[1] Cândido Batista briefly recognised the need for amplifying his proposals but was out of office before he had time to do so. Nevertheless, Lord Palmerston at the Foreign Office decided to accept Cândido Batista's memorandum as a basis for the negotiation of a completely new Anglo-Brazilian anti-slave trade treaty, which would settle once and for all the disputes arising from the ambiguities inherent in the treaty of 1826. What he had in mind was an agreement whereby any ship engaged in slaving activities and belonging to a Brazilian or to a foreigner resident in Brazil, whatever flag it was flying, and whether or not it was carrying slaves, would be liable to visit and search by British cruisers and adjudication by British admiralty courts instead of by Anglo-Brazilian mixed commissions. In the event of a ship's being condemned it would be broken up or converted for use as a British cruiser; any slaves it was carrying would be sent to a British colony and there liberated. At the same time, Palmerston did not want a new treaty to release the Brazilian government from their existing obligations. The Emperor of Brazil would once again have to engage to bring to justice and punish all traders whose ships eluded the British net and to free any slaves they landed. After waiting in vain for confirmation that Cândido Batista's views were shared by the Brazilian government as a whole, on 31 December 1839 Palmerston sent to Rio the draft of a new treaty along these lines.[2]

Cândido Batista's successor, Caetano Maria Lopes Gama, professed a willingness to do all in his power to fulfil Brazil's obligations to abolish the slave trade. But his political position was no less precarious than that of his predecessor, and he enjoyed little real power. For the third year in succession the additional articles of 1835 were not even mentioned in the Foreign Minister's annual *Relatório*, and, moreover, Lopes Gama showed no inclination to follow up Cândido Batista's overtures for an entirely new treaty: if the Chamber continued to withhold ratification of the additional articles, he argued, it was hardly likely to accept Lord Palmerston's new treaty proposals.[3] After a short spell during which he had

[1] Ouseley to Cândido Batista, 10 August, enclosed in Ouseley no. 42, 17 September 1839, F.O. 84/287.
[2] Draft of treaty enclosed in Palmerston to Ouseley, no. 38, 31 December 1839, F.O. 84/288.   [3] Ouseley no. 35, 17 September 1840, F.O. 84/325.

been optimistic of securing a new treaty, Ouseley had now subsided into his mood of two years earlier. No Brazilian government, he decided, could ever be trusted to co-operate willingly in suppressing the trade. Unless they were 'continually watched, urged and in some measure controlled' by the British legation in Rio de Janeiro, they were not even prepared to go through the motions of checking the importation of slaves into the country. And every improvement to the system of suppressing the trade at sea had to be imposed upon them by force. 'The employment or perhaps the mere display of force on our part', he wrote to Palmerston in May 1840, 'is, I am sorry to say, the only efficacious mode of enabling the well disposed part of the administration to outweigh their opponents . . . on this question; of course the naval force is that to which I allude.'[1] However, Ouseley's hopes were again raised, if only partially, by the political and constitutional changes which took place in Brazil in July 1840. Led by Antônio Carlos de Andrada, the Cabinet of the Majority seemed more disposed towards co-operation with Britain for the suppression of the trade than had any Brazilian administration for the past decade. Moreover, with the proclamation of the Emperor's majority came a curtailment of the powers of the legislature: for example, it was no longer necessary to secure the approval of the Chamber of Deputies before agreements with foreign powers would be ratified—which prompted Ouseley to believe that there was at last 'a fair prospect of success' in Britain's treaty negotiations with Brazil.[2] He lost no time in asking the new Foreign Minister, Aureliano Coutinho, to open negotiations for a new anti-slave trade treaty based on Lord Palmerston's draft of the previous December, at the same time taking particular care to point out that overtures had come from Brazil in the first instance. (On this occasion, Ouseley thought, the Brazilians—'so suspicious of any interference with their much boasted independence and so jealous of any appearance of dictation'—could hardly accuse Britain of making unreasonable demands upon them.) Realising that negotiations would obviously be delayed until the new government had consolidated their position, a week later Ouseley demanded

---

[1] Ouseley no. 22, 28 May 1840, Conf., F.O. 84/324.
[2] Ouseley no. 34, 21 August 1840, Conf., F.O. 84/324.

the immediate ratification of the additional articles of 1835 so that in the meantime the existing treaty might be more effective and future disputes in the mixed courts over the legality of British captures avoided.[1]

Whatever their abolitionist inclinations, however, this Brazilian government, like every other, had to move with extreme circumspection. They still had to take account of the interests and prejudices of the vast majority of influential Brazilians who equated the abolition of the slave trade with agricultural ruin. Moreover, there now seemed every reason for exercising caution in any future treaty negotiations whose purpose would be to extend further the powers of the British navy. Since 1839 British cruisers had in practice been searching and capturing ships as they left Brazilian ports—and Brazilians had found it a salutary experience. Already several vessels engaged in legitimate trading activities had been captured by mistake and subsequently acquitted by the Rio de Janeiro mixed commission. Brazil's coastal trade had been extensively interrupted by the British navy's exercise of the right of search, and Brazilian territorial waters had frequently been violated. There had even been cases of Brazilian ships being taken before British tribunals—where there was no Brazilian judge to see that their interests were protected. The new treaty which Lord Palmerston proposed would not only legalise all these activities but would lead to their adoption on an even greater scale.[2] No Brazilian government, however much it wished to see an end to the slave trade, could countenance arbitrary interference by the navy of a foreign power in legitimate commerce, especially along the coast of Brazil. Consequently, Aureliano and his colleagues in the Cabinet were disinclined to open fresh negotiations along the lines suggested by Lord Palmerston. Ouseley heard that Aureliano had commented to an intimate friend: 'Snr Cândido Batista de Oliveira nous a compromis horriblement en proposant de telles bases.'[3] Indeed it now seemed to the Brazilians that even the additional articles of 1835 failed to protect

[1] Ouseley to Aureliano, 23 August, 2 September, enclosed in Ouseley no. 35.
[2] Aureliano to Francisco Acaiaba de Montezuma, 25 September 1840, A.H.I. 218/4/2 (Montezuma, a former Foreign Minister, was leaving for London to take up his post as Brazilian minister); Aureliano to Antônio Carlos de Andrada, 2 September 1840, A.H.I. 55/4.   [3] Ouseley to Palmerston, 12 January 1841, Private, F.O. 84/364.

Brazilian shipping sufficiently from the depredations of the British navy.

For five months, Aureliano went on assuring Ouseley of his goodwill, but made one excuse after another—illness, holidays, the demands on his time made by the young Emperor, the reluctance of the government to declare themselves too decidedly on so controversial an issue before the forthcoming elections—for not replying to British overtures until, eventually, Ouseley began to suspect 'a pre-meditated system of procrastination'.[1] Under instructions from London, however, he persisted in his demands for a positive response to Britain's latest treaty proposals and in February 1841 forced Aureliano to come out into the open and announce that they were unacceptable. No Brazilian government, Aureliano declared, could allow Brazilian ships—even suspected slave ships—to be adjudicated by exclusively British tribunals, and no equipment clause would ever be acceptable to Brazil which did not make absolutely clear what would constitute *prima facie* proof of a ship's illegal purpose.[2] So rebuffed, a month later Ouseley asked the Brazilian government to submit counter-proposals for a treaty, thereby indicating how far they were prepared to go towards meeting Palmerston's own proposals. Aureliano agreed, and announced that as soon as they had been prepared either the Marquês de Barbacena or Senator Lopes Gama would be empowered to open negotiations.

Because of his intimacy with young Dom Pedro II, Aureliano was retained as Foreign Minister in the government which followed the resignation of the Cabinet of the Majority in March 1841. The new government, however, were, on the whole, more sympathetic to the labour needs of the Brazilian planters and therefore to the traders who supplied them with African slaves. Moreover, the activities of British cruisers off the Brazilian coast during 1841—especially incidents like that which occurred at Campos in May[3]—combined with yet more acquittals by the Rio commission of captured Brazilian coastal vessels, confirmed Aureliano in his determination to work for the restriction, rather than

[1] Ouseley no. 16, 13 March 1841, F.O. 84/364.
[2] Aureliano to Ouseley, 3 February, enclosed in Ouseley no. 16.
[3] See above, ch. 7, pp. 206–7.

the extension, of the powers of the British navy.[1] Ouseley realised that there was little chance of securing the ratification of the additional articles, much less the negotiation of an entirely new treaty, unless a new factor were introduced into the situation. This, he thought, might take the form of an internal threat—a major slave insurrection like that of 1835—or possibly a threat from outside—the adoption by the British government of 'coercive measures', if not open hostilities. For two years (April 1839 to March 1841) Brazilian governments had been relatively amenable on the slave trade question and Ouseley had therefore been reluctant to bring too much official pressure to bear, trying instead to make progress by what he called 'essentially fair means'. In some ways he almost welcomed the change of government in March 1841, since it meant that 'no delicacy need now restrain H.M. Government or agents in pushing to the utmost any means that it may be expedient to employ in furtherance of their views'. In May, during an interview in which he used 'somewhat strong language', Ouseley warned Aureliano that the Brazilian administration 'must choose between the line they had now taken to conciliate certain parties and the friendly feelings of H.M. Government'; if they continued to favour slave trade interests, he solemnly declared, they must be prepared for the consequences. In June Ouseley suggested to Palmerston that tougher measures 'whether by extending the Bill against the Portuguese slave trade to Brazil, or putting into execution part of its provisions' would be fully justified unless the Brazilian government immediately ratified the additional articles of 1835 and agreed to open negotiations for a new treaty.[2] Palmerston himself had been thinking along similar lines. In July he instructed Ouseley to warn the Brazilian government that summary proceedings, similar to those employed since 1839 against slave ships under the Portuguese flag, would soon be adopted in respect of slave ships sailing under Brazilian colours unless Brazilian co-operation for the suppression of the slave trade were forthcoming.[3]

[1] *Relatório do Ministério dos Negócios Estrangeiros* (Rio de Janeiro, May 1841).
[2] Ouseley to Palmerston, 17 May 1841, Private and Conf., F.O. 84/365; Ouseley no. 66, 15 June 1841, F.O. 84/365; Ouseley 15 June 1841, Separate and Conf., F.O. 84/365. Similar views were again expressed in Ouseley no. 81, 7 July 1841, Conf., F.O. 84/365.
[3] Palmerston to Ouseley, 23 July 1841, F.O. 84/364.

All these warnings went unheeded. The Brazilian government resented Ouseley's 'insults' and threats no less than the overbearing way in which, in their view, the British navy already showed its contempt for Brazil's rights as an independent nation. The continuation of the slave trade was becoming increasingly—and dangerously—linked in the public mind with the question of national sovereignty as well as economic survival; even those ministers who were anxious to co-operate with Britain on the slave trade question had to avoid at all costs the appearance of bowing to the dictation of the British government. At the same time, all Brazilian ministers, whatever their attitude towards the slave trade, were fully aware that the British government were in certain circumstances prepared to adopt even more extreme preventive measures. It was therefore imperative, at the very least, to keep open the possibility of agreement being reached on a more effective slave trade treaty. Early in June 1841 Lopes Gama had at last been instructed to open fresh treaty negotiations with Ouseley with a view to securing a clearer definition of the treaty of 1826 in order that the slave trade might more rapidly be suppressed—but by 'proper and friendly means'.[1] The additional articles of 1835—a continuing source of embarrassment to the Brazilian government—were quietly dropped. Palmerston's treaty proposals of December 1839 were simply ignored: the Brazilian government, Aureliano said, had never recognised the Cândido Batista memorandum as 'a formal engagement to which [they] must strictly adhere'.[2] Instead, on 26 August 1841 the Brazilian Foreign Minister produced, with a long explanatory note, some carefully formulated counter-proposals for supplementary articles to the Anglo-Brazilian treaty of 1826. The Brazilian government accepted, as they had in 1835, the need for the addition of an equipment clause, but this time with certain safeguards; a Brazilian ship should not be liable to capture and condemnation because of a single piece of slaving equipment for which the master had no satisfactory explanation: the onus of proof of criminal intent should lie with the captor, and a ship should be condemned only if *all or a considerable number* of the usual equipment articles were

[1] Instructions to Lopes Gama, 3 June 1841, A.H.I. 218/4/2.
[2] Aureliano to Ouseley, 26 August, enclosed in Ouseley no. 96, 31 August 1841, F.O. 84/366.

found on board. Furthermore, British cruisers must stay clear of the Brazilian coast and out of Brazilian territorial waters; a ship equipped for slaving would be liable to capture only on the high seas (article 1). The Brazilian government were also prepared to concede the addition of the other article long sought after by Britain, that requiring the break-up and sale of condemned vessels other than in cases where they were purchased by either of the two governments for public service (article 4). But they refused to allow Brazilian subjects to be tried and punished by laws and tribunals other than those of Brazil, nor could they permit Brazilian ships to come under the jurisdiction of any but Brazilian or Anglo-Brazilian courts. Moreover, all captured ships which were believed to have set off from a Brazilian port should, they insisted, be taken before the mixed commission in Rio de Janeiro where a Brazilian judge was always available (article 2). In all other cases ships should be taken before the nearest mixed commission and two additional commissions should be established at Demerara and the Cape of Good Hope (article 3). The Brazilian government again agreed that Britain should be entitled to dispose of the liberated slaves (article 6). The proceeds from the sale of condemned ships (after break-up) should be used to help finance free European immigration to Brazil, which the British government should encourage by all possible means (article 7). When a ship was acquitted, however, the Brazilian government insisted that the commissary judges should be able to draw bills of compensation on the appropriate government in favour of the owners and payable at sight (article 5).[1] Naturally, Ouseley was far from satisfied. He was, moreoever—and the Brazilian government could not have been unaware of this—authorised to negotiate only on the basis of the British treaty draft of December 1839. Resigned to further delays, he therefore forwarded Aureliano's treaty proposals to London where, in the meantime, Lord Aberdeen had replaced Lord Palmerston at the Foreign Office.

It was at this point that complicated questions of commercial policy imposed a further strain upon Anglo-Brazilian relations.[2]

[1] Aureliano counter-proposals 26 August, enclosed in Ouseley no. 96.
[2] The following discussion of British and Brazilian commercial policy and Anglo-Brazilian commercial relations is based, primarily, on A. J. Pryor, 'Anglo-Brazilian Commercial

Slave trade, slavery and sugar duties, 1839–1844

The commercial treaty of 1827 which, like the anti-slave trade treaty, had been negotiated during the period of Brazil's weakness and dependence upon Britain following her declaration of independence from Portugal, was proving increasingly irksome to the Brazilians. In the first place, they resented the extra-territorial privileges it conferred on Britain, especially the right to appoint judges conservators, which they considered incompatible with Brazil's independence and sovereignty. Secondly, and of more immediate importance, the treaty was held largely responsible for Brazil's not inconsiderable financial difficulties: duties on imported goods, the bulk of which were British, were a major source of government revenue, but they could not be raised above 15% *ad valorem* because of the Anglo-Brazilian commercial treaty and the most favoured nation treaties Brazil had subsequently signed with other powers. And despite the fact that *laissez faire* ideas still prevailed amongst both the Brazilian landowners and the commercial classes of the coastal cities, the first signs were becoming apparent of an awareness in some circles that, by providing protection for home manufacturing and thus decreasing Brazil's overwhelming dependence on British goods, higher tariffs could be an instrument of economic change as well as a valuable source of revenue. Moreover, the low duties on British goods contrasted most unfavourably with the virtually prohibitive duties on Brazilian produce entering the English market. Whereas colonial sugar from the British West Indies, the East Indies and Mauritius was subject to a duty of only 24 s per cwt, foreign sugar paid 63 s per cwt; similarly, the duty on colonial coffee was 6 d per lb while that on foreign coffee was 1 s 3 d per lb. Only cotton from Pernambuco

Relations and the Evolution of Brazilian Tariff Policy, 1822–50' (unpublished Ph.D. thesis, Cambridge, 1965); A. K. Manchester, *British Preeminence in Brazil* (Durham N.C., 1933); Celso Furtado, *The Economic Growth of Brazil* (Univ. of Calif. Press, 1963); Lucy Brown, *The Board of Trade and the Free Trade Movement, 1830–42* (Oxford, 1958); W. P. Morrell, *British Colonial Policy in the age of Peel and Russell* (Oxford, 1930); R. L. Schuyler, *Fall of the old colonial system: a study in free trade* (New York, 1945); *Cambridge History of the British Empire*, vol. ii. *The Growth of the New Empire, 1783–1870* (Cambridge, 1940); E. Williams, *Slavery and Capitalism* (Durham, N.C., 1944); G. R. Mellor, *British Imperial Trusteeship, 1783–1850* (London, 1951); W. L. Burn, *The West Indies* (London, 1951); Elsie I. Pilgrim, 'Anti-slavery sentiment in Great Britain, 1841–54, its nature and its decline; with special reference to its influence upon British policy towards its former slave colonies' (unpublished Ph.D. thesis, Cambridge, 1952); N. Deerr, *The History of Sugar* (2 vols., London, 1949–50).

and Maranhão was imported into Britain on any great scale, and cotton was now much less important to the Brazilian economy than was either coffee or sugar, which were exported for the most part (albeit in British ships very often) to the United States and continental Europe. Brazil's adverse balance of trade with Britain and her inability to gain a foothold in the British market were particularly irritating during the early 1840s when the Brazilian economy was going through rather a lean period (in reality more the consequence—at least in the case of sugar—of antiquated techniques of production, poor quality produce and competition from sugar beet than simply the result of British colonial preference). An earlier attempt to put Anglo-Brazilian commercial relations on a more equal footing—the Barbacena mission of 1836 —had completely failed. However, an opportunity for Brazil finally to assert her independence and at the same time to extract vital trading concessions from Britain was about to present itself. The treaty of 1827 was due to expire in November 1842, or so it seemed, fifteen years after its ratification, and there was widespread feeling throughout Brazil that it should not be renewed without radical revision. Indeed, there were indications that if Britain proved unwilling to modify her commercial policy Brazil might not even be prepared to sign a most favoured nation treaty, and threats that higher and differential duties would be levied on British goods entering Brazil.

The Brazilians were encouraged in their attitude towards the commercial treaty of 1827 by the knowledge that in England there was now considerable and mounting opposition to the old system of colonial preference. The interests of the consumer, particularly during years of depression, were a major consideration of those who were demanding lower duties on imported foreign foodstuffs, especially sugar: stationary since the end of the Napoleonic wars, in decline since the emancipation of the slaves, West Indian production was proving totally inadequate to satisfy the growing demand for sugar in the expanding urban areas; the level of sugar prices in Britain was far higher than in most other European countries and would be lowered only if foreign sugar were more readily admitted into the domestic market. By enabling them to keep wages down, lower food prices would also, it was hoped, improve the competitive position of British manufacturers in overseas markets at a difficult period in world trade. Furthermore, it now seemed that unless Britain abolished or lowered the differential duties on foreign sugar and coffee an attempt might soon be made to impose increased, indeed discriminatory, duties on British goods entering the important Brazilian market which was worth more than three million pounds each year to the British manufacturer. More than half the manufactured goods imported into Rio de Janeiro, Bahia and Pernambuco were British. Indeed Brazil was one of the biggest markets for Lancashire cottons, besides a whole range of consumer goods from hardware, earthenware and glass to hats, umbrellas and musical instruments. Moreover, it was a market with great potential for expansion (unlike the West Indies, for example, which took a declining proportion of British exports) and one that Britain could not afford to lose.[1]

There was, however, one complicating factor: slavery. Brazilian sugar and coffee were slave-grown and it was this that enabled the West Indian interest—planters, brokers, shippers, refiners and those who sympathised with them—to defend the existing system of colonial preference on more respectable grounds than those of economic self-interest. In the first place, they could argue that, until slavery was abolished in Cuba and Brazil or at least until the slave trade was abolished and Cuban and Brazilian planters were denied their regular supply of cheap slave labour, West Indian sugar, which had long ago lost its European market, would be unable to compete on equal terms in the home market with Brazilian and Cuban sugar, and the Great Experiment of Emancipation in the West Indies, which was to demonstrate the superiority of free over slave labour, would be irreparably damaged. Moreover, it could even be argued that lower duties on foreign sugar would serve to encourage more intensive and more extensive production in Brazil and Cuba which in turn would both sharpen and prolong the evils of the slave system and act as a powerful stimulus to the trade in slaves which Britain was trying so desperately to suppress. Thus severe fiscal discrimination against foreign, slave-grown

---

[1] It should also be remembered that, besides Brazil's importance as an export market, British commercial houses and British shipping companies handled half of Brazil's exports and a large proportion of her domestic trade (Manchester, *op. cit.*, pp. 314–16).

sugar was defended by the former defenders of slavery and the slave trade, whose interests now coincided with international abolition, as an essential element in Britain's policy of discouraging the slave trade and undermining the slave system throughout the world.

It was not difficult for free traders to demonstrate that the real purpose of the sugar duties, like that of the Corn Laws, was to protect the interests of the landed aristocracy (in the case of sugar, the colonial landed aristocracy) at the expense of the working-class consumer and the middle-class manufacturer. Nor was it difficult to make capital out of the inconsistencies in the protectionist case—not least the fact that there was little concern about the importation into the home market of slave-grown cotton and slave-grown tobacco. It was less easy, however, to refute the contention that the removal of the protective duties on sugar would, first, completely undermine the West Indian economy whose other two props, the slave trade and slavery, had already been removed, and, secondly, serve in the long run as a stimulus to the slave trade to Brazil and Cuba. Some free traders were frankly untroubled about the fate of the West Indies: John Roebuck, for example, was ready to 'consign Jamaica to the bottom of the sea and all the Antilles after it'.[1] There were others who pointed out that the West Indian planters had been given more than adequate compensation for the losses they sustained as a result of emancipation and had been granted ample time in which to adjust themselves to a more competitive situation. Some, however, tried to argue—and it was not easy—that, although painful initially, to remove the crutches of protection would in the long term actually prove advantageous to the West Indies since free labour (augmented perhaps by free African immigration) must always be more productive than slave labour. As for the point that slavery and the slave trade would be positively encouraged by a reduction in the sugar duties, many free traders were no more interested in this than they were in the economic well-being of the West Indies: for them the interests of the British consumer and the British manufacturer came before those of either the West Indian planter or the African slave in Brazil. Those, however, like

[1] Quoted by Morrell, *op. cit.* p. 181.

Slave trade, slavery and sugar duties, 1839–1844

Lord Palmerston, Lord John Russell and other leading Whigs who were opposed both to colonial preference and to slavery denied that the trade could in fact be suppressed by discriminatory duties against slave produce ('fiscal coercion'). Indeed, they convinced themselves that far from encouraging slavery and the slave trade the admission of Brazilian (and Cuban) sugar, by lessening hostility to Britain in Brazil (and Spain), would facilitate more friendly and therefore more successful negotiations for improving the more traditional methods of combating the trade.

It was the financial crisis of 1840–1, combined with the need to secure a larger proportion of the middle-class and working-class vote, which proved decisive in finally converting the Whig government to the virtues of freer trade.[1] The Report of the 1840 Select Committee on Import Duties had demonstrated that less prohibitive duties would lead to an increase in government revenue besides lessening the heavy burden of indirect taxation, and in his budget of May 1841, the Chancellor of the Exchequer, Sir Francis Baring, proposed a reduction of the duty on foreign sugar from 63s per cwt to 36s per cwt (colonial sugar to remain at 24s) together with lower duties on corn, timber and a number of other items. The ensuing debate spread over several days and the Melbourne government were twice defeated—281 votes to 317 and 311 votes to 312—by an alliance of the West Indian interest, Corn Law Protectionists, old-fashioned Imperialists—and, significantly, a large number of abolitionists.[2] (The sugar question had already begun to divide the members of the Anti-Slavery Society inside and outside Parliament. Most of them were Anti-Corn Law Leaguers, supporters of free trade in general and, of course, traditionally enemies of the West Indian interest. At this early stage in the struggle for cheap sugar, however, the majority reluctantly came down on the side of protection so as not to encourage the slave trade and strengthen slavery in Cuba and Brazil.[3])

[1] Brown, *op. cit.* pp. 214–22.
[2] *Ibid.*, pp. 222–4; Morrell, *op. cit.* pp. 171–2; Burn, *op. cit.* p. 128.
[3] See Duncan E. Rice, 'Critique of the Eric Williams Thesis: The Anti-Slavery Interest and the Sugar Duties, 1841–53', in *The Transatlantic Slave Trade from West Africa* (Edinburgh, 1965), pp. 44–60. Also the *Proceedings* of the General Anti-Slavery Conventions called by the British and Foreign Anti-Slavery Society, June 12–23, 1840, June 13–20, 1843 (London, 1841, 1843). There was open dissent at the second convention culminating in the secession of a minority of Cobdenite free traders.

Slave trade, slavery and sugar duties, 1839–1844

Sir Robert Peel's Conservative government, which in September 1841 succeeded the Melbourne administration, were no less preoccupied with the country's financial deficit than their predecessors, and Peel himself was favourably disposed towards many of the arguments in favour of an all-round reduction in import duties, at least to the level at which tariffs would become mildly protective instead of positively prohibitive. He was, however, personally disinclined to facilitate the entry into Britain of slave-grown produce and, moreover, at least two of his colleagues —Henry Goulburn, the Chancellor of the Exchequer, and Gladstone, Vice-President of the Board of Trade—had strong West Indian connexions. One of the problems Peel inherited from the Whigs was that of the Anglo-Brazilian commercial treaty.[1] Britain was now insisting that the treaty was due to expire in November 1844 and not, as the Brazilians seemed to believe, in November 1842: Article 28 stipulated that the treaty would remain in force for fifteen years after ratification (in November 1827) and thereafter until one of the parties gave notice of their wish to terminate it; in the event of such a notification being given at the end of the fifteen-year period, the treaty would only expire after a further two years.[2] But even this interpretation of the treaty only gave the British government a breathing space of two years and if British manufacturing and shipping interests were not to suffer it was imperative either to renew the existing treaty or, at the very least, to sign a new most favoured nation treaty. The Brazilians, however, continued to demand reciprocity in the shape of lower import duties on Brazilian sugar and coffee. In the circumstances Peel could see only one way out of the dilemma—and one that was not very practicable at that: Britain would lower the the duties on Brazilian produce but as a *quid pro quo* Brazil would make its produce eligible for the British market by agreeing to take the first steps towards the abolition of slavery as well as more effective measures against the slave trade. 'If we are to make a

---

[1] 'This matter has a more immediate bearing on our financial measures than any other within the range of the Foreign Office', Peel wrote to Aberdeen on 28 October 1841, B.M. Add. MSS 40453 (Peel Papers). Treaty negotiations with Brazil were more than a political and a commercial question, he added; they were 'one of the elements of any extensive *financial* scheme which can be proposed' (Peel to Aberdeen, 1 November 1841, B.M. Add. MSS 43061 (Aberdeen Papers).

[2] *B.F.S.P.* xiv, 1024–5.

concession in favour of Brazilian sugar and coffee', Lord Ripon, President of the Board of Trade, wrote to Gladstone in October 1841, 'it must be in return for some stringent and really efficient regulation on their part in respect of slave trading and even slavery'.[1] By the end of the year the decision had been taken to submit to the Brazilian government proposals for a new commercial treaty similar to that already in existence (with its favourable tariffs on British manufactures) but with important and striking additions: the British government would agree to reduce import duties on Brazilian sugar; in return Dom Pedro would agree to declare free all children born of slave parents after a date to be determined (subject to negotiation) and give consideration to the emancipation of all slaves in Brazil at the earliest possible moment.

It was never intended that a new commercial treaty should provide a substitute for the more orthodox type of anti-slave trade treaty. The Conservative government had every intention of vigorously enforcing existing treaties and of pursuing, quite separately, negotiations for their improvement. Lord Aberdeen at the Foreign Office was, however, prepared to drop Palmerston's earlier draft for an entirely new treaty if agreement could be reached on the counter-proposals for supplementary articles to the treaty of 1826 which Aureliano Coutinho himself had put forward in August. He thought the wording ought in places to be made rather more precise and he felt that a few alterations were necessary. In particular, the kind of equipment clause Aureliano had proposed would in Aberdeen's view be all too easily evaded: it was essential that *any one or more* of the specified equipment articles found on board or proved to have been on board a ship should constitute *prima facie* evidence of slaving and that the onus of proving that the article or articles were indispensable to some lawful enterprise should be placed squarely on the shoulders of the ship's owners and master. Lord Aberdeen also repeated the British view that the owner of a ship proved to have been involved in the trade but acquitted on some technical ground could never be entitled to compensation for losses, damages and expenses to the owners. He was agreeable to the proposal that two new Anglo-

[1] Ripon to Gladstone, 14 October 1841, quoted in Jones, *Lord Aberdeen and the Americas*, p. 41.

Brazilian mixed commissions should be set up, but felt that the Rio commission should enjoy no precedence: all four should have equal authority. Finally, Aberdeen felt that there should be one further supplementary article in addition to those proposed by Aureliano: the Emperor of Brazil should engage to establish an Anglo-Brazilian commission to investigate the whereabouts of all Africans illegally landed in Brazil since 1830 and should guarantee the freedom of any who might be landed in the future. In February 1842 Aberdeen's anti-slave trade treaty proposals were despatched to Rio de Janeiro together with the draft of a new commercial treaty which was to include articles relating to the British sugar duties and the future of slavery in Brazil.[1]

The situation in Brazil could hardly have been less favourable for the opening of fresh treaty negotiations. As a result of further irregular captures by British warships on the Brazilian coast and the direct clashes which had occurred with Brazilian local authorities, animosity to Britain, fanned by a violently nationalistic press campaign, had reached fever pitch. 'Uncompromising aversion', reported Hamilton Hamilton, who had recently resumed his duties as British minister, 'is proclaimed towards England and all intimate connexion with her by treaty' as well as to any negotiations 'tending to the continuance of that connexion'.[2] The one hopeful sign was the fact that the Brazilian Chamber of Deputies, an important platform for the expression of anti-British feeling, was not in session at the time: the Conservative Cabinet of March 1841 had declared the elections conducted by the Liberal Cabinet of the Majority to have been fraudulent and had taken steps to prevent the Chamber from meeting. As a result, however, the Brazilian government found itself facing Liberal revolts in the provinces of São Paulo and Minas Gerais and had little time to spare for treaty negotiations with Britain. The realisation that Britain had no intention of allowing the commercial treaty to expire for at least another two years proved a further stimulus to latent nationalist feeling in Brazil; the British attitude, Hamilton

[1] Aberdeen to Hamilton no. 1, 2 February 1842, F.O. 84/410; Aberdeen to Hamilton, no. 2, 1 February 1842, F.O. 13/178.

[2] Hamilton to Aberdeen, no. 45, 12 October 1842, F.O. 84/408. Also Hamilton no. 7, 20 October 1841, Conf., F.O. 84/366; Hamilton no. 29, 9 April 1842, F.O. 13/180.

wrote, was considered 'tyrannous in the extreme'.[1] Nevertheless, in September the government conceded that the commercial treaty would continue in force until November 1844 although Aureliano declared himself unwilling to enter into negotiations either for its renewal or for its replacement until it had actually expired and again hinted that Brazil was considering the possibility of tariff discrimination against British goods unless reciprocity were forthcoming. At the same time, he made it clear that he was not prepared to make major concessions in order to secure lower duties on Brazilian produce: the Brazilian government fully realised that freer trade was in Britain's own interests and that a relaxation of the sugar duties could not for long be delayed in any case.[2] (In March 1842 the British government had lowered the duties on coffee, now Brazil's major export, to 9*d* per lb foreign and 4*d* per lb colonial—yet another example of their inconsistency: if coffee, why not sugar?—thereby weakening Hamilton's bargaining position in Rio.) As for the supplementary articles to the anti-slave trade treaty, Britain's proposals, which had been presented to the Brazilian government in April, were finally returned to Hamilton in October. Aureliano had found his own proposals of August 1841 'essentially altered' and Aberdeen's 'objectionable on the same grounds as obliged the Imperial Government to decline ratifying the additional Articles [of 1835] . . . that is to say [they threatened] to oppress and annihilate the lawful commerce of the Empire'.[3] The Brazilian government showed no inclination to pursue the matter further.

In the meantime, Lord Aberdeen had decided, in spite of Hamilton's unfavourable reports, to send a special mission to Brazil headed by Henry Ellis, Lord Ripon's brother-in-law. His instructions were, however, by no means clear. While being given to understand on the one hand that his principal object was to persuade the Brazilian government to take the steps necessary to make the abolition of slavery in Brazil certain 'at no distant period' and

1 Hamilton to Aberdeen, 20 September 1842, B.M. Add. MSS 43124 (Aberdeen Papers).
2 Aureliano to Hamilton, 6 September, enclosed in Hamilton no. 85, 20 September 1842, F.O. 13/184.
3 Hamilton to Aureliano, 11 April, enclosed in Hamilton no. 22, 23 April 1842, F.O. 84/407; Aureliano to Hamilton, 17 October, enclosed in Hamilton no. 51, 26 November 1842, F.O. 84/409.

that this was the one condition upon which the British market could be opened to Brazilian sugar, Ellis was instructed on the other, as Aberdeen had by now instructed Hamilton, that the proposed articles concerning slavery and the sugar duties (articles 9 and 15) were not regarded as essential to any new commercial treaty—they could just as well be negotiated separately later—and if it proved impossible to reach agreement upon them a straightforward continuation of the existing commercial treaty would suffice. Failing that, he should at least try to secure a most favoured nation treaty in its place. Indeed, the British government could now see a positive advantage in terminating the 1827 treaty provided they could secure the necessary safeguards against the imposition of discriminatory duties on British goods. The treaty guaranteed Brazilian sugar the benefit of any reduction in the duties on foreign sugar entering the British market. Once the treaty was terminated it would be possible for Britain to lower the duties on *free-grown* foreign sugar (from Java, for instance) while continuing to exclude that cultivated by slave labour in Brazil and Cuba. Ellis was also ordered to bring to a speedy conclusion the negotiations for supplementary articles to the anti-slave trade treaty of 1826. These rather than a new treaty were now Britain's objective, he was told, unless the Brazilian government could be induced to accept as a whole and without significant alteration a treaty modelled on the Anglo-Spanish treaty of 1835 and the recent Anglo-Portuguese treaty (July 1842)—'by far the best and most satisfactory settlement of the question', Aberdeen thought.[1]

With great pomp and ceremony, on 10 November 1842, Henry Ellis arrived in Rio de Janeiro, where he too found both the Brazilian press and public opinion 'absurdly violent and impertinent' in their attitude towards 'enslaving Brazil with treaties'. Nor were the government any more favourably disposed towards Britain. It did not take Ellis long to realise that any agreement affecting the future of slavery in Brazil was 'quite out of the question'.[2] While perhaps no longer prepared to fly in the face of

[1] Aberdeen to Ellis, no. 7, 28 September 1842, F.O. 13/199; Aberdeen to Ellis, no. 1, 31 August 1842, F.O. 84/410. Cf. Aberdeen to Hamilton, no. 14, 6 July 1842, F.O. 13/183.
[2] Ellis no. 11, 26 November, no. 16, 16 December 1842, F.O. 13/199; Ellis to Aberdeen, 20 November 1842, Private, B.M. Add. MSS 43124 (Aberdeen Papers). Ellis's arrival

enlightened world opinion by openly defending the slave system, Brazilians of all shades of opinion recognised the necessity of slave labour in Brazil, at least until free European immigrants could be attracted in sufficient numbers. No Brazilian government would dare bring the question of slavery before the Chamber of Deputies. An offer from Britain to reduce her sugar duties and facilitate the entry of foreign sugar into the British market, however important this might be to Brazil, was in itself not a sufficient inducement for Brazilians to consider changing not only their economic system but indeed their entire way of life. At the same time Ellis realised that without an unconditional offer to lower the duties, or some other major concession, there was little hope of renewing the treaty of 1827 as it stood, so critical was the state of the country's finances, so great the need to raise additional customs revenue, and so widespread the resentment at Brazil's position of semi-dependence on Britain. When the Chamber assembled in January 1843, the government came under heavy fire for having capitulated over the terminal date of the Anglo-Brazilian commercial treaty and there were noisy demands for its immediate termination—even for a declaration of war—before moderate elements were able to persuade the extremists to accept the *fait accompli*. Clearly the Chamber could not be expected to swallow any extension of the treaty beyond November 1844 without positive benefits in return. When he consulted British merchants in Rio Ellis found they no longer attached much importance either to their judicial privileges in Brazil or to the 15% preferential tariff; these had been useful in the past when Britain was establishing its position in the Brazilian market but, provided no special favours were now granted to other nations, Britain's economic superiority over its nearest rivals would ensure the continuation of Britain's pre-eminence in Brazil. He therefore decided to settle for a new commercial treaty which simply guaranteed that British merchants and their goods would be treated on a par with those of other nations. To secure even this, however, would not be easy: as late as September Aureliano had flatly refused to discuss any new treaty

is described in J. M. Pereira da Silva, *Memorias do Meu Tempo* (Rio de Janeiro, 1898), i. 98–9. Reflections on Brazilian attitudes to slavery can also be found in Ellis no. 23. 14 January 1843, F.O. 13/200.

which did not specifically facilitate the entry of Brazilian exports into Britain.[1]

In December Ellis presented Aureliano and Senator Miguel Calmon du Pin e Almeida, the Minister of Finance, with a private memorandum setting out what he felt might be the broad basis of a new Anglo-Brazilian commercial treaty. They did not reject it out of hand; it was referred to their Cabinet colleagues and eventually submitted to the Council of State.[2] However, Aureliano again expressed the view that the proposed treaty would run into opposition unless Britain were prepared to offer some positive reciprocal advantage for Brazilian produce entering the British market. He also re-introduced the question of the activities of the British navy on anti-slave trade patrol in Brazilian territorial waters and intimated that, unless British warships were more strictly controlled, the Brazilian government would withhold co-operation over both the anti-slave trade treaty and the commercial treaty—which prompted Ellis to complain of Aureliano's 'unreasonable disposition' to mix up the negotiations for two entirely separate treaties.[3] On 15 January 1843 the foreign affairs sub-committee of the Council of State submitted a report on Ellis's memorandum: Lopes Gama alone favoured the opening of negotiations for a new commercial treaty;[4] the other members, notably Honório Hermeto Carneiro Leão, now Conservative Senator for Minas Gerais, demanded the admission of Brazilian produce into the British market on the same basis as colonial produce, or with only a small differential, as a prior condition for negotiations.

[1] For the commercial aspects of Ellis's mission I have relied heavily on A. J. Pryor's unpublished thesis, 'Anglo-Brazilian Commercial Relations', pp. 200–23; also Manchester, *British Preëminence in Brazil*, pp. 290–3.

[2] The Council of State (*Conselho de Estado*), abolished by the *Ato Adicional* of 12 August 1834, had been re-established by the law of 23 November 1841. Nominally an advisory body, its twelve members were appointed by the Emperor, who presided over its deliberations. In fact major policy decisions, for example, the decision to end the slave trade in July 1850 (see below, ch. 12, pp. 332–5), were usually taken by the Council of State, attended, if necessary, by appropriate ministers.

[3] Ellis no. 15, 10 December 1842, F.O. 13/199.

[4] Councillor Lopes Games, Senator for Rio de Janeiro, a former Minister of Empire and Foreign Minister and a former British judge conservator, had been bribed by Ellis to press for a limited commercial treaty with Britain in the Council of State (see Pryor, *op. cit.* p. 204). During the next few years he frequently served British interests—and the cause of the abolition of the slave trade—in the Council of State.

Slave trade, slavery and sugar duties, 1839–1844

On 19 January, however, after Ellis had brought forward his treaty proposals officially,[1] the full Council of State decided in favour of negotiations. But four days later there was a change of administration which put Honório in charge of Foreign Affairs in a Conservative government which was even more closely identified with the sugar interests, more protectionist in outlook, more favourable to slave trade interests and more hostile to Great Britain than its predecessor had been. (Part of the reason for Aureliano's fall after two and a half years as Foreign Minister lay in his apparent willingness to negotiate with Britain for supplementary articles to the anti-slave trade treaty and his acceptance of the continuation of the commercial treaty until November 1844.) Ellis decided that there was no longer any point in pressing for na agreement on the anti-slave trade proposals: Honório, he believed, would simply use the opportunity to contest many of the points that Britain had already gained in practice.[2] Nevertheless, Ellis continued to hope for progress on the commercial question, and in the event Honório agreed to negotiate. Confident, however, that Britain needed Brazilian foodstuffs and the Brazilian market almost as much as Brazil needed British manufactures and the British market, he continued to demand 'positive reciprocity': in return for most favoured nation status for British manufactures, Brazilian sugar together with coffee, tobacco and other agricultural produce should enter Britain at duties no more than 10% higher than those levied on colonial produce and where possible on equal terms.[3] Ellis replied, in confidence, that he was only empowered to make such a concession in return for the eventual abolition of slavery in Brazil; he did not develop the point, however, either verbally or in writing, because he was well aware that agreement on this issue was impossible. Indeed, he regretted having raised the matter at all.[4] His remark was received by Honório 'with a shrug of disgust and a positive refusal',[5] and he soon took the opportunity to remind Ellis that there were more slaves than free men in Brazil (a

[1] Ellis to Aureliano, 16 January 1843, A.H.I. 273/1/9.
[2] Ellis no. 4, 20 February 1843, F.O. 84/467. Honório and Vasconcelos had already declared that no anti-slave trade treaty would be acceptable which did not permit the introduction of free African labour into Brazil (Ellis no. 16, 16 December 1842, F.O. 13/199).
[3] Ellis no. 28, 20 February, Conf., F.O. 13/199; Ellis no. 31, 18 March 1843, F.O. 13/200.
[4] Ellis no. 31, F.O. 13/200; Ellis to Honório, 23 February, 16 March 1843, A.H.I. 273/1/9.
[5] Ellis no. 31.

235

doubtful proposition) and that the entire economy of the country was founded upon slavery. (In contrast, Honório argued, in 1833 the British government had only to emancipate 'a few hundred thousand slaves in a few small colonies'.) 'The abolition of slavery in Brazil', he went on, 'is a question for the future and not for the present . . . to determine the epoch and the manner in which for the future this question may be resolved is an object for the internal government of the country and is in the special competence of the nation represented by the general assembly and cannot form part of a treaty with any nation.'[1] An article in the *Jornal do Comércio* signed *Um deputado ministerial* (probably Honório himself or else someone writing under his direction) then made public the fact that Britain ('so excessively generous') would reduce the duties on Brazilian sugar when Brazil could no longer produce any and, deliberately exaggerating the gravity of the situation, called for Brazilians to resist any attempt by Britain to impose her demands by force. 'I had my doubt', the writer concluded, 'whether Brazil was an independent nation or whether it ought not to be considered an English colony.'[2] By the end of March 1843 negotiations had completely broken down and, shortly after, Ellis left for home with not one of his objects achieved and conscious of the fact that his mission had generated a fresh wave of ill-feeling against Britain. He had, however, at least succeeded in getting negotiations for a commercial treaty started and the Brazilian government agreed that the talks should continue in London later in the year.

As far as the slave trade treaty was concerned Hamilton was convinced that negotiations for a new treaty were futile, not, he believed, because of the Brazilian government's frequently expressed anxiety to prevent British interference in Brazilian affairs, and to protect Brazil's legitimate trade, but simply because, in his view, the Brazilian government were hand in glove with the slave trade interests.[3] Lord Aberdeen himself had by now become almost as impatient with Brazil as Lord Palmerston had been during his last months as Foreign Secretary, and in July he decided that the time had come to give the Brazilian government clear warning

[1] Honório to Ellis, 15 March, enclosed in Ellis no. 31.
[2] *Jornal do Comércio*, 15 March 1843.
[3] Hamilton no. 10, 12 April 1843, F.O. 84/467.

that, under article 1 of the treaty of 1826, Britain was obliged to suppress the Brazilian slave trade, and that if the Brazilian government persisted in refusing to concede a treaty which would enable the British navy to act with greater effectiveness then the British government would have to take the necessary steps 'alone and by her own means'.[1] On 1 September Aberdeen's warning was conveyed to the Brazilian Foreign Minister, now Paulino José Soares de Sousa (who had taken over from Honório in June) but, although Hamilton repeatedly called his attention to it, Paulino failed to comment for over four months. He then strongly denied that any Brazilian administration, past or present, had ever refused to adopt measures that would make the suppression system more efficient; indeed on more than one occasion—in August 1841, for example —they had themselves put forward concrete proposals. If the lengthy negotiations had so far proved fruitless, the reasons, Paulino suggested, were the same as they had always been: the nature of the propositions made by the British government, the manner in which they were trying to impose them on Brazil and, in particular, the outrageous—and, in his view, illegal—activities of the British warships in Brazilian waters, which could scarcely be expected to reassure the Brazilian government about the consequences of conceding them yet wider powers. He made it clear that the Brazilian government was 'not disposed to give its sanction and acquiescence to that which has been done without it, by force and against the clear and express disposition of the treaties', and wearily he repeated that any abolition treaty must respect Brazil's rights and dignity as an independent nation and must include safeguards and guarantees in respect of the property of Brazilian citizens engaged in legal trade. In particular, since impartiality was a virtue rarely found amongst over-zealous British naval officers, commissary judges and commissioners of arbitration, there were, he insisted, two *sine quibus non* of any treaty: a clause strictly defining the extensive circumstantial evidence which was necessary before any ship suspected of slaving could be condemned; and a clause establishing the means whereby compensation would be paid when a ship was acquitted. Paulino claimed that no proposals put forward by Britain at any time had dealt

[1] Aberdeen to Hamilton, no. 10, 5 July 1843, F.O. 84/468.

satisfactorily with these crucial issues, and whenever a Brazilian government had tried to clarify them, the British government had fallen back on arrogant threats.[1]

In the autumn of 1843 José de Araújo Ribeiro, the Brazilian minister in Paris and a personal friend and political ally of Honório, was sent as special envoy to London for talks with the British government. He carried, however, no new instructions on the slave trade question. Moreover, with regard to the commercial treaty, he could still only offer a most favoured nation treaty, and this in exchange for the admission of Brazilian sugar to the British market at a duty no more than 10% higher than that on colonial sugar. For their part, Aberdeen and Gladstone (who was now President of the Board of Trade) refused to divorce the question of the sugar duties from that of slavery and the slave trade and since Araújo Ribeiro had been instructed that, so as not to embarrass future Brazilian governments, he was to give no hint of when the slave system in Brazil might eventually be abolished, the deadlock remained unbroken. In January 1844 yet another round of negotiations broke down.[2] The correspondence between Aberdeen and Peel at this time suggests that the former was now prepared to permit the entry of Brazilian slave-grown sugar provided that the slave trade at least could be contained and he had great hopes that the plans afoot for strengthening the British preventive squadron and for a more systematic blockade of the west African coast might go a long way towards achieving this. Time alone would tell, however, and, as Peel reminded him, experience had shown that they could not afford to be too sanguine as to the success of their efforts for the repression of the slave trade. In the meantime, Peel continued, much as they might wish to see the sugar duties reduced, the British government could hardly adopt a commercial policy which might serve as a positive encouragement to the slave trade.[3]

---

[1] Hamilton to Paulino, 1 September 1843, Paulino to Hamilton, 11 Jan. 1844, enclosed in Hamilton no. 9, 27 February 1844, F.O. 84/523. Paulino's reply has been printed in Pereira Pinto, i. 445–62, and Perdigão Malheiro, ii. 244–52.

[2] For details of the Araújo Ribeira mission, see Pryor, *op. cit.* pp. 240–56; Manchester, *op. cit.* pp. 293–5.

[3] Aberdeen to Peel, 17 January, Peel to Aberdeen, 19 January 1844, quoted in W. D. Jones, 'The Origins and Passage of Lord Aberdeen's Act', *H.A.H.R.* xlii (1962), pp. 505–6.

In manufacturing and commercial circles with interests in Brazil there nevertheless remained a great deal of apprehension about the consequences for British trade of the termination of the 1827 treaty before it had been replaced by a most favoured nation treaty. As for the Whig opposition, they felt that the government had irritated the Brazilians unnecessarily by making the abolition of slavery rather than a simple fulfilment of their obligations to suppress the slave trade the *sine qua non* for the admission of Brazilian sugar into Britain. On 7 March 1844 the issue was debated in the House of Commons. Henry Labouchere, who had been President of the Board of Trade during the last two years of the Melbourne administration, supported by prominent free traders like John Bright, William Ewart and Thomas Milner Gibson, as well as by Lord Palmerston, urged the end of the sugar monopoly as the measure best calculated to maintain and increase Britain's already substantial trade with Brazil.[1] However, the government stood by their policy which, they claimed, not only served to protect the West Indian colonies but also, in Gladstone's words, 'powerfully and effectually aided the vigilance of our cruisers in suppressing the slave trade'.[2] Labouchere's motion was defeated by 205 votes to 132.

A month later—in April—Hamilton was instructed to make a final bid to sign a commercial treaty which would at least guarantee British merchants parity with those of other nations.[3] But by this time it was clear that the Brazilian government had definitely decided that the treaty of 1827, which so restricted their power to adjust tariffs to meet the financial needs of the country, must be terminated before any consideration could be given to fresh British proposals. A Brazilian Tariff Commission, however, appointed in December 1843 to adjust the tariffs on imported goods in anticipation of the ending of the treaty, proved surprisingly responsive to *laissez-faire* ideas. Moreover, a change of administration in February 1844 had brought in a coalition government in which the Minister of Finance, Manuel Alves Branco, a Liberal, was a leading figure. As a result, the new tariffs finally announced in August 1844 proved much less protectionist in their nature than

---

[1] Hansard, lxxiii. 606–90.   [2] *Ibid.* 632.
[3] Pryor, 'Anglo-Brazilian Commercial Relations', p. 300.

many people in Britain had anticipated.[1] Nevertheless, British commerce no longer enjoyed a privileged position and Brazilian governments now had the power to retaliate against British goods if, for example, the restrictions on Brazilian produce entering Britain were not relaxed. The Conservative government in England, however, did little to allay the fears of those who would be affected by the imposition in Brazil of discriminatory duties on British manufactures; although Peel further reduced the coffee duties to 6*d* per lb foreign and 4*d* per lb colonial, he took advantage of the impending termination of the Brazilian treaty to lower the duty on *free-grown* foreign sugar to 34*s* per cwt while leaving that on *slave-grown* sugar at 63*s* per cwt. (A year later the duty on colonial sugar was reduced to 14*s* and that on foreign free-grown sugar to 23*s*.) Thus Peel alienated both die-hard protectionists and extreme free traders but managed to satisfy the moderates in both camps, as well as many abolitionists; two opposition amendments in favour of equalising all sugar duties were heavily defeated.[2] Naturally, this latest British move did nothing to improve relations with Brazil, though with her exports showing signs of expansion again and her economy more dependent now on coffee than on sugar, Brazil was rather less concerned with the state of the British sugar duties.

There was one other area in which Britain might have been able to give Brazil sufficient assistance to secure in return both a satisfactory commercial treaty and a more effective anti-slave trade treaty. The Brazilian government was becoming increasingly alarmed at political instability in the Río de la Plata, resulting from the war between Buenos Aires and Montevideo, and at the growing and disturbing influence of Rosas, the Argentinian dictator, who quite clearly had designs not only on Uruguay and Paraguay, but also on the adjoining Brazilian province of Rio Grande do Sul which was in revolt against the central government in Rio de Janeiro. Ellis had earlier suggested to Aberdeen that if the British government wanted concessions from Brazil they would be better advised to offer to guarantee Brazil's southern boundary and the territorial integrity of the Empire rather than to reduce the

[1] Pryor, *op. cit.* pp. 258 ff; for Aberdeen's comments, see Jones, *op. cit.* p. 506.
[2] Schuyler, *op. cit.* pp. 138–40; Morrell, *op. cit.* pp. 182–5.

sugar duties.[1] During the summer of 1843 the Brazilian government had sounded out Hamilton on the possibility of Anglo-Brazilian co-operation for the pacification of the Río de la Plata and the maintenance of the territorial *status quo* and the balance of power there.[2] A year later the antagonism between Buenos Aires and Brazil had reached menacing proportions and the Marquês de Abrantes (Miguel Calmon du Pin e Almeida), who was on the point of leaving for Berlin in the hope of negotiating a commercial treaty with the Zollverein, was instructed to stop *en route* in London and Paris and seek the help of Britain and France whose governments, because of their own commercial involvement, also had an interest in maintaining peace and stability in the Río de la Plata. In the course of discussions with Abrantes during November and December 1844 Lord Aberdeen showed some interest in the prospect of tripartite Anglo-French-Brazilian intervention provided that a satisfactory settlement could be reached immediately on both the commercial and the slave trade treaties. Abrantes, however, could hold out no hope of any change in the Brazilian government's position on either treaty.[3] By the end of the year, all negotiations between the two countries had apparently ground to a halt.

[1] Ellis no. 16, F.O. 13/199; Ellis no. 28, F.O. 13/200. Cf. Stevenson to Hamilton, 21 April 1842, Conf., enclosed in Hamilton no. 46, 18 May 1842, Conf., F.O. 13/182.

[2] Jones, *Lord Aberdeen and the Americas*, p. 41.

[3] On the Abrantes mission, see *A Missão Especial do Visconde de Abrantes* (2 vols., Rio de Janeiro, 1853); Jones, *Lord Aberdeen*, pp. 42–3; Jones, *H.A.H.R.* (1962), pp. 502–3. In the event Brazil was excluded from the joint Anglo-French intervention of 1845–6 which proved such a dismal failure. See John F. Cady, *Foreign Intervention in the Río de la Plata, 1838–50* (Univ. of Pennsylvania Press, 1929), pp. 132–3, 139–40, 144–59; H. S. Ferns, *Britain and Argentina in the Nineteenth Century* (Oxford, 1960), ch. 9; José Honório Rodrigues, 'The Foundations of Brazil's Foreign Policy', *International Affairs*, XXXVIII (1962), pp. 328–9.

CHAPTER 9

LORD ABERDEEN'S ACT OF 1845

In a letter to Peel on 18 October 1844, Lord Aberdeen forecast that Britain's relations with Brazil would soon become 'unpleasant and complicated'.[1] Partly as a demonstration of her independence from Britain, Brazil had insisted—as she had the right to do—on terminating the Anglo-Brazilian commercial treaty of 1827, one of the two treaties which had been imposed upon her more than fifteen years earlier as the price of British recognition of her independence from Portugal. The other treaty, the Anglo-Brazilian abolition treaty of 1826, was of indefinite duration and could not therefore be terminated unilaterally by Brazil. However, the treaty of 1817, which formed part of the treaty of 1826—and a crucial part, since it was under this treaty that the British navy exercised the right of search and the Anglo-Brazilian mixed commissions adjudicated upon captured Brazilian vessels—was not permanent. Indeed, it would have been brought to an end as early as March 1830 when the Brazilian slave trade first became entirely illegal had not Lord Palmerston taken advantage of the separate article of 11 September 1817 which permitted it to continue in force for a further fifteen years.[2] In May 1842 David Stevenson, the English lawyer resident in Rio de Janeiro who frequently acted for British naval officers in the Rio mixed commission as well as for British merchants with claims against the Brazilian government and whose advice on slave trade matters was frequently sought by the British legation, had drawn attention to the disturbing fact that the fifteen-year period since March 1830 was now drawing to a close, and in March 1843, after consultations with John Samo, the British commissary judge, both Henry Ellis and Hamilton Hamilton had privately acknowledged in their despatches to Lord Aberdeen that in March 1845 the Brazilian government might well insist upon the termination of the mutual right of search and the dissolution of the mixed com-

[1] Aberdeen to Peel, 18 October 1844, B.M. Add. MSS 43064 (Aberdeen Papers).
[2] See above, ch. 4, p. 94.

242

missions.[1] With classic British understatement, Ellis had described this possibility as a 'contingency of no trifling importance'. In fact it would mean that the British preventive squadron on the West African naval station, which was shortly to be strengthened, would be rendered almost powerless at a time when there were clear signs that the slave trade to Brazil (after several years of reduced activity) was beginning to revive once again. Brazilian ships, even those packed with slaves, would be free to pursue their traffic in human lives, untroubled by the fear of search and capture by British warships and condemnation in the courts of mixed commission. Moreover, traders of other nationalities, too, would inevitably take advantage of the complete security which the Brazilian flag would henceforth offer. Ellis could not believe that Britain would readily give up its rights in this matter in deference to the 'illusory pretensions' of the Brazilian government to suppress the slave trade themselves. But if no new treaty were signed —and both Hamilton and Ellis were agreed that negotiations were unlikely to be brought to a successful conclusion before March 1845—on what grounds could British cruisers legally continue to capture Brazilian slave ships, and which courts would be competent to adjudicate upon them? Ellis found himself arguing that the British government might have no alternative but to carry out immediately the threats they had been making on and off for years to 'deal summarily with the Brazilian government . . . and take such measures for preventing the landing of slaves on the coast of Brazil as the naval power of Great Britain supplies'. He thought it highly probable that such a course of action would quickly induce the Brazilian government to make proposals for a new anti-slave trade treaty in order to control the operation of the British navy on the Brazilian coast (Lord Palmerston's Act of 1839 had soon persuaded the Portuguese of the wisdom of signing a new treaty).[2]

Throughout 1843 and 1844, the Brazilian government had

[1] Stevenson's 'Observations in reference to the proposed supplementary articles to the Convention of 1826 for the abolition of the slave trade', 16 May 1842, F.O. 84/407; Ellis to Aberdeen, no. 5, Conf., 4 March 1843, F.O. 84/467; Hamilton to Aberdeen, 22 March 1843, Secret and Conf., F.O. 84/467.
[2] Ellis to Aberdeen, no. 5; cf. Ellis to Aberdeen, 22 March 1843, B.M. Add. MSS 43124 (Aberdeen Papers): 'we must I am sure rely entirely upon our own means for its [the slave trade's] suppression'.

given no indication that they were aware of the state of the treaties and naturally Aberdeen had no intention of jogging their memory.[1] At the same time, Hamilton continued to seek guidance in the event of the Brazilians seizing the opportunity to terminate the treaty of 1817 in March 1845. No clear instructions, however, were forthcoming. By the autumn of 1844 time was running out and it was becoming urgently necessary to decide upon a course of action. Aberdeen had until then given very little attention to the matter: he apparently believed that it was the treaty of 1826 that was due to expire in March 1845 and that Britain would be thrown back upon the treaties of 1815 and 1817! However, he now began to toy with the idea of adopting coercive measures against Brazilian slave ships, similar to those which had been taken against Portuguese ships in 1839, and which he had himself brought to an end in 1842. In October 1844 he wrote to Peel:

I should propose to offer to Brazil the Portuguese Treaty of 1842 or something like it and to follow it up with an intimation that if they refuse to concur in effectual measures for the abolition of the Trade, they will be treated in the same manner as Portugal. The Law [of 1839] was certainly a great stretch of power, and open to many objections in principle; but having been once sanctioned by Parliament, the difficulty of applying it in a similar case is in great measure removed.[2]

Three weeks later, however, in a long memorandum in which he contrasted Brazil's treaty engagements with those of Portugal in 1839, Lord Canning, Under-Secretary of State at the Foreign Office, made it clear that Britain could not simply extend the Act of 1839 to Brazilian vessels: many of the charges of violating the

[1] In July 1843, in the original draft of a despatch to Hamilton, Aberdeen had threatened unilateral British action against the Brazilian slave trade if the Brazilians continued to reject the idea of reinforcing or replacing the anti-slave trade treaty and, more specifically, if they allowed the right of search to lapse before the slave trade had become extinct. In the event, however, it had been thought prudent to omit any reference to the fact that the Brazilians had the right to terminate the right of search in March 1845 (Aberdeen to Hamilton, no. 10, 5 July 1843, draft, F.O. 84/468).

[2] Aberdeen to Peel, 18 October 1844, quoted in W. D. Jones, 'The Origins and Passage of Lord Aberdeen's Act', *H.A.H.R.* xlii (1962), 510–11. A number of documents relating to the origins of Aberdeen's Act are quoted extensively in this interesting article which appeared when my own work was in progress; some aspects of the subject are, however, inadequately treated and some important documents which help explain the nature of the Act and, in particular, the extent to which it differed from the Palmerston Act have been completely overlooked.

treaties of 1810, 1815 and 1817 which had been levelled against Portugal in order to justify the Palmerston Act were not applicable to Brazil. If coercive measures were to be adopted against the Brazilian slave trade they would have to be justified on different grounds—that is, Brazil's failure to fulfil her engagements under the treaty of 1826. In conclusion Canning raised two questions of some importance: first, before taking matters into their own hands should the British government allow the Brazilians a trial period in the hope, however remote, that they might themselves take vigorous action against the slave trade once they were freed from what they clearly regarded as an odious treaty and one under which they had discharged their duties 'sulkily and imperfectly'? secondly, should the British government give Brazil advance warning of what their intentions were if the treaty of 1817 were allowed to expire?[1]

Reluctant to use coercive methods against Brazil if they could be avoided, Lord Aberdeen decided to make a last-minute bid to avoid a crisis. At the beginning of December 1844, in a typically indecisive and ambiguous despatch, he instructed Hamilton to propose once again a new treaty on the lines of that signed by Portugal in 1842—'the best as it is the most recent of our slave trade treaties, and our new Code of Instructions to our officers renders any abuse in the execution of it scarcely possible'—but only if the Brazilian government seemed likely to agree without prolonged negotiation and appeared strong enough to withstand the opposition such a treaty would inevitably create. Aberdeen was now prepared to admit that past Brazilian governments had probably gone as far as they were able towards meeting British demands, and he was afraid that too much pressure at this critical juncture might jeopardise the chance of at least prolonging the existing treaties after March 1845. He was still not entirely clear in his own mind about the state of the treaties and had still to concede that the treaty of 1817 did in fact expire in March 1845: 'it is', he insisted obscurely, 'a question of how far the practical adoption by Brazil of the measures necessary to give efficiency to the treaties has invested them with a permanent character'. To Aberdeen's

---

[1] 'Memorandum on the present position of Brazil as regards the slave trade treaties with Great Britain compared with that of Portugal in 1839', 11 November 1844, F.O. 96/29.

mind the best way of avoiding the impending difficulties seemed to be for Britain 'to continue to act tacitly as at present'. 'This we conceive we have a right to do', he wrote to Hamilton, 'in virtue of the treaties with Portugal of 1815 and 1817, and of the obligations contracted with us by Brazil [in 1826]. We shall consequently send no new instructions to our officers and continue to act in all respects as heretofore.' If the Brazilians preferred, he was prepared to agree to a formal renewal, for two years, of existing treaty engagements, together with the modifications which had been made to them during recent years—he was thinking in particular of the addition in practice of the equipment clause—with a view to the immediate reopening of negotiations for a new treaty. In the course of his discussions with the Brazilian government, Hamilton was instructed to adopt as conciliatory and friendly a tone as possible, being 'particularly careful to avoid anything like menacing language or a harsh or dictatorial manner'. He was, however, given permission to issue a warning that if a satisfactory agreement on the slave trade question were not reached, Britain would not enter the proposed concert, recently discussed in London by Lord Aberdeen and the Marquês de Abrantes, for dealing with the problems of the Río de la Plata. And if the Brazilians proved obstinate and insisted that the treaty of 1817 expire, Aberdeen suggested to Hamilton that it might be advisable to 'hold out the possibility of our being compelled to have recourse to a law similar to that enacted against Portugal in 1839 ... We should consider that the permanent engagement of Brazil would justify us in having recourse to such a measure of necessity, as in the case of Portugal. I should regret it very much, and it would undoubtedly be a proceeding of a very unfriendly character; but with this recent example, I do not see how we could help following the precedent.'[1]

In Rio de Janeiro, Hamilton was not at all clear how he should act. He had no doubt that agreement on a treaty similar to the Anglo-Portuguese treaty of 1842 was out of the question: both collectively and individually, he believed the Brazilian govern-

[1] Aberdeen to Hamilton, no. 15, 4 December 1844, Conf., F.O. 84/525; Aberdeen to Hamilton, 4 December 1844, B.M. Add. MSS 43124. Extracts from the latter (private) despatch are quoted in Jones, *op. cit.* pp. 511–12.

ment at the time to be on the whole averse to the slave trade—
Alves Branco, the Minister of Finance, for example, was the minister responsible for the additional articles of 1835—but 'they would
not, because they dare not, make any forward move towards its
suppression—unless under compulsion'. On the other hand, he
continued to hold out some little hope that in the event they might
allow the treaty of 1817 to continue in force after March 1845 and
thus avoid taking a step backwards. However, loath to precipitate
any action by the Brazilian government Hamilton appears to have
made no attempt to reach a formal agreement on this point. Nor
did he threaten the Brazilians with Lord Aberdeen's alternative
which, in the circumstances, was perhaps a more serious omission.[1]
John Samo, the British commissary judge, however, had little
doubt that the British navy would soon be called upon to adopt
extreme measures against the Brazilian slave trade, perhaps even
in Brazilian territorial waters. He was reported to have enquired
of Mr Slocum, a friend and neighbour who had once served as
U.S. consul, whether he would still be in Rio de Janeiro in April,
remarking, 'If you are here then, you will see some fun.'[2]

Encouraged by the stand they had taken over the Anglo-Brazilian
commercial treaty (and also by the knowledge that Britain had
recently failed to persuade the United States to concede the right
of search and was now prepared to consider the repeal of the
Anglo-French right of search treaties of 1831 and 1833[3]), the
Brazilian government were in fact secretly planning to take
advantage of the opportunity about to be presented for terminating the right of search treaty of 1817. By doing so they could at
a stroke remove the teeth from an anti-slave trade treaty which

[1] Hamilton to Aberdeen, 31 January 1845, B.M. Add. MSS 43124. Hamilton to Aberdeen,
no. 5, 15 February 1845, F.O. 84/581.
[2] Henry A. Wise to John C. Calhoun, Secretary of State, 25 February 1845, printed in
Manning, *Diplomatic Correspondence*, ii, 274–5.
[3] In view of the growing popular pressure on the French government for the termination
of the right of search, Britain had agreed to establish a commission to investigate whether
alternative means could be found to prevent a reappearance of the French flag in the
slave trade. On the controversy between Britain and France over the right of search, see
Douglas Johnson, *Guizot: aspects of French history 1787–1874* (London, 1963), pp. 286–91.
The Duc de Broglie and Stephen Lushington took evidence from a number of British
and French naval officers during March–April 1845 (Minutes, B.M. Add. MSS 43357
(Aberdeen Papers).

they and their predecessors had always claimed had been signed by
Dom Pedro I in 1826 under extreme pressure, which had never
been acceptable to the Brazilian people as a whole and which in
the event had proved highly prejudicial to national sovereignty
and national interests. On 4 March the foreign affairs sub-committee of the Council of State consisting of three Conservative politicians, the Marquês de Monte Alegre (José da Costa Carvalho),
Bernardo Pereira de Vasconcelos and Honório Hermeto Carneiro
Leão (all of them known to favour the landed interest and the last
two, in particular, well known for their hostility to Britain) was
asked as a matter of urgency to look into the state of the anti-slave
trade treaties with Britain.[1] Five days later they reported that the
treaty of 1817 could and should be terminated immediately.[2]
Moreover, they were at pains to point out that Brazil's right to do
so could not be contested by Britain in view of the position
adopted by Lord Palmerston in his negotiations with Mello Mattos,
the Brazilian *chargé* in London, fifteen years earlier.[3] On 10 March
the report was approved by an extraordinary meeting of the full
Council of State presided over by the young Emperor.[4] On
12 March Ernesto Ferreira França, Minister of Foreign Affairs
(February 1844 to May 1845), who in the great debate of 1827 on
the Anglo-Brazilian treaty had declared that 'if we should wish
to make a law concerning this [the slave trade] we would do well
to call in the English to make it with us',[5] officially notified
Hamilton that as from the following day the treaty of 1817 would
expire, that the mutual right of British and Brazilian cruisers to
visit, search, detain and send for adjudication British and Brazilian
slavers would consequently come to an end, and that the Anglo-
Brazilian mixed commissions sitting in Rio de Janeiro and Freetown would continue to function for a further six months only,
in order to conclude the adjudication of ships captured before
13 March. At the same time the Brazilian government, apprehensive about Britain's reaction to this move, assured Hamilton that
they intended, as soon as possible, to introduce more rigorous

---

[1] *Aviso*, 4 March 1845, A.H.I. 342/3/17.
[2] *Paracer*, 9 March 1845, A.H.I. 342/2/12.
[3] See above, ch. 4, pp. 94–5.
[4] *Acta*, 10 March 1845, A. N. Códice 307/1.
[5] Quoted in Rodrigues, *Brazil and Africa*, p. 163.

legislation of their own for the suppression of the slave trade, which, of course, remained illegal. And in the meantime a determined attempt would be made to enforce the anti-slave trade law of November 1831.[1] (On 15 March the Minister of Justice informed the presidents of the maritime provinces that the ordinary courts of Brazil would henceforth be competent to adjudicate on slave ships captured by Brazilian military and naval forces.[2]) Two weeks later, in the Chamber of Deputies, Ferreira França again emphasised that the government's decision to end the 1817 treaty should not be taken to mean that the illegal slave trade would now be tolerated and that since the government believed peaceful and friendly relations with Britain to be highly desirable they were still prepared to try and reach agreement on a new anti-slave trade treaty, always provided it was 'just and reasonable'—that is, on Brazil's terms.[3]

The Brazilian deputies were given an opportunity to express their views on the recent turn of events during a debate on foreign affairs (31 March to 2 April 1845).[4] While no member openly or even implicitly came out in defence of the slave trade, even on the grounds of Brazil's short-term economic needs, the Chamber was virtually unanimous in its condemnation of the anti-slave trade measures that Britain had lately adopted and wholeheartedly supported the government's determination to withdraw the right of search. At the same time the debate produced one of the greatest abolitionist speeches ever heard in the Brazilian Chamber. Antônio Carlos de Andrada e Silva (São Paulo), the late José Bonifácio's brother and the man who had led the short-lived abolitionist Cabinet of the Majority (1840–1), stated categorically,

I am an enemy of the traffic in slaves. I see in this commerce all possible evils, an attack on Christianity, humanity and the true interests of Brazil. I am a man, a Christian, a patriot, and I cannot allow it. This commerce carried on for the benefit of one race is anti-Christian and I

---

1 Ferreira França to Hamilton, 12 March, enclosed in Hamilton to Aberdeen, no. 8, 22 March 1845, F.O. 84/581.
2 Ministry of Justice circular, 15 March, enclosed in Hamilton no. 8, 22 March 1845; see also Livro de registro dos alvarás, decretos, nomeações e correspondência expedida pelo Ministério dos Negócios Estrangeiros, A.H.I. 341/1/6, pp. 191–200.
3 *Anais do Parlamento Brasileiro. Câmara dos Deputados*, first session, 1845, vol. ii, pp. 342–3.
4 *Ibid.* pp. 340–3, 345–58, 371–99.

do not believe that man was born for slavery. I believe that the blacks, the mulattos, the greens if there are any, are quite as good as we are and as worthy of being free.

On the grounds of expediency, too, he considered it unwise to people the continent with enemies 'because truly deplorable will be the epoch, should it ever arrive, of reprisals'. He bore no dislike for the English; he thought Brazil herself was largely responsible for her difficulties because he felt that past governments should have enforced the law of November 1831. Instead, he asserted, they had secretly countenanced the trade: 'members of past ministries have their estates full of Africans, they are the culprits'. Furthermore, he believed that 'all the ill-feeling that has been raised against England proceeds from the extinction of the traffic'. Yet even Antônio Carlos, a staunch patriot ('infamy and Brazil can have no connexion!'), felt bound to join the majority of deputies in supporting the government's action of 12 March: he too disliked the manner in which Britain had arrogantly imposed laws and treaties upon them; he liked even less the activities of the British navy on the coast of Brazil. The debate produced only one wholly uncritical defence of Britain and that came from Nicolau Rodrigues dos Santos França Leite, a deputy for Paraíba and later president of the Brazilian Anti-Slave Trade Society (founded in 1850): he deplored the 'great odium heaped upon the English nation' and thought 'her pretensions [had] been greatly exaggerated'. Britain did not claim the right of search in order that she might consolidate her maritime supremacy, nor that she might ruin Brazilian agriculture, as most Brazilians believed; it was needed, he argued, for the 'sublime task' of abolishing the slave trade which Brazilian governments tolerated and protected in violation of their own laws and the treaties they had contracted with Britain.

But if most Brazilian deputies supported the government in its move to end the right of search treaty, they were also apprehensive about the consequences. Francisco de Sousa Martins (Piauí) reminded the Chamber that in 1839, in violation of the Anglo-Portuguese treaties, British warships had been ordered to visit and capture Portuguese slave ships in any latitude, even within the territorial waters of Portuguese Africa, and to take them for adjudication before British admiralty courts. There was ample evidence in the activities of the British navy on the Brazilian coast since 1839, and in the repeated threats of the British government, that similar action might now be taken against Brazilian ships. As Angelo Muniz da Silva Ferraz (Bahia) commented gloomily, 'England does not respect either treaties or conventions.' Yet the Chamber was divided on the question of what action the government should take if Britain refused to accept that the treaty of 1817 had expired. Ferreira França, the Foreign Minister, announced that Brazil would stand firm in maintaining the rights she enjoyed under international law. But Sousa Martins and José Ildefonso de Sousa Ramos (his colleague from Piauí) could see that Brazil was likely to suffer further humiliations unless the government were able to withstand British pressure; they therefore demanded that the money should somehow be found in order that the number of ships in the Brazilian navy could immediately be quadrupled in the event of a declaration of war. Antônio Carlos de Andrada, on the other hand, while promising his support if the government did decide to go to war in defence of their interpretation of the anti-slave trade treaty, was reluctant to do battle with 'a colossus' like Great Britain, except as a last resort. And he was not alone: indeed there were few deputies who doubted that the government would be wise to offer to negotiate a new treaty as soon as possible.

Two weeks after this debate, on 15 April, the foreign affairs sub-committee of the Council of State produced a second, rather confused, report on the slave trade question. They recognised Brazil's permanent treaty obligations to suppress the trade, but they expressed the hope that no effort would be spared to find a means of doing so other than the mutual right of visit and search which was, by its very nature, subject to abuse. At the same time, however, the members of the committee seemed prepared in certain circumstances to accept a continuation of this right, provided there could be adequate safeguards: in order to protect Brazil's coastal trade there should be a line of longitude within which vessels leaving a Brazilian port could not be searched; captured vessels should be taken for adjudication before their own national tribunals instead of before mixed commissions; ships should be captured only if there were absolutely positive indications that they were engaged in the trade—and equipment alone would probably not constitute sufficient evidence; merchant vessels travelling in convoy protected by a warship should not be liable to visit; and only high-ranking British officers, with Brazilian authorisation, should be allowed to search suspicious vessels.[1] The sub-committee's report was approved on 12 June at a meeting of the full Council of State. However, there was by no means unanimity of opinion about its recommendations. Francisco de Paula Sousa, a senator from São Paulo, rejected the sub-committee's compromise over the right of search. The former Regent, Pedro de Araújo Lima, now Visconde de Olinda, found the report satisfactory as far as it went and was anxious that the government should make immediate overtures for a new anti-slave trade treaty acceptable to Brazil. It was Lopes Gama (himself an advocate of a much tougher policy against the slave trade) who introduced a gloomy note into the proceedings by arguing that by terminating the treaty of 1817 before a new treaty had been negotiated Brazil's position *vis-à-vis* Britain had been weakened, not, as the Brazilian government seemed to think, strengthened. The British government, he reminded his colleagues, were now free from any obligation to work for an agreement with Brazil and, far from either relinquishing their efforts or signing what they would regard as a less effective treaty, they would probably resort to even stronger measures than those adopted in the past and might even decide to treat the Brazilian slave trade as piracy.[2]

It was already beginning to look as though Lopes Gama might be right. To begin with, Hamilton had still not replied to Ferreira França's note of 12 March. (Unknown to the Brazilians he had in fact suggested to Aberdeen 'a little gentle coercion . . . as the only effective means yet at our command . . . a few days blockade of the port of Rio de Janeiro would be amply sufficient to open their eyes and enlighten their judgement'.[3]) Commodore Purvis, senior naval officer on the Brazilian coast, still awaiting instruc-

---

[1] *Paracer*, 18 April 1845 (submitted 7 May), A.H.I. 342/2/13.
[2] *Acta*, 12 June 1845, A. N. Códice 307/1.
[3] Hamilton to Aberdeen, 28 May 1845, B.M. Add. MSS 43124 (Aberdeen Papers). In his despatch no. 8, 22 March, commenting on Ferreira França's note of 12 March, Hamilton had written that it was an 'admissible question whether . . . the convention on the slave trade . . . ought not to be considered as remaining in full vigour'.

tions from London, had not yet countermanded the orders previously issued to his officers concerning the capture of Brazilian slavers—although as it happened the squadron was still very much occupied in the Río de la Plata and no Brazilian vessel had been captured on the Brazilian coast for several months.[1] And on 18 June the British commissioners in the Rio mixed court, also awaiting fresh instructions, positively refused in the meanwhile to accept the validity of the Brazilian interpretation of the anti-slave trade treaties, declaring themselves competent to deal with any Brazilian prizes which might be brought before the court.[2] Moreover, Britain's apparent reluctance to co-operate with Brazil against Rosas in the Río de la Plata was now seen in a new light: the Brazilian government had come to believe, reported Henry Wise, the American minister, that it was Britain's policy 'to bring Rosas down upon this country and then to dictate a new slave trade treaty in the midst of new difficulties, precisely as she dictated the old treaty in the times of old troubles'.[3]

At the beginning of July Antônio Paulino Limpo de Abreu, who on 26 May had taken over from Ferreira França as Foreign Minister in a reshuffled Liberal administration, felt it advisable to reiterate in a note to Hamilton that the Brazilian government were not refusing outright to enter a new anti-slave trade convention, and would be willing to do so provided the terms were right. And in an effort to persuade Britain to give way to Brazilian demands he tried to link negotiations for a new slave trade treaty with those for a new commercial treaty. When the old treaty had finally expired in November 1844 the Brazilian government had appointed a plenipotentiary to treat with Hamilton on this question. They had, however, made two prior conditions: a satisfactory settlement of the boundary dispute with British Guiana and the payment of compensation for Brazilian vessels illegally seized by British warships in the past. To these two conditions Limpo de Abreu now added a third, a mutually acceptable agreement on the slave trade question, and he offered to instruct the Brazilian plenipotentiary to draw up a number of anti-slave trade

1 Purvis to Admiralty, 18 March 1845, F.O. 84/610.
2 Extract of minute, enclosed in Samo and Grigg to Hamilton, 18 June 1845, F.O. 131/7.
3 Wise to Buchanan, Secretary of State, no. 23, 2 July 1845, printed in Manning ii, 283.

articles which could be added to a new commercial treaty. In the meantime he expressed the hope that the British government would do nothing unilaterally which might damage the chances of agreement being reached.[1]

It was at the beginning of May that Lord Aberdeen first received news from Hamilton that the Brazilian government had given notice to terminate the treaty of 1817. Neither he nor Peel was in any mood to abandon lightly the struggle for the suppression of the Brazilian slave trade. They were already smarting under several blistering attacks delivered by Lord Palmerston on what he called unfairly the Conservative record of 'indifference' on slave trade matters: Aberdeen's 'misguided' letter to the Admiralty of May 1842 concerning the navy's blockading tactics on the west African coast, the partial suspension of the Act of 1839, the 'capitulation' to the United States on the right of search question, the decision to concentrate the navy almost exclusively on the west African coast, the government's apparent readiness to relinquish the right of search treaties of 1831 and 1833 with France, and their overall failure to use 'political influence and . . . physical coercion with a steady and firm determination'—all these were responsible, in Palmerston's view, for the revival of the slave trade after it had been brought under some measure of control during the last years of his own period at the Foreign Office.[2] Having already failed to persuade the Brazilians to renew or replace the commercial treaty of 1827, the Conservative government could not afford a second retreat in the face of pressure from Brazil, a weak and formerly dependent state, particularly since it was bound to lead to a further expansion of the Brazilian slave trade by placing it 'beyond the reach of the only means of repression which have hitherto been found effective', namely, the mutual right of search and the courts of mixed commission.[3] At the same time,

---

[1] Limpo de Abreu to Hamilton, 2 July, enclosed in Hamilton to Aberdeen, no. 25, 4 July 1845; Manchester, *op. cit.* p. 296; Pryor, 'Anglo-Brazilian Commercial Relations', pp. 335-7.

[2] E.g. Hansard, lxxvi, 922-48 (16 July 1844), lxxx, 199-209 (5 May 1845), lxxx, 466-81 (16 May 1845). Cf. Eric Williams, *Capitalism and Slavery* (Chapel Hill, 1944) p. 174: 'In office Palmerston accomplished little. Out of office he goaded the government to greater efforts to accomplish what he had failed to do.'

[3] Aberdeen to Hamilton, no. 9, 14 May 1845, F.O. 84/583.

since the treaty of 1817 had always been less than satisfactory and had given rise to interminable wrangles with Brazil, an opportunity to discard it was not entirely unwelcome, always provided it was possible to find other equally, and preferably more, effective means of suppressing the trade.

In spite of his earlier threats of unilateral action against Brazilian slavers Lord Aberdeen was anxious to avoid a repetition of the events of 1839. Many Tory peers had protested against Lord Palmerston's Act to the bitter end. Moreover, both he and Peel had repeatedly asserted in the past that, unlike Palmerston and the Whigs, they were not prepared to overstep the limits of existing treaties in their efforts to suppress the slave trade. The Conservative government had every intention of dealing with the slave trade problem, Peel told Palmerston in the House of Commons on 16 May 1845, 'within the terms of existing treaties and the framework of international law, and without taking any action which might endanger amicable relations with other states whose goodwill and co-operation were essential to the attainment of Britain's object'. Indeed, he wondered whether Britain's difficulties 'instead of being diminished would not be increased if we were to place ourselves decidedly in the wrong even in enforcing the admitted rights of humanity'.[1]

The situation was, Aberdeen and Peel agreed, 'most complicated and embarrassing',[2] but happily a way out of it was quickly found. Lord Aberdeen was by this time rather better acquainted with the Anglo-Brazilian treaties than he had been six months earlier and he was now aware that, even though the treaty of 1817 had expired, the treaty of 1826, the first article of which declared that slaving by Brazilian subjects was to be 'deemed and treated as piracy', still continued in full force. It was in the word 'piracy' that Aberdeen discovered what he was looking for. By the common consent of all civilised nations the warships of any nation could search and capture on the high seas pirate vessels, whatever flag they were flying. Aberdeen realised that if it were possible to interpret the first article of the treaty of 1826 as giving Britain the

---

[1] Hansard, lxxx, 489–90. Cf. lxxvi, 957, 966 (16 July 1844).
[2] Peel to Aberdeen, 11 May 1845, Aberdeen to Peel, 12 May 1845, quoted in Jones, *op. cit.* p. 513.

right to treat the Brazilian slave trade as piracy, then *without exceeding its treaty rights* the British navy could not only continue but intensify its efforts for the suppression of the Brazilian slave trade. Thus the problem of Britain's rights under the first article of the treaty of 1826, first posed fifteen years earlier and subsequently shelved, had now to be faced once again. During the years which followed the signing of the treaty, it had in fact been widely understood that, after 1830, Brazilian slave ships could be treated as pirates by British warships, and it was possible to argue, though this was debatable, that the Brazilian government themselves had at the time concurred in this interpretation of the treaty. For their part the British government had actually considered introducing legislation which would have enabled British courts to deal with cases of Brazilians suspected of slave trading and therefore of piracy. In the event, however, Lord Palmerston had preferred to prolong the treaty of 1817, and with it the mutual right of search and the Anglo-Brazilian mixed commissions, into the period after 1830,[1] contenting himself with periodic demands (for example, in 1838) that the Brazilians themselves treat slave traders as pirates.[2] For fifteen years it had seemed that successive Brazilian governments had contrived to prove how wrong that decision had been: they had permitted the slave trade to expand to an unprecedented extent and had consistently refused to co-operate with Britain in making the treaty of 1826 a more effective weapon. They had been warned often enough of the consequences of their behaviour. Now, in 1845, with the termination of the 1817 treaty the British government seemed to be faced with the choice either of allowing the slave trade to flourish without restriction or of resorting to what they conceived to be their right, under the first article of the

---

[1] The Palmerston–Aberdeen–Mello Mattos correspondence (1830–1) was re-examined in a confidential Cabinet memorandum, 7 July 1845, B.M. Add. MSS 43125 (Aberdeen Papers) and by Peel in the House of Commons on 31 July 1845 (Hansard, lxxxii, 1288–94).

[2] See above, ch. 3, p. 85. It had been George Jackson's opinion at the time that no piracy law was needed: article 1 of the 1826 treaty was not 'promissory or prospective but positive and final—not engaging that a law declaring it [the slave trade] unlawful etc., *shall* be passed but decreeing at once and for ever the illegality of the act and the penalty attached to it' (Jackson to Bandinel, 10 August 1838, Private and Conf., F.O. 84/242). Palmerston had disagreed (memorandum, 7 November 1838, F.O. 84/242).

treaty of 1826, to treat the Brazilian slave trade as piracy—a right which, Aberdeen was to tell Hamilton in June, had been 'long allowed to lie dormant but not forfeited'.[1]

On 13 May a full and detailed statement on the situation, together with all the relevant papers (including the Palmerston–Mello Mattos correspondence of 1830–1) had been submitted to the Law Officers of the Crown, Sir John Dodson, Queen's Advocate and Judge of the Prerogative Court, Sir William Follett, Attorney General and a close friend of the Prime Minister, and Sir Frederick Thesiger, Solicitor General.[2] Aberdeen told Peel that he was confident they would produce 'such an opinion as we desire' but that it would probably be necessary to go to Parliament 'to provide the means of meeting the difficulty'.[3] On 15 May *The Times*, which invariably supported Aberdeen's policies, predicted that

unless the Brazilians think fit to solicit a renewal of these conventions which they allege to be extinct, with the addition of all the more recent provisions, Her Majesty's cruisers will no doubt be instructed that the subjects of His Imperial Majesty being engaged in the African slave trade are pirates, and as such entitled to no protection from their own government, and exposed to the utmost rigour of the maritime law of nations.

If every nation had declared the slave trade piracy *from the outset*, *The Times* continued, it might have been effectively suppressed; instead the whole complicated machinery of rights of search and mixed commissions had been created 'to supply the want of a more direct and effectual mode of proceeding'. Brazil, however, had by treaty made slave trading a piratical offence and Britain could therefore let the unsatisfactory treaty of 1817 lapse and revert to 'the plain language' of the first article of the treaty of 1826.[4] Two weeks later, on 30 May, the Law Officers duly

---

1 Aberdeen to Hamilton, no. 10, 4 June 1845, F.O. 84/583; see also Aberdeen no. 12, 2 July 1845. Hamilton warned Limpo de Abreu on 23 July (Hamilton to Aberdeen, 29 July 1845, B.M. Add. MSS 43124).

2 Canning to Law Officers, 13 May 1845, F.O. 83/2352.

3 Aberdeen to Peel, 11 May, 12 May 1845, B.M. Add. MSS 40455 (Peel Papers).

4 *The Times*, 15 May 1845; cf. *The Times*, 26 July: the British government ought to feel 'no more compunction in adopting rigorous proceedings against them [the Brazilian slave traders] than in waging war with the pirates of the Barbary coast'.

reported on the state of the treaties. The government, they said, were bound to concede that the treaty of 1817 had expired. Under the first article of the treaty of 1826, however, the Crown had 'acquired the right to order the seizure of all Brazilian subjects found upon the High Seas engaged in the slave trade, of punishing them as pirates, and of disposing of their vessels in which they may be captured together with the goods on board belonging to them as *bona piratoram*'.[1] On the strength of this opinion the government decided to issue fresh warrants for the search and capture of Brazilian ships in the illegal slave trade— and, moreover, at any stage of their voyage, since in Britain's eyes any equipment articles found on board constituted conclusive proof of slaving intentions. Like their predecessors in 1830 when the question had first arisen, the Law Officers had, however, advised the government that before the Crown could exercise its rights legislation would be necessary to establish which courts should adjudicate upon captured ships and how they should deal with vessels, crews, cargoes and slaves. For almost a month the Law Officers, in consultation with Stephen Lushington, who was now Judge of the High Court of Admiralty and unrivalled in his experience of slave trade matters, and Sir Herbert Jenner, who as Advocate General in 1830-1 had had experience of this particular problem, worked on the preparation of the necessary legislation. In the end they decided that the simplest procedure would be to amend the Act of 2 July 1827 authorising Anglo-Brazilian mixed commissions to adjudicate Brazilian slavers captured under the Anglo-Portuguese treaty of 1817, which had been incorporated into the Anglo-Brazilian treaty of 1826. The completed bill repealed that part of the Act which had specifically debarred the High Court of Admiralty and vice-admiralty courts from exercising jurisdiction in cases of Brazilian slave ships found contravening the treaty of 1826; the mixed commissions were authorised to function only until 13 September 1845, for the adjudication of ships taken before 13 March, and Admiralty courts were authorised to deal with all Brazilian ships captured after that date as they already dealt with

---

[1] Law Officers' opinion, 30 May 1845, F.O. 83/2352; quoted at length in Jones, *op. cit.* pp. 513-14.

Lord Aberdeen's Act of 1845

British-owned vessels and ships without nationality, and as they had dealt with Portuguese ships for three years after August 1839; condemned ships were to be taken into British service or broken up and sold publicly in separate lots; naval officers were to be rewarded with the usual bounties and indemnified against possible actions brought against them by Brazilian traders. This was the notorious Slave Trade (Brazil) bill, known in Brazil as *o bill Aberdeen* or *o bill inglês*.

Aberdeen was all along anxious that the Duke of Wellington should realise that his bill was essentially different from the bill Palmerston had introduced six years before. The Act of 1839 had given British warships the power to suppress the slave trade carried on under the Portuguese flag which the Portuguese government had repeatedly refused to concede by treaty. Wellington and the Tory peers had opposed it because it seemed that Parliament was being asked to usurp the Crown's prerogative and authorise British officers to adopt hostile measures against a friendly power. In Aberdeen's view his own bill, though in some respects modelled on that of 1839, was not open to the same objection: it simply enabled the Executive to exercise powers which Brazil had conceded to Britain under the first article of the treaty of 1826.[1] In the end Wellington, like other members of the Cabinet, allowed himself to be persuaded that the proposed bill was perfectly legitimate, that the Brazilians had brought it upon themselves, and that there was no other course of action open to the British government.[2]

At the beginning of July, Lord Aberdeen's bill was ready to go before Parliament. It was important that it should come into

---

[1] Aberdeen to Wellington, 5 June, 14 June, 30 June 1845, B.M. Add. MSS 43060 (Aberdeen Papers). Enclosed in the note of 30 June was a long and detailed memorandum by Lushington comparing the two bills (Lushington to Aberdeen, 30 June, B.M. Add. MSS 43244 (Aberdeen Papers). On this point see also unsigned (Jenner?), undated memorandum on the Law Officers' opinion of 30 May in which it was argued that in 1839 it was a case of 'either *casus belli* or nothing at all' whereas in 1845 'it is not *casus belli* but *casus federis* . . . the Act [of 1845] would be in furtherance of the treaty [of 1826]. The Portugal Act of 1839 was avowedly not in furtherance of the Treaties with Portugal'. Peel used this line of argument in his speech in the House of Commons on 24 July at the committee stage of the bill (Hansard, lxxxii, 1050–7).

[2] Wellington to Aberdeen, 2 July, B.M. Add. MSS 43060. The Cabinet memorandum of 7 July (see above, p. 256, n. 1) was circulated to explain the legal grounds on which the government were proceeding and the nature of the bill.

force as quickly as possible in order to shorten the period during which the Brazilian slave trade was free from interference by the British navy and, as the parliamentary session was already well advanced, there was no time to lose. Between 3 and 10 July Aberdeen successfully steered his bill through the House of Lords without a division, or even a debate. It had been Peel's idea to introduce the bill in the Lords[1] because, in marked contrast with the situation in 1839, opposition was more likely to come from the Commons where there had recently been disturbing signs of dissatisfaction with Britain's traditional anti-slave trade policies amongst radical free traders, especially those interested in fostering trade with Brazil. In the late 1830s, Thomas Fowell Buxton and his friends had suggested several new lines of approach to the slave trade question, but they had been in favour of retaining and strengthening the existing preventive system.[2] With the continued and costly failure of the West African squadron to curb, much less suppress, the foreign transatlantic slave trade, the question had recently arisen of whether Britain's efforts should not now be abandoned. Viscount Howick (later Earl Grey and a distinguished Colonial Secretary) had suggested as much in a speech to the House of Commons in February,[3] as had William Hutt, the member for Gateshead and a leading free trader, as recently as 24 June.[4] These and other critics of government policy were fortified by the knowledge that the British and Foreign Anti-Slavery Society—founded in 1839 and the leading abolitionist society since the collapse in 1843 of Buxton's Society for the Extinction of the Slave Trade and the Civilisation of Africa—had always officially disapproved of the use of armed force by Britain for the suppression of the slave trade.[5] Thus Lord Aberdeen found himself on the brink of authorising a more extensive and vigorous assault by the British navy on the Brazilian slave trade at the very time when the morality and expediency of Britain's anti-slave trade policies were beginning to be seriously questioned.

[1] Peel to Aberdeen, 25 June 1845, B.M. Add. MSS 40455.
[2] See above, ch. 6, pp. 152–3.   [3] Hansard, lxxvii, 129 (4 February 1845).
[4] Hansard, lxxxi, 1156–72. After a short debate the House adjourned with only twenty-nine members present. See Mathieson, *Great Britain and the Slave Trade*, pp. 88–9.
[5] See above, ch. 6, pp. 153–4 and below, ch. 11, pp. 296–7.

When, on 24 July, the bill reached the committee stage in the Commons, the government were not surprised to find its passage strongly resisted by Thomas Milner Gibson, one of the two members for Manchester, a doctrinaire free trader and, on this occasion as on so many others, like Hutt, a spokesman for Northern manufacturing and commercial interests.[1] In the first place, Milner Gibson questioned the government's interpretation of the treaty of 1826: in his view, article 1 obliged only the Brazilians themselves to treat the Brazilian slave trade as piracy. However strongly the British government might feel about Brazilian violations of the treaty, he argued, they were now powerless to enforce it themselves because, with the termination of the treaty of 1817, the British navy no longer had the right to visit and search Brazilian vessels. Whatever the government might say, he insisted, their bill was therefore in every respect similar to that introduced by Lord Palmerston in 1839 and, like Wellington on that occasion, he objected to the fact that Parliament was being asked in effect to authorise acts of hostility against a friendly power: 'let them [the government] make war openly upon their own responsibility', he declared, 'and come next year to Parliament for a Bill of Indemnity'. Peel attempted to explain to the House the legal basis of the bill and the extent to which it differed from Lord Palmerston's bill (which Peel himself had in fact approved of), but there was no hope of his satisfying Milner Gibson whose basic objection was to the proposed measures themselves, whatever they might be called and however they might be justified on legal grounds: they were, he declared, scarcely calculated to influence favourably 'the only power that could put down the slave trade—Brazilian public opinion'. He believed that the Brazilian government was already doing more than Britain had any right to expect in dealing with a problem which was so closely involved with the feelings, prejudices and financial interests of the Brazilian propertied classes. (At this point he compared the Brazilian government's policy on the slave trade question with that of the British government

---

[1] Milner Gibson, M.P. for Manchester (1841–57) and Ashton-under-Lyne (1857–68), was to be Vice-President of the Board of Trade (1846–8) and President of the Board of Trade (1859–66). William Hutt, M.P. for Hull (1832–41) and Gateshead (1841–74), was to be Paymaster-General and Vice-President of the Board of Trade (1865).

on the Corn Laws—an unfortunate example since the Corn Laws were, of course, repealed a year later.) Patriotic Brazilians were no longer prepared to tolerate British armed interference, Milner Gibson believed. Moreover, the resentment to which it gave rise could have serious repercussions on British trade; indeed, with William Hutt, he believed that Aberdeen's bill, following so closely on the failure to secure a new commercial treaty, would finally destroy all trade with Brazil within two years. 'How long', Milner Gibson demanded, 'were the great manufacturing interests of this country to be jeopardised, how long were the property and the lives of British subjects to be endangered, in order to carry out the peculiar views of a small section of the anti-slavery party in this country?'[1]

Milner Gibson's opinion, however, did not command sufficient support in the House of Commons seriously to impede the passage of Aberdeen's bill. Although the Whig leaders believed that the Conservative government had to some extent brought the present crisis upon themselves as a result of their hostile commercial policy towards Brazil and their clumsy attempt to introduce the question of slavery into negotiations for the renewal of the Anglo-Brazilian commercial treaty—an action which had angered the Brazilians to no purpose[2]—they were nevertheless both ready and eager to give the bill their support. In the past some of Lord Palmerston's sharpest criticism had been reserved for the government's 'kid glove' treatment of Brazil. The Brazilians, he believed, should long ago have been compelled to fulfil the obligations they had 'freely' contracted. (Towards the end of his previous term of office he had himself seriously considered extending his Act of 1839 to cover Brazilian vessels.) When news of the termination of the 1817 treaty reached London, Palmerston had been one of the first to point out that, under the treaty of 1826, Brazilian slave traders could be treated as pirates 'and this, of course, not by their own government only, but by either of the contracting parties'.[3] He was therefore

---

[1] Hansard, lxxxii, 1043–50.
[2] The Opposition always exaggerated the significance of the Ellis mission and its relevance both to the Brazilian government's refusal to sign a new anti-slave trade treaty and to their determination to terminate the treaty of 1817.
[3] Hansard, lxxx, 477–8 (16 May 1845).

delighted to hear that the government were at last going to take some positive action. He warned them, however, that the measures they were now proposing might not of themselves be sufficient to suppress the Brazilian slave trade since the traders might in the short term find shelter under another flag—for example, the American or, now that the right of search treaties of 1831 and 1833 had finally been suspended, the French.[1] Nevertheless, it would be a great step forward if the trade could be driven from under the Brazilian flag. His one complaint was that Aberdeen's bill fell short of what the treaty would justify: the bill referred to ships and their cargoes, the treaty to the traders as well.[2] The government, however, had felt that, at least in the first instance, it would be inexpedient to ask Parliament for authority to try Brazilian subjects in British courts: it would be sufficient to hand them over, where possible, to their own authorities.

Supported by a majority of the opposition the passage of the bill seemed assured, and the government were completely unprepared for a formidable speech from Sir Thomas Wilde, a former Solicitor General and Attorney General (and, as Lord Truro, a future Lord Chancellor), in which, so late in the day, he cast grave doubts upon the bill's legality: 'It applied an interpretation and a law to piracy', he declared, 'which was not applicable by the law of nations.' Referring back to a point made by Milner Gibson, he reminded the House that the Brazilian legislature had never passed a law declaring the slave trade piracy and he very much doubted whether the treaty of 1826 alone gave Britain the right to subject Brazilians and their property to proceedings in British admiralty courts, to which British-owned vessels were subject by virtue of British statutes.

They [the British] might punish their own subjects as pirates for any offence they pleased, but could they pass a law to punish as pirates the

---

[1] An Anglo-French treaty of 29 May 1845 (*B.F.S.P.* xxxiii, 4–18) suspended the right of search treaties of 1831 and 1833 for ten years in the first instance and, like the Webster-Ashburton treaty of 1842, instituted a policy of joint anti-slave trade cruising. Britain and France agreed to station not less than twenty-six cruisers on the west African coast between Cape Verde and 16° 30′ S. Captured ships and their crews were to be dealt with in their own courts. In May 1849 the French West African squadron was reduced, but the French flag never reappeared in the slave trade on any significant scale.

[2] Hansard, lxxxii, 1059–60 (24 July 1845).

subjects of another nation, for committing an act against the subjects of a third nation? They had no more right to make a law binding on the subjects of Brazil than they had on the subjects of China or any other nation; and they had no right to punish them for an alleged act of piracy which was not piracy by the law of that country.[1]

Remarkably the Attorney General was unable to answer Wilde's fundamental objection to the bill, the validity of which he was forced to admit, and it was left to Peel to promise that serious consideration would be given to the points Wilde had raised.

Both Aberdeen and Peel were now thoroughly confused by the legal complexities of the case. '*Can* you constitute Slave Trading by Brazil *Piracy*?' Peel asked Aberdeen in despair.[2] It is clear from Aberdeen's memorandum referring the matter back to Stephen Lushington that he did not know and was, if anything, even more bewildered than before.[3] Lushington had few doubts on the subject, however, and drew up a lengthy memorandum on the origins and nature of the bill. On 31 July, the three of them met to discuss the matter, a few hours before Peel was due to report back to the House. Lushington's memorandum,[4] although by no means entirely convincing, came to form the basis of the British government's subsequent justification, both at home and abroad, of their right to take the action they proposed in respect of the Brazilian slave trade.

Lushington was in no doubt that the Brazilian government had every right to terminate the convention of 1817. The first article of the treaty of 1826, however, continued in force, and the British government therefore had to examine closely the rights it conferred upon them. First, Brazil had engaged with Britain to abolish the slave trade carried on by Brazilian subjects: 'this is a subsisting obligation which Great Britain has a right to require to be fulfilled and to enforce the fulfilment of'. Secondly, Brazil had contracted that the trade should be 'deemed and treated as piracy'; he observed that

this clause does not say by whom it shall be treated as piracy, nor is there to be found any words shewing that the only meaning of the

[1] Hansard, lxxxii, 1066-7, 1069-70.
[2] Peel to Aberdeen, 25 July 1845, B.M. Add. MSS 43064 (Aberdeen Papers).
[3] Memorandum, 29 July 1845, B.M. Add. MSS 40455 (Peel Papers), quoted, not entirely accurately, in Jones, *op. cit.* p. 516, n. 47.   [4] Memorandum, 31 July, F.O. 97/430.

Convention was that the Brazilians should pass a law to that effect—in short, that the first article was simply a compact that the Brazilians should effect the abolition of the trade by *municipal regulation*—had that been intended other and different words must have been used and it was especially incumbent on the Government of Brazil to have taken care of this, as Brazil was the granting party.

The correct construction of the first article of the treaty, Lushington concluded, was that 'the slave trade shall be deemed and treated as piracy by both contracting parties'. On the assumption, therefore, that the treaty had conferred on Britain the right to treat the Brazilian slave trade as piracy, it was then necessary to consider the meaning of the word in this particular context. Under the law of nations the slave trade was not deemed to be piracy, and although some states had made the trade piratical by municipal law, this was something that no other state could enforce, neither could any agreement between two powers render the trade piracy in respect of other nations. Britain and Brazil, however, were perfectly entitled to declare by treaty that *inter se* the trade would be treated as piracy when carried on by Brazilian subjects. Consequently, 'whatever right the Crown of Great Britain had by the Law of Nations as to pirates it has by virtue of the Convention [of 1826] over Brazilian subjects engaged in the slave trade'. It was generally agreed that the warships of every state were entitled to exercise the right of search and detention on the high seas where there were grounds for suspecting piracy. 'The *same* right', Lushington contended, 'has been conceded to Great Britain as to the Brazilian slave trade.' (Like the Law Officers in their report of 30 May, he was prepared to argue that Britain could try and punish Brazilian subjects as well as confiscate their property.) It was doubtful, however, whether the Crown had the power to exercise its rights simply by virtue of its own prerogative; legislation would be necessary, for instance, to empower British courts to adjudicate upon Brazilian slave vessels captured by the British navy. Nevertheless, Lushington was quite clear that Great Britain 'by virtue of the exercise of the prerogative of the Crown *and by Act of Parliament*' had 'full right and power' to treat the Brazilian slave trade as piracy.

When Peel faced the House of Commons on 31 July, he was

able to declare that, in the opinion of 'the highest authority' on the subject, there was 'nothing inconsistent with the law of nations in the bill as it stood', and he repeated the British government's view that in 1830 the Brazilian government had in fact admitted that, under the treaty of 1826, Britain had the right to take the measures they were now proposing to take.[1] The bill had an uneventful third reading the following day when Sir Thomas Wilde, who later described it as 'a national disgrace manifesting either great ignorance of the law of nations or monstrous assumption, calculated either to lead to war or to our rendering ourselves contemptible',[2] was conveniently absent in Newcastle. A week later, on 8 August 1845, Lord Aberdeen's bill, Britain's answer to the termination by Brazil of the right of search treaty of 1817, received the royal assent.[3] In his book *Explorations of the Highlands of Brazil*, published in 1869, the explorer and scholar Richard Burton called the Aberdeen Act 'one of the greatest insults which a strong ever offered to a weak people',[4] and Joaquim Nabuco, the future leader of the Brazilian anti-slavery movement, described it a year later, in an early and for long unpublished essay on slavery and the slave trade, as 'an insult to our dignity as an independent people'[5]— judgements echoed ever since in numerous books and articles by Brazilian historians.

[1] Hansard lxxxii. 1288–94.
[2] Wilde to Hutt, 12 March 1849, quoted by Milner Gibson in the House of Commons, Hansard, civ, 765–6 (24 April 1849).
[3] 8 and 9 Vict. cap. 122; printed in Pereira Pinto, i, pp. 419–26.
[4] Richard F. Burton, *Explorations of the Highlands of Brazil* (London, 1869), i. p. 5.
[5] Joaquim Nabuco, 'A Escravidão', *R.I.H.G.B.* vol. 204 (1949), p. 65.

CHAPTER 10

THE AFTERMATH OF THE
ABERDEEN ACT

In 1845 Lord Aberdeen had felt compelled to seek authorisation for the kind of high-handed anti-slave trade measures more readily associated with the name of Lord Palmerston. He had, however, shown a much greater concern than his predecessor for at least the façade of legality: in instructing British warships to seize all Brazilian ships engaged in the slave trade and British vice-admiralty courts to adjudicate upon them the British government, it was claimed, were merely exercising their treaty rights. And as Peel was at pains to explain to the House of Commons, it was 'the mildest measure to which they [the British government] could resort';[1] they were deliberately not seeking authority from Parliament for British courts to punish Brazilian subjects engaged in the slave trade as under article 1 of the treaty of 1826 they had every right to do. Moreover, the decision to introduce the Brazil (Slave Trade) bill had been taken 'with pain and only under the last necessity'.[2] At the time of its passage Aberdeen offered to repeal it, either when the slave trade had finally ceased or when the Brazilian government signed an anti-slave trade treaty acceptable to Britain.[3]

When in March 1845 the Brazilian government had professed a willingness to enter negotiations for a new anti-slave trade treaty they had done so in the belief that by terminating the right of search treaty of 1817 they had seized the diplomatic initiative and put themselves in a strong position to dictate its terms: the British government would now have to accept Brazil's treaty

---

[1] Hansard, lxxxii, 1293, 31 July 1845. Cf. ibid. 150–7, 24 July.
[2] Ibid. 1288, 31 July 1845. Many years later, after Aberdeen's death, Lord Malmesbury revealed that Aberdeen 'had never felt satisfied in his mind that he was right in proposing that act', quoted in W. D. Christie, Notes on Brazilian Questions (London, 1865), p. 64. Christie, however, doubted the accuracy of this statement.
[3] Aberdeen to Hamilton, no. 10, 4 June, no. 12, 2 July 1845, F.O. 84/583; Aberdeen to Hamilton, 4 June 1845, B.M. Add. MSS 43124 (Aberdeen Papers); Aberdeen to Lisboa, 6 August, 8 August 1845, F.O. 84/583.

proposals, they reasoned, or else abandon entirely their efforts to suppress the Brazilian slave trade. They were to realise their mistake, however, and on 25 July and again on 5 August, José Marques Lisboa, the Brazilian minister in London, found himself trying to avert the passage of Lord Aberdeen's bill by warning him that it would destroy any chance that the two governments might reach agreement on a new treaty *satisfacory to both parties*. On the latter occasion he had even offered to try and persuade his government to permit the 1817 treaty to continue in force until a replacement had been negotiated, provided the British government dropped its plan to give jurisdiction over Brazilian ships to British vice-admiralty courts.[1] Once the bill had become law and Britain had thus ensured that the initiative would be hers in any future treaty negotiations—Brazil would have to put up with Lord Aberdeen's Act or, like Portugal in 1842, accept an anti-slave trade treaty dictated by Britain—Aberdeen suggested to Lisboa that if the Brazilian government signed an agreement re-establishing the treaty of 1817 *as it had functioned in practice before 13 March*, pending the negotiation of a new treaty similar to those signed by Spain in 1835 and Portugal in 1842, it would be ratified at once and, without waiting for Parliament to reassemble, the British government would immediately and 'most joyfully' recommend by Order in Council the transfer of jurisdiction over captured Brazilian slavers from vice-admiralty courts back to the courts of mixed commission.[2] Aberdeen sent word to Hamilton Hamilton in Rio de Janeiro that the British government were very anxious to reach a speedy settlement along these lines. He warned him, however, that 'no admission must be made either in the articles [of the agreement] . . . or in any negotiation of them which can in any degree affect the right H.M. Government had asserted or the practice which H.M. cruisers and H.M. commissioners have observed in dealing with Brazilian vessels equipped for the slave trade as liable under the treaty of 1826 to seizure and confiscation'. And should the Brazilian government renew the treaty of 1817, only to abrogate it again

[1] Lisboa to Aberdeen, 25 July, 5 August 1845, F.O. 84/583.
[2] Aberdeen to Lisboa, 8 August 1845; Lisboa to Limpo de Abreu, no. 22, August 1845, Reservado, A.H.I. 217/3/4.

before the treaty negotiations had been brought to a close, or fail to fulfil their engagements under a new treaty, 'Her Majesty', Aberdeen wrote, 'will of course be free to revert to her rights under the first article of the treaty of 1826'.[1]

At the end of June Hamilton Hamilton, the British minister in Rio de Janeiro, had taken steps to prepare the Brazilian government for the advent of Lord Aberdeen's bill.[2] By the second week in September the precise nature of its contents had become widely known.[3] In the event of any threat to British lives or property, Hamilton had permission to call upon the navy in the Río de la Plata, but despite 'the excited state of public feeling in the capital . . . and argument, virulence, invective in the public press' there was only one minor incident, involving a group of British seamen.[4] The foreign affairs sub-committee of the Council of State had had the situation under review for some time and now that the British government had actually carried out its threats the full Council of State was convened for a series of urgent meetings. They had one consolation: in its final form the Act was not quite as severe as had at first been anticipated in that at least it contained no threat to Brazilian lives. On 16 September the Council met to discuss three questions put to them by the Foreign Minister, Antônio Limpo de Abreu: first, should the Brazilian government protest against the bill and in what terms? secondly, should they open negotiations with the British government for an anti-slave trade treaty to replace the bill? thirdly, on what basis should any new treaty rest? There was a clear division of opinion between a minority led by Bernardo Pereira de Vasconcelos and Francisco de Paula Sousa, who favoured a protest couched in the strongest possible terms coupled with a complete severance of diplomatic relations and a total rejection of any new treaty, and the majority of councillors who, accepting Brazil's continuing obligation to suppress the slave trade, fearful

---

[1] Aberdeen to Hamilton, no. 20, 9 August 1845, F.O. 84/583.
[2] On 23 July Hamilton informed Limpo de Abreu of the contents of Aberdeen's despatch no. 10, 4 June (note enclosed in Hamilton to Aberdeen, 29 July 1845, B.M. Add. MSS 43124 (Aberdeen Papers).
[3] The Act was printed in *Jornal do Comércio*, 15 September 1845.
[4] Aberdeen to Hamilton, no. 21, 9 August 1845, F.O. 84/583; Hamilton no. 55, 22 December 1845, Conf., F.O. 84/582.

of the lengths to which Britain might be prepared to go, and perhaps still hoping for British support in the Río de la Plata, were in favour of issuing a more moderate protest against the illegality of the Act while leaving the door open for future treaty negotiations—although they continued to insist, unrealistically, that any new treaty should impose severe restrictions on the anti-slave trade operations of the British navy.[1] After some lengthy discussions approval was finally given to a statement of protest drawn up by Limpo de Abreu.[2] It was a principle of international law, Limpo de Abreu began, that the ships of one state could not in peace-time search the ships of another, except where the right to do so had been conceded by treaty; the treaty of 1817 alone had given British warships the right to search Brazilian vessels suspected of slaving and that treaty had now expired. The first article of the treaty of 1826, he insisted, obliged the Brazilian authorities, and only the Brazilian authorities, to treat Brazilian slave traders as pirates; it did not confer on Britain any rights whatsoever over Brazilian nationals or their ships: 'the intervention of the British government . . . is limited to the right of demanding from the Imperial Government an exact and punctual observance of the treaty and nothing more'. Further-more, he denied categorically that, when the question had first arisen in 1830, the Brazilian government had accepted the British view of the 1826 treaty; on the contrary, he argued, Lord Palmerston had accepted the Brazilian view of the treaty and, significantly, there had never been any mention of Britain's so-called rights to treat the Brazilian slave trade as piracy during the entire period since 1830. In short, the interpretation of the first article of the 1826 treaty now put forward by Britain was 'absurd and dangerous'. Brazil, he went on, was unlikely to have conceded to Britain the right to try and punish Brazilian subjects

---

[1] *Acta*, 16 September 1845, A. N. Códice 307/1.
[2] Limpo de Abreu to Hamilton, 22 October 1845, enclosed in Hamilton no. 49, 11 November 1845, F.O. 84/582 and Lisboa to Aberdeen, 27 December 1845, F.O. 83/583. The full text appeared in *Jornal do Comércio*, 29 October 1845 and *Relatório do Ministério dos Negócios Estrangeiros* (May 1846). Limpo de Abreu's note was published separately as a pamphlet in Portuguese, English and French and widely distributed. Also printed in Perdigão Malheiro, ii, 253–61; Pereira Pinto, i, 426–45. For the Brazilian view of the Aberdeen Act see also *Inglaterra e Brasil: Trafego de escravos* (Rio de Janeiro, 1845) by José Justiano da Rocha, the editor of the conservative, anti-British, pro-slave trade Rio newspaper *O Brasil*.

and Brazilian vessels under British law and in British courts without 'a very express, clear and positive delegation of this power'. The Aberdeen Act, Limpo de Abreu declared, 'cannot be based either upon the letter or the spirit of the said article, is opposed to the most clear and positive principles of the Law of Nations, and, finally, is an infringement of the sovereignty and independence of Brazil'. The Brazilian government flatly refused to recognise the validity of the 'unjust and offensive' Act and gave notice that they would claim compensation for any injury that Brazilian commerce might suffer as a result of its execution. Nevertheless, Limpo de Abreu's protest against the Act ended on a moderate, conciliatory, note and the Minister of Justice, Senator Manuel Antônio Galvão, was given full powers to open negotiations with Hamilton for a new treaty which would replace it. Galvão, however, was 'an individual proverbially indolent and dilatory on all occasions'[1] and Limpo de Abreu, who did not enjoy the full support of his colleagues, could do little to speed up the preparation of a draft convention. The little Hamilton did learn in advance about the form Brazilian demands were likely to take was not encouraging: it seemed likely that Brazil would again seek substantial indemnities for Brazilian ships previously acquitted by the Anglo-Brazilian mixed commissions, an extension of the area off the coast of Brazil in which the right of search could in no circumstances be exercised and an agreement which would permit the importation from Africa of 'free colonists' to meet the lack of fresh supplies of slaves.[2] (The last point was one which had been raised on more than one occasion in the past. It was still the view of the British government, however, that until slavery had been abolished, the importation into Brazil of free Africans would constitute, as Hamilton put it, 'a covert and insidious means of continuing the slave trade'.[3])

Clearly there was no hope of progress on these terms. More-

[1] Hamilton no. 49, 11 November 1845.
[2] Hamilton no. 40, 22 September, no. 42, 8 October, no. 50, 6 December, no. 52, 22 December, no. 55, 22 December 1845, F.O. 84/582; Hamilton no. 92, 22 December 1845, F.O. 13/227; Hamilton no. 4, 24 January, Conf., no. 19, 21 February, Conf., F.O. 13/234. Limpo de Abreu promised to draw up, privately, a draft treaty (Hamilton, no. 55); see below, pp. 276–7.
[3] Hamilton no. 50, 6 December 1845.

over, thanks to information regularly supplied by Senator Lopes Gama, who was in the pay of the British government, Aberdeen was well aware that the Brazilian Council of State inclined to the belief that serious treaty negotiations on any basis would be impossible until the Act had first been repealed.[1] In the event, therefore, nothing came of these early attempts to find a satisfactory substitute for the Aberdeen Act. Hamilton and Galvão never even met officially. In April 1846, Aberdeen recalled the British commissioner of arbitration who had remained in Rio in the hope that negotiations would lead to a re-opening of the mixed commission there.[2] At the beginning of May another change of government in Brazil removed Limpo de Abreu, the minister most sympathetic to the British viewpoint, from the Foreign Ministry. The leading figure in the new administration, Antônio Francisco de Paula e Holanda Cavalcanti de Albuquerque, Finance Minister and chief adviser to the young Emperor, was not entirely opposed to the idea of a new anti-slave trade treaty—on the right terms—and was, according to James Hudson, British *chargé d'affaires* in Rio, contemplating 'some great and sweeping measure' for the abolition of slavery itself within twenty-five or thirty years.[3] At the same time, however, he was adamant that Britain should rescind the offending Act before Brazil took any action: 'You cannot expect us to assist England or consent to stop the trade', he told Commodore Charles

[1] The intermediary between Lopes Gama and the British government was John George Young, a British citizen with financial claims against the Brazilian government: see, for example, Report no. 5, January 1846, enclosed in Young to Aberdeen, Private, 28 February 1846, B.M. Add. MSS 43245 (Aberdeen Papers); Report no. 6, February 1846, enclosed in Young 16 April 1846, Private, Report no. 7, April 1846, enclosed in Young 10 June 1846, Private, B.M. Add. MSS 43246 (Aberdeen Papers). See also Jones, *H.A.H.R.* (1962), *op. cit.* p. 518. In August and again in October 1846, when the issue came before the foreign affairs sub-committee of the Council of State, Vasconcelos and Honório rejected without hesitation the idea of signing a new treaty imposed by Britain while the Act remained in force and thus isolated the third anti-slave trade, pro-British, member of the committee, Lopes Gama (*Parecer* no. 93, 10 August 1846, *Parecer* no. 101, 10 October 1846, A.H.I. 342/1/6).
[2] Aberdeen to Grigg, no. 1, 2 April 1846, F.O. 84/622; Aberdeen to Hamilton, no. 2, 3 April 1846, F.O. 84/632. The court house had been closed since 25 September 1845.
[3] 'Memorandum on the present temper of the government of Brazil regarding negotiating a slave trade treaty with England', 22 June 1846, B.M. Add. MSS 43124; Hudson to Palmerston, 17 October 1846, Broadlands MSS GC/HU/1. James Hudson was secretary to the Rio legation 1845–50 (acting as *chargé d'affaires* August 1846 to August 1847, April 1848 to July 1850) and minister July 1850 to December 1851 before being transferred to Turin where he was to play a leading role in the Italian Question.

Hotham, who was visiting Rio de Janeiro before taking up his post as commander-in-chief on the West African naval station, 'while you are seizing Brazilian vessels, insulting our flag and illegally condemning them.'[1] In Britain, in the meantime, the Whigs had replaced the Conservatives in office, bringing back to the Foreign Office Lord Palmerston who immediately ordered Hamilton to suspend all treaty negotiations.[2] As it happened, Hamilton had already left Rio de Janeiro for home following a severe stroke.

One issue that was settled by the fall of Peel's Conservative government at the end of June 1846 was the fate of the British sugar duties. Within three weeks of taking office, the new Prime Minister, Lord John Russell, proposed the gradual reduction of the differential in favour of colonial sugar over a period of five years until the final equalisation in 1851 of the duties on sugar 'of all sorts, of whatever growth and whencesoever imported'— that is to say, including Brazilian and Cuban slave-grown sugar. Peel, and those of his supporters who had already accepted the repeal of the Corn Laws, did not oppose the government's Sugar Bill: propaganda against 'monopoly' and dear sugar had succeeded in winning over public opinion to the view that philanthropy was being bought at too high a price—and public opinion could not permanently be resisted. Moreover, free trade ideas had by now so thoroughly infiltrated the Anti-Slavery Society that of the leading abolitionists in the House of Commons, only the Tory member for Oxford University, Sir Robert Inglis, put up real opposition to the government's proposals on the sugar duties. It was left to Bentinck, Stanley and the Protectionists to argue most effectively that a reduction in the duties on slave-grown sugar would lead to an increased demand for slaves in Brazil and Cuba and thus act as a stimulus to the slave trade. In the House of Lords, old-guard abolitionists like Lord Brougham, Chief Justice Denman (the father of Captain Joseph Denman) and Samuel Wilberforce, the Bishop of Oxford, protested bitterly

[1] Recalled in Hotham to Admiralty, no. 395, 5 December 1848: 'Remarks and Observations on the final extinction of the slave trade', F.O. 84/782.
[2] Palmerston to Hamilton, no. 9, 13 August 1846, F.O. 84/632.

but without success that the bill would encourage the slave trade: they were defeated by twenty-eight votes to eleven.[1]

Following on the abolition of the slave trade in 1807 and the emancipation of the slaves in 1833, the Sugar Duties Act of 1846 constituted the West India interest's final defeat. Would it also prove to be the first retrogressive step in the history of the British anti-slave trade campaign? Lord Palmerston did not think so: 'The argument against the measure, as tending to increase the slave trade, would be good and conclusive', he wrote, 'if that slave trade were free and unimpeded and if it could be increased at the will of the trader . . . but if our repressive system is good to such an extent against existing inducement, it is not likely that the small additional inducement which would arise from opening British markets to Brazilian sugar would sensibly increase the importation of Negroes.'[2] In other words, the volume of the illegal Brazilian slave trade was determined more by the effectiveness of Britain's anti-slave trade measures than by Britain's commercial policy, and the Whig government which had lowered the discriminatory duties on Brazilian slave-grown produce entering the British market and thereby discarded the policy of 'fiscal coercion' had not the slightest intention of giving up the struggle to bring the slave trade to an end by means of 'physical coercion'. In particular, Palmerston was determined to enforce vigorously his predecessor's anti-slave trade Act of which he had so heartily approved—despite the fact that serious doubts were again being expressed about its legality. In July 1845 at Exeter Assizes seven of the crew of the Brazilian slave schooner *Felicidade* (an unfortunate name), who had murdered a British prize crew after the vessel had been captured by H.M.S. *Wasp*, had been

[1] 9 and 10 Vict. cap 63, 18 August 1846. See Schuyler, *Fall of the old colonial system*, pp. 151–5; Morrell, *British colonial policy*, pp. 222–3. Also some half a million words in Hansard. Richard Cobden asserted in the Commons (16 June 1848) that 'nearly all the men who led the agitation for the emancipation of the slaves . . . are against those Hon. Gentlemen in this House who advocate a differential duty on foreign sugar with a view to put down slavery abroad', quoted in Williams, *Capitalism and Slavery*, pp. 161–2. But for a different view, see Rice, 'Critique of the Eric Williams Thesis' in *Transatlantic Slave Trade from West Africa*, p. 46. Many abolitionists aided the Protectionists in securing, in 1848, the extension of the period before the complete equalisation of the sugar duties from 1851 to 1854, and gave their support to the frequent but fruitless Commons motions of Sir Edward Noel Buxton for the restoration of differential duties on slave-grown sugar.

[2] Cabinet minute, 23 July 1846, F.O. 97/430.

sentenced to death. Later in the year, however, they were acquitted in the Court of Criminal Appeal on the grounds that since it was only equipped for the slave trade the *Felicidade* was not in the lawful possession of the Crown at the time. The fact that the appeal court judges deliberately chose to disregard the piracy clause in the treaty of 1826 was taken to mean that they disagreed with the Law Officers' opinion of 30 May 1845 which formed the legal basis of the recently enacted Aberdeen bill.[1] When in February 1846 Lord Aberdeen asked the Law Officers whether in the light of the Brazilian government's protest at the illegality of the Act they had any reason to revise their opinion on Britain's rights under article 1 of the treaty of 1826, they significantly chose to remain silent.[2] While this might have disturbed Aberdeen, who had never been entirely happy with his Act, it was of little concern to Lord Palmerston. For him the question had always been much more straightforward than the Conservative government had made it appear with their elaborate, legalistic, arguments about the meaning of the first article of the 1826 treaty and their insistence that their Act was essentially different from his own Slave Trade (Portugal) Act of 1839. It seemed to Palmerston that Brazil, like Portugal on that earlier occasion, was unquestionably guilty of not fulfilling her treaty engagements and that the British government had therefore a perfect right to adopt any measures they chose to ensure that the purpose of the 1826 treaty was no longer frustrated. 'We should ourselves have proposed and passed it' [the Act of 1845], he told James Hudson, 'if our predecessors had not done so for us.'[3] Indeed, he warned the Brazilian government that if they continued to connive at

---

[1] Lisboa to Limpo de Abreu, no. 14, Reservado, 5 May 1846, A.H.I. 217/3/5; Eddisbury (Under Secretary at the F.O.) memorandum, 12 August 1848, F.O. 97/430; Sir Joseph Arnould, *Memoir of Thomas, First Lord Denman* (London, 1873), ii, 199–206. Also see W. Senior, *Naval History in the Law Courts* (London, 1927), pp. 78–88; Clowes, *Royal Navy*, vi, pp. 363–71; Lloyd, *Navy and Slave Trade*, pp. 85–8.

[2] Aberdeen to Law Officers, 5 February 1846, F.O. 83/2353. On 27 March 1847 and 10 September 1847 Palmerston demanded an answer to Aberdeen's note. Finally on 15 October 1847 he was told that a report was ready but that an interview would be desirable first. Palmerston met the Law Officers on 22 October. Afterwards he decided that the report in which, it is reasonable to assume, the Law Officers expressed doubts, to say the least, about the validity of their earlier opinion, could 'stand over for the present'. Palmerston memorandum, 23 October 1847, F.O. 83/2354. No written report by the Law Officers has been located.

[3] Palmerston to Hudson, 5 January 1847, Broadlands MSS, GC/HU/43.

the trade 'still sharper measures of coercion' might be found necessary.[1]

Palmerston was much less eager than Aberdeen had been to replace the Act of 1845 with a treaty. As he told Hudson, he was 'quite indifferent [to the idea] . . . We like our Act of Parliament much better than a treaty': it placed no restriction on the navy's anti-slaving operations and 'just and impartial' decisions in favour of the condemnation of captured ships were more likely in British admiralty courts than they could ever be in courts of mixed commission. For his part, Palmerston was 'quite content to remain as we are'.[2] On the other hand, since the Brazilian government had objected so strongly to the Act, and the British government did not want to perpetuate unnecessarily a source of friction between the two countries, Palmerston was prepared to accept an *efficient* anti-slave trade treaty in its place; but it would, he insisted, have to be one similar in all important respects to that signed by Portugal in 1842 in exchange for the partial repeal of the Act of 1839 and it would have to be both signed and ratified before any steps could be taken to suspend the operation of the Aberdeen Act.[3]

In February 1847, José Marques Lisboa sent Palmerston a draft treaty which had been drawn up by Limpo de Abreu when he was Foreign Minister and submitted privately to Aberdeen for his consideration and which Lisboa believed had the approval of Abreu's successor, Barão de Cairu (Silva Lisboa).[4] It suggested, for example, that while Brazilian ships which were carrying slaves, which had just landed slaves or which were carrying all or not a small number of equipment articles should be liable to search and capture, it should be made absolutely clear in order to protect the free movement of Brazilian subjects and their goods between Brazilian ports that British cruisers could not search or capture Brazilian ships in Brazilian ports and roadsteads, within range of shore batteries and in territorial waters (that is, three

[1] Palmerston to Hudson, no. 1, 13 January 1847, F.O. 84/677; cf. statement in House of Commons on 8 March 1847, Hansard, xc, 1,023.
[2] Palmerston to Hudson, 5 January 1847.
[3] Palmerston no. 9, 13 August 1846; Hansard, xc, 1023 (8 March 1847).
[4] Enclosed in Lisboa to Aberdeen, 3 July 1846, B.M. Add. MSS 43124, and Lisboa to Palmerston, 10 February 1847, F.O. 84/677.

miles from the Brazilian coast) other than when Brazilian authorities asked for assistance. Again it was suggested that all captured vessels which were known to have cleared from a Brazilian port should be taken before the mixed commission in Rio de Janeiro and that in all cases there should be a right of appeal to Rio from other mixed commissions sitting in Demerara and the Cape (Sierra Leone was deliberately omitted). A mixed commission should be able to draw bills payable at sight on the appropriate government to cover costs and damages resulting from 'arbitrary and illegal detentions', and it was proposed that the British government should promise to pay the indemnities already claimed by Brazilian subjects for losses resulting from previous arbitrary acts by British cruisers. Finally, Limpo de Abreu's draft treaty contained an entirely new proposal: the treaty should be terminated 'the moment the Brazilian government can establish and maintain in service on the African coast sufficient naval force of ships completely prepared and fitted out for the effective repression of the slave trade'—otherwise after ten years. Palmerston was not prepared to enter into negotiations on the basis of this draft, if only because it had not come officially from the Brazilian government, although as a reflection of current Brazilian thinking on the treaty question he found it worthy of study and set out in detail his objections to it.[1] In the first place he was opposed to the omission of any reference to article 1 of the 1826 treaty and considered it imperative that Brazil should not be released from existing engagements with Britain to abolish the slave trade and that Britain should not waive any of its existing rights to treat the Brazilian slave trade as piracy. The article stipulating extensive areas within which Brazilian ships were not liable to search and capture was, in Palmerston's view, 'totally inadmissible'; it would render the operations of the British navy on the coast of Brazil 'entirely nugatory'. It was quite sufficient, he thought, to provide, as previous treaties had done, that vessels should not be searched and captured in any port or roadstead or within cannon shot of a shore battery. He also insisted yet again that ships should be liable to capture if *any one or more* equipment articles were found on board. As for

[1] Enclosed in Palmerston to Howden, no. 1, 4 June 1847, F.O. 84/677.

payment of indemnities, it was quite enough for each country to engage to make good any justifiable claims within a year. No previous awards were still outstanding. And since most Brazilian ships were captured on the African coast, it would be not only inconvenient but often inhumane to send them all to Rio de Janeiro for adjudication; the real object of the Brazilian government in making such a recommendation, he believed, was to 'increase the probabilities of unjust acquittal'. Finally, a maximum period of ten years for the operation of the right of search was completely out of the question: 'H.M. Government will not consent to abrogate the treaty', Palmerston wrote, '*until slavery is abolished in Brazil*; the treaty must be as unlimited in its duration as the Act of Parliament for which it is to be a substitute.'

At the beginning of the year, Lord Howden had been sent on a special mission to Buenos Aires and Montevideo with instructions to proceed to Rio de Janeiro to replace Hamilton as British minister. In June, Palmerston sent him a copy of a draft anti-slave trade treaty which was essentially the same as the Anglo-Portuguese treaty of 1842 apart from a few minor changes and the inclusion in the preamble of a reference to Brazil's existing obligations under the treaty of 1826 and the law of 1831. Howden was instructed that since it contained nothing which was not considered by the British government as 'absolutely essential' for the effective suppression of the slave trade, no alteration could be permitted: 'the treaty must be adopted such as it purposed to be by the draft; and upon no other condition whatever can H.M. Government recommend to Parliament the repeal of the Act of 1845'.[1] Howden was also told to re-open negotiations for a commercial treaty (the negotiations which had been opened soon after the old treaty had expired in November 1844 had been suspended in July 1845 when the Brazilian government were informed about the nature of Aberdeen's anti-slave trade bill). Palmerston's feeling was that Britain could manage very well without a commercial treaty—British trade had not suffered since 1844, even as a result of the Aberdeen Act, and

---

[1] Palmerston no. 1, 4 June 1847. John Hobart Caradoc, 2nd Baron Howden, was in Buenos Aires, May–June 1847 and Montevideo, August 1847; he was minister in Rio de Janeiro, August 1847 to April 1848.

there was much less likelihood of retaliatory duties against British manufactured goods now that the sugar duties had been reduced—but the protection that a treaty would afford British economic interests in Brazil might be worth having in the long run.[1]

When Lord Howden arrived in Rio de Janeiro, he found, like so many of his predecessors, considerable anti-British feeling—and not only on account of Britain's efforts to suppress the slave trade which, as Hudson had acknowledged, were 'interfering, visibly, with the daily bread of every human being in the capital'.[2] Hostility to Britain also arose, Howden later recalled, because of 'the tone which their indifference to their engagements [had] obliged us to assume towards them: they are proud and sensitive like all South American colonies who have lately assumed nationalities'; the Aberdeen Act, in particular, he thought, had 'offended their nationality', and it was his belief that 'they dislike it still more for that reason than for the obstruction it causes to the slave trade'.[3] Shortly before his arrival, there had been further ministerial changes in Brazil, and two members of the Cabinet of May 1847 (led by Manuel Alves Branco), the Foreign Minister, Saturnino de Sousa e Oliveira, and the Minister for the Navy, Cândido Batista de Oliveira, were known to be particularly anxious to reach an understanding with Britain on the slave trade question.[4] The prospects for a settlement, however, were not encouraging. 'Your Bill', Howden wrote privately to Lord Aberdeen, 'is a dead stop here to a treaty.' The Brazilian government, it appeared, had no intention of conceding a commercial treaty until agreement had been reached on an anti-slave trade treaty to replace the Act of 1845. And a number of distinguished Brazilians, including some of the slave trade's more

---

[1] Palmerston to Howden, no. 2, 4 June 1847, F.O. 13/243. For the commercial aspect of Howden's mission, I have again relied heavily on A. J. Pryor's unpublished thesis, 'Anglo-Brazilian Commercial Relations', pp. 356–81.

[2] Hudson memorandum, 22 June 1846, B.M. Add. MSS 43124.

[3] *P.P.* 1850 (Lords), XXIV (35), House of Lords Select Committee on Slave Trade, par. 334–5.

[4] Hudson to Palmerston, 25 June 1847, Broadlands MSS, GC/HU/4; Howden to Palmerston, 10 December 1847, Broadlands MSS, GC/HO/907; Howden to Aberdeen, 12 December 1847, B.M. Add. MSS 43124 (Aberdeen Papers). See Pryor, *op. cit.* pp. 359–60; *História Geral da Civilização Brasileira*, II, ii, pp. 531–2.

outspoken opponents, believed Brazil should refuse to open negotiations on either treaty until the Act had *first* been repealed. Moreover, if the slave trade negotiations were to have any chance of success, Britain would have to modify its latest treaty proposals and bring them more into line with Brazil's own demands.[1]

After several months of waiting in the vain hope that Saturnino and Cândido Batista might win over their Cabinet colleagues, Lord Howden, never the most patient of men, decided that it was time to adopt a tougher line. On 23 December he submitted for official consideration drafts of two treaties—one commercial, the other anti-slave trade. If the Brazilian government persisted in making the commercial treaty dependent on a prior agreement on the slave trade question and if they continued to demand modifications of the slave trade treaty draft, then he warned that 'serious consequences' would follow: there was in his warning a clear hint of a possible break in diplomatic relations and a thinly veiled threat that force might have to be used.[2] Six weeks later, when the Brazilian government had still not replied, he demanded an immediate and unequivocal answer if they wished to avoid 'imminent collision' with Britain; he was not prepared, he said, to tolerate the 'dilatory and temporising manner' of transacting business which the Brazilian government had been in the habit of adopting in their dealings with his predecessors—a manner 'so strong, so tardy, sometimes so inconsistent with diplomatic usage, often so supercilious in its inefficiency and almost always so unsatisfactory'.[3] Howden's tactics seem extraordinary in the light of Palmerston's repeated claim that the commercial treaty was not absolutely necessary for Britain, and that the British government had 'no wish for a [slave trade] treaty beyond the natural desire which we have that our relations with Brazil should be placed on a footing more like the usual mutual relations of

---

[1] Howden to Aberdeen, 1 March 1848, B.M. Add. MSS 43124 (Aberdeen Papers). Like Ouseley before him (see above, ch. 4, p. 20) Howden believed a few handsome bribes might produce results. Every man in Brazil, including members of the government and the legislature, was 'venal by nature and education', he declared (Howden to Palmerston, 30 September 1847, Broadlands MSS, GC/HO/904).

[2] Howden no. 51, 3 December, no. 53, 23 December, no. 55, 23 December, no. 58, 30 December 1847, F.O. 13/246; Pryor, *op. cit.* pp. 369–71.

[3] Howden to Pimenta Bueno, 8 February 1848, A.H.I. 284/4/3.

friendly States'.[1] As recently as October 1847 Palmerston had written to Howden (as he had already told Hudson), 'I prefer our Act of Parliament to any treaty, and so you may tell them.'[2]

In the event Lord Howden was to discover, as Henry Ellis had done five years earlier, that the situation in Brazil in the middle of the nineteenth century was very different from what it had been in 1810 and in 1825-7 when Lord Strangford, Sir Charles Stuart and Robert Gordon had held the necessary 'political lever' with which to extract from the Portuguese and Brazilian governments the treaties that Britain required. As Howden himself admitted, Brazil 'hopes nothing, fears little from England. Brazil believes that in Lord Aberdeen's bill England has expended all its powers of evil, and she sits sullen and motionless under the infliction... Never was Brazil more deaf and never was England's voice less calculated to make itself heard.'[3] Unwilling to provoke a break with Britain because of the situation in the Río de la Plata, the Brazilian government was nevertheless prepared to call Howden's bluff, relying on British commercial and financial interests in Brazil to restrain the British government should they consider using force. 'English Gold', Alves Branco believed, 'would always protect Brazil against English Iron.'[4] Backed by a majority in the Council of State, the Brazilian government (unlike the Portuguese government in 1842) thus refused to negotiate while the Aberdeen Act remained in force and in any case rejected the British terms for a new anti-slave trade treaty. In February, José Antônio Pimenta Bueno, who had replaced Saturnino as Foreign Minister, following the latter's serious illness (he died in April), returned to Howden both British treaty drafts which, he still contended, were interdependent.[5] In March, a change of government brought Limpo de Abreu back to the Foreign Ministry, but when, on the eve of his departure for

---

[1] Palmerston to Howden, 2 October 1847, Broadlands MSS, GC/HO/955. Cf. Palmerston to Hudson, no. 9, 13 August 1846, F.O. 84/632; Hansard, xc, 1023, 8 March 1847; Palmerston to Howden, no. 1, 4 June 1847, F.O. 84/677.

[2] Palmerston to Howden, 2 October 1847.

[3] Howden to Palmerston, 12 November 1847, quoted in Pryor, *op. cit.* p. 366.

[4] Quoted in Howden to Palmerston, 1 March, enclosed in Howden to Aberdeen, 1 March 1848, B.M. Add. MSS 43124. Cf. Honório's views in 1843, see above, ch. 8, p. 235.

[5] Pimenta Bueno to Howden, 19 February, enclosed in Howden, no. 7, 20 March 1848, F.O. 84/725.

home, Howden made a last offer to reopen talks, Limpo de Abreu replied coldly that he had not the slightest wish to negotiate with Howden and that in future he proposed to act through the Brazilian minister in London.[1] Lord Howden left Brazil at the end of April 1848, thus concluding 'a most unpleasant and, I may add, hopeless duty'.[2] '[The] Brazilians', he wrote to Aberdeen, 'have no anxiety whatever (except by an *inefficient* slave treaty) to make any arrangements . . . for the object of getting rid of the bill against which they cry out.'[3] Once again, Britain had failed to persuade Brazil to sign either a new commercial treaty or new anti-slave trade treaty. As Palmerston had realised, Britain's commercial pre-eminence in Brazil was not adversely affected by the lack of a commercial treaty—the tariffs on British manufactured goods remained reasonably low and in no way discriminatory—but Britain's position would henceforth be dependent not so much on privilege and preference but on her continuing economic superiority over her rivals. The Brazilian slave trade would be virtually suppressed (although only after it had reached unprecedented heights) before negotiations for an Anglo-Brazilian anti-slave trade treaty were eventually reopened in London.[4] In the event, no new treaty was ever signed and only after the trade had been extinct for many years was Lord Aberdeen's Act finally repealed.

In the meantime British warships on anti-slave trade patrol had never before been armed with such extensive powers: they could capture both Brazilian and 'stateless' slave ships (the latter mostly Portuguese and, following the passage through the Spanish Cortes in March 1845 of more stringent anti-slave trade legislation, Spanish[5]) anywhere on the high seas and at any stage of

[1] Howden to Palmerston, London, 8 June 1848, Broadlands MSS, GC/HO/911; *Relatório do Ministério dos Negócios Estrangeiros* (May 1848).
[2] Howden to Palmerston, 8 June.
[3] Howden to Aberdeen, 1 March.   [4] See below, ch. 13, pp. 369–70.
[5] For the origins and passage of the Spanish anti-slave trade law of 4 March 1845, which had been promised when Spain and Britain signed the anti-slave trade treaty of June 1835, see David Robert Murray, 'Britain, Spain, and the slave trade to Cuba, 1807–1845' (unpublished Ph.D. thesis, Cambridge, 1967), pp. 295–330, and Arthur F. Corwin, *Spain and the Abolition of Slavery in Cuba, 1817–1886* (Univ. of Texas Press, 1968), pp. 84–5. The law did not, of course, end the Cuban slave trade, although for a few years the trade was carried on less extensively (Corwin, *op. cit.* pp. 88–9).

their voyage. Moreover, during the period 1845–50, the British squadron on the west African coast, which had been considerably strengthened in 1844, never numbered fewer than twenty-six ships—in 1847, thirty-two ships were stationed there—and, in addition to the flagship *Penelope*, usually included half a dozen other steamships.[1] The period after 1845 was by far the most successful the British navy had every enjoyed. In a little over five years, ships of the West African station, together with those of the Cape station which were from time to time available for anti-slave trade duties on the east African coast, captured almost 400 ships engaged in the Brazilian slave trade alone—27 during the last quarter of 1845; 49 in 1846; 78 in 1847; 90 in 1848; 54 in 1849; 80 in 1850—besides many others trading to Cuba.[2] Captured ships were despatched for adjudication to British vice-admiralty courts—more than half went to St Helena, the rest to Sierra Leone and the Cape of Good Hope. (The Aberdeen Act thus completed the process, begun in 1839, whereby the work previously undertaken by British and foreign commissioners in the courts of mixed commission passed almost entirely into the hands of the Chief Justices of British colonies in their capacity as judges in British vice-admiralty courts.[3]) And with very few exceptions these vessels were condemned quickly and with the minimum of fuss: in a British vice-admiralty court there was no foreign judge present to ensure that justice—or, as the British would have argued from their experience of the mixed commissions, injustice—was done; many traders did not even go to the trouble of arranging for legal representation in court, which was generally thought to be expensive and futile, much less of appealing to the High Court of Admiralty in London. And although Brazilian consuls or vice-consuls were maintained at St Helena, Sierra Leone and the Cape throughout the period they had no instructions other than that they should protest

[1] Lloyd, *Navy and Slave Trade*, Appendix C; Bartlett, *Britain and Sea Power*, Appendix II. On the significance of the change-over from sail to steam for the suppression of the slave trade, see Lloyd, *op. cit.* pp. 126–9 and J. Holland Rose, *Man and the Sea* (Cambridge, 1935), ch. 12.

[2] For cases before vice-admiralty courts 1845–50, see for St Helena, F.O. 84/651, 696, 738, 748, 776, 817; for Sierra Leone, F.O. 84/556, 619, 665–6, 712–13, 752, 788; for the Cape, F.O. 84/284, list of vessels adjudicated August 1839 to September 1849.

[3] See Bethell, *Journal of African History* (1966), p. 92.

formally against the illegality of the capture whenever Brazilian ships alleged to have been engaged in the slave trade were brought in for adjudication. When in 1847, for example, Saul Solomon, who from August 1846 acted as Brazilian consul in St Helena (as well as consul of Hamburg and Lübeck and commercial agent of France and Holland), was asked by José Gregorio Pereira, master of the *Rolha*, to provide money for his defence, Solomon felt obliged to refuse on the grounds that that was the job of a moneylender, not a consul (*este é a occupação de um cambista e não de um consul*).[1] The most the Brazilian government ever did was to send the occasional vessel to St Helena to transport back to Rio the sick and the destitute crew members of condemned Brazilian ships.

Despite the record number of slave ships captured by the British navy and subsequently condemned in British vice-admiralty courts—a number which ten years earlier would probably have brought the trade to a standstill—the Brazilian slave trade was by no means crushed. On the contrary, during the late forties it actually exceeded all previous levels. The reason can be found in the continued development of the plantation sector of the Brazilian economy in response to the demand for Brazilian produce in Europe and North America. The quantity of coffee exported during the period 1846–50 was 40% up on 1841–5. Sugar exports, too, expanded, and sugar exports as a proportion of total exports rose from 22% (1841–5) to 28% (1846–50), in part as a result of the opening up of the British market following the Sugar Act of 1846.[2] At the same time schemes for free white European immigration, both government-sponsored and, like those of Senator Vergueiro of São Paulo, private, failed to provide Brazilian plantation agriculture with the

---

[1] Solomon to Cairu, 6 February 1847, A.H.I. 263/2/9. In this same despatch Solomon wrote: '*he inutil de tentar fazer qualquer causa aqui contra o julgamento*'.

[2] Pryor, *thesis* pp. 388–93; Stanley J. Stein, *The Brazilian Cotton Manufacture, 1850–1950* (Harvard, 1957), p. 7; Stein, *Vassouras*, p. 53, Table 4; Furtado, *op. cit.* pp. 114–24; S. Ferreira Soares, *Notas estatisticas sobre a producção agricola e carestia dos generos alimenticios no imperio do Brazil* (Rio de Janeiro, 1860), pp. 28–9, 45. On the effects of the British Sugar Act, see for example, S. Cave, *A Few Words on the encouragement given to Slavery and the Slave Trade by recent measures and chiefly by the Sugar Bill of 1846* (London, 1849) and H. V. Huntley, *Free Trade, the Sugar Act of 1846 and the Slave Trade* (London, 1849).

additional labour force it required.[1] The demand for African slaves (*instrumentos de trabalho*) therefore showed no signs of abating, and with slave prices high—at least until 1848-9—the trade became more lucrative than ever. No less than 50,000–60,000 slaves were imported into Brazil each year during the period 1846-9.[2] Two-thirds were landed along a 200-mile stretch of the Brazilian coast north and south of Rio de Janeiro; the remainder were deposited in Rio itself (where in 1846 it was still possible openly to visit auctions of newly imported slaves),[3] in Bahia, whose trade grew steadily in the late forties, and to the south of Santos, especially near Paranaguá.

In order to out-manoeuvre the British preventive system the trade was more highly organised than ever before. 'All the appliances of this trade', Lord Howden later recalled, '[were] brought to a degree of perfection that is astonishing and which nothing but the immense profit can explain.'[4] More careful studies were made of the movements of British cruisers since even a squadron of some thirty ships could not effectively blockade the entire slave coasts of west and east Africa. The British West African squadron, now under the command of Sir Charles Hotham, reduced its own effectiveness by again pursuing 'off shore' tactics instead of blockading well-known points of embarkation and river mouths.[5] These tactics were forced upon it, however, by the fact that the African chiefs on the Guinea coast most involved in the slave trade (notably the King of Dahomey) refused to sign anti-slave trade treaties with Britain,[6] and in Portuguese Africa south of the equator, where the Brazilian trade was still largely carried on, the authorities

---

[1] On the efforts to stimulate European immigration, see Carneiro, *Imigração e Colonização no Brasil*, pp. 10–12. Also Djalma Forjaz, *O Senador Vergueiro* (São Paulo, 1924); Thomas Davatz, *Memórias de um colono no Brasil (1850)* ed. Sérgio Buarque de Holanda (São Paulo, 1941). [2] See Appendix.

[3] T. Ewbank, *Life in Brazil; or a journal of a visit to the land of the cocoa and the palm* (New York, 1856), p. 284.

[4] *P.P.* 1850 (Lords), XXIV (35), Select Committee of the House of Lords on the Slave Trade, 1st Report, Howden evidence, par. 301. See also, T. R. H. Thomson, *The Brazilian Slave Trade and Its Remedy* (London, 1850), pp. 19–24.

[5] Hotham to Admiralty, 17 August, 5 December 1848, F.O. 84/782. See Lloyd, *op. cit.* pp. 119–22.

[6] See K. Onwuka Dike, *Trade and Politics in the Niger Delta, 1830–85* (Oxford, 1956), pp. 81–96; Curtin, *Image of Africa*, pp. 466–8.

co-operated only intermittently; indeed in 1847 British naval officers were denied the right to make captures in Portuguese African territorial waters even along those parts of the coast outside the area of effective Portuguese control.[1] It was also still unfortunately true that some of the slowest ships in the service ended their days on anti-slave trade patrol; most if not all of them certainly fell a long way short of James Hudson's requirement that they should be able to 'spring upon their prey like greyhounds from a leash'.[2] For their part the traders increasingly made use of fast, American-built sailing ships which could easily elude the cruisers. And towards the end of 1846 they began to employ steamships, their engines, Hudson tartly observed, 'the best England could manufacture':[3] the *Tereza* owned by Tomás da Costa Ramos ('Maneta') and built to carry over a thousand slaves was said to be the first;[4] the *Serpente* and the *Providentia* proved to be the most famous and successful. Alternatively, the traders used old unseaworthy vessels which were, in the last resort, expendable. Inevitably, a great many of the vessels actually captured by the British navy fell into this category. During the late forties there was a striking increase in the number of slave ships destroyed on the spot by their captors. This was not only due to the fact that British officers could now afford to act more arbitrarily since cases now came before British rather than mixed courts and that with the increase in the number of captures prize crews could not always be spared; it was also true that more ships than hitherto were regarded as totally unfit to undertake the long journey to the nearest vice-admiralty court. There is evidence to suggest that many vessels of this kind were actually acting as decoys for the bigger, faster and more costly slave ships, which makes the number of British captures rather less impressive than may appear at first sight. Some of the traders formed themselves into associations which could more easily withstand losses while continuing to insure their vessels—at exorbitant rates. Most important, many Brazilian traders continued to make good use of the American flag, as they had done since the late thirties.[5]

---

[1] Frere and Surtees (Cape commissioners) to Aberdeen, no. 8, 13 January 1848 (Report on 1847), F.O. 84/717.
[2] Hudson to Palmerston, 24 March 1849, Private, F.O. 84/767.   [3] *Ibid.*
[4] Rodrigues, *Brazil and Africa*, p. 182.   [5] See above, ch. 7, pp. 189–93.

Under the terms of the Webster-Ashburton treaty of 1842 the United States was obliged to station a naval squadron on the west African coast. The squadron consisted of no more than half a dozen ships, however, and its base was Porto Praia in the Cape Verde Islands, far from the most important slave trading areas; few American cruisers ever ventured as far as the Congo or Angola. Moreover, American naval officers had no confidence that any slave vessels they captured would be condemned in American courts. The American anti-slave trade patrol of the coast of Africa was always therefore a 'sham patrol'.[1] At the same time the U.S. government continued to deny British warships the right to visit and search suspected slave ships flying the American flag. Consequently, the proportion of slaves landed in Brazil in vessels which were or had been or were pretending to be American rose steadily during the late forties, from 20% in 1848 (itself a remarkable figure) to almost 50% in 1850.[2]

Across the Atlantic on the Brazilian coast there was little likelihood during this period of outward bound slave vessels being prevented by the British navy from leaving Brazilian ports, nor of homecoming vessels which had successfully eluded the West African squadron being prevented from landing their slaves. Until 1849 all but one or two of the ships attached to the south-east coast of America naval station were fully occupied in the Río de la Plata. When, for example, Lord Howden arrived in Rio de Janeiro in August 1847, there was not a single British cruiser on the entire Brazilian coast and only one, the *Grecian*, when he left in April 1848.[3] Not that naval operations would have been easy even if more ships had been available. In addition to the many obstacles encountered by the British navy during an earlier period of anti-slave trade operations off the Brazilian coast (1839-42)—not least local armed opposition and the need to avoid unnecessary interference with legitimate coastal trade and to show some token respect for Brazilian sovereignty in Brazilian territorial waters[4]—the Brazilian authorities now took

---

[1] Howard, *American Slavers and the Federal Law*, pp. 105-7; Soulsby, *The Right of Search and the Slave Trade in Anglo-American Relations*, pp. 130-7.
[2] Howard, *op. cit.* pp. 46, 282, Appendix G.
[3] P.P. (Lords), xxiv (35), Select Committee of the House of Lords on the Slave Trade. 1st Report, Howden evidence, par. 219.   [4] See above, ch. 7, pp. 200-13.

the view that the navy's attempts to put down the slave trade under the Aberdeen Act were entirely illegal and on the rare occasions when a slaver was captured, they refused to co-operate in fitting it out with water and provisions for the long voyage to St Helena. Early in 1848, the Bahian authorities went further and actually turned a blind eye on an attempt from the shore to recapture the *Bella Miguelina* which the *Grecian* had taken with 500 slaves.[1] At the end of the year, Hudson felt compelled to advise the commander-in-chief, Sir Thomas Herbert (who was himself in Montevideo), that no protection from piratical attacks could be expected from the local authorities: 'the ports of Brazil to a certain extent', he wrote, 'are not the ports of a friendly but of a *hostile* power'.[2]

In March 1845, besides offering to negotiate a new treaty with Britain, the Brazilian government had announced that henceforth the Brazilian authorities would themselves make more determined efforts to curb the illegal Brazilian slave trade.[3] From the way the trade expanded in the late forties, however, it is clear that they failed to do so. Brazilian administrations during the *qüinqüênio liberal* (1844–8) were weak and short lived—no government before that of 29 September 1848 was sufficiently strong nor in power for long enough to conceive and execute unpopular anti-slave trade measures—and although there were ministers who genuinely wished to see the trade put down, there were undoubtedly more who, like the majority of councillors of state, senators and deputies, were either positively in favour of the trade (and in some cases as planters and slave owners themselves even indirectly engaged in it) or else, mindful of its importance for the Brazilian economy, preferred to leave it well alone. As James Hudson had reminded Lord Palmerston in June 1846: '*Brazil lives upon slave labour.* The government is carried on by the daily receipts of the Customs Houses. Foreign trade depends upon exports and they cannot be obtained at present unless by that most expensive of all systems of production, the

[1] Howden to Palmerston, no. 17, 5 May 1848, F.O. 84/725.
[2] Hudson to Herbert, 4 December, enclosed in Hudson no. 22, 16 December 1848, F.O. 84/726.   [3] See above, ch. 9, pp. 248–9.

labour of the slave.'[1] Moreover, any government which did attempt to curtail the slave trade would have to contend not only with plantation owners thirsty for fresh supplies of slaves but with the traders themselves who by this time constituted a powerful pressure group. The Brazilian slave trade had become big business and traders like Manuel Pinto da Fonseca and José Bernardino de Sá who ten years earlier had both served in small provision stores now commanded impressive financial resources and wielded considerable political influence. Many observers testified to the wealth and power of the slave traders in Brazil. '[They] are the nabobs of the Brazils', wrote T. Nelson, a naval officer who had served as Senior Assistant Surgeon on the *Crescent* in Rio harbour, in his book *Remarks on the Slavery and the Slave Trade of the Brazils* (1846), 'they form the dazzling class of the parvenus millionaires.'[2] The U.S. minister in Rio de Janeiro, Henry A. Wise, wrote to Secretary of State James Buchanan in 1846:

There are only three ways of making a fortune in Brazil—either by the slave trade, or by slaving, or by a coffee commission house. The foreign merchants alone engage in the latter, and to be a Brazilian 'man of consequence' all have to partake more or less, directly or indirectly, in the two former. And *all who are of consequence* do partake in them both. Here you must be rich to profit by usury and to be rich you must engage in the slave trade. The slave traders, then, are either the men in power, or those who lend to the men in power and hold them by the purse strings. Thus the government itself is in fact a slave trading government against its own laws and treaties.[3]

The dealers were 'tolerated, petted, fostered, flattered', Lord Howden wrote to Palmerston in March 1848, '. . . they make the government which makes them', and two years later he told the House of Lords Select Committee on the slave trade, 'put a dozen Rothschilds together and you will soon see how variegated is their influence'.[4]

[1] Hudson memorandum, 22 June 1846, B.M. Add. MSS 43124 (Aberdeen Papers).
[2] Nelson, *Remarks on Slavery and the Slave Trade*, p. 64.
[3] Wise to Buchanan, 9 December 1846, quoted in Rodrigues, *op. cit.* p. 186.
[4] Howden to Palmerston, 1 March, enclosed in Howden to Aberdeen, 1 March 1848, B.M. Add. MSS 43124 (Aberdeen Papers); *P.P.* 1850 (Lords), xxiv (35), House of Lords Select Committee on Slave Trade, par. 232. A good deal more is known about the

Aftermath of the Aberdeen Act

In January 1847, Barão de Cairu, Brazilian Foreign Minister (May 1846–May 1847) and himself an opponent of the slave trade on account of its extreme cruelty and because he feared that Brazil ('this fair country') was being delivered up to Africa, told Hudson that he frankly could not see how any Brazilian government could enforce the law of 1831 or indeed any other legislation aimed at the suppression of the slave trade. He described his own feelings of helplessness in the most striking terms:

I know of none who could or would attempt it, and when 99 men in every 100 are engaged in it, how is it to be done? . . . The vice has eaten into the very core of society. Who is so sought after, who is so feasted in this city as Manuel Pinto [da Fonseca]? You know him to be the great slave trader *par excellence* of Rio. Yet he and scores of minor slave dealers go to the Court—sit at the tables of the wealthiest and most respectable citizens—have seats in the Chamber as our Representatives and have a voice even in the Council of State. They are increasing in vigilance, perseverance, audacity—those whom they dare not put out of the way, they buy. No people make money so easily or spend it so lavishly—what they touch turns to gold—they carry all before them. You know my individual abhorrence of this cursed traffic—but with such men to deal with, what am I to do, what can I do? . . . where am I to begin? With my colleagues—useless. With the Council, they would not listen to me. In the Chamber, they would call me traitor. In the streets, I would be stoned. I cannot consent to be *The* Man in Brazil from whom all his countrymen would turn away with contempt and aversion. *I will not Bell the Cat.*[1]

Eighteen months later, however, an enlightened, far-sighted minority in Francisco de Paula Sousa's Liberal Cabinet of 3 May 1848, in the Senate and in the Chamber of Deputies was becoming increasingly concerned at the almost unprecedented number of Africans being imported into Brazil, tens of thousands of 'ignorant

Brazilian slave traders on the west African coast, and especially at Whydah (Dahomey), than in Brazil. See, for example, J. F. de Almeida Prado, *O Brasil e o Colonialismo Europeu* (São Paulo, 1956), pp. 115–226; Pierre Verger, *Les Afro-Américains: Influence du Brésil au Golfe du Bénin* (Ifan-Dakar, 1953); David A. Ross, 'The Career of Domingo Martinez in the Bight of Benin, 1833–64', *Journal of African History*, vi (1965), pp. 79–90; Rodrigues, *op. cit.* pp. 177–9, 183. On the slave dealers in Brazil, see the report by the informer 'Alcoforado', October 1853, A.N. IJ6–525 (summarised in Rodrigues, *op. cit.* pp. 179–82).

[1] Quoted in Hudson to Palmerston, 12 January 1847, Private, F.O. 84/678. Cf. Henry A. Wise to Buchanan, 12 April 1847, Manning, *Diplomatic Correspondence*, ii, p. 380.

savages'—'*milhares de defensores das instituições de Haiti*', as Lopes Gama described them[1]—perhaps as many as 150,000 during the three years since the passage of the Aberdeen Act, all of them legally free but held in slavery. As in other periods of unusually heavy slave importation fear of 'Africanisation' produced something of a reaction, however transient, against the slave trade, and as in 1835 at the time of the Bahia slave revolt the belief that the racial balance in Brazil was being upset, thereby endangering life and property, was reinforced by the discovery at Pelotas (Rio Grande do Sul) in February and in various municipalities of Rio de Janeiro province in July of well-laid plans for armed slave uprisings.[2] By the middle of 1848 there was also rather more concern than there had been hitherto at the capture of Brazilian ships by the British navy and their adjudication in British vice-admiralty courts. A majority of the Council of State had always taken the view that any vessel captured off the coast of Africa could reasonably be presumed to be guilty of illegal slave trading and therefore unworthy of protection. As long as the British navy concentrated its activities on the other side of the Atlantic Brazilian governments had not found it too difficult to live with the Aberdeen Act. Indeed, as Lord Howden was to explain, however much they might have wished it to be repealed, most leading Brazilian politicians positively preferred it to the only available alternative—an anti-slave trade treaty on Britain's terms:

Its action is comparatively noiseless, it is distant, it saves the ministers . . . the odium of making treaties with an abhorred power like England, and the onus of carrying out a slave treaty if they had one. Moreover, it does not in the least prevent slaves from coming into Brazil . . . and it gives ministers and all the members of the Assembly an opportunity of abusing foreigners.[3]

However, with the sharp increase in the number of British captures and with the capture of the *Bella Miguelina* on the coast

---

[1] *Parecer* no. 93, foreign affairs sub-committee of the *Conselho de Estado*, 10 August 1846, A.H.I. 342/1/6.
[2] Morgan (Rio Grande do Sul) to Palmerston, 15 February 1848, F.O. 84/727; Howden no. 12, 20 March 1848, F.O. 84/725; report of special committee of Rio provincial assembly, 8 July 1848, enclosed in Hudson no. 7, 20 February 1850, F.O. 84/802.
[3] Howden to Aberdeen, 1 March 1848, B.M. Add. MSS 43124.

of Brazil, the first to take place there for almost two years, there was a shift of opinion towards the view, frequently expressed by Lopes Gama, that for Brazil to permit such a state of affairs was tantamount to renouncing her sovereign rights; no nation whose flag was not universally respected on the high seas and whose laws were executed by foreign agents could possibly regard itself as completely independent.[1] And by no means least the Brazilian government was becoming increasingly anxious about the situation in the Río de la Plata where the independence of Uruguay and the territorial integrity of the Brazilian empire were under constant threat from Rosas. In the event of war with Buenos Aires Brazil would require the benevolent neutrality, and preferably the active support, of Britain, and it could reasonably be assumed that this would be secured only by a settlement of the slave trade question.

Thus for a number of reasons the Paula Sousa administration was coming round to the idea that it was time to take some positive steps towards curbing the illegal Brazilian slave trade. They realised, however, that such was the power of the landowners in the rural areas that it was not practicable simply to enforce the existing law of November 1831 which had declared all slaves entering Brazil free and which had made the purchaser as well as the importer liable to punishment. They decided therefore to concentrate on the effective suppression of the slave trade at sea and at points along the Brazilian coast where slaves were actually disembarked and slave ships fitted out for the trade; no action was proposed once a cargo of slaves had been successfully landed and transferred inland. The simplest procedure seemed to be to resurrect the Marquês de Barbacena's bill of 1837 which had prohibited the importation of slaves into Brazil, made ships equipped for the trade as well as those taken carrying slaves liable to confiscation, imposed heavier penalties for transporting and importing slaves, offered bigger rewards to informers and captors, provided for the careful inspection of all shipping in and out of Brazilian ports and the payment of bond

[1] E.g. Bahia legislative assembly representation to Chamber of Deputies, 31 July 1848, enclosed in José Pedro Dias de Carvalho (Minister of Empire) to Bernardo de Sousa Franco (Foreign Minister), 13 September 1848, A.H.I. 300/3/1.

by ships in the African trade—and at the same time repealed the existing law of 1831.[1] 'I hope the measures we contemplate', Bernardo de Sousa Franco, the Brazilian Foreign Minister, told Hudson, 'will prove to Lord Palmerston that we are in earnest— that he will no longer need cruisers and that the "bill" will be unnecessary.'[2]

Early in August a rare event took place. Under pressure from the Minister of Justice, Antônio Manuel de Campos Melo, the President of Rio de Janeiro province ordered the Chief of Police and a detachment of troops to the Saco de Jurujuba (Niterói), one of the most notorious slave deposits near the capital, where they seized nearly one hundred recently imported slaves.[3] Less than a month later on 1 September Campos Melo reintroduced into the Chamber Barbacena's bill of 1837. It had been suitably streamlined and amended: potential loopholes in the equipment article, for example, had been tightened up and both the 'principals' and the 'accomplices' in cases of slave trading more clearly identified; for the first time slaving was accorded the stigma of piracy, though the penalties remained those laid down in the law of 1831 and the Criminal Code; bounties were increased; liberated slaves were to be re-exported at the expense of the state and in the interim kept out of the hands of private individuals. Despite opposition at every stage during a debate which lasted several days, all the articles were finally approved with the exception of the thirteenth and last, that which sought to repeal the law of November 1831. At this point, Gabriel José Rodrigues dos Santos (São Paulo), speaking on behalf of the government, persuaded the Chamber to go into secret session because article thirteen involved *graves questões de ordem internacional e interna*. During two days of tormented debate (25–26 September) the Chamber seems to have been hopelessly divided, as it had been twelve years earlier, about whether the existing law should be kept in existence and enforced along with the new measures or whether it should be repealed. The former

---

[1] For the terms of Barbacena's bill of 1837, see above, ch. 3, p. 82.
[2] Hudson to Palmerston, 5 August 1848, Private, F.O. 84/726.
[3] Hudson no. 8, 5 August 1848, F.O. 84/726; Eusébio de Queiroz to Olinda, 24 October 1848, Reservado, A.H.I. 301/1/11; Olinda to Lisboa (London), no. 48, 26 October 1848, A.H.I. 268/1/17.

course would menace the 'property' of the most influential men in the country; the latter would seriously weaken any attempt to put down the slave trade and indeed deprive of their liberty thousands of Africans—not only those who had already been illegally imported but those which might be successfully imported in future.[1] Moreover, the repeal of the 1831 law could not fail to anger the British government. Like his predecessor when the issue was first raised in 1837, Hudson had already protested against the bill which, he declared, contained 'the deadliest blow ever levelled by a Brazilian statesman at the only remedy which Brazilian law affords to the slave to assert his rights to freedom . . . in three short lines [it] condemns to perpetual slavery thousands of men and their descendants without a hope, without a chance that their doom can be changed'. The existing law, Hudson reminded the Brazilian government, presumed an illegally imported African to be free, the new bill presumed him to be a slave: it was impossible and absurd to expect 'a little barbarian speaking a sort of monkey dialect' to send to Africa for proof that he had not been born a slave, but there was always a chance, admittedly slight, that he might at some future date establish his unlawful importation into Brazil.[2] In the event, in an effort to appease as far as possible the landed interest, the government stood firm on the necessity of including article thirteen in the bill. However, a motion to postpone the vote on this article and thus defer a final decision on the bill until the following session (scheduled to begin on 1 January 1850) was carried by thirty-two votes to twenty-nine. It was a victory for the more enlightened critics of the bill's final article—but also, and more immediately important, for the die-hard opponents of the bill as a whole. The first attempt by a Brazilian government for almost a decade to get to grips with the problem of the illegal slave trade had come to nothing. On 29 September 1848 the Paula Sousa government fell—to be replaced by a Conservative

---

[1] *Anais do Parlamento Brasileiro: Câmara dos Deputados.* 1848 session, vol. ii, pp. 323–52, 407–12; Alves, *R.I.H.G.B.* (1914), pp. 234–6; Hudson no. 10, 12 September, no. 11, 11 October 1848, F.O. 84/726; Olinda to Lisboa, no. 47, 14 October 1848, A.H.I. 268/1/17. Also Eusébio de Queiroz's recollections in his speech of 16 July 1852 (*Anais,* 1852 session, vol. ii, pp. 241–58).

[2] Hudson to Sousa Franco, 4 September, enclosed in Hudson no. 10, 12 September 1848, F.O. 84/726; Hudson to Palmerston, 12 September 1848, Private, F.O. 84/726.

administration led by the Visconde de Olinda.[1] The new government was expected to be much more sympathetic to the landed interest and therefore willing to connive at the illegal slave trade —a not unreasonable expectation in the light of the Conservative record during the years 1837–9 and 1841–4.

[1] *História Geral da Civilização Brasileira* II, iii, p. 12.

CHAPTER 11

CHANGING ATTITUDES AND PLANS
OF ACTION, 1845–1850

As the illegal slave trade to Brazil continued to expand throughout the late forties in the absence of any really effective preventive
action by the Brazilian authorities and in defiance of the most
extreme measures so far adopted against it by the British navy,
opposition in England to what John Bright called Lord Palmerston's 'benevolent crotchet for patrolling the coasts of Africa and
Brazil' gathered considerable momentum both inside and outside
Parliament. It was towards the end of the previous decade that a
degree of dissatisfaction with Britain's traditional anti-slave trade
policies had first become apparent.[1] Considerably strengthened
and extended the British preventive system had nevertheless been
given a further period in which to prove itself. If, however, its
raison d'être was the suppression of the illegal transatlantic slave
trade, or at the very least a substantial reduction of it, with the
Cuban trade as well as the Brazilian still flourishing its failure
could no longer be denied and there was evidence of a growing
conviction that it ought now therefore to be dismantled.

Since its foundation in 1839 the British and Foreign Anti-
Slavery Society, very much Quaker dominated, had been
opposed to the use of armed force for the suppression of the slave
trade and, consequently, completely out of sympathy with the
anti-slave trade efforts of successive British governments, both
Whig and Tory. Although the question of the use of force
against the slave trade, like that of differential duties on slave-
grown sugar, had produced deep divisions within the abolitionist
movement, the official policy of the Society remained unchanged
throughout the 1840s.[2] In March 1845 (before the slave trade had

---

[1] See above, ch. 6, pp. 152–4.
[2] For a discussion of some of the issues which divided British abolitionists during the 1840s,
see, for example, Elsie I. Pilgrim, 'Anti-Slavery Sentiment in Great Britain, 1841–54'
(unpublished Ph.D. thesis, Cambridge, 1952) and Duncan E. Rice, 'Critique of the Eric
Williams Thesis: The Anti-Slavery Interest and the Sugar Duties, 1841–53', in *The
Transatlantic Slave Trade from West Africa* (Edinburgh, 1965), pp. 44–60.

reached its peak) the veteran abolitionist Thomas Clarkson, now eighty-five years old and President of the Anti-Slavery Society, had presented Lord Aberdeen, then Foreign Secretary, with a remarkable memorial in which, after reaffirming the Society's pacifist principles, he explained why he felt that the policies hitherto pursued for the suppression of the slave trade had failed and, more important, would continue to fail. In the first place, there was no hope of negotiating comprehensive anti-slave trade treaties with every foreign power involved in the trade. Secondly, even if the existing treaty system could be strengthened Britain would never have sufficient naval resources to patrol effectively the vast area in which the trade was carried on. Thirdly, the object of the treaties would inevitably be defeated 'either by a want of cordiality in their execution or by the positive bad faith of foreign powers': in the absence of any moral feeling against such an apparently necessary trade neither international agreements nor anti-slave trade legislation would be enforced. Fourthly, while the demand for slaves continued and profits from the slave trade remained high the efforts of the navy would be 'continually overmatched by the cunning, fraud and audacity of slave dealers'. Clarkson's advice to the government, therefore, was to abandon their existing policies and instead, like the Society, direct their energies against the slave system itself by 'creating where it does not exist and fostering where they see germs of it a sense of humanity and moral rectitude'. Clarkson concluded that only by the total abolition of slavery in the Americas could the slave trade be annihilated. 'Destroy the demand of the slave holder', he argued, 'and there will be no longer a traffic carried on to supply wants which shall no longer exist.'[1]

The attack on Britain's long established methods for suppressing the foreign slave trade was taken up in the House of Commons on a much broader front by the radical free traders led into battle on this occasion by William Hutt, M.P. for Gateshead, and Thomas Milner Gibson, M.P. for Manchester. It was their contention that since Britain's efforts over a period of forty years

---

[1] Clarkson to Aberdeen, 7 March 1845, F.O. 84/616. Cf. John Scoble (Secretary, Anti-Slavery Society) to Peel, 12 July 1845, B.M. Add. MSS 40570 (Peel Papers).

had proved completely unequal to the task it was futile to persevere with them. Not 'ten men out of Bedlam', Hutt declared in
February 1848, any longer believed that laws, treaties and warships could suppress so profitable a trade and he called upon the
government to abandon its 'blundering and ignorant humanity'
and 'leave to a higher authority . . . the moral government of
the world'.[1] Many free traders inclined to Richard Cobden's
view, expressed in 1842, that free trade and international peace
were 'one and the same cause'[2] and, like the Anti-Slavery
Society, strongly objected to the bellicose nature of Britain's
anti-slave trade policy—described by Thomas Anstey, radical
member for Youghall, as 'the pacification of Africa by making
war against the rest of the world'[3]—as well as many other aspects
of 'Palmerstonianism'. It was John Bright's firm conviction that
it was in any case absolutely impossible to 'dragoon' a free and
independent nation like Brazil into suppressing a trade which it
felt to be necessary for its economic survival.[4] As well, the free
traders were able to adduce more positive reasons for Britain's
abandoning its self-appointed role as the world's anti-slave trade
policeman. In the first place, it was proving increasingly expensive. The possibility of a saving in government expenditure had
considerable appeal for those like Cobden, Bright, Hume and
Molesworth, whose watchword was 'retrenchment' and who
were already, on more general grounds, seeking to curb naval
expenditure by reducing what they regarded as an excessive peace-
time naval establishment: the money saved on the West African
squadron could be better spent at home—or, better still, not spent
at all.[5] A second and perhaps more telling criticism levelled at the
slave trade preventive system was that it had an adverse effect on
Britain's foreign trade. Representatives of northern and midlands

[1] Hansard, xcvi, 1091–1101, 22 February 1848. The opponents of British policy were able
to quote a statement Russell (Prime Minister, 1846–51) had made in 1839 (when he was
Colonial Secretary): 'to repress the foreign slave trade by a marine guard would scarcely
be possible if the whole British navy could be employed for that purpose. It is an evil
which can never be adequately encountered by any system of mere prohibition and
penalties' (Russell to Treasury, 26 December 1839, printed in Thomas Fowell Buxton,
The African Slave Trade and its Remedy (2nd ed. London, 1840), Appendix F).
[2] Quoted in Oliver Macdonagh, 'The Anti-Imperialism of Free Trade', *Economic History
Review*, 2nd ser. xiv (1962), p. 492.
[3] Hansard, civ, 789, 24 April 1849.   [4] *Ibid.* 786.
[5] See Bartlett, *Britain and Sea Power*, pp. 257–9, 268–9.

constituencies, notably Milner Gibson, Cobden and Bright, voiced the anxiety at the steady deterioration in Anglo-Brazilian relations felt by manufacturers and merchants in Manchester, Liverpool, Glasgow and elsewhere who had a stake in the important and growing trade with Brazil.[1] One of the two major obstacles in the way of improved relations with Brazil—the British differential sugar duties—had been removed. Why not now get rid of the Aberdeen Act and the anti-slave trade squadrons? It was not that the free traders wished to see the slave trade flourish (although some of the more doctrinaire amongst them went so far as to argue that no artificial barriers whatsoever should be erected against the free movement of goods, including slaves). It was simply that they believed that the trade should and could be suppressed by other means. Several lines of argument were used, none of them particularly convincing: anti-slavery propaganda and 'moral pressure' alone would eventually produce in Brazil a climate of opinion more favourable to abolition; allowing the slave trade to continue without restriction for a short period would produce a glut in Brazil which would inevitably lead to a natural reduction in the trade; legitimate trade with West Africa would by itself eventually undermine the slave trade at its source; free labour in the West Indies would prove more productive than slave labour and stiffer competition would force the sugar and coffee planters of Brazil and Cuba to turn abolitionist.

Paradoxically, there were also Protectionists and spokesmen for the West India interest in Parliament who, having previously supported the policy of suppressing the foreign slave trade, had now become its critics, embittered as they were by the passage of the Sugar Act. Their viewpoint found expression in *The Times* (which had supported the Aberdeen Act in 1845); at a time of pinching economy, it declared in one notable editorial, Britain could ill afford to spend £1 million a year on 'a philanthropic sham . . . doing at one side of the Atlantic what we deliberately undo at the other . . . we encourage a trade for our convenience in order that we may make a virtue of pretending to suppress it . . . we are either hypocrites or fools'.[2] Many West Indian planters—

[1] See A. Redford, *Manchester Merchants and Foreign Trade, 1794–1858* (Manchester, 1934), p. 106.   [2] *The Times*, 19 March 1850.

especially those in less developed colonies like Trinidad and British Guiana where labour was in extremely scarce supply—believed their best hope of economic prosperity lay not in relying on the preventive squadrons to suppress the slave trade of their competitors—this now seemed hopeless—but in putting themselves as far as possible on equal terms with their rivals by securing free immigrant labour from Africa on a much bigger scale than ever before (some were even to be found advocating the reopening of a regulated slave trade under British control). And this they believed would be facilitated by a withdrawal of the West African naval squadron. Again *The Times* spoke for them:

Were we to apply our money and ships in buying on the African coast 50,000 head of Negroes a year, and landing them free in our West Indian ports, it would tend far more to the prosperity of our Islands, and to the suppression of the slave trade, than all that our settlements and cruisers have done, with the balance of expense very much in our favour.[1]

Uncomfortably aware, however, that Jamaica and Barbados could be finally ruined as much by increased competition from Trinidad and British Guiana as from Cuba and Brazil, those whose concern was the future of the older West Indian sugar colonies continued to put their faith in the existing policy of suppressing the slave trade rather than in large-scale free immigration. The launching in 1849 of a powerful campaign in support of the West African squadron in Kingston, Jamaica, by David Turnbull, a former Consul and Superintendent of Liberated Africans in Havana and commissary judge in Jamaica, served to underline this point.[2] The demand for the retention of the West African squadron was also voiced by the older generation of Buxtonite abolitionists—for example, Lord Chief Justice Denman, Lord Brougham, Samuel Wilberforce (Bishop of Oxford) and Sir Robert Inglis—who could not agree with the official views of the Anti-Slavery Society on the best means of suppressing the slave trade and by those interested in the development and civilisation of Africa, a cause

[1] *The Times*, 5 February 1848, quoted in the Rev. George Smith, *The Case of our West African cruisers and West African settlements fairly considered* (London, 1848), p. 4.
[2] See David Turnbull, *The Jamaica Movement for promoting the enforcement of the slave trade treaties and the suppression of the slave trade* (London, 1850).

which once again attracted growing support during the 1840s.[1] In August 1842 Lord Palmerston had declared in the House of Commons:

Let no man imagine that [slave trade] treaties . . . are valuable only as being calculated to promote the great interests of humanity and as tending to rid mankind of a foul and detestable crime. Such is indeed their great object and their chief merit. But in this case as in many others virtue carries with it its own reward; and if the nations of the world could extirpate this abominable traffic (and vast populations of Africa left free for trade) the greatest commercial benefit would accrue not to England only, but to every civilised nation which engages in maritime commerce. These slave trade treaties therefore are indirectly treaties for the encouragement of commerce.[2]

And in 1849 he again declared his belief that

if the slave trade could be entirely put down there would be a very great increase of legitimate trade with the coast of Africa: the natives are much in want of commodities with which we can furnish them, and they possess very ample means of paying for them in commodities which we require.[3]

Finally, and of decisive importance in the debate over the future of Britain's anti-slave trade policies, the leaders of both Whigs and Peelites—Palmerston, Russell, Peel, Aberdeen—were determined to resist any attempt to weaken, much less dismantle, the suppression system based on anti-slave trade treaties and naval power to which they and their parties were so deeply committed. Called upon to justify their faith in the system they claimed that if the trade had not yet been completely crushed it was simply because, despite the progress made since 1839, it had not yet proved possible to bring Britain's maritime police force into fully effective operation and give it a fair and extended trial. As it was, the trade had been seriously impeded and was carried on less extensively than would otherwise have been the case. They were convinced, moreover, that no better or quicker way of putting down the

---

[1] See Philip D. Curtin, *The Image of Africa. British Ideas and Action, 1780–1850* (Wisconsin, 1964); R. J. Gavin, 'Palmerston's Policy towards East and West Africa, 1830–1865' (unpublished Ph.D. thesis, Cambridge, 1960).
[2] Hansard, lxv, 1251–2, (10 August 1842).
[3] Quoted in Roger Anstey, 'Capitalism and Slavery—a Critique', in *Transatlantic Slave Trade from West Africa*, p. 27.

slave trade had yet been devised and that if Britain gave up its efforts at this stage with (as they saw it) complete success close at hand the slave traders would be left in undisturbed possession of the African coast, legitimate African trade would suffer and the illegal slave trade would actually expand, to the further advantage of Brazilian and Cuban planters at the expense of their British West Indian rivals. As for the argument that Britain would do better to concentrate its efforts on the abolition of slavery in America, Lord Canning, Under Secretary for Foreign Affairs (1841–6), had the answer to this: replying on behalf of Aberdeen to Clarkson's memorial of March 1845, he did not deny that 'to rob the slave traders of their market by a general emancipation of the Negro race would be a higher and worthier victory over them than any that can be gained by physical force', but, he added, 'the influence of one country on the domestic institutions of another, those institutions being recognised and upheld by the laws and closely interwoven with the habits and interests of the people, can scarcely be otherwise than slow and uncertain'. Far better, he thought, to deal with the slave trade at sea.[1] And a few months later from the opposition benches Palmerston, at his most persuasive, made a brilliant, sustained attack on the views of both the Anti-Slavery Society and many of the supporters of Free Trade when he told the House of Commons that while it was undoubtedly and obviously true that slavery was 'the cause, the object and the purpose of the slave trade' and that if it could be abolished all over the world the trade would necessarily cease, it was equally true that the trade was

the root which gives life, spirit and stability to the condition of slavery
... Seek to upheave the vast living tree whose mighty roots are strongly, vigorously and deeply embedded in the soil, it will baffle the utmost exertion of your strength; but lay your axe to the root, cut off the supply of nourishment and the tree will sicken and decay and you will no longer find any difficulty in bringing it to the ground.[2]

In July 1845 Milner Gibson had gathered little support in the House of Commons for his opposition to the passage of Lord

[1] Lord Canning to Clarkson, 20 March 1845, F.O. 84/615.
[2] Hansard, lxxxii, 143–4, 8 July 1845.

Aberdeen's bill, of which so much was expected,[1] and when, during the same session, William Hutt had launched, rather prematurely, the parliamentary campaign for the withdrawal of the West African squadron with a motion stating that Britain's policy had resulted in vast expenditure and serious loss of life without in any way mitigating the horrors or diminishing the extent of the slave trade, the House had adjourned after a short debate with only twenty-nine members present.[2] Yet in March 1848, less than three years later, as the Brazilian slave trade reached new heights, Hutt forced a division on a similar motion and, though heavily defeated, as many as eighty members voted for the withdrawal of the squadron.[3] In April 1849 the Aberdeen Act itself—'an aggression upon Brazil—unjust, impolitic and destructive of the objects for which it was professedly framed', as Milner Gibson persisted in calling it—came under attack. Thirty-four members of the Commons, including Cobden and Bright, supported a motion for its repeal, but they were easily defeated by a majority of 103.[4]

By 1848, however, sufficient public doubt and anxiety had been expressed on the slave trade question for the House of Commons to establish a Select Committee under Hutt's chairmanship to examine how it might best be suppressed and, in particular, whether Britain's existing anti-slave trade methods had succeeded in reducing or at least containing it—or, as *The Times* succinctly put it, whether 'the difference between what the slave trade is now and what it would be if our squadron were withdrawn is worth what it costs us to keep the squadron where it is'.[5] In the following year the House of Lords set up its own Select Committee on the slave trade under the chairmanship of the Bishop of Oxford. Both committees were reappointed for a second session, and there passed before them a succession of witnesses—ministers, members of parliament, diplomats and consuls, colonial officials, naval officers, West Indian planters, merchants in the West African trade, African missionaries, even a former slave trader—whose

---

[1] See above, ch. 9, pp. 261–3.
[2] Hansard, lxxxi, 1156–72, 24 June 1845; W. L. Mathieson, *Great Britain and the Slave Trade 1839–1865* (London, 1929), pp. 88–9.
[3] Hansard, xcvii, 1004–6.
[4] Hansard, civ, 806–7.   [5] *The Times*, 24 October 1849.

evidence, reflecting as it did the entire spectrum of British attitudes towards the slave trade and its suppression, provided material for any and every argument. No clear verdict emerged in favour of either the "coercionists" or the "anti-coercionists" (to use W. L. Mathieson's useful terms). Whereas, however, the reports of the Lords Committee came out strongly in support of government policy, the first report of the Commons Committee, published in August 1848, was indecisive and contained several flatly contradictory conclusions; then in June 1849 the Committee accepted a series of recommendations in favour of the withdrawal of the West African squadron, although only after the Chairman (Hutt) had used his casting vote.[1]

It was becoming increasingly clear to the supporters of the British preventive system that if the illegal foreign slave trade were to be reduced and eventually destroyed rather than merely impeded further measures must be devised to reinforce those already in use. But what measures still remained to be taken? Various suggestions were made during the public debate on the slave trade question which took place during the late forties; all, however, presented difficulties. There were still, for example, those who advocated the exclusion of all slave produce from the English market. Indeed the Prime Minister himself, Lord John Russell, considered suspending the Sugar Act and re-establishing differential duties until such time as the slave trade to Cuba and Brazil had been suppressed. But the realisation that both Whigs and Peelites were now committed to free trade and that such a proposal would meet with little support compelled him to drop the idea.[2] Another suggestion was to despatch an even bigger, faster squadron to the west African coast: as Palmerston had said

[1] The House of Commons Committee produced four reports in 1848 and two in 1849: *P.P.* 1847–8, xxii (272), (366), (536), (623); *P.P.* 1849, xix (309), (410). The House of Lords Committee produced one report in 1849 and one in 1850: *P.P.* (Lords) 1849, xviii (32); *P.P.* (Lords) 1850, xxiv (35). The evidence submitted by Palmerston, Denman, Matson, Howden, Hotham, Lushington, Bandinel, Ouseley and many others to these committees constitutes one of the most valuable sources for the history of British policy towards the slave trade in the nineteenth century. For a selection of the numerous books and pamphlets on the slave trade question which appeared during the late forties, see Bibliography. See also Mathieson, *op. cit.* pp. 85–113; Curtin, *op. cit.* pp. 341 (n. 53), 444–8; Lloyd, *Navy and the Slave Trade*, pp. 104–14.

[2] Russell to Palmerston, 24 November 1849, 22 January 1850, Broadlands MSS GC/RU/ 306, 312.

in 1845, 'unless the coasts are guarded by constables that can run instead of Old Charlies we can't expect to succeed . . . we ought therefore to have recourse to the new police'.[1] But a sizable force, including several steamers, was already deployed on the coast and there was a limit to the number of ships that could be made available for anti-slaving duties. Experienced naval officers like Joseph Denman and Henry Matson tended to favour a more rigorous policy of destroying slave barracoons on the African coast.[2] But this, too, gave rise to difficulties: even where African chiefs could be persuaded to co-operate complicated questions of international law could arise—as the Gallinas incident (1841) had shown all too clearly.[3] And in any case it was Portuguese or Portuguese-claimed territories south of the equator that still supplied the overwhelming majority of slaves for Brazil. Was Britain prepared to go to war with Portugal for the suppression of the slave trade? An effective right of search treaty with the United States, others argued, would increase considerably the powers of the British West African squadron, but negotiations had always failed in the past and there was no reason for thinking they would succeed now. Especially persistent was the demand that those engaged in the trade should be dealt with far more severely. Crime, it was argued by some opponents of the slave trade, was prevented not by the presence of officers of the law but by fear of the punishment which would be inflicted were violations of the law to be detected. Under the provisions of the Aberdeen Act British courts had no right to try and punish persons found on board captured Brazilian vessels and slave traders faced only pecuniary losses—which they could well bear—with the result that the same men were often taken over and over again. In March 1848 Lord Palmerston, who had become Foreign Secretary once again in 1846, declared before the Select Committee of the House of Commons: 'I think they [the Brazilian traders] ought to be punished and I wish that the law gave us the power to punish them', and in July he declared that Parliament would be fully justified under article 1 of the treaty of 1826

[1] Hansard, lxxxii, 155, 8 July 1845.
[2] See evidence of Denman and Matson to the House of Commons Select Committee; also J. Denman, *The Slave Trade, the African Squadron and Mr. Hutt's Committee* (London, 1850); H. J. Matson, *Remarks on the Slave Trade and the African Squadron* (London, 1848).
[3] See above, ch. 7, pp. 185–6.

in extending the Aberdeen Act to Brazilian subjects if Brazil failed to enforce its own legislation.[1] But nothing was done. It would have been an extreme step, and it was doubtful whether even Brazil, which of necessity had put up with so much, would allow British courts to deal summarily with Brazilian subjects.

A more realistic policy frequently advocated by the 'coercionists' and one more likely to bring immediate results, was that of naval action on the other side of the Atlantic. A stronger and more active anti-slave trade squadron on the Brazilian coast, it was argued, would severely hinder the Brazilian trade and might also compel the Brazilian authorities themselves to take decisive steps to bring it to an end. In February 1847, for instance, John Hook, the British commissary judge in Freetown, had called for 'some bold measures' to be taken if the Brazilian government failed to adopt a more rigorous anti-slave trade policy. 'I would plant a *military police* on the whole coast of Brazil,' Hook wrote. 'Nay . . . I would at once go to war with Brazil and thereby probably within twelve months put a *final end* to the slave trade.'[2] Jackson and Gabriel, the British commissioners in the Anglo-Portuguese mixed court in Luanda, insisted that 'no naval force on the west coast of Africa, however numerous, can suffice to suppress the traffic unless a corresponding force, even though it should not be so great an amount, be contemporaneously stationed on that of Brazil and the egress of vessels from her ports be again narrowly watched'.[3] The men who were, or had recently been, on the spot, Lord Howden and James Hudson, also argued in favour of operations on the Brazilian side of the Atlantic, Howden because he thought it might force the Brazilians into giving the co-operation he considered essential if the slave trade were ever to be suppressed, Hudson because he believed that by blockading Brazil's major

---

[1] *P.P.* 1847–8, xxii (272). 1st Report, par. 134; Palmerston to Hutt, 20 July 1848, F.O. 96/30; Palmerston to Hudson, no. 10, 25 August 1848, F.O. 84/726. The punishment of Brazilian slave traders as pirates had been frequently advocated in the past: e.g. Weiss (Bahia consul) no. 5, 25 February 1830, F.O. 84/112; Ouseley memorandum, 24 April 1838, F.O. 84/252; Macaulay and Doherty (Sierra Leone), General no. 111, 31 December 1838, F.O. 84/231; Frere and Surtees (Cape), no. 18, 25 April 1844, F.O. 84/515; Jackson and Gabriel (Luanda), no. 9, 18 February 1847, F.O. 84/671.

[2] Hook to Stanley (F.O.), General no. 6, 9 February 1847, F.O. 84/665.

[3] Jackson and Gabriel to Palmerston, no. 9, 14 February 1848, F.O. 84/719.

ports a bigger squadron could itself substantially reduce the trade.[1] James Bandinel, who had been head of the Slave Trade Department of the Foreign Office for over twenty-five years until his retirement in 1845, was another of those who believed that force could be successful against the slave trade although only if British cruisers prevented slave ships leaving Brazilian ports and the co-operation of the Brazilian authorities could be secured; should the Brazilians refuse to co-operate and continue to break their treaty engagements, Bandinel thought that Britain had ample justification for 'making redress by force of arms'.[2] Sir Charles Hotham, commander-in-chief on the West African station from October 1846 to March 1849, judged the existing anti-slave trade measures 'perfectly futile' and he, too, advocated naval action off the Brazilian coast. But he was convinced, too, that it was essential to enlist the co-operation of the Brazilian government against the trade—perhaps even by allowing it to function on a strictly regulated basis for a brief period of years; otherwise, he agreed, Britain had no alternative but to resort to war, although he was personally reluctant 'to extirpate slavery on the ruin of a young and rising nation'.[3]

Lord Palmerston himself often contended that the Brazilian slave trade could be substantially reduced only if, in addition to maintaining the West African squadron, half a dozen cruisers were sent to blockade the Brazilian coast to the north and south of Rio de Janeiro.[4] He frequently asked the Admiralty to station more ships there, but the reply was always the same: it was

---

1 *P.P.* 1849 (Lords), xviii (32), House of Lords Select Committee, 1st Report, Howden evidence, 25 April 1849, pars. 252–3, 266; Hudson to Palmerston, 4 May 1847, Private, F.O. 84/678; Hudson to Palmerston, 24 March 1849, Private, F.O. 84/767.
2 *P.P.* 1847–8, xxii (272), House of Commons Select Committee, 1st Report, pars. 3278–85, 3322, 3333–7, 3387.
3 Hotham to Admiralty, no. 395, 5 December 1848: 'Remarks and Observations on the final extinction of the slave trade', F.O. 84/782; *P.P.* 1849, xix (309), House of Commons Select Committee, 1st Report par. 508, 671, 714, 725, 731; *P.P.* 1849 (Lords), xviii (32), House of Lords Select Committee, 1st Report, par. 1932.
4 Palmerston minute, 22 June 1847 (on Hesketh no. 4, 26 April 1847) F.O. 84/679; Palmerston minute, 18 September 1849 (on Cape commissioners no. 18, 20 July 1849) F.O. 84/755; *P.P.* 1847–8, xxii(272), House of Commons Select Committee, 1st Report, pars. 76, 80, 161. Palmerston had opposed the decision of 1844 to concentrate Britain's anti-slave trade efforts on the west African coast; it would have been better, he had argued, to blockade Rio de Janeiro and Havana for a short time than to blockade the entire coast of Africa (Hansard, lxxvi, 942, 945, 16 July 1844).

impossible to send *additional* cruisers to Brazil, and ships could not be transferred from west Africa because of Britain's treaties with France and the United States. Directly peace was restored in the Río de la Plata, however, the Admiralty promised to move the squadron there up the coast for anti-slave trade duties, and at the same time to replace some of its less useful vessels with steamers.[1] Palmerston had also come round to the belief that British measures were bound to remain to a considerable extent ineffective while the Brazilian authorities continued to afford the slave traders protection: the slave trade would be completely and finally suppressed, he believed, only when the Brazilian government fulfilled to the letter their treaty obligations.[2] He was convinced they could put down the trade within six months if they chose, but clearly would do so only if compelled. Palmerston had always felt that the Act he inherited from Aberdeen was a less drastic measure than the circumstances justified and on more than one occasion he had threatened to order naval officers to adopt tougher measures, especially on the coast of Brazil.[3] If Brazil were to allow a 'running account of grievances' to accumulate, he told James Hudson in January 1847, in terms notably reminiscent of those he had used in reference to Portugal during the years 1838-9, he would be obliged before long 'to send a British Admiral to settle the bill; our navy wants exercise and practice in time of peace, and Rio would do . . . well for that purpose'.[4] The most effective means of coercing Brazil, Palmerston came to believe, would be to institute a blockade of Rio and Bahia—and not simply an anti-slave trade blockade. Asked for his opinion, Hudson in a fifty-four-page report agreed such a blockade would be practicable—'no port in the world is capable of being so easily blockaded than Rio' —and that to interrupt all trade in and out of Brazil's major ports (he preferred to see the whole of Rio province blockaded as well as Santos and Bahia) would not only put an end to the slave trade

[1] Admiralty memorandum, 28 June 1847, F.O. 84/704; Admiralty to F.O., 31 June 1847, F.O. 84/708; Sir Francis Baring (First Lord of the Admiralty) to Palmerston, 21 May 1849, F.O. 84/767.
[2] Hansard, xcvi, 1123, House of Commons, 22 February 1848.
[3] E.g. Palmerston to Hudson, no. 1, 13 January 1847, (see above, ch. 10, p. 276); Hansard, lxxxii, 1060 (24 July 1845), xc, 1023 (8 March 1847). Also Palmerston to Hudson, no. 6, 23 April 1849, F.O. 84/765.
[4] Palmerston to Hudson, 7 January 1847, Broadlands MSS, GC/HU/43.

but would quickly bring the Brazilian government to its knees, dependent as they were on the customs house for five-sixths of their revenue, and compel their future co-operation. To ensure that Brazil would fulfil its obligations once such a blockade were lifted Hudson agreed with Palmerston that, at least until the slave trade had been completely suppressed, one or more Brazilian islands should be occupied and he suggested Santa Catarina and Itaparica (Bahia) for the purpose.[1] In the autumn of 1848 and again a year later Palmerston discussed the possibility of such a blockade with Russell and his colleagues in the Cabinet. The Prime Minister was personally agreeable to a blockade of Rio (and also of Havana) but the Cabinet, it seems, was strongly opposed to the whole idea and he feared, not unreasonably, that the House of Commons would be even more so. Nevertheless, if the Brazilian government persisted in its refusal to fulfil its anti-slave trade obligations, Russell told Palmerston in January 1850, the day would surely come when Brazil would be treated 'as the government of 1816 treated Algiers'.[2]

During 1849 Britain did finally settle its differences with Rosas in the Río de la Plata with the result that, as the Admiralty had always promised, part of the South American squadron was at last transferred to the coast of Brazil after an interval of more than six years.[3] Commodore Sir Thomas Herbert, who remained in Montevideo, was never enthusiastic about the anti-slave trade patrol,[4] but the steamer *Hydra* (Commander Skipwith) and the steamer *Rifleman* (Lieutenant Crofton), supported by the *Tweed* and the *Harpy*, immediately succeeded in making five captures and for several months established a partial blockade of the port of Santos and successfully prevented two notorious steam slave ships —the *Serpente* and the *Providentia*—from leaving for the African

[1] Palmerston to Hudson, 4 August, Hudson to Palmerston, 10 October 1848, Broadlands MSS, GC/HU/45, 6.
[2] Russell to Palmerston, 18 November 1848, 24 November 1849, 22 January 1850, Broadlands MSS, GC/RU/230, 306, 312.
[3] See Cady, *Foreign Intervention in the Río de la Plata*, pp. 244–6, 253.
[4] Commander Skipwith of the *Hydra* was reprimanded for using too much coal between March and July (Hudson to Palmerston, no. 17, Conf., 13 August 1849, F.O. 84/765) and later ordered not to leave Rio (Hudson no. 29, Conf., no. 33, Conf., 10 October, 13 November, 1849, F.O. 84/766).

coast (the latter having carried many thousands of slaves across the Atlantic over the previous two or three years).[1] In October 1849, Rear Admiral Barrington Reynolds replaced Herbert at Montevideo, and when at the end of the year the *Hydra* left for home, he immediately sent to Rio de Janeiro H.M.S. *Cormorant*, a 1,050 ton steamer which had recently arrived from England. In the meantime, James Hudson had renewed contact with the British legation's chief informer, a former slave trader known as 'Alcoforado', who once again began to supply, as he had done on several occasions in the past, regular information about imminent departures of slave ships and landings of slaves in the provinces of Rio de Janeiro, Espírito Santo and São Paulo, including such details as the name, class and build of the vessel, its owner, past history and expected time and place of arrival and departure.[2] This information was then relayed to British naval officers. As a result, January 1850 proved the British navy's most successful month on the Brazilian coast for almost exactly a decade. On the 5th, just south of Rio de Janeiro, the *Cormorant* captured the *Santa Cruz* suspected of having recently landed nearly seven hundred slaves at São Sebastião and emitting an 'abominable stench'. Captain Herbert Schomberg considered that his prize was not in a fit state to be sent to the vice-admiralty court at St Helena and ordered its destruction. On the 10th the *Rifleman* finally captured the *Providentia* (now called the *Paquete de Santos*) as it tried to leave Santos on a slaving enterprise, and despatched it with a prize crew to St Helena. On the 12th the *Cormorant* made another capture—the Brazilian barque *Paulina* leaving Rio de Janeiro under the American flag; ostensibly bound for Paranaguá and Montevideo, its real purpose—slaving—seemed clear to Schomberg who had no hesitation about despatching it to St Helena.[3] In recognition of his services, Alcoforado received 10% of the bounty money paid,

---

[1] Hudson no. 16, 13 August, no 31, 13 November, no. 32, 13 November 1849, F.O. 84/765–6. See also *P.P.* 1850 (Lords), xxiv (35), House of Lords Select Committee, Skipwith evidence.

[2] Hudson to Palmerston, 13 August 1849, Separate and Secret, F.O. 84/767. It is possible, though by no means certain, that 'Alcoforado' was the man who assisted the British legation during an earlier period of British naval activity on the Brazilian coast (1840–3), see above, ch. 7, p. 209.

[3] Hudson no. 7, 20 February, no. 9, 20 February, no. 10, 20 February, no. 21, 12 May 1850, F.O. 84/802–3.

in addition to his monthly allowance from the British legation. Many other ships were stopped and searched by British cruisers during January, frequently in territorial waters—the searching by mistake of the mail steam packet *São Sebastião* by officers from the *Rifleman* within range of the guns of the Santa Cruz fortress was only one of several incidents which caused considerable resentment in Brazil.[1] During the next few months the *Rifleman*, the *Cormorant* and other British warships continued to patrol the Brazilian coast to the north and south of the capital but, although occasional captures were made and clashes with the Brazilian authorities were not entirely avoided, on the whole Rear Admiral Reynolds tended to favour a cautious policy, at least until January's proceedings had been approved in London and instructions received as to precisely how far the squadron under his command could proceed with their efforts to drive the slave trade from the Brazilian coast.

The resumption of anti-slave trade operations on the Brazilian coast by the British navy coincided with certain tentative steps which the Brazilian government themselves were taking in preparation for an attempt to end the illegal slave trade. The Conservative Cabinet of 29 September 1848 was led by Visconde de Olinda, President of the Council of Ministers, Minister of Foreign Affairs and Minister of Finance. When in October 1849 Olinda was forced to retire he was replaced as President of the Council by Visconde de Monte Alegre, as Minister of Foreign Affairs by Paulino José Soares de Sousa, and as Minister of Finance by Joaquim José Rodrigues Tôrres. In the Council of State the government was strongly supported by Bernardo Pereira de Vasconcelos and Honório Hermeto Carneiro Leão. All these men had been associated with previous Conservative administrations which had been closely identified with the interests and prejudices of the Brazilian landowners, openly favoured the slave trade and consequently adopted a strongly anti-British standpoint. Once back in power, however, the more far-sighted of them—like certain of their predecessors in the Liberal government of Paula Sousa—became not a little disturbed by the proportions the illegal slave trade had

[1] Hudson no. 11, 20 February 1850, F.O. 84/802.

311

now reached—60,000 in 1848 and another 54,000 in 1849:[1] such massive imports, they were forced to admit, constituted a threat to the country's long-term economic interests, its racial equilibrium and its internal stability—besides encouraging widespread contempt for the law. It was also clear that despite a gradual change which seemed to be taking place in British public opinion, the British government was unwavering in its determination to put an end to the Brazilian trade; the transfer of part of the British South American squadron from the Río de la Plata to the Brazilian coast, combined with apparently well-founded rumours that Britain would soon adopt more extreme measures to coerce Brazil into fulfilling its treaty obligations, served to create a degree of disquiet in Brazilian government circles. Moreover, the situation in the Río de la Plata was becoming critical (Olinda was removed in October 1849 because he preferred diplomacy to outright intervention[2]), and, as the Liberals, too, had realised, there could be no hope of a successful showdown with Rosas if relations with Britain over the slave trade were to deteriorate to the point of open conflict. The Liberals in opposition had taken up the slave trade question in a big way, partly out of conviction and partly because it was a convenient stick with which to beat the government. Since the young Emperor was beginning to play a more influential role in government—he intervened decisively in the ministerial crisis of October 1849—and was known to favour abolition, it also presented a possible road by which to return to power.[3] Liberal politicians like Alves Branco, Lopes Gama and Leopoldo Muniz Barreto, the late vice-President of the Chamber of Deputies, castigated the slave trade as the prime source of all the country's difficulties, both internal and external, and the leading Liberal newspaper, the *Correio Mercantil*, persistently raised the question whether it was not time 'to take some steps seriously to put a stop to a traffic which had sacrificed so many victims and which . . . contributes to the moral and material backwardness of the country'.[4] For a number of reasons, therefore, the Conserva-

[1] See Appendix.
[2] Heitor Lyra, *História de Dom Pedro II* (São Paulo, 1938–40), i, 303–13.
[3] See Paula Beiguelman, 'Aspectos da organização político-partidária no Império Brasileiro'. *Revista de História* (São Paulo) xxv (1962), no. 51. p. 7; *História Geral da Civilização Brasileira*, ii, iii, pp. 198–9.   [4] *Correio Mercantil*, 3 July 1849.

tive cabinet of 28 September 1848 was obliged to give serious consideration to the problem of the illegal slave trade.

There were signs, too, of a change in Brazilian public opinion on this issue. Since August 1848, when Hudson had first detected 'a very satisfactory change . . . taking place in the mind of the Brazilian government *and public* on the importation of slaves . . . more rapidly than I dared hope or could . . . have believed possible', the movement of opinion in favour of abolition—on political, economic and social, rather than humanitarian, grounds—had gained a little ground:[1] abolitionist speeches were heard rather more frequently in both the Chamber of Deputies and the Senate; abolitionist newspapers like *O Monarchista, O Contemporâneo, O Grito Nacional* and, most notably, from April 1849 *O Philanthropo* (the first two, like the *Correio Mercantil*, financed in part by the British legation, with Lord Palmerston's approval, from the Secret Service Fund[2]) made their appearance in Rio de Janeiro, though most were short-lived; by the end of 1849 there were also small abolitionist newspapers in other parts of Brazil—for example, *O Seculo* (Bahia), *Revista Commercio* (Santos), *Tamandica* (Ouro Preto), *Argos Pernambucano, Commercial* (Pernambuco), *Observor* (Maranhão), *Reformista* (Paraíba). However, only a tiny, essentially urban, minority of Brazilians had yet been converted to abolition. As slave prices rose steadily during the forties (they only began to level off in 1848–9)[3] there were, it is true, progressive planters who began to see more clearly the advantages of free labour and mechanisation. And no doubt the vast majority of *fazendeiros* resented the ostentatious wealth, power and influence of the slave traders, especially since so many of them were foreign and, worse still, Portuguese.[4] More important, as a result of buying

---

[1] Hudson to Palmerston, 5 August 1848, Separate and Secret, F.O. 84/726; Hudson to Palmerston, no. 38, 27 July 1850, F.O. 84/805; W. G. Ouseley, *Notes on the Slave Trade* (London, 1850), pp. 10–13.

[2] Hudson to Palmerston, 5 August, 9 September, 18 October, Separate and Secret, F.O. 84/726; Hudson to Palmerston, 10 July, 15 August 1849, Broadlands MSS, GC/HU/14, 15; Hudson to Palmerston, 13 August 1849, Separate and Secret, F.O. 84/769; Hudson to Palmerston, 12 May 1850, Secret, F.O. 84/801. 'Do your best and as cheaply as possible', wrote Palmerston in March 1850 (Palmerston to Hudson, 31 March 1850, Broadlands MSS, GC/HU/48).

[3] See Stein, *Vassouras*, p. 229, figure 6: Average price of male and female slaves aged twenty to twenty-five years, 1822–88.

[4] According to Robert Hesketh, the British consul in Rio de Janeiro, of 38 prominent slave dealers in Rio in 1850, 19 were Portuguese, 12 Brazilian, 2 French, 2 American,

slaves on long-term credit at exorbitant interest rates over a period of many years, a great many were heavily indebted to, or had even partially mortgaged their estates to, the slave traders.[1] Moreover, in the short run some planters, particularly in the stagnant or declining areas of the north and north-east, stood to gain from the ending of the transatlantic slave trade if they were prepared to sell slaves to the developing coffee areas, where the demand for slaves and, consequently, slave prices could be expected to rise sharply. Too much, however, should not be made of such considerations. There is little evidence for thinking that in the years 1849–50 the landed interest, or indeed any important section of the landed interest, was demanding the abolition of the African slave trade. The habits and prejudices of centuries persisted, and there was still no real alternative to slave labour for large-scale plantation agriculture in Brazil. Nevertheless, the task of any Brazilian government seeking to put down the slave trade would undoubtedly be facilitated by the fact that more Brazilians than hitherto recognised the evils and dangers inherent in the trade, by the growing awareness of Brazil's international isolation on this question, by the hatred now felt for the traders and, most important, by the glut in the slave market which had satisfied the immediate needs of the Brazilian planters and thus, at least temporarily, lessened their dependence on the trade.

Although firmly of the opinion that no self-respecting Brazilian government could accept the legality of the Aberdeen Act or sign a new anti-slave trade treaty with Britain while the Act remained in force, Eusébio de Queiroz Coutinho Matoso da Câmara, Minister of Justice in the Cabinet of 28 September 1848, had personally

---

1 Spanish, 1 Italian and 1 Anglo-American; of 16 well-known dealers in ports near Rio, 12 were Portuguese and 4 Brazilian (Hesketh to Palmerston, no. 3, 14 March 1850, F.O. 84/808). 'Political hatred is . . . mixed with the wish to abolish slavery (*sic*)', Hesketh told the House of Lords Select Committee on the Slave Trade. 'They [the Brazilians] hate the Portuguese party and the influence which, as foreigners, they have assumed in the country' (*P.P.* (Lords) 1850, xxiv (35), par. 3194). Lord Howden estimated that there were approximately 40,000 Portuguese in the coastal towns of Brazil, many of them prominent in commerce, finance and the slave trade (*ibid.* pars. 229–32).

1 As early as 1845 the British Commissioners in Rio de Janeiro had made the point that 'the planters as a body may be said to cultivate their estates more for the advantage of the slave dealers than themselves' (Hesketh and Grigg to Aberdeen, Report on 1844, 21 March, 1845, F.O. 84/563). See also Hesketh to Palmerston, no. 3, 14 March 1850, F.O. 84/808; Hudson to Palmerston, 10 July 1849, Broadlands MSS, GC/HU/14.

come round to the view that the Brazilian government themselves should and could take steps to halt the trade.[1] He had inherited from his Liberal predecessor a modified version of Barbacena's anti-slave trade bill of 1837, which, he believed, constituted a step in the right direction and which, conveniently, had already been more or less agreed to by the Chamber of Deputies in September 1848.[2] Further modifications, however, were required before it could be re-introduced. In particular, it was necessary, in Eusébio's view, not only to improve the methods of detecting crime but also to take cases of slave trading out of the hands of local elected juries, members of which—like most witnesses—were interested, prejudiced and, indeed, open to corruption and intimidation; that is to say, special courts would need to be established to deal exclusively with slave trade offences. There remained the difficult problem of whether to reaffirm or revoke the existing anti-slave trade law of November 1831. Eusébio agreed with his predecessors that at plantation level it was simply unenforceable. However, he also believed that it would be unjust to the Africans who had been illegally imported into Brazil and, in view of the inevitable British reaction, inexpedient to repeal it. He therefore took the realistic view that the Brazilian government should omit article 13 from Barbacena's original anti-slave trade bill, thereby leaving the law of 1831 on the statute book, but at the same time conveniently forget all past and ignore all future illegal purchases of slaves while they got on with the immediate job of preventing the importation of yet more slaves into Brazil. In this way Eusébio hoped to appease the Brazilian planters, since in practice the threat to their existing property would be removed and their plantations were in any case well stocked against future needs, and, simultaneously, satisfy both Brazilian and British opponents of the slave trade. Only the slave traders on the one hand and the 'ultra-philanthropists' on the other would be likely to oppose the Bill after these further modifications; 'neither of these parties are of any

---

[1] Speech in Chamber, 1 August 1848, quoted in Alfredo Valladão, *Eusébio de Queiroz e os centenários do Código Commercial, do Regulamento 737 e da Supressão do Tráfico Africano* (Rio de Janeiro, 1951), pp 22–3. Eusébio, born in Luanda in 1812, had been Chief of Police in the capital from March 1833 (at the age of twenty) to March 1844 (except during the short period July 1840 to March 1841).

[2] See above, ch. 10, pp. 292–4.

importance', Eusébio wrote in 1849, in a cabinet memorandum on the slave trade question, 'nor do they merit any attention'.[1]

Towards the end of 1849, on instructions from Eusébio de Queiroz, the Chief of Police in Rio de Janeiro warned slave traders that tougher anti-slave trade measures were being prepared by the Brazilian government. To give point to his warning, some two hundred slaves were seized in two raids, one in Rio and the other in Niterói, and at the same time some of the better known slave depots on the outskirts of the capital were closed down.[2] When the Chamber of Deputies reassembled in January 1850, Eusébio declared in his *Relatório*: 'A bill exists in this Chamber the discussion of which is already far advanced; it certainly requires important modification which the government promises to submit to your consideration whenever the subject is brought forward.'[3] And on 7 February (a month after the captures made by the British cruisers *Cormorant* and *Rifleman* close to the Brazilian capital) Paulino, the Foreign Minister, outlined to Hudson—whose views on Barbacena's bill had been made plain only eighteen months earlier—the nature of the modifications which, he said, the government had now agreed upon and which included the omission of the controversial article 13.[4] The Brazilian government, however, were afraid, or claimed to be afraid, that their plans for the suppression of the slave trade might be jeopardised by the British navy's recently resumed anti-slave trade operations in Brazilian territorial waters. Apart from the occasional mild protest, they had virtually ignored the capture—in their view the illegal capture—of literally hundreds of Brazilian vessels by British cruisers on the west African coast, and their subsequent condemnation in British vice-admiralty courts, during the years since the termination of the right of search treaty of 1817 and the passage of the Aberdeen Act in 1845. But what they could not overlook was the visit, search, detention and in some cases outright destruction of Brazilian vessels on their very doorstep, in Brazilian territorial

[1] Cabinet memorandum (1849) read to the Chamber of Deputies in a speech, 16 July 1852 (*Anais do Parlamento Brasileiro: Câmara dos Deputados*, 1852, vol. ii, pp. 241–58).
[2] *Relatório do Ministério da Justiça* (Rio de Janeiro, 11 January 1850).
[3] *Ibid.* See also *Relatório do Ministério dos Negócios Estrangeiros* (Rio de Janeiro, 7 January 1850).
[4] Reported in Hudson no. 6, 20 February 1850, F.O. 84/802.

waters; at stake now were vital questions of national sovereignty and independence. The Brazilian government, Paulino told Hudson, were anxious to co-operate with Britain for the suppression of the slave trade, but unless the recent 'acts of vandalism' in territorial waters ceased such co-operation might prove impossible and their common goal unattainable. The conduct of the British navy on the coast of Brazil, Paulino declared, 'wounds deeply every feeling of dignity and national spirit in the country and raises a general cry of indignation against such oppression and violence, and will operate as a reaction in the opinion pronounced against the slave trade and without which assistance the means of repression will be nearly always set at nought'.[1]

James Hudson, however, who had nothing but contempt for Brazilian governments—they were all 'equally vicious, corrupt and abominable', he told Palmerston a year later[2]—and who believed that they would do nothing to fulfil their treaty engagements unless coerced, remained sceptical of this sudden conversion to the cause of abolition; if the Brazilian government were now intent on ending the trade, he asked, why did they not as a first step do more to enforce existing Brazilian legislation? It remained his view that the trade could be suppressed by 'a few simple measures of police' along the three hundred mile coast of Brazil between Campos and Santos where three-quarters of the slaves imported from Africa were landed. If further legislation were indeed necessary, Hudson had no confidence in the ability of the Brazilian government to secure or enforce it: the planter interest still dominated the Legislature and Vasconcelos, described by Hudson as the 'Slave Dealers' Friend', still wielded enormous influence in the Council of State.[3] Nor did Hudson believe that the activities of the British navy were responsible for alienating

[1] Paulino to Hudson, 12 February, enclosed in Hudson no. 7, 20 February 1850, F.O. 84/802. Cf. Olinda to Hudson, 3 September, 3 October, enclosed in Hudson no. 27, 10 October 1849, F.O. 84/766; Paulino to Lisboa (Brazilian minister in London), no. 2, 30 January, no. 5, 7 February 1850, A.H.I. 268/1/17; Paulino to Hudson, 16 April, enclosed in Hudson no. 21, 12 May 1850, F.O. 84/803.
[2] Hudson to Palmerston, 11 January 1851, Broadlands MSS, GC/HU/29.
[3] Hudson to Palmerston, 10 October 1849, Broadlands MSS, GC/HU/18; Hudson no 1, 17 January, no. 5, 20 February 1850, F.O. 84/802; Hudson to Palmerston, 21 February 1850, Private, F.O. 84/801. Hudson expressed the view that 'Vasconcelos ought to be destroyed as a politician or driven to the wall at once' if progress were to be made on the slave trade question (Hudson no. 1, 17 January).

abolitionist opinion in Brazil and thus adding to the Brazilian government's difficulties. On the contrary, he believed that leading abolitionists in Brazil looked to a British blockade of the Brazilian coast as the only means of ridding Brazil of the slave trade, and that without British support they might be tempted to desert the cause; indeed many were already disheartened by the change apparently taking place in British public opinion on the slave trade question.[1] Lopes Gama, for example, a Senator and Councillor of State, an enemy of the slave trade and, in Hudson's view, 'one of the few respectable men in this country'—and one, it might be added, who had for many years been in the pay of the British government—had written to Hudson, 'If your government will cruise against the slave trade on this coast vigorously, you may now put down the slave trade and force us to do as you please, but we all feel that it is a deliberate insult to attempt to crush the slave trade and coerce us with two slow steam sloops.'[2] Furthermore, a group of Brazilians—officers in the Brazilian navy, men of independent means, customs officers, pilots—had offered to provide further information on a regular basis about the movements of slave ships in and out of Brazilian ports, provided a sufficient number of British cruisers were stationed on the Brazilian coast to make use of it.[3] Throughout January, it was true, numerous angry speeches directed against Britain and the British navy had been delivered in the Chamber of Deputies and equally violent editorials defending Brazilian sovereignty and attacking 'Lord Palmerston's Piracy' had appeared in such anti-British, pro-slave trade newspapers as *O Brasil* and the *Correio da Tarde*:[4] the latter, Hudson later recalled, abused Palmerston personally in language 'such as Billingsgate never heard and would blush to hear'.[5] But the Brazilian government, too, had been censured, and not only by the sole Liberal opposition deputy and former Foreign Minis-

[1] Hudson no. 38, Conf., 13 November 1849, F.O. 84/766; Hudson no. 7, 20 February 1850, F O 84/802. Cf. *P.P.* 1850 (Lords), xxiv (35), House of Lords Select Committee, Skipwith evidence, pars. 544–60.
[2] Quoted in Hudson to Palmerston, 21 February 1850, Private, F.O. 84/801.
[3] Hudson no. 3, 17 January 1850, Secret and Private, F.O. 84/801; Hudson to Palmerston, 17 January 1850, Broadlands MSS, GC/HU/20.
[4] Extracts from speeches in Chamber of Deputies, 18, 22, 25, 31 January, 1 February, and copies of *O Brasil*, 22 January, and *Correio da Tarde* 16 January, 21 January, enclosed in Hudson no. 7, 20 February 1850, F.O. 84/802.
[5] Hudson to Palmerston, 3 August 1850, Broadlands MSS, GC/HU/25.

ter, Bernardo de Sousa Franco, and the Liberal newspaper *Correio Mercantil*, for failing to act more energetically to remove the cause of renewed British aggression in Brazilian territorial waters. It seemed to Hudson that as a direct result of the reappearance of the British navy on the Brazilian coast, increasing numbers of deputies, irrespective of their attitudes for or against the slave trade, were beginning to realise, first, that Britain would not readily relinquish the struggle for its suppression, a policy which José Martins da Cruz Jobim (Rio Grande do Sul) declared sprang from 'a religious feeling tainted with fanaticism . . . engraved on the hearts of all Englishmen',[1] secondly, that Brazil could not resist British 'aggression' without inflicting even more harm upon herself, and thirdly, that only by fulfilling her treaty engagements and suppressing the slave trade could Brazil hope to secure respect for her national sovereignty. 'If we are weak', declared Father Resende (Pernambuco), 'we have still a force . . . capable of making England lower her flag . . . sincerity and good faith, reason and justice. Let the government take the lead and be the first to repress the traffic.'[2] In the circumstances, therefore, Hudson communicated to Paulino Lord Palmerston's opinion—expressed before the events of January 1850, with reference to British captures made during 1849—that it would be impossible to discontinue the 'necessary and unavoidable proceedings' of the British navy on the coast of Brazil until the Brazilians had fulfilled their engagements and their promises to co-operate with Britain in suppressing the trade.[3]

Indeed, it remained Hudson's view that British naval operations should be extended and intensified in order both to obstruct the slave trade at its Brazilian as well as its African end and, at the same time, to coerce the Brazilian government into adopting the measures they talked so much about. He had in mind the establishment of a small, highly mobile squadron on the Brazilian coast comprising four small steamers and two schooners equipped with small boats capable of remaining absent from the parent ship for several days at a stretch. Such a force, he believed, could be built

[1] Quoted in Hudson no. 7.   [2] *Ibid.*
[3] Hudson to Paulino, 3 March, enclosed in Hudson no. 13, 23 March 1850, F.O. 84/803 (based on Palmerston to Hudson, no. 7, 31 December 1849, F.O. 84/766).

up either by transferring more ships from the Río de la Plata to Brazil or else by sending out reinforcements from England.[1] Hudson wrote directly to Rear Admiral Reynolds begging him to move his flagship to Rio de Janeiro:

The Brazilian Government and Legislature are powerless and helpless . . . face to face for the first time with the British Commander-in-Chief in their waters. They have . . . discovered that you are the real arbiter of their fate and of the slave trade, and of the amount of consideration which shall be allotted to their own ships and their own flag in their own waters and this without a resort to any belligerent right whatever, but simply by adhering to and acting up to the spirit and letter of the treaty for the suppression of the slave trade between Great Britain and Brazil of 1826 . . . Your presence here at this most critical juncture would encourage our friends, dishearten our enemies and aid this government to escape from the pressure imposed upon them by Vasconcelos and the slave dealing interest and would serve as an excuse to that interest for their adopting active measures against the slave trade . . . It requires but little foresight to perceive where is the weak point of all Brazilian administrations and that they will suppress the slave trade rather than abandon power, while at the same time past events prove that no Brazilian Government will ever suppress the slave trade if left to themselves.[2]

And to Lord Palmerston Hudson wrote:

There is nothing you cannot do, at this moment, with the Brazilian Government, who . . . hampered by the first Article of the treaty of 1826 are entirely at your mercy.[3]

Although he recognised there might well be an attempt to provoke incidents by those interested in the continuation of the slave trade in order to raise a popular, nationalistic outcry which would force the Brazilian government to abandon their own anti-slave trade efforts and take positive measures to prevent British warships patrolling Brazilian waters, Hudson did not anticipate any serious confrontation between the Brazilian people and the British navy.

[1] Hudson no. 3, 17 January 1850, Secret and Private, Hudson to Palmerston, 21 February 1850, Private, F.O. 84/801.
[2] Hudson to Reynolds, 3 February, enclosed in Hudson 21 February 1850, Private, F.O. 84/801.
[3] Hudson 21 February 1850, Private, F.O. 84/801. Also Hudson to Palmerston, 21 February 1850, Broadlands MSS, GC/HU/21.

'Courage', he told Reynolds, 'whether animal, or moral, is not a Brazilian virtue'.[1]

In England, meanwhile, the movement of opinion in favour of Britain's abandoning her anti-slave trade campaign, or at least her naval operations against the trade, showed no signs of running out of steam. On the contrary, encouraged by the findings of the House of Commons Select Committee on the Slave Trade William Hutt and his supporters were preparing to renew the Parliamentary struggle. Yet another motion had been put down for debate on 19 March 1850, this time urging the government to release themselves from all treaty engagements with other powers (that is, France and the United States) which required them to maintain a squadron on the African coast and to desist from the use of force for the suppression of the slave trade. By this time important sections of the press, too, had become openly hostile to the government on the slave trade question—not only *The Times* ('this most stupendous folly') but also the *Morning Chronicle* ('a cruel, hopeless and absurd experiment'), the *Daily News*, the *Spectator* ('this costly failure, this deadly farce'), the *Economist*, the *Quarterly Review*, and the *Westminster Review*. (Only the *Morning Post* felt impelled to attack *The Times* for its advocacy of 'free trade in human blood'.)[2] Moreover, government whips reported that very few of the government's supporters were disposed to vote against Hutt's motion when it came to a division—even so prominent an abolitionist as Stephen Lushington had come out against the West African squadron—and that the Protectionists, more eager to bring down the government than to defend what little remained of the West Indian interest, were determined to give them, in Stanley's own words, 'a run for their money'.[3] The government were thus sufficiently apprehensive about the outcome of the forthcoming debate for them to resort to drastic measures: letters —'five lines of a dry threat'[4]—were written to wavering supporters; some received personal calls from leading ministers; and,

---

[1] Hudson to Reynolds, 3 February. [2] Mathieson, *op. cit.* p. 110.

[3] Hobhouse diary, vol. xi (16 March to 18 March), B.M. Add. MSS, 43754; Sir Charles Wood (Chancellor of the Exchequer) to Russell, 17 March, Palmerston to Russell, 17 March 1850, P.R.O. 30/22/8D (Russell Papers).

[4] J. E. Denison, M.P. to Russell, 18 March 1850, P.R.O. 30/22/8D.

finally, on the morning of the debate, a meeting of the Whig party was called at Downing Street where Russell warned 160 M.P.s that if Hutt's motion were carried both he and Palmerston would resign rather than execute policies which they regarded as a betrayal of party policy and their own personal principles.[1] In the discussion which followed Russell's statement little criticism of the government was expressed, although according to some reports many members left the meeting surprised and indignant that Russell had taken such a strong line on 'so unpopular a question and one so entirely fallen into disrepute' and that they were being forced to jettison strongly held convictions in order not to bring the government down.[2] *The Times* reported the occasion with some relish: 'Massa Russell' had gathered his captives 'in the above mentioned barracoon' (10 Downing Street) and instructed them 'shortly and sharply' in the terms of their servitude.[3]

After so much preliminary excitement the debate itself was rather dull, because it was so predictable.[4] Hutt produced all the familiar arguments against the use of the West African squadron as an instrument for the suppression of the slave trade and the advantages which would follow its withdrawal. For the government Henry Labouchere, President of the Board of Trade, declared that while nobody ever expected the squadron *alone* to put down the trade, to withdraw it would be to sanction a further expansion of the inhuman trade and at the same time deal a fatal blow to the prospects for legitimate commerce with Africa and destroy any chance of restoring to prosperity the 'long suffering [West Indian] colonies' which were already at such a grave disadvantage *vis-à-vis* their slave trading competitors.[5] The Prime Minister himself spoke in a similar vein against Hutt's motion, concluding (amid cheers, it might be noted) that Britain would have no right to further blessings from the Almighty if 'this high and holy work'

[1] Hobhouse diary (19 March); *Greville Memoirs 1814–1860*, Ed. Lytton Strachey and Roger Fulford (London, 1938), vol. vi, pp. 211–12 (19–20 March); Russell speech, 19 March (P.R.O. 30/22/8D); *The Times*, 20 March, 21 March 1850.
[2] *Greville Memoirs*, vi. 211–12.
[3] Quoted in Mathieson, *op. cit.* p. 110.
[4] Hansard, cix, 1093–1186, 19 March 1850. See also Hobhouse diary (19 March); *Greville Memoirs* (20 March); Mathieson, *op. cit.* pp. 106–11.
[5] Hansard, cix, 1121.

were abandoned before reaching a successful conclusion.[1] The debate was notable in one respect only: for the first time a member of ministerial standing came out against Britain's traditional anti-slave trade policies. In a remarkable speech made towards the end of the debate Gladstone, a prominent Peelite and former President of the Board of Trade, declared his belief that it was not 'an ordinance of providence that the government of one nation should correct the morals of another' and that it was downright impracticable to try and put down 'a great branch of commerce'. If the government wished to suppress the slave trade, Gladstone argued, they must first repeal the Sugar Duties Act, secondly double the number of ships on the West African station, thirdly secure right of search agreements with France and the United States, fourthly obtain the power to treat slave trading as piracy, and lastly compel Spain and Brazil to fulfil their treaty obligations; 'the first two you might do', he considered, '[but] you cannot do the last three'. On the fifth and final point, Gladstone did not deny the government's right to demand the fulfilment by Brazil of their treaty engagements under the treaty of 1826 which had been broken 'every day for the last twenty years', and if they had the right to demand it they had the right to do so 'at the point of the sword in case of refusal'. Nevertheless, he expressed the fervent hope that Palmerston would not in the event resort to outright coercion. In conclusion, he warned the House that the slave trade preventive system was in danger of being perpetuated unquestioningly on a permanent basis, thereby becoming 'one of the institutions of the country', and beyond rational criticism.[2]

When, in the early hours, the House divided, almost twice as many members as in 1848—a total of 154, comprising 48 Liberal Whigs, 17 Peelites and 89 Protectionists—voted against the continuation of Britain's efforts to suppress the foreign slave trade (at least by the means hitherto used), but 232 (176 Liberal Whigs,

[1] *Ibid.* 1183. In a similar vein, in the House of Commons eight years later, Palmerston declared, 'the world is governed by a Divine Providence, and good deeds and bad deeds meet with their appropriate reward or punishment . . . nations are made to suffer for their misdeeds and derive advantages from the good deeds which they perform'. It was, he added, a curious coincidence that since Britain had abolished the slave trade and used her influence for its international abolition the country had prospered to a degree never before known! (Hansard, cli, 1340, 12 July 1858).

[2] Hansard, cix, 1160–70; Mathieson, *op. cit.* pp. 108–9.

11-2

23 Peelites and 33 Protectionists, including, after much hesitation, Stanley their leader) remained loyal to the work of the West African squadron.[1] It was, in the view of a modern historian, 'the last important stand of humanitarian politics'.[2] How much closer the voting figures would have been or whether the result would have been different had Russell not made the issue one of confidence in his administration it is impossible to say; in any case some Whigs, it was suggested, stayed away from the House; others, notably Lushington, abstained.[3]

For the time being, however, the British preventive system had been saved. But despite this 'signal triumph' (as Palmerston described it[4]) clearly the next time the issue was debated it might not be possible to carry the House unless in the meantime some impression had been made on the slave trade, and especially the slave trade to Brazil. To *The Times*, which continued to denounce those who identified 'the promotion of an unimpeachable principle with the maintenance of a particular scheme of violence, rude and barbarous in its essence, costly in its practice, ineffective in its operation, convicted by its results and formally condemned by those who were most instrumental in bringing it into being', the government's long amendment to Hutt's motion praising the work of the navy and demanding that even greater pressure should be brought to bear on slave trading powers suggested the alarming idea of an 'armed apparition in the Tagus or perhaps in the harbour of Rio'. *The Times* found it difficult to suppose that 'so prudent and far-seeing a man as our Foreign Secretary, with such an instinctive hatred of war, should not have that vision before his eyes'.[5]

Within a few weeks of the House of Commons debate which had demonstrated so clearly how widespread the opposition to Britain's anti-slave trade policies had become, but which at the same time had strengthened the government's determination to justify their faith in them, Lord Palmerston heard of the recent activities of the *Cormorant* and the *Rifleman* on the Brazilian coast

---

[1] Hansard, cix, 1184–6; Hobhouse diary (19 March).
[2] Curtin, *Image of Africa*, p. vii.
[3] Letter to *The Times*, 21 March 1850.
[4] Palmerston to Hudson, 31 March 1850, Broadlands MSS, GC/HU/48.
[5] *The Times*, 20 March, 21 March 1850.

and of Hudson's subsequent exchanges with Paulino Soares de Sousa, the Brazilian Foreign Minister. He also had a chance to consider Hudson's analysis of the situation in Brazil and his forth-right proposals for bringing the Brazilian slave trade to an end, once and for all. Palmerston, who had long been an advocate of naval operations on the Brazilian side of the Atlantic directly sufficient ships were made available, was happy to approve all that the *Cormorant* and the *Rifleman* had already done. He was, too, in agreement with Hudson that of all the measures that could now be taken the continuation and, if possible, the intensification of British naval pressure on the coast of Brazil was the most likely finally to cripple the slave trade. The Brazilian government should be advised, he immediately wrote to Hudson, 'calmly and seriously to consider the extreme nature of the rights which Great Britain has acquired against Brazil by the deliberate, systematic and long continued violation by the government of Brazil of the treaty engagements . . . [and] the great moderation and forbearance which the British government has hitherto displayed by availing itself of these rights *only in so limited a degree*'.[1] And he specifically warned Joaquim Tomás do Amaral, the Brazilian *chargé d'affaires* in London, that the British government was prepared, if necessary, to resort to even more rigorous measures against the Brazilian slave trade than those already taken.[2]

In 1843 the Law Officers of the Crown had advised that under the right of search treaty of 1817 British naval operations in Brazilian territorial waters were illegal.[3] Since then, however, the treaty of 1817 had been terminated. Strictly interpreted, the Act of 1845 which replaced it also confined the operations of the British navy to the high seas but, based as it was on article 1 of the treaty of 1826 which declared the Brazilian slave trade piracy, it could always be stretched so as to afford British warships any powers they required. On 22 April 1850, the Foreign Office advised the Admiralty, which had already promised to reinforce the squadron

---

[1] Palmerston to Hudson, no. 10, 13 April 1850, F.O. 84/801. Also Palmerston to Hudson, 31 March 1850, Broadlands MSS, GC/HU/11; Palmerston no. 12, 13 April 1850, F.O. 84/801.

[2] Amaral to Paulino, no. 8, Reservado, 24 April, no. 9, Reservado, 26 April 1850, A.H.I. 217/3/6; Amaral to Paulino, no. 27, 30 April 1850, A.H.I. 216/2/14. Palmerston threatened to occupy a section of the Brazilian coast as a guarantee of Brazilian co-operation against the slave trade. [3] See above, ch. 7, p. 212.

on the Brazilian coast,[1] that the anti-slave trade Acts of 1839 and 1845 contained 'no restrictions as to the limits within which the search, detention and capture of slave traders under the Brazilian flag or without any nationality are to take place and therefore such proceedings may be had *at any place within the Brazilian waters* as well as on the high seas'; the British government, the note went on, would therefore not feel any 'greater difficulty in replying to representations from the Brazilian government against captures of slavers made in Brazilian waters *or ports* than they would in replying to representations against such captures made on the high seas'—although it might be expedient to limit naval operations to places where there was no likelihood of successful resistance (my italics).[2] Essentially these instructions were designed to reassure Rear Admiral Reynolds that, despite the fact they had been operating inside Brazilian territorial waters, the actions in January of the *Cormorant* and the *Rifleman* were in the British government's view perfectly legal and should be continued. But did they not also constitute a positive encouragement to Reynolds to go even further? The Foreign Office note of 22 April 1850 had far reaching consequences which at the time were perhaps not entirely foreseen.

[1] Baring to Palmerston, 25 March 1850, Broadlands MSS, GC/BA/279; Palmerston to Hudson, no. 7, 4 April 1850, F.O. 84/801.

[2] Stanley (F.O.) to Hamilton (Adm.), 22 April 1850, F.O. 84/823—following consultations with the Law Officers to the Crown.

CHAPTER 12

CRISIS AND FINAL ABOLITION, 1850–1851

In the middle of June 1850 when the steamer *Sharpshooter*, des-patched from England to reinforce the British naval squadron on the Brazilian coast, arrived off Rio de Janeiro and immediately made its presence felt in the vicinity of the capital by capturing two Brazilian vessels—the *Malteza* which was destroyed on the spot and the *Conceição* which was sent to St Helena[1]—the Brazilian slave trade was already being carried on less extensively than at any time for almost a decade. The frequently repeated declaration by the Brazilian government of their intention to introduce fresh measures to combat the trade, the activities of British warships along the Brazilian coast during the previous twelve months (in addition to the continued vigilance of the British West African and Cape squadrons) and, perhaps most important, the glut in the Brazilian slave market after several years of exceptionally heavy imports, had combined to reduce the Brazilian slave trade to a mere shadow of its former self. Only 8,000 slaves had been landed along the coast between Santos and Campos during the period January–June 1850, less than a third of the number imported in any comparable period during recent years. Bahia alone, where significantly not a single British cruiser had put in an appearance for almost a year, had imported its usual quota of slaves—a little over 4,000.[2] James Hudson, the British *chargé*, and Rear Admiral Reynolds, who had by now moved the flagship *Southampton* from Montevideo to Rio de Janeiro, were eager that the British navy should come to grips with the Brazilian trade while it was in such a weakened state, and Hudson was not slow to see the significance of the note of 22 April 1850 from the Foreign Office to the Admiralty which was among the correspondence and instructions brought out by the *Sharpshooter*. On 18 June, at a conference at sea, the two men agreed upon a plan of action.[3] Two days later,

[1] Rear Admiral Reynolds to Admiralty, 22 June 1850, F.O. 84/827.
[2] See Appendix. Also Porter (consul in Bahia) to Palmerston, no. 7, 13 July 1850, F.O. 84/808.
[3] Reported in Hudson to Palmerston, no. 38, 27 July 1850, Secret, F.O. 84/805.

Hudson warned Paulino Soares de Sousa, the Brazilian Foreign Minister, of the measures he had, he said, been authorised to adopt.[1] Paulino, Hudson reported, was thunderstruck. The Brazilian government, Paulino reminded him, were planning to introduce new legislation which, it was hoped, would make it easier for the Brazilian authorities themselves to put down what remained of the trade. And this was indeed the case: in a second *Relatório* to the Chamber of Deputies in May, Eusébio de Queiroz, the Minister of Justice, had declared hopefully that public opinion was running strongly for abolition and that so grave was the danger to internal security from the large-scale importation of slaves that *in the present session* the government would 'promote with all its efforts the examination of the Bill which for that purpose was submitted to the legislative body [in September 1848] and which has already been discussed'.[2] The fact remained, however, that they had still failed to act. Far from united themselves on the slave trade question, the Brazilian government remained apprehensive as to how far they could carry with them the country's great landowners, the Legislature (in particular the Senate since, following the elections of 1849, the government had almost complete control of the Chamber), and the Council of State. Influential voices were still to be heard arguing that immediate abolition was completely impossible: on 13 May, for example, Holanda Cavalcanti had introduced a bill into the Senate for the renegotiation of the Anglo-Brazilian treaty of 1826 in order to permit a regulated slave trade—although on the very same day Cândido Batista de Oliveira had also introduced a bill aimed at strengthening the law of 1831.[3] Moreover, the government were naturally concerned

---

[1] Reported in Hudson to Palmerston, no. 38, 27 July 1850, Secret, F.O. 84/805.

[2] *Relatório do Ministério da Justiça* (Rio de Janeiro, May 1850).

[3] *Jornal do Comércio*, 14 May, 15 May 1850; Alves, *R.I.H.G.B.* (1914), pp. 243–4; Tavares Bastos, *Cartas do Solitario* (Rio de Janeiro, 1863), p. 175. On 1 July a special Senate committee consisting of Paula Sousa, Limpo de Abreu and Visconde de Abrantes reported on the two bills before the Senate. British naval operations on the Brazilian coast, they declared, constituted 'a permanent . . . obstacle which will prevent the success of whatsoever measures the Government may adopt to repress the traffic. This new difficulty comes to unite itself with others previously existing'. They came to the conclusion, however, that repressive measures against the slave trade could no longer be avoided, although rather than endorse Cândido Batista's bill they were content to remind the Senate that there was before the Chamber an anti-slave trade bill, an earlier version of which the Senate had already adopted (Hudson no. 35, 27 July 1850, F.O. 84/804; Alves *op. cit.* pp. 244–6).

that any forward move against the slave trade should not appear the result of capitulation to British pressure as the Liberals, hoping to discredit the government's efforts, were bound to suggest. On 27 May in the Senate, during a debate on the Emperor's *Falla do Throno*, the former Liberal President of the Council of Ministers, Francisco de Paula Sousa, insisted that they should 'act and legislate as our interests dictated, by our own self will, for the benefit of our country and not for the foreigner'. He did not see how the government could take any measures to suppress the trade whilst they endured 'all the evils of war without war having been declared'. Brazil should first show she had 'blood in her veins', he declared, and by demanding that the British navy respect the Brazilian flag and, if necessary, by taking steps to resist British aggression in Brazilian waters, the government should demonstrate that they were not acting out of fear.[1] Nevertheless, as recently as 11 June Paulino had sent Hudson a copy of the anti-slave trade bill the Brazilian government proposed to bring before the Chamber. And it was in order to discuss its provisions that he had himself arranged the 20 June meeting at which Hudson had warned him of the additional anti-slave trade measures about to be adopted by the British navy.[2]

On 22 June Rear Admiral Reynolds ordered British warships under his command to enter Brazilian ports as well as Brazilian territorial waters and flush out any ships they found being fitted for the trade.[3] The very next day the *Sharpshooter* proceeded up the coast to the port of Macaé. Under cover of the *Sharpshooter*'s guns, two boats entered the harbour and twenty minutes later—through a blaze of musket fire and shots from the shore batteries—emerged with the brigantine *Polka*.[4] The *Sharpshooter* went on to inspect the neighbouring coast line but, although several suspicious vessels were boarded, no more captures were made. On the

---

[1] Extracts from Senate debates, 27 May, 2 July 1850, enclosed in Hudson no. 35; also Alves, *op. cit.* p. 246.
[2] Hudson to Paulino, 3 July 1850, Private, A.H.I. 284/4/3; Hudson to Palmerston, no. 38, 27 July, Secret, F.O. 84/805. Hudson contrived to give the impression that at the meeting of 20 June he forced Paulino to remove from the bill the final article repeating the law of 1831; in fact this had already been decided upon by the Brazilian government (cf. above, ch. 11, pp. 315–6).
[3] Standing order no. 16, 22 June 1850, enclosed in Hudson no. 38, Secret.
[4] Bailey to Reynolds, 25 June, enclosed in Reynolds to Admiralty, 26 June 1850, F.O. 84/827.

26 June, with the guns of the *Cormorant* trained on the fort, two British boats entered Cabo Frio and burned the brigantine *Rival* whilst angry but impotent crowds gathered on the shore.[1] The *Cormorant* then moved down the coast to Paranaguá, about two hundred miles south of Santos, where several ships were known to be fitting out for the trade. On the 29th Captain Schomberg sent a note to the commander of the fort at the mouth of the river, informing him of the new instructions he had received from the Admiralty 'to examine all vessels *suspected* and seize all that are *engaged* in the traffic of slaves *wherever I may meet them* in further-ance of the *Perpetual Joint Convention* of 1826', and asking for the commander's co-operation. Apparently the note was never opened: Schomberg was asked only about his destination and courteously waved on. He found a cluster of ships at anchor. Among those clearly ready to embark on slaving voyages were the brig *Sereia* which had already landed 800 slaves at Macaé in July 1848, 840 at Dois Rios in May 1849, 900 at Campos in November 1849 and 986 at Santos in March 1850, the brig *Leonidas* (alias *Donna Anna*) which had landed 800 slaves at Dois Rios in March 1850, the brigantine *Astro* which had made two landings in 1849 and a third of 600 slaves at Macaé in February 1850, and the *Lucy Ann* (alias *Campaneja*) which, it was said, was capable of carrying 1600 slaves. The *Astro* was scuttled by its crew during the night in order to avoid capture, but on the following day the other vessels were boarded despite protests from the municipal authorities about Schomberg's 'iniquitous preposterous assumption', his 'unmeasured arrogance', and his acts of 'pure piracy'. As the three ships were being towed out to sea the fort opened fire and, in the short engagement which ensued, one British seaman was killed, two more were wounded and the *Cormorant* was slightly damaged. On 1 July, however, Schomberg burned the *Leonidas* and the *Sereia* in full view of the fort, sent the *Lucy Ann* to St Helena, and moved back up the coast after 'this interesting service'.[2]

On Friday 5 July the *Cormorant* called in Rio de Janeiro before

[1] Schomberg to Reynolds, 5 July, enclosed in Hudson no. 30, 27 July 1850, F.O. 84/804.
[2] Schomberg to Paranaguá fort commander, 29 June, enclosed in Paulino to Hudson, 31 January 1851 (in Hudson to Palmerston, no. 18, 11 February 1851, F.O. 84/843); memorandum on slave ships at Paranaguá, enclosed in Hudson to Paulino, 12 July 1850

going on to search the creeks, anchorages and bays of Rio das Ostras, Guarapari, Santa Anna, Armação and Cabo Frio to the north. Over the week-end the capital seethed with wild accounts of what had occurred at Paranaguá—and elsewhere. It was even rumoured that the fort had been completely destroyed, with heavy loss of life, and that the British navy was now preparing to bombard the capital itself, remove from the bay all ships suspected of slaving—and even make off with the Crown Jewels! Angry crowds gathered in the Largo do Paço and in the square in front of the Hotel Pharoux, but no serious incidents occurred. A group of Brazilians broke into Mr Wood's boarding house and beat up some English sailors, the chief engineer of the *Harpy* was pelted with mud, and several officers and men were insulted—but that was all.[1]

As a result of a series of questions tabled by Deputy Silveira da Mota (São Paulo) on 28 June,[2] it had already been arranged that on the following Monday, 8 July, the Brazilian Foreign Minister would address the Chamber on the government's attitude towards the British navy's incursions into Brazilian territorial waters and their effect on Brazil's coastal trade. With the invasion of Brazilian ports and the exchange of shots between a Brazilian fort and a British warship, the situation had clearly taken a much more serious turn and when the day came for Paulino's promised statement the galleries, corridors, staircases, as well as the Chamber itself, were packed with those anxious to hear what he had to say. In the course of a tumultuous debate more than one deputy expressed marked hostility towards the slave trade, which all were agreed was controlled by foreigners and therefore 'not properly

(in Hudson no. 32, 27 July 1850, F.O. 84/804); Filastrio Nunes Pires (municipal judge, Paranaguá) to Schomberg, 30 June, enclosed in Reynolds to Admiralty, 6 July 1850, F.O. 84/827; Schomberg to Hudson, 5 July 1850, enclosed in Hudson no. 30, 27 July 1850, F.O. 84/804; *Relatório do Ministério dos Negócios Estrangeiros* (Rio de Janeiro, May 1851). The incident has attracted a great deal of attention amongst *paranaense* historians. See, for example, David Carneiro, *A História do Incidente Cormoran* [*sic*] (Curitiba, 1950) for a description of the fort, the cruiser and the main protagonists. (The significance of the incident in the events of 1850 is rather exaggerated by Carneiro, however: see a review article, José Antônio Soares de Sousa, 'Documentação para uma Tese sôbre o Tráfico de Escravos', *R.I.H.G.B.* vol. 219 (1953), pp. 266–86.)

[1] *Jornal do Comércio*, 8 July 1850; Hudson no. 33, 27 July 1850, F.O. 84/804. There were similar scenes in Bahia (Porter to Palmerston, no. 10, 20 August 1850, F.O. 84/808).

[2] *Jornal do Comércio*, 1 July 1850; Hudson no. 36, 27 July 1850, F.O. 84/805.

speaking a Brazilian interest' and which, moreover, was directly responsible for recent British outrages against Brazilian sovereignty. The majority, however, were rather more concerned to ensure that British aggression in Brazilian waters and ports should be strongly resisted; one deputy even believed that the time had at last come to consider, calmly and seriously, the possibility of going to war with Britain.[1] In the event, Paulino deferred his statement for another week—until Monday 15 July—so that more complete information could be gathered and proper consideration given to the latest disturbing developments.

In the meantime, a full meeting of the Council of State—the first to be held since February—was called for the afternoon of Thursday 11 July and, after consultations with the young Emperor, Paulino drew up and circulated for the Council's attention a memorandum on the slave trade question. It concluded with a rather hastily compiled series of questions designed to determine how Brazil could extricate herself with the minimum of embarassment from what Paulino saw as an extremely dangerous situation:[2] should Brazil resist British 'aggression', seek the mediation of a third power, or negotiate a new anti-slave trade treaty to replace the Act of 1845 which apparently placed no restrictions on the operations of the British navy? if the Brazilian government chose to negotiate, was it likely that they would be able to secure better terms than those (based upon the Anglo-Portuguese treaty of 1842) which had been presented by Lord Howden as Palmerston's last word and rejected by Brazil in February 1848? would *any* treaty protect Brazil from British 'hostilities' if the slave trade to and from Brazilian ports were allowed to continue? was it practicable for the Brazilians themselves to suppress or at least substantially reduce the trade? and, finally, if British cruisers continued to police Brazilian territorial waters and ports, visiting, searching, burning and destroying vessels suspected of trading in slaves, what instructions should be issued to the commanders of Brazil's coastal forts and Brazilian warships?

With the Emperor himself in the chair, the meeting of the Coun-

---

[1] *Anais do Parlamento Brasileiro: Câmara dos Deputados*, 1850, 2nd session, vol. ii, 112–20; *Jornal do Comércio*, 9 July 1850; Hudson no. 36; Soares de Sousa, *R.I.H.G.B.* (1953), *op. cit.* p. 272.
[2] Enclosed, for example, in Paulino to Lopes Gama, 8 July 1850, A.H.I. 55/4.

cil of State—also attended by leading ministers—took place in an atmosphere of crisis:[1] it was in the view of Paula Sousa probably the most grave situation ever to face the Council. Exaggerating both the scale of the British navy's recent operations and the degree of deliberate planning in London which lay behind them, it now seemed evident to the Brazilians that the British government had finally abandoned all hope of persuading Brazil herself to put an end to the slave trade and had decided to end it themselves, whatever the cost. And despite a good deal of fighting talk —from, for example, General Lima e Silva who wanted to discuss the possibility of war and argued that, at the very least, preparations should be made to repel aggression within or near the capital —it seemed equally clear that Brazil was virtually powerless to resist the British navy and that any attempt to do so could only aggravate the situation: Brazilian commerce would be completely paralysed with serious consequences for the entire Brazilian economy and for public revenue, the slave population might be dangerously inflamed, the recently established internal stability would be threatened and, always a most important consideration, Brazil's position would be seriously weakened in the coming confrontation with Rosas in the Río de la Plata if she were at the same time involved in a conflict with Britain. Moreover, since to resist British pressure would be tantamount to an open defence of the slave trade, Brazil could expect no outside support in her hour of need now that the slave trade was so universally condemned (although Paula Sousa did wonder whether Brazil could appeal to the United States on the grounds that Britain was violating the Monroe Doctrine).[2] The suggestion was made that Brazil might offer immediately to enter fresh treaty negotiations with Britain on condition that the 'violences' ceased, but this the Council realised would entail soliciting under pressure the kind of treaty they had in the past consistently refused to accept and, in any case, it was difficult to believe that having gone so far the British government,

[1] The following summary of the proceedings of this most important meeting of the Council of State is taken from A. N. Códice 307/1, pp. 101–11. For a brief account, see José Antônio Soares de Sousa, *A Vida do Visconde do Uruguai, 1807–66* (Rio de Janeiro, 1945), pp. 208–10: the author had access to Paulino's private papers.
[2] France was later approached for her support, but St George, the French minister, made it absolutely clear that on this issue Brazil stood alone (St George, 23 July, quoted in Lyra, *História de Dom Pedro II*, i. 321–2).

with or without a new treaty, would now ease the pressure until the slave trade was finally suppressed. Thus, like it or not, even Councillor Honório Hermeto Carneiro Leão, previously a staunch·defender of the slave trade interest, eventually came round to Paulino's view of the situation and the solution he had hinted at in his thirteen questions: since the slave trade was in any case about to be crushed the Brazilian government might just as well fulfil Brazil's treaty obligations and push through their own plans for its suppression as quickly as possible; only then could they enter negotiations with Britain from a position of relative strength and demand that Brazil's rights be respected. (Bernardo Pereira de Vasconcelos, the other great opponent of Britain on the slave trade question, had been a yellow fever victim two months earlier; his death removed a major obstacle to the Council of State's reaching agreement on measures to combat the trade[1]). Several members of the Council were quick to point out that the government's task had been made somewhat easier by the fact that the scale of the trade was already considerably reduced and by the fact that abolitionist sentiments continued to gain ground: only a few days earlier a preliminary meeting of a Brazilian abolitionist society—*A Sociedade contra o trafico e promotora da colonização*—had been held.[2] However, if the government had approached the

[1] At the time of Vasconcelos's death Hudson had written: 'his death will remove one of the chiefest obstacles [*sic*] to the suppression of the slave trade in this country' (Hudson no. 26, 12 May 1850, F.O. 13/275). Consul Ryan (Pará) and vice-consul Goring (Pernambuco) also died from yellow fever early in 1850. The outbreak of the terrible yellow fever epidemic in Brazil (1849–50) was eventually traced back to a slave ship, and this discovery proved a powerful weapon in the hands of opponents of the trade (Hudson no. 46, 2 September 1850, F.O. 84/806: press cuttings enclosed). The slave trade was also blamed for the spread of syphilis, elephantiasis, ophthalmia, smallpox and almost every other known disease.

[2] In his inaugural address on 7 September the Society's first president, Dr Nicolau Rodrigues dos Santos França Leite, a defender of Britain's anti-slave trade policies in 1845 (see above, ch. 9, p. 250), pledged his support for the government's anti-slave trade efforts not least because they removed the cause of Britain's 'exaggerated pretensions'. He also drew attention to the fact that 'the independence of Brazil was illusory so long as Portuguese were allowed to remain in the land turning the population into a vicious mass of slaves and slave masters' (quoted in Hesketh to Palmerston, no. 13, 9 September 1850, F.O. 84/808. Also *O Philanthropo*, which became the official organ of the Society, 13 September 1850; Hudson no. 57, 10 October 1850, F.O. 84/806). On 11 July, the very day the Council of State met to discuss the slave trade question, an article in the *Jornal do Comércio* argued that 'the slothful and impure civilisation imported from Africa is increasingly more discredited, opinion is clearly changing, and now it requires some courage for anyone to boast of the profession of slave trader' (quoted in Rodrigues, *Brazil and Africa*, pp. 193–4).

problem with a certain amount of apprehension earlier in the year because of their uncertainty as to how the population at large, and especially the landowners, would react to abolition, they now had yet another cause for concern—growing popular indignation at the British navy's persistent violation of Brazilian sovereignty. Could the government hope to carry through its own plans for suppression if Britain continued its anti-slave trade efforts on the Brazilian coast? As it was, the government were bound to incur the odium not only of those who favoured the continuation of the trade but also of those who, like Paula Sousa, preferred abolition to be *por própria vontade, por próprio interesse, e não por obrigação.* Any decision to act could not help but appear the outcome of British compulsion rather than the result of conviction. Indeed they would be adopting the policy advocated by their political opponents, who would certainly claim that by failing to suppress the trade at an earlier date the government themselves were to blame for the crisis. It was too late now, however, for spontaneous action: the government were paying the price for their earlier procrastination and timidity. They were being subjected to two conflicting pressures, Lopes Gama declared, one exerted by traders and their supporters for the continuation of the trade, the other by Britain for its suppression; 'only with the cessation of the first', he concluded, 'can we obtain the cessation of the second'.[1] After many hours of discussion, the Council of State in the end decided that whatever the difficulties and whatever the consequences Brazil now had no choice but to suppress the illegal slave trade. The very next day, 12 July 1850, Eusébio de Queiroz did what he had been promising to do for months: he invited the Chamber of Deputies to resume, in secret session, its consideration of the anti-slave trade bill first introduced in September 1837, reintroduced in September 1848 and since then substantially modified.[2]

In the meantime, Paulino had approached Hudson. They met on 13 July, two days before Paulino was due to make a full explanation of government policy to the Chamber. At this meeting

---

[1] Quoted by Soares de Sousa, *Vida do Uruguai*, pp. 209–10, and Rodrigues, *op. cit.* pp. 167–8.
[2] Alfredo Valladão, *Eusébio de Queiroz* (Rio de Janeiro, 1951), pp. 44–5; Alves, *R.I.H.G.B.* (1914), p. 249. At the end of the day an official statement declared that the Chamber had rejected article 13 for the repeal of the 1831 law *com quasi unanimidade.*

Hudson was informed of the Brazilian government's decision to take effective measures for the suppression of the slave trade—measures, Paulino was at pains to remind him, which they had all along intended to take and about which he had been fully informed. At the same time Paulino emphasised that Brazil could not tolerate the continuation of the British navy's recent activities—she would prefer to go to war—and, moreover, without some prior understanding about the future conduct of British warships on the coast of Brazil, the Brazilian government's own plans could not succeed. A repetition of such incidents as that at Paranaguá, Paulino declared, could only lead to an eruption of nationalistic sentiment so violent that it would swamp any feelings of hostility to the slave trade, embarrass the government *vis-à-vis* the opposition and jeopardise the passage of the anti-slave trade legislation the government required. Paulino therefore asked Hudson to arrange, at the very least, for the immediate suspension of those naval operations which might lead to further collisions with Brazilian coastal authorities.[1] Aware that at last Brazil had a government capable of putting down the slave trade—and in the knowledge, too, that with the limited naval resources at his disposal it was in any case impossible to 'play the Paranaguá game' again—and on the assumption that the British government wanted 'to suppress the slave trade and not war with Brazil' Hudson agreed to ask Rear Admiral Reynolds partially to suspend his standing orders of 22 June.[2] For his part, Reynolds was reluctant to act without instructions from London. At the same time, however, he had been surprised and not a little concerned by what had happened at Paranaguá; after all the Foreign Office note of 22 April upon which his orders were based had advised caution and the

[1] For Hudson's view of this meeting, see memorandum on the interview of 13 July, enclosed in Hudson no. 38, 27 July 1850, Secret, F.O. 84/805; for Paulino's recollections, see Paulino to Hudson, 28 January 1851, enclosed in Hudson no. 27, 11 February 1851, F.O. 84/843. Paulino's initial approach to Hudson (on 11 July) was made through Irineu Evangelista de Sousa, the future Barão de Mauá, Brazil's most famous nineteenth-century entrepreneur and a friend of Britain, who the following year distributed in London 10,000 copies of a pamphlet explaining Brazil's attitude to the slave trade, *The Case of England and Brazil and the Slave Trade, stated—by a Brazilian merchant* (London, 1851). See Richard Graham, 'Mauá and Anglo-Brazilian Diplomacy, 1862–1863', *H.A.H.R.* xlii (1962), p. 202.

[2] Hudson no. 38, Secret; Hudson to Palmerston, 27 July 1850, Broadlands MSS, GC/HU/22.

avoidance of incidents. He therefore agreed on 14 July to call a halt to the search and capture of Brazilian vessels close to Brazilian forts. But he insisted that the cruisers under his command should continue their operations elsewhere in Brazilian territorial waters and along the Brazilian coast and, moreover, that operations would be resumed *in full* should the Brazilian government prove slow to take effective action against the trade and, in particular, if Brazilian forts were permitted to afford the trade protection.[1]

On 15 July, in an atmosphere of suppressed excitement and great anxiety, Paulino, a Conservative whose political support, it should be remembered, came from Rio de Janeiro province, one of the great slave areas of the country, addressed a crowded Chamber of Deputies and sought support for the government's momentous decision to suppress the slave trade.[2] As a first step he felt bound to deny that the government were responsible for the crisis. It was, he said, a national not a party issue: the Conservatives were no less opposed to the trade than the Liberals now claimed to be; in the past Liberal administrations had done no more than Conservative to end it—all governments had in the main reflected the interests and prejudices of the Brazilian landed and slave-owning classes. As for the recent incidents in Brazilian ports and waters, these were not, as the opposition had suggested, a consequence of the present government's connivance at the slave trade but rather of the failure of *all* Brazilian governments to fulfil the treaty engagements of 1826; indeed, seen in their true perspective, they clearly had their origin in Lord Aberdeen's

[1] Reynolds to Hudson, 14 July, enclosed in Hudson no. 38. The navy continued to make the occasional capture during the next few months and clashes with the Brazilian authorities were not entirely avoided: the *Harpy* at Guarapari in August and the *Cormorant* and *Sharpshooter* at Salvador in September–October, for example, were involved in incidents arising from their anti-slave trade patrols.

[2] *Anais do Parlamento Brasileiro: Câmara dos Deputados,* 1850, 2nd session, ii, pp. 192–208; *Jornal do Comércio,* 16 July; also printed in *Três Discursos do Ilmo. e Exmo. Sr. Paulino José Soares de Souza* (Rio de Janeiro, 1852), pp. 1–37. Extracts in Hudson no. 36; Soares de Sousa, *R.I.H.G.B.* (1953), pp. 211–15; Rodrigues, *op. cit.* pp. 168–70. Paulino's speech of 15 July produced a marked movement against the slave trade in the press, including such formerly anti-British, pro-slave trade newspapers as *Correio da Tarde* and *O Brasil*; many papers took the opportunity to reprint the Bishop of Bahia's famous anti-slave trade speech of July 1827 in the Chamber of Deputies (see above, ch. 3, pp. 64–5). For the charges and counter-charges of Liberals and Conservatives in June–July 1850 as to which party had been most responsible for permitting the slave trade to continue in the past, see Rodrigues, *op. cit.* pp. 187–9.

illegal Act which came into force in 1845 when the Liberals were in power. (Speaking in 1852 in a similar vein Eusébio de Queiroz described the Act of 1845 as 'the true insult offered to our sovereignty because all the others are only more or less remote consequences therefrom arisen'.[1]) However, Paulino made no attempt to disguise the fact that it was British pressure that had finally compelled Brazil to end the slave trade—he said little about the growth of Brazilian abolitionism—and he presented to the Chamber a lengthy, detailed, and remarkably fair account of Britain's campaign over the preceding half century for the international abolition of the trade and of the vicissitudes which had beset Anglo-Brazilian relations on the slave trade question. 'Brazil', he declared, 'is now the only nation which has not acquiesced in this [anti-slave trade] system . . . The traffic is now almost exclusively carried on under our flag . . . The greater the facilities are for covering these speculations with our flag the greater will be the number of insults which we shall have daily to suffer . . . It is natural that England should on each occasion press us more in order to render her system complete.' With the whole of the civilised world now opposed to the slave trade, and with a powerful nation like Britain intent on ending it once and for all, 'Can we resist the torrent?' he asked—and answered, 'I think not.' The slave trade was doomed and before long the Brazilian economy, and especially Brazilian agriculture which, Paulino admitted, was in the short run still dependent on the importation of slaves, would have to adapt itself to the new situation, however difficult this might prove to be. It was, however, necessary for the government to take *immediate* steps for the suppression of the trade, he argued, because this was the only way of bringing to an end the incidents on the Brazilian coast which, if they were permitted to continue—and possibly to escalate—were bound eventually to lead to war with Britain, and this could only result in the ruin of Brazil.[2] At the same time,

---

[1] Speech of 16 July 1852, for reference see p. 361, n. 4.

[2] Two years later, in a conversation with Henry Southern, the British minister, Paulino said the government had found it useless to argue with influential slave holders, buyers and sellers on grounds of philanthropy or political economy. They were prevailed upon to support, or at least not to oppose, the government by pointing out the serious consequences for Brazil of war with Britain (Southern no. 78, 10 May 1852, F.O. 84/878).

in the knowledge that Rear Admiral Reynolds had agreed to suspend naval operations close to Brazilian forts, Paulino was able to appease those nationalist feelings which were bound to be affronted by this capitulation in the face of British coercion: he announced that the commanders of Brazilian coastal forts would be ordered to prevent by force any further seizures of Brazilian ships by foreign aggressors in Brazilian waters.[1] Hudson, who in a series of despatches to London dated 27 July suggested, misleadingly, that the Brazilian government's decision to act was exclusively the consequence of his single-handed efforts and, in particular, of his persuading Reynolds to issue the orders of 22 June, and who even now remained sceptical about the Brazilian government's determination and ability to end the slave trade, nevertheless commented:

The speech made by His Excellency will form an epoch in the history of Brazil. It is a most creditable performance . . . a brilliant peroration . . . I believe it to be the first time that the Brazilian nation has been informed correctly and publicly of its position and of its engagements. The proof that the heart of the Brazilian people and their Representatives is sound is to be found in the fact that the Chamber of Deputies received the speech of Senhor Paulino with the gravest, the deepest attention. At his conclusion there was not a dissentient voice to any of the propositions it contained. It was received with unanimous marks of cordial approbation and the warmest congratulations greeted the Minister whose courage had enabled him to achieve a great victory over that worst enemy of Brazil—the slave dealer.[2]

Eusébio de Queiroz's anti-slave trade bill now passed quickly through the Chamber, where deputies who were rash enough to make a last-ditch defence of the slave trade were shouted down; it was adopted on 17 July. Some opposition was encountered in the Senate, but after a series of debates in secret session the bill

---

[1] Following an Imperial circular to presidents of maritime provinces, 31 July 1850 (enclosed in Reynolds to Admiralty, 9 September 1850, F.O. 84/828), orders were indeed issued to fort commanders, e.g. orders of Bahia president, 19 August (enclosed in Porter no. 11, 7 September 1850, F.O. 84/808).

[2] Hudson no. 36; quoted in Soares de Sousa, *R.I.H.G.B.* (1953), pp. 280–1. Hudson was elated at, as he saw it, his own personal triumph. Besides his despatches, nos. 26–38, 27 July 1850, see, in particular, Hudson to Palmerston, 27 July 1850, Broadlands MSS, GC/HU/22. Also Hudson to Palmerston, 9 September 1850, Private, F.O. 13/275.

was accepted on 13 August.[1] A week later, it was sent to the Emperor who, through his Chamberlain, José de Mascaranhas, had already, perhaps decisively, made known to both Chamber and Senate his support for it, and who resisted a last minute bid by Conservative die-hards to force a change of ministry.[2] On 4 September 1850 the bill became law.[3] Henceforth Brazilian vessels, wherever they were found, and foreign vessels in the ports, bays, anchorages and territorial waters of Brazil, which were carrying slaves whose importation into Brazil was prohibited by the law of 1831, or which had landed slaves, or which were fitted out for the slave trade, were liable to seizure by the Brazilian authorities and Brazilian warships (article 1); the importation of slaves into Brazil was declared to be piracy and the 'principals' in the crime—the owner, captain or master, mate and boatswain of a slave vessel—as well as the 'accomplices'— members of the crew and individuals who assisted in the landing or who concealed newly imported slaves or who in any way obstructed the authorities—were liable to punishment under the law of 1831 and the Criminal Code (articles 3 and 4); all captured vessels were to be sold and the proceeds divided between the captors and the informers (if any), while the government would award the captors an additional bounty of 40 *milreis* for each African liberated (article 5); captured slaves would eventually be re-exported at the state's expense and in the meantime employed in work supervised by the government and *not*, as in the past, hired out to private individuals (article 6); passports would not be given to ships bound for the African coast until the owners had signed a declaration that they would not engage in the slave trade and given bond equal to the value of the ship and its cargo, which would be cancelled only after a period of

[1] Paulino to Amaral, no. 38, 29 August 1850, A.H.I. 268/1/17; *Jornal do Comércio*, 14 August, 21 August 1850; Alves, *op. cit.* p. 249.

[2] Hudson no. 38, 27 July 1850; St George (French minister), 4 September, quoted in Lyra, *op. cit.* i, p. 324. It has been argued that the coming together of moderate Conservatives with moderate Liberals at the expense of the ultra-Conservatives on the slave trade issue in 1850 marks the beginning of what became known in the fifties as the politics of *conciliação* (see, for example, Vicente Licínio Cardoso, *A margem da história do Brasil* (São Paulo, 1933), pp. 135–6).

[3] Law no. 581, 4 September 1850. Printed in E. Bradford Burns (ed.), *A Documentary History of Brazil* (New York, 1966), pp. 231–4; Perdigão Malheiro, ii. 241–2; Pereira Pinto, i, 462–6.

eighteen months (Article 7); all cases concerning vessels captured on suspicion of slave trading would be tried in the first instance before specially appointed judges in maritime courts (*auditoria da marinha*), although persons named in Article 3 of the 1831 law, but not included in Article 3 of the new law (that is, the *purchasers* of newly imported slaves), would as before be tried and sentenced in the ordinary courts of Brazil (Articles 8 and 9). On 14 October 1850 the government issued a decree regulating the proceedings in the maritime courts and setting out in detail the circumstantial evidence on which a vessel would be presumed guilty of attempting to engage in the illegal slave trade (it constituted a formidable list of items). Finally, a decree of 14 November 1850 regulated the manner in which appeals could be made to the Council of State's *Secção de Justiça*.[1]

Thus, after the law of November 1831 had been virtually a dead letter for almost twenty years, a second and more comprehensive Brazilian anti-slave trade law was enacted. Both sprang to a considerable extent from British pressure and both were introduced at a time when the Brazilian slave trade was already being carried on at a greatly reduced rate. There were, however, important differences between the situation in 1850 and that in 1831; not only was it more urgent from every point of view that the remaining vestiges of the trade be stamped out and its revival made impossible but, in 1850, Brazil had for the first time a government with sufficient authority and power to enforce its will. The Conservative government of 29 September 1848 was the strongest and most stable that Brazil had known since independence. Designed to strengthen the hand of the central government in Rio de Janeiro, certain constitutional, administrative and judicial reforms, beginning with the reinterpretation of the *Ato Adicional* of 1834 in May 1840, *A Maioridade* in July 1840, and the reform of the Criminal Code in December 1841, were at last in the late forties beginning to bear fruit, and what proved to be the last of the provincial revolts—*a insurrecção*

---

1 Printed in Pereira Pinto, i. 466–86, 487–90. See also Minister of Justice's *avisos* of 17 October, 31 October 1850, A. N. Códice 302/1; and *resoluções* of 30 October, 14 November 1850 in *Imperiais Resoluções tomadas sobre Consultas da Secção de Justiça do Conselho de Estado*, Part 1 (1842–63), pp. 237–9, 242–6.

praieira (1848–9) in Pernambuco—had recently been successfully overcome. The National Guard and the provincial police forces were by this time more numerous and better organised and, with the continued expansion of Brazilian exports and the termination in 1844 of the Anglo-Brazilian commercial treaty which had limited the tariffs which could be imposed on imported goods, the financial position of the Brazilian government had improved considerably with the result that funds were now available for, among other things, the development of the Brazilian navy which was once again available for anti-slave trade duties. In July 1850 the Brazilian navy comprised thirty-five ships—six stationed between Rio and Pará, twenty-two (including one steamer) between Rio de Janeiro and Rio Grande do Sul, and four in the Río de la Plata;[1] during the next six months several more steamers, including ex-slavers like the *Serpente*, were purchased and the government entertained plans for a rapid build-up of naval forces (with Rosas as well as the slave trade question in mind). Brazilian warships—including the *Urania*, the *Golphino*, the *Don Affonso* and the *Fidelidade*—now patrolled the coast between Cabo Frio and Ilha Grande, examining the creeks and bays and searching suspicious vessels; several captures were made, including that of the slave ship *Rolha* (belonging to Joaquim Pinto da Fonseca, brother of the notorious Manuel Pinto), which on 4 October was seized by the Macaé authorities and the war steamer *Urania* with two hundred slaves on board. In the meantime, as they had promised, the government had established courts in Rio de Janeiro, Belém(Pará), São Luís (Maranhão), Recife, Salvador and Porto Alegre, to deal with captured vessels. At the same time strict orders were issued to presidents of coastal provinces to close down all slave depots, seize any slaves they found there and ensure that no ships fitted out for the trade. And, for the most part, these orders were speedily and energetically carried out.[2] Indeed, in some provinces they had been anticipated: on 15 July, for example, the very day that Paulino delivered his famous address to the Chamber of Deputies,

[1] Minister of Marine, *Relatório*, May 1850, quoted in Hudson no. 31, 27 July.
[2] Hudson no. 60, 10 October 1850, F.O. 84/806; *Relatório do Ministério da Justiça*, 13 May 1851; *Relatório do Ministério dos Negócios Estrangeiros*, 14 May 1851.

Vicente Pires da Mota, the President of São Paulo, had ordered the seizure of all ships fitting out or landing slaves in the province. The 'insolent foreigners' who directed the Brazilian slave trade, he explained, were the cause of, or rather served as a pretext for, English attacks on national vessels in Brazilian waters and ports. 'It is necessary to curb these half dozen individuals who, caring for nothing but their own gains, involve the nation in great difficulties . . . a faithful co-operation of the authorities is indispensable to the government, who can do nothing without their valuable assistance.'[1] It was also made clear to all chiefs of police, their sub-delegates, magistrates and municipal authorities throughout Brazil, that in future the road to promotion would lie in suppressing the trade and that connivance at it would now bring dismissal. And, as a final proof of their good intentions, although the law of 1850 failed to make adequate provision for dealing with the men behind the slave trade—'that gang of ruffians and kidnappers who for so long a time had lorded it over the Brazilian authorities', as Hudson described them[2]—some of the leading foreign traders, for example Joaquim Pinto da Fonseca (who had retained Portuguese nationality), and the Sardinian Pareto, were arrested, imprisoned and finally ordered to leave the country. By the middle of November Hudson was able to report that in the provinces of Rio de Janeiro, São Paulo, Espírito Santo and Santa Catarina the slave trade had been brought almost to a standstill. Only 5,000 slaves were imported into these provinces between June and December 1850—and very few of these were landed after October. Moreover, he was also able to report that there were no ships fitting out anywhere along the entire Brazilian coast from fifty miles south of Bahia to Rio Grande do Sul. He suspected, however, that the slave traders were shifting their operations to the north-east where there had not yet been any evidence of a decline in the trade. Quite the reverse: between July and December 1850 5,000 slaves were landed in Bahia (more than in any previous six-month period since 1847) and during the year as a whole 2,300 were landed in Pernambuco compared with an estimated 300 in 1847, none in

[1] 15 July circular, enclosed in Hudson no. 49, 2 September 1850, F.O. 84/806.
[2] Hudson no. 83, 17 December 1850, F.O. 84/807.

1848 and 450 in 1849.[1] Nevertheless, the Brazilian slave trade had suffered its most serious reverse since it had first been declared illegal twenty years ago.

It was September 1850 before news of the events which had taken place in June and July reached London from Rio de Janeiro. Not a little surprised at the course and speed of developments in Brazil, Lord John Russell and his senior colleagues in the Cabinet nevertheless readily approved Rear Admiral Reynolds's orders of 22 June: matters had clearly arrived at the point where a final settlement of the slave trade question had to be reached and, in view of Brazil's flagrant and systematic violation of her treaty engagements—to say nothing of what Palmerston called 'the common principles of humanity and the fundamental precepts of Christian religion'—it was agreed that any action, not excluding the use of force within the territorial waters and ports of a friendly power, was fully justified.[2] Lord Palmerston was personally delighted with the way things had turned out; naval operations on the Brazilian coast, he wrote to Sir Francis Baring, First Lord of the Admiralty (who himself thought Reynolds's officers had acted 'right merrily'), had apparently accomplished in a few weeks what diplomatic notes and treaty negotiations had failed to achieve over a period of many years.[3] Not for one moment did it cross Palmerston's mind that the Brazilian government had spontaneously and sincerely set foot upon the path of righteousness—that would have amounted to a 'modern miracle'; he never questioned that they had been forced along it by the British navy. The Brazilian slave trade question served to confirm Palmerston's belief that, where the interests and prejudices of foreign governments were involved, 'persuasion seldom succeeds unless there is [behind it] compulsion of some sort'.[4] On another occasion, with reference to China, Portugal, and Spanish America, he wrote in a similar vein:

---

[1] See Appendix; Hudson no. 78, 11 November 1850, F.O. 84/807; Hudson to Palmerston, 11 November 1850, Private, F.O. 84/801.
[2] Baring to Palmerston, 29 August 1850, Broadlands MSS, GC/BA/286; Baring to Russell, 18 September 1850, P.R.O. 30/22/8E; (Russell Papers); Palmerston to Baring, 3 September 1850, Broadlands MSS, GC/BA/310; Russell to Palmerston, 24 September 1850, Broadlands MSS, GC/RU/363.
[3] Palmerston to Baring, 3 September.   [4] *Ibid.*

These half civilised governments . . . all require a dressing down every eight or ten years to keep them in order. Their minds are too shallow to receive any impression that will last longer than some such period and warning is of little use. They care little for words and they must not only see the stick but actually feel it on their shoulders before they yield to that only argument which to them brings conviction, the *Argumentum Baculinum*.[1]

Since, like Hudson, Palmerston believed that the British South American squadron, far from being an obstacle in the path of Brazilian co-operation, had shown itself to be the countervailing force necessary to offset the influence of the slave traders over the Brazilian government, he reasoned that to ease the pressure on Brazil prematurely, that is, before the slave trade had actually been suppressed, would be to permit the Brazilian government to relapse into its former state of indifference towards the trade. Palmerston found Paulino's speech of 15 July immensely gratifying but, ever cautious, he wanted 'actual payment, not an I.O.U.'—in short, action not words. Even were the promised anti-slave trade legislation enacted (as indeed it already had been), its existence, he wrote, was one thing, its enforcement another; after all, the law of 1831 had been a dead letter for twenty years.[2] Thus when José Marques Lisboa, the Brazilian minister in London, communicated a request from Paulino Soares de Sousa for the total suspension of British naval operations in Brazilian waters, to be followed by the negotiation of a new and mutually satisfactory anti-slave trade treaty, Palmerston replied that he was willing to sign a treaty only on his own terms (which now included the right of search and capture *within the Brazilian three-mile limit*) and that the only sure way for Brazil to secure the cessation of the operations of British warships in her waters was for the Brazilian authorities to ensure that there were no slave ships for them to search and capture.[3] As for the arrangement

[1] Palmerston 29 September 1850, quoted in Bartlett, *Britain and Sea Power*, pp. 261–2.
[2] Palmerston to Baring, 3 September; F.O. to Adm., 27 September 1850, F.O. 84/823.
[3] Lisboa to Palmerston, 2 October, Palmerston to Lisboa, 3 October, Private, enclosed in Lisboa to Paulino, 4 October 1850, Reservado, A.H.I. 217/3/6. On the Brazilian desire to negotiate a treaty to replace the Act of 1845, see also Paulino to Hudson, 24 October, enclosed in Hudson no. 68, 11 November 1850, F.O. 84/807; 'Memorandum on the state of the slave trade in Brazil and the proposal of the Brazilian government to treat

which Hudson had already made for the *partial* suspension of
British naval operations in Brazilian territorial waters, Palmerston
grudgingly accepted in his dispatches to Hudson that in the circumstances such a course of action might have been justified in
order to prevent clashes with the Brazilian authorities (although
privately he felt Hudson had been too ready to put his trust in
verbal promises whose sole aim was the removal of the British
navy from Brazilian waters). He was relieved, however, that
Rear Admiral Reynolds had insisted on limiting both the extent
and duration of the suspension. And on 15 October Palmerston
instructed Hudson that unless the Brazilian government had
begun to execute the law of 1831 together with any new legislation 'actively, effectually and without favour or partiality' and,
in particular, unless the Brazilian authorities were now seizing
all slave ships at those points on the Brazilian coast where
Reynolds had agreed not to interfere (that is, close to Brazilian
forts), and prosecuting all those involved, the temporary and
partial suspension of the orders of 22 June should be immediately
rescinded. Furthermore, he should require the Brazilian government to issue express instructions to all coastal authorities to
co-operate with British warships on anti-slave trade patrol and
on no account to open fire on them. It was this, Palmerston
believed, not the withdrawal of British cruisers, which was the
obvious and proper way to avoid collisions like that at Paranaguá
without at the same time giving tacit encouragement to the slave
trade.[1]

In the light of Lord Palmerston's instructions of 15 October 1850
(which arrived in Rio de Janeiro in December, three months after
the passage of the Brazilian law of 4 September), and in response
to pressure exerted by Rear Admiral Reynolds who was eager to
deliver the *coup de grâce* to the ailing Brazilian slave trade, Hudson,
who was now British minister, warned Paulino at the end of the
year that he might be obliged to order the resumption *in full* of

---

with Great Britain for its suppression', enclosed in Hudson to Palmerston, 11 November
1850, Private, F.O. 84/801; Amaral to Paulino, no. 22, 23 December 1850, A.H.I.
216/2/14.
[1] Palmerston to Hudson, no. 28, 15 October 1850, F.O. 84/801. Extracts printed in
W. D. Christie, *Notes on Brazilian Questions* (London, 1865), pp. 193–5.

British anti-slave trade operations on the Brazilian coast.[1] He argued without much conviction that such a move would be justified on the grounds that the Brazilian government had failed to fulfil the engagement to suppress the trade which they had entered into on 13 July in return for the partial suspension of Reynolds's orders of 22 June. And by way of substantiating this charge, Hudson enumerated some of the Brazilian government's more outstanding sins of omission: several thousand slaves landed in the Rio area since July of which only a few had been seized; local authorities, especially in Bahia where the slave traders had now made their headquarters, still permitting ships to be fitted out for the trade; regular slave depots still not broken up; and some of the worst offenders—importers and receivers—still at large. Hudson was nevertheless anxious to avoid a renewal of hostilities between British cruisers and Brazilian forts and on 23 December, on his own initiative, put forward a scheme for ensuring Anglo-Brazilian co-operation along the Brazilian coast: British naval officers would henceforth invite Brazilian fort commanders to join in the search of vessels lying within range of shore batteries. And if Brazilian civilian authorities were prepared to co-operate, he added, a similar procedure might possibly be adopted in Brazilian ports, bays and anchorages.

Paulino was astonished that Britain was considering the adoption of tougher measures against a government which was now faithfully fulfilling Brazil's treaty engagements. If the trade were still not quite extinct, Paulino argued, it was simply because there had not yet been sufficient time for the government to amass the necessary information about slaving enterprises, build up and perfect its suppression system along the vast coast line of

[1] The following account of the discussions between Hudson and Paulino, December 1850–January 1851, is based on: Hudson to Paulino, December 1850 (draft), enclosed in Hudson no. 6, 11 January 1851, F.O. 84/843; Hudson to Paulino, 11 January, enclosed in Hudson no. 7, 11 January 1851, F.O. 84/843 and printed in Christie, *op. cit.* pp. 196–202; Hudson to Palmerston, 11 January 1851, Broadlands MSS, GC/HU/29; memorandum on the conferences of 10 January 1851, enclosed in Paulino to Dom Pedro II, A.M.I.P. maço cxv, doc. 5701; Paulino to Hudson, 28 January, enclosed in Hudson no. 27, 11 Febuary, 1851, F.O. 84/843, printed in *Jornal do Comércio*, 31 January and *Relatório do Ministério dos Negócios Estrangeiros*, 14 May 1851, Annex B; two notes from Paulino to Hudson, 8 February, enclosed in Hudson no. 30, no. 39, 15 March 1851, F.O. 84/844; Paulino to Amaral, no. 2, 8 January, no. 5, 11 January 1851, A.H.I. 268/1/18; Paulino's speech in the Senate, 29 May 1852, (see below, p. 361, n. 4).

Brazil, and begin to re-educate public opinion. It was an immense job and a delicate one: the slave trade was a deeply rooted evil in which formidable interests—not all of them illegitimate—were involved. Since the new anti-slave trade legislation had been brought into force in October, a great deal had been done. It was perhaps true, Paulino was prepared to concede, that the trade was still systematically carried on in Bahia (although fresh orders for its suppression had recently been sent to the President there) and no doubt there were isolated slave depots still in existence and a few ships fitting out in ports up and down the coast. But this did not amount to a breach of the July agreement. It seemed to Paulino, therefore, that the threat of renewed hostilities against Brazil could only be understood in terms of past frustration and scepticism about the future and not in the context of the present conduct of the Brazilian government. Untimely as well as illegal, a renewal of full-scale naval operations could only lead to a further series of incidents which, Paulino insisted, by once again confusing the defence of the slave trade with the defence of national independence, might well make it impossible for the Brazilian government to pursue its own measures against the trade. Anxious as he was to co-operate with Britain and acutely aware of how hard pressed Hudson was by both Lord Palmerston and Rear Admiral Reynolds, Paulino could not however agree to Hudson's scheme for avoiding future conflicts on the Brazilian coast. It would mean recognising the right of British cruisers to search Brazilian ships in Brazilian ports and territorial waters, which was more even than Lord Howden had demanded of Brazil during the years 1847–8 when the Brazilian slave trade was at its height. As Paulino well knew, neither his colleagues, nor the legislature, nor the Brazilian people would be prepared to sanction the scheme; on the contrary, they expected Brazilian forts to resist British aggression. Indeed, as Paulino had promised in his speech of 15 July 1850, orders to this effect had been issued to fort commanders, although they had been given in the belief that they would never have to be executed. 'If you have one Admiral on your back', Paulino remarked to Hudson at one point in their discussions, 'the Brazilian government has hundreds.'

At the same time Paulino was well aware of the disastrous consequences for Brazil of renewed hostilities with Britain— both internally and externally (in the struggle against Rosas Brazil was now giving financial aid to Montevideo and had recently signed a defensive alliance with Paraguay). It was beginning to look like the crisis of July 1850 all over again. Already, as a first step towards ending the suspension of his orders of 22 June, Rear Admiral Reynolds had despatched the now notorious *Cormorant* (an unhappy choice from the Brazilian point of view) to join the *Sharpshooter* in Bahia where, on 9 January, Schomberg was to threaten the President of the province with 'disastrous consequences' if the slave ships lying in the Bahia de Todos os Santos were not immediately taken into custody.[1] It was in these circumstances that at midday on 10 January, at the end of one of a number of meetings with Hudson, Paulino tentatively produced a counter-proposal to Hudson's own scheme which, although imperfect, he believed could help prevent a further outbreak of hostilities on the Brazilian coast without actually empowering British officers to exercise jurisdiction in Brazilian territorial waters. Personally, he told Hudson, he could see no objection to making one change in the procedure governing the search and capture of ships along the Brazilian coast, at least in the small ports and anchorages and under the guns of Brazilian fortresses: when they were informed by a British officer of the presence of a slave ship, he suggested, Brazilian authorities, civilian and military, should invite the officer to be present while they searched the ship and, if the suspicion as to its character proved well founded, to observe its despatch to a Brazilian maritime court. Paulino then consulted his colleagues and at 6 p.m. offered Hudson (subject to the Emperor's approval) an 'unwritten understanding' along these lines. Such an arrangement could continue for six months, he said, during which time the Brazilian government would give further evidence of their good faith by completely suppressing the trade; at that point it might then be possible to reopen

[1] Porter to Hudson, 11 January, Francisco Gonçalves Martins (Pres. of Bahia) to Porter, 11 January, Schomberg to Reynolds, 13 January, enclosed in Hudson no. 26, 11 February 1851, F.O. 84/843; Reynolds to Admiralty, 4 January, 13 January, enclosed in Adm. to F.O., 10 March, 15 March, F.O. 84/863; Porter no. 1, 13 February 1851, F.O. 84/848.

negotiations for a new treaty to ensure that the trade could never revive. When Hudson asked what would happen if at any time the Brazilian authorities refused to co-operate in this way with a British naval officer, Paulino was reported by Hudson to have airly responded, 'Oh, in that event you may take slave ships on your own responsibility—you may do what you think proper.'[1]

Whatever Hudson might have thought of it, this 'emasculated proposition' was evidently unacceptable to Rear Admiral Reynolds, and on 11 January Hudson told Paulino that the partial and temporary suspension of the orders of 22 June had been revoked.[2] Shortly after, Paulino was warned that if the Brazilian government failed to instruct their authorities along the coast not to engage in 'piratical attacks' on British cruisers engaged in the suppression of the slave trade under the terms of the treaty of 1826, they would bear the responsibility for any 'signal retributive calamity' which might be suffered by any town from which such attacks were made.[3] Again there was a large element of bluff in all this. Even now British naval officers were under orders to avoid unnecessarily provoking the Brazilian authorities where there was any likelihood of successful resistance and in all cases they were required to communicate with the Brazilian authorities before making a capture inside the limits of a Brazilian port.[4] The cautionary note in these instructions was further underlined when in February fresh orders arrived from London to the effect that, where ships were found within range of forts and shore batteries, application must be made to the local commander before they were searched and seized and, in the event of refusal, no action was to be taken apart from informing the British legation in Rio; since his despatch to Hudson of 15 October Palmerston had heard about the orders issued to Brazilian fort commanders and, in the circumstances, felt it

[1] Hudson no. 6, 11 January 1851.
[2] Hudson to Paulino, 11 January 1851. The decision was approved in London: F.O. to Adm., 19 March 1851, F.O. 84/863; Palmerston to Hudson, no. 24, 29 March 1851, F.O. 84/842.
[3] Hudson to Paulino, 15 January, 30 January, enclosed in Hudson no. 19, 11 February 1851, F.O. 84/843. Hudson was echoing Palmerston's own words (Palmerston no. 35, 9 November 1850, F.O. 84/801).
[4] Reynolds to Admiralty, 13 January 1851, F.O. 84/868.

wise to modify his earlier instructions.[1] Moreover, until the small fast steamers persistently asked for by both Hudson and Reynolds could be transferred to Brazil, either from Lisbon or from west Africa, the British squadron was hardly in a position to resume active operations on any really effective scale: the *Cormorant* and the *Geyser* were in need of major repair and minor repairs were required on the *Rifleman* and the *Sharpshooter*; as for the *Conflict* and the *Harpy*, they were too large and cumbersome for inshore patrol.[2]

Nevertheless, Paulino's unwillingness to revoke his orders to fort commanders, combined with his apparent failure to prevent the resumption in full of British naval operations on the Brazilian coast, left the Brazilian government with no alternative but to remove any possible pretext for conflict by pressing ahead with their efforts to stamp out what remained of the Brazilian slave trade. The effect of his note to Paulino of 11 January, Hudson reported, was 'magical and ludicrous'.[3] The very next day every available Brazilian steamship, a party of armed police on board each one of them, was despatched on anti-slave trade duties; and the pride of the Brazilian navy, the steamer *Don Affonso*, together with the *Recife*, was immediately sent to Bahia carrying strict orders to President Gonçalves Martins to seize all slave ships in the bay and destroy all slave depots in the area before the *Cormorant* was ordered into action.[4] Moreover, it was now, in an effort to improve their rudimentary Intelligence Service, that Paulino, Eusébio and Rio's Chief of Police, Bernardo Augusto Nascentes de Azambuja, asked Hudson how the British legation managed to gather such remarkably accurate and detailed information about the activities of the slave traders in the provinces of Rio de Janeiro and São Paulo. Hudson put them in touch with 'Alcoforado', on condition that his life would be fully protected[5] —an action for which Hudson was later criticised by Palmerston

---

[1] Palmerston minute, 5 November, on Adm. to F.O. 3 November, enclosed in F.O. to Adm., 26 November 1850, F.O. 84/828; Palmerston to Hudson, no. 38, 30 November 1850, F.O. 84/823.
[2] Hudson to Palmerston, 11 January, 11 February, 15 March 1851, Broadlands MSS, GC/HU/29, 31, 32.
[3] Hudson to Palmerston, 11 February 1851.
[4] Paulino to Dom Pedro II, 13 January 1851, A.M.I.P. maço cxv, doc. 5759.
[5] Hudson no. 64, 11 April 1851, Secret, F.O. 84/844.

who argued that, since Hudson believed that some members of the Brazilian Cabinet and Council of State were still far from totally committed to abolition, he had no business divulging the name of the British legation's main informer.[1] Hudson, however, had every confidence in Eusébio and gladly supplied him with the means whereby the law of September 1850 could be more effectively enforced. Henceforth, 'Alcoforado' was to feed information to the Brazilian Ministry of Justice as well as to the British legation, and apparently so satisfied his new employers that after only three months (in April 1851) he was given a gratuity of £2,500.[2]

On 1 February 1851 Reynolds was able to report that there was 'more earnestness on the part of this government for the repression of the slave trade than has ever been evinced before. It does not amount to a cordial co-operation with us so much as an independent movement in the same direction.'[3] The policing of the coast by Brazilian warships prevented any landings taking place and, more important, deterred slave ships from leaving for Africa. Local military and civilian authorities, including those in Bahia,[4] were now making even more determined efforts to prevent ships fitting out for the trade—and those who failed were frequently dismissed, like, for example, the commander of the Macaé fort. Local officials and the Brazilian navy also co-operated in occupying and closing down the deposits for slaving equipment and freshly imported slaves which were still maintained in such notorious spots as Periqué, Marambaia, Dois Rios,

[1] Palmerston minute, 16 May, on Hudson no. 64.

[2] Hudson no. 64, 11 April 1851. Alcoforado continued to serve both the Brazilian government and the British legation, earning from British sources alone over £5,000 during the years 1850–1 and over £2,000 during 1852 (Howard, British minister in Rio, to Palmerston, 22 September 1855, F.O. 84/968). In February 1852 Southern, Hudson's successor, wrote, 'he is well known and feared by the slave traders . . . he has established a police which extends its ramications to every slave trading port in the country' (Southern to Granville, no. 14, 13 February 1852, Conf., F.O. 84/878). His report of October 1853 to the Brazilian police is the most detailed 'inside story' available on the nineteenth-century illegal Brazilian slave trade and the traders engaged in it (A.N. I j⁶-525; for a summary, see Rodrigues, *op. cit.* pp. 179–82). He was paid a regular monthly allowance by the British legation in Rio at least until the end of 1855 by which time the trade had been suppressed.

[3] Reynolds to Admiralty, 1 February, enclosed in Adm. to F.O., 10 March 1851, F.O. 84/864.

[4] Schomberg to Reynolds, 22 January, 25 January, enclosed in Hudson no. 26, 11 February 1851, F.O. 84/843.

Sombrio and Mangaratiba. A number of foreign slave traders were either deported or forced to retire from the trade under threat of deportation.[1] (It proved more difficult to deal with Brazilian traders who were still liable to be taken for trial before the ordinary courts of Brazil and therefore always likely to be acquitted by local juries.) One result of so much Brazilian anti-slave trade activity during the first half of 1851 was that there were no clashes between Brazilian authorities and the British navy, which continued to police Brazilian waters to the north and south of Rio de Janeiro and to the north and south of Bahia but which now came across very few slavers. 'The slave trade', wrote Edward Wilberforce, a midshipman on H.M.S. *Geyser* at this time, in his book *Brazil viewed through a naval glass*, 'is in the position of Tom Jones when he called Partridge to examine his wound. It is progressing so favourable that the poor doctor's occupation's gone.' And he expressed his disappointment at his failure to earn any prize money (even though the *Geyser* stopped and searched almost every ship it came across): 'the navy prefers cure to prevention', Wilberforce wrote, 'because it gets its fee for the one, and not for the other.'[2] British naval officers were, however, full of praise for the way in which the Brazilians were executing the law of September 1850 and, moreover, reported the Brazilian authorities as being unusually friendly and hospitable: indeed, it was now not unusual for provincial presidents and leading citizens publicly to demonstrate their goodwill by paying official visits to British cruisers when the opportunity arose.[3]

During the first quarter of 1851 only two successful landings of slaves were reported along the entire coast of Brazil from Pará

[1] Hudson to Palmerston, 15 March 1851, Broadlands MSS, GC/HU/32, 33. The British consul in Lisbon calculated that 300–400 individuals involved in the slave trade had voluntarily returned to Portugal between March 1850 and March 1851 bringing capital amounting to £400,000 (Smith no. 1, 19 March 1851, F.O. 84/841).

[2] E. Wilberforce, *Brazil viewed through a naval glass: with notes on slavery and the slave trade* (London, 1856), pp. 219, 220. In Wilberforce's view it was of no importance what Brazilians thought of Britain's anti-slave trade policies: 'the ox can afford to despise the spiteful comments of the frog' (*ibid.* p. 223).

[3] E.g. Tatham (of the *Geyser*), 6 April, enclosed in Hudson no. 61, 11 April 1851, F.O. 84/844 (quoted in Wilberforce, *op. cit.* pp. 233–5); Tatham, 30 June, enclosed in Hudson no. 87, 14 July 1851, F.O. 84/845; Drake (of the *Conflict*) to Reynolds, 5 March, enclosed in Hudson no. 58, 11 April 1851, F.O. 84/844.

to Rio Grande do Sul: one near Rio de Janeiro and one in Pernambuco. In the period April–June 1850 three further landings —in Rio de Janeiro, Rio Grande do Sul and Alagoas—came to the attention of the local authorities, but in each case most of the slaves were traced and taken into custody.[1] Several factors served to confirm that the trade had been reduced to a very low level: slave prices in Brazil had almost doubled over the previous twelve months while prices on the African coast had collapsed;[2] various schemes for encouraging European colonisation were once more in the air; and there were signs that a more extensive internal trade in slaves was beginning to develop, principally from the relatively depressed north-east to the still expanding coffee areas of the Paraíba valley: 1,000 slaves were moved down the coast to Rio de Janeiro province in 1849, a further 1,000 in 1850, 3,000 in 1851 and increasing numbers thereafter.[3] Rear Admiral Reynolds, however, like most of his officers and the majority of British consuls up and down the coast, believed that the transatlantic trade was only in abeyance.[4] The Brazilian market had been glutted during the late forties, as it had been in the late twenties, with the result, he argued, that there had been a temporary lull in the demand for slaves. But since there was still no real alternative source of labour this situation could not last: slave prices were rising once more, as they had in the early thirties, traders would be tempted by the enormous profits to be made, and the Brazilian government would be unable or unwilling to prevent a renewal of the trade—unless of course the British navy remained on the spot to encourage and, if necessary, coerce them. For this reason Reynolds was disinclined to suspend any part of his squadron's operations, much less to withdraw

---

[1] Hudson no. 62, 11 April 1851, F.O. 84/844; Hudson to Palmerston, 11 April, Private, Broadlands MSS; Hudson no. 70, 12 May, no. 80, 14 July 1851, F.O. 84/845; Reynolds 28 March, enclosed in Adm. to F.O., 15 May 1851, F.O. 84/869; Paulino to Hudson, 30 June, enclosed in Hudson no. 85, 14 July 1851, F.O. 84/845; *Relatório do Ministério dos Negócios Estrangeiros*, 14 May 1851; *Relatório do Ministério da Justiça*, 13 May 1851.
[2] Stein, *Vassouras*, p. 229, Fig. 6: Average price of male and female slaves aged twenty to twenty-five years, 1822–88.
[3] *Relatório do Ministério da Justiça*, 1 May 1852; Morgan (consul in Bahia) to Russell, no. 31, 17 February 1853, F.O. 84/912.
[4] Reynolds 10 May 1851, enclosed in Adm. to F.O. 11 June 1851, F.O. 84/865; Hudson to Palmerston, 15 March 1851, Broadlands MSS, GC/HU/32, 33; Tatham 30 June, enclosed in Hudson no. 87; Wetherall (vice consul in Bahia) no. 15, 30 June 1851, F.O. 84/848.

altogether from Brazilian waters. And both he and Hudson were still concerned about the feeble condition of the squadron: most ships were either unsuitable for anti-slave trade duties or in a state of near collapse, although the squadron had been to some extent strengthened by the recent arrival of two excellent steamers, the *Plumper* and the *Locust*.[1]

An apparent revival of slaving activity in the middle of the year seemed to justify Reynolds's caution, and in June and July 1851 British warships enjoyed their period of greatest activity since June of the previous year. Within the space of a few days H.M.S. *Cormorant* captured and sank near Rio de Janeiro the steam tug *Sarah* on her way to the Sardinian-registered *Valarozo*, with the latter's crew and slaving equipment on board; H.M.S. *Plumper* captured and sank the *Flor do Mar*, also carrying equipment for the *Valarozo*; and H.M.S. *Sharpshooter* captured the *Valarozo* itself—which apparently had been chartered by a group of notorious dealers including Tomás da Costa Ramos (Maneta) and Manuel Pinto da Fonseca.[2] (Initially despatched to St Helena, the *Valarozo* was eventually handed over to the Sardinian authorities at Genoa.) A few weeks later the slaver *Sylphide* successfully landed a cargo of Africans in the province of Alagoas north of Bahia; two hundred suffocated or were drowned in the course of a terrifying disembarkation, but four hundred were successfully put ashore. When Hudson heard that it was planned to ship some of them down the coast first to Bahia and then to São Sebastião, he arranged for the *Sharpshooter* to intercept them and, on 22 July, she detained a Brazilian coastal trader, the *Piratinim*, with one hundred and two Africans on board. It transpired that all the slaves carried by the *Piratinim* had been given passports by the authorities at Bahia. Nevertheless, on his own initiative—and, indeed, going far beyond the letter of his instructions—Lieutenant Bailey of the *Sharpshooter* decided that some of them at least had been recently imported into Brazil and that the rest had almost certainly been illegally imported since 1831. Thus, he reasoned, both vessel and cargo were liable to

[1] Hudson to Palmerston, 14 July 1851, Broadlands MSS, GC/HU/36/2.
[2] Hudson no. 91, 14 July 1851, F.O. 84/845; Hudson to Palmerston, 1 July 1851, Broadlands MSS, GC/HU/36/1.

12-2

seizure; he therefore transferred the slaves to the British hulk, *Crescent*, anchored in Rio bay, and ordered the destruction of the *Piratinim* since it was unfit to undertake a journey to St Helena half way across the Atlantic.[1] At about the same time Hudson received information which led him to suspect that the slave traders who had been driven first from the area immediately north and south of the capital and subsequently from the vicinity of Bahia were now planning to make their base down the coast from Paranaguá on the Ilha de Santa Catarina; apparently two successful landings had already been made and more were expected at any time. The *Locust* and the *Plumper* were sent there at once and, towards the end of July, Captain Curtin of the *Locust* was responsible for the destruction of vast stocks of slaving equipment (worth over £3,000) and the seizure of several ships claiming to be engaged in legitimate coastal commerce.[2]

Meanwhile, the arrival in Rio of the *Sharpshooter* with its prize the *Piratinim* created almost as much of a sensation as the news of the incident at Paranaguá had done the year before. The Rio press, in Hudson's words, 'vomited forth abuse and slander of Great Britain'[3] and, in the Chamber of Deputies on 26 July, Eusébio de Queiroz indignantly condemned Lieutenant Bailey's action and the enormous extension of the British navy's powers over Brazil's coastal trade which it implied, promising, amid cheers, to do all within his power to prevent its repetition.[4] A week later, on 2 August, the Brazilian deputies, who had by now learned of the events in Santa Catarina as well, heard a speech from Joaquim José Rodrigues Tôrres, the Minister of Finance, which, according to Hudson, was unusually 'inflammatory, ill-advised and unjust', even for him, and which 'exhausted the vocabulary of vituperation'.[5] With the Brazilian slave trade

[1] On the *Piratinim* affair, see Hudson no. 104, 14 August 1851, F.O. 84/846; *Relatório do Ministério dos Negócios Estrangeiros* 14 May 1852; *Cartas ao Amigo Ausente* ed. José Honório Rodrigues (Rio de Janeiro, 1953) pp. 211–13: these 'letters' were first published, on a weekly basis, in the *Jornal do Comércio* (1851–2) by José Maria da Silva Paranhos, the future Visconde do Rio Branco, for whom Palmerston and Rosas were the arch-enemies of the Brazilian people.
[2] Hudson no. 113, 13 September 1851, F.O. 84/847; *Correio Mercantil*, 4 September, 5 September, 6 September, 7 September, 10 September 1851; *Relatório*, 14 May 1852.
[3] Hudson to Palmerston, no. 104, 14 August 1851, F.O. 84/846.
[4] *Jornal do Comércio*, 27 July 1851.
[5] Hudson to Palmerston, no. 104.

virtually at an end, Rodrigues Tôrres told the Chamber, there was no longer any pretext for the arbitrary capture and destruction of Brazilian vessels by British cruisers anywhere, least of all in Brazilian territorial waters. Yet they continued. 'We have arrived at such a pitch', he declared (and his words were almost drowned in the general uproar), 'that it is not possible nowadays to ship in the port of Rio de Janeiro a copper boiler for the use of the sugar houses in this province or in that of São Paulo because the masters of our merchant vessels refuse to receive them fearing that this might be sufficient motive for the sinking or burning of their vessels by the English cruisers.' Rodrigues Tôrres went on to announce that, if further remonstrances failed, the government would avail themselves of any legal means of preventing the annihilation of Brazilian mercantile navigation and, amidst the cheers and embraces of his colleagues, added that they would not shrink from covering Brazil's coastal trade with the flag of a nation whose rights would be better respected (the Brazilian government had on more than one occasion—in July 1850, for example—already considered making use of either the American or the French flag). Under Article 309 of the Customs House Regulations the government had the power to resort to such a measure only in wartime; a motion authorising its extension to cover a situation which amounted to one of undeclared war was now carried by seventy votes to fifteen.[1] For the time being, however, Paulino merely lodged yet another formal protest against the 'warlike acts' of the British navy. It seemed ironical, he observed, that 'the more this country proceeds in the career of repression, the more frequent becomes the injustice and the violence which is committed upon her'.[2] There was, however, as Paulino well knew, nothing the Brazilian government could do that would make Britain respect Brazil's rights as a sovereign and independent nation apart from maintaining their efforts against the slave trade. Henry Southern, the new British minister, transferred from Buenos Aires when Hudson moved to Turin towards the end of 1851, had something to say about the suggestion

[1] *Jornal do Comércio*, 3 August 1851; Hudson to Palmerston, 13 September 1851, Broadlands MSS, GC/HU/38.
[2] Paulino to Hudson, 8 August, enclosed in Hudson no. 113, 13 September 1851, F.O. 84/847.

that Brazil might act as though a state of war already existed and proceed with the plan of putting its coastal trade under a foreign flag: 'If the relations between Great Britain and Brazil were ever unfortunately to become those of war', he declared during his first interview with Paulino in December, 'there are naval measures belonging to such a state of things the employment of which by Great Britain would put a stop to *all* the coasting trade between the ports of Brazil, whatever might be the nationality of the vessels by which the Brazilians might attempt to carry that coasting trade on.'[1]

Threats and counter-threats of this kind were unnecessary since within a short time British naval operations on the Brazilian coast had again come to a standstill. The Foreign Office eventually ruled that British cruisers had no authority to interfere with the legitimate coastal trade of Brazil—which included legitimate trade in slaves; vessels suspected of transporting newly imported slaves were liable to detention, but not those transferring slaves already owned by Brazilians from one part of the country to another, even though it could be argued that most of these had probably been imported since 1831 and, strictly speaking, were therefore not legally owned.[2] Thus any recurrence of incidents like that involving the *Piratinim* became highly improbable. Henceforth British cruisers could search and detain only those vessels suspected of engaging directly or indirectly in the transatlantic slave trade and few cargoes of slaves were now being shipped across the Atlantic to Brazil. Only an estimated 3,200 Negroes were known to have been imported into Brazil during 1851 in nine separate landings, and only two of these—both in Bahia—occurred during the last four months of the year.[3] Early in September 600 Negroes were landed at Ilheus, ninety miles south of Salvador, but as the result of prompt action by President Gonçalves Martins, who immediately despatched to the scene two ships and a detachment of police, led by the vice-president of the province, at least some of the slaves were rounded up.[4] Then, at the end of October, the *Relampago*, an American-built

[1] 21 December interview, quoted in Southern no. 15, 15 January 1852, F.O. 84/878.
[2] Malmesbury to Southern, no. 14, 17 June 1852, F.O. 84/877, following Southern no. 19, 10 April 1852, F.O. 84/878.   [3] See Appendix.
[4] Wetherall (Bahia) no. 19, 17 September 1851, F.O. 84/848.

vessel of two hundred and twenty tons, owned by an Italian with connexions in Bahia and sailing under the Sardinian flag, was chased ashore about twenty miles south of Salvador by the Imperial war steamer *Itapagipe*. Many of the Africans she carried had died on the voyage, many more were drowned while disembarking and the chief of police of the province, Dr João Mauricio Wanderley, assisted by the National Guard and sub-delegates of police from the surrounding area, recovered over three hundred of those successfully landed. President Gonçalves Martins then asked the Captain of H.M.S. *Locust* to help move the vessel itself to Salvador.[1] Although there were to be three further known landings of slaves in Brazil (two in 1852 and one in 1855), as well as at least one well-authenticated unsuccessful attempt (in January 1856),[2] by the beginning of 1852 there was general agreement that the Brazilian branch of the transatlantic slave trade had been completely crushed.[3]

Although the Brazilian slave trade had been brought to an end during the years 1850–1, the controversy surrounding the way in which this had come about—and in so short a time—was only just beginning. Lord Palmerston was now prepared to concede that the Brazilian government were at last fulfilling their long standing treaty engagements with Britain,[4] but he remained convinced that in the last analysis the British squadron on the South American station had played a role at least equal in importance to that of the Brazilian navy and the Brazilian coastal authorities in the final suppression of the trade. But, it remained the British government's

---

[1] Wetherall to Hudson, 7 November, enclosed in Hudson no. 128, 11 December 1851, F.O. 84/847; Wetherall no. 23, 14 November 1851, F.O. 84/848; Wanderley report, 18 November 1851, published in *Jornal do Comércio*, 3 January 1852.

[2] See below, ch. 13, pp. 367, 370, 373–4.

[3] In February 1852 Southern wrote that the trade was 'utterly destroyed' (Southern no. 14, 13 February 1852, Conf., F.O. 84/878). In May Eusébio referred to its 'almost total extinction' (*Relatório do Ministério da Justiça*, 1 May 1852). The British West African squadron now came across very few Brazilian slave ships: 18 were captured in 1851, 4 in 1852, 3 in 1853 (adjudications in Freetown, F.O. 84/831, 869, 897; adjudications in St Helena, F.O. 84/859, 887, 921). Many Brazilian traders in the Bight of Benin were ruined by the sudden ending of the trade (see Ross, *Journal of African History* vi (1965), p. 84). When David Livingston visited Angola in May 1854 he found the slave trade virtually extinct (see Duffy, *Question of Slavery*, p. 5).

[4] E.g. report of interview with Palmerston in Amaral to Paulino, 8 May 1851, no. 9, Reservado, A.H.I. 217/3/6; statement by Palmerston in House of Commons, 14 July 1851 (Hansard, cxviii. 683–91).

view that it was the decision to send the navy into Brazilian territorial waters and ports, *and this alone*, which had first prompted the Brazilian government to act (they had done little enough during the previous twenty years when British anti-slave trade activities had been largely confined to the west African coast).[1] Palmerston believed that had this important decision been taken two years earlier, when it was first proposed, the Brazilian slave trade would have been suppressed that much sooner.[2] As James Hudson wrote in June 1851, repeating the view he had first expressed in his despatches of 27 July 1850, *l'affaire Paranaguá* had 'scattered like chaff the slave dealers, their apologists and their protectors' and compelled the Brazilian government to introduce more effective anti-slave trade legislation.[3] And it was a remarkable coincidence, Palmerston observed to José Marques Lisboa, referring to the partial suspension of British naval operations on 14 July 1850 and their resumption in full on 11 January 1851, that 'exactly in proportion as the activity of the British cruisers ceased exactly in that same proportion were the efforts of the Brazilian government against the slave trade discontinued' and vice versa.[4] 'Nothing would or could have been done by the Brazilian government alone', Henry Southern commented in August 1852.[5] Such was the official British view of how the Brazilian slave trade had finally been suppressed. In 1864, only a year before his death, Palmerston was to write, 'the achievement which I look back on with the greatest and the purest pleasure was forcing the Brazilians to give up their slave trade, by bringing into operation the Aberdeen Act of 1845'.[6]

Eager to discredit the Conservatives while, at the same time, dissociating themselves from the slave trade interest, the Liberal opposition in Brazil also claimed that the Brazilian government

[1] E.g. Palmerston to Lisboa, 10 October 1851, enclosed in Lisboa to Paulino no. 56, 27 October 1851, A.H.I. 216/2/15; quoted in Richard Graham, *Britain and the Onset of Modernization in Brazil, 1850–1914* (Cambridge, 1968), p. 165.
[2] Palmerston to Russell, 15 March 1851, P.R.O. 30/22/9B. Recent events in Brazil, Palmerston wrote, demonstrated the effect of 'vigorous and decisive action where Right and Might are both on our side'.
[3] Hudson no. 71, 11 June 1851, F.O. 84/845.
[4] Palmerston to Lisboa, 10 October 1851.
[5] Southern no. 47, 10 August 1852, F.O. 84/879.
[6] Palmerston to Sir John Crampton, 17 February 1864, quoted in A. E. M. Ashley, *Life of Henry John Temple, Viscount Palmerston, 1846–1865* (London, 1876), ii, 263–4.

had acted solely through fear of Britain. 'The Minister of Foreign Affairs was sleeping soundly on a bed of roses', Senator Costa Ferreira declared in May 1851, referring to the events of June–July 1850, 'without feeling the thorns and without dreaming that England . . . would not allow herself to be joked with or laughed at . . . The Minister was only awakened by the thunder of the English cannon.'[1] A year later useful ammunition came into the hands of the opposition as a result of the British government's publication in a Blue Book of a good deal of the correspondence which had passed between Hudson and Palmerston, Hudson and Reynolds, and Hudson and Paulino during the period April 1850– March 1851, and especially during July 1850—this despite Hudson's plea at the time that his despatches should not be published on the grounds that the Brazilians already felt they had been 'driven into the measures [for the suppression of the slave trade]' and it would require all his efforts to 'soothe their wounded vanity'.[2] In April 1852 the British legation in Rio furnished the opposition newspaper, the *Correio Mercantil*, with a copy of the Blue Book, and those parts of the correspondence most damaging to the Brazilian government appeared in the issues of 7, 9 and 12 April.[3] As a result, Paulino Soares de Sousa (in the Senate on 29 May) and subsequently Eusébio de Queiroz (in the Chamber on 16 July during a debate on the third reading of a government bill to provide additional steamships for anti-slave trade duties) felt themselves obliged to put forward a coherent alternative account of how the suppression of the Brazilian slave trade had been accomplished.[4] While freely admitting that between 1830

[1] Quoted in Hudson no. 72, 11 June 1851, F.O. 84/845.
[2] Hudson no. 38, Secret, 27 July 1850, F.O. 84/805.
[3] See Soares de Sousa *R.I.G.H.B.* (1952), pp. 268–9. Paulino commented that the correspondence was *cheio de falsidades* (Paulino to Macedo, no. 7, 10 April 1852, Reservado, A.H.I. 268/1/18). Macedo, the Brazilian minister in London, also sent to Rio de Janeiro a copy of the Blue Book which, in his view, contained *as communicações inexactas e malevolas* (Macedo to Paulino, no. 15, 18 June 1852, Reservado A.H.I. 217/3/7).
[4] Paulino's speech of 29 May 1852, printed in *Jornal do Comércio*, 31 May, 1 June 1852 and in *Três Discursos do Ilmo. e Exmo. Sr. Paulino José Soares de Souza* (Rio de Janeiro, 1852), pp. 38–62; extracts in Southern no. 33, 11 June 1852, F.O. 84/878. Eusébio's speech of 16 July 1852, *Anais do Parlamento Brasileiro, Câmara dos Deputados*, 1852, vol. ii, pp. 241–258; published as *Questão do Trafico* (Rio de Janeiro, 1852); extracts in Southern no. 47, 10 August 1852, F.O. 84/879; also printed in Perdigão Malheiro, ii, pp. 262–87. Alfredo Valladão refers to this speech as *discurso sensacional pela beleza de sua forma, pela elevação e sabedoria de seus conceitos, pela defesa do nome, da dignidade do Brasil, e*

and 1850 Brazilian governments had made only weak and intermittent attempts to suppress the trade, they argued that in 1850–1 the measures taken by the Brazilian government had been responsible, *solely and exclusively responsible*, for the ending of the trade: the British navy, they argued, had long ago proved itself incapable of even diminishing, much less suppressing it. Moreover, the Brazilian government's decision to act had been a *spontaneous* one, not, as Hudson had reported, the result of British coercion. There had been, Eusébio claimed, a 'revolution in public opinion'. Even the Brazilian planters had finally been persuaded that their real long-term interests lay in abolition and that in any case, as Paulino was fond of saying, it was no longer possible for Brazil 'to resist the pressure of the ideas of the age in which we live'. Eusébio was able to demonstrate that stiffer measures against the slave trade had been conceived and legislation drafted long before the English cannon had been heard at Paranaguá and elsewhere along the Brazilian coast. Both Eusébio and Paulino argued that it was in spite of, not because of, the British navy's 'acts of aggression', which simply succeeded in rousing opposition to the anti-slave trade cause, that the Brazilian government went ahead with their own measures as planned and carried them through to a successful conclusion. So ran the official Brazilian account of how the slave trade question had finally been resolved. And just as the Brazilian opposition preferred the British view of events, so the English opponents of Palmerstonian methods—the radical free traders and the leaders of the Anti-Slavery Society—through their (and the Brazilian government's) mouthpiece the *Daily News* chose to accept the Brazilian government's version in which final abolition resulted from a change of heart in Brazil, as they had always insisted that it would, rather than acknowledge the possi-

pelo vigor de sua lógica irrespondível, constituindo uma das maiores vitórias que registram os nossos Anais Parlamentares (*Eusébio de Queiroz, op. cit.* p. 45). The *Jornal do Comércio*, 28 July 1852, published extracts from the British Blue Book more favourable to the Brazilian government. For the Brazilian view of how the slave trade came to be finally suppressed, see also Paulino to Hudson, 28 January 1851, enclosed in Hudson no. 27, F.O. 84/843; Paulino speech in Senate, 24 May 1851, quoted in Soares de Sousa, *Vida do Uruguai, op. cit.* pp. 221–3; Olinda speech in Senate, 28 May 1851, *Jornal do Comércio*, 31 May 1851; Lisboa to Palmerston, 27 September 1851, enclosed in Lisboa to Paulino, no. 49, 30 September 1851, A.H.I. 216/2/15; *Relatório do Ministério dos Negócios Estrangeiros*, May 1851, May 1852.

bility that Britain's traditional anti-slave trade policies, which they had so vigorously opposed and which had almost been reversed in March 1850, might have triumphed in the end.[1]

Both sides thus claimed the credit for having suppressed the trade. And, in so doing, both exaggerated the extent of their own responsibility. By the middle of 1850 there had already been a marked reduction in the scale of the Brazilian slave trade thanks in part to the efforts of the British West African and South American squadrons but more particularly because of a glut in the Brazilian slave market following several years of unusually heavy imports. The trade was finally and completely crushed during the ensuing twelve months largely, though not entirely, because for the very first time a Brazilian government decided to take effective action against it and, more important, had the authority and the resources to implement this decision. There is evidence to show that for a variety of reasons (which included the reappearance of a British preventive squadron in Brazilian territorial waters and the deteriorating situation in the Río de la Plata, as well as purely domestic political considerations) the Brazilian government had for some time been cautiously considering what steps could be taken to put down the trade. And, as they later claimed, legislation had actually been drafted before the middle of 1850. It is clear, however, that it was the sudden extension in June and July of the British squadron's anti-slave trade operations into Brazilian inland waters and ports which, by provoking a major political crisis in Brazil, led directly to the passage of a new anti-slave trade law and to its vigorous enforcement. It is fruitless to speculate when, or even whether, such a law would have been passed—much less enforced—had not Britain intervened decisively at this critical juncture. At the very least, British naval action could be said to have greatly accelerated, if it did not alone precipitate, Brazil's own, ultimately successful, efforts to suppress the slave trade.

[1] *Daily News*, 11 February, 13 March, 17 July 1851; also Milner Gibson speech, 10 March 1851, Hansard, cxiv. 1219–20. Hudson later criticised these 'garbled statements' and asked what was the use of an Anti-Slavery Society which expressed similar views (Hudson to Stanley, 13 September 1851, Private, F.O. 84/842). Palmerston wrote in the margin, 'none whatever'.

CHAPTER 13

THE AFTERMATH OF ABOLITION

The final suppression of the Brazilian slave trade during the years 1850-1—twenty years after it had been declared illegal by treaty with Britain and more than forty years after Britain had abolished her own share of the transatlantic trade and made her first official abolitionist overtures in Lisbon and Rio de Janeiro—did not immediately remove the slave trade question from Anglo-Brazilian relations. On the contrary, both the memory and the legacy of a conflict so protracted and at times so bitter poisoned relations between the two countries for many years to come. And serving most effectively to keep the slave trade controversy alive was the continued existence of the Aberdeen Act long after the trade had been abolished.

At the time of its passage in 1845, Lord Aberdeen had looked upon his Act, like the Palmerston Act before it, as an exceptional, temporary measure; it would be repealed, he had indicated, either when Brazil signed an effective anti-slave treaty with Britain—as Portugal had done in 1842—or when Brazil co-operated with Britain and herself abolished the trade. Towards the end of 1851, believing that by their actions they had now clearly demonstrated their desire and their ability to put down the slave trade and to prevent its revival, the Brazilian government made a second attempt—the first had been made, prematurely, in October-November 1850—to persuade Britain to repeal the Act which had always been deeply resented in Brazil or, at the very least, not to enforce it in Brazilian inland and territorial waters.[1] As usual, the Brazilian government found support in England amongst radical free traders who were anxious to reduce the cost of the British preventive system and to re-establish amicable Anglo-Brazilian relations in the interests of British trade and investment in Brazil.[2]

---

[1] Lisboa to Palmerston, 27 September, enclosed in Lisboa to Paulino, no. 49, 30 September 1851, A.H.I. 216/2/15.

[2] See, for example, petitions of Manchester Commercial Association and Liverpool Brazilian Association, September–October 1851, F.O. 84/860.

Lord Palmerston at the Foreign Office, however, had no intention of removing the British naval squadron from the Brazilian coast; if, as he believed, the Brazilian government had finally taken action against the slave trade only as a result of British naval pressure, they could be trusted to keep the trade down (particularly when the shortage of labour again became acute) only for as long as that pressure was maintained.[1] Unlike Aberdeen, Palmerston had been prepared to repeal the Act of 1845 only when a suitable anti-slave trade treaty of unlimited duration had been signed to replace it. The negotiation of a new treaty was included in the instructions sent by Paulino José Soares de Sousa, the Brazilian Foreign Minister, to Sérgio Teixeira de Macedo who was to replace José Marques Lisboa as Brazilian minister in London. But since Paulino felt that, with the trade virtually eliminated, the British government ought to be ready to meet Brazil's long-standing demands for proper guarantees for her legitimate commerce and territorial rights, and since Palmerston remained unyielding in his opposition to these demands—the distrust of twenty years could not easily be overcome—there seemed no point in trying to open negotiations.[2] In the meantime, Lord Palmerston, totally insensitive to Brazilian feelings on this question, took the view that if, as the Brazilians claimed, the trade had been completely and permanently extinguished, there could in future be no slavers for British warships to capture and therefore no cause for complaint from the Brazilian government.[3]

In December 1851, after more than five years at the Foreign Office, Lord Palmerston was replaced by Lord Granville who shared his belief that the Brazilian slave trade would quickly revive if any part of the existing British preventive system, and especially Rear Admiral Reynolds's orders of 22 June 1850, were prematurely relaxed.[4] However, Granville was in office for only a few weeks and Lord Malmesbury, Foreign Secretary in Lord Derby's short-lived Conservative government (February–December 1852),

---

[1] Palmerston to Lisboa, 25 September, 13 November 1851, F.O. 84/842; Palmerston to Lisboa, 10 October, enclosed in Lisboa to Paulino, no. 56, A.H.I. 216/2/15.
[2] Paulino to Macedo, no. 31, 13 November 1851, A.H.I. 268/1/18; Hudson to Palmerston, 14 October 1851, Broadlands MSS, GC/HU/40.
[3] Palmerston to Lisboa, 13 November.
[4] Granville to Southern, February 1852, draft, F.O. 96/31.

viewed the situation in a different light: while quick to point out that he was no less anxious than his predecessors to bring the transatlantic slave trade to an end, he disliked Palmerston's method of conducting foreign policy which he was reported to have described as a 'system of violence, angry acts and ill humour'. Malmesbury thought Palmerston had irritated and humiliated the Brazilians by legalising 'a kind of piracy' for the suppression of the trade. Perhaps this had been necessary at an earlier date, he conceded, when the slave trade still flourished and Brazilian governments were indifferent to their obligations. But times had changed; Brazil was now prepared to co-operate with Britain and some gesture of confidence in the Brazilian government was called for if relations between the two countries were ever to be improved.[1] On 27 April 1852, Malmesbury therefore requested the Admiralty to suspend all previous instructions and order naval officers of the South American station once again to confine their activities under the Acts of 1839 and 1845 to the high seas; there should be no further cruising inside Brazilian territorial waters, he said, so long as the Brazilian slave trade was effectively kept down by the Brazilians themselves[2]—although two months later he was to tell Henry Southern in Rio de Janeiro that if the trade showed signs of reviving the British government would, at his request, immediately resume naval operations in full.[3]

It so happened that in April 1852, soon after Rear Admiral Henderson, Reynolds's successor as commander-in-chief on the south-east coast of America, had confirmed that the slave trade was no longer being carried on anywhere along the Brazilian

[1] Malmesbury to Southern, no. 6, 24 March 1852, F.O. 84/877; Macedo to Paulino, no. 9, Reservado, 7 April 1852, A.H.I. 217/3/7. Some years later Malmesbury elaborated on the 'very peculiar style' of Palmerston's diplomatic correspondence: 'whatever the circumstances', he said, 'the stereotyped despatch opened by expressing the unqualified displeasure of Her Majesty's Government and concluded with some menace' (Hansard, cxliii. 1070–9, House of Lords, 21 July 1856).

[2] Addington (F.O.) to Hamilton (Adm.), 27 April 1852, F.O. 84/891. This important decision was immediately sent to Rio de Janeiro (Malmesbury no. 9, 27 April 1852, F.O. 84/877; Macedo no. 13, Reservado, 1 May 1852, A.H.I. 217/3/7).

[3] Malmesbury to Southern, no. 15, 18 June 1852, F.O. 84/877. There were, however, at the time only two British warships fully operational on the Brazilian coast—the *Plumper* and the *Rifleman*. The *Sharpshooter*, the *Cormorant*, the *Geyser* and the *Tweed* had all returned to England at the end of 1851; the *Conflict* and the *Locust* had been moved to the Río de la Plata.

coast,[1] a landing of slaves was made by the *Palmeira* in Rio Grande do Sul.[2] It was the first for almost six months and the Brazilian government, supported by the authorities on the spot, took immediate action to frustrate a plan to send the slaves north, by means of small coasting vessels, to Santa Catarina and thence to the province of São Paulo. Within a month of this reminder that the possibility of the Brazilian slave trade's reviving could still not be entirely discounted, some long expected changes in the Brazilian Cabinet were announced, and among those retiring from office was the Minister of Justice, Eusébio de Queiroz, 'the most strenuous, energetic and unbending friend of the suppression of the trade in Negroes that Brazil has yet produced' as Southern described him, a man whose very name 'infused terror into Brazilian slave traders'.[3] Eusébio, however, assured Southern that he had complete confidence in his successor, José Ildefonso de Sousa Ramos and in the new Minister for Internal Affairs, Francisco Gonçalves Martins who, as President of Pernambuco and President of Bahia respectively, had demonstrated their determination to end the slave trade once and for all.[4] Paulino, who continued as Foreign Minister, expressed his deep satisfaction at the suspension of British naval operations in Brazilian waters, and assured Southern, who had taken the opportunity to lecture him on the Brazilian government's increased responsibilities so far as the slave trade was concerned, that Lord Malmesbury's 'act of justice' had strengthened his resolve that no one should be given an opportunity to reopen the trade.[5] Moreover, with the defeat of Rosas by General Urquiza (with Brazilian and Uruguayan support) at Monte Caseros in February 1852, Brazilian warships had been released from the Río de la Plata for anti-slave trade patrol: by the middle of the year 16 ships (8 of them steamers) were stationed between Campos and Rio Grande do Sul, another 3 at Bahia, 3 at Pernambuco and 5 at Maranhão. And in August

---

[1] Henderson to Admiralty, 12 April 1852, F.O. 84/894.
[2] Southern to Malmesbury, no. 32, 11 June 1852, F.O. 84/878; Southern no. 40, 12 July 1852, F.O. 84/879; *Relatório do Ministério dos Negócios Estrangeiros*, 14 May 1853.
[3] Southern to Malmesbury, no. 29, 13 May 1852, Conf., F.O. 84/878; Southern to Henderson, 21 May, enclosed in Southern no. 32, 11 June 1852, F.O. 84/878.
[4] Southern no. 30, 14 May 1852, Conf., F.O. 84/878.
[5] Southern no. 31, 8 June 1852, F.O. 84/878; Paulino to Southern, 12 June, enclosed in Southern no. 38, 7 July 1852, F.O. 84/879.

1852 the government was authorised by Congress to purchase additional steamships for this service.[1]

While realising that it might be unwise to put too much faith in the durability of what could prove to be only a temporary reaction against the slave trade in Brazil, and reluctant to give up altogether Britain's powers to obstruct the slave trade on the high seas and to compel Brazil to enforce her own ban on the trade, at the same time Lord Malmesbury wanted to encourage the Brazilian government's independent efforts to stamp out the last vestiges of the slave trade. With this in mind, he was prepared to consider not only the withdrawal of British cruisers from Brazilian waters but also the dismantling—perhaps for three years in the first instance—of 'any part of the system now in force which may be felt by Brazilians as wounding their national dignity or tending to lower the dignity of their flag'.[2] When Teixeira de Macedo took the initiative and sounded him out on the possibility of negotiating a treaty to replace the Aberdeen Act,[3] Malmesbury therefore showed some interest in the idea. Before making a decision, however, an opinion was sought from James Hudson, now British minister in Turin, who strongly advised the government to approach any negotiations with the greatest circumspection. Twelve months absence from Brazil had done nothing to soften Hudson's views on the Brazilian people and their predilection for the slave trade. 'No living Brazilian', he wrote in September 1852, 'will refuse to buy an African at a low figure on a long credit whenever the chance is offered to him by a slave dealer.' It followed therefore that in any final settlement of the slave trade question Britain should secure adequate guarantees against a possible return to the situation which prevailed during the years 1830–50, when Brazilian governments so blatantly connived at the illegal trade. In Hudson's view, no new treaty would be com-

---

[1] *P.P.* 1852–3, xxxix (920), Report of House of Commons Select Committee on the Slave Trade Treaties, Appendix A, no. 16; Paulino to Macedo, no. 30, 8 June, no. 38, 9 July 1852, A.H.I. 268/1/17; Perdigão Malheiro, ii. 62. Also memorandum enclosed in Moreira (Brazilian minister) to Malmesbury, 3 July 1858, F.O. 84/1051.

[2] Stanley (F.O.) to Hudson (Turin), 31 August 1852, Private, F.O. 84/877.

[3] Macedo to Malmesbury, 19 August, enclosed in Malmesbury to Hudson, 3 September, F.O. 84/877, following Paulino to Macedo, no. 10, 12 April 1852, Reservado, A.H.I. 268/1/18. Also Macedo to Paulino, no. 17, 8 September 1852, Reservado, A.H.I. 217/3/7.

plete without, first, a renewal of the first article of the treaty of 1826 which, by declaring the slave trade piracy, provided the means whereby Britain could if necessary again coerce Brazil into suppressing the trade; secondly, the inclusion of the Brazilian laws of 7 November 1831 and 4 September 1850; thirdly, an agreement guaranteeing the freedom of the Africans emancipated by the mixed commission in Rio de Janeiro between 1819 and 1845; fourthly, an agreement guaranteeing the freedom of Africans illegally imported since the passage of the 1831 law and therefore *ipso facto* free. If Brazil refused to accept these conditions, Hudson argued, the British government could be sure 'they [the Brazilians] mean to carry on such a slave trade as circumstances will permit'.[1] Hudson's successor in Rio de Janeiro, Henry Southern, whose advice was also sought, died in January 1853 but William George Jerningham, the *chargé d'affaires*, for whom all treaty negotiations with Brazil were 'a snare', offered, unsolicited, similar (if rather more colourful) advice. The Brazilian government's sole purpose, he wrote, was 'to get their necks out of the halter of the bill of 1845 sanctioned by the everlasting provision of that charming old document of 1826'; he therefore advised the British government to

treat that old Act well for it has worked well upon these shores and though odious to the malignant eye of the slave dealer is nevertheless regarded by him with fear and trembling. As long as that exists Brazil is like a toad under a harrow, she must go along whether she will or not. But stop and lift up the harrow for an instant and the toad will easily jump off and spit in your face . . . Do you imagine . . . this reclaimed old sinner who now looks very devout will easily withstand the temptation of backsliding into her former wickedness, especially if the fear and apprehension of the 'Sword of Damocles' be removed by the repeal of the worthy old Act of 1845?

Brazil, Jerningham concluded, should not be allowed 'the shadow of a chance of slipping her wily head out of the noose which, though not tight, holds her so securely and gently for the present'.[2] Meanwhile, treaty negotiations had in fact been opened in London and continued intermittently for the next twelve

---

[1] Hudson to Stanley, 12 September 1852, Private, F.O. 84/877. 'We have undertaken a job which is beyond our strength', Hudson wrote in a separate letter of the same date, 'unless we use extraordinary means of coercion with a friendly state.'

[2] Jerningham to Clarendon, 14 August 1853, Private, F.O. 84/910.

months. However, since in the event Britain required that Brazil sign at the very least an anti-slave trade treaty based on the Anglo-Portuguese treaty of 1842 before the Act of 1845 could be repealed, and since Brazil was not even willing to concede the right of search now that the Brazilian slave trade had ceased, there was no question of any agreement being reached.[1] In October 1853, Lord Aberdeen's Peelite–Whig coalition government (with Lord Clarendon at the Foreign Office and Lord Palmerston as Home Secretary) finally decided to abandon negotiations with Brazil and—it seemed to Macedo—to pursue a policy of officially forgetting the Act while maintaining it in existence as an insurance against the future.[2]

One reason for the uncompromising attitude adopted by the British government was the fact that in the course of the negotiations news had reached London of another landing of slaves in Brazil—even though this was only the second in twelve months. In December 1852, the American brig *Carmargo* had successfully put ashore at Bracuhy, Ilha Grande (south of Rio de Janeiro), between 500 and 600 Africans from Quelimane in Moçambique and was then immediately set on fire by its crew. On this occasion the Brazilian government had been let down unexpectedly by the local magistrate who, pleading sickness, waited two weeks before reporting the landing with the result that, when the Chief of Police arrived on the scene from Rio with a force of sixty men, the slaves had been taken inland to the municipality of Bananal (São Paulo province), sold and dispersed to a number of different coffee plantations, notably those belonging to Joaquim José de Sousa Breves, the wealthiest landowner in the district. The Brazilian government for the first time ordered a systematic search of local *fazendas* for newly imported slaves—an order which the police and the National Guard found extremely difficult to carry out. Powerful *fazendeiros* like Breves, most of whom commanded the support of small private armies, fiercely defended their hitherto

---

[1] On the treaty negotiations 1852–3, see Macedo–Malmesbury correspondence, F.O. 84/877 (e.g. Macedo, 17 September, 15 November 1852) and Macedo–Paulino correspondence, A.H.I. 217/3/7 (e.g. Macedo no. 18, 8 October 1852, Reservado, no. 2, 7 February 1853, Reservado). Also Clarendon to Macedo, 23 May 1853, F.O. 84/910.
[2] Macedo to Paulino, no. 22, 21 October 1853, Reservado, A.H.I. 217/3/7. Also Clarendon to Howard, 7 October 1853, F.O. 84/910.

unchallenged authority on their own estates, and only thirty-eight of the *Carmargo*'s slaves were recovered by the authorities. The *fazendeiros* and their representatives in the municipal chamber of Bananal, and in both the Chamber of Deputies and Senate in Rio de Janeiro, lost little time in protesting against illegal armed invasions of private estates which, they claimed, had the effect of stirring up a spirit of insurrection amongst the Negro slaves. And when a charge of purchasing illegally imported slaves was eventually brought against Breves at Angra dos Reis in Rio de Janeiro province, the jury brought in a unanimous verdict of Not Guilty.[1]

Although the events following the landing of slaves at Bracuhy in December 1852 strengthened the Brazilian government's determination to avoid further direct confrontations with the planters, instructions went out to all Brazilian naval officers, presidents of maritime provinces, chiefs of police, port authorities and local magistrates in coastal towns to maintain their efforts to prevent any further importations of slaves. In June 1853 Luís Antônio Barbosa, a former President of Minas Gerais and successor to Sousa Ramos as Minister of Justice, promised to resign if a single slave were imported into Brazil during his term of office—a promise he did not have to keep.[2] Even more energetic was José Tomás Nabuco de Araújo, Minister of Justice in the strong all-party Government of Conciliation (*Conciliação*), led by the Marquês de Paraná (Honório Hermeto Carneiro Leão) which was formed in September 1853 and which remained in power until May 1857. The new government was responsible for the introduction into the Senate of a Bill—which became law on 5 June 1854—extending the powers of the special maritime courts set up under the anti-slave trade law of September 1850. Hitherto, it had been difficult to prosecute Brazilians thought to be involved in the trade unless they were actually caught in the act of importing slaves and even then the law required that they should be brought

---

[1] Southern no. 1, 4 January, no. 2, 7 January, no. 7, 13 January 1853, F.O. 84/911; Jerningham no. 3, 7 February, no. 7, 4 March, no. 11, 2 April, no. 17, 11 June, no. 28, 27 August 1853, F.O. 84/911; *Relatório do Ministério do Negócios Estrangeiros*, 14 May 1853; *Jornal do Comércio* 18 May, 19 May 1853. At one point Jerningham wondered whether it might not be necessary to send the British navy once again into 'inner Brazilian waters' (Jerningham no. 3, F.O. 84/911).

[2] Quoted in Jerningham no. 21, 27 June 1853, F.O. 84/911.

371

for trial before a local jury, which invariably acquitted them. Brazilian maritime courts were now empowered to try and punish any Brazilian—and any foreigner resident in Brazil—suspected of having an interest in the slave trade.[1]

During the years 1854–5, the Brazilian government—through their legation in London—and the English free traders—both in the columns of the *Daily News* and, led by Milner Gibson, in the House of Commons—stepped up the pressure for the repeal of the Aberdeen Act. The British government, however, still feared that without a satisfactory Anglo-Brazilian treaty to replace it, there would be nothing to prevent the Brazilians from one day reverting to their old habits. When, in a debate on 26 June 1854, John Bright objected to the government's 'holding this Act over the Brazilian government as a security for its good behaviour', Palmerston solemnly replied that abolition had conferred such moral and material benefits on Brazil that the repeal of the Act of 1845 would be 'the greatest injury to the Brazilian people which it would be possible for us to inflict upon them'. He would only concede that the government might review the situation 'after a long series of years'.[2] Sir Henry Howard, the British minister in Rio de Janeiro (1853–55), agreed that there was no better guarantee against a resumption of the trade than the knowledge, both in government and in slave trading circles, that Britain retained the power to prevent it.[3]

Towards the end of 1855—after three years in which not a single importation of slaves is known to have been made—a last attempt was made to revive the transatlantic slave trade to Brazil. The circumstances seemed unusually propitious: both the British West African and South American preventive squadrons had been considerably reduced in numbers as a result of the demands for ships in the Crimean War; a labour shortage was again beginning to make itself felt in Brazil—particularly since a cholera epidemic in

---

[1] Law no. 731, 5 June 1854, printed in Pereira Pinto, i, 490–2. The bill had been introduced into the Senate within a few days of the government's taking office. See *Jornal do Comércio*, 16 September 1853; Jerningham no. 35, 1 October 1853, F.O. 84/911; Joaquim Nabuco, *Um Estadista do Império, Nabuco de Araújo: Sua Vida, Suas Opiniões, Sua Época* (2nd ed., São Paulo, 1936), i, pp. 165–7.   [2] Hansard, cxxxiv. 723, 725.
[3] Howard to Clarendon, no. 11, 28 May 1855, F.O. 84/968. Cf. two despatches from Howard to Clarendon, 4 June 1854, printed in Christie, *Notes on Brazilian Questions*, pp. 208–14.

1855 had made inroads into the existing slave population[1]—and slave prices in the areas of greatest demand (the Paraíba Valley and the province of São Paulo) had soared since the end of the slave trade; and slave barracoons in Benguela, Ambriz and the Congo estuary were full and prices lower than they had been for more than twenty years. Early in September a rumour began to circulate in Rio de Janeiro that 250 Negroes had been landed at Angra dos Reis, on the mainland behind Ilha Grande, to be followed a month later by a rumour that 300 had been deposited on the border between the provinces of Rio de Janeiro and Espírito Santo; both were thoroughly investigated but neither was ever completely substantiated.[2] On 13 October, however, a successful landing of between 200 and 240 Negroes certainly took place near Serinhaém in the province of Pernambuco. The majority were eventually rounded up and liberated—only sixteen were never recovered—but subsequent investigation revealed not only negligence on the part of the local authorities but also the fact that the president of the province, the chief of police and several leading families had been implicated in the landing.[3] Lord Palmerston, who had recently become Prime Minister at the head of a new Whig-Liberal government, infuriated the Brazilian government by issuing 'a friendly warning' that unless steps were taken to deal with the offenders and prevent future landings, it might prove necessary for British warships to resume anti-slave trade operations under the Aberdeen Act—as he believed they had a perfect right to do—'on the coast, in the rivers and in the harbours of Brazil'.[4]

---

[1] Jerningham no. 2, 12 January 1856, F.O. 84/993; *Falla do Throno*, 3 May 1856.

[2] Jerningham no. 13, 15 October, no. 15, 9 November, no. 17, 13 November 1855, F.O. 84/968.

[3] Jerningham no. 15, 9 November, no. 16, 12 November, no. 22, 14 December 1855, no. 7, 12 February, no. 19, 14 March 1856, F.O. 84/993; Cowper (Pernambuco) no. 9, 21 April 1856, F.O. 84/994; *Relatório do Ministério dos Negócios Estrangeiros*, May 1856; Nabuco, *op. cit.* i. pp. 169–76; Manchester, *British Preeminence in Brazil*, p. 264.

[4] Clarendon to Jerningham, no. 2, 9 January 1856, F.O. 84/993, based on Palmerston minute 31 December 1855 (printed in Christie, *op. cit.* pp. 221–2); Jerningham to Paranhos, 7 March, enclosed in Jerningham no. 19, 14 March 1856 (approved by Clarendon, no. 22, 28 April, no. 38, 26 June 1856, F.O. 84/993). '*Não há nota mais dura na triste história diplomática do tráfico*', commented Joaquim Nabuco in *Um Estadista do Império*, i, p. 170. Sérgio Teixeira de Macedo in London had already complained bitterly to Lord Clarendon (in May 1854) that 'it was always with a threat on its lips that the English government spoke to Brazil' (quoted in Manchester, *op. cit.* p. 288). Following the Serinhaém affair Jerningham's successor in Rio de Janeiro, Campbell Scarlett, asked for authority to enforce the orders of June 1850 again should it ever prove necessary

In the event, the Brazilian government had already punished those involved in the affair and had redoubled their efforts to prevent its repetition—but the fact that the trade was clearly still not entirely dead further hardened Palmerston's resolution not to repeal the Act. 'The bill of 1845', he wrote in April 1856, 'is the only security against the revival of the Brazilian slave trade and *it ought never to be repealed*. The sincerity of the Brazilian government against the slave trade is the sincerity with which a pickpocket keeps his hands from a bystander's coat flaps while he sees a policeman's eyes fixed upon him.'[1] And in July Lord Aberdeen in the House of Lords, while admitting that he had been reluctant to introduce the Bill in the first place and, indeed, had always been looking for an opportunity to repeal it, in the light of recent events in Brazil now hesitated to advocate its immediate repeal.[2] The slaves landed at Serinhaém, however, proved to be the last which are known to have been imported into Brazil directly from Africa. When, in January 1856, the *Mary E. Smith* of New Orleans, carrying nearly 400 slaves aged between fifteen and twenty, arrived off the port of São Mateus on the border between Espírito Santo and Bahia, the Imperial steam brig *Olinda* was on the spot waiting for it. The vessel was taken to Bahia where it was found that 106 Africans had already died; the remainder were liberated after the vessel had been condemned but so bad was their condition that few survived for very long.[3] There were rumours in July 1857 that an attempt was about to be made to land slaves on the coast north of Pernambuco—in Rio Grande do Norte or even Paraíba—but the Brazilian government kept the area under careful surveillance and no evidence of any landing came to light.[4] By this time the traders had finally abandoned all hope of re-opening the Brazilian trade and were instead concentrating their energies on the illegal Cuban trade, which was to continue for another decade.

without reference home (Scarlett, 30 May 1856, F.O. 84/994), and believed Britain should demand a treaty giving her 'the right of search and of visiting without interruption and at all times every port in Brazil' (Scarlett no. 17, 15 December 1856, F.O. 84/994).

[1] Memorandum, 30 April 1856, F.O. 84/993.
[2] Hansard, cxliii. 1078–9, 21 July 1856.
[3] Jerningham no. 5, 8 February 1856, F.O. 84/993; Pierson, *Negroes in Brazil*, p. 37; Howard, *American Slavers and the Federal Law*, pp. 47, 124–6.
[4] Unsigned memorandum (Nabuco?), Informação sobre tráfico escravo, 21 July 1857, A.M.I.P. maço cxxiv, doc. 6208.

Aftermath of abolition

By the late 1850s, the Brazilian slave trade could be said to be well and truly dead.[1] Brazil's manpower problems, however, remained very much alive, although considerably less acute than they had been in the thirties and forties or than they were to become in the seventies and eighties with the spread of coffee plantations to the *terra roxa* of north-west São Paulo. In the long run, the cutting off of plentiful supplies of cheap slaves from Africa was bound to produce a serious *falta de braços* in Brazil and deal a major blow to the slave system itself. In the short term, however, the consequences of abolition on the supply of labour were mitigated by a number of new developments. In the first place, as abolitionists had always hoped and anticipated, the collapse of the slave trade convinced many plantation owners of the advantages to be gained by improving the conditions of life and work for the slaves they already owned. (They were also obliged to pay more attention to slave breeding, but this was never very successful if for no other reason than that seven out of every ten slaves in Brazil were male.[2]) Of more immediate importance, the ending of the transatlantic slave trade acted as a stimulus to the trade in slaves within Brazil, from urban to rural areas, from subsistence agriculture to the cultivation of export crops (coffee, sugar and cotton) for the international market and, despite all the efforts of the provincial authorities in Maranhão, Ceará, Pernambuco and Bahia to prohibit the inter-provincial slave trade, from the impoverished north and north-east (the 'new African coast') to the developing south. In his *Notas Estatisticas* published in 1860, Sebastião Ferreira Soares calculated that 26,622 slaves had been imported into Rio de Janeiro, city and province, from northern provinces during the years 1852–9:

1852	4,409	1856	5,006
1853	2,090	1857	4,211
1854	4,418	1858	1,993
1855	3,532	1859	963

[1] See, for example, the replies of British consuls and vice-consuls in Brazil—Vereker (Rio Grande do Sul), Callander (Santa Catarina), Westwood (Rio de Janeiro), Morgan (Bahia), Cowper (Pernambuco), Wilson (Maranhão)—to a circular requesting information on the state of the slave trade and the likelihood of its revival, collated in Christie to Russell, 2 June 1860, *B.F.S.P.* li, 1012–15.

[2] Stein, *Vassouras*, p. 76.

It was his view, however, that these figures were, if anything, rather conservative: an average annual influx of 5,500 slaves would, he felt, be a more accurate estimate.[1] In September 1862, W. D. Christie, the British minister in Rio de Janeiro, reported that 34,688 slaves had been imported by sea from northern provinces into the capital alone during the ten and a half years from January 1852 to July 1862 and he believed that many more had been transported by land.[2] This internal movement of the Brazilian slave population eventually led to a heavy concentration of slaves on the large plantations, and in particular on the coffee plantations of Rio de Janeiro, Minas Gerais, and São Paulo (*as provincias negreiras da nação*, as they came to be called) and this in turn, by reducing slightly the importance of slave labour to the Brazilian economy as a whole, was one of the factors, along with the progressive decline in the size of the slave population of working age and the decline in the slave population as a proportion of the total population, which combined to make the institution of slavery more vulnerable to attack in the second half of the nineteenth century.

Although during the 1850s the British government frequently protested at the inhumanity of the Brazilian coastal slave trade, since the *Piratinim* case (1851) the British navy had made a point of not interfering with the *legitimate* transfer of slaves from one part of Brazil to another. When, however, attempts were made to revive the old idea of importing free labour from Africa—a bill to promote free African immigration and the gradual extinction of slavery was introduced into the provincial legislature of Pernambuco in 1857, for example—the British government made it clear, as they had done on more than one occasion in the past, that such a move would be regarded, and treated, as a covert renewal of the slave trade, since 'the free African' would almost certainly be reduced to slavery when he arrived in Brazil. 'Vessels bringing such cargoes of [free] Africans to Brazil', Lord Clarendon empha-

---

[1] *Notas Estatisticas sobre a producção agricola e carestia dos generos alimenticios no imperio do Brazil* (Rio de Janeiro, 1860), pp. 135–6. Also Stein, *Vassouras*, p. 65: Estimated slave imports into Province of Rio from other provinces, 1852–9; Rodrigues, *Brazil and Africa*, p. 171, n. 142. Steamships of the Anglo-Luso-Brazilian Navigation Co. conveyed slaves from Northern ports to Rio (see Christie, *op. cit.* p. lvi).

[2] Christie, *op. cit.* p. 93.

tically declared in June 1857, 'would, unavoidably, be dealt with as slavers by British cruisers.'[1] Attempts to attract European immigrants to Brazil were an entirely different matter. European immigration was always seen by abolitionists in Britain as well as in Brazil as the ultimate solution to Brazil's labour problem. Once the slave trade had been finally abolished many coffee planters began to show an interest for the first time in the *parceria* system (a kind of share cropping) initiated in the forties by Senator Vergueiro in São Paulo, and, while trying to preserve and increase their slave labour force, at the same time set about recruiting and financing the transportation of European contract labourers.[2] The *parcerias* were eventually discredited—the Brazilian landowners, used only to slave labour, inevitably abused the system, and the immigrants themselves, unused to labour on semi-tropical plantations, were quickly disillusioned—and these early, tentative experiments in large-scale European immigration proved a failure. Nevertheless, during the 1850s, more than 130,000 Europeans—many of them German and Swiss (the most prominent immigrant groups in the days before abolition), but now more than half of them Portuguese—emigrated to Brazil:[3]

1850	2,072	1856	14,008
1851	4,425	1857	14,334
1852	2,731	1858	18,529
1853	10,935	1859	20,114
1854	18,646	1860	15,774
1855	11,798		

Most of them had contracts with *fazendeiros* in Rio de Janeiro province, but a considerable number went to São Paulo: whereas fewer than 50 European immigrants annually entered São Paulo during the period 1830–51, on average almost a thousand arrived each year from 1852 to 1857.[4] Thus, with a redeployment of the existing slave population and a marked increase in European

[1] Clarendon to Cowper, 8 June 1857, *B.F.S.P.* xlviii, 1135–6.
[2] See Viotti da Costa, *Da Senzala à Colônia*, pp. 78–83; *História Geral da Civilização Brasileira*, II, iii, pp. 158–62, 245–60; Thomas Davatz, *Memórias de um colono no Brasil (1850)* ed. Sérgio Buarque de Holanda (São Paulo, 1941).
[3] Statistics from José Fernando Carneiro, *Imigração e colonização no Brasil* (Rio de Janeiro, 1949), Appendix.
[4] Richard Morse, *From Community to Metropolis. A biography of São Paulo, Brazil* (Gainsville, 1958), p. 114.

immigration, the abolition of the slave trade did not have the immediately disastrous effect on the supply of labour available for the growth sectors of Brazilian agriculture, and therefore on the economy as a whole, that had been universally anticipated. On the contrary, with the continuing boom in Brazilian coffee production and exports, the 1850s was a golden decade for the Paraíba Valley.[1] There was an increase, too, in Brazilian sugar and cotton production, although less than that in coffee.[2] And it is frequently argued that, by releasing capital for investment in agriculture, commerce, transportation, urban services and manufacturing, the abolition of the slave trade actually provided a considerable stimulus to all-round economic development in Brazil during the period 1850–64.[3] This thesis, however, is one which demands more detailed investigation than it has hitherto been afforded.

In July 1858 the Brazilian minister in London again raised the issue of the Aberdeen Act which, though now entirely inoperative for many years, remained on the statute book—a major obstacle to improved Anglo-Brazilian relations. However, Lord Malmesbury, Foreign Secretary in a second and equally short-lived Derby administration (1858–9), informed him that only when a new anti-slave trade treaty had been signed and ratified would the British government propose to Parliament the repeal of the offending Act.[4] An attempt to force the government's hand was made by William Hutt who introduced into the House of Commons yet another motion urging the government finally to dismantle the anti-slave trade preventive system by withdrawing the West African squadron and by repealing the Act of 1845. It was generally

[1] See Stein, *Vassouras*, p. 53.
[2] See Ferreira Soares, *Notas estatísticas*, pp. 17–61 and Perdigão Malheiro, ii, pp. 67–8.
[3] On this interesting question, see Stein, *Vassouras*, pp. 20, 29, 52; Rodrigues, *Brazil and Africa*, pp. 192–3; Roberto Simonsen, 'As conseqüências econômicas da abolição', *Jornal do Comércio*, 8 May 1938; João Cruz Costa, *A History of Ideas in Brazil* (Univ. of Calif. Press, 1964), pp. 69, 77, 80 ('After 1850', Cruz Costa wrote, 'Brazil was on a completely new economic footing . . . [the suppression of the slave trade] unleashed forces of renewal in Brazil'). Important sources are Ferreira Soares, *Notas estatísticas* (1860), *Elementos do estatística* (1865), *Esboço ou Primeiros Traços da Crise Commercial do Rio de Janeiro em 10 de Setembro de 1864* (1865); *Relatório da comissão encarregada pelo Govêrno Imperial . . . de proceder a um Inquérito sôbre as causas principais e acidentais da crise do mês de setembro de 1864* (1865).
[4] Moreira to Malmesbury, 3 July, Malmesbury to Moreira, 7 July 1858, F.O. 84/1051.

felt, however, that the squadron was still needed for the suppression of the slave trade to Cuba (if no longer to Brazil) as well as for the protection of Britain's expanding commerce with west Africa. As for the Aberdeen Act, there was considerable support for the view again expressed by Lord Palmerston (temporarily in opposition) that any British government would be well advised to 'reserve it in power to be used in case the Brazilians should revert to their bad courses. So long as you have that Act in reserve, so long will the government of Brazil pursue the policy which you compelled them to adopt.'[1] Hutt's motion was defeated by 223 votes to 24, and for the time being Lord Aberdeen's Act continued in existence—to the intense irritation of Brazil.

In addition to the Aberdeen Act, two other aspects of the slave trade question continued to sour relations between Britain and Brazil for more than a decade after the trade itself had been suppressed. In the first place, Brazilian governments persisted with their claims for damages in a number of cases where Brazilian merchant vessels had in the past been illegally searched and captured by British cruisers. (Many of these claims referred back to the period before 1830 when several vessels equipped for the trade had been acquitted by the mixed commission in Sierra Leone, but never compensated for the losses they sustained; others concerned vessels captured since 1845 and condemned in British vice-admiralty courts—although the Brazilian government never carried to its logical conclusion their argument that *every* capture made under the Aberdeen Act was *per se* illegal.) In the course of the negotiations for a new treaty during the years 1852–3, Teixeira de Macedo, the Brazilian minister in London, had raised the question of Brazilian claims, but the British government as usual refused to recognise that they had any validity. At the same time there were other, miscellaneous Brazilian claims still outstanding against the British government, and Britain for its part was claiming damages totalling £250,000 in respect of losses sustained by British merchants as a result of the *Guerra da Independência* (1822–3), the Brazilian blockade of the Río de la Plata (1825–7),

---

[1] Hansard, cli. 1338, 12 July 1858. Lord Aberdeen was still not sure that the time was ripe to repeal his Act of 1845 although he remarked that Brazil's recent conduct entitled her to some consideration (Hansard, cl. 2211, House of Lords, 17 June 1858)

and the numerous provincial revolts during the thirties and forties, as well as excess duties which on occasion had been levied on British imports. It was in an effort to settle these claims that in June 1858 a Convention was signed establishing an Anglo-Brazilian mixed commission in Rio de Janeiro to which they could all be referred—although from the very outset there was a certain amount of uncertainty as to whether the Commission was empowered to deal with slave trade cases. In the event, Brazil submitted ninety-nine claims, most of them arising out of the slave trade, and totalling two million pounds. The British Commissioner, however, was instructed that no case of slave trading which had been dealt with originally either by an Anglo-Brazilian mixed commission or by a British vice-admiralty court could now be reviewed and, as a result, in March 1860 the Claims Commission was obliged to suspend its work almost before it had begun. Two years later the British government announced that it regarded the Commission as defunct since the Convention of 1858 had specified that all claims should be settled within a period of two years.[1]

The other issue which continued to bedevil Anglo-Brazilian relations during the fifties and early sixties was the fate of the *emancipados* or *Africanos livres*.[2] These—and there were several thousand of them—fell into two categories: first, illegally imported slaves who had been seized and liberated by the Brazilian authorities and, while awaiting repatriation, had been hired out as apprentices to private individuals; secondly, slaves who had been brought into Rio de Janeiro on board captured slave vessels, liberated by the mixed commission sitting there and, while under the protection of the Brazilian government, employed in public works or apprenticed to private individuals as servants and free labourers. It was a notorious fact that most *Africanos livres* ended up as slaves, and the unceasing efforts of the British legation in Rio to secure for them the freedom to which they were entitled and for which, at least in the case of those liberated by the mixed commission, Brazil was responsible to Britain, brought little

[1] The claims question has been dealt with in some detail in Christie, *op. cit.* pp. 140–54 and Manchester, *British Preeminence*, pp. 266–73.
[2] On the *emancipados* question, see Christie, pp. xxxiv–xlv, 1–50; Tavares Bastos, *Cartas do Solitario*, pp. 123–46.

result. By the late forties it was no longer possible to discover with any degree of certainty the number still alive, their whereabouts or their status. In 1851 the Brazilian government rejected a proposal put forward by Lord Palmerston for a mixed commission to investigate the whole question,[1] although in December 1853 they relented sufficiently to announce that 'free Africans' who had served as apprentices for fourteen years could now petition their masters for their release and their return to Africa.[2] But in practice this meant very little and further British representations on the subject went unheeded. What the decree of December 1853 did mean, however, was that by 1859 every African 'liberated' by the Rio mixed commission could demand his complete freedom (the commission had ceased to function in 1845, fourteen years previously), and the British legation took the opportunity to step up the pressure for their discovery and speedy release.

Of even greater concern to the Brazilian government than Britain's representations on behalf of a relatively small number of *emancipados* was the fact that the British government from time to time showed interest in the fate of the hundreds of thousands of slaves who had been imported into Brazil during the last twenty years of the Brazilian slave trade; not only was their importation into Brazil illegal under the terms of the Anglo-Brazilian abolition treaty which came into force in March 1830 but, according to the first article of the Brazilian law of November 1831, they—and their children—were legally free. In March 1850 during the House of Commons debate on the future of the West African squadron, Gladstone had declared 'we have . . . a perfect right to go to Brazil and call upon her to emancipate every slave imported since 1830 and, upon refusal, to make war with them (*sic*) even to extermination' (although he went on to express the hope that this right would not be exercised).[3] And, as we have seen, the inclusion of an agreement guaranteeing the freedom of Africans imported into Brazil after 1830 was for James Hudson a *sine qua non* of any new anti-slave trade treaty with Brazil.[4] Indeed, it became one of Britain's formal demands when treaty negotiations

[1] Palmerston to Hudson, 5 July 1851, printed in Christie, *op. cit.* pp. 203–5.
[2] Decree no. 1303, 28 December 1853, printed in Perdigão Malheiro, ii. 288.
[3] Hansard, cix. 1170, 19 March 1850.
[4] See above, p. 369.

were opened in London at the end of 1852. Teixeira de Macedo, however, pointed out that for Brazil to give way on this point would be equivalent to her emancipating the vast majority of Brazilian slaves of working age and could not fail to 'produce general revolution and annihilate the Brazilian Empire'. He therefore stated categorically that, regardless of the pressure exerted by Britain, 'in slavery they must remain (*na escravidão hão de ficar*)'.[1] When, in 1854, a Brazilian judge threatened to apply the law which declared the holding of slaves imported after 1831 illegal, Nabuco de Araújo, the Minister of Justice (1853–7), who was largely responsible for ensuring that the slave trade did not revive, made it known that the government were determined not to meddle in an issue which would undermine the very foundations of Brazilian society.[2] In the meantime, however, Britain continued to irritate the Brazilian government by raising the matter on every possible occasion.

Thus Anglo-Brazilian relations left much to be desired when in 1860, soon after Palmerston's resumption of the premiership in a new Whig-Liberal administration, William Dougal Christie arrived in Rio as British minister and made matters a good deal worse. A Palmerstonian diplomat—impulsive, arrogant, self-assertive, hostile towards 'inferior' and weaker nations who needed to be 'taught how to live', convinced that 'fear is the only effectual security for justice' and force the only instrument of political control[3]—Christie adopted a tough line on all the issues of the day: freedom for the *emancipados*, freedom for the slaves imported into Brazil since 1830, the rejection of Brazilian claims against the British government, and the continuation in force of the Aberdeen Act. But it was two relatively minor incidents (the first involving a merchant vessel, the *Prince of Wales*, and the second H.M.S. *Forte*)—both of which, to Christie's mind, demonstrated the inability of the Brazilian authorities to afford British lives and property adequate protection—which led first to a diplomatic quarrel and eventually to British reprisals in the shape of a six-day naval blockade of Rio de Janeiro (31 December 1862 to 5 January 1863) and the seizure of five Brazilian merchant vessels in Brazilian

[1] Macedo to Paulino, no. 18, 8 October 1852, Reservado, A.H.I. 217/3/7.
[2] Nabuco, *Um Estadista do Império*, i, 177.   [3] Christie, *op. cit.* liii, lxvii.

territorial waters. On this occasion, as on so many others in the past, Brazil had no alternative but to yield to British pressure, but when later in the year the British government refused either to make reparations or to apologise for the navy's violation of Brazilian sovereignty, the Brazilian government took the extreme step of breaking off diplomatic relations, a move which is usually regarded as marking a further stage in Brazil's gradual assertion of her independence from British political domination.[1] It was in the middle of the 'Christie Affair' that the Brazilian government at last took up the case of the *emancipados*—although whether, as Christie claimed, they acted in response to British pressure is not clear. Over 1,000 *emancipados* were released in the twelve months from September 1863 to August 1864 (more than had been freed during the entire period 1854–63).[2] The next step forward came in September 1864 when a law was passed emancipating all those who had served their fourteen years apprenticeship (that is, every slave freed by the Rio mixed commission and of those liberated by the Brazilian authorities all but a handful seized after the passage of the law of September 1850).[3] Unfortunately, by this time it was in practice almost impossible to differentiate between *emancipados* and slaves.

It was also in 1864 that the debate on the Aberdeen Act was resumed. In June in the House of Lords, Lord Brougham recommended the repeal of the Act; almost ten years had elapsed, he reminded the House, since a landing of slaves was known to have taken place in Brazil and he saw no reason to anticipate that there would be any more.[4] Even now, however, Lord Russell, Foreign Secretary in the Palmerston administration, was not to be persuaded that Brazil had spontaneously suppressed the trade and therefore remained convinced that 'if the Act were repealed the Brazilian slave trade would be revived'. And he was disinclined to grant Brazil any favours now that her government had chosen

[1] On the 'Christie Affair', see Manchester, *British Preeminence*, pp. 273–84 and Richard Graham, 'Os Fundamentos da Ruptura de Relações Diplomáticas Entre o Brasil e A Grã-Bretanha em 1863: "A Questão Christie"', *Revista de História* (São Paulo), no. 49 (1962), pp. 117–38, no. 50 (1962), pp. 379–402.
[2] Christie, *op. cit.* pp. xxxiv–xxxv.
[3] Law no. 3310, 24 September 1864, printed in Perdigão Malheiro, ii. 289; Pereira Pinto, i. 493–5.
[4] Hansard, clxxvi. 411, 28 June 1864.

to suspend diplomatic relations with Britain.[1] The matter was raised in the House of Commons the following month when John Bright again argued that the repeal of Aberdeen's 'offensive and illegal Act' would go a long way towards restoring the good Anglo-Brazilian relations which manufacturers, merchants, bankers and investors believed were essential if Britain's economic pre-eminence there were to continue and be further consolidated.[2] Replying for the government, Lord Palmerston conceded that the Act was 'a thorn in her [Brazil's] side', but he affirmed his belief that the slave trade could still revive and declared that, much as he valued Brazilian friendship and trade, 'if that were put in one side and the suppression of the slave trade in the other I should prefer the latter'.[3] It was at this time that W. D. Christie, who had returned to London in 1863, was writing his controversial *Notes on Brazilian Questions* which was published in the following year. Addressed to Lord Palmerston, it raised in a manner which could not fail to offend Brazilians many old issues including the fate of the 'free Africans', and the incidents which culminated in the British blockade of 1862-3, as well as, inevitably, the Aberdeen Act itself. On the future of the Act, Christie sided with those who claimed that Britain had promised to repeal it only when an effective anti-slave trade treaty was signed and argued that in the absence of such a treaty it should be retained as Britain's only insurance against a resumption of the slave trade, at least as long as slavery existed in Brazil and Brazilians showed no apparent disposition towards its abolition or even the mitigation of its more cruel features. 'Where slavery prevails', Christie pronounced, 'the slave trade is likely.'[4] It was a view which the British government seems to have shared. In March 1865 Palmerston stated categorically in the House of Commons that the government had no intention of introducing a bill for the repeal of the Aberdeen Act,[5] and neither a petition from the British Anti-Slavery Society in June[6] nor the restoration of diplomatic relations with Brazil in November induced them to alter their decision.

Times, however, were changing. Aberdeen, the author of the

---

[1] Hansard, clxxvi. 412–13. [2] *Ibid.* 1380–1, 12 July 1864.
[3] *Ibid.* 1385. [4] Christie, *op. cit.* xlv–xlvi, 51–66.
[5] Hansard, clxxvii. 1369–70, 9 March 1865.
[6] 30 June 1865, Broadlands MSS, SLT/37.

Act of 1845, died in 1860, Palmerston, its great champion, in 1865. A year later, Russell retired from political life. It was now fifteen years since the Brazilian slave trade had been crushed and in 1865, following the signing at long last of an Anglo-American right of search treaty (7 June 1862) and the rigorous enforcement by the Lincoln administration of American anti-slave trade legislation, the Cuban trade was also finally suppressed: the last remaining branch of the once flourishing transatlantic slave trade, it had, in its later stages, been pursued almost exclusively by American ships under the American flag.[1] At the same time the European powers continued to penetrate west Africa politically as well as commercially—Lagos was annexed by Britain in 1861—making a revival of the slave trade north of the equator increasingly difficult, and in Portuguese Africa, traditionally the main supplier of slaves to Brazil, efforts were being made to encourage legitimate commerce and to stamp out slavery (a decree of 1858 abolished slavery *after twenty years* throughout all Portuguese territories) although there remained a considerable gap between law and reality. Across the Atlantic slavery had been abolished in the United States during the Civil War and in Brazil, where there were still more than a million and a half slaves (half of them concentrated in the provinces of Rio de Janeiro, Minas Gerais and São Paulo), there were during the Paraguayan War (1865–70) encouraging signs that abolitionist sentiment was gaining ground in influential political circles. In August 1866, in response to a petition addressed by French abolitionists to the Emperor Dom Pedro, the Brazilian government announced that 'the emancipation of the slaves, *a necessary consequence of the abolition of slave trade*, is only a question of form and opportuneness'[2] (my italics). And the following May, in his *Falla do Throno*, Dom Pedro himself declared that while it was essential that existing property rights be respected and agriculture, 'our premier industry', not disrupted, the issue of slave emancipation

---

[1] See Warren S. Howard, *American Slavers and the Federal Law, 1837–1862* (Univ. of Calif. Press, 1963). For the abolitionist movement in Spain and the origins and passage of a new anti-slave trade law on 9 July 1866, see Arthur F. Corwin, *Spain and the Abolition of Slavery in Cuba, 1817–1886* (Univ. of Texas Press, 1967), pp. 177–81. Despite rumours that the Cuban slave trade was still being carried on, no slave ships were in fact captured after 1865 (*ibid.* pp. 182–3).

[2] Quoted in Percy A. Martin, 'Slavery and Abolition in Brazil', *H.A.H.R.* xiii (1933), p. 173. The reply had been drafted by Dom Pedro.

385

deserved careful consideration 'at an opportune time'.[1]
Indeed, prompted by the Emperor, the Council of State had
already begun to examine a number of proposals for the gradual
extinction of slavery in Brazil. At the end of the War the Conservative Rio Branco administration was to introduce a bill which
ensured that all children born of slave mothers would eventually
be free.[2] The Law of Free Birth,[3] finally enacted on 28 September
1871, after one of the most prolonged and passionate parliamentary battles of the nineteenth century, destroyed twenty years
after the suppression of the slave trade from Africa the second
vital source of slave supply, and for the first time made certain,
although by no means immediate, the end of slavery in Brazil.

It was in these circumstances that the Gladstone administration
which took office in 1868 came to the conclusion that the time
was now ripe to dismantle the system Britain had erected for the
suppression of the transatlantic slave trade. The West African
squadron, which had not captured any slave vessels for some years,
was not actually withdrawn—it still had an important role to play
in protecting British settlements from Gambia to Lagos and British
commercial interests along the west African coast, especially in
the Niger Delta and the Congo—but in 1869 it suffered a further
reduction in size and in 1870 was again merged with the Cape
squadron.[4] The few remaining mixed commissions were either
formally dissolved by treaty (as was the case with the Anglo-
Portuguese and Anglo-American commissions) or else they were
simply allowed to cease functioning. The mixed court at Freetown
which had dealt with only seven cases—four Spanish, two Uru-

[1] *Falla do Throno*, 22 May 1867.
[2] For the origins and passage of the Law of Free Birth, see Nabuco, *Um Estadista do Império*, i. 565–70, ii. 15–54; Viotti da Costa, *op. cit.* pp. 387–93; *História Geral da Civilização Brasileira* II, iii, pp. 206–10; Graham, *Britain and the Onset of Modernization in Brazil*, pp. 167–71. Among other aspects of the question, I hope to examine Professor Graham's interesting thesis that British pressure was largely responsible for the passage of the Law of 1871 and that the law was not so much 'the first evidence of an abolitionist campaign [in Brazil]' as 'the conclusion of the British phase of the story which had begun forty years earlier' in a second volume on the struggle for the abolition of slavery in Brazil.
[3] Law of 28 September 1871 printed in E. Bradford Burns, *Documentary History of Brazil*, pp. 257–63. Until they were eight years old children born of slave mothers were to remain with their mother's owners who then had the option of releasing them with indemnification or of retaining them as apprentices until they became twenty-one.
[4] See Newbury, *British Policy Towards West Africa*, pp. 595–600; Fyfe, *History of Sierra Leone*, p. 332.

guayan and one Dutch—since 1845 (compared with over five hundred between 1819 and 1845) was closed in 1871.[1] Despite the fact that Brazil had refused to the end to sign a new anti-slave trade treaty acceptable to Britain the British government, in April 1869, also repealed the Aberdeen Act. This gesture can be usefully taken to mark the end of the slave trade question and an important chapter in the history of Anglo-Brazilian relations,[2] although the dispute over Brazilian claims for damages arising from Britain's anti-slave trade blockade dragged on for several years (it was never satisfactorily settled) and many of the slaves illegally imported into Brazil after 1830—and their descendants—had to wait another twenty years before the law of 13 May 1888, which finally abolished slavery in Brazil, gave them their freedom.

[1] See Bethell, *Journal of African History* (1966), pp. 92–3.
[2] Although the Aberdeen Act had been repealed, the first article of the Anglo-Brazilian anti-slave trade treaty of 1826 upon which it was founded continued in force. It was 1921 before, by mutual agreement, it was finally abrogated. See Hugo Fischer, 'The Suppression of Slavery in International Law', *International Law Quarterly* iii (1950), pp. 47–8.

ESTIMATES OF SLAVES IMPORTED INTO BRAZIL, 1831–1855

No accurate estimate has ever, or can ever, be made of the number of slaves imported into Brazil after the entire slave trade had been declared illegal in 1830–1. One set of figures (relating to the period 1840–51 only) has, however, appeared again and again in books and articles dealing with, or touching upon, the Brazilian slave trade question in the nineteenth century:

1840	30,000	1846	50,324
1841	16,000	1847	56,172
1842	17,435	1848	60,000
1843	19,095	1849	54,000
1844	22,849	1850	23,000
1845	19,453	1851	3,287

Total (1840–51) 371,615

See, for example Alves, *R.I.H.G.B.* (1914), p. 232; Adams, *Journal of Negro History* (1925), p. 633; Manchester, *British Preeminence in Brazil* (1933), pp. 239–40, 256, 264; Taunay, *Subsídios Para a História do Tráfico* (1941), p. 292; Gomes, *R.I.H.G.B.* (1949), p. 34; Goulart, *Escravidão Africana no Brasil* (1950), pp. 249–63; Gouveia, *História da Escravidão* (1955), p. 118; Buarque de Holanda, *Raízes do Brasil* (3rd ed. 1956), p. 92; Stein, *Vassouras* (1957), p. 25; Sodré, *História da Burguesia Brasileira* (1964), p. 90; Rodrigues, *Brazil and Africa* (1965), pp. 159–60.

The history of these by now well-known statistics is of some interest. The figures for the years 1842–51 were first cited by three Brazilian authors writing in the 1860s soon after the suppression of the trade: Sebastião Ferreira Soares, *Notas Estatísticas* (1860), pp. 134–5 and *Elementos de Estatística* (1865), vol. I, pp. 227–8; Antônio Pereira Pinto, *Apontamentos para o Direito Internacional* (1864–9), vol. I, p. 365; Agostinho Marques Perdigão Malheiro, *A Escravidão no Brasil* (1867), vol. III, p. 49. Their immediate source was the *Relatório do Ministério dos Negócios Estrangeiros* (May 1853) p. 8. The Brazilian Foreign Ministry had taken them from British Parliamentary Papers, 1852, LV (201), p. 337, Return of the number of slaves embarked on the coast of Africa

Appendix

and landed in Cuba and Brazil, 1842–51. The figures for the years 1840–1 were first cited by another Brazilian writer of the sixties, A. C. Tavares Bastos in his *Cartas do Solitario* (1863), p. 175. He also gave figures for the years 1842–7 which were different from those presented by Ferreira Soares, Pereira Pinto and Perdigão Malheiro:

1842	12,200	1845	22,700
1843	30,500	1846	52,600
1844	28,000	1847	57,800

Tavares Bastos's sources were Paulino José Soares de Sousa's famous speech to the Chamber of Deputies on 15 July 1850 and Paulino's *Relatório* of May 1852. He was, however, guilty of some slight errors of transcription. The figures quoted by Paulino were

1840	30,000	1844	26,000
1841	16,000	1845	22,700
1842	14,200	1846	52,600
1843	30,500	1847	57,800

Paulino himself had taken these figures from British Parliamentary Papers, 1847–8, xxII (623), Select Committee of the House of Commons on the Slave Trade, 3rd Report, Appendix 4, Number 2, Memoranda of the number of slaves computed to have been exported and imported westward from Africa 1840–1848 (the work of James Bandinel, former superintendent of the Slave Trade Department of the Foreign Office). Thus most historians have taken one complete set of figures for the years 1842–51 and, for want of any others, figures for the years 1840–1 from another slightly higher and apparently less convincing set relating to the period 1840–7. Rodrigues, who, like Taunay, presents both sets of figures, refers to those used by Ferreira Soares *et al.* as 'Brazilian statistics' and those used by Tavares Bastos as 'English statistics', when in reality *all* these figures first appeared in British Parliamentary Papers. The Brazilian government produced no slave trade statistics of their own; they simply reproduced British estimates of slaves illegally imported into Brazil.

A third, earlier, calculation by the Slave Trade Department of the Foreign Office of the slaves landed in Brazil between 1817 and 1843 (16 July 1844, F.O. memorandum, F.O. 97/430) has not been given the attention it deserves. It provides different and lower figures for the years 1840–1 from those widely accepted and, even more important, valuable estimates of slaves imported during the eighteen thirties:

389

Appendix

1831	138	1838	40,256
1832	116	1839	42,182
1833	1,233	1840	20,796
1834	749	1841	13,804
1835	745	1842	17,435
1836	4,966	1843	19,095
1837	35,209		

In 1864, long after the trade had been suppressed, a final estimate of the number of slaves landed in Brazil since 1817 was made (4 August 1864, F.O. memorandum, Broadlands MSS, SLT/36). The last official word on the subject, it took the figures for 1831–1843 put forward in the Memorandum of July 1844, the figures for 1842–51 from the 1852 parliamentary return (with slightly more precise estimates for 1849–50) and added figures for the years after 1851.

1831	138	1839	42,182	1847	56,172
1832	116	1840	20,796	1848	60,000
1833	1,233	1841	13,804	1849	54,061
1834	749	1842	17,435	1850	22,856
1835	745	1843	19,095	1851	3,287
1836	4,966	1844	22,849	1852	800
1837	35,209	1845	19,453	1853	—
1838	40,256	1846	50,324	1854	—
				1855	90

Total (1831–55) 486,616

Lloyd, *The Navy and the Slave Trade* (1949), Appendix A, took the 1864 figures for the years after 1847 but for some reason almost alone clung to Bandinel's estimates for the years 1840–7 which the Foreign Office had now repudiated.

These various estimates of the size of the Brazilian slave trade made by the Slave Trade Department of the Foreign Office were all based (although occasionally it would seem only very loosely based) on information sent in from time to time by members of the British legation in Rio de Janeiro, the British commissioners in the mixed court at Rio de Janeiro and British consuls and vice-consuls, especially those in Rio de Janeiro, Bahia and Pernambuco. Despite the remarkably open nature of the illegal slave trade and the efforts made to gather information on slaves landed from every possible source (including the use of paid informers) it should be noted that this information was always, of course, necessarily less than complete and, where the informants ventured beyond the known (or strongly rumoured), often highly speculative.

Appendix

Abstract of information on the importation of slaves sent to the Foreign Office in London from the British legation, the mixed commission and British consulates in Brazil

1831–6. After the trade had almost come to a standstill in the middle of 1830 only a few successful landings of slaves were reported during the next three years and it was impossible to estimate even the approximate number. From the end of 1833 a sharp increase in the number of imports was reported (e.g. Jackson and Grigg to Palmerston, 12 November 1833, F.O. 84/138; Fox to Palmerston, 24 July 1834, F.O. 84/157). 32 ships were reported to have left Rio de Janeiro for Africa during 1834 (Jackson and Grigg, no. 15, 23 March 1835, F.O. 84/174). Throughout 1835–6 the trade all along the coast, and especially between Santos and Campos, was reported to be growing rapidly (e.g. Ouseley to Palmerston, no. 2, 31 January 1836, F.O. 84/204; Jackson and Grigg, no. 13, 18 May 1836, F.O. 84/198). Between July 1835 and June 1836 over 100 ships were said to have left the Rio area for Africa and at least 20 were known to have landed slaves (Jackson and Grigg, no. 24, 30 September 1836, F.O. 84/199). In the last quarter of 1836, 36 ships left for Africa and 29 were known to have landed slaves (Hamilton to Palmerston, no. 12, 11 November 1836, F.O. 84/204). In the last six weeks of 1836, 14 ships landed 6,150 slaves in the Rio area (Hamilton no. 15, 19 December 1836, F.O. 84/204; Hamilton no. 1, 17 January 1837, F.O. 84/222). No precise figures for Bahia, Pernambuco, Maranhão etc. [It would seem, therefore, that official British statistics considerably underestimated the trade during the years 1831–6, and especially 1835–6.]

1837. 41,917 slaves landed from 93 ships between Campos and Santos, and at least 3,500 more estimated to have been landed during the third quarter of the year (British legation, monthly returns, F.O. 84/222–4, 252).

90 landings of slaves (British commissioners, monthly returns, F.O. 84/218–19).

Approximately 46,00 landed to the north and south of Rio de Janeiro from 92 ships (Gordon no. 4, 28 February 18,8, F.O. 84/252). No figures for Bahia etc. [Again the official statistics seem to have underestimated the trade.]

1838. 36,974 slaves between Campos and Santos from 84 ships (British legation, monthly returns, F.O. 84/252–4, 285). Ouseley, however,

391

Appendix

regularly commented on the fact that ships were now landing slaves in more remote spots and refitting in smaller ports along the coast rather than in Rio. In August he wrote of his July return: '[it] by no means embraces the whole number of slave vessels that have probably succeeded in landing their cargoes in the province of Rio de Janeiro, but those only which have been ascertained to have landed in the immediate neighbourhood of this capital'.

24,790 slaves between Campos and Paranaguá from 59 ships, but probably as many as 18,000 more (Samo and Grigg, no. 25, 17 July 1843: Report on 1838–42, F.O. 84/454; also Hesketh no. 10, 8 August 1843, F.O. 84/470).

No figures for other areas.

1839. 28,643 slaves between Campos and Santos from 66 ships, more than half between January and April, and none in August or September (British legation, monthly returns, F.O. 84/285–8, 323).

35,000 between Campos and Santos from 68 ships, estimated from the tonnage of the ships known to have arrived from Africa (Jackson and Grigg, no. 5, 20 January 1840, F.O. 84/314).

30,290 between Campos and Paranaguá from 64 ships (Samo and Grigg, Report on 1838–42, F.O. 84/454).

No figures for other areas.

1840. 14,910 slaves between Campos and Paranaguá from 28 ships (Samo and Grigg, Report on 1838–42, F.O. 84/454).

3,800 between Campos and Santos from 10 ships, and probably at least 1,000 more, January–August (British legation, monthly returns, F.O. 84/323–5).

5,322 between Campos and Santos from 18 ships, July–December, estimated from tonnage of ships arriving from Africa (British commissioners, monthly returns, F.O. 84/315–16).

1,413 slaves landed in Bahia (Porter no. 14, 31 December 1847, F.O. 84/679).

1841. 8,370 slaves between Campos and Paranaguá from 20 ships, and probably more (Samo and Grigg, Report on 1838–42, F.O. 84/454).

1,470 in Bahia (Porter no. 14, F.O. 84/679).

[Bandinel for the House of Commons Select Committee on the Slave Trade (1848) would certainly seem therefore to have overestimated the size of the trade during the years 1840–1 and thus to have misled later historians.]

Appendix

1842. 8,894 between Campos and Paranaguá from 20 ships (Samo and Grigg, Report on 1838–42, F.O. 84/454). There is some evidence, however, that the trade had begun a considerable revival before the end of the year (e.g. in April 1843 Hamilton told the Brazilian Foreign Minister that from November 1842 to March 1843, 39 ships were known to have landed between 11,700 slaves, if they carried approx. 300 each, and 17,550 slaves if, as seemed more likely, they carried 450 each (Hamilton to Honório, 7 April 1843, enclosed in Hamilton no. 10, 12 April 1843, F.O. 84/467).

2,520 slaves in Bahia (Porter no. 14, F.O. 84/679).

1843. 14,891 slaves between Campos and Santos from 37 ships, but a more accurate figure might be at least 30,000 and possibly 40,000 (Samo and Grigg, no. 8, 20 February 1844: Report on 1843, F.O. 84/510).

3,111 in Bahia (Porter no. 14, F.O. 84/679).

[If the British commissioners' speculations were correct Bandinel's figure of 30,500 for 1843 may be nearer the truth than the modified (1852) figure of 19,095 given in the 1852 Parliamentary Return.]

1844. 16,218 slaves between Campos and Santos from 43 ships, but many landings had been missed and the trade was probably more extensive than in 1843 (Hesketh and Grigg, 21 March 1845: Report on 1844, F.O. 84/563).

6,501 landed in Bahia (Porter no. 14, F.O. 84/679).

[The 1852 figure of 26,000 allows for landings not reported; Bandinel's figure of 22,849 does not.]

1845. 13,459 slaves between Campos and Santos from 36 ships but 16,000 would be a more accurate estimate; the trade was less extensive than in 1844 (Hesketh and Grigg, 11 March 1846; Report on 1845, F.O. 84/622).

5,582 in Bahia (Porter no. 14, F.O. 84/679).

[Again the 1852 Return allows for landings not reported; Bandinel does not.]

1846. 42,500 slaves between Campos and Santos with a large proportion landed during the last quarter (Hesketh to Palmerston, 19 February 1847: Report on 1846, F.O. 84/679).

7,354 in Bahia (Porter no. 14, F.O. 84/679).

Appendix

1847. 46,000 slaves between Campos and Santos and probably more (Westwood 17 February 1848: Report on 1847, F.O. 84/727).

23,500 between Campos and Santos, July–December (Hudson no. 8, 11 January 1851, F.O. 84/843).

10,064 in Bahia (Porter no. 14, F.O. 84/679; Porter no. 1, 13 February 1851, F.O. 84/848).

300 in Pernambuco (Christophers no. 1, 29 January 1851, F.O. 84/849).

60,000 imported into Brazil (Howden no. 6, 9 February 1848, F.O. 84/726).

1848. 22,307 slaves between Campos and Santos from 40 ships, but probably 35,000 or more (Westwood no. 4, 28 February 1849: Report on 1848, F.O. 84/767).

27,750 between Campos and Santos July–December (Hudson no. 8, F.O. 84/843).

7,299 in Bahia (Porter no. 17, 31 December 1849, F.O. 84/767; Porter no. 1, 13 February 1851, F.O. 84/848).

60,000 imported into Brazil (Hudson no. 12, 9 June 1849, F.O. 84/765).

1849. 40,980 slaves between Vitória and Paranaguá from 72 ships, but probably at least 5,000 more (Hesketh no. 3, 14 March 1850: Report on 1849, F.O. 84/808).

22,098 between Campos and Santos, July–December (Hudson no. 8, F.O. 84/843).

8,081 in Bahia (Porter no. 17, F.O. 84/767; Porter no. 1, F.O. 84/848).

450 in Pernambuco (Christophers no. 1, F.O. 84/849).

1850. 13,372 slaves between Campos and Santos from 25 ships—8,012 during the first half of the year, 5,360 during the second (Hesketh no. 2, 8 February 1851: Report on 1850, F.O. 84/848; Hudson no. 11, 11 February 1851, F.O. 84/843).

9,451 in Bahia—4,292 during the first half of the year, 5,159 during the second, 8,301 between January and September (Porter no. 1, F.O. 84/848).

2,300 in Pernambuco—800 during the first half of the year, 1,500 during the second (Christophers no. 1, F.O. 84/849).

1851. 3,200 slaves imported into Brazil from 9 ships—2 landings (one in Rio de Janeiro, one in Rio Grande do Sul) January–March, 3 landings

394

Appendix

(one in Rio, one in Rio Grande do Sul, one in Alagoas) April–June, 3 landings (two in Rio de Janeiro, one at Ilheus, Bahia) July–September, 1 landing in Bahia (the *Relampago*) October–December (Hudson no. 62, 11 April, no. 70, 12 May, no. 80, 14 July, no. 116, 14 October, no. 128, 11 December 1851, F.O. 84/844–7). Also rumours of landings at Santa Catarina.

1852. 700–800 slaves imported into Brazil from 2 ships—one landing in April in Rio Grande do Sul (the *Palmeira*), one landing in December at Bracuhy, Ilha Grande, Rio province (the *Carmargo*).

1853. None.

1854. None.

1855. Rumours of landings in September never completely substantiated. 200–240 slaves landed near Serinhaém (Pernambuco) in October.

From the above statistics—the only statistics available—the fluctuations in the volume of the illegal Brazilian slave trade become clear: after a slow but steady growth during the first quarter of the nineteenth century followed by a sudden acceleration during the years 1827–30 (prior to total prohibition), the trade almost came to a standstill during the early thirties, expanded again during the mid-thirties until it reached a peak during the years 1837–9, suffered a setback during the period from the middle of 1839 to the middle of 1842, grew steadily during the mid-forties until it reached another peak during the years 1846–9, and was finally suppressed during the years 1850–1.

500,000, and possibly more, slaves would seem to have been imported into Brazil (all of them illegally) after 1830. At least an equal number—and probably as many as 750,000—had been imported (after 1815 those originating from Africa north of the equator illegally imported) between 1800 and 1830. Thus Brazil imported well over one million slaves (half of them illegally) during the first half of the nineteenth century compared with an estimated three million slaves during the previous 300 years.

BIBLIOGRAPHY

A. PRIMARY SOURCES

(i) MANUSCRIPT

Public Record Office, London

Foreign Office 84 (Slave Trade)

Brazil: legation and consular, 1823–56, vols. 24, 31, 42, 55–7, 71, 84, 95, 111–12, 122, 130, 141, 156–7, 179–80, 204, 222–3, 252–5, 285–9, 323–6, 364–8, 406–11, 467–70, 523–6, 581–4, 632–4, 677–9, 725–7, 765–7, 801–9, 842–9, 877–80, 910–12, 941–4, 968–9, 993–4.

Portugal: legation, 1834–42, vols. 158, 178, 202–3, 215, 248–51, 281–4, 320–2, 361–3, 403–5.

Admiralty, 1839–53, vols. 301–3, 338–40, 383–5, 436–43, 492–8, 547–51, 606–12, 655–60, 701–6, 744–9, 781–5, 823–8, 863–6, 891–5, 924–6.

Sierra Leone mixed commission (General, Brazil, Portugal) and Sierra Leone vice-admiralty court, 1819–54, vols. 3–4, 9–11, 14–16, 21–2, 28, 38, 48–9, 63–4, 65–6, 76–7, 79, 87–8, 90, 101–3, 105, 116–18, 127, 134–5, 146–7, 149, 165–6, 169, 188–9, 194, 211–12, 214, 230–1, 235–8, 266–73, 307–11, 343–6, 390–3, 448–50, 503–7, 556–60, 618–19, 664–6, 711–13, 752, 788, 831, 869, 897, 928.

Rio de Janeiro mixed commission, 1819–46, vols. 5, 12, 17, 23, 30, 40, 53, 69, 82, 93, 108, 120, 129, 138, 152–3, 173–5, 198–9, 218–19, 241–2, 275–7, 313–16, 350–1, 397–8, 453–4, 510–11, 563–4, 622.

Loanda mixed commission, 1843–53, vols. 461, 517, 569–72, 626–7, 671–2, 719–20, 757–9, 792–5, 834–5, 872, 902.

Cape of Good Hope mixed commission and vice-admiralty court, 1843–53, vols. 457–8, 514–15, 566–7, 623, 669, 717, 755, 790, 833, 871, 901.

St Helena vice-admiralty court, 1846–53, vols. 651, 696, 738, 776, 817, 859, 887, 921.

Domestic various, 1829–30, vols. 96–100, 113–15, 1837–42, vols. 227–9, 261–5, 305, 342, 388–9, 446–7, 1845, vols., 615–16.

Foreign and Domestic, 1844–6, vols. 542, 600, 650, 1849–52, vols., 777, 818–19, 860, 887.

Slave Trade Returns and Memoranda, vol. 445.

Bibliography

Slave Trade Estimates (mixed commission expenses), 1846–64, vol. 1234.

Foreign Office 97 (Supplementary to General Correspondence: Slave Trade)
Abstracts and memoranda, 1845–52, vol. 430.
Drafts of Brazilian (1847–52) and U.S. (1862) slave trade treaties, vol. 431.
Treaties with native chiefs, 1818–61, vol. 432.

Foreign Office 96 (Cabinet and Slave Trade memoranda)
Minutes, memoranda etc.: Palmerston, 1830–50, vols. 17–23.
Draft despatches, memoranda, 1833–51, vols. 28–30.

Foreign Office 83 (Great Britain and General)
Law Officers' Reports: Slave Trade, 1817–55, vols. 2343–56.

Foreign Office 63 (General Correspondence: Portugal)
Correspondence between London and Consulate in Rio de Janeiro, 1822–4, vols. 245–7, 257–61, 275–9.

Foreign Office 13 (General Correspondence: Brazil)
Correspondence between London and Rio de Janeiro, 1825–6, vols. 1–11, 17–26.
Domestic various, 1825–6, vols. 14–16, 32–4.
Correspondence between London and Rio de Janeiro, 1842–3, vols. 178–85, 193–5, 199–200; 1845–8, vols., 227, 234, 244–6, 250, 255, 257; 1850, vols., 274–5.

Foreign Office 128 (Rio de Janeiro legation archives: correspondence)
Letters and papers relating to slave trade, 1842–3, vol. 39.
Letters and papers relating to slave trade, 1847–60, vol. 48.

Foreign Office 129 (Rio de Janeiro legation archives: letter books)
Mixed commission: slave trade, 1819–46, vols. 3–13.

Foreign Office 131 (Rio de Janeiro legation: miscellanea)
Slave Trade etc. various, 1820–45, vols. 1–12.

Foreign Office 315 (Slave Trade: Sierra Leone)
Mixed commission archives, 1819–59, vols. 1–9, 12–15, 17–19, 24

Gifts and Deposits 30/22 (Russell Papers)
1838–40, vols. 3 A–E, 1848–51, vols. 7 A–F, 8 A–G, 9 A–K.

Bibliography

British Museum
Aberdeen Papers

Add MSS. 43124, Brazil 1841–8.

Add MSS. 43125, Slave Trade with Brazil, 1825–46.

Add MSS. 43357, Confidential Cabinet memoranda and papers: slave trade.

Add MSS. 43061–5, Peel correspondence, 1841–6.

Add MSS. 43158–60, Letter Books, Brazil, 1842–5.

Add MSS. 43243–6, General correspondence, 1844–8.

Peel Papers

Add MSS. 40453–5, Aberdeen correspondence, 1841–6.

Add MSS. 43754, Hobhouse diary, vol. XI (March–September 1850).

National Register of Archives, London
Palmerston Papers

Broadlands MSS. GC/HO/362–655, 748–854. Correspondence with Lord Howard de Walden, 1834–1842.

Broadlands MSS. GC/HO/877–914, 951–5. Correspondence with Lord Howden, 1847–8.

Broadlands MSS. GC/HU/1–40, 43–52. Correspondence with James Hudson, 1846–51.

Broadlands MSS. GC/OU/17–41. Correspondence with William Gore Ouseley, 1833–9.

Broadlands MSS. GC/RU/171–459, 1033–101. Correspondence with Lord John Russell, 1848–51.

Broadlands MSS. GC/BA/275–306, 310–15. Correspondence with Sir Francis Baring, 1849–51.

Broadlands MSS. SLT/1–37. Slave Trade Memoranda.

City Library, Leeds
Canning Papers

Box 70, correspondence with Lord Liverpool, November 1822–February 1823.

Box 104, correspondence with Duke of Wellington, October–November 1822.

Box 80a, correspondence with William Wilberforce, October–November 1822.

Box 106, correspondence with Lord Bathurst, 1822–7.

Bibliography

Box 109, correspondence with Sir Charles Stuart, 1825–6.
Box 126, correspondence with Robert Gordon, 1826.
Box 80, correspondence with Lord Amherst, 1823.
Boxes 117, 118, 119, correspondence with William A'Court, 1824–6.
Box 68, correspondence with William Huskisson, 1825–6.
Box 130, correspondence with Duc de Palmella and Conde de Villa Real, 1824–5.
Box 132, correspondence with General Brant, 1823–6.

Arquivo Histórico do Itamaratí, Rio de Janeiro

Correspondence to and from legation in London, 1822–56, vols. 216/1/1–15, 216/2/1–16, 218/4/1, 2, 6, 7, 219/1/1.
Confidential correspondence, vols., 217/3/1–10.
Letter books, vols. 268/1/14–18.
Correspondence with British legation in Rio de Janeiro, 1830–51, vols. 284/2/14, 15, 284/3/1–16, 284/4/1–7, 285/3/9–15.

Special mission archives (Brazilian and foreign):
Sir Charles Stuart (1825–6), vols. 273/1/6–8, Marquês de Barbacena (1828–36), vol. 271/4/5, Henry Ellis (1842–3), vol. 273/1/9, José de Araújo Ribeiro (1843), vol. 271/4/6, Visconde de Abrantes (1844–6), vols. 217/1/2–4.

Correspondence with mixed commission in Rio de Janeiro, 1819–46, vols. 51/4, 5, 52/1–3, 53/1–3, 54/1–4, 55/1–4, 56/1–4, 57/1.
Correspondence with mixed commission in Sierra Leone, 1819–46, vols. 57/2, 3.
Correspondence with Brazilian consuls in St Helena, 1846–52, vols. 263/2/9, 263/2/11.
Council of State, *Consultas*, 342/1/1–6, 12, 15, 342/2/1, 6, 11–13, Correspondence, 342/3/11, 12, 14, 17, 19–21.

Arquivo Nacional, Rio de Janeiro

Códice 184, vols. 1–2, Rio mixed commission, minute books, 1819–40.
Códice 307, vols. 1–2, *Actas* of the full Council of State, 1842–57.
Códice 50, vols. 1–2, Correspondence of ministers with the Council of State, 1841–52.
Códice 302, vol. 1, Register of *Avisos* to Councillors of State, 1844–55.
IJ⁶–525 (Report of 'Alcoforado' on the slave trade, October 1853.

Bibliography

Arquivo do Museu Imperial, Petrópolis
Miscellaneous papers, especially correspondence between Paulino Soares de Sousa and Dom Pedro II, January 1851, maço 115.

Instituto Histórico e Geográfico Brasileiro, Rio de Janeiro
Arq. 2. 3. 12, Coleção de documentos (transcrições manuscritas, impressos, recortes de jornal) de providências legislativas, tratados, convenções e negociações diplomáticas (principalmente com a Inglaterra) sôbre a abolição do tráfico de escravos (1690–1865).

(ii) PRINTED

Anais do Parlamento Brasileiro. Câmara dos Deputados.
Anais do Senado do Império do Brasil.
Archivo Diplomatico da Independencia (6 vols., Rio de Janeiro, 1922–5).
Aurora Fluminense (Rio de Janeiro), 1829–34.
Bandinel, James, *Some account of the trade in slaves from Africa, especially with reference to the efforts of the British government for its extinction. A memoir to Lord Aberdeen* (London, 1842).
Biker, Julio Firmino Judice, *Supplemento a Collecção dos Tratados, Convenções, Contratos e Actos Publicos celebrados entre a Coroa de Portugal e as mais Potencias desde 1640 compilado pelo Visconde de Borges de Castro* (Lisbon, 1872–9).
British and Foreign State Papers, 1812– (London, 1841–).
Burns, E. Bradford, *A Documentary History of Brazil* (New York, 1966).
'Cartas sôbre a Independência, 1822–3', *Publicações do Arquivo Nacional* no. 7 (Rio de Janeiro, 1907), pp. 235–359.
Complete Collection of the Treaties and Conventions, and Reciprocal Regulations at present subsisting between Great Britain and Foreign Powers . . . compiled by Lewis Hertslet (8 vols., London 1835–51).
Correio Mercantil (Rio de Janeiro), 1848–52.
Correspondence of William Wilberforce ed. R. I. and S. Wilberforce (2 vols., London, 1840).
Daily News (London), 1850–1.
Despatches, Correspondence and Memoranda of the Duke of Wellington ed. by his son (8 vols., London, 1867–80).
Dodson, J., *Reports of cases argued and determined in the High Court of Admiralty* (2 vols., London, 1815–28).

Bibliography

Early Correspondence of Lord John Russell, 1805–1840 (2 vols., London, 1913).

Fallas do Throno desde o anno de 1823 até o anno de 1889 (Rio de Janeiro, 1889).

Hansard's *Parliamentary Debates*, 3rd series.

Imperiais Resoluções tomadas sobre consultas da Secção de Justiça do Conselho de Estado. Part I, 1842–63 (Rio de Janeiro, 1884).

Instructions for the Guidance of Her Majesty's Naval Officers employed in the Suppression of the Slave Trade (London, 1844).

Jornal do Comércio (Rio de Janeiro), 1837–53.

Manning, W. R., ed., *Diplomatic Correspondence of the United States. Inter-American Affairs, 1831–60* (12 vols., Washington, 1932–9).

Missão Especial do Visconde de Abrantes, 1844–6 (Rio de Janeiro, 1853).

Newbury, C. W. (ed.), *British Policy towards West Africa. Select Documents, 1786–1874* (Oxford, 1965).

Organizações e Programmas Ministeriais. Regime Parlamentar no Império (1889: 2nd ed., Rio de Janeiro, 1962).

Paranhos da Silva, José, *Cartas ao Amigo Ausente*, ed. José Honório Rodrigues (Rio de Janeiro, 1953).

Parliamentary Papers, 1847–8, XXII (272), (366), (536), (623). Four Reports of the House of Commons Select Committee on the Suppression of the Slave Trade.

P.P. 1849, XIX (309), (410), Two further reports of the House of Commons Select Committee.

P.P. (Lords) 1849, XVIII (32), Report of House of Lords Select Committee on the Slave Trade.

P.P. (Lords) 1850, XXIV (35), Second report of House of Lords Select Committee.

P.P. 1852–3, XXXIX (920), Report of the House of Commons Select Committee on the Slave Trade Treaties.

Pereira Pinto, Antônio, *Apontamentos para o Direito Internacional, ou Collecção Completa dos Tratados celebrados pelo Brazil com differentes Nações Estrangeiras* (4 vols., Rio de Janeiro, 1864–69).

Proceedings of the General Anti-Slavery Conventions called by the British and Foreign Anti-Slavery Society (London, 1841, 1843).

Relatórios do Ministério dos Negócios Estrangeiros apresentados à Assembléia Geral Legislativa, Rio de Janeiro, 1833–56.

Relatórios do Ministério da Justiça, Rio de Janeiro, 1832–52.

Some Official Correspondence of George Canning, ed. Edward J. Stapleton (2 vols. London, 1887).

The Times, 1839–1852.

Bibliography

Webster, C. K., ed., *Britain and the Independence of Latin America, 1812–1830. Select Documents from the Foreign Office Archives* (2 vols., London, 1938).

Contemporary Memoirs, Books, Pamphlets and Speeches

Allen, W., *Plan for the Immediate Extinction of the Slave Trade* (London, 1849).

Almeida, Tito Franco de, *O Brazil e a Inglaterra: ou o trafico de Africanos* (Rio de Janeiro, 1868).

Andrada e Silva, José Bonifácio de, *Representação a Assembleia-Geral Constituinte e Legislativa do Imperio do Brazil sobre a Escravatura* (Paris, 1825).

Armitage, John, *The History of Brazil from the Period of the Arrival of the Braganza Family in 1808 to the Abdication of Dom Pedro the First in 1831* (2 vols., London, 1836).

Arnould, Sir Joseph, *Memoir of Thomas, First Lord Denman* (2 vols., London, 1873).

Ashley, A. E. M., *The Life of Henry John Temple, Viscount Palmerston, 1846–1865* (2 vols., London, 1876).

Azeredo Coutinho, J. J. da Cunha de, *Analyse sobre a justiça do commercio do resgate dos escravos da Costa da Africa* (2nd ed., Lisbon, 1808).

Barreto, Domingos Alves Branco Moniz, *Memoria sobre a abolição do commercio de escravatura* (Rio de Janeiro, 1837).

Brasahemeco, Ananias Dortano, *Rights of Portugal, in reference to Great Britain, and the Question of the Slave Trade* (2 vols., Lisbon, 1840).

Burlamaque, F. L. C., *Memoria analytica acerca do commercio de escravos e acerca dos males da escravidão domestica* (Rio de Janeiro, 1837).

Buxton, C. (ed.), *Memoirs of Sir Thomas Fowell Buxton* (2nd ed., London, 1849).

Buxton, Thomas Fowell, *The African Slave Trade and its Remedy* (2nd ed., London, 1840).

Candler, John, and Burgess, William, *Narrative of a Recent Visit to Brazil to present an address on the Slave Trade and Slavery* (London, 1853).

[The] *Case of England and Brazil and the slave trade, stated—by a Brazilian merchant—with introduction and notes by an English merchant* (London, 1851).

Cave, S., *A Few Words on the encouragement given to Slavery and the Slave Trade by recent measures and chiefly by the Sugar Bill of 1846* (London, 1849).

Christie, W. D., *Notes on Brazilian Questions* (London, 1865).

Bibliography

Clarkson, T., *History of the Rise, Progress and Accomplishment of the Abolition of the African Slave Trade by the British Parliament* (1808: 2nd ed., London, 1839).

Costa, J. Severiano Maciel da, *Memoria sobre a necessidade de abolir a introducção dos escravos africanos no Brazil* (Coimbra, 1821).

Davatz, Thomas, *Memórias de um colono no Brasil (1850)*, ed. Sérgio Buarque de Holanda (São Paulo, 1941).

Denman, Capt. Joseph, *Practical Remarks on the slave trade with the west coast of Africa, with notes on the Portuguese treaty* (London, 1839).

West Indian Interests, African Emigration and the Slave Trade (London, 1848).

The Slave Trade, the African Squadron and Mr. Hutt's Committee (London, 1850).

Denman, Lord (Thomas), *A Letter to Brougham on the Final Extinction of the Slave Trade* (London, 1848).

A Second Letter to Brougham on the Final Extinction of the Slave Trade (London, 1849).

Ewbank, Thomas, *Life in Brazil; or a journal of a visit to the land of the cocoa and the palm* (New York, 1856).

Ferreira Soares, S., *Elementos de estatistica comprehendendo a theoria da sciencia e a sua applicação a estatistica commercial do Brazil* (2 vols., Rio de Janeiro, 1865).

Notas estatisticas sobre a producção agricola e carestia dos generos alimenticios no imperio do Brazil (Rio de Janeiro, 1860).

Forbes, F. E., *Six months service in the West African Blockade* (London, 1849).

[The] *Foreign Slave Trade, a brief account of its state, of the treaties which have been entered into, and of the laws enacted for its suppression, from the date of the English abolition act to the present time* (London, 1837).

Gardner, George, *Travels in the interior of Brazil, principally through the northern provinces, and the Gold and Diamond districts, during the years 1836–41* (London, 1846).

Greg, W. R., *Past and Present efforts for the extinction of the African Slave Trade* (London, 1840).

Greville Memoirs, 1814–1860, ed. by Lytton Strachey and Roger Fulford (London, 1938), vol. VI.

Hill, P. G., *Fifty days on board a slave vessel in the Mozambique Channel in April and May 1843* (London, 1844).

A voyage to the slave coasts of West and East Africa (London, 1849).

Hobhouse, J. C. (Lord Broughton), *Some account of a long life* (London, 1867), vol. V.

Bibliography

Huntley, Sir H. V., *Free Trade, the Sugar Act of 1846 and the Slave Trade* (London, 1849).

Seven Years' Service on the Slave Coast of West Africa (2 vols., London, 1850).

Kidder, D. P., *Sketches of residence and travels in Brazil* (2 vols., Philadelphia, 1845).

Kidder, D. P., and Fletcher, J. C., *Brazil and the Brazilians* (Philadelphia, 1857).

Laird, McGregor, *The effect of an alteration in the sugar duties* (London, 1844).

Lawrence, W. B., *Visitation and Search* (Boston, 1858).

Leonard, Peter, *Records of a voyage to the west coast of Africa in HMS "Dryad" and of the service on that station for the suppression of the slave trade in the years 1830, 1831 and 1832* (Edinburgh, 1833).

Mansfield, J. S., *Remarks on the African Squadron* (London, 1851).

Matson, H. J., *Remarks on the Slave Trade and the African Squadron* (London, 1848).

Nabuco, Joaquim, *A Escravidão* (1870), published in *Revista do Instituto Histórico e Geográfico Brasileiro* vol. 204 (1949), pp. 10–106.

Nelson, T., *Remarks on the slavery and the slave trade of the Brazils* (London, 1846).

Ouseley, W. G., *Notes on the Slave Trade, with remarks on the measures adopted for its suppression* (London, 1850).

Perdigão Malheiro, Agostinho Marques, *A escravidão no Brasil: Ensaio histórico-jurídico-social* (1867: 2nd ed., 2 vols., São Paulo, 1944).

Pereira da Silva, J. M., *Memorias do Meu Tempo* (2 vols., Rio de Janeiro, 1898).

Queiroz Coutinho Matoso da Camara, Eusébio de, *Questão do Trafico* (Rio de Janeiro, 1852).

Representation of the Brazilian Merchants against the Insults offered to the Portuguese flag and against the violent and oppressive capture of several of their vessels by some officers belonging to the English navy (London, 1813).

Richard, Henry, *Memoirs of Joseph Sturge* (London, 1864).

Richardson, J., *The Cruisers, being a letter to the Marquis of Lansdowne in defence of armed coercion for the extinction of the slave trade* (London, 1849).

Ritchie, J. E., *Thoughts on Slavery and Cheap Sugar* (London, 1844).

Rocha, José Justiano da, *Inglaterra e Brasil: Trafego de escravos* (Rio de Janeiro, 1845).

Bibliography

Sá da Bandeira, Bernardo de, *O Trafico da escravatura e o bill de Lord Palmerston* (Lisbon, 1840).

Saldanha da Gama, A. de, *Memoria histórica e politica sobre o commercio da escravatura* (Lisbon, 1880).

Silva, José Eloy Pessoa da, *Memoria sobre a escravatura e projeto de colonização dos Europeus e pretos da Africa no Imperio do Brazil* (Rio de Janeiro, 1826).

Smith, George, *The Case of our West African Cruisers and West African Settlements fairly considered* (London, 1848).

Stapleton, Augustus Granville, *The Political Life of George Canning* (3 vols., London, 1831).

Stewart, C. S., *A visit to the South Seas, in the United States ship "Vincennes", during the years 1829 and 1830; including scenes in Brazil, Peru, Manilla, the Cape of Good Hope and St. Helena* (2 vols., London, 1832).

Stokes, R., *A Regulated Slave Trade* (London, 1850).

Systhema de medidas adoptaveis para a progressiva e total extincção do trafico e da escravatura no Brazil (Rio de Janeiro: Sociedade contra o trafico de africanos e promotora da colonisação e civilização dos indigenas, 1852).

Tavares Bastos, A. C., *Cartas do Solitario* (Rio de Janeiro, 1863).

Thomson, T. R. H., *The Brazilian Slave Trade and its remedy, shewing the futility of repressive force measures* (London, 1850).

Thorpe, R., *A view of the present increase in the slave trade* (London, 1818).

A Commentary on the Treaties (London, 1819).

Três Discursos do Ilmo e Exmo Sr Paulino José Soares de Souza (Rio de Janeiro, 1852).

Turnbull, David, *The Jamaica Movement for promoting the enforcement of the slave trade treaties and the suppression of the slave trade* (London, 1850).

Travels in the West. Cuba: with notices of Puerto Rico and the Slave Trade (London, 1840).

Velloso de Oliveira, Henrique, *A substituição do trabalho dos escravos pelo trabalho libre no Brasil, por um meio suave e sem difficuldade* (Rio de Janeiro, 1845).

Walsh, R., *Notices of Brazil in 1828 and 1829* (2 vols., London, 1830).

Wilberforce, E., *Brazil viewed through a naval glass: with notes on slavery and the slave trade* (London, 1856).

Wilberforce, R. I. and S., *The Life of William Wilberforce* (5 vols., London, 1838).

Wilson, J. L., *The British Squadron on the coast of Africa* (London, 1851).

Yule, Sir H., *The African Squadron Vindicated* (London, 1850).

Bibliography

B. SECONDARY SOURCES

Adams, Jane Elizabeth, 'The Abolition of the Brazilian Slave Trade', *Journal of Negro History*, x (1925), pp. 607–37.

Aguiar, Antônio Augusto de, *Vida do Marquez de Barbacena* (Rio de Janeiro, 1896).

Alden, Dauril, 'The Population of Brazil in the late Eighteenth Century: a preliminary study', *Hispanic American Historical Review*, XLIII (1963), pp. 173–205.

Almeida Prado, J. F. de, *O Brasil e O Colonialismo Europeu* (São Paulo, 1956).

Alves, João Luís, 'A Questão do Elemento Servil. A Extinção do Tráfico e a Lei de Repressão de 1850. Liberdade dos Nascituros', *Revista do Instituto Histórico e Geográfico Brasileiro*, Tomo Especial ... Primeiro Congresso de História Nacional, 1914, Part IV, pp. 187–257.

Amaral, Luís, *História Geral da Agricultura Brasileira* (2 vols., São Paulo, 1958).

Anstey, R. T., *Britain and the Congo in the Nineteenth Century* (Oxford, 1962).

'Capitalism and Slavery—A Critique', in *The Transatlantic Slave Trade from West Africa* (Centre of African Studies, Univ. of Edinburgh, 1965), pp. 13–29.

Bandeira de Mello, Afonso Toledo, 'A escravidão—da supressão do tráfico à lei Aurea', *Revista do Instituto Histórico e Geográfico Brasileiro*, Tomo Especial, 1922, vol. III, pp. 379–406.

Bartlett, C. J., *Great Britain and Sea Power* (Oxford, 1963).

Bastide, Roger and Fernandes, Florestan, *Brancos e Negros em São Paulo* (2nd. ed., São Paulo, 1959).

Beiguelman, Paula, 'Aspectos da organização político-partidária no Império Brasileiro', *Revista de História* (São Paulo), XXV (1962), no. 51, pp. 3–12.

Bell, H. C. F., *Lord Palmerston* (2 vols., London, 1936).

Besouchet, Lidia, *José Ma. Paranhos, Visconde do Rio Branco. Ensaio Histórico-Biográfico* (Rio de Janeiro, 1945).

Bethell, Leslie, 'Britain, Portugal and the suppression of the Brazilian slave trade: the origins of Lord Palmerston's Act of 1839', *English Historical Review*, LXXX (1965), pp. 761–84.

'The mixed commissions for the suppression of the transatlantic slave trade in the nineteenth century', *Journal of African History*, VII (1966), pp. 79–93.

Bibliography

Boxer, C. R., *Race Relations in the Portuguese Colonial Empire, 1415–1825* (Oxford, 1963).

The Golden Age of Brazil, 1695–1750. Growing Pains of a Colonial Society (Univ. of Calif. Press, 1962).

Some Literary Sources for the History of Brazil in the Eighteenth Century (Oxford, 1967).

Brown, Lucy, *The Board of Trade and the Free Trade Movement, 1830–42* (Oxford, 1958).

Burn, W. L., *The West Indies* (London, 1951).

Cady, John F., *Foreign Intervention in the Río de la Plata, 1838–50* (Univ. of Pennsylvania Press, 1929).

Caio de Freitas, *George Canning e o Brasil* (2 vols., Rio de Janeiro, 1958).

Calógeras, João Pandiá, *Formação Histórica do Brasil* (Rio de Janeiro, 1930). Eng. trans. *A History of Brazil* ed. Percy Alvin Martin (Univ. of North Carolina Press, 1939).

A Política Exterior do Império (2 vols., Rio de Janeiro, 1927–8).

Da Regência à Queda de Rozas (São Paulo, 1933).

O Marquês de Barbacena (São Paulo, 1932).

Cambridge History of the British Empire, vol. II. *The Growth of the New Empire, 1783–1870* eds. J. Holland Rose, A. P. Newton, E. A. Benians (Cambridge, 1940).

Cardoso, Fernando Henrique, *Capitalismo e escravidão no Brasil meridional* (São Paulo, 1962).

Cardoso, Vicente Licínio, *A margem da história do Brasil (Livro póstumo)*, (São Paulo, 1933).

Carneiro, David, *A História do Incidente Cormoran* (Curitiba, 1950).

Carneiro, Edison, *Ladinos e Crioulos. Estudos sôbre o Negro no Brasil* (Rio de Janeiro, 1964).

Carneiro, José Fernando, *Imigração e colonização no Brasil* (Rio de Janeiro, 1949).

Cesarino Júnior, Antônio Ferreira, 'A intervenção da Inglaterra na supressão do tráfico de escravos africanos para o Brasil', *Revista do Instituto Histórico e Geográfico de São Paulo*, XXXIV (1938), pp. 145–66.

Clowes, Sir W. L., *The Royal Navy. A History from the Earliest Times to the Present* (London, 1903), vol. VI.

Corwin, Arthur F., *Spain and the Abolition of Slavery in Cuba, 1817–1886* (Univ. of Texas Press, 1967).

Coupland, R., *The British Anti-Slavery Movement* (London, 1933).

William Wilberforce (Oxford, 1923).

Bibliography

Cruz Costa, João, *Contribuição à história das idéias no Brasil* (*O desenvolvimento da filosofia no Brasil e a evolução histórica nacional*) (Rio de Janeiro, 1956). Eng. trans. *A History of Ideas in Brazil* (Univ. of Calif. Press, 1964).

Curtin, Philip D., *The Image of Africa. British Ideas and Action, 1780–1850* (Wisconsin, 1964).

Curtin, Philip D., and Vansina, Jan, 'Sources of the Nineteenth Century Atlantic Slave Trade', *Journal of African History*, v (1964), pp. 185–208.

Davidson, Basil, *Black Mother* (London, 1961).

Deerr, Noel, *The History of Sugar* (2 vols., London, 1949–50).

Dias Tavares, Luís Henrique, 'As Soluções Brasileiras na Extinção do Tráfico Negreiro', *Journal of Inter-American Studies*, ix (1967), pp. 367–82.

Dike, K. Onwuka, *Trade and Politics in the Niger Delta, 1830–85* (Oxford, 1956).

Dornas Filho, João, *A escravidão no Brasil* (Rio de Janeiro, 1939).

DuBois, W. E. Burghardt, *The Suppression of the African Slave Trade to the U.S.A., 1638–1870* (Harvard, 1896).

Ducasse, André, *Les Négriers, ou le Trafic des Esclaves* (Paris, 1948).

Duffy, James, *Portuguese Africa* (Harvard, 1959).

A Question of Slavery. Labour Policies in Portuguese Africa and the British Protest, 1850–1920 (Oxford, 1967).

Duignan, Peter and Clendenen, Clarence, *The United States and the African Slave Trade, 1619–1862* (The Hoover Institution on War, Revolution and Peace, Stanford, 1963).

Duque Estrada, Osório, *A Abolição, 1831–88* (Rio de Janeiro, 1919).

Ferns, H. S., *Britain and Argentina in the Nineteenth Century* (Oxford, 1960).

Fischer, Hugo, 'The Suppression of Slavery in International Law', *International Law Quarterly*, iii (1950), pp. 28–51, 503–22.

Fladeland, Betty, 'Abolitionist Pressures on the Concert of Europe, 1814–1822', *Journal of Modern History*, xxxviii (1966), pp. 355–373.

Forjaz, Djalma, *O Senador Vergueiro* (São Paulo, 1924).

Freyre, Gilberto, *Casa Grande e Senzala* (8th ed., 2 vols., Rio de Janeiro, 1954). Eng. trans. *The Masters and the Slaves* (2nd ed., New York, 1956).

Sobrados e Mucambos (2nd ed., 3 vols., Rio de Janeiro, 1951). Eng. trans. *The Mansions and the Shanties* (New York, 1963).

408

Bibliography

Furtado, Celso, *Formação Econômica do Brasil* (Rio de Janeiro, 1959). Eng. trans. *The Economic Growth of Brazil* (Univ. of Calif. Press, 1963).

Fyfe, Christopher, *A History of Sierra Leone* (London, 1962). *Sierra Leone Inheritance* (London, 1964).

Gallagher, J., 'Fowell Buxton and the New African Policy, 1838–1842', *Cambridge Historical Journal*, x (1950), pp. 36–58.

Gomes, Alfredo, 'Achegas para a história do tráfico africano no Brasil. Aspectos Númericos'. *Revista do Instituto Histórico e Geográfico Brasileiro*, IV Congresso de História Nacional (1949), vol. v, pp. 25–75.

Goulart, Mauricio, *Escravidão Africana no Brasil: Das origens à extinção do tráfico* (São Paulo, 1950).

Gouveia, Maurílio de, *História de escravidão* (Rio de Janeiro, 1955).

Graham, G. S., *Great Britain in the Indian Ocean. A Study of Maritime Enterprise, 1810–1850* (Oxford, 1967).

Graham, Richard, 'Causes for the Abolition of Negro Slavery in Brazil: An Interpretive Essay', *Hispanic American Historical Review*, XLVI (1966), pp. 123–37.

Britain and the Onset of Modernization in Brazil, 1850–1914 (Cambridge, 1968).

Hammond, R. J., *Portugal and Africa, 1815–1910: a study in uneconomic imperialism* (Stanford, 1966).

Hancock, W. K., *Survey of British Commonwealth Affairs* (London, 1942), vol. II.

Haring, C. H., *Empire in Brazil* (Harvard, 1958).

Hill, Lawrence F., *Diplomatic Relations between the United States and Brazil* (Duke Univ. Press, 1932).

'The Abolition of the African Slave Trade to Brazil', *Hispanic American Historical Review*, XI (1931), pp. 169–97.

História Geral da Civilização Brasileira, ed. Sérgio Buarque de Holanda: I i *A Época Colonial. Do Descobrimento à Expansão Territorial* (São Paulo, 1960); I ii *A Época Colonial. Administração, Economia, Sociedade* (São Paulo, 1960); II i *O Brasil Monárquico. O Processo de Emancipação* (São Paulo, 1962); II ii *O Brasil Monárquico. Dispersão e Unidade* (São Paulo, 1964); II iii *O Brasil Monárquico. Reações e Transações* (São Paulo, 1967).

Howard, Warren S., *American Slavers and the Federal Law, 1837–1862* (Univ. of Calif. Press, 1963).

Ianni, Octavio, *As metamorfoses do escravo: apogeu e crise da escravatura no Brasil meridional* (São Paulo, 1962).

Bibliography

Jackson, M. V., *European powers and South-East Africa 1796–1856* (London, 1942).

Johnson, Douglas, *Guizot: Aspects of French History, 1787–1874* (London, 1963).

Jones, W. D., *Lord Aberdeen and the Americas* (University of Georgia, 1958).

'The Origins and Passage of Lord Aberdeen's Act', *Hispanic American Historical Review*, XLII (1962), pp. 502–20.

King, J. F., 'The Latin American Republics and the Suppression of the Slave Trade', *Hispanic American Historical Review*, XXIV (1944), pp. 387–411.

Klingberg, F. J., *The Anti-Slavery Movement in England* (New Haven, 1926).

Lewis, Michael, *The Navy in Transition. A Social History, 1814–64* (London, 1965).

Livermore, H. V., *A New History of Portugal* (Cambridge, 1967).

Lloyd, Christopher, *The Navy and the Slave Trade* (London, 1949).

Lopes, Edmundo Correia, *A Escravatura: Subsídios para a sua história* (Lisbon, 1944).

Lyra, Heitor, *História de Dom Pedro II* (3 vols., São Paulo, 1938–40).

Macdonagh, Oliver, 'The Anti-Imperialism of Free Trade', *Economic History Review* 2nd ser., XIV (1962), pp. 489–501.

Macedo, Sergio T. D. de, *Apontamentos para a história do tráfico negreiro no Brasil* (Rio de Janeiro, 1942).

Manchester, Alan K., *British Preeminence in Brazil: Its Rise and Decline* (Univ. of North Carolina Press, 1933).

'The Rise of the Brazilian Aristocracy', *Hispanic American Historical Review*, XI (1931), pp. 145–68.

'Paradoxical Pedro: First Emperor of Brazil', *Hispanic American Historical Review*, XII (1932), pp. 176–88.

'The Recognition of Brazilian Independence', *Hispanic American Historical Review*, XXXI (1951), pp. 80–96.

Mannix, Daniel P., and Cowley, Malcolm, *Black Cargoes. A History of the Atlantic Slave Trade, 1518–1865* (London, 1963).

Martin, Percy A., 'Slavery and Abolition in Brazil', *Hispanic American Historical Review*, XIII (1933), pp. 151–96.

Mathieson, W. L., *Great Britain and the Slave Trade, 1839–1865* (London, 1929).

Mellor, G. R., *British Imperial Trusteeship, 1783–1850* (London, 1951).

Moraes, Evaristo de, *A escravidão africana no Brasil: Das origens à extinção* (São Paulo, 1933).

Bibliography

'A escravidão—da supressão do tráfico à lei Áurea', *Revista do Instituto Histórico e Geográfico Brasileiro*, Tomo Especial (1922), vol. III, pp. 243–313.

Morrell, W. P., *British colonial policy in the age of Peel and Russell* (Oxford, 1930).

Morse, Richard, *From Community to Metropolis. A biography of São Paulo, Brazil* (Gainsville, 1958).

Nabuco, Joaquim, *Um Estadista do Império, Nabuco de Araújo: Sua Vida, Suas Opiniões, Sua Época* (2nd ed., 2 vols., São Paulo, 1936).

Nelson, B. H., 'The Slave Trade as a Factor in British Foreign Policy, 1815–62', *Journal of Negro History*, XXVII (1942), pp. 192–209.

New, C. W., *Henry Brougham (to 1830)*, (London, 1961).

Newbury, C. W., *The Western Slave Coast and its Rulers* (Oxford, 1962).

Oliveira Lima, Manuel de, *Dom João VI no Brasil, 1808–1821* (2nd ed. 3 vols., Rio de Janeiro, 1945).

O Movimento da independência, 1821–1822 (São Paulo, 1922).

História Diplomática do Brazil. O Reconhecimento do Império, 1822–1827 (Rio de Janeiro, 1902).

Padua, Ciro T. de, 'Um capítulo da história econômica do Brasil', *Revista do Arquivo Municipal de São Paulo*, XI (1945), pp. 135–90.

Palmer, T. W., 'A Momentous Decade in Brazilian Administrative History, 1831–40', *Hispanic American Historical Review*, XXX (1950), pp. 209–17.

Pierson, D., *Negroes in Brazil: a study of race contact at Bahia* (Chicago, 1942).

Prado Júnior, Caio, *Formação do Brasil Contemporâneo (Colônia)* (5th ed. São Paulo, 1957). Eng. trans. *The Colonial Background of Modern Brazil* (Univ. of Calif. Press, 1967).

Evolução Política do Brasil e Outros Estudos (2nd ed., São Paulo, 1957).

História Econômica do Brasil (6th ed., São Paulo, 1959).

Ramos, Arthur, *O Negro na Civilização Brasileira* (Rio de Janeiro, 1956).

Redford, A., *Manchester Merchants and Foreign Trade, 1794–1858* (Manchester, 1934).

Rice, E. Duncan, 'Critique of the Eric Williams Thesis: The Anti-Slavery Interest and the Sugar Duties, 1841–53' in *The Trans-atlantic Slave Trade from West Africa* (Centre of African Studies, Univ. of Edinburgh, 1965), pp. 44–60.

Rodrigues, José Honório, *Brasil e África: Outro horizonte* (2nd ed. 2 vols., Rio de Janeiro, 1964). Eng. trans. *Brazil and Africa* (Univ. of Calif. Press, 1965).

Bibliography

'The Foundations of Brazil's Foreign Policy', *International Affairs*, XXXVIII (1962), pp. 324–38.

Rodrigues, Raymundo Nina, *Os Africanos no Brasil* (Rio de Janeiro, 1932).

Rose, J. Holland, *Man and the Sea* (Cambridge, 1935).

'The Royal Navy and the Suppression of the West African Slave Trade', *Mariner's Mirror*, XXII (1936), pp. 54–64, 162–171.

Ross, David A., 'The Career of Domingo Martinez in the Bight of Benin, 1833–64', *Journal of African History*, VI (1965), pp. 79–90.

Sayers, R. S., *The Negro in Brazilian Literature* (New York, 1956).

Schuyler, R. L., *Fall of the old colonial system—a study in free trade* (New York, 1945).

Senior, W., *Naval History in the law courts* (London, 1927).

Siqueira, Sônia Aparecida, 'A Escravidão negra no pensamento do bispo Azeredo Coutinho. Contribuição ao estudo da mentalidade do último inquisidor geral', *Revista de História* (São Paulo) XXVII (1963), no. 56, pp. 349–65, XXVIII (1964), no. 57, pp. 141–76.

Soares de Sousa, José Antônio, *A Vida do Visconde do Uruguai, 1807–66* (Rio de Janeiro, 1945).

'Documentação para uma Tese sôbre o Tráfico de Escravos', *Revista do Instituto Histórico e Geográfico Brasileiro*, vol. 219 (April–June 1953), pp. 266–86.

Sodré, Nelson Werneck, *As Razões da Independência* (Rio de Janeiro, 1965).

História da Burguesia Brasileira (Rio de Janeiro, 1962).

Soulsby, H. G., *The Right of Search and the Slave Trade in Anglo-American Relations, 1814–62* (Baltimore, 1933).

Sousa, Octavio Tarquinio de, *Bernardo Pereira de Vasconcelos e seu tempo* (Rio de Janeiro, 1937).

José Bonifácio, 1763–1838 (Rio de Janeiro, 1945).

Sousa Vianna, Manuel Alvaro de, 'O Tráfico e a Diplomacia Brasileira', *Revista do Instituto Histórico e Geográfico Brasileiro*, Tomo Especial, 1914, Part V, pp. 537–64.

Stein, Stanley, J., *The Brazilian Cotton Manufacture, 1850–1950* (Harvard, 1957).

Vassouras: A Brazilian Coffee County, 1850–1900 (Harvard, 1957).

'The Historiography of Brazil, 1808–1889', *Hispanic American Historical Review*, XL (1960), pp. 234–78.

Taunay, Affonso d'Escragnolle, *História do café no Brasil* (Rio de Janeiro, 1939–43).

Subsídios para a história do tráfico africano no Brasil (São Paulo, 1941).

Bibliography

'Notas sôbre as últimas décadas do tráfico' *Mensário do Jornal do Comércio*, (Rio de Janeiro) 24 July 1938, III, i, pp. 115–19.

'As últimas décadas do tráfico', *Mensário*, 31 July 1938, III, i, pp. 181–4.

'Cessão do Tráfico', *Mensário*, 7 August 1938, III, ii, pp. 295–9.

Temperley, H. V., *The Foreign Policy of Canning, 1822–7* (London, 1925).

Valladão, Alfredo, *Eusébio de Queiroz e os centenários do Código Comercial, de Regulamento 737 e da Supressão do Tráfico Africano* (Rio de Janeiro, 1951).

Verger, Pierre, *Les Afro-Américains: Influence du Brésil au Golfe du Bénin* (Institut Français d'Afrique Noire, Ifan-Dakar, 1953).

Bahia and the West African Trade, 1549–1851 (Ibadan Univ. Press for Institute of African Studies, 1964).

Vianna Filho, Luís, *O Negro na Bahia* (Rio de Janeiro, 1946).

Viotti da Costa, Emília, *Da Senzala à Colônia* (São Paulo, 1966).

Wanderley Pinho, José, *Cotegipe e seu tempo: primeira phase, 1815–1867* (São Paulo, 1937).

Webster, Sir Charles K., *The Foreign Policy of Castlereagh, 1812–15* (London, 1931).

The Foreign Policy of Castlereagh, 1815–22 (2nd ed., London, 1934).

The Foreign Policy of Lord Palmerston, 1830–41 (2 vols., London, 1951).

Williams, E., 'Laissez faire, sugar and slavery', *Political Science Quarterly*, LVIII (1943), pp. 67–85.

Capitalism and Slavery (University of North Carolina Press, 1944).

Williams, M. V., 'The Treatment of Negro Slaves in the Brazilian Empire. A comparison with the United States', *Journal of Negro History*, xv (1930), pp. 313–36.

Wilson, Howard H., 'Some Principal Aspects of British Efforts to crush the African slave trade, 1807–1929', *American Journal of International Law*, XLIV (1950), pp. 505–26.

C. UNPUBLISHED THESES

Gavin, R. J., 'Palmerston's policy towards East and West Africa, 1830–1865' (Ph.D., University of Cambridge, 1958).

Herrington, E. I., 'British measures for the suppression of the slave trade from the West Coast of Africa, 1807–1833' (M.A., University of London, 1923).

Bibliography

Murray, D. R., 'Britain, Spain and the slave trade to Cuba, 1807–1845' (Ph.D., University of Cambridge, 1967).

Pilgrim, Elsie I., 'Anti-slavery sentiment in Great Britain 1841–54; its nature and its decline; with special reference to its influence upon British policy towards its former slave colonies' (Ph.D., University of Cambridge, 1952).

Pryor, A. J., 'Anglo-Brazilian Commercial Relations and the Evolution of Brazilian Tariff Policy, 1822–50' (Ph.D., University of Cambridge, 1965).

INDEX

415

Index

416

Index

Captured ships, *see* Ships

Caravelas, *see* Carneiro de Campos, José

Carneiro de Campos, João, 135, 138, 141, 147,148,168, 170,173,174,201,205, 212

Carneiro de Campos, José Joaquim (Marquês de Caravelas), 46, 68 n.

Carneiro Leão, Honório Hermeto (Marquês de Paraná), 69, 83, 234–6, 235 n., 238, 248, 272 n., 311, 334, 371

Carta Régia, 7

Carvalho e Melo, Luís José de, 47

Castlereagh, Lord, x, 14, 22, 31; and first treaty of Paris, 12; and Congress of Vienna, 12–13; and right of search, 17–18, 21; and recognition of Spanish American republics, 30

Cayenne, 73

Ceará, 375

Cerqueira Lima, José and Manoel, 117

Chamber of Deputies, 56–7, 58, 195, 217, 230, 290, 313, 318, 371; and 1826 treaty, 62–6, 89–90; and 1831 bill, 69–70; and 1831 law, 80; and 1837 bill, 82–3; and repeal of 1831 law, 80, 87; and additional articles of 1835, 112, 113, 114, 116, 118–19, 120, 214, 216; and renewal of commercial treaty, 232; and termination of 1817 treaty, 249–51; and 1848 bill, 293–4, 315, 316, 328; and debate of 8 July 1850, 331–2; and 1850 bill,335, 335 n.,339–40; Paulino's speech of 15 July 1850, 337–9, and *Piratinim* affair, 356–7; Eusébio's speech of 16 July 1852, 361–2

Chamber of Deputies: *Comissão de Diplomacia*, and 1826 treaty, 62–3; and 1837 bill, 83; and additional articles of 1835, 116, 119

Chamber of Deputies: *Comissão de Legislação e de Justiça*, 56–7

Chamberlain, Henry, 15, 37–8, 42, 43–4, 45, 46, 52, 55–6

Cholera, epidemic of 1855, 372–3

Christie, W. D., 267 n., 376, 382–3, 384

Claims: Portuguese, 13; Brazilian, 114, 115, 117, 119, 253, 271, 379, 382, 387; British, 379–80

Claims Commission of 1858, 380

Clarendon, Lord, 370, 373 n., 376–7

Clarkson, Thomas, 151 n., 297, 302

Clemente Pereira, José, 56, 64, 66

Cobden, Richard, 274 n., 298, 299, 303

Coffee, 15, 41, 73–4, 76, 184–5, 284, 375, 378; British coffee duties, 223, 231, 240

Collier, Sir George, 20

Colonists, Colonisation, *see* Immigration

Commercial (Recife), 313

Conciliação, 340 n., 371

Congo, 1, 79, 85, 127, 150, 181, 182

Congo river, 9, 182, 373, 386

Consequences of abolition, 375–8

Constitutent Assembly (1823), 43, 45–6, 46

Constitution of 1824, 46, 52

O Contemporâneo (Rio de Janeiro), 313

Correio Brasiliense (London), 36

Correio Mercantil (Rio de Janeiro), 312, 313, 319, 361

Correio da Tarde (Rio de Janeiro), 318, 337 n.

Costa, Hipólito José da, 36

Costa Carvalho, José da (Visconde de Monte Alegre), 68 n., 83, 248, 311

Costa da Mina, see Guinea Coast

Costa Ferreira, Antônio Pedro da, 361

Costa Ramos, Tomás da, 286, 355

Cotton, 3, 15, 41, 72, 223–4, 378

Council of State, 44, 58, 234 n., 290, 291, 311,317,328; and renewal of commercial treaty, 234–5; and termination of 1817 treaty, 248, 251–2; and Aberdeen Act, 269, 272, 272 n., 281; and suppression of slave trade, 332–5, 341; and abolition of slavery, 386

Coutinho, José Lino, 63, 70

Crimean War, xii, 372

Cruz Costa, João, 378 n.

Cruz Jobim, José Martins da, 319

Cuba, slave trade to, xii, xiii, 9 n., 20, 25, 71 n., 103, 125–6, 126 n., 151, 175, 183, 184, 189, 282 n., 283, 296, 374, 379, 385, 385 n.

Cunha Matos, Raimundo José da, 63–4, 65, 66

Curtin, Captain, 356

Dahomey, 1, 9, 285, 289–90 n.

Daily News, 321, 362, 372

Denman, Lord, 164 n., 273, 300

Denman, Captain Joseph, 136 n., 180, 186 n., 199, 305; and Gallinas incident, 183, 185–6

Denmark and the slave trade, xi, 1, 15

Diario Fluminense, 53 n.

Dodson, Sir John, 100, 139 n., 177–8, 180, 195 n., 195–6, 205 n., 212, 257

Dois Rios, 75, 330, 352

Dudley, Lord, 88

Economist, 321

Eldon, Lord, 10

Index

Index

Index

Paine, Lieutenant John S., 191
Paiva, José de, 95, 133
Palmella, Conde (then Duc) de, 13, 18–19, 21, 28–9, 99, 101 n., 187
Palmerston, Lord, x, 95, 96, 97, 101, 115, 166, 167, 186, 189, 191, 201, 236, 301, 313, 322, 323 n., 324, 332, 351–2, 365, 370, 381, 385; and talks with Mello Mattos, 93, 248; and Portuguese treaty negotiations, 98, 101 n., 104–11, 155–6; and Brazilian treaty negotiations, 111–21, 216, 217, 273; and Admiralty, 124; and cases before Rio mixed court, 139, 146, 147–8, 177–8; and Buxton, 154; and Act of 1839, 155–66; and naval operations in African waters, 180, 185–6; and Campos incident, 207–8; and sugar duties, 227, 239, 274; and Conservative record, 254; and Aberdeen Act, 262–3, 274, 275–6, 275 n.; treaty proposals of 1847, 277–8; and Howden mission, 278, 280–1; and legitimate African trade, 154, 301; and tougher measures against the Brazilian slave trade, 220, 262, 304–5, 307–9, 324–6, 325 n., 344–6, 350–1; and suppression of the Brazilian slave trade, 359–60; and Anti-Slavery Society, 302, 361 n.; and repeal of Aberdeen Act, 365, 372, 373–4, 379, 384
Palmerston Act: origins of, 155–9; passage of, 159–64; Portuguese reaction to, 164–6; and territorial waters, 180, 212, 366; captures under, 182, 189, 202–4; Conservative attitude towards, 186–7; partial repeal of, 187–8; and treaty of 1842, 276, 364; Brazilian attitude towards, 204; threat to extend it to Brazil, 220, 243, 244, 244 n., 246; compared with Aberdeen Act, 255, 259, 259 n., 261, 275
Pará, 73, 77
Paraguay, 240, 349
Paraguayan War, 385, 386
Paraíba (province), 374
Paraíba river, see Paraíba valley
Paraíba valley, 73, 74, 75, 76, 373, 378
Paraíba do Sul, 76
Paranaguá, 76, 285, 310, 356; Paranaguá incident, 330, 331, 336, 346, 356, 360, 362
Paranaguá, Visconde de, 51
Paranhos, José Maria da Silva (Visconde do Rio Branco), 356 n., 386
Parati, 76
Paula Sousa e Melo, Francisco de, 87, 252, 269, 290, 294, 311, 328 n., 329, 333, 335
Paulino, see Soares de Sousa

Pedro I, and independence, 27–8, 32; and abolition, 33, 40–2, 44, 44 n., 45, 55, 67; and Constitution of 1824, 46; and Portuguese Africa, 49; and treaty negotiations, 50–2, 57, 58, 60, 248; and Portuguese succession, 98, 98 n; see also Abdication
Pedro II, 68, 79, 86, 184, 217, 219, 248, 272, 329, 332, 349; and abolition, 312, 340, 385–6, 385 n.
Peel, Sir Robert, 113, 160, 301; and import duties, 228, 238, 240, 273; and Aberdeen bill, 254–66, 267
Pelotas, 3, 291
Peninsular War, 13
Pennell, Charles, 41–2, 67, 86 n.
Pereira da Cunha, Antônio Luís (Marquês de Inhambupe), 57
Pereira da Silva, J. M., 210, 210 n.
Periqué, 76, 352
Pernambuco, 3–4, 5, 11, 14, 41, 71, 76, 126, 184, 211 n., 205–6, 223, 225, 341–2, 343, 354, 367, 373, 374, 375, 376
Perry, Commodore Matthew, 191
O Philanthropo (Rio de Janeiro), 313, 334 n.
Pimenta Bueno, José Antônio (later Marquês de S. Vicente), 78 n., 281
Pinto da Fonseca, Joaquim, 342, 343
Pinto da Fonseca, Manuel, 289, 290, 342, 355
Piracy, 21, 21 n.; see also Treaties, Anglo-Brazilian, 23 November 1826, interpretation of article 1
Pires da Mota, Vicente, 343
Piumas Islands, 206
Portaria of 4 November 1829, 91–2
Porto Alegre, 3, 342
Portuguese Africa and slave trade, xi, 1–2, 9, 26, 99, 102, 103, 285–6, 305, 385, see also Congo, Angola, Moçambique; Portuguese claims in Africa, 9, 11, 18, 49, 104–5; demand for British guarantee for Portuguese claims in Africa, 104, 106–7, 107 n., 107–8
Portuguese flag, use of, in the slave trade, 96–7, 103, 111, 113, 126, 134, 188
Príncipe, 1
Profitt, George H., 192
Protectionists, 227, 240, 273, 274 n., 299, 321, 323–4
Puerto Rico, 9, 25, 103
Purvis, Commodore, 252

Quarterly Review, 321
Queiroz Coutinho Matoso da Câmara, Eusébio de, 315 n., 338, 351–2, 356,

421

Index

Index

Index

Index